BRAZIL

A BIOGRAPHY

© Renato Parada

A NOTE ABOUT THE AUTHORS

LILIA M. SCHWARCZ was born in 1957 in São Paulo, Brazil. She is a professor of anthropology at the University of São Paulo, a visiting professor in the Department of Spanish and Portuguese Languages and Cultures and the Program in Latin American Studies at Princeton University, and the author of *The Emperor's Beard* and *The Spectacle of the Races*.

HELOISA M. STARLING is a professor of history at the Federal University of Minas Gerais and the author of *Memories of Brazil* and *The Lords of Gerais*.

BRAZIL

A BIOGRAPHY

Lilia M. Schwarcz *and* Heloisa M. Starling

TRANSLATED FROM THE PORTUGUESE

PICADOR | FARRAR, STRAUS AND GIROUX | NEW YORK

Picador
120 Broadway, New York 10271

Originally published in Portuguese in 2015 by Companhia das Letras,
Brazil, as *Brasil: Uma Biografia*
English translation originally published in 2018 by Allen Lane,
an imprint of Penguin Books, Great Britain
Published in the United States in 2018 by Farrar, Straus and Giroux
First Picador paperback edition, April 2020

The Library of Congress has cataloged the Farrar, Straus and Giroux
hardcover edition as follows:
Names: Schwarcz, Lilia Moritz, author. | Starling, Heloisa Maria Murgel, author.
Title: Brazil : a biography / Lilia M. Schwarcz and Heloisa M. Starling.
Description: First American edition. | New York : Farrar, Straus and Giroux,
[2018] | Includes index. | Originally published: Brasil: uma Biografia :
Companhia das Letras, Brazil, 2015. | Translated from Portuguese.
Identifiers: LCCN 2018021716 | ISBN 9780374280499 (hardcover)
Subjects: LCSH: Brazil—Civilization. | Brazil—History.
Classification: LCC F2510 .S38713 2018 | DDC 981—dc23
LC record available at https://lccn.loc.gov/2018021716

Picador Paperback ISBN: 978-0-374-53848-4

Our books may be purchased in bulk for promotional, educational,
or business use. Please contact your local bookseller or the Macmillan
Corporate and Premium Sales Department at 1-800-221-7945, extension 5442,
or by e-mail at MacmillanSpecialMarkets@macmillan.com.

Picador® is a U.S. registered trademark and is used by Macmillan Publishing Group,
LLC, under license from Pan Books Limited.

For book club information, please visit facebook.com/picadorbookclub or
e-mail marketing@picadorusa.com.

picadorusa.com • instagram.com/picador
twitter.com/picadorusa • facebook.com/picadorusa

P1

MINISTÉRIO DAS RELAÇÕES EXTERIORES

MINISTÉRIO DA CULTURA
Fundação BIBLIOTECA NACIONAL

Obra publicada com apoio do Ministério das Relações Exteriores do Brasil em
cooperação com a Fundação Biblioteca Nacional / Ministério da Cultura.
(Published with the support of the Ministry of Foreign Affairs, Brazil, in cooperation
with the National Library Foundation / Ministry of Culture.)

For Luiz and Otávio, because, as Guimarães Rosa used to say:
'A book may be worth all that could not be written therein.'

Contents

List of Illustrations

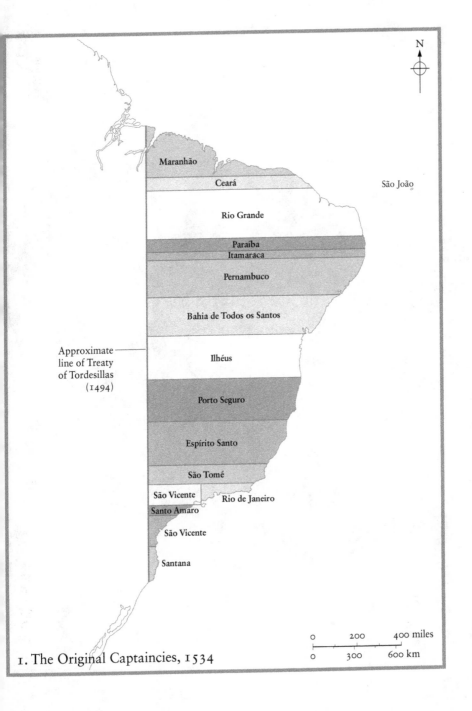

N

Maranhão

Ceará

Rio Grande

São João

Paraíba

Itamaraca

Pernambuco

Bahia de Todos os Santos

Approximate line of Treaty of Tordesillas (1494)

Ilhéus

Porto Seguro

Espírito Santo

São Tomé

São Vicente

Santo Amaro

Rio de Janeiro

São Vicente

Santana

0   200   400 miles

0   300   600 km

1. The Original Captaincies, 1534

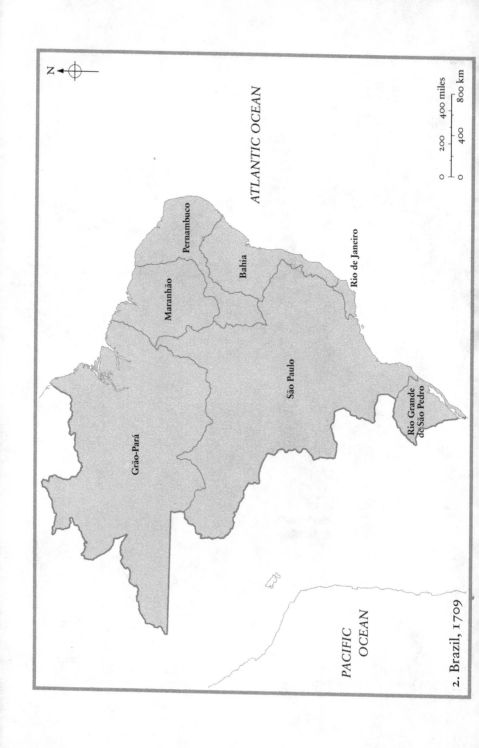

PACIFIC OCEAN

ATLANTIC OCEAN

Grão-Pará

Maranhão

Pernambuco

Bahia

São Paulo

Rio de Janeiro

Rio Grande
de São Pedro

| 0 | 200 | 400 miles |
| 0 | 400 | 800 km |

2. Brazil, 1709

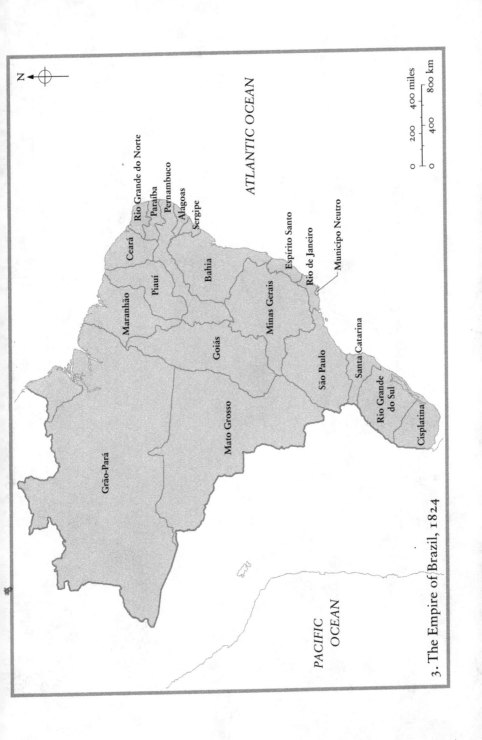

3. The Empire of Brazil, 1824

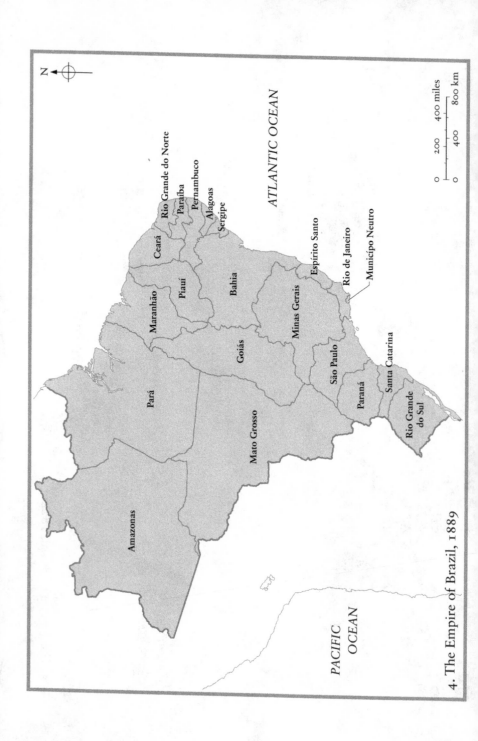

4. The Empire of Brazil, 1889

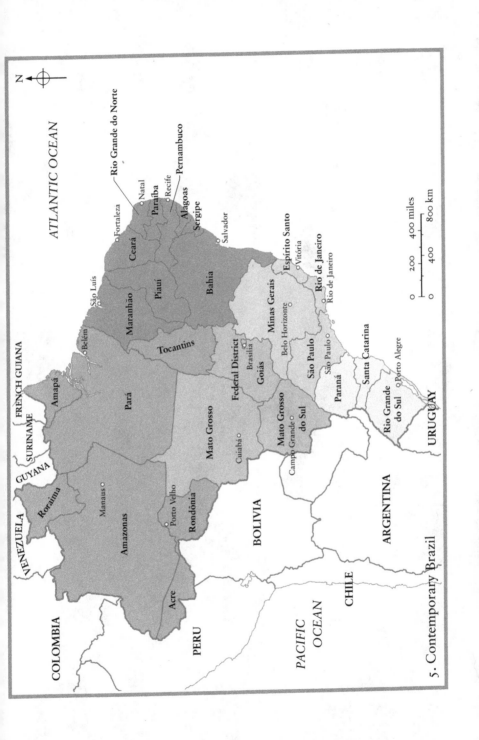

5. Contemporary Brazil

Introduction: 'Brazil Is Just Nearby'

It's good to know the joyful reaction in the city [Rio de Janeiro] to the abolition of slavery, in 1888, was felt all over the country. It could not have been otherwise, as in everyday life the injustice of its origins was felt by all. Where I went to school, a state-run institution in Rua do Rezende, the children were delighted. I recall that our teacher, D. Tereza Pimentel do Amaral, a highly intelligent woman, explained to us what it really meant; but with the simplicity of a child, all that I could think was: free! free! I thought we could all now do as we liked; that from then on there would be no limits to the progress we dreamt of. But how far we are from that! Still so trapped in the cobwebs of prejudice, the rules and the laws! [. . .] These memories are good; they have a whiff of nostalgia and lend us a feeling of eternity. Inflexible time, the offspring and brother of Death, gradually kills aspirations, destroying our hopes, leaving us with only sorrow and our recollections of the past – often mere trifles, but which are always a consolation.

The author of this passage is Lima Barreto. Journalist, essayist and columnist of the city, he was one of the few Brazilian writers to define himself as black – both as a man and in his writing – and this despite living in a country where the censuses showed that the majority of inhabitants were black and mestizo. The passage does not appear to have been written for posterity. This emotional outburst was scribbled on the back of a piece of paper in the War Ministry, where the writer worked as a clerk; a government employee, relatively low in the hierarchy of civil servants.

His father, João Henriques de Lima Barreto, who had connections to the monarchy, was one of the first to lose his job under the new republican government; he found employment in a warehouse and was subsequently put in charge of an asylum. In 1902 he was diagnosed as 'mentally insane' and forced to retire from his government post. Insanity, which at the time was thought to be a result of a racial degeneration resulting from miscegenation, was to pursue his son throughout his life; Lima Barreto was interned in the National Hospital for the Insane on two occasions, in 1914 and 1919. The words 'madness', 'despondency' and 'exclusion' frequently appear in the writer's work and to a large extent define his generation.

There seems to be nothing random or arbitrary about the passage. It reveals some of the persistent traits of Brazil's short history; at least, the history that begins in 1500 with the country's 'discovery', as it is referred to by some, though 'invasion' would be a more accurate term. Although these five centuries of the nation's existence have been marked by a wide diversity of events, in differing political and cultural contexts, certain stubbornly insistent traits can be observed. Among these has been precisely the challenging and tortuous process of building citizenship. As this book will demonstrate, there have been occasions when the public has demonstrated civic-mindedness and enthusiasm, for example when slavery was abolished in 1888, as mentioned by Lima Barreto. When Princess Isabel announced the long-awaited decree from the balcony of the *Paço Imperial*, people crowded into the square below. Although eventually enacted by the government, the law, known as the *Lei Áurea*, was largely the result of the pressure of public opinion. As important as it was, the law nonetheless did very little to integrate those Brazilians who had enjoyed neither citizenship nor rights for so long. It illustrates a recurring pattern. Many such acts were followed by political and social setbacks: projects that failed to produce an inclusive society; a Republic devoid of republican values, as described by Lima Barreto.

This is the reason why comings and goings, advances and setbacks are so much a part of Brazilian history, a history that might be characterized as 'mestizo', in a sense, like the Brazilian people. It is a history providing multiple, and at times ambivalent answers, one that cannot be interpreted in terms of the traditionally celebrated dates and events; nor can it be traced through objective considerations alone, nor in terms of a clear-cut evolution. Brazil's history is an amalgam generating different forms of 'memory'. It is 'mestizo' not only because it is a 'mixture', but also, clearly, a 'separation'. In a country characterized by the power of the landowners – many of whom own immense estates, each the size of a city – authoritarianism and personal interest have always been deeply rooted, undermining the free exercise of civic power, weakening public institutions and consequently the struggle for people's rights. There is a popular Brazilian proverb, 'if you steal a little you're a thief, if you steal a lot you're a chief', as if to legitimize the notion – highly controversial and much discussed today – that the wealthy and powerful are exempt, citizens above suspicion.

There is a further trait which, as a social rather than a natural construction, is not endemic, but is nevertheless shockingly resistant to improvement and a constant presence in Brazilian history. The logic and language of violence are deeply embedded determinants of Brazilian culture. Violence has characterized Brazilian history since the earliest days of colonization, marked as they were by the institution of slavery. This history of violence has permeated Brazilian society as a whole, spreading throughout, virtually naturalized. Although slavery is no longer practised in Brazil, its legacy casts a long shadow. The experience of violence and pain is repeated, dispersed, and persists in modern Brazilian society, affecting so many aspects of people's lives.

Brazil was the last Western country to abolish slavery and today it continues to be the champion of social inequality and racism, which, albeit veiled, is equally perverse. Although there is no legal form of discrimination, the poor, and above all black people, are the most harshly treated by the justice system, have the shortest life span, the least access to higher education and to highly qualified jobs. The indelible mark of slavery conditions Brazilian culture; the country defines itself on the basis of gradations of skin colour. Whereas those who achieve success become 'whiter', those who become impoverished become 'darker'. But Brazilians' self-identity does not end with this porous sense of ethnicity, for there is racial inclusion in many of the country's best-known cultural activities: capoeira, candomblé, samba, football. Brazilian music and culture are 'mestizo' in both their origin and singularity. Nevertheless, the numerous processes of social exclusion cannot be ignored; they are reflected in the limited access to entertainment and leisure, to the employment market and to health services (affecting birth rate), and in the daily intimidation by the police, where racial profiling is the norm.

To a certain extent, this amalgam of colours and customs, the mixture of races, has formed the image of Brazil. On the one hand, this mixture was consolidated by violence, by the forced importation of peoples, cultures and experiences into the country. Far from any alleged attempt at social harmony, the different races were deliberately intermingled. This resulted from the purchase of Africans brought to Brazil by force in far larger numbers than to any other country. Brazil received more than 40 per cent of all slaves that were brought from Africa to work on the plantations in Portuguese America – a total of around 3.8 million individuals. Today, 60 per cent of the country's population is made up of blacks and 'browns'; it could thus be ranked as the most populated 'African' country, with the exception of Nigeria. Furthermore, despite the numerous controversies, it is estimated that in 1500 the native population was between 1 million and 8 million, of which between 25 per cent and 95 per cent were decimated after the 'meeting' with the Europeans.

On the other hand, it is undeniable that the same mixture of races, unequalled in any other country, generated a society that was defined by mixed marriages, rhythms, arts, sports, aromas, cuisine and literary expression. It could be said that the 'Brazilian soul' is multicoloured. The variety of Brazilian faces, features, ways of thinking and seeing the country are evidence of how deeply rooted the mixture of races is, and of how it has produced new cultures born from its hybrid nature and variety of experiences. Cultural diversity is perhaps one of the most important aspects of the country, deeply marked and conditioned by 'separation' but also by the 'mixture' resulting from the long process of mestiçagem.

Although the result of centuries-old discriminatory practices, Brazil's mixed-race soul – born of the mixture of Amerindians, Africans and Europeans – provides for new perspectives. There is a multiplicity of meanings in the culture produced by a country that does not obey the established correlations between the dominator, on the one hand, and the dominated on the other – European and Amerindian, white and African. As Riobaldo Tatarana, one of Guimarães Rosa's most important fictional characters, once said, 'held captive inside its little earthy destiny, the tree opens so many arms' – so too, with its hybrid soul, Brazil has many arms. Brazil cannot be categorized, by way of blurring the most obvious cultural practices; the country is both a part of and distinct from the rest of the world – but always Brazilian.

And the country has many characteristics. Lima Barreto concludes his text with a sarcastic outburst: 'We keep on living stubbornly, hoping, hoping . . . For what? The unexpected, which may occur tomorrow or sometime in the future; who knows, a sudden stroke of luck? A hidden treasure in the garden?' This is Brazil's national obsession, which the historian Sérgio Buarque de Holanda wrote about in his 1936 seminal work *Raízes do Brasil*, a country on the lookout for the daily miracle, or some unexpected saviour. He called the trait 'Bovarism', using the concept in reference to 'an invincible disenchantment with our own reality'. Since then, the idea has been adopted by the *Carioca* (inhabitant of Rio) literati to describe the Brazilian addiction to 'foreignisms', to 'copying everything as if it were its own raw material'.

The term 'bovarismo' originates with Gustave Flaubert's *Madame Bovary*, and defines the altered sense of reality when a person thinks of himself or herself as someone else. This psychological state generates chronic dissatisfaction, produced by the contrast between illusions and aspirations, and, above all, by the continuous disparity between these illusions and reality. Now imagine this same phenomenon transferred from an individual to an entire community that conceives itself as something that it is not and is waiting for some unexpected event that will transform its dismal reality. According to Buarque de Holanda (and Lima Barreto), all Brazilians have an element of Madame Bovary.

At football matches, an iconic metaphor for Brazilian nationality, everyone waits for 'something to happen' that will save the game. People cross their fingers in the hope that some magical intervention will fall from the skies (alleviating malaise and solving all problems). Immediatism takes the place of planning substantive, long-term changes. The current fashion is for Brazilians to identify themselves as members of the BRICS, and to cling to the belief that the country has joined the ranks of Russia, India, China and South Africa because of the extraordinary economic growth of recent years, and with a greater degree of autonomy.[1] If Brazil has truly achieved such remarkable economic growth – and is really the seventh largest economy in the world, not to mention the country's enormous, and little exploited, natural resources – it should not be ignoring serious social problems in the areas of transport, health, education and housing which, although there has been considerable progress, are still woefully inadequate.

'Bovarism' is also implicit in a very Brazilian form of collective evasion, which allows Brazilians to reject the country as it really is and imagine a quite different one – since the real Brazil is unsatisfactory and, worse still, citizens feel impotent regarding their ability to make changes. In the void between what Brazilians are and how they perceive themselves, nearly all possible identities have been explored: white, black, mulatto, savage, North American, European, and now, BRICS. The tropical version of Hamlet's 'To be or not to be' is 'To be is not to be'. Or, in the words of film critic Paulo Emílio Sales Gomes, 'the arduous construction of ourselves [that] develops in the rarefied dialectic between not being and being someone else'.

This concept also explains another local obsession: looking at ourselves in the mirror and always seeing something different. At times more French, at others more American; at times more backward, at others more advanced: but always different. In various phases of Brazilian history, this type of idealized construction of the country served to foment Brazilian nationalism.

At any rate, despite the ambiguities of the national discourse, colonial nations of the recent past, like Brazil, are obsessed with creating an identity that is comparable to an inflatable mattress. For these countries, national identity is always in question. We know, however, that identities are not essential phenomena and, far less, atemporal. On the contrary, they are dynamic, political and flexible representations, reactions to negotiations in given situations. This is perhaps the reason why Brazilians cling to the idea that this plasticity and spontaneity are an integral part of their national practices and ethos. From this viewpoint, Brazil becomes the land of improvisation where things always turn out well, and the popular proverb (with its ill-concealed certainty), 'God is Brazilian', can be understood. Whether by witchcraft, invoking the aid of the saints or through prayers and incantations, beliefs and religions intermingle for the desired miracle to materialize.

Brazilian Bovarism is implicit in another characteristic that defines nationality: 'familyism' – the deep-rooted custom of transforming public issues into private ones. A good politician becomes a 'member of the family' who is always referred to by his Christian name: Getúlio, Juscelino, Jango, Lula, Dilma. It seems no coincidence that during the dictatorship the generals were referred to by their surnames: Castello Branco, Costa e Silva, Geisel, Médici and Figueiredo. As Buarque de Holanda argued, Brazil has always been characterized by the precedence of affection and emotion over the rigorous impersonality of principles that organize society in so many other countries. 'We will give the world a cordial man', as Buarque de Holanda said, not in a celebratory tone, rather regretting and criticizing Brazil's tortuous entry into modernity. The word 'cordial' derives from the Latin 'cor, cordis', semantically linked to the Brazilian word for 'heart' (*coração*) and to the supposition that, in Brazil, intimacy is the norm (even the names of saints are used in the diminutive), revealing an extraordinary lack of commitment to the idea of the public good and a clear aversion to those in power. Worse still, Buarque de Holanda's argument has been rejected in most circles, and his notion of 'cordial' widely misinterpreted. It was seen as a parody of Brazil's cordiality, a harmonious, receptive people who reject violence. It was not understood in the critical sense, as a reference to the difficulty in being proactive in establishing effective institutions. Another example of Bovarism is how lasting Brazil's self-image has been: a peace-loving country, one that rejects radicalism, despite the innumerable rebellions, revolts and protests that have punctuated Brazilian history since the outset. Brazil is and is not: an ambiguity far more productive than a handful of stilted official images.

Sound ideologies, therefore, can be compared to tattoos or an *idée fixe*; they appear to have the power of imposing themselves on society and generating reality. Hearing them constantly, Brazilians end up believing in a country where hearsay is more important than reality. Brazilians have constructed a dreamt-up image of a different Brazil – based on their imagination, happiness and a particular way of confronting difficulties – and have ended up as its mirror image. All this is well and good. But the country continues to be the champion of social inequality and is still struggling to construct true republican values and true citizens.

Once this internal dialectic has been recognized, the next step is to understand that it is not in fact exclusively internal. The country has always been defined by those looking on from outside. Since the sixteenth century, before Brazil was Brazil, when it still constituted an unknown Portuguese America, it was observed with considerable curiosity. The territory, the 'other' of the West, was either represented through what it *did not* possess – neither laws, rules nor hierarchy – or else by what it demonstrated in excess – lust, sex, laziness and partying. Seen from this angle the country would merely be at the margins of the civilized world, a gauche culture filled with uncouth people, who are nevertheless peace-loving and happy. In advertising, and according to foreigners, Brazil is still seen as hospitable, with exotic values, and home to a type of 'universal native', since the country is apparently inhabited by an amalgam of 'foreign peoples' from around the world.

Although Brazil is undeniably blessed by a series of 'miracles' – a temperate climate (sixteenth-century travellers called it 'the land of eternal spring'), an absence of natural catastrophes (hurricanes, tsunamis or earthquakes) and of institutionalized and official antagonism towards certain groups – it is certainly neither the promised land nor 'the land of the future'. There are those who have attempted to cast Brazil as representing an alternative solution to the impasses and contradictions of the West. Inspired by the idea of cannibalism, as witnessed by the first visitors, later developed by Montaigne, and even later reinterpreted in the twentieth century by Oswald de Andrade in his 'Manifesto antropófago' (1928), Brazilians have an obsession with reinventing themselves, with transforming failings into virtues and omens. Cannibalizing customs, defying conventions and upsetting premises is still a local characteristic, a ritual of insubordination for nonconformists that perhaps sets Brazilians apart, or at least keeps the flame of utopia alive.

Ever since the arrival of Cabral and his fleet of caravels, Brazil has been a paradise for some, an endless hell for others, and for the rest, a kind of purgatory on earth. Despite these characteristics being identified with the past, they are still alive and well. Around 1630, Vicente do Salvador, a Franciscan friar, considered Brazil's first historian, wrote in his short *History of Brazil*: 'There is not a single man in this land who is republican, who cares for or administers the public wealth; instead, it is every man for himself.'

Since the very beginning of the country's short history, of five hundred years or so, from the establishment of the first plantations in the territories that were later to constitute Brazil, the difficulty in sharing power and engendering a sense of common good was evident. However, despite Frei Vicente's comment, republican values do exist in Brazil. Inventing an imaginary construction of public life is a typically Brazilian way of avoiding the impasse generated in the interior of a society that has been a success in some aspects while a failure in others.

Thus Brazil's development was born of ambivalence and contrast. On the one hand, it is a country with a high degree of social inequality and high rates of illiteracy, whereas on the other its electoral system is one of the most sophisticated and reliable in the world. Brazil has rapidly modernized its industrial parks, and it has the second-highest number of Facebook users in the world. At the same time, vast geographical regions lie abandoned, particularly in the north, where the chief means of transport is by rudimentary sailboats. Brazil has an advanced constitution that forbids any kind of discrimination, yet in reality, silent and perverse forms of prejudice are deeply ingrained and pervade everyday life. In Brazil the traditional and the cosmopolitan, the urban and the rural, the exotic and the civilized, walk hand in hand. The archaic and the modern intermingle, the one questioning the other in a kind of ongoing interrogation.

No single book can relate the history of Brazil. In fact there is no country whose history can be related in linear form, as a sequence of events, or even in a single version. This book does not set out to tell the story of Brazil, but to make Brazil the story. In the words of Hannah Arendt, both the historian and her or his reader learn to 'train the imagination to go out on a visit'. This book takes her notion of 'a visit' seriously. It does not intend to construct a 'general history of the Brazilian people', but rather opts for a biography as an alternative form of understanding Brazil in a historical perspective: to learn about the many events that have shaped the country, and to a certain extent remain on the national agenda.

A biography is the most basic example of the profound connection between the public and the private spheres: only when articulated do these spheres constitute the fabric of a life, rendering it forever real. To write about the life of this country implies questioning the episodes that have formed its trajectory over time and learning from them about public life, about the world and about contemporary Brazil – in order to understand the Brazilians of the past, and those that should or could have been.

The imagination and the diversity of sources are important prerequisites in the composition of a biography. A biography includes great figures, politicians, public servants and 'celebrities'; it also includes people of little importance, who are virtually anonymous. But constructing a biography is never an easy task: it is very difficult to reconstitute the moment that inspired the gesture. One must 'walk in the dead man's shoes', according to the historian Evaldo Cabral, to connect the public to the private, to penetrate a time which is not our own, open doors that do not belong to us, be aware of how people in history felt and attempt to understand the trajectory of the subjects of the biography – in this case the Brazilian people – during the time they lived: what they achieved in the public sphere, over the centuries, with the resources that were available to them; the fact that they lived according to the demands of their period, not of ours. And, at the same time, not to be indifferent to the pain and joy of everyday Brazilians, but to enter into their private world and listen to their voices. The historian has to find a way of dealing with the blurred line between retrieving experience, recognizing that this experience is fragile and inconclusive, and interpreting its meaning. Thus a biography is also a form of historiography.

For similar reasons this book does not go beyond the year that marked the final phase of democratization after the dictatorship, with the election of President Fernando Henrique Cardoso in 1995. It is our view that the effects of the governments of Cardoso and his successor Lula are yet to be fully felt and that they mark the beginning of a new phase in the country's history. The present has been influenced by both presidents, and perhaps it is the task of the journalist to register the effects of their governments.

It is evident, then, that this book does not attempt to cover the entire history of Brazil. Rather, bearing in mind the issues mentioned above, it narrates the adventure of the construction of a complicated 'society in the tropics'. As the writer Mário de Andrade said, Brazil explodes every conception that we may have of it. Far from the image of a meek and pacific country, with its supposed racial democracy, this book describes the vicissitudes of a nation which, with its profound *mestiçagem*, has managed to reconcile a rigid hierarchy, conditioned by shared internal values, with its own particular social idiom. Seen from this angle, in the words of the songwriter and composer Tom Jobim, 'Brazil is not for beginners.' It needs a thorough translation.

BRAZIL

A BIOGRAPHY

I

First Came the Name,
and Then the Land Called Brazil

*Pedro Álvares Cabral, a young man escaping from tedium,
found pandemonium; in other words he found Brazil.*
Stanislaw Ponte Preta[1]

ON THE VICISSITUDES
OF A NEW WORLD

It is hard to conceive the impact and the significance of the 'discovery of a new world'. New, as it was uncharted on existing maps; new, as it was populated with unknown wildlife and plants; new, as it was inhabited by strange people, who practised polygamy, went about naked, and whose main occupations were waging war and 'eating each other'. They were 'cannibals', according to the earliest reports, which were fanciful, exotic and brimming with imagination.

It was the Genovese explorer himself, Christopher Columbus,[2] who coined the term *canibal*, a corruption of the Spanish word *caribal* ('from the Caribbean'). The term originated from the Arawak language spoken by the *caraíba*, the indigenous people of South America and the Antilles, and soon became associated with the practices reported by European explorers, who were disturbed by the anthropophagical[3] habits of the local people. It was also associated with the word *can*, the Spanish for 'dog', and with the biblical figure *Cam* (in English spelt 'Ham' or 'Cham'). In the book of Genesis *Cam*, Noah's youngest son, mocked his father's nakedness as he lay drunk in his tent. For this Noah cursed him to be his brothers' 'servant of servants'.[4] Thus the seeds were sown for the Church's future justification of the enslavement of black Africans – and, by association, the

Indians – both of whom were considered to be descendants of the cursed line of Ham.[5]

In the diary of his first expedition to the Caribbean (1492–3), Columbus, with a mixture of curiosity and indignation, comments on the fact that the island's natives were in the habit of eating human flesh, and uses the adjective *caribes* (or *canibes*) to describe them. It was on his second expedition to the Antilles (1493–6) that the term first appears as an adjective, *canibal*. The spreading of the news that the indigenous peoples of the Americas practised cannibalism would provide a convenient justification for the monarchy's new proposal: the implementation of slavery. In his letter to their Catholic Majesties Ferdinand and Isabella of Spain, Columbus declared that the natives were lazy and lacking in modesty – they covered their bodies in war paint and wore no clothes, using only necklaces, bracelets and tattoos to cover their intimate parts. The argument went that although the cannibals were devoid of the values of Western civilization, they could be put to good use as slaves.

In his letters, Amerigo Vespucci also mentioned the presence of cannibals in America. One letter, allegedly from Vespucci to Lorenzo di Pierfrancesco de' Medici,[6] which was printed in book form in 1504 under the title *Mundus Novus*, immediately became a great success and was published in various parts of Europe. Vespucci's observations had an even greater impact than Columbus's, as they described scenes of cannibalism the author had witnessed first-hand and were illustrated with graphic prints. Vespucci's persuasive arguments, accompanied by equally persuasive images, made a decisive contribution to the demonization of the indigenous peoples of the Americas. They were portrayed as a people with no social order or religious faith and with no notion of property, territory or money, ignorant of institutions such as the family and marriage.[7] His image of the New World was inextricably associated with a decadent people. They were seemingly another part of humanity, oblivious to the values of the Old World.

The news that arrived from this Portuguese part of the Americas, replete with tales of its paradisiacal natural abundance and the diabolical practices of its people, ignited the imagination of Europeans. The realization that an unknown, unfathomed territory existed marked the beginning of a new chapter in the history of humanity. The canon of Brazilian history begins with the achievement of the 'discoverers', who not only founded the new Portuguese territory but also had a clear perception of its value. Paradoxically though, this official, metropolitan narrative would always be altered when indigenous peoples were included in the story – those apparently forgotten by humanity, impossible to classify, name or understand.

But if the tone of these descriptions was marked by surprised reactions – the logs described sea monsters, gigantic animals, warriors and cannibals – historians no longer contend that the Americas were discovered by chance. After Vasco da Gama established the sea route to the Indies in 1499, the Portuguese monarchy immediately planned a further expedition based on the information he brought back. This, clearly, was the best way forward for the kingdom of Portugal, a tiny nation located at the mouth of the Atlantic Ocean. The country had finally unified its territory after years of fighting against the Moors, who had occupied the Iberian Peninsula. The unification was completed by Dom Afonso III[8] with the reconquest of the Algarve in 1249. The unification, along with the development of its navy and of maritime instruments, placed Portugal in a privileged position to undertake the great explorations. And it is no coincidence that the first conquest by the Portuguese Empire, the longest-lasting colonial empire with domains on four continents, was that of Ceuta, on the West African coast, in 1415.

From the outset Portugal's impulse to expand was based on a combination of commercial, military and evangelizing interests. During the fourteenth and fifteenth centuries, for example, the market for spices had motivated the Portuguese to discover new routes to the East. The term 'spice' referred to a group of vegetable products with either a strong aroma or flavour, or both. These were used to season and to conserve foods, but also in oils, ointments, perfumes and medicine. Their consumption began to increase after the Crusades, with tropical spices such as black peppercorns, cloves, cinnamon and nutmeg in highest demand in the fourteenth century. These spices were indigenous to Asia and commanded a very considerable price. They were used as currency, included in the dowries of aristocrats and royalty, in bequests, in capital reserves and in revenues of the Crown. They were also used for bartering – in exchange for services, in agreements, for meeting religious obligations and obtaining tax exemption – as well as for bribing high-ranking officials.

When the Ottoman Turks took Constantinople, on 29 May 1453, however, the spice routes came under Turkish control and were closed to Christian merchants. As a result, the Spanish and Portuguese embarked on exploratory expeditions to discover new routes, by land and sea, with the aim of monopolizing the spice trade. They attempted to circumnavigate the African continent, a hazardous venture that had never been undertaken before. Success would take a century, but the delay would prove advantageous. Portugal set up trading posts along the African coast, which became strategic locations for present and future colonization.

The route was consolidated with the arrival of the Portuguese in the East, and became known as the 'African Periplus'. Originally, the term implied a good omen: a long journey undertaken and a successful return. But with time, since language is always subject to the oscillations and moods of any given period, the term acquired a more negative connotation, associated with failed ventures and the 'curse of Sisyphus'. It was used to refer to all those who had undertaken adventures that had proved beyond their powers to complete, just as Sisyphus, in Greek mythology, had cheated Death, but only for a time. In Portuguese, a 'periplus' came to mean a journey without end that led to nowhere. But such scepticism proved to be unfounded. The new route generated extraordinary dividends and served as a symbol for Portugal's entry into the modern era. It was the departure point for the construction of an extensive and powerful empire.

Spain was also undergoing a process of colonial expansion. The Spanish kingdom, which had been unified as the National State in 1492, had set out to discover a new route to the East by travelling west. To prevent further battles in a Europe perpetually embroiled in conflict, on 7 June 1494 the Treaty of Tordesillas was signed, dividing 'discovered or yet-to-be discovered' territories between the crowns of Portugal and Spain. The agreement was the immediate response to the Portuguese Crown's challenge to a claim made by the Spanish Crown. A year and a half earlier the Spanish had arrived at what they believed to be the Indies, but was in fact the New World, officially laying claim to it for the Catholic Queen Isabella. Although no one yet knew where these lands would lead, through the Treaty of Tordesillas they now had an owner and a certificate of origin.[9]

There was a forerunner to the Treaty of Tordesillas: the papal bull

Inter Caetera, signed by Pope Alexander VI on 4 May 1493, which divided the New World between Portugal and Spain. In practice, this meant that all lands situated up to 100 leagues to the west of the Cape Verde Islands would belong to Portugal, and those further than 100 leagues to Spain. Fearing it could lose potential conquests, Portugal proposed a revision of the bull and managed to have it amended. The Treaty of Tordesillas, signed by both monarchies, defined the dividing line as the meridian located 370 leagues to the west of an unspecified island in the Cape Verde archipelago (a Portuguese domain), at the halfway mark between Cape Verde and the Caraíbas, discovered by Columbus. The treaty also stipulated that all territories east of the meridian would belong to Portugal, and all those to the west, to Spain. It was signed by Spain on 2 June and by Portugal on 5 September 1494, as if the world – real, or as they imagined it to be – could simply be divided into two, with no further dispute.

Brazil, for example, which did not yet appear on any world map, was already included in the agreement: the line established in the treaty cut vertically down the country from approximately the present-day location of Belém, the capital of the northern state of Pará, to the town of Laguna in the southern state of Santa Catarina. However, at the time Portugal showed little interest in exploring this putative territory, mainly because the profits from its trade with the East were sufficient to meet its needs. Nevertheless, a further expedition was organized in 1500, this time under the command of Captain-General Pedro Álvares de Gouveia, a member of the minor aristocracy who had inherited his name from the family of his mother, Dona Isabel de Gouveia. He later changed his name to Pedro Álvares Cabral, adopting the surname of his father, Fernão Cabral, commander of the fortress in the town of Belmonte. As is the case with the other major explorers, very little is known about him. In 1479, at the age of about twelve, he had been sent to the court of the Portuguese king, Dom Afonso V.[10] He was educated in Lisbon, where he studied humanities, and was brought up to fight for his country.

On 30 June 1484, when he was about seventeen, Cabral received the title of junior cavalier of the first order of nobility at the court of Dom João II[11] – a title of no great significance that was generally conferred on young aristocrats – and received an annuity from the Crown of 26,000 réis in recognition of his services. In 1494 he was promoted to

Knight of the Order of Christ, Portugal's most prestigious chivalric order. He received a further annuity of 40,000 réis, probably, as in the case of other young members of the aristocracy, as remuneration for the journeys he undertook to North Africa. Although no pictures of him have survived, Cabral is known to have been a man of sturdy build and tall, almost six feet three inches in height (the same as his father). There are accounts that describe him as learned, courteous, tolerant with his enemies and also vain, as was often the case with nobles who achieved such high-ranking posts. He was generally thought to be wise and canny, and despite his lack of experience, he was placed in command of the largest fleet that had ever set sail from Portugal, to lands that were as distant as they were unknown.

Very few documents survive that shed light on the criteria for choosing who was to command the expedition to the Indies. The decree appointing Cabral as captain-general mentions only his 'merits and services'. But it is known that the king was well acquainted with the members of his court, and that the Cabral family was famous for its loyalty to the Portuguese Crown. Cabral was also a member of the King's Council, and his appointment may have helped to resolve a complex political intrigue. There are those who see it as a deliberate manoeuvre to balance two factions of the nobility, because, despite his personal qualities, Cabral lacked the experience to command such an important expedition. It is interesting to note that more experienced Portuguese navigators, such as Bartolomeu Dias, Diogo Dias and Nicolau Coelho, were appointed as ship captains and sailed under Cabral's command.

The captain-general's salary was high: Cabral received 10,000 cruzados (the equivalent of 35 kilos of gold) and the right to buy 30 tons of pepper and ten crates of any other spice, at his own expense, and to resell them in Europe free of taxes. Thus, although the journey was extremely hazardous, it would ensure that on his return Cabral would be a very rich man, as, despite the high demand, the spices were extremely rare.[12] The captains received a thousand cruzados for every hundred barrels of storage space aboard, as well as six 'unencumbered'[13] crates and fifty 'quintais'[14] of pepper.[15] Sailors earned ten cruzados a month and ten 'quintais' of pepper, cabin-boys half of this, and swabbers a third. In addition there were the boatswain and the ship's guardian, who received the wages of 'one and a half sailors'. There were also priests aboard, who acted not only as spiritual guides but also as doctors – as well as the inevitable prostitutes, often concealed among the crew. This very masculine world was not inclined to dispense with its women of 'dubious repute' who sometimes got pregnant on the high seas and gave birth to their children on-board.

The expedition crew was made up of around a thousand men. Seven hundred of these were designated as soldiers, although in fact they were untrained men from peasant families, many of whom had been press-ganged. And there was no lack of problems on this veritable floating citadel. A priest, Fernando Oliveira, who travelled on many such expeditions, gave the following cautious advice: 'On the sea there are no shops, no comfortable lodgings on enemy territory; for this reason each man brings provisions from his home.'[16] Only the captain was allowed to bring chickens aboard – which were mostly used for feeding the sick – as well as goats, pigs and even cows. But the livestock was never shared with the crew, who generally went hungry.

On a journey without incident, the food on-board was barely enough to satisfy the sailors' basic needs. The situation worsened considerably during the calms, or when, due to the ineptitude of the steersman, the ship sailed off course, unexpectedly prolonging the journey. Dry biscuits, present from the earliest days of navigation, were the main food item on-board. There was also a good supply of wine. The daily ration was a quarter of a litre, the same amount as for the water used for drinking and cooking. However, the water was often stored in unhygienic casks, which led to a proliferation of bacteria and outbreaks of diarrhea and other infections among the crew. The distribution of meat was highly controlled, handed out every other day; on the alternate days meals consisted of cheese or fish with rice, when available. Storage also presented a frequent problem. Since most of the food came on-board with the crew, infestations of rats, cockroaches and beetles were a common occurrence, all competing for the food with equal voracity. There were no bathrooms on these ships – small seats were suspended over the side, causing a permanent stench on deck.

With so many hygiene problems, illnesses were frequent during the crossings. Scurvy, caused by a lack of vitamin C (later known as gum or Luanda sickness), was among the most common, along with pleural and pulmonary diseases. As deaths occurred almost daily, the only solution was to lay the bodies out on deck, summon the priest to say a quick prayer, and cast them overboard.

During these journeys across unchartered waters, violence, theft, and every conceivable type of corruption abounded. Crimes, assaults and fights tended to increase in direct proportion to the degree of general uncertainty on-board ship. There were very few activities to alleviate the tension: card games, collective theatre, reading profane and religious books, and processions around the deck.

Strictly speaking, maritime exploration was a private enterprise. But it was also entirely financed by the royal family and closely supervised by the king himself. It required massive investment as well as representing enormous personal risk, which had to be highly remunerated to make it worthwhile. In return the monarchy reserved the right to control all territories conquered, to distribute lands and monopolize the profits. Thus the departure of such an expedition demanded a ritual commemoration.

The fleet that sailed from the Tagus at midday on 9 March 1500 was a very fine sight – thirteen vessels, probably ten sailing ships and three caravels. The year, marking the turn of the century, was promising, and the season was a good one for crossing the South Atlantic. The previous day the crew had received a resounding send-off with public celebrations and a Mass in the presence of the king. Ever since Bartolomeu Dias in 1488 had rounded the Horn of Africa, which he named the Cape of Torments in a deprecative reference to St Cosmas' disease[17] (fetid rains had stained the sailors' clothes and provoked abscesses on their skin) – and especially since Dom João II had changed the name to the Cape of Good Hope – the Portuguese saw themselves as the Lords of the Seas, protected by the blessings of Fortune.

After all, whatever its name, this cape offered the only route that connected the Atlantic and Indian Oceans. The world had never appeared so navigable to the Portuguese, or so small. Nevertheless, the Atlantic was 'an unknown sea', concealing every conceivable type of danger: monsters, torments, seas that ended in massive waterfalls. As described by Valentim Fernandes in an official statement dated 20 May 1503, the Atlantic was an 'unknown ocean'.[18] But the mysteries of the oceans were constantly being probed: during the nine years between Bartolomeu Dias's rounding of the Horn of Africa and the departure of Vasco da Gama's fleet in 1497, the ocean had become a laboratory for experimentation and lessons had been learnt. And so, although there were no certainties, things were not entirely left to chance. Cabral's fleet headed straight for the Cape Verde Islands, avoiding the African coast to escape being trapped in the equatorial calms. Everything points to precision and the notion that the commander was following a recognized route.

On the morning of 14 March 1500 the fleet sailed past the Canary Islands and headed towards Cape Verde, a Portuguese colony off the West African coast, where they arrived on 22 March. The following day, one of the ships, with 150 men on-board and under the command of the experienced captain Vasco de Ataíde, simply disappeared without a trace. A pall of gloom descended on the crews, who now began to dread these unknown, virtually unchartered waters. In general the men knew very little about the purpose of the expedition. With only scanty information about these parts of the world, they developed inordinately fanciful notions about treasure and mountains of gold awaiting the explorers, but also about terrible monsters – any large fish assumed mythical proportions – and every sort of nameless danger.

In fact such losses were commonplace. According to Crown data, between 1497 and 1612, 381 of the 620 ships that sailed from the Tagus did not return to Portugal; of these, 285 remained in the East, 66 were shipwrecked, 20 were driven off course, 6 caught fire and 4 were seized by enemies.[19] Storms, excess cargo, bad conditions for navigation, the poor quality of the wood used for building the caravels – most of which could only withstand one long journey – were largely responsible for this litany of woes.

But despite setbacks, the Portuguese fleet, sailing southwest away from the African continent, crossed the equator on 9 April. They used a Portuguese sailing technique that consisted of describing a large arc, skirting the central area of the calms and thus taking advantage of the favourable currents and winds. The manoeuvre was a success. As early as 21 April, Pêro Vaz de Caminha[20] recorded 'signs of land': seaweed and debris in the sea. On 22 April, Cabral's fleet sighted land to the west. At first they saw birds, probably petrels, then a large, rounded hill of considerable altitude, which they named 'Monte Pascoal' as it happened to be Easter week. They called the new land 'Terra de Vera Cruz'.[21] The initial reaction was both wonder at this 'new world, which this expedition has found', and the desire to take possession, with the Portuguese creating names for everything they had 'discovered'.

We have two surviving early descriptions of this new land, located in what we now know as the state of Bahia.[22] They were both written between 26 April and 1 May. The Spanish astronomer João Faras, more commonly known as Mestre João, was the first person to describe the sky and the stars of the New World. He considered the stars to be entirely new, 'especially those of the Cross'. This was the first recorded European observation of the Southern Cross, the constellation that would become the symbol of Brazil. The other extant document is the famous 'Letter' addressed to the King of Portugal, which is regarded as a kind of 'birth certificate' for Brazil: the founding document that marks the origin of Brazil's history. The author was Pêro Vaz de Caminha, who had travelled with the fleet to record events. Already fifty years old when he was appointed for the task, Vaz de Caminha was a trusted servant of the Crown, having served as a knight in the courts of Dom Afonso V, João II and Manuel I.[23] He gave an exultant witness report of 'the discovery of Your New World which this expedition has found'. In the eyes of the crew and their spokesman there was no doubt that this was a new land that had just been 'discovered'. As a case of 'finders keepers', the idea was to register the property at once, even though they had no clear notion of what it was that they had actually found.

And what they 'found' was a supposedly 'new' human race. A number of bizarre theories began to circulate about the origin of the Indians. In 1520, Paracelsus[24] expressed his belief that they were not descended from Adam, but were akin to giants, nymphs, gnomes and pigmies. In 1547, Gerolamo Cardano[25] stated that they were a spontaneous generation that had emerged from decomposing matter, like worms or mushrooms. Vaz de Caminha reported what he saw:

> And Nicolau Coelho signalled to them to put down their bows. They laid them down. But it was not possible to hear them or understand anything of use, as the waves were breaking on the shore. He only gave them a *biretta*, a linen skullcap that he wore on his head, and a black straw hat. And one of them gave him a headband made of birds' feathers, very long, with a crown of red and brown feathers, like a parrot's.

The exchange described here remains widely debated in Brazil: what was the tone of this seminal moment of conquest? Was it perceived as a 'friendly encounter', a case of give-and-take, despite the political, cultural and linguistic differences?

Vaz de Caminha was fascinated by these new people:

> They are brown skinned, with a reddish complexion, with handsome
> faces and well-formed noses. They go about naked, without clothing.
> They feel no need to cover their private parts, which they show as readily
> as they show their faces. In this matter they are of great innocence.[26]

He was amazed by their 'red skin and silky hair', and by their beauty, both of body and of soul. This was the origin of the somewhat over-used cliché of the Brazilian 'noble savage', a trope frequently used by French explorers, and later adopted by Rousseau in the eighteenth century. But whereas for the Enlightenment philosopher the concept served as a useful foil in criticizing Europe and its civilization – and bore no relation to any direct observation – for the first arrivals in Brazil the perception was real. Here were good heathens who could be catechized and converted to the true faith. Thus, on Easter Sunday 1500 a wooden altar was erected for the priests to celebrate Mass. The captain-general displayed the flag of Christ – linking the prowess of men to the powers of the divine – 'and a solemn, salutary sermon was given, narrating the story of Christ; and at the end, the story of our arrival and the discovery of this land, in the name of the Cross.'

Next, on the Friday, the first day of May, they searched upriver for the best place to raise a cross so that it could be seen from all around. Once the cross and the royal crest had been erected, the priest, Friar Henrique, celebrated Mass, which, according to Vaz de Caminha, 'was attended by fifty or sixty of them, all on their knees', in addition to the other members of the fleet. At the moment when the Gospel was read and everyone stood and raised their hands, Vaz de Caminha noted that the Indians followed suit. He was amazed when they actually took communion: 'One of them, a man of about fifty-five, stood among those who were taking communion [. . .] and walking among them, speaking to them, pointed a finger at the altar and then up at the sky, as if they were a portent of good things to come: and so we took them to be!'

Vaz de Caminha was clearly entranced by what he saw, and his report became the source of another recurrent myth – that of a peaceful conquest, a communion of hearts united in religion. It was the start of a curious process by which Brazil came to be seen as a country without conflict, as if the tropics – by some miracle or by divine intervention – could melt tensions and avert war. While Europe was divided by wars and immersed in bloodshed, in the New World, according to the Europeans, if wars existed they were only small internal ones. The first encounter was supposed to have been unequalled and between equals, however much time proved the opposite: a story of genocide and conquest.

By this time the Portuguese already saw themselves as the owners of the new land and the lords of its destiny, frontiers and names. Nevertheless, the discovery did not initially redirect the interests of the Portuguese, who only had eyes for the East. Thus, for some time, the vast new area was reserved for the future. But international competition, the menace of other nations and quarrels over the bilateral Treaty of Tordesillas did not permit this state of affairs to last for long. The Spanish were already occupying the northeastern coast of South America, while the British and the French, who rejected the division of the globe between Spain and Portugal, made incursions at various points along the coast. Francis I of France[27] commented tersely: 'I'd like to see the clause of Adam's will that divided the world between Portugal and Spain and denied me my share.'

By 1530 it was already evident to Dom João III[28] that the papal sovereignty legitimizing the treaty would not be enough to scare away the French corsairs who were settling with increasing frequency in his American domains. The solution was to create a number of colonizing fronts, basically independent, that frequently communicated more with Lisbon than between themselves. The administrative system adopted was that of hereditary captaincies, which the Portuguese had already successfully used in their colonies of Cape Verde and the island of Madeira. The concept was simple: as the Crown had limited financial and human resources, so it delegated the task of colonizing and exploiting vast areas of territory to private citizens, granting them tracts of land with hereditary rights.

In 1534 the Portuguese government began the process of dividing Brazil into fourteen captaincies that were granted to twelve men, known as donees. Since the interior of the country was completely unknown, it was decided to imagine parallel strips of coastline that stretched inland as far as the *sertão*.[29] All the beneficiaries were members of the minor nobility; seven had served with distinction in the African campaigns and in India, and four were high-ranking court officials. The system granted them jurisdiction over their captaincies with supreme powers to develop the region and enslave the Indians. The extreme isolation, however, proved to be highly detrimental. So much so that in 1572 the Crown divided the country into two departments: the Northern Government, with its capital in Salvador, was responsible for the region that went from the captaincy of the Bahia de Todos os Santos to the captaincy of Maranhão. The Southern Government, based in Rio de Janeiro, was responsible for the region that stretched from Ilhéus[30] to the southernmost point of the colony. In this way territories within territories were created, regions that barely recognized each other as belonging to a single political and administrative unit.

Actually, once this strange world, along the route to the Indies, had been 'discovered', it was decided it should at least be named. For many years the Portuguese did not quite know what to make of this new territory, and there was plenty of indecision. To offset this, after 1501 the expeditions sent to explore the coast had started to name geographical features and to measure and classify latitudes, based on the premise that it really was a new continent. Despite their lack of interest in the territory – especially because, at the outset, they had failed to find the vast quantities of silver and gold that had gladdened the hearts of the Spaniards – they needed to give it a name.[31] In their letters both Mestre João and Vaz de Caminha called it *Vera Cruz* or *Santa Cruz*. But there was no general agreement; after 1501, at times the territory was called *Terra dos Papagaios* (Land of the Parrots), in a reference to the multicoloured birds that could talk (even though no one understood what they said), and at others *Terra de Santa Cruz* (Land of the Holy Cross). This latter was used by Dom Manuel I in the letter he sent to the King of Spain. It was also the name of the place where the first Mass had been celebrated, described at length by Vaz de Caminha and seen as the location of the military and Christian inauguration of the territory. According to the contemporary report of João de Barros, Cabral had dedicated the possession of Santa Cruz to the cause of the Holy Cross, and associated the celebration of the Mass to the sacrifice of Christ, transported to the land they had 'found'. It should, therefore, be entirely dedicated to God, to whom the greatest service would be the conversion of the heathens.

The rumours and conflicting reports of the early days were followed by a growing awareness of the need to protect the new territory from foreign attacks. It had to be peopled and colonized and some sort of economic activity had to be stimulated. Apart from parrots and monkeys, the only tradable product was a 'dye wood', well known in the East as a valuable pigment that could fetch high prices in Europe. Thus, shortly after Cabral's expedition, other Portuguese navigators set sail to explore the new territory and extract this native plant.

Brazilwood,[32] which grew abundantly along the coast, was originally called 'Ibirapitanga' by the Tupi Indians. Often growing as high as 15 metres, the tree has a large trunk, sturdy branches and thorn-covered pods. It was in high demand for making quality furniture, and for its reddish resin that was used for dyeing cloth. It is thought that about 70 million of these trees existed when the Portuguese arrived. In the years that followed, the species was decimated by Portuguese loggers, with the aid of Indian labour, which they bartered. As early as 900 CE the wood can be found in the records of the East Indies, listed among a number of plants that produced a reddish dye. Both the tree and the dye went by many different names: *brecillis, bersil, brezil, brasil, brazily*, all of which were derived from the Latin word *brasilia*, meaning a glowing red, 'the colour of embers'. The first recorded arrival of a '*kerka de bersil*' in Europe was in France, as far back as 1085. During Gaspar de Lemos's expedition in 1501, Amerigo Vespucci had noted a cargo of this beautiful wood.

In 1502 the colonizers were already starting to exploit brazilwood more systematically. Although it was not considered as valuable as the merchandise from the East, it generated considerable interest: indirectly, the Portuguese had gone back to the spice trade. The Portuguese Crown immediately declared it a royal monopoly, only permitting its exploitation via the payment of taxes. The first concession was granted in 1501 to Fernando de Noronha,[33] who was also granted an island, the island of São João, later converted into a captaincy that took the donee's name. Labour was provided by the Indians in exchange for trinkets. They cut down the trees and carried them to the Portuguese ships anchored near the shore; in return they received knives, penknives, pieces of cloth and other knick-knacks. The first ship carrying brazilwood to Portugal, the *Bretoa*, sailed in 1511, with five thousand logs, as well as monkeys, cats, a large quantity of parrots, and forty Indians, who excited great curiosity among the Europeans.[34]

In 1512, or thereabouts, with the product established on the international market, the term *Brazil* became the official name for Portuguese

America. But other names, or combinations of names, remained in parallel use. These included both *Terra Sante Crusis de lo Brasil* and *Terra Sante Crusis del Portugal*. Behind this divergence in terminology lay a more complex dispute, between the secular and the spiritual powers. The cross erected on that distant hilltop had experienced a short reign; it was the Devil who now held sway. Christian chroniclers deplored the fact that, as the shiploads of merchandise increased, material interests were replacing those of the Holy Cross in this new kingdom. João de Barros, for example, lamented that more importance was given 'to the name of a wood for dyeing cloth' than to 'that wood that gave its colour to the Eucharist by which we were saved, dyed in the blood of Christ that was shed upon it'.[35]

Thus began the struggle between the red 'blood of Christ' and the 'red dye' that would become increasingly associated with the Devil. This was further fuelled by the work of Pero de Magalhães Gândavo,[36] who was probably a copyist at the National Archive in Lisbon.[37] In his *História da província de Santa Cruz*, published in 1576, he called for a return to the original name, arguing that trying to extinguish the memory of the Holy Cross was the work of the Devil. It was an uphill struggle; colonization was well under way, with the colonizers increasingly linking the role of trade with the Church's religious and catechizing mission. Although the Devil might continue to be present, they argued their work was also that of the Lord. The new colony's contested name captures an ambivalence and discomfort that came to be reflected in the expression of deeper concerns about the place.

It was at this time that reports on the New World began to cease distinguishing between the land, its products and the native people. Sérgio Buarque de Holanda, in *Visão do Paraíso*,[38] recalls an ancient Celtic myth that could provide an alternative explanation for the origin of the name. According to the myth, there were islands in the Atlantic that were lost in space and time and covered in lichens and other dye-producing plants such as 'Dragon blood', both of which produced a red-coloured resin. The historian concludes that the name has its origins in the Irish expressions *Hy Bressail* and *O'Brazil*, meaning 'Island of Good Fortune'.

Islands are ideal places for projected utopias. The Irish 'Isle of Brazil' was originally a phantom island, lost in time, that re-emerged near the Azores in the fifteenth century. It was also associated with Saint

Brendan's 'Isle of the Blessed'. The paradise Vaz de Caminha described recalls the utopian 'Isle of Brazil'. This would also explain why the name *Obrasil* appears on a number of maps from the beginning of the sixteenth century. The Irish myths were part of a religious and Edenic tradition that greatly appealed to the cartographers of the period. The name first appeared in 1330, as the designation of a mysterious island, and in 1353 it was still present on an English map. At any rate, during the period of the 'discoveries' there was a clear association between the Indians, their longevity and Edenic living conditions, and these other mysterious lands. And the mystery was to remain untouched for a long, long time, just like the ambivalence regarding the (glowing coal) red brazilwood and the wood of Christ. Perhaps the best thing to do was to light one candle for God, and blow out another for the Devil.[39]

HEAVEN OR HELL: NATURE AND NATIVES IN SIXTEENTH-CENTURY ACCOUNTS

Along with its chosen name, whether it be Brazil, Land of the Holy Cross, Land of the Parrots, or Portuguese America, there came a certain ambivalence, but there was also one certainty: the place had taken on the role of an 'other', both its nature and its natives.[40] And while its natural surroundings were seen as a paradise – an eternal spring inhabited by harmless animals – its peoples were increasingly becoming a cause for concern. Soldiers, commanders, corsairs, priests and the merely curious avidly traded florid stories. These fantasies built on the venerable tradition of travellers' extravagant accounts, tales going beyond what the eye could behold or what the intellect could accept, like those found in *Navigatio Sancti Brendani Abbatis*,[41] Aethicus Ister's *Cosmographia*,[42] Pierre d'Ailly's *Imago Mundi*,[43] *The Travels of John Mandeville*[44] and other writings popular in the early sixteenth century.[45]

In such traveller's tales, these wonderful regions were sometimes described as earthly paradises, with fertile plains and fountains of youth; at other times, they were portrayed as godforsaken terrains populated by misshapen monsters. Such was the insistence of the literature that these places were inhabited by men with four arms or one eye at the centre of the forehead, by hermaphrodites, pigmies and enchanted mermaids, it is hardly surprising that in one of his first letters home, Columbus, relieved but a little disappointed, admitted to having seen no human monsters and that, to the contrary, the natives' bodies were very well formed.[46] Nevertheless, monsters were still depicted in drawings and maps and associated with the practice of cannibalism. This in turn led to philosophical and religious discussions about the nature of these pagan peoples. For some they were the descendants of Adam and Eve; for others they were ferocious beasts.

This kind of literature was to proliferate in the sixteenth and seventeenth centuries. In European thought, this meeting with America was to be the most grandiose achievement in modern Western history, considered with both trepidation and wonder. This explains in part why travel narratives recreated within the New World a myth that had once been held to be true: the presence of a heaven on earth. Still, the customs of the heathens were hardly compatible with a terrestrial paradise. Although the impact of negative images was perhaps on balance not as strong as the Edenic portrayals, nevertheless fantasies about the natives came close to depicting them as the inhabitants of an anti-paradise, or even hell. These people, with their cannibalism, witchcraft and uncontrolled lust, must be condemned.[47]

From the sixteenth century onwards this new frontier for humanity was the subject of numerous texts. Since the concept of authorship did not really exist, often one report was reproduced and expanded by another, reinforcing fanciful notions and spreading them wider afield. The first letter about the country, written by Pêro Vaz de Caminha in 1500, was to remain unpublished until 1773. However, Amerigo Vespucci's letters to Lorenzo di Pierfrancesco de' Medici mentioned not only the Land of the Holy Cross but also its inhabitants. These documents were based on the thoughts expressed in the first of Columbus's diaries, which in turn revealed the influence of Marco Polo's and Mandeville's travel narratives. The idea began to spread that heaven on earth and the fountain of youth were located somewhere close by, as were the brave female warriors, the Amazons, who dwelt there. The travellers of various nationalities who visited the country were already well acquainted with the writings of the Italian Pigafetta,[48] who in 1519 summarized his findings as follows: 'Brazilian men and women go about naked and live to be 140.'

It was only in the 1550s that a wider range of literature about Brazil began to appear: on the one hand, the Iberian writers whose focus was on colonization; and on the other, the 'non-Iberians', mainly the French, whose interest lay in reflecting on Native Man. Among the Portuguese texts, the best known was by the previously mentioned Pero de Magalhães Gândavo, Servant and Knight of the Royal Chamber of Sebastião I,[49] Secretary of the Royal Treasury and (probably) copyist of the National Archive, who made what was generally considered to be the most authoritative contribution to the debate that had begun with Vaz de Caminha and Vespucci. Was Brazil a heaven or a hell? Were its inhabitants innocents or degenerates? While Gândavo praised the fertility of the land with its temperate, hospitable climate, he was also one of the first to describe its people as a 'multitude of barbarous heathens'. In the 1570s he wrote his *Tratado da Terra do Brasil* and in 1576 *História da província de Santa Cruz*.[50] Both were works intended to encourage the Portuguese to emigrate to and invest in their American colony, much as the British had done in Virginia. Whereas the attention of the Portuguese was still focused on the East, that of the Spanish, English and French was now directed towards the New World,[51] albeit to different regions: Peru and Mexico were to become the America of the Spanish; Florida that of the English; and Brazil that of the French.[52]

Gândavo was effusive in his praise: 'This land is so delightful and temperate that one never feels either excessive heat or cold.' It was indeed the land of abundance and eternal spring. He was less encouraging, however, about the Indians of the land: 'The language of these people who inhabit the coast is simple to describe: it lacks three letters. There is no F, no L, no K,[53] something worthy of astonishment; there is therefore neither Faith, Law nor King, and thus they live without justice or order.'[54] The native peoples were encapsulated not by the values they had, but by those they lacked. Although the natural abundance was paradisiacal, the customs of the natives were, at the very least, strange: they lived in villages 'crowded with people' and used hammocks where 'they all slept together without the existence of rules'. What is more, according to Gândavo, they were 'extremely bellicose', killing and eating their prisoners 'more out of vengeance and hatred than to satisfy their hunger'. As the book progresses, the writer shows less and less sympathy for these 'savages'. 'These Indians are extremely inhuman and cruel, they are never moved by pity. They live like wild animals without order or harmony, are very dishonest and give themselves over to lust and vice as if they possessed no human reason.'[55]

Gândavo repeated these arguments in his *História da província de Santa Cruz a que vulgarmente chamamos Brasil*.[56] Here he describes 'natives of the land' at length; with their copper-coloured skin and straight black hair, their flattened faces and 'Chink-like' features. He insists that 'they live lazily and are fickle and erratic', and 'worship nothing, having no respect for their king or any kind of justice'. Their laziness and lustfulness were symbolized by the hammock, always present in engravings of the period, as if the Americans had awaited the arrival of the Europeans lying down. In the eyes of the Church, their rituals were idolatrous, full of practices such as human sacrifice; these were false religions, practised by these devil-worshipping peoples, in complete opposition to the message of salvation and sacrifice of the Son of God, who had redeemed mankind. Indigenous beliefs were regarded as a serious instance of retrogression; they were dangerous and perfidious for the moral state of these recently conquered peoples.[57]

While Portuguese accounts of the natives were generally unfavourable, they were extremely positive when promoting the territory's natural abundance; after all, they were often written with the intention of encouraging immigration. The travellers' journals left by the French, on the other hand, created more of a commotion. Although the question of 'lack of faith' was mentioned in the texts of Norman navigators who prospered from trading in brazilwood and bartering with the Tupinambá, the French in general seemed little concerned with the natives' lack of rules and religion. Pierre de Ronsard,[58] in his *Complainte contre Fortune* (1559), describes a Golden Age of America, where he wanted to settle, and 'Where the uncultured people wander innocently about, always naked; without malice, without virtues, without vices . . .'[59] Here the word 'without' refers to the presence of qualities rather than to a lack of them. The heathens of Brazil had captured the French imagination.

An example of this was a *fête brésilienne* that was held in Rouen in 1550, in the presence of the French king, Henri II,[60] and his wife, Catherine de' Medici.[61] The city planned a magnificent reception for the royal couple, erecting grandiose monuments, including obelisks, temples and a triumphal arch, to celebrate the New World. It had been half a century since the Portuguese had arrived in America, and presenting 'the men of Brazil' – the courageous Tupinambá who fought alongside the French – was the height of fashion. Fifty Tupinambá simulated combat on the banks of the River Seine observed by the local aristocracy. To make the display more impressive, 250 'extras', dressed as Indians, joined the performers, who presented hunting expeditions, love trysts and scenes of war, as well as appearing loaded down with parrots and bananas.[62]

In contrast to such idyllic representations, a very different image – that of the Indians as cannibals – was emerging as emblematic of the way they lived. The spectre of cannibalism had haunted the European imagination since the Middle Ages, albeit with no specific location. The first place where the practice was known to occur was in Columbus's Antilles; its people were still listed as such in Diderot's *Encyclopaedia*.[63] In 1540 an edition of Ptolemy's *Geographia*[64] included a map by Sebastian Münster,[65] which had the single word 'cannibals' written across the whole of Brazil, from the Amazon Basin to the River Plate. The Indians were said to be 'dogs who kill and eat each other', evoking Renaissance images,[66] particularly that of Rabelais: 'Cannibals, monstrous people in Africa who have faces like dogs and bark instead of laughing.'[67]

The French later provided two different interpretations by creating the crucial semantic distinction between 'cannibalism' and 'anthropophagy'. Even though both terms referred to the custom of eating human flesh, in the case of the latter the practice was only adopted when the motive was highly ritualized *vengeance*. The idealization of the Brazilian Indians in eighteenth-century humanist France and by the Romantic Indianist School in nineteenth-century Brazil[68] was based on this concept, which emerged in sixteenth-century thinking.

Michel de Montaigne's 1580 essay 'The Cannibals', one of France's most celebrated humanist texts, and which uses the Tupinambá as a model, is a fine example of this strand of thought. The philosopher said the ideas for his essay had come to him after speaking to Indians who had settled in France after the *fête brésilienne* in Rouen. His essay is an exercise in relativity, in which he finds more logic in the Tupinambá methods of waging war than in those of the Europeans: 'Now, returning to the subject, I don't see anything barbaric or savage about these peoples; except that everyone considers barbaric that which is not practised in his own country.' There have been many interpretations of

Montaigne's famous essay. Perhaps what is most important to keep in mind, however, is that he expressed a more laudatory view of the native peoples, especially against the backdrop of the religious wars that assailed Europe in the sixteenth century. Nevertheless, he concludes: 'In plain truth these men are very savage in comparison to us; of necessity, they must either be absolutely so or else we are savages; for there is a vast difference between their manners and ours.'[69] But here were the beginnings of a humanist vision that questioned not so much the Indians' values as those of the Europeans.

Philosophical considerations were far from the only interest. A large number of the French reports from the sixteenth and seventeenth centuries were more concerned with France's attempts to create a colonial settlement in Brazil. In flagrant disregard of the Treaty of Tordesillas, which they refused to accept, the French made a number of incursions into the colony, of which two were more lasting. The first project for a colonial settlement – France Antarctique – was undertaken by Nicolas Durand de Villegaignon, who disembarked in Rio de Janeiro in 1555 accompanied by a large number of soldiers and artisans. However, the following year Villegaignon wrote to John Calvin, one of the leaders of the Protestant Reformation, who had been his fellow law student in Orleans, asking him to send a contingent of believers of the new faith to control the rebellions that were undermining the colony. Thus in 1557 fourteen Calvinists arrived in Rio de Janeiro. It soon became clear that their presence only made the conflicts worse. When the antagonism came to a head the Calvinists were forced to flee the island in Guanabara Bay and take refuge among the Tupinambá.

Several accounts of the experience, describing the land and its people, survive. Villegaignon himself, who stayed in Brazil from 1555 to 1558, left a number of letters describing the region. In a letter dated 1556, signed N. B. (Nicolas Barré, one of the Calvinists sent from France), Villegaignon is full of praise for the natural beauty of Brazil but describes the 'Brazilian savages' with slight suspicion: 'They walk around naked with their bows and arrows, ready for making war.' The letters contain a mixture of religious and philosophical considerations as well as plans for exploring the country. Barré said he was certain they would find precious metals, 'because the Portuguese [had] found silver and copper fifty leagues upriver'.

These letters were to influence future reports, such as those of André

Thevet (1516–1590/2), a Franciscan friar who, after travelling around the East and some of the Mediterranean islands, disembarked in 1555 with Admiral Villegaignon to found the colony of France Antarctique. Thevet only spent three months in the colony in Guanabara Bay, alleging that he was ill and returning to France in June the following year. In Europe, where there was great curiosity about the New World, he saw an opportunity for a work combining humanism with a voguish account of recent discoveries. In 1577 he published *Les Singularitez de la France Antarctique*,[70] which was highly successful within his lifetime. Thevet's text is long, rambling and frequently interspersed with rather self-serving observations intended to show his erudition. Despite its extravagant style, this is the first detailed description of Brazil's natural beauty and, more importantly, of the Tupinambá Indians, who, although they fought alongside the French, Thevet described as 'cannibals – naked and feathered'. Discussion of Brazil is found starting in Chapter 27, with a paridisiacal description of the land. Once again, however, Thevet has a very different opinion of the peoples. In fact, his comments on the Indians are on the whole distinct from those of a previous work, *Cosmographie*, where he sympathetically described them as 'these poor people, living without religion or law'. In *Les Singularitez de la France antarctique* he expresses outrage at 'their noxious religions, magic and witchcraft' and the never-ending wars between these 'unbelievably vengeful'[71] savages who practised the 'barbarity of cannibalism'.

Two other writers who lived among the Tupinambá during this period – one as an ally, another as an enemy to be devoured – were to end up as enemies of Thevet. Hans Staden, an artillery soldier from Hesse, was imprisoned by the Indians and narrated his experience in a book that was published in 1557 and ran to four editions in a single year. Jean de Léry's book,[72] *Histoire d'un Voyage Faict en la Terre du Brésil*, written in 1563 but only published in 1578, was equally well received. In the two books Brazil became famous as the 'other side of the world'. Both works were republished in France in 1592 as part of the *Great Journey* series, illustrated by Théodore de Bry, a goldsmith, engraver and Huguenot propagandist who had never been to the Americas but nevertheless became the most famous painter of the period to portray them.[73] What the eye could not see the imagination invented.

Jean de Léry's *Histoire d'un Voyage Faict en la Terre du Brésil*[74] ran to five editions after its publication in 1578, and to a further ten, in both French and Latin, by 1611. According to the author, the aim of the book was to correct the 'lies and errors' contained in Thevet's account. Léry, a minister of the Church during the initial phase of the Reformation, was a shoemaker and student of theology in Geneva when Villegaignon requested Calvinist reinforcements. In 1558, Léry set out to join the founders of France Antarctique with a group of Protestant ministers and artisans. He witnessed the disintegration of the French colony and during the rest of his time in Brazil he lived with the Tupinambá. It was the 'difference' of the Indians, rather than their ungodly practices, that interested this sixteenth-century traveller, who became the most widely known and imitated commentator on the newly discovered land of Brazil.

Opposing other reports, Léry shows that the wars waged by the 'caraíbas' were based on internal rules and that vengeance was a shared value among them: 'There is a different manner of thinking here, very different from that of the fables that have been spun so far.'[75] Despite the enormous impact of the natural beauty of the country, with its parrots and monkeys, multicoloured birds, butterflies, giant turtles, caymans, armadillos and coatis, the impression the Indians left on him was even greater. He described how the 'savages' prepared flour, made bread, produced wine and dried meat.

Léry went to great lengths to understand the role of war and vengeance among the Indians and how their 'rules' prevailed over 'gluttony'.[76] On his return to Geneva, he learnt of the Massacre of Saint Bartholomew's Day, when, on 24 August 1572, Catholics murdered Protestants in France, initiating a brutal civil war that was to divide the country and immerse it in bloodshed.[77] Jean de Léry did not believe the wars waged by the Indians and their practice of cannibalism were motivated by the need for food. Rather, they represented forms of internal communication, and were symbolic of exchanges of values and goods.[78] Thus a new chapter in this story of conflicting opinions about the New World began.

To return to Hans Staden, the artillery soldier was to write two books, the first entitled *Two Journeys to Brazil* and the second *Brave Adventures in the Sixteenth Century among the Cannibals of the New World*. Staden made two journeys to South America – one on a Spanish ship and the other on a Portuguese ship. While he was working in a small fort on the island of Santo Amaro,[79] one of the most important captaincies at the time, he was captured by the Tupinambá, who were allies of the French and enemies of the Portuguese. They forced him to live in captivity for ten and a half long years of hardship. During his struggle to avoid being eaten by the Indians – pretending to be a witch doctor or using his medical knowledge to help cure an epidemic that debilitated the group – he found time to note down the daily life of the village and the Tupinambá who lived there, people who, in his own words, haunted him 'with their hideous customs'.[80]

Very little is known about Staden's life, despite the fact that *Two Journeys to Brazil* ran to over fifty editions in German, Flemish, Dutch, Latin, French, English and Portuguese. The attraction of the book was that the author had been a captive of the Tupinambá, not to mention its lurid wood engravings, designed under his supervision. The account is straightforward with Staden explaining the tricks he used to avoid being eaten. The writer, who had witnessed a number of massacres, lived with the 'savages' and treated their diseases, is only released in the final chapters of his book, when he was rescued by French traders aboard the ship *Catherine de Vetteville*.

Hans Staden corrected a number of Vespucci's observations, providing information about the family structure of the Indians, their sexual life, material culture, spiritual beliefs, and their methods of classifying animals, fruits and flowers. All this is described in colloquial language, including the practice of cannibalism and cutting up human meat. He ends the book with an uncompromising declaration: 'All this I saw and witnessed.'[81] This was a way of conferring credibility on a book that might otherwise be construed as a fantasy. 'Who is to blame?' he asks, and concludes: 'I have given you in this book sufficient information. Follow the trail. For those whom God helps, the world is wide open.'[82] At one level Staden was of course entirely right: the world had never been closed.

A PORTION OF HUMANITY TO BE CATECHIZED OR ENSLAVED

There is still much controversy about the antiquity of the peoples of the so-called 'New World' (which was only 'New' because the Europeans thought of their own civilization as 'Old'). Most traditional estimates consider their origins to go back 12,000 years, but more recent research puts this between 30,000 and 35,000 years. Very little is known of the history of these indigenous people, or of the innumerable peoples who disappeared as a result of what we now euphemistically call the 'encounter' between the Old World and the New. A massacre of genocidal proportions began at the time of a pacific first Mass: a population that was estimated at several million in 1500 was reduced to little over 800,000 – the number of Indians who live in Brazil today.[83] There are several explanations for this catastrophe. First, these peoples had no immunity to European diseases, and were attacked by pathogenic agents that included smallpox, measles, whooping cough, chickenpox, diphtheria, typhus, bubonic plague, and even what would today be considered a relatively inoffensive cold. It was the opposite of what took place in Africa, where Caucasians died by the thousands, as if there were some sort of invisible poison thread running through them. In the Americas, in contrast, the natives died. But the lack of immunity is not enough to explain entirely the massive death rate. This biological cataclysm only had the effects it did because it occurred within a specific context with specific social characteristics, which up until then had been in balance.

Colonization led to the exploitation of Indian labour, which was a major factor in the massive mortality rates. The colonists also aggravated the wars between Indian groups. Although these enmities had already existed, they were now fuelled by the colonizers, who made strategic alliances with indigenous groups, then broke them at will. This frequently led to Indians in the villages being allied to the Portuguese, whereas those in the unknown interior (*sertão*) became their enemies. These two groups – 'friendly' and 'savage' Indians – were defined by law. The village Indians, the allies, were guaranteed freedom in their villages and put in charge of maintaining and protecting the borders. The process of making contact with the 'friendly Indians of the villages' was always the same: first they were 'brought down' from their villages to the Portuguese settlements; then they were catechized, civilized and thus transformed into 'useful vassals'.[84]

The village Indians were also assigned the task of fighting in the wars waged by the Portuguese against groups of hostile Indians. The participation of both 'the villagers and the allies' – the latter, Tapuia

Indians – is mentioned in virtually all colonial war documents of the time. They formed a line of defence to protect the *sertão* and block the passage of strangers. It was this contingent that was mobilized to expel Villegaignon and his men, who in turn joined forces with the Tupi-nambá, the allies of the French. And thus, if 'liberation' – meaning catechism – was the 'reward' of the allied village Indians, slavery was the destination of the enemy Indians.

In this context, the Portuguese Crown revived the old concept of a 'righteous war' – 'Guerra Justa' – that could be waged against peoples who had no knowledge of the faith and therefore could not even be treated as infidels. There were a number of causes that legitimized a 'righteous war': refusal to be converted, hostility towards Portuguese subjects and allies, breaking agreements, and cannibalism. Cannibalism was an 'offence against natural law'; war against it was considered both a right and a duty in order to save the souls of those who would be sacrificed or eaten.

At the time, a heated debate took place between two religious men – Bartolomé de Las Casas and Juan Ginés de Sepúlveda – over two ways of understanding the native people. Their difference of opinion generated distinct models of domination: for Las Casas, the natives were like herds that should be controlled; in Sepúlveda's view, they were not yet human and should be forced to achieve humanity through baptism, and through work, to become men. Although war was considered a last resort by the Portuguese Crown, the settlers constantly resorted to it and used it as proof of the 'enmity of these people' and the 'ferocity of the enemy'. The Crown itself was aware of abuses and made laws to control illicit enslavement, which did not, however, prevent the elimination of many indigenous peoples in what, according to European logic, were 'righteous wars'. These wars, waged according to that logic, resulted in a random renaming of opponents, and the creation of both allies and enemies.

The concentration of the indigenous population in villages controlled by missionaries proved to be equally disastrous, as it led to the proliferation of diseases and epidemics. Catechism and civilization were central to the whole colonial project, the justification for confinement to missions near villages and for the use of Indian labour under a Jesuit administration. This system was first set in place by the Society of Jesus (Companhia de Jesus), founded by Ignacio Loyola in 1534 and a typical example of a religious order born in the context of the Catholic Reformation. Shortly prior, Pope Paul III had issued a papal bull in which he recognized the Indians as men, made in the image of God, and thus deserving of catechization. In Europe the Jesuits were focused on the teachings of Catholicism, but the 'discoveries' saw them travelling the world, spreading the 'true faith' through catechism. They were eventually called 'the soldiers of Christ', and that is how they ended up, a veritable army of cassock-clad priests, fighting the Devil and at the ready to save souls.

As soon as Pope Paul III approved the foundation of the Order, the Jesuits set out for the Portuguese East, travelling as far as China and Japan. On the southwest coast of Africa they founded a Jesuit college in Luanda and translated Christian texts into Bantu. They arrived in Brazil in 1549 under the leadership of Manoel da Nóbrega, and by 1557 had established a plan to confine the Indians to missionary villages, which in effect meant transferring them to locations controlled by the Order. Missionary work in Brazil was seen as dangerous – after all Pedro Correia had been devoured by the Carijó Indians in 1554, and Dom Pero Fernandes Sardinha, known as Bishop Sardinha, had been eaten by the Caeté Indians in 1556 on the coast of the present-day state of Alagoas. The best thing to do was to indoctrinate these people, who, unlike the natives of the East, 'lacked any faith or religion'. The Jesuits were instructed to achieve their conversion through kindness and good example, and to 'adapt' Catholicism to the local culture, adjusting terms and concepts to the realities of the region. An early example of this was the *Grammar of the Tupi-Guarani Language* written by José de Anchieta[85] in 1556, which became mandatory reading for virtually every citizen in the colony.

With so many conflicting aims, the enmity between the Jesuits and the settlers soon came to the surface. Whereas the latter were ever ready to enslave the Indians as a part of their 'righteous war' against them, the former tried to protect their newly converted Catholics, appealing to the Crown for more effective measures to do this. This pressure resulted in the Royal Charter of 1570, which forbade the enslavement of Indians, except when motivated by a 'righteous war'. The king had to constantly arbitrate in conflicts, with the Jesuits accusing the settlers of greed, and the settlers accusing the Jesuits of wanting to control the country.

The Society of Jesus was, over time, to transform itself into a veritable economic powerhouse. Although initially it depended on the generosity of the Crown, the Jesuits gradually grew rich, renting out houses, leasing land, and controlling the lucrative trade in spices that were cultivated in the villages they controlled. Their hegemony was such that in the eighteenth century the Crowns of Spain and Portugal banned the Order. The Jesuits were expelled from Portugal and its colonies in 1759, from France in 1762, from Spain and the Kingdom of Naples in 1767, until finally in 1773 Pope Clement XIV abolished the Order. It was only to be restored in 1814 in the wake of the sweeping changes created by Napoleon Bonaparte. But that is another story. At the time of colonial expansion the history of the Jesuits was inextricably linked to the Indian peoples.

LONG BEFORE CABRAL

The colonial metropoles soon understood the strategic potential of the rivalries between indigenous groups, whether longstanding or recently provoked. For this reason, in the sixteenth century, the Portuguese made an alliance with the Tupiniquim while the French allied themselves to the Tamoios and the Tupinambá. Later, in the seventeenth century, the Dutch were to join forces with the Tapuia against the Portuguese. The Tamoio, the Tapuia, the Tupiniquim – whatever name the Portuguese had given the groups they encountered – had their own reasons for making these alliances, which they interpreted within the context of their customs. In the words of the Brazilian modernist poet Oswald de Andrade,[86] 'Before the Portuguese discovered Brazil, Brazil had discovered happiness.' Indeed, the native peoples already had their own societies, values, languages, customs and rituals.

When Christopher Columbus landed in the Antilles in 1492, the islands were densely populated by the Arawak-speaking Taino people, who were soon to be almost annihilated by epidemics and inhuman treatment. These indigenous groups, known as *kasiks* in Arawak (corrupted to *cacicazgos* in Spanish), were subordinated to a tribal chief or *cacique*. In America a centralized political system existed where the *caciques* were the supreme leaders with powers over the villages and districts, which were also hierarchically structured. Unlike European countries, however, there was no body of administrators and no permanent army. All disputes were resolved by the chief, who summoned his warriors in cases of conflict.[87]

As this model began to expand across the colony, it was given the name *cacicado*. The term referred to settlements that had a regional centre, public works, collective and agricultural labour, dwellings of varying sizes, a commercial network for the exchange of produce, and technical procedures for burial. There were many regions with differing hierarchical structures, but all these societies did have a faith and the rule of law, despite their values being very different from those of the Europeans. The geographical divisions of the modern era, which led to the creation of distinct nation states, were also based on the logic of colonization and 'discovery', with no respect for pre-existing borders. Thus today these people are generically known as Amerindians, because, despite their linguistic differences, they were united by cultural ties and by the continent that was later to be called America.

The continent was named as a tribute to Amerigo Vespucci, the Italian merchant, navigator, geographer and cartographer who wrote about the 'new lands' to the west of Europe, and considered himself to be the first person to set foot in a land that had in fact been inhabited for approximately 35,000 years. Of this very distant past very little is known. It is known, however, that about 12,000 years ago milder temperatures led to the gradual separation of the two continents and to the ocean coming between them. For this reason the hypothesis most generally accepted is of a terrestrial migration from the northeast of Asia via the Bering Straits, from where the migrants gradually spread across the entire length of the American continent. A more recent, highly controversial hypothesis suggests that the first migrants arrived by sea and landed on the northeastern coast of Brazil. It is certain, however, that on the eve of the European conquest the differing social indigenous systems did not exist in a state of isolation, but were linked at both local and regional levels. There were also commercial networks connecting groups that lived in regions wide distances apart.

The first of these immense areas was formed by the Amazon basin. Aside from the more florid reports fantasizing about a lost Eldorado and a land inhabited by the Amazons, the sixteenth- and seventeenth-century chroniclers provide us with some valuable information. By all indications there were intermittent occupations along the banks of the Amazon river, villages interspersed between uninhabited stretches of land. The villages varied in size and in the number of inhabitants. It is known that the largest of these extended along the river for as much as seven kilometres, and had a hierarchical system as well as political and ceremonial activities. The records also mention a wealth of natural resources, including an abundant supply of fish and agricultural products such as corn and manioc. In many of these villages the art of pottery was already developed, as in the Marajoara culture. Based on the island of Marajó, located off the coast of the present-day state of Pará, at the mouth of the Amazon river, it prospered from 400 to 1400 CE. Its political systems varied widely. Records show the prevalence of *cacicados*, or chiefdoms, and groups of descendants formed by matrimonial alliances. Contradicting the official version of Brazilian history, violence was very much present from the beginning of the 'encounter', with the colonizers seizing ports and sacking villages, where they were received by warriors armed to the teeth, with fleets of canoes and poisoned arrows.

Another area that is much studied today lies along the Xingu river, one of the main southern tributaries of the Amazon. In this region a multi-ethnic, multi-linguistic but culturally homogeneous society emerged. It was non-migratory, based on fishing and the cultivation of manioc. Abundant natural resources meant that a large population existed in the fifteenth and sixteenth centuries, which enjoyed regular interaction with other cultures, very different from the traditional image of these peoples as isolated groups who only made sporadic contact with outsiders. The political system of the Xingu people included a chief and different social groups with a remarkable degree of political autonomy.

There was also a third area, bordering the Amazon Forest to the south and east: the grasslands of the *cerrado*.[88] This was a vast area of scrubland dotted with bush, home to the Macro-Jê people. On that population fell a certain cultural myopia, distorted by the Andean viewpoint – with its great civilizations – but also by a lens of the Tupinambá, the Tupi-Guarani and the Portuguese who degraded these groups. Hence, for many years the Macro-Jê were described as 'barbaric people', who possessed neither villages, agriculture, transport nor ceramics.

Actually, it was the coastal Tupi-Guarani who named the people of the *sertão* Tapuias, thus obliterating their individuality. However, the supposed marginalization of the Jê of the scrublands has been revisited in studies by major anthropologists such as Curt Nimuendajú, Claude Lévi-Strauss and more recently Eduardo Viveiros de Castro, among many others. The Jê are no longer seen only as nomadic hunter-gatherers, but have become studied and acknowledged as a people who possessed a sophisticated economy and cosmology. There are records of horticultural practice in the region going back millennia, as well as of the art of ceramics, known as *una*, present in the entire region from prehistoric times until the ninth century, when it was replaced by other traditional forms of ceramics, such as *aratu* and *uru*.[89] Villages laid out in circular form, characteristic of the central plateau, date from approximately 800 to 1500 CE. There the Indians cultivated corn and sweet potatoes. These villages consisted of between one and three circles of houses, sometimes called *ocas*,[90] with a circular communal area at the centre[91] where ceremonies and rituals were conducted. The population of these villages was larger than those of the present day, with between eight hundred and two thousand inhabitants. The structure of Jê society in Brazil was very different from that of the peoples of the tropical rainforest. They were travellers; they lived in large villages; their subsistence technology was simple and their body adornments elaborate. There were no supreme chiefs, although a certain hierarchical order existed alongside community institutions and imposing ceremonies.

Although the Jê, like the Amazonian peoples and Amerindians in general, did not leave the kinds of monumental constructions associated with those of the Andes that have become the benchmark for evaluating the indigenous people of the Americas, their cosmology was truly sophisticated. Anthropologists like Eduardo Viveiros de Castro and Philippe Descola borrowed a term from philosophy – 'perspectivism', employed by Leibniz and Nietzsche – to describe certain aspects of the Amerindian peoples' cosmology. The concept is based on the idea that perception and thought result from a 'perspective' which alters according to the context and situation. This is a very complex cosmology, but can be simplified by examining two of its major premises: first, that the world is populated by many species, both human and nonhuman, all of whom possess consciousness and culture, and second, these species perceive themselves and each other in a very particular way. Each group sees itself as human and all the others as non-human, in other words, as animals or spirits. According to

Amerindian myths, at the 'beginning' all beings that were human became the animals of today. Whereas according to Western science, humans were animals who became humans, for the Amerindians all animals were previously humans. The consequence of this was a different interpretation of the interaction between humans and animals, all of whom are 'citizens' with social relations. This model also questions basic Western parameters such as 'nature' and 'culture'. For Westerners, there is Nature (which is a given and universal) and different cultures (which are constructed). For the Amerindians, on the other hand, there was one culture but different 'natures': men, animals and spirits.

In this interaction between 'natures' the shaman plays a vital role; he was the equivalent of a political, social and spiritual leader. An appreciation of this role is essential for understanding societies that do not discriminate between humans and nonhumans. He was the only one who could 'transport bodies' and had the powers to perceive these different states of being (human, animal or spirit). These Amerindian theories question our widely held prejudices which suppose that the Indians had 'myths', whereas we have 'philosophies'; that they had 'rituals', whereas we have 'sciences'. These are the vestiges of the legacy of the writings of sixteenth-century travellers, who saw as inferior what was in fact different. Taking seriously these groups that lived in America before the arrival of the Portuguese implies not only thinking of their history in our own terms, but also understanding that there existed and continue to exist other ways of comprehending the land we now call Brazil.[92]

In order to give a complete overview of these indigenous people, we need to mention the group that inhabited Brazil all along the coast at the time when the Portuguese arrived: from north to south, the coastline was occupied by a people widely considered homogeneous, the Tupi-Guarani. The group can be divided into two subgroups, based on linguistic and cultural differences. In the south, the Guarani lived in the basins of the Paraná, Paraguay and Uruguay rivers, and along the coast from the *Lagoa dos Patos*[93] to Cananeia, in the present-day state of São Paulo. The north coastline, from Iguape to what is today the state of Ceará, was mostly inhabited by the Tupinambá, some of whom also lived inland, in the area between the Tietê[94] and Paranapanema[95] rivers.[96]

As in the Amazonian cultures, the Tupi-Guarani lived from fishing and hunting. They also practised the traditional agricultural technique known as *coivara*, cutting down native brush, then burning the vegetation to clear the land for planting rotating crops. The staple food of the Guarani was corn, whereas the Tupinambá grew bitter manioc from which they made flour. Both groups benefited from the fluvial and maritime resources of the region, and were expert canoeists, a fact duly noted by sixteenth-century chroniclers. The wealth of natural resources provided sustenance for a large population. It is thought that the total population in the area inhabited by the Tupinambá was one million, or nine inhabitants per square kilometre. In the southern regions occupied by the Guarani the total population was one and a half million, or four inhabitants per square kilometre. In this region a particularly large number of Indians lived in villages established by Jesuit missionaries. They were often mobilized for war (especially in the case of the Tupinambá), or enslaved by the so-called *bandeirantes* (adventurous settlers, who ventured into unmapped regions in the pursuit of fortunes from slave-hunting and precious metals), for use on expeditions into the interior, during which large numbers of Guarani were captured from the sixteenth century on. As explained before, the term *sertão* was first employed by Vaz de Caminha to refer to the vast unknown interior of the colony, far from the sea. From the fifteenth century on, as the colony expanded, the word (originally used to designate regions in Portugal that were distant from Lisbon) was used to refer to areas about which little or nothing was known.

With time, however, the name came to indicate a symbolic space rather than a geographical one. Whereas 'settlement' referred to a location where order was imposed by the Catholic Church, *sertão* referred to vast areas where no such order existed – areas that were soon to be explored for the exploitation of their resources (wood, minerals and Indians). It was thanks to the alliances that the Portuguese made with Indian groups that they were able to conquer the interior of the continent. Piratininga[97] is a particularly significant example.[98] The introduction of sugar production from the middle of the sixteenth century – the subject of the next chapter of this book – led to a significant increase in the demand for labour to sustain the emerging economy, a situation that was exacerbated by the wars between rival groups of Indians.

In 1548, when São Vicente was founded, there were three thousand Indian slaves working along the coast of the captaincy, all available for work at the six local sugar mills. The conflict between the local sugar planters and the Jesuit missionaries, who arrived in the region in 1553, began during this period. The Jesuits demanded that the Indians from the interior should be settled in the missionary villages. The immediate outcome of this was the Freedom of Indians Act, passed in 1570, which forbade the enslavement of indigenous people except for in cases of a 'righteous war'. Thus, between 1580 and 1590, the expeditions that brought back large numbers of captured Indians from the interior were all conducted under the guise of 'righteous wars'.

Between 1600 and 1641 the Carijó Indians, part of the Guarani linguistic group living in areas to the south and southwest of São Paulo, became the main target. These 'hunting expeditions' reached a peak in the 1620s and 1630s, when, in flagrant disrespect of the law and in spite of the Jesuits' protests, they began to resemble paramilitary groups such was their size and the scale of resources at their disposal. *Bandeiras* – expeditions to the interior of the land – under the command of Manuel Preto, Antônio Raposo Tavares and Fernão Dias Paes, to mention only a few, decimated the local populations, creating considerable tension between the explorers, the Jesuits and the Crown.

The *Bandeirantes* were so heroically depicted in Brazilian history that their image was used by the state of São Paulo, as recently as the beginning of the twentieth century, to symbolize the 'adventurous and intrepid spirit of the region'. Whereas the benefits of their exploits were exalted – the fearless explorers of the 'dangerous *sertão*' and its wealth of mineral resources – the violence that characterized these expeditions, with the capture and enslavement of the Indians, was conveniently forgotten. The truth is that the vicious circle, set in motion during the sixteenth and seventeenth centuries, was brutally perverse. The lack of native labour on the coast led to more and more expeditions that penetrated further and further into the interior, resulting in the decimation of the Indian population from both epidemics and attacks by the explorers.

However, while many of these groups suffered a drastic reduction in numbers, during the sixteenth century the Tupi-Guarani sustained a remarkable political and economic system. Organized in villages each with a population of between about five hundred and two thousand, they maintained close links with other groups with whom they had ties of kinship. Great Tupi-Guarani shamans, known as *karaí* or *karaíba*, travelled around the land healing and prophesying. It was within this context that the millenarist movements of the Tupi emerged, which foresaw the coming of a time without evil. After the arrival of the Europeans the movement would adopt a distinctively anti-Portuguese bias.

Besides this, some of the villages were allied with each other and formed multi-community groups. They had no regional centres or chiefs whose powers went beyond their village. Power was not hereditary; it had to be earned in battle. There were chiefs who became famous for their leadership in war, when they mobilized large military forces by bringing together a number of local groups. Jean de Léry, for example, cites a confrontation between the Maracajá and the Tupinambá, in which the forces of the latter totalled four thousand men. The aims of these wars were not, however, the customary ones: sacking villages and conquering their lands. They were motivated by 'vengeance' and intended to capture prisoners, whose destiny was not slavery but death. They were to be eaten in the *ocara*, the circular communal meeting place at the centre of the village.[99] All the reports from the time agree. No writer of the period fails to mention the wars and cannibalism practised by the Tupinambá. We now know these practices were central to the beliefs of these groups, which created lively systems of trade and cultural exchange but abhorred centralization and any form of overarching state.[100]

Prior to the arrival of the colonizers there was a vast contingent of peoples spread across the continent, with a large variety of social, economic and political systems, at local and regional levels. If Cabral's arrival was a disaster for these populations, there is no reason to describe the losses only in terms of lives, land and culture. There is no static history, and contact and changes continue to be made today. Amerindian practices, religions and beliefs have been gaining greater space as social actors within Brazil, despite still representing a largely ignored political voice. Although we know too little about their history, there is no reason to believe that they were passive subjects of indoctrination by the Jesuits. Padre Antonio Vieira – a Portuguese orator and philosopher of the Society of Jesus, and great defender of the 'rights of the Indians'[101] – attempted in one of his famous sermons to describe the natives he had met in Brazil. After lamenting the modest success of the evangelizing mission, he went on to compare the difference between Europeans and Indians to the difference between marble and a myrtle bush. The Europeans, he said, were like marble: difficult to sculpt, but once the statue had been concluded, it remained intact forever. The Amerindians, on the other hand, were the opposite. They were like a myrtle bush: at first sight easy to sculpt, only to later return to its original form.[102] This was the reality that evangelization would have to face. Although the Amerindians appeared to accept the new religion without reacting, they were 'inconstant', or 'worse, ill-disposed towards the new faith and laws', always returning to their own social mores and cosmologies.

Nevertheless, five hundred years ago, the inhabitants of this immense territory – which had been given a name, but whose frontiers and interior were as yet unknown – seemed to encapsulate everything that was 'New': a new and strange form of humanity. To the public in Europe everything about these new lands was exciting and exotic: the people, the animals, the climate and the plants.

Padre Cardim's treatise, *On the Climate and Land of Brazil*, was written between 1583 and 1601, translated into English in 1625 (anonymously), and finally published in full in Portuguese in the nineteenth century. Clearly, it took a while to catch on. However, as at the turn of the sixteenth century documents in circulation frequently alluded to one another, the priest's comments may well have added fuel to the fire of public imagination, according to which 'Brazil', the Brazils, the Land of the Holy Cross, the Land of the Parrots, had now become the fascinating land of cannibalism. Padre Cardim made further exotic additions: after enumerating the wealth of Brazil's natural resources, he went on to reveal the existence of mermaids and mermen, among other imaginary creatures indispensable to Portuguese writers of the time. Cardim concludes, to great effect: 'This Brazil is another Portugal.' It was, however, much more than that. Brazil was a different world.

2

The Sugar Civilization: Bitter for the Many, Sweet for a Few

He who beholds in the blackness of night those terrible fur-
naces perpetually burning [. . .] the noise of wheels, of chains,
of people the colour of the very night, arduously toiling and all
the while groaning, without a moment's rest or relief; he who
beholds the thunder and chaos of this machinery of Babylon
shall not doubt, though he has looked into the very depths of
Mount Etna or Vesuvius, that he has seen the likeness of hell.

Padre Antônio Vieira

SO BITTERSWEET: A SUGAR CIVILIZATION

It is hard to understand how this land – located somewhere between heaven and hell – was to gradually become a major centre for sugar production, selling 'sweetness' produced by labour derived from the 'infamous trade in human souls'. It is time to revisit this story, for no chain of events is simply natural – nor a mere gift from the gods. Our propensity to like places, products and sensations is learned, and some-times these tastes were created or invented at some specific date in history; we identify them and they become familiar. Europeans created companies and colonial societies in the Caribbean and in Brazil; they also created sugar. Humans make food out of almost anything, but their choice and preparation of it varies considerably according to region, social class, generation and gender. Sugar was not only a *prod-uct*, but also a *producer* of codes and customs. And in the sixteenth century the invention of a desire for sweets was widely cultivated. It is true that fruits and honey had been used as sweeteners long before this, but the new taste for sweets, its transformation into a universal need, occurred at a very specific time in the history of the Western world. It was only after 1650 that sugar, mainly cane sugar – previously the rarest of luxuries – became commonplace, a basic need.

Whereas honey has been known since the early days of human history, sugar, and especially sucrose – a substance extracted from sugarcane – appeared much later and has only been widely consumed for the past five hundred years.[1] In 1000 CE only very few people were aware of the existence of sugar, but by the seventeenth century the aristocracy and wealthy middle classes had become 'addicted' to it. It was adopted by Western medicine because it was thought to have healing properties, it penetrated the literary imagination of the time, and was a constant presence on the tables of 'good society'.

The first known references to sugarcane come from New Guinea, dating back to around 8000 BCE. Two thousand years later it reportedly found its way to the Philippines, India and possibly Indonesia. References to actual sugar-making only began to appear with regularity after 350 CE, in India, becoming more frequent around 500 CE. The Arabs brought sugarcane to Europe with their invasion of Spain in 711. They established the art of sugar-making and the taste for different 'types of sweetness'. In addition to its use in medicine and cooking, sugar began to be used to simply 'sweeten' everyday items such as tea, bread and pies. By that time, sugarcane plantations could be found in northern Africa and on a number of Mediterranean islands, most notably Sicily. But with the Crusades sugar consumption increased markedly, largely due to the expansion of the sugar trade between Africa and Europe.[2] From then on, sugar was on the list of precious trading goods – which included pepper, cloves and cinnamon. It became a staple for monarchs, essential to princesses' dowries, to nobles' wills, and so on and so forth.

The development of the spice trade and the routes along which the traders travelled have mainly been well documented. It is less clear, however, why these products became so popular and what led the rich and powerful of Europe to develop a taste for piquant foods, seasoned with pepper, smoked, aromatic, cured, oily, spicey, or, quite simply, sweet. The most convincing explanation is that before the arrival of these products food was in general dull and monotonous. Thus, more varied and exotic flavours, to satisfy even the most unusual tastes, were welcomed. Sugar was also easy to preserve. It was this combination that ensured its place as an object of desire and power in the hands of kings and merchants. Before long it had become a staple, with investment in the production and sale of sugar increasing to meet the growth in demand.

This was the case for the Kingdom of Portugal, which saw in this market a solution to the problems it faced in both Africa and America. An additional factor that led to the Portuguese monarch's decision to promote sugar production was that the industry that had previously flourished in the Mediterranean, especially in Sicily and Moorish Spain, had begun to wane. And so, under the auspices of Prince Henry of Portugal,[3] the first sugarcane saplings were brought from Sicily and initially planted on the island of Madeira, which soon became the largest single producer of sugarcane in the West. By the early sixteenth century it was producing over 177,000 arrobas[4] of white sugar and 230,000 of Muscovado sugar,[5] as well as other inferior grades.[6]

But the growth of the sugar trade on the island was as swift as its decline. From there it rapidly spread to the Azores, Cape Verde and São Tomé. Initially it was the Genoese and Venetians who controlled the trade from these Atlantic islands. Around 1472, however, Flemish merchants, who by then controlled the distribution of commodities to the Portuguese market, took over the trade. For some time Portugal had been establishing commercial and financial ties with Genoese and Flemish bankers who provided them with access to credit for essential investments. The Netherlands, in fact, had taken an interest in Brazil long before the creation of the West India Company in 1621. There was considerable trade between Portugal and the Low Countries, with Dutch ships supplying Portuguese ports with merchandise from northern Europe – wheat, timber, metal and manufactured goods – as well as Dutch products, including fish, butter and cheese. On the return journey they carried cargoes of timber, rock salt, wine, spices and medicinal herbs from East Africa, to which, later on, they added sugar from Brazil. Not infrequently, under Philip II and III[7] of Spain, a country hostile to Protestant Holland, Spanish fleets blockaded the Portuguese ports to prevent Dutch ships from entering. But despite these temporary disruptions the trade continued.

After the decline of the plantations on Madeira, sugarcane production was to flourish in São Tomé. By this time slaves were already being used to work on the plantations. In 1516 alone 4,000 slaves disembarked on the island and by 1554 the local population consisted of 600 whites, 600 mulattoes and 2,000 slaves. With its proximity to the African coast the island later became an Atlantic market for the trafficking of slaves to the New World. When its sugar industry declined in the mid-sixteenth century, São Tomé turned entirely to the trafficking of slaves, receiving 'supplies' from Senegambia, Angola and Benin.

Sugar production in São Tomé turned out to be an excellent training ground for future activities in Brazil. Production methods, internal organization, the proportion of slaves to colonists – all the lessons learnt on the island – were assimilated and later applied. Even slave uprisings, especially in 1574, weighed heavily on the minds of the plantation owners as they headed towards the colony in America. Nevertheless, the Portuguese had learned from the experience. Although they had no precise idea of the extent of the territory of the New World, they knew the coastline relatively well and they understood the need for it to be populated, if only to prevent the foreign invasions that were starting to occur along the coast. On the other hand, by that time sugar, along with other spices, was fetching increasingly higher prices in an expanding European market.

Thus, combining business with pleasure – the need to populate the colony and the desire to make handsome profits – the policy of merely populating the territory was replaced by a new form of colonization, with a different purpose. Until that time Portugal had limited itself to selling the commodities it had found in its new domains (as it had done with brazilwood in the early days of the colony). But now the colonial enterprise aimed at achieving more substantial results, which required a production system that would serve the European markets on an ongoing basis. The need to populate the land went hand in hand with the desire to exploit it for profit. And nothing could be more profitable than the monoculture of sugarcane. Portugal had ample experience in its cultivation, as well as how to market and distribute it. Although the Crown was still very far from controlling the whole of its territory, it was clear that the abundant availability of land would attract large investments.

Thus the primary goal, rather than settling the population, became the large-scale production of specific products to be traded in Europe. A new type of tropical colony came into being, directed at the cultivation of crops that thrived in the temperate climate and for which there was constant demand in Europe. Their economies were entirely directed at supplying European, rather than domestic, demand, so that at times there was not an ounce of sugarcane left for consumption in the colony.

At any rate, a system was developed based on huge landholdings – the plantations – specializing in the large-scale production of a single export crop. In this new modern era, economic survival required highly specialized production in dependent economies, a system designed to maximize the colony's resources and secure profits abroad. Sugar was ideally suited to all of these requirements, to the delight of European consumers with their insatiable appetite for the new powdered sweetness. As we know, demand can be created, and consumption is often dictated by fashion. Black tea, for example, which contains caffeine, was consumed as a stimulant in Asia, but in the West for its calming effects. It was taken at five in the afternoon in preparation for a good night's sleep.[8] Now sugar became the craze, no longer as a medicine, but as an extravagance: more sweetness, more flavour, more calories and more happiness.

SUGAR ARRIVES IN BRAZIL

The earliest record of sugar and plans for its production in Brazil date back to 1516, when Dom Emmanuel[9] ordered hoes, axes and other tools to be distributed to 'those who were to populate Brazil', and that 'a capable and skilful man be found to establish a sugar mill there . . .'[10] As can be seen, the idea was to profit from the new land before it could become a problem. This was, after all, the 'whole point of colonization': populate the new land, but always with Lisbon's interests in mind.

Although premature, the monarch's plans would slowly consolidate. An expedition under the command of Martim Afonso de Sousa left Portugal for Brazil in December 1530 with the first saplings of sugarcane aboard. They were planted along the coastline of São Vicente, where Martim Afonso built the first sugar mill in 1532. It became known as the *Engenho do Governador*. A few years later it was sold to a Flemish merchant and renamed the *Engenho São Jorge dos Erasmos*, the ruins of which exist to this day. In 1534 the king, Dom João III,[11] established the system of hereditary captaincies. He divided the coastline of his American colony into fifteen segments, which he donated to twelve Portuguese aristocrats to administer. Martim Afonso received the captaincy of São Vicente where the sugarcane plantations thrived. In general, however, the outcome was disappointing: some of the captaincies were never even colonized, while others suffered from isolation and attacks by the Indians.

In fact, ever since the beginning of the Brazilian colonization, indigenous groups had tried to resist Portuguese domination, either by fleeing or by taking up arms. The latter strategy provided the Europeans with the pretext to wage a so-called 'righteous war' to enslave them. But, since they were on their 'home turf', opportunities for individual flight were innumerable, and preventing the slaves from escaping proved to be truly difficult. Although rare, there were also records of occasional uprisings, in which the Indians murdered their owners and escaped en masse.

Towards the end of the sixteenth century these uprisings became a clear indication that the contrasting cultures and economies were set on a collision course. The Portuguese called this type of collective slave, and mainly indigenous, revolt *Santidade*.[12] Behind these uprisings lay a messianic cult that promised an end to slavery and white rule and the coming of a future when peace would reign. As the process of colonization progressed, these prophecies of a time without evil had become explicitly anti-Portuguese in spirit. Indians began launching attacks on the sugar plantations and taking in runaway slaves.

The most important of these insurrections erupted in the *Recôncavo baiano*[13] – the *Santidade de Jaguaripe* in the 1580s.[14] The insurgents combined elements of Tupinambá ritual, which promised an earthly paradise, with Roman Catholic symbols that held out the promise of future redemption. Despite the expeditions the Portuguese sent against them, the group continued to grow. In 1610 the governor of the wealthy captaincy of Bahia reported the group to be 20,000 strong. In 1613 the Portuguese began a war of extermination against the *Santidades*, and all references to them cease after 1628.[15]

The few regions that were successful under the captaincy system combined sugarcane production with (at least an attempt at) peaceful coexistence with the Indians. Sugarcane was planted in all the captaincies that had been colonized – from São Vicente to Pernambuco – with saplings brought from Madeira and São Tomé. Mills were erected in Porto Seguro[16] and Ilhéus in the captaincy of Bahia, as well as in São Vicente. The efforts of Martim Afonso de Sousa to introduce the cultivation of sugarcane were so successful that by the end of the sixteenth century more than a dozen sugar plantations had been established in the *Baixada Santista*.[17]

However, the difficulty of obtaining labour was considerable. Among the causes of this were the Jesuits' increasingly ostentatious protection of the Indians, and the frequency with which the latter managed to escape. Other important factors were the substantial investments required and the constant need to stave off foreign invasions. The outcome was that only two of the captaincies were successful: Pernambuco and São Vicente. But not even the thriving sugar plantations of the latter were to last. With the departure of the donee, who returned to Portugal in 1533, the captaincy of São Vicente was governed directly from Lisbon and became the target of a series of foreign attacks. In January 1615 the Dutch admiral Joris van Spilberg delivered the *coup de grâce*: he invaded the shores of São Vicente (now the state of São Paulo) and proceeded to raid, sack and then torch the emblematic and once imposing *Engenho São Jorge dos Erasmos*. With such constant setbacks and so few incentives, its owners thought it best to abandon the venture.

These events marked the beginning of the migration of sugarcane production to the northeast, and the consequent dramatic increase in the volume of exports to Europe. Areas of fertile alluvium soil in the region, known locally as *massapê*, were found to be ideal for the production of sugarcane. Many years later, in 1930, Gilberto Freyre[18] was to describe it in poetic fashion: 'It's a gentle soil [. . .] The gentleness of the *massapê* contrasts with the terrible, wrathful creaking of the dry sands of the scrublands [. . .] The *massapê* is noble and resistant. It has depth.'[19] Freyre, in his usual style, presents the soil as predestined for the plantation of sugarcane, and thus for nurturing the distinctive culture of Brazil's northeast. And in fact he was right: the *massapê* did have the right characteristics for the successful cultivation of sugarcane. The hot climate of the region, the high humidity, and the vast network of natural waterways for transporting the product to the coast, in addition to its relative proximity to Portugal – the favourable winds and shorter distance greatly curtailed the journey – turned sugarcane into the champion of the Portuguese Empire. The centre of gravity shifted. The attention and strategic measures of the Portuguese Empire were no longer directed at India, but at Brazil.

The first sugar mills began to operate in Pernambuco in 1535, under the direction of the owner of the captaincy, Duarte Coelho. From then on their numbers grew: 4 plantations in 1550; 30 in 1570; and 140 by the end of the sixteenth century. The production increased both numerically and geographically, spreading across the entire region, southwards to Bahia and northwards to Paraíba and Rio Grande do Norte. But it was in Pernambuco and Bahia, above all in the region of the Recôncavo, that sugar production really prospered. Thus began the golden years of Brazilian sugar production. By the end of the sixteenth century production had reached 350,000 arrobas[20] a year, with the colony virtually monopolizing the market. Sugarcane became an intrinsic part of the identity of Brazil: the entire colony was directed at its production and the Crown established it as a royal monopoly.

However, the sugar trade very soon became dependent on Dutch cargo ships transporting goods to the northern hemisphere.[21] It is even arguable that the sugar boom in Brazil was only possible due to the commercial and financial know-how of the Dutch, who were also the main providers of the capital indispensable for the establishment and expansion of the country's sugarcane industry. What is known for certain is that the use of Dutch ships grew steadily year by year as they were faster and better equipped than Portuguese ones. They disguised themselves as Portuguese vessels and thus accounted for most of the traffic between Brazil and Europe.

The Portuguese had no alternative. No matter how hard they tried to control every stage of the operation, command of the trade in sugar was to escape their hands, or rather, those of the owners of the land where the crops were produced. The major importers were located in Amsterdam, London, Hamburg and Genoa,[22] and they had the power to establish prices. Thus Brazil's sugarcane economy became increasingly international, and, in its own way, globalized.

ANOTHER BRAZIL: THE FRENCH AND DUTCH

Between the sixteenth and seventeenth centuries, as soon as the other European countries found out that another American colony had been 'discovered', the Brazilian coast became a target for frequent invasions. First by Algerian and Moroccan pirates on their way from the island of

Madeira to Lisbon, and then by French, Dutch and English corsairs, who patrolled the coast on both sides of the Atlantic, attacking any ship carrying sugar cargo. Vessels that set sail from Brazil loaded with merchandise also fell victim to pirates. Between 1588 and 1591 alone thirty-six of these ships were captured.[23] The Portuguese caravels were small and light, weighing between 80 and 120 tons, and with their small crews they became an easy prey. The Jesuit writer Padre Vieira referred to these ships as 'cowards' schools', since their only act of defence was to flee – a rarely successful tactic, since they were usually so overloaded with cargo. In 1649, in an attempt to reduce the vulnerability of their maritime transport, the Portuguese passed a law obliging the vessels to travel in fleets. From then on the caravels, now larger and heavier, were escorted by galleons that were lighter, faster and well equipped with artillery.

Pirates were not the only problem the Portuguese had to face. In defiance of the Treaty of Tordesillas, as referred to in Chapter 1, on two occasions France attempted to establish a colony in Brazil. The first attempt – France Antarctique – was led by Nicolas Durand de Ville-gaignon, who disembarked in Rio de Janeiro in 1555 with an extensive group, and stayed there for three years. Although his stay was short, it was to have broad repercussions. From the writings of André Thevet and Jean de Léry to those of Montaigne, Indian civilization was held up as a model, more as a criticism of European civilization than from any real knowledge of Brazil's indigenous peoples.

France constantly fought against Portugal to gain control of the trade with the Tupinambá and Tupiniquim. After the failure of France Antarctique, the French returned in 1612, this time invading São Luís in Maranhão, where they attempted to establish the colony of Equinoctial France.[24] The adventure was hardly new for the French, whose experience of the region dated from several years prior. In 1594, Captain Jacques Riffault had set out on an expedition to Brazil that ended in failure. However, part of the crew stayed behind in the Portuguese colony, including Charles des Vaux, who later returned to France and convinced Henry IV of the need for a colonial campaign. Shortly afterwards he set out on an expedition to the 'Island of Maranhão'.[25] By this time the French had already established an outpost on the island of São Luís (Upaon-Açu) and gained the confidence of the local Indian population, even learning their language.

Equinoctial France was created with the support of the French monarchy and the collaboration of the Queen Regent, Mary of Medici, who granted the concession for the establishment of a colony south of the equator, stretching fifty leagues on either side of the fort that had been constructed on the 'Island of Maranhão'. She also appointed Capuchin missionaries to evangelize the Tupinambá in the region. The colony was founded in March 1612, under the command of Daniel de la Touche, an aristocrat who had become famous eight years earlier for exploring the coast of Guiana. With three ships and five hundred settlers on board he set out in the direction of what is today the state of Maranhão. When they arrived in Equinoctial France they founded a settlement that they named Saint Louis, after King Louis XIII. On 8 September 1612, Capuchin friars conducted the first Mass, symbolically claiming the location as a Christian domain.

The territory they occupied was vast, stretching from the coast of Maranhão to the north of the present-day state of Tocantins. The French also controlled almost all the eastern part of Pará and a large amount of what is today Amapá. They established several settlements, including Cametá, on the banks of the Tocantins river, and others around the mouth of the Araguaia river. Portugal's reaction was proportional to the size of the invasion. They gathered their troops in the captaincy of Pernambuco from where they marched on the settlement of Saint Louis. The expedition ended with the capitulation of the French on 4 November 1615. Portuguese settlers then occupied the area and introduced the cultivation of sugar. The French, however, did not give up. Their next attempted colonization was at the mouth of the Amazon river, from where they were once again expelled by the Portuguese. In 1626 they colonized the territory of what is today French Guiana, where they finally met with success. Although its capital city Cayenne was founded in 1635, the French only acquired control of the region in 1674; the region has been administered by the French state ever since.[26] Nonetheless, after 1615 the French made no further attempt at establishing colonial settlements in Brazil.

If the French attempts at colonization were circumstantial, those of the Dutch were very different. Relations between Portugal and Holland had never been easy, and they were seemingly destined to confront each other directly in the New World.[27] With the end of the Avis dynasty in 1580, the succession crisis in Portugal came to a head, and the throne passed to the Spanish Crown, during the period now known as the

Iberian Union. During the period known as the 'Philippine Dynasty' it was not only the two Crowns that were shared, but also the respective colonies of Spain and Portugal. Although the 'Iberian Union' is a term that was coined by modern historians, it appropriately describes the situation in which Portugal not only came under Spanish rule but also 'acquired' Spain's enemies, which included, of course, the Netherlands.

The Netherlands had only recently become independent; previously the country had been a part of the Habsburg Empire that was ruled from Spain. Since Spain refused to recognize Dutch independence, relations between the two countries were strained. Holland and the Low Countries, previously allies of the Portuguese, now became enemies. And with the new status quo the Dutch felt justified in invading Portugal's wealthiest colonies. After all, as an ally of Portugal, the Dutch had previously controlled the commercialization and refinement of sugar from Brazil; they would now, at least theoretically, have to relinquish them.

They did not delay. In 1595 the Dutch pillaged the African coast and, in 1604, launched an attack on the city of Salvador, then Brazil's capital city.[28] They were confident they could count on the inexperience of the local military defence and imagined (wrongly as it turned out) that after conquering the city the Portuguese inhabitants would accept them. They were, however, in doubt as to whether their military forces would be able to defend the vast extent of the colony's entire coastline.[29] Apart from these strategic considerations, the Dutch relished the prospect of the profits they could make in Brazil. They also thought that a Dutch conquest would weaken the Spanish Crown, and consequently the Iberian Union. The plan was simple: attack the capital, the head of the colony. However, this first assault in 1604 failed, and it would be some time before the Dutch tried again.

After relative tranquillity for several years, tensions rose again for Portugal. In 1621 the Dutch West India Company was founded, an event that was to alter the status quo and mark the end of the truce between the two countries. The company was financed with state money as well as by private financiers, and its principal aims were to take over sugar production areas in Brazil and control of the supply of slaves from Africa: two highly complementary activities. As Padre Antonil,[30] one of the most important chroniclers of Portuguese America, stated at the beginning of the eighteenth century, the slaves were 'the hands and feet' of the sugar-mill owners, and without them there would be no sugar.

The population of Salvador was aware of Dutch intentions and expected an attack. Since the end of the truce, a recommencement of the conflict between Spain and the Netherlands was thought to be highly plausible and it seemed likely that it would spill over into Portuguese America. The next Dutch attack on the capital came on 9 May 1624, on which occasion they held the city for twenty-four hours. According to the historian Charles Boxer, 'such was the panic, and so generalised, that neither whites nor Indians were of any use at all, each looking for a safe place to hide without even thinking of fighting back'.

However, the Dutch didn't manage to go beyond the limits of the city. Led by Matias de Albuquerque – the new Portuguese governor of the colony – and by Bishop Marcos Teixeira, the so-called 'good men' organized the resistance and prevented the farms from being taken. They used guerrilla tactics until the arrival of a surprisingly large contingent of reinforcements from Portugal – 56 man-of-wars, 1,185 pieces of artillery and 12,463 men from Castela, Portugal and Naples – who managed to prevent the expansion of the invasion. Portugal was determined not to lose its richest colony; after suffering prolonged fighting, ambushes and going without food, the Dutch surrendered. They had been in Bahia for almost a year. There was to be another attack in 1627, but on that occasion the Dutch force was smaller and the city was better fortified. The Dutch seemed more interested in sacking the city than invading it, to the extent that they took 2,654 crates of sugar (approximately one-sixth of the annual production of the Recôncavo), as well as leather, tobacco, cotton, gold and silver.[31]

But the Dutch refused to give up. They set their eyes on the prosperous captaincy of Pernambuco, which at that time rivalled Bahia in wealth. With its 121 sugar mills the captaincy had awakened the interest of the directors of the Dutch West India Company.[32] In addition, the journey from Salvador to Luanda took thirty-five days, whereas from Recife it took only twenty-nine, a difference that the Dutch would have been well aware of.[33] They launched the attack in early 1630, with sixty-five vessels and 7,280 men. Olinda, the capital, fell on 14 February.

The first reaction from Madrid, when it heard of the catastrophe, was to send an order to Lisbon to pray 'that a greater evil be avoided'. The Inquisition was told to redouble its efforts and apply harsher punishments, as the event could only be understood as 'punishment from God', who must have been angered by the freeing of the Jews and heretics. But the prayers did not do the job and a resistance army had to be formed. At the same time a guerrilla campaign – the *guerra brasílica* – was organized. Nevertheless, between 1630 and 1637 the Dutch consolidated their control of the region between Ceará and the São Francisco river. At this time a local plantation owner named Domingos Fernandes Calabar became notorious in Portugal and Brazil for his treachery. Calabar left the Portuguese forces and joined the Dutch, using his knowledge of the local terrain to facilitate the enemy's advance. In the end he was arrested and executed. Today he is still seen as a paradoxical figure in Brazil: a hero for some, a villain for others. Traitor of the Portuguese interests or defender of another Brazil: a Dutch Brazil.

Rather than casting the deciding vote, it would be wiser, perhaps, to describe the period of peace that followed the wars of resistance. Although the Portuguese continued fighting in the interior, abandoning the cities and fortresses to the enemy, the Dutch were already certain of their victory and began to invest in the colony they had conquered. The Council of Nineteen, which governed the West India Company responsible for the administration of Dutch Brazil, invited a young army colonel to become governor-general from 1637 to 1644: the German count Johann Moritz von Nassau-Siegen, who was thirty-two at the time. When Nassau arrived in the captaincy the situation was extremely disheartening: the sugar mills were destroyed and abandoned and the population terrified and dismayed, both at the destruction that had been wrought and at the idea of being ruled by a foreign conqueror.

With the aim of reinvigorating the economy and gaining credibility, Nassau had the abandoned sugar mills sold on credit, the owners having fled to Bahia. He re-established the slave traffic to the region (the Dutch had invaded a number of slave markets in Africa); provided credit for the purchase of factories and equipment; and solved the food supply crisis by obliging landowners to plant 'the bread of the country' – manioc – in proportion to the number of slaves they owned. A Calvinist, the count decreed freedom of religion, was tolerant towards the Catholics and, according to documents of time, also towards the so-called 'Crypto-Jews', the New Christians,[34] who until then had practised their religion in secret. Traders of Jewish origin were active in Recife, which, in the 1640s, boasted two synagogues. Nassau also encouraged artists, botanists and academics to come to Pernambuco.

The few depictions of Dutch Brazil were painted by artists invited by

Nassau to Pernambuco during this period. Since the majority of Portuguese paintings were religious in nature, intended for churches, artists such as Frans Post (1612–1680) and Albert Eckhout (1610–1666) are essential references for this period. Post was only twenty-four when he arrived in Brazil, a member of Nassau's retinue. Very little is known about him, except that he was born in 1612 in the city of Leiden, where there was a concentration of important artists who had been trained at the local university. He painted innumerable views of ports and fortifications, and appears to have been enchanted with the placid tropics of Pernambuco, Maranhão and Bahia. With the dearth of pictures of daily life of the time, his paintings have become part of the Brazilian imaginary, as if they faithfully depicted Dutch Brazil of the seventeenth century. But they do not. Whereas in Holland most of the painters illustrated family and urban scenes, Frans Post preferred Brazilian landscapes. Cloudy skies, magnificent waterfalls, isolated houses, boats on paradisiacal rivers, exotic fruits and animals – all depictions of the harmonious, unchartered tropics.

Albert Eckhout also visited Nassau's Dutch captaincy, where he concentrated on depicting the Indians and fruits of the region. Initially seen as a reliable, ethnographic source, the details of this Dutchman's paintings actually reveal a number of folkloric elements. The artist gave his viewers what they wanted to see: 'the exotic practices of these cannibal people'. This must have been the reason why, in a painting of a tranquil Tapuia couple, Eckhout insisted on including the hands and feet of their dead enemies, deposited in baskets which the couple carried on their backs, in an obvious allusion to cannibalism and the stories that surrounded it. In addition to Eckhout and Post, Zacharias Wagenaer (1614–1688) left a rich legacy of drawings representing a dance of the African cult of Xangô, the sugar mill at Maciape and the slave market in Recife.

The importance of the name Nassau goes beyond the incentives he gave to the arts and commerce. The count undertook far-reaching improvements to the city of Recife, which the Dutch elevated to the capital of the colony, replacing Olinda. Near to the rundown area of the port, Nassau constructed the *Cidade Maurícia*, designed by the architect Pieter Post; a tropical replica of the Dutch capital, built on a grid system intersected by canals. The new town greatly improved the precarious hygiene and housing conditions of the population, estimated at around 7,000. This is the town that appears as Mauritz-Stadt on the maps and panoramas included in the work of Gaspar Barlaeus, published in Amsterdam in the year 1647. The governor also built palaces, a Calvinist temple, and installed Brazil's first observatory (which registered a solar eclipse in 1640). He went on to pave some of the streets and create a sewage system. He ordered that all the streets be covered with sand to prevent flooding. The operation had to be repeated twice a day, or risk a fine of six florins. The same fine was charged to anyone who 'threw rubbish on the streets'[35] or sugarcane bagasse[36] into the rivers or reservoirs, as it prevented the proliferation of freshwater fish, which was the basic diet of the population. Nassau also ordered the construction of three bridges, the first ones of major proportions to be built in Brazil.

Maurice of Nassau created a large 'recreation garden' in Recife, which was also an orchard for rare plants, with 852 orange trees, 5 lemon trees, 80 sweet lime trees and 66 fig trees. Seven hundred coconut palms were planted specifically as habitat for animals brought from all over the world. These included many types of birds: Alagoas curassows,[37] parrots, peacocks, pigeons, turkeys, ducks, swans and guinea fowl. There were also spiders, tortoises, coatis, anteaters, howler monkeys and marmosets, large cats including tigers and pumas, goats from Cape Verde, sheep from Angola, as well as fish, for which two breeding tanks were built. The park was used as a kind of laboratory by the scientists who were part of Nassau's retinue. Among these was the doctor Willem Piso – who studied the natural environment, the tropical climate and disease – and the botanist and cartographer Georg Marcgrave. In his palace the count built up a collection of curiosities that included bows, arrows, spears, hammocks, indigenous ornaments made from feathers, furniture made from jacaranda and ivory – all of which were made in Brazil.[38]

Nassau was extremely popular in Brazil, nicknamed 'The Brazilian' due to his fascination with the colony. Nonetheless, he was pressured by the Dutch authorities to return to Europe in 1644, the same year that marks the beginning of the decline of Dutch Brazil – a colonial project conceived to last forever.

The following year the so-called *guerras brasílicas* against the Dutch started once again. These wars that were known as 'The Reconquest' were to continue until 1654, with Portuguese and Brazilian troops once again joining forces to expel the 'invaders'. The terms *coloniseres* and *invadors* are indicative of the mood and the local temperature. During peacetime, the Dutch had been referred to as 'colonizers'; now they once again became 'intrusive invaders'. The international situation was also extremely complex: in 1640 the Portuguese had risen up against the Spanish Crown and restored the Portuguese monarchy. John IV,[39] the first monarch of the House of Bragança, was placed on the throne and acclaimed by the *Cortes*.[40] Although this marked the end of the Iberian Union, relations between Portugal and Holland continued to be hostile; the peaceful relations between the two nations that had existed before 1580 were not to be re-established. The Dutch had occupied a considerable part of Brazilian territory and gave no indications that they intended to leave. A revolt was organized in Pernambuco under the leadership of André Vidal de Negreiros and João Fernandes Vieira, one of the most prosperous landowners in the area, and they were joined by the Afro-Brazilian military leader Henrique Dias and the Indian Filipe Camarão.

The two battles of Guararapes, fought between 1648 and 1649, ten kilometres south of Recife, are seen as a sort of cornerstone for the creation of the Brazilian nation, above all in Pernambuco. The story was further elaborated by future generations, glorifying the multi-ethnic people of the region who had united to fight for Brazil's emancipation. With time the term 'Reconquest' acquired an emotive force, and even today the event is celebrated by Portuguese and Brazilians as a triumph of 'the just'.[41] Most of the time history is written by the winners, and, in this case, the Dutch were the losers. Today we know that, in addition to Calabar, many sugar-mill owners, cane-cutters, New Christians, black slaves, Tapuia Indians, poor mestizos and others among the poorest classes supported the Dutch. The forces that confronted the Dutch in no way demonstrated a united front made up of the country's three races: Indians, blacks and Portuguese.

The wars continued for several years: while the insurrectionists occupied the interior, the Dutch maintained control of Recife. The uprising of the Brazilians was not, however, the only reason for the collapse of the Dutch: the West India Company itself was in crisis and could no longer find investors. Besides the lack of funds, there was also a culture shock: while the Portuguese tended to be dogmatic about religion, and rather unorthodox when it came to politics and economics, the Dutch were the exact opposite. They were tolerant in religious practices, but extremely harsh when dealing with landowners in debt. In the end, after so many years of conflict, the resources required for financing the military operation in Brazil were simply no longer forthcoming.

The Dutch finally capitulated in 1654, when a Portuguese squadron arrived and blockaded Recife. The Portuguese resistance movement, which became known as the 'War of Divine Freedom', concentrated on making alliances throughout the region, especially with landowners who were discontent with the high taxes demanded by the Dutch. On 6 August 1661, with the intervention of the British monarchy, the details of the Treaty of The Hague were finally agreed: the Portuguese would keep all the invaded territories in Africa and America and would pay the Dutch compensation of four million cruzados. The Brazilian government introduced a tax to help pay for it; to have an idea of how long a shadow was cast by this tax, it remained in force until the nineteenth century (although the sum had been fully paid off long before). The Pernambucans were indignant at the idea of having to pay for a war that they had won. Perhaps the seeds had already been sown for the future uprisings that were to take place in this state, most ferociously in the nineteenth century.[42]

But, at least for the time being, peace had been re-established and the captaincy of Pernambuco could get back to the laborious task of producing sugar. The war against the Dutch was just one example of the warlike atmosphere in Brazil during this period, 'everyone against everyone'. In addition to the fear of another foreign occupation, there was also the smouldering anger of the Amerindians and the enslaved Africans.[43] In such a society every citizen carried a weapon and never laid it down.

IN THE LAND OF FORCED LABOUR

Brazil had now established a major enterprise based entirely on the monoculture of sugarcane. Other minor activities developed around the plantations, such as the production of subsistence food – especially manioc – and cattle-raising. Cattle were indispensable for the cultivation of the land, the grinding and transportation of sugarcane, as well as for providing food for the population. Alongside the sugar-based society, a 'leather society' developed in the interior of the northeast, due to both the abundance of cattle and of men available for work.

In Bahia, the cultivation of tobacco was developed in Cachoeira and in the Recôncavo, as well as further north in the captaincy; combined, these areas were responsible for around 90 per cent of national production. A variety of tobaccos were produced, of which the most refined were exported to Europe. The coarser varieties were used as barter for slaves on the African coast. Tobacco production was to complement the production of sugarcane. It could be produced on a small scale, so that many smallholdings developed, mostly run by manioc farmers or Portuguese immigrants who had arrived in the colony with hardly any money. Tobacco also helped to stabilize Portugal's trade balance, as its production in the colony was a Crown monopoly. There was no risk, however, of tobacco competing with sugarcane in terms of importance, or of funding the emergence of a landowning class who might rival the sugarcane planters.

For the sugar system to function, to keep the mill wheels turning, it was vital to maintain the supply of labour. As was noted, the use of indigenous workers had already become a thorny problem in the previous century around the production of brazilwood. In the era of sugarcane production, the situation became even more serious. The religious orders, above all the Jesuits, did all they could to discourage the use of slave labour. Among other arguments, they alleged that the indigenous people were 'rebels', 'idle', and refused to settle on the land. Today we know the Amerindians were no more rebellious nor 'less inclined to work' than any other human beings submitted to a system of slavery that presupposes the ownership of one man by another and uses violence as its *modus operandi*. But in truth the Church and the colonizers had widely diverging views when it came to policies regarding the treatment of Indians on the one hand and Africans on the other.

The fight between the settlers and the Church over the question of enslaving the Indians was never-ending, as were the myths surrounding the issue of forced native labour. The Church's argument, based on moral considerations, was that the Indians were 'unsuited' for agricultural work. However, this supposed 'lack of ability to adapt' actually revealed the very different ways in which Europeans and Native Americans conceived of their daily life. The Indians were entirely indifferent to the concept of 'surplus'; their concern was for the welfare of the community, for reciprocity in cultivation and consumption. This was domestic production. In indigenous society, status was not derived from economic capacity. This different understanding of labour was interpreted by the Portuguese as a lack of energy or aptitude. In reality, it was the consequence of an entirely different concept of the world, of social relations, and of the management of life's basic necessities.

Beyond these differences, diseases such as smallpox and even their deep knowledge of the land were contributing factors to the Indians' fleeing from the advancing colonists. Above all, their goal was to avoid being seized and enslaved. Meanwhile the Church continued preaching that its evangelizing mission was a moral and Christian duty. The Indians were 'flocks' of potential converts to the faith of Reformed Christianity.

However, in contrast to the traditional view popularized by history books – that the demise of the Indians prompted the importation of African slaves – we now know that the Indians in fact continued to be enslaved for a very long period of time. For example, the *Paulistas*[44] continued to imprison Indians until the eighteenth century, either selling them or using them as slave labour for plantations on the Piratininga plateau. The *Paulistas* not only attacked the Jesuit missions established in the region of the Paraguay river, but also, starting in 1640, they virtually decimated the Indian populations from the whole of the northeastern scrublands, before the advance of the colonizers into the region. This campaign against the Indian population, known as the Barbarians' War, continued until the middle of the eighteenth century.[45] The interests of the *Paulistas* and those of the Jesuits were diametrically opposed, leading to the constant undermining of each other's initiatives.

In fact, the maintenance of a prosperous market, for an industry like sugarcane, required long-term, stable solutions, completely separate from religious and moral controversies. Thus, the marriage of the profitable trade in sugarcane with that of the traffic of human beings. On the one hand, the Portuguese Empire had trading posts along the entire western coast of Africa; on the other, by controlling the internal wars on the South American continent, the Portuguese traders could turn the conquered into captives, replicating the slavery of the African continent.[46]

It is true that various forms of slavery have existed in Africa. The critical difference, however, is the scale and systematic nature of the process, which involved the introduction of a mercantile system that generated enormous profits, first for the African negotiators, then for the Portuguese, and finally for the Brazilian traders. The purchase and distribution of slaves constituted a kind of advanced payment against the income generated by the colony. Both the supply of labour and the sale of sugarcane were monopolies of the Portuguese Crown. Almost none of the wealth remained in the colony: neither the sugarcane nor the profits it produced.

Gradually, more and more Brazilians began to traffic in slaves. Records show that around this time many slave traders began to be referred to as 'Brazilian', probably to distinguish them from colonists of Portuguese origin. On several occasions, particularly in the eighteenth century, the African slave markets controlled by the Dutch refused to trade with the Portuguese while continuing to trade with the Brazilians. The Brazilians, after all, were equipped with *cachaça*,[47] tobacco and leather, with which they bartered for slaves.

Parodoxically, the long history of African slavery on the Iberian Peninsula, which increased during the expansion of the Atlantic sugar trade, had allowed the Portuguese to become very familiar with the Africans and for them to get to know their particular strengths. As early as the sixteenth century, the ability of many African peoples to learn the techniques of making sugar was carefully recorded in Portuguese documents. This is the reason why the first Africans to arrive in Brazil, coming from Angola and Guinea, were immediately assigned specialized tasks, such as purging and boiling the sugar and overseeing the production process. Actually, a number of slaves from western Africa were already experienced in blacksmithing, agriculture, and in branding and caring for cattle. This did not imply they were 'willing slaves': very much to the contrary.

As time passed, African slavery became increasingly associated with the process of sugar production, until the two phenomena were regarded as virtually inseparable. The embeddedness of slavery in Brazilian colonial culture at this time is reflected in the terms that were used – Indians were referred to as 'natives' or 'negroes', and Africans as 'Guinea' negroes or 'native' negroes. The word *negro* had thus become a generic term that signified 'slave', marking the polarity between black and white on which the economy of the colony depended. The range of words adopted by the Portuguese language to indicate gradations of skin colour, far from indicating a lack of discrimination, constituted a veritable exercise in linguistic engineering to distinguish physical features, behavioural characteristics and differing mentalities. The structure was complex and at first sight appears to have been more flexible than it was. Native Americans, after being catechized, became vassals of the Crown, whereas slaves were converted to Christianity. But in reality the colony adopted slavery throughout the whole of its territory, creating a dichotomous society that opposed landowners to slaves, whites to blacks and natives to Africans.

Although, for the palate, sweetness and bitterness are two different things, in the logic of the sugarcane business they were inseparable. The slave ships were never idle. Ships crossed and recrossed the Atlantic, laden with white sugar – the whiter it was the greater its purity – and cargoes of black-skinned slaves from the various nations of Africa. Slave labour was decreed by the *Cortes* of Lisbon, the commercial establishments of Amsterdam and London, the forests of the Amazon, the trading posts of Africa, and above all by the sugar plantations of America.[48] As Padre Vieira said, a new hell had been created in the distant lands of Brazil. A hell that was no longer made from the red dye of brazilwood, but from the furnaces of the sugar mills and the bleeding bodies of slaves.

A NEW 'SUGAR LOGIC'

From the beginning of the sixteenth century every aspect of the colonial enterprise depended on the production of sugarcane: from the formation of settlements, towns and the defence of territories, to the division of properties, relations between differing social groups, even the choice of the capital. In 1548, Dom João III established by Royal Charter the appointment of a governor-general and other representatives of the Crown who would reside in the colony. The following year the first governor, Tomé de Souza, disembarked in the then almost deserted captaincy of Bahia and immediately set about building the capital on the coast. Baptized as *Salvador da Bahia de Todos os Santos*, the city was to remain Brazil's capital until 1763, when it was transferred to Rio de Janeiro. Salvador became the seat of government, of the Supreme Court and of the principal Crown Inspectors. It became a centre for exportation, first of brazilwood and later of sugarcane. But not all the captaincies were as lucky. Most of them were sorely afflicted by isolation and Indian attacks, so that little advantage could be taken of the incentives provided by the Crown: exemption from taxes such as the 10 per cent tithe as well as other fiscal advantages.

Despite the Crown's attempts to control the colony, decentralization was evident. Power was retained, both literally and symbolically, in the *casa-grande* and the *engenho*;[49] these were the centres of colonial life, of command and of hierarchy. The word *engenho*, which initially referred to the sugar mill itself, later came to signify the entire sugar production complex: the mills, the land, the plantations and the outbuildings.

The *casa-grande* was located near the sugar mills. Not only was it the landowner's residence, it also served as a fortress, guesthouse and office. Some of these houses had a second floor, but even so, in most cases, they were by no means imposing. Until the seventeenth century their appearance was modest; the walls were made out of wattle covered with mud and the roofs were thatched with *sapê*.[50] Nevertheless, the landowners, especially the owners of *engenhos* near the coast, made these houses icons of the social importance and economic and political power they had acquired in the colony. Padre Antonil described these landowners as having the position to which everyone aspired, saying that they were 'served, obeyed and generally respected'. They constituted a kind of aristocracy of wealth and power rather than the hereditary nobility of European countries.

In the colony, titles of nobility were conferred in recognition of services rendered but could also be bought. However, those who aspired to nobility did not have the enduring power that the sugar barons enjoyed. As the traveller Alexander von Humboldt noted: 'In America, every white man is a gentleman.' In a territory where the workforce was made up of African slaves, the mere fact of being white was considered a merit in itself with the right to be treated as nobility. In 1789 an employee of the Crown noted that the colony was a place where 'a person with few possessions and modest origins gives himself airs of the grandest noble'.[51] Even learned magistrates and wealthy tradesmen aspired to become aristocrats.

Members of the nobility in Brazil were defined by what they *did not* do. Manual labour, running a shop, working as an artisan and other such activities were all carried out by natives or slaves. This may explain why the prejudice against manual labour, considered an 'inferior' activity and generally treated with contempt, has persisted in Brazil. The 'nobles', on the other hand, lived off their income from rents and government posts. The best thing of all, however, was to be a sugar baron and surround oneself with a large number of relatives, servants and hangers-on. Capital, power, authority, ownership of slaves, engagement in politics, being the head of a large household with numerous relatives – these were the collective trappings of this new 'nobility' that dominated colonial society. This model, based on the extended family, was to last throughout the sugarcane cycle. Although the biological family formed the nucleus of the *engenho*, the master's entourage also included adopted children and others to whom the household offered a home,[52] as well as relatives, servants and slaves.

Furthermore, taking these landowning families as a whole, very few of them were Portuguese nobility, and even fewer Old Christians. Ever since the establishment of the Inquisition in Portugal, during the reign of Dom Manuel I, the distinction had been made between the descendants of Roman Catholics – 'Old Christians' – and those of recently converted Jews – the 'New Christians'. Despite their airs and graces, many of the sugar barons were in fact New Christians, descended from wealthy immigrant tradesmen who had invested their time and capital in the production and sale of sugarcane. After a few generations of marrying into Old Christian families, these landowners set about the task of creating a mythical genealogy, establishing distant links to noble families.

However, whether they were descended from nobility or not, they 'reinvented' themselves as though they were. There are many reports describing how the landowners ceremoniously paraded around the streets in their fine clothes, white hats and polished boots. Early risers, by daybreak they would have already examined the property, given work orders, and checked that the previous day's tasks had been satisfactorily completed. They also liked to be associated with a certain type of sociability, maintaining their salons and tables generously replete, and entertaining and organizing outings. The local villagers and the workers who crushed the sugarcane would greet them with filial reverence, often being bestowed with nicknames as part of the display of paternalistic dominance.

An important part of this spectacle of power involved dressing the master's family in the finest clothes originating from abroad, offering lavish hospitality and showing off the luxurious interiors of the *casas-grandes*, whose architecture during the seventeenth century became more and more imposing. These two-storey houses varied in style and size. All of them, however, had large windows, verandas that ran all around the house, and elegant pillars. They were usually built on the highest point of the *engenho* so that they could be seen from afar. They contained a large number of bedrooms – for the family and those it had taken in: parents-in-law, nephews, grandchildren, political allies, tradesmen, family friends and the household's parson – as well as a reception room, a dining room, an oratory, an office, a larder and a kitchen. Adjoined to the *casa-grande*, and virtually an extension of it, was the chapel: modest, entirely white, but big enough for baptisms, marriages and funerals. These were normally low brick buildings with only one altar. The landowners were often greatly attached to their small chapels and frequently stated in their wills their wish to be buried there.

Whether built inside the *casa-grande* or set apart, these chapels were an essential element of this universe. On Sundays and public holidays the few wooden benches and chairs they contained were not enough to seat all of the people who came for Mass: the master's extended family, local farmers, neighbours and others whose lives gravitated around the *engenho*. The slaves were also summoned to attend religious services, and those who had not been previously christened in Africa were ritually baptized. The Roman Catholic religion was central to this world of sugarcane and forced labour; it was therefore an established tradition for the master to choose one of his sons for a life of celibacy in the priesthood. The oldest son would be the heir to the *engenho*. The second was usually destined for service to the Crown, in administration, law, or in war. And if the master, whose virility was measured by the number of offspring – preferably male – he sired, was 'blessed by fortune', the third son would become a priest. And so the landowners ensured their ties both to the government and to the Church, both of which supported the sugar industry.

Another symbol of opulence was the abundant quantities of food served at the master's table. The household was never without sugar, large quantities of which were delivered to the kitchen, above all for making deserts – made from corn, coconut, passion fruit, banana, geni-pap and mangaba[53] – as well as cakes and sweets. Many of these desserts were given sentimental names, indicating intimacy, such as 'love rings', 'love ties', 'love cake', 'husband fattener' or 'flirty'; while others had religious overtones such as 'Eve's pudding', 'Manna from heaven' or 'nun's dream'.[54] By the way, these pious names are an indication that housewives in the colony continued the Portuguese tradition of the confectioner nuns (and may be related to the fact that some of the larger *engenhos* had convents built on their land).[55] Perhaps it is no coincidence that the expression 'winning friends through the stomach' is still used in Brazil today.[56]

But there was no *casa-grande* without the *senzala* – the slave quarters. It was these two, apparent opposites – which were in fact intimately connected – that became the subject matter of Gilberto Freyre's iconic account of the formation of Brazilian society, *Casa-grande & Senzala*, published in 1933, in which he discusses the contradictions surrounding the relationship between masters and slaves. The '&' in the title, linking the two, shows that the Pernambucan anthropologist understood the importance of the co-relation between these two extremes. 'Balancing the economic and cultural antagonism' were the words he used to indicate how paternalism and violence, but also negotiations between the two sides, coexisted in daily life.[57]

Senzala is a Kimbundu[58] word that means 'residence for workers on an agricultural property' or 'a dwelling separate from the main house'. The sugarcane *senzalas* housed dozens or even hundreds of slaves, frequently with their hands and arms chained, lying on the dirt floor in appalling hygienic conditions. As owning large numbers of slaves was a sign of prestige and prosperity, the masters preferred quantity to quality. The circumstances varied: on some plantations the slaves were lodged collectively, on others there were separate lodgings for men and women, and in a few cases separate lodgings for couples and children. In the northeast, most of the *senzalas* consisted of adjoining huts laid out in rows at a certain distance from the *casa-grande*. The overseers padlocked them at night in order to prevent escape, to impose discipline, and to control what time the slaves woke up and went to sleep. Rest was scarce, as was sanitation. The *senzalas* had neither light nor windows, so not only was there permanent darkness, but overcrowding made them stifling. The huts usually consisted of mud walls and roofs thatched with *sapê*, and were very fragile, leading many travellers of the time to comment on their rudimentary appearance.[59] There was no *casa-grande* without a *senzala*, two sides of the same coin.

In contrast, the masters surrounded themselves with symbols of their 'aristocracy': fine clothes, rich furniture, thoroughbred horses, literacy in a land of illiterates, and above all the power of command. Another aspect of Brazilian life that differed from that of Lisbon was the coexistence of various cultures that were classified by the colonizers in terms of gradation of colour. Since both Africans and Indians were seen as pagans (even though they had been baptized or transformed into vassals), neither group had any rights. The divisions between 'natives' and 'village Indians', or, among Africans, *boçais* and *ladinos*,[60] thus represented cultural categories that marked the divisions within internal hierarchies of inclusion and exclusion.

Colour became a basic social indicator. The categories were fluid and varied according to time and place: but they always defined social status. Mixed-race groups that originated, from the early days of the colony, from intercourse between Portuguese and Indians or between whites and blacks, were classified separately. And there were further subdivisions in the day-to-day life of the colony: children born from intercourse between masters and slaves were called *mestizos*; those from intercourse between Indians and blacks were called *cabras*; *moreno* (originating from the word 'Moor') referred to a person with 'dark-coloured' skin, and lastly came *pardo* (something akin to 'a pale-skinned mestizo'). The colour *pardo* is still included in the Brazilian census, in practice meaning something along the lines of 'none of the above', a sort of *et cetera* or a wildcard in the classification. In other words, those who are not white, yellow (the colour used in Brazil to refer to peoples from the East), red (the Indians) or black are usually called *pardo*.

Even today the meaning of this word varies according to social context and the person it is used to classify. The word is thought to have come from Portugal, originating from the name *pardal* (sparrow), known for its dark feathers of an undefined colour on the one hand and its common presence on the other.[61] There were further ethnic and racial subdivisions of *mestizos*: *mamelucos* (resulting from intercourse between Indians and whites); *caboclos* (Indians who spoke the language taught by the Jesuits – the *lingua franca*); *carijós* (the term originally used to classify the inhabitants of southern Brazil, but which in Tupi designated the descendants of the union between a white man and a black bird with white wings); and *curibocas* (mestizos with copper-coloured skin, and straight hair).[62]

During the 'sugarcane era' this was the complex human 'mapping system' by colour and by parentage. 'Coloured people', a word still current in Brazil (used as a sort of euphemism – 'colour' means 'black', whereas 'white' is a non-colour), were submitted to every possible type of discrimination. Firstly, the shade of their skin colour indicated that their forebears were slaves, with the consequent implications of forced manual labour that was treated with such contempt. Secondly, it indicated a morally doubtful social standing, since these people were born of 'unofficial' unions (cases of slave-owners officially registering their illegitimate children were very rare). And lastly, mestizos were typecast as greedy, devious and not be trusted.

As some slaves were gradually released by their masters, a heterogeneous group of free blacks gradually emerged and surrounded the *casa-grande*. Again, this group was shaped by gradations of colour: the lighter a person's skin colour, the easier it was for her or him to achieve their release (the so-called *alforria*) and employment, even a domestic job inside the slave-master's residence. Freed slaves with sufficient resources immediately acquired slaves of their own, as did poor farmers. In the sugarcane culture, having slaves was a symbol of social distinction, a virtual guarantee that the owner was a prosperous, reliable citizen.

A complex combination of racial, cultural and personal considerations existed. 'Mulattoes' and 'Creoles' – the latter referring to slaves born on their owners' property, in other words, not African – were those who got closest to the *casa-grande* itself. They constituted a type of elite who undertook domestic and specialized tasks, although they were often referred to as lazy. *Pardos* were considered capable of mastering specific assignments, whereas 'Africans' were seen as 'foreign pagans' – or at best recent converts – who were, with rare exceptions, dangerous and unstable. Slavery became increasingly associated with Africans and their descendants. Over time, this concept was to become deeply rooted in Portuguese America.

Although slave-owners and their slaves formed the heart of the sugarcane complex, there was a wider social world, made up of *agregados* (retainers) and farmers, which revolved around them. The former often comprised a large group whose living depended on the favour of the master. Although these retainers had little economic power, they did have some political and social significance because their numbers and loyalty bolstered their master's influence. This group was made up of freed slaves, local politicians and tradesmen, and relatives who had no land, and thus were dependent. The dispensation of favours by the local master became a kind of currency that further increased his dominion, and fed the economic, political and cultural centralization of the plantation complex.[63] Meanwhile, the farmers were divided into two groups: those who leased land from the owner; and small landowners who depended on the sugar mills of the *engenho* to grind their sugarcane. In neither case did they escape the sovereignty of the master.

Thus a sugarcane aristocracy was created, commanded by the slave-owner around whom political and social life centred. In the 'distant world of the Brazils' the main landowner of the region reigned virtually uncontested. The Crown was reluctant to intervene in what it considered internal matters. However, the day-to-day business of sugarcane was by no means secure. There were many risks. The business was at the mercy of oscillations in international market prices, and the size of the harvest; it depended on good management, on adequate control of the slaves, and the wise administration of paternalistic favours to a vast extended family.

THE SUGARCANE BUSINESS

The idea of a sugarcane 'culture' is appropriate because sugar production permeated the social, economic and cultural life of the colony. The production process occupied the entire year, without intervals. Planting began with the first rains of February and continued until May. In some regions it extended into July or August. Preference was given to higher land due to the weeds – the great enemy of the sugar plantations – that proliferated in low-lying areas. The land was prepared by burning, a technique inherited from the Indians and based on the premise that there was no lack of land in these Brazils. First the trees were cut down and then the vegetation was set alight. Ploughs were not used; the slaves turned the earth with hoes. The cane that was introduced into Brazil originally came from India – the same plant that had been successful in Sicily – and was popularly known as *cana-crioula*. It was a slender plant with short stems whose productivity was considered to be poor in relation to other varieties. Once again the name is no coincidence; it denotes a moral judgement on the Creoles. After twelve or at most eighteen months, the harvest began, always programmed to coincide with the availability of the mills for grinding. The process had to be fast and efficient, because twenty-four hours after the cane was cut its sucrose content diminished significantly.

Once the cane had been cut it was taken from the plantation to the mill by boat or on ox-drawn carts. Transport by boat was much faster. Consequently land that was close to rivers commanded the highest prices. Rivers also powered the large-scale watermills, which were known as 'water mills' or 'royal mills' because they were superior to the others, not because of any connection to the Crown. But very few landowners could afford the luxury of such a mill. Most were operated by oxen, horses, or even by human beings, and were popularly known as *trapiches*, *molinetes*[64] or *almanjarras*. In the last named it was the slaves who inserted the sugarcane into the rollers, an extremely dangerous job that led to frequent accidents.

There were further distinctions that separated the *engenhos* located on the coast – considered to be the oldest and most aristocratic – from those 'in the woodlands' or 'the interior'. The latter were in general smaller and poorer. The technique used for sugar production was relatively primitive. Until the seventeenth century most of the mills worked with two horizontal wooden cylinders and the grinding process was slow. It was only after 1610 that more advanced installations began to be used, in the so-called 'stilt mills', which adopted a new system for grinding: three metal-lined cylinders that not only required fewer workers but also produced faster results.

Another item that was essential for operating the mills was wood. It has been calculated that one ox-drawn cartload of wood per hour was needed to feed the furnaces. The Jesuit Padre Antonil described them as 'mouths that devour forests, dungeons of fire and smoke, the perpetual, living images of volcanoes'.[65] One of the consequences was the devastation of the forests on Brazil's northeastern coast, which had already suffered greatly from the removal of its brazilwood.

No matter what type of sugar mill, after this initial process the sticks of sugarcane were prepared for feeding into the rollers to extract the juice. The fluid was stored in barrels before being transported to the furnace where it was boiled and purged in large copper boilers. Once it was free of impurities it was turned into molasses, which was poured into moulds or clay vessels with a capacity of around thirty-two litres. The long process did not end there. Next the sugar was taken to the 'purge house', where it went through a forty-day process of 'whitening'. Lastly, it was dried, after which, with a thin-bladed knife, the whitest part was separated from the darker portion called *muscovado*.

The price of sugar varied enormously. Four types were obtained from the first boiling. These were known as the *macho* or 'male' sugars: refined white, granulated white, low-quality white and muscovado – the prices they fetched depending on the degree of whiteness. The treacle that oozed from the vats during the purging process was also collected and reprocessed, but went for a lower price. There was also a thinner syrup that oozed from the moulds. This was used as the raw material for producing *aguardente* – *cachaça* or *pinga* – a spirit that was consumed throughout the colony and also widely used in Africa as barter for slaves. Although the three terms are used interchangeably to refer to the same drink, they are not, in fact, synonymous. *Aguardente*[66] is the generic name for any spirit distilled from sweet vegetables; *cachaça* is the specific name for *aguardente* made from sugarcane, for which *pinga* is a popular nickname. The word (which means 'drip' in Portuguese) is said to have originated from the slaves who distilled the *cachaça*: while the liquid sugarcane boiled, the steam condensed on the roof and dripped down onto their heads.

Cachaça was so popular that the importation of the product to Portugal was banned, and restrictions were even imposed on the amount that could be produced in the colony, in an attempt to protect the interests of Portuguese wine-growers. However, as an essential item for barter in the slave traffic, the spirit remained a very important product in Brazil. In the eighteenth century the city of Rio de Janeiro exported more *cachaça* than sugar. It was the city's number one export, a large amount of which was destined for use in the slave trade in Angola. In fact, every by-product of the sugar-making process was utilized, including *rapadura*, a form of unrefined cane sugar, similar to jaggery. Along with dried meat and coarse flour, with which it is often associated, it formed the basis of the workers' diet.

It is important to bear in mind a crucial and very characteristic aspect of Brazil's sugar economy: the lack of refineries. There were none in Brazil, nor in Portugal. This meant that not only the trade in sugar but also the final production stage were left in the hands of the Dutch. Brazil was best known for its unrefined sugar (the *pardo* or *muscovado*). This type of sugar, also produced in the Antilles, accounted for most of the country's production and provided the raw material for the refinery industry of northern Europe.[67]

As a matter of fact, Brazilian sugar was always treated with suspicion in Europe. The weight of the crates was frequently falsified, as was the declaration of the product's quality. The price of the sugar varied according to colour. Since the crates were sealed and thus the contents could not be verified, it was common practice to put stones in the bottom to increase their weight. European traders constantly complained about these forms of deception, saying that its 'dark sugar' and 'darker practices' would be the death of Brazil's sugar trade. The comparison between white sugar – the whiter it was, the purer – and the darker varieties, reputed to be of lower quality, became a metaphor that was to endure for many years in Brazilian society.

Soon the social hierarchy, with white landowners at the top and black slaves at the bottom, was seen as stemming from nature itself. The contrast between the status of the two groups was not explained by historical, economic or political arguments, but rather by comparison to the two colours of the sugarcane and the supposedly 'natural' supposition that white was superior to darker shades. Even today Brazilians are inclined to describe each other according to gradations of colour that correspond to different levels of the social hierarchy, in expressions such as *branco melado, branco sujo, quase branco, puxado para branco* and *mestiçado*.[68] The use of these terms shows that perceptions of social status according to colour still exist in Brazil today.[69]

Thus the combined forces of sugarcane and slavery had both an extensive and intensive impact. The cultivation and harvesting of the sugarcane took up half the year, while fabricating the sugar took up the other half. Both entailed continuous, arduous work. To give an idea of the size of the undertaking, at one seventeenth-century plantation, Sergipe do Conde, located in the Recôncavo in Bahia, there were approximately 203 tasks undertaken every day – all related to the production process. These same tasks would have taken a single worker around three hundred working days to complete. The workers toiled day and night, in two shifts, grinding and boiling the sugarcane. The purging, drying and packaging only required one shift, which, however, lasted for eighteen hours or more. On Sundays and holidays, on most plantations, the slaves worked to grow food for their own consumption or fish in a nearby river. These provisions were essential additions to a diet that was not only rationed but also had very little nutritional value.

In every sector a single day's work pushed the slaves to the edge of exhaustion. To alleviate the fatigue and maintain the frenetic rhythm, the work was accompanied by singing, which, as well as uniting the group, helped to raise morale during the long hours of uninterrupted labour. According to the Reverend Wash, a cleric who visited Brazil at the time, the slaves woke at five in the morning, said their prayers, and went straight to the plantations. Without leaving the fields they had a small breakfast at nine, followed by lunch at midday. Then they took to their hoes again and worked until nightfall. During the harvest everything had to go faster. At that time the *engenhos* operated for twenty hours non-stop, of which only four were allocated for rest and cleaning equipment.

There were four basic sectors: processing the sugarcane, transport, maintenance and administration. The *engenho* was administered by the master with the aid of a priest and the chief overseer. The master very rarely left the *engenho* during the harvest period, during which he required the help of professionals to verify legal documents and the accounts. As mentioned above, it was usual for the second son to graduate as a lawyer in order to protect his family's commercial interests and to deal with legal papers and other administrative matters. The 'royal' *engenhos* often employed a surgeon and a local clerk, who dealt with the commercial side of the operation.

Non-slave labour was used for specialized tasks, and these individuals were considered technicians. The chief overseer acted as manager, dealt with any 'personal' problems, and was responsible for applying collective and individual punishments. The slaves were terrified of him. He was also in charge of the upkeep of equipment. As the master's right-hand man, he earned the highest wages on the *engenho*. Next in the hierarchy came the clerk from the local town, who acted as a commercial agent: he received the sugar, deposited it in the warehouse on the docks, and was responsible for its sale and embarkation. Then came the 'income collector' who was responsible for receiving the rent money owed by the farmers who leased their land from the master. The copyist and stock-keeper, who controlled expenses, were paid a similar amount, as was the solicitor who acted as a sort of legal representative for the *engenho*.

Then there were the 'men of letters' who were hired to deal with lawsuits, and the 'cauldron skimmers' responsible for skimming the foam off the sugarcane juice. But perhaps the most valuable of all the sugarcane professionals, the one on whom the success of the *engenho* depended, was the 'sugar master'. Virtually an engineer, he was in charge of all the technical procedures. He oversaw the grinding, avoiding any excess of liquid, and attempted to achieve the ideal conditions for boiling. He was responsible for overseeing the entire boiling process, as well as the work of the boilers and the other mill workers. He was a highly respected professional, hard to find and very well paid.

With so many areas of specialization, the Brazilian *engenhos* adopted the manufacturing standards of the time, which tended to involve sequences of interlinked, complex activities. The requirement for large-scale production obliged Brazil to organize its sugar production units within a rigid hierarchical structure. But the rigour of the enterprise should not be overrated: documents from the period attest that scientific methods were ignored in favour of individual and group experience. Travellers used to comment that in Brazil everything was 'done by eye'. This was the way that the volume of sugarcane transported by boat or by ox-drawn cart was assessed. Tools were rudimentary: pickaxes and hoes were used for preparing the soil; ploughs were not regularly used. Ultimately, the productive cycle depended on the sweat of the slaves and the use of the whip.

This type of organization gradually evolved across the seventeenth century as slaves took the place of the few free workers. Actually, the sugar production in Brazil's northeast led to the population of African slaves outnumbering that of the Native Americans. In the 1550s and 1560s there were virtually no Africans working on plantations in the northeast. The workforce was made up of Indian slaves, and, to a lesser extent, Indians brought from the Jesuit villages. But this situation was to radically change as African slaves began to replace both the Indian slaves and the free Indian villagers. In 1574 Africans represented just 7 per cent of slave labour; in 1591 they represented 37 per cent, and by 1638, together with Afro-Brazilians, they accounted for virtually the entire workforce.[70] In 1635, for example, the aforementioned Sergipe do Conde *engenho* had eighty slaves and thirteen paid workers. By the beginning of the eighteenth century the number of slaves had risen to 200 and the number of paid workers had declined to just six. The predominance of African labour also created a paradox: the most prestigious and essential positions could be highly beneficial to slaves capable of fulfilling them, with freedom being the most valuable form of payment.

Investment in these establishments was spread between the construction of buildings, the grinding mill and the 'coppers' (boilers), as well as being used for the acquisition of cattle, carts, boats, pasture, land for planting and, most importantly, slaves. Investment in slaves varied between 7 per cent and 37 per cent of the landowner's total capital, with the majority spending around 25 per cent on the acquisition of slaves. These purchases thus represented a significant part of total expenses, and the imperative was to make the maximum use of resources and to avoid any possible 'losses'.

By the seventeenth century, the slave traffic had become a highly profitable business, and many slave-owners began to take more interest in 'replacing' their dead slaves than in helping in the long and costly task of rearing any child that 'belonged' to them. The popular assumption that slavery in Brazil was less harsh than in North America, where special ranches for 'breeding' slaves existed, is more hypothetical than true. The behaviour of Brazilian slave-owners was in no way humanitarian; it stemmed from commercial and pragmatic considerations. Maintaining a child slave until she or he had reached a productive age was expensive. Thus it was better to purchase a 'new one' in one of the open markets, where slaves were put on display alongside household goods and items of decoration. Prices also varied according to 'use': women and children were cheaper than adult men. Slaves were classified as children until they were eight; after thirty-five they were seen as old and of little use for the heavy work on the *engenhos*. Ageing occurred early, as did the end of adolescence: by the age of eight, or at most twelve, a slave's childhood was over. There are records that show slaves of eight years old being registered as fully grown men. The excessive workload aged them prematurely, depriving them of a normal lifespan. As we shall see in greater detail, the sugar culture produced a land of extremes. A genuinely new world was being created. A world that extracted the sweetness demanded by Europe from the bitter toil of those it enslaved.

3
Tit for Tat: Slavery and the Naturalization of Violence

THE TRAFFIC IN HUMAN BEINGS

The Italian Jesuit Padre Antonil was famous for making statements that were as logical as they were cruel. He defined the slaves as 'the hands and feet of their masters. Without them it is not possible to create Brazil, maintain and increase its revenues, or to keep the sugar mills running.' The slaves, who in regions like the Recôncavo in Bahia constituted as much as 75 per cent of the population, were the real foundation of society. From the sixteenth century until the prohibition of the slave traffic in 1850, the decline in slave numbers – due to premature deaths and the low birth rate – meant that new slave labour had to be constantly imported from Africa. This led to the rise of an influential class of human traffickers headed to America, and an increasing demand for products to sell on the African coast, including tobacco and *aguardente.*

Since antiquity, various forms of slavery had been known in Europe, a system that was far from extinct at the time of the great navigations, albeit less intensive and widespread than the slave trade adopted from the sixteenth century onwards. Almost all societies had coexisted with slavery at one time or another, with the common denominator that they treated their slaves as 'foreigners', as individuals who had no history or family. And it is true that peasants and serfs in Europe also lived in conditions very similar to slavery. However, it was the lack of roots, of rights and of ties to the community that distinguished slavery from these other forms of forced labour.

The Greek cities and the Roman Empire can be considered the most significant examples of slave societies in antiquity – at the height of the Roman Empire there were between two and three million slaves, representing 35 to 40 per cent of the entire population. Nonetheless, unlike slavery in modern times, forced labour was not the main source of production for goods and services. Even with the decline of the Roman Empire and the concentration of slaves in domestic duties, the system remained in place. In the fifth and sixth centuries, during the barbarian invasions, there are constant references to the existence of slaves and the use of slave labour. The practice of slavery increased with the Muslim invasions of the Iberian Peninsula and the Mediterranean islands, assuming a more significant role particularly in Spain and Portugal. It was only with the Crusades, however, from the tenth to the thirteenth centuries, that the use of slave labour became more generalized. Also between the tenth and thirteenth centuries, with the arrival of the Genoese and the Venetians in the Black Sea, the Balkans, Syria, Palestine, Cyprus and Crete, there was another wave of slave labour, a flourishing trade in captured Slavs, from where the word *slave* originates.

At the end of the Middle Ages, slaves were already working in sugar production on the Mediterranean islands, the region of Europe where the use of slave labour was at its most intense. It should be noted, however, that although a number of peoples adopted the use of slave labour, it was very rarely used in agriculture. The slaves were above all artisans. Local peasant labour remained essential for agricultural production,[1] that is, until the Portuguese arrived on the coast of Guinea in the fifteenth century.

Slavery was also used in Africa, but within a very different context: one of lineage and kinship. Without any far-reaching political or religious systems, Africans were free to sell, buy and even export their slaves. Caravans undertook the long journey into the Sahara Desert, where, since the seventh century, Islamic merchants had traded in human beings. The main trade routes were to the north of Africa, as well as to the Red Sea and to the east of the continent, where slavery also existed, although it was not fundamental to the local economy. In general, slaves were mostly used for household tasks; only in a few cases were they used for the production of goods or for agricultural labour. They also carried out domestic and religious tasks. Female slaves were often forced into working as concubines and at times were subjected to acts of ritual sacrifice. In spite of this, the slave trade flourished for eight centuries, not only domestically, but also on the international market, where Europeans were its largest clientele.

Portuguese contact with black Africa has an equally long history, pre-dating the colonization of Brazil by almost half a century. In 1453, for example, in his *Crônica de Guiné*, the Portuguese chronicler Gomes Eanes de Zurara described the activities of the Portuguese at the mouth of the Senegal river. At this time the Portuguese were mainly interested in gold, with only a secondary interest in slaves, ivory and pepper. When they first began to traffic in slaves it was to meet the demand for domestic labour in Europe. However, this was to drastically change with the growth of sugar plantations. Portuguese interest in pepper was entirely superseded by the demand for human beings. Trafficking now became the priority. By the middle of the sixteenth century, Lisbon was the European city with the largest number of African slaves, followed by Seville. Out of an overall population of a hundred thousand inhabitants, ten thousand were either black or mulatto captives.[2]

In the sixteenth and seventeenth centuries veritable Luso-African societies developed in Cape Verde, São Tomé and Madeira. The Portuguese presence grew out of transatlantic commerce, and, after 1492, the sudden increase in contact between the continents. By 1582 the population of these islands was around sixteen thousand, of whom the great majority were slaves, who accounting for 87 per cent of the total. Due to the new maritime routes and the discovery of favourable currents, the oceans that had previously separated peoples and cultures now brought them together. By 1520 the Portuguese had established a number of trading posts in Africa, from where slaves from Benin and the lower Congo river were taken to São Tomé and, from around 1570, to the flourishing market in Brazil. The traders, most of whom were Sephardi, began to take charge of the 'Brazilian sugar trade'. On the other hand, the enormous plantations in America saw the Portuguese creating a large-scale market to supply that ever increasing demand.[3]

Furthermore, at that time the concept of 'Africa' as a territorial reality did not exist, not even for the inhabitants of the continent. Prior to nineteenth-century pan-Africanism, Western societies viewed the populations residing to the south of the Sahara as 'waiting to be enslaved'. In truth, for at least six centuries Africans were exported to Asia, Europe and the Middle East. It is estimated that the number of Africans sold into slavery was around six million.

The arrival of the Portuguese on the sub-Saharan Atlantic coast in the early fifteenth century was to radically alter the slave trade, both in terms of scale and the increasing resort to violence. The Portuguese presence also affected the domestic wars between Africans, and their network of relationships in the interior of the continent. If, as we have previously noted, Portugal was initially only marginally interested in obtaining slaves, the Portuguese radically altered their position when sugarcane became one of the major products of the empire – notably after the occupation of São Tomé and the establishment of friendly relations with the Congolese. The Portuguese maintained a strong presence in the region, acting as clerks, soldiers and traffickers. They were also missionaries for the Catholic faith, which was embraced by the Congolese royal family, the region's elites and its urban population. This friendly relationship, however, was only to last until 1665.[4]

In the early years of colonization, black workers, who had been converted to Christianity and had adapted to the culture of the Iberian Peninsula, were re-exported to work on the sugar plantations in Brazil, but with the rapid expansion of sugar production slaves began to be exported directly from Africa to the New World. The numbers also increased: whereas in the first half of the sixteenth century the number of Africans brought to Brazil was just a few hundred, this number soon increased to around a thousand 'imports' a year, and by the 1580s had reached three thousand.[5] From then on Africans who had no privileged position, who were not Christians and who spoke none of the Romance languages, nicknamed *boçai*, were exported en masse to Brazil. The new trading post that the Portuguese established in Luanda on the west African coast played a central role in this increase in trade, becoming a major centre for the transport of slaves after 1575. The Portuguese trade centres were to be concentrated in Luanda for another two centuries, in the region of the Cuanza and Benguela rivers. The number of white men employed in the area never exceeded five hundred.

By this time the Portuguese considered themselves familiar with the peoples of Africa, classifying them either as friends or enemies, Muslims or pagans, never characterizing them according to colour or to what today we would refer to as 'race'. It was in part their specific use for labour that rendered slaves relatively less expensive than other workers. Other contributing factors were the increasing cost of labour brought on by the rise of the Ottoman Empire and the consolidation of an independent Moroccan Empire and the resulting restrictive use of these peoples, plus the opening of the maritime routes to sub-Saharan markets.

Furthermore, with the increase in the gold and ivory trade from western Africa and the growth of Portuguese economic activity in Asia, contact with the Africans became more frequent. At the same time, the Atlantic traffickers were becoming more efficient at providing labour for the Americas and transporting slaves with greater security. Slaves became cheaper as ever greater numbers were uprooted by force and taken to the colonies. Gradually, in the eyes of sixteenth-century Europeans the term 'African' became synonymous with 'slave labour'. Between 8 and 11 million Africans would be enslaved during the years of the trade. Of these, 4.9 million were taken to Brazil. Furthermore, the great success of the Brazilian plantation system was to influence the slave-based agricultural regimes of other European nations, with the French, British and Spanish adopting the Portuguese model, albeit on smaller estates.

The operation began by either ambushing the prospective slaves or capturing them in war. This was followed by an often lengthy journey through the African interior. The captives were forced to cover long distances to reach the port of embarkation, with many failing to survive the journey, either because of disease or else the enormous strain of the voyage. These operations were undertaken by African kingdoms allied to the Portuguese, the latter never involving themselves directly in such internal activities. In return for this traffic, some African elites were given access to weapons and popular consumer goods such as *aguardente* and tobacco. In the ports, the captives were squeezed together in barracks, for days and sometimes even months, until the corresponding human cargo for the ship was complete; in those precarious, insalubrious and airless conditions, the mortality rate was high. They would then enter the *tumbeiros*,[6] as the slave ships were called, and be sent to an unknown world. Usually, before boarding, they were branded with a hot iron on the chest or the back, as a sign to identify the trafficker to whom they belonged, for it was common practice to transport captives belonging to a number of different owners aboard the same ship.

Contrary to commonly held beliefs, it was not just a question of seizing the Africans. They had to be exchanged for cloth, tools, metal bars, gunpowder, or for spirits like *cachaça* or rum. In the hands of the slave traffickers these products were transformed into an important currency for barter. The African merchants were by no means ingenuous or passive partners in the trade. On the contrary, they did business with the traffickers who best suited the conditions of their local markets. Brazilian slave-owners preferred to purchase workers from a variety of ethnic and cultural groups; without their being able to communicate with one another, there was a reduced risk of uprisings. The traffickers, however, who generally determined the terms of these transactions, preferred to transport people from the same region, as a matter of logistical convenience.

Slave trafficking was a complex business. It required trading posts, ships that navigated along the coast, fortresses built on the beaches, and ports that were well located. There were various different types of African merchants: some were merely agents, while others were employees of state monopolies or similar, stable organizations belonging to kings and nobles. In some places no taxes were levied, while others were subject to the intervention of governments and other groups. Another widely held, false belief is that slaves were so cheap that wanton destruction of life was commonplace on the slave ships. Although the conditions were appalling, the traffickers wanted to avoid mortality rates that would compromise their profits. This is the reason why calculations of how many slaves a vessel would hold were made on the same basis as those used for the transportation of soldiers or prisoners. But the objective was always the same: to get 'the cargo' to its destination.

Between the sixteenth and eighteenth centuries a Portuguese caravel could transport 500 slaves, and a small brig up to 200. In the nineteenth century the journeys were made by steamships, which travelled faster and had an average capacity of 350 slaves. It is often said that the Europeans conducted a 'triangular' trade, taking cargoes of European goods to Africa, cargoes of slaves to America, and American sugar back to Europe. This idea is refuted by the fact that the traffickers' ships were generally smaller and their holds were specially designed to transport a human cargo.[7]

Everything was done to maximize cost-effectiveness. The hold was filled to capacity, frequently obliging a reduction in food supplies. In such circumstances enslaved people, who usually ate once a day, had to survive the entire journey on corn and olive oil alone, with tiny amounts of drinking water. Outbreaks of scurvy were common as from the time of their imprisonment their diet was deficient in vitamin C; scurvy became known as 'Luanda disease'.

Over the years the shortages of food supplies and livestock were gradually remedied, at least as far as basic necessities were concerned. As the crossings became more frequent the mortality rate began to fall. From the beginning of the eighteenth century, general standards were imposed, requiring the traders to restrict the number of slaves to one and a half per ton, maintain the same diet and observe the same basic standards as for the transport of captives. Health requirements included hygiene procedures, exercise and daily sunbaths.[8] The slave traders vaccinated the crew against smallpox and, when space permitted, divided the slaves according to sex and age.[9] Nevertheless the death rate remained high in all cases: an average of 10 per cent of healthy adolescents and adults perished during the thirty-five-day journey. To put this in perspective, in France at this time such a mortality rate would have been classified as epidemic.

Most of the deaths resulted from various types of gastroenteritis caused by the poor quality of the food and water. Dysentery was common, as were outbreaks of the 'bloody flux', an epidemic of intestinal infections that resulted in mass deaths. Infectious diseases such as smallpox, measles, yellow fever and typhus also contributed to the death rate. In addition, Africans from different regional groups were placed in close proximity aboard the ships, with the result that many died from illnesses with which they had had no previous contact. There are also records of suicides, captives who threw themselves overboard or who systematically rejected food. And let us not forget the constant overcrowding, which also led to deaths during the crossing to America.

Few accounts of the horrors of these crossings have survived. In 1649, Friar Sorrento, an Italian Capuchin who travelled on a slave ship, counted 900 captives aboard. He described the experience thus: 'that ship [. . .] with its intolerable stink, the lack of space, the continual cries and infinite woes of so many wretched people, appeared to be hell itself'.[10] And on the topic of hell, some of the imprisoned passengers were even further traumatized, worried about the destiny of their souls, because in the religions of the Congo and Angola regions, people believed that at death they must be surrounded by 'their living' and their descendants. Dying at sea aboard a slave ship meant that their spirit would not be able to rejoin the people of their village; this contributed to a general atmosphere that prevailed on board the ship, oscillating between sorrow, non-conformity, melancholy and anger.

Some benefits did result from the crossing, albeit very few. Captives who travelled aboard the same ship sometimes formed bonds of friendship and referred to each other as *malungos* (fellow travellers). Despite the adverse conditions, ties of loyalty were created that could last a lifetime on the rare occasions when *malungos* were purchased by the same landowner. It was not only diseases that were exchanged on a slave ship, but also social practices, beliefs, rituals, methods of healing, religious secrets and above all friendship.[11] It was these relationships that the traffickers most feared and were responsible for the atmosphere of wariness and suspicion on board. The captives were often chained because the traffickers were afraid of revolt. In the sixteenth century the crossing from Angola to Pernambuco took an average of thirty-five days, to Bahia an average of forty days, and to Rio de Janeiro an average of fifty days. When the winds were unfavourable, the crossings took longer, with the result that food supplies became scarce and the death rate could be as high as 20 per cent of the captives.

Despite these 'setbacks', slave trafficking was considered a good investment. The flow of vessels across the Atlantic was determined by the needs of the plantation owners in Brazil, not by any meteorological or even geographical considerations, such as the rounding of the Cape of Good Hope. And European traffickers, with the exception of the Portuguese – who had overseers in the Congo, Angola and Mozambique – knew very little about their African captives, since their first contact only took place on board. Furthermore, captives frequently did not speak the same language or dialect, and very little was known about the groups to which they belonged.

The traffickers either did not know or did not want to know what might happen once the slaves were a few miles out to sea. The stable relationship between the captaincy of Bahia and the Bay of Benin in the sixteenth century was a flagrant exception to the rule. Nor did they have control over the proportion of males to females. These were dictated by the conditions of the African market rather than by American demand. Men generally accounted for 65 per cent of the captives, many of whom, however, were children, whereas demand from the plantations was mostly for adults. The women, who had less physical strength, were nonetheless put to work alongside the men on the sugar, coffee and cotton plantations. They were considered good 'specialists' for certain activities.

In Africa, however, where the economic, social and cultural organization was structured according to regional and matrilineal kinship, there was a greater demand for women, which accounted for the fact that more men than women were taken captive. In some societies women were highly valued due to the status acquired by men who 'accumulated wives', as well as due to the kinship rules that resulted in the formation of powerful networks within these societies. In polygamous societies, female slaves conferred greater power on the local lords. In Africa women were also in great demand as agricultural workers, especially during the planting season. With so many important roles in African society, it is no wonder that, in general, the women who disembarked in Brazil were older than the men.

Very few children were put aboard the slave ships as the price they fetched on the American markets was so low. According to the logic of the traffickers it was better not to use up space with 'merchandise' that produced little profit. These factors contributed to the low growth rate of the slave population in the colony, above all in the first generation. They also contributed to the intensification of the slave traffic, which gradually became a thriving business. Before 1700, 2.2 million slaves were exported from Africa, and by the eighteenth century, slaves had become the continent's leading 'export'.[12]

As previously mentioned, the slaves who arrived in America spoke different languages and captives with family and cultural ties were frequently separated and sold to different masters. African religious practices were also altered on the new continent, combining elements of Catholicism with traditional cults. Although the Catholic Church systematically prohibited the practice of these religions, the Africans displayed considerable skill in disguising their rituals under the mantle of Catholicism. The most common forms of religious expression in the Americas were *candomblé*, *voodoo* and *santeria*.[13] Voodoo was most common on the island of St Domingo, mostly in the form that originated with the Fon people of Dahomey. However, it was *candomblé nagô*, brought by the Yorubas, which was to provide the basis for the many forms of these religions that were practised by the Dahomey, Angola and Congo nations, above all in Bahia.

Candomblé is a religion derived from African animism, of totemic and family origin, in which the deities – known as *orishas* – are worshipped. As a means of disguise and protection the captives linked the orishas to the Catholic saints. As far as is known, in Africa each nation worshipped only one orisha, thus the joining together of different cults was a specific characteristic of religions brought to the colony by the enslaved. Generally a 'custodian of the Saints' was appointed (known as 'babalorisha' when a man and 'ialorisha' when a woman), who was responsible for conducting the rites. Some of these were African priests who were among the captives and who brought their orishas, rituals and regional languages to Brazil. It was from this rich combination of cultures that a new form of candomblé emerged in the Americas, a religion that is still widely disseminated and influential in Brazil today.[14]

Through the transference and adaptation of African cults, with their traditional chants, music, drum-beating, food and vestments, a process of hybridization occurred in the New World. This was especially the case in Brazil where, from the beginning of forced immigration, the Africans recreated their traditions and cults under the adverse conditions of slavery; something that was neither intended nor expected by the Portuguese, whose plan for them was simply to work en masse on the sugar plantations of the northeast. In the prosperous captaincies of Pernambuco and Bahia alone, between 1580 and 1590, 6,000 Africans were imported to the former and a further 4,000 to the latter. Although the figures may be approximate, it is estimated that in 1584 the total population of Brazil was made up of 25,000 whites, 18,000 domesticated Indians and 14,000 African slaves.[15] The country was thus living a sort of new black Rome, a forced exodus of heretofore unknown proportions.

Thus, after a long and traumatic crossing, the Africans arrived at the Brazilian ports. Initially Rio de Janeiro, Salvador, Recife, Fortaleza, Belém and São Luís were the main importers and distributors. During the seventeenth century, Salvador and Recife also became major ports from which slaves were distributed to the northern captaincies of Maranhão, Pará and the Amazon. With the discovery of the gold mines in the eighteenth century, Rio de Janeiro became the busiest port, from where the captives were re-exported to Minas Gerais, Mato Grosso and the Colônia do Sacramento[16] (in present-day Uruguay).

As soon as they arrived the slaves were classified by the local authorities according to sex and age. The number of children who had been brought along with their mothers was also verified. After the registration of their 'merchandise' the traffickers paid the taxes due on all slaves over three years old. The new arrivals were then taken to be auctioned. If there were clients present, they were auctioned off right there in front of the customs house; if not they were taken to warehouses near the port. After the journey the captives were thin and debilitated and covered in sores. Drawings of the period always show the children with swollen stomachs, the result of worms and malnutrition. Many were suffering from scurvy and conjunctivitis, an ailment that commonly spread during the journey due to the lack of hygiene and sun.

With the goal of making the slaves more valuable, prior to exposing them at auction, great efforts were made to improve their appearance. The captives were cleaned and bathed; the men's beards and heads were shaved and oil was rubbed into their skins to conceal the sores. They were also given larger quantities of food to make them look healthier; and to avoid the downcast aspect that the traders called '*banzo*' – also known by the Brazilian traffickers as '*saudade* sickness', a kind of longing – they were given stimulants such as ginger and tobacco.

After advertisements had been placed in the newspapers, the Africans were put on display, arranged according to sex, age and nationality. Slave-owners and traffickers bargained aloud over conditions and prices – men were more expensive. There were also rules: if within a fortnight of purchase the slave contracted an illness, was discovered to have a physical disability, or displayed a 'lack of morality', he or she could be returned. Those who were not sold immediately were negotiated by trading companies or by small-scale local traffickers, muleteers and hawkers who travelled throughout the colony. This was how the long journey from the African savannas ended: on the sugarcane plantations, the farms, or in the houses of the few towns that existed.

Thus, various points on the map were connected to strengthen and increase a trade that led to the banishment and exile of millions of people. The efficacy of the system was exploited by the traffickers in what was to become one of the greatest holocausts known to humanity. This most oppressive of all migration models provided the workforce for the growing sugarcane industry and, in the following century, for the excavation of gold and diamonds. The slave trade, at least in Brazil, was to continue until 1850 (when trafficking, but not the ownership of slaves, was outlawed), and even beyond, such were its economic advantages.

Most of the slaves who entered the colony in the sixteenth century came from the region of Senegambia on the west coast of Africa. They belonged to different groups, including the Balantas, Manjacos, Bijagós, Mandingas and Jalofos. The trade that had traditionally been controlled by the Muslims in Mauritania, Senegambia and the Ivory Coast now shifted to the Portuguese-controlled trading posts located strategically along the coast. Further south, the Congolese now entered the trade. The arrival of the Portuguese dramatically altered the nature of the slave trade, partly because of the expanse of their operations, but also because of the great mixture of cultures and non-Christian beliefs they encountered.

The first contacts with the King of the Congo were made between 1480 and 1490, with an exchange of ambassadors and the conversion of local leaders to Catholicism. King Nzinga a Nkuwu himself was converted and baptized with the name of Dom João.[17] At this time there was also ritual destruction of the 'idols' worshipped in the Kingdom of the Congo. From then on there was a constant flow of soldiers, teachers, Christian books, liturgical vestments, European cloth, weapons, horses and even farming tools into the kingdom. The Portuguese were agile, and by 1567 they had managed to establish several stable bases of operations in the Congo and at the port of Luanda. Thirty-three years later, trade with America was greater than the trade taking place in the interior of the African continent.

In 1575, with the Portuguese colonization of Angola and the founding of Luanda, the numbers in slave-trafficking doubled. By 1600 it is calculated that a total of 50,000 Africans had disembarked in Brazil. In the 1620s Dutch records show that 4,000 slaves were imported per year into Pernambuco alone. During the sixteenth century it is calculated that between 10,000 and 15,000 Africans from Guinea, the Congo and Angola were exported as slaves to Brazil. Estimates for the seventeenth century mention 6,000 slaves per year being shipped from the Gulf of Guinea alone.[18] At the same time, Luanda, Benguela, Cabinda and Ouida were the most important ports for the slave trade during the sixteenth century, with Luanda exporting a total of 2,826,000 Africans, and Benguela a total of 1,004,000, between 1502 and 1867. The numbers would increase according to the extent of the Portuguese presence in the area.[19] In the early days of the colony the association between Brazil and Angola was so evident that Padre

Vieira commented: 'Say sugar, and you say Brazil. Say Brazil, and you say Angola.'[20]

Initially the slaves from Angola were mostly taken to captaincies in the south. In the northeast the majority of the slaves came from the Bay of Benin (the southeast of present-day Nigeria) or from the Ivory Coast. Slaves from the Ivory Coast were generically referred to as *minas*. African traffickers and later slave traders from Bahia imported Dagomés, Jejes, Hausa, Bornus, Tapas and Nagôs from the ports of Ajudá, Popó, Jaquin and Apá in the Bay of Benin, and later also from the port of Onim (near present-day Lagos).[21] While the proximity of linguistic groups helped to build networks of solidarity and friendship, the diversity of customs added to the cultural wealth of the African diaspora in America. Brazil was becoming a kind of 'new Africa', or, in the words of Ambrósio Fernandes Brandão, a merchant in Goa and Lisbon who established himself as master of an *engenho* in Paraíba, a 'New Guinea'.[22]

IN BRAZIL, A MIXTURE

Although the slave trade was affected by the Spanish-Dutch Wars, in the seventeenth century they in fact only helped to strengthen the role of the traffickers who guaranteed a constant supply of workers for the colony. St George's fortress in what is now Ghana became the centre from which vast numbers of captives from Guinea, Angola, Mozambique and the *Costa da Mina* were exported to America. The Portuguese created closer ties with the King of Dahomey, and they built a fortress there in São João Baptista de Ajudá, which was to become the largest supply centre for slaves later in the century. In Brazil, as previously mentioned, there was always a substantial mixture of African cultures among the enslaved: they came from Senegal, Angola, the Congo, the *Costa da Mina* and the Bay of Benin. There were also thousands of Jejes, Nagos (Yorubas), Tapas (Nupes), Hausas and Sudanese peoples. Nearly one-third of the slaves, however, came from the Bantu peoples of Angola and Central Africa.

The slave masters usually preferred the 'blacks from Angola', who were considered 'good workers'. The 'blacks from Mozambique' were not so 'highly esteemed'. One landowner went as far as to say that they rebelled so much 'they were like the devil himself'. Nevertheless, the continuous requirement for new workers meant that the masters purchased whatever was on the market. There are many descriptions of the places where the 'products' were sold; their bodies, now covered in whale oil and gleaming in the sun, were submitted to a careful examination of their teeth, hair and muscles, in order to assess their value. In addition to gender and age, health was also an essential concern in evaluating the price.

Brazil received fewer women than men. Among the reasons for this was that women's reproductive capability was not considered important. What mattered was masculine strength. Children under fourteen years of age made up 2 per cent to 6 per cent, while women accounted for 20 per cent to 30 per cent of the total number. It is not easy to calculate the exact age of the new arrivals, as this was usually rounded up or down in the registries. While the ages of children up to ten were carefully noted down, the same did not apply to the 'old', the term used for slaves over forty.

There was an enormous difference between the slaves who worked inside the *casas-grandes* – domestic servants about whom every type of personal detail was known – and those who worked on the plantations, selected on the basis of quantity rather than quality. The traffickers used a series of terms to identify the age group of their 'merchandise': 'breastfeeders' for babies of up to one year old; 'boy' or 'girl' for children up to the age of eight; *'moleque'* or *'moleca'* for captives between eight and fourteen; and 'youngsters' for adolescents.[23] In the early days of the colony most of the slaves were recent arrivals. Around 1600 they accounted for 70 per cent of the total. The *engenho* owners preferred new arrivals who were not adapted to the customs of the country and were thus less likely to escape.

The 'breeding' of slaves, as occurred in the United States, did not appeal to slave masters in Brazil because the mortality rate among children was particularly high and fertility rates were low. The latter was due to malnutrition (retarded menstruation), the excessive workload and the scarcity of women. There were also cultural reasons. The Yoruba believed in postpartum abstinence because they thought a child's health would be compromised should there be another pregnancy. It is at the very least paradoxical that, instead of the alleged 'sexual promiscuity', in fact there appears to have been voluntary abstention from sexual intercourse. 'Promiscuity' is always a term used to describe and condemn the sexual habits of 'others'. Very few registries of marriages exist because the masters preferred not to recognize these common-law unions, so that they could sell one or the other of the partners whenever they chose.[24] However, children usually lived with one of their parents or both, or in groups under the surveillance of adults.

But in practice there was usually an attempt to ignore this type of familial relationship. Slaves were generally known by the Christian names they received at baptism, as well as by their colour and place of birth. As there were a large number of slaves called João, it was common practice to identify them by their country of origin: *João Angola, João Cabinda* or *João da Guiné*. The name of their owners was often added, for example 'slave of Antonio dos Santos'. When they were given their freedom it was not unusual for them to keep the name of their last owner – Felix Maciel had been Belchior Maciel's slave. Actually, the adoption of the former master's surname was an indication that, even after a slave's release, she or he still depended on the master's protection. This was regarded as a deep-rooted tradition of patronage that created family ties between the 'godparents' and the 'godchild'. It meant that loyalty and subservience to the master were still expected, as if slavery in Brazil was an irrevocable destiny.

SLAVERY IS SYNONYMOUS WITH VIOLENCE

The creation of an institution on the scale of modern slavery can only be understood in the context of the development of overseas colonies and their vast production geared toward an external market. Monoculture demanded a large contingent of workers who were required to submit to a gruelling regime, with neither pay nor personal motivation. Slavery in the New World was thus recreated with the use of the forced labour of workers who had been alienated from their origins, and had neither freedom nor any connection with the work they undertook. They were labourers who were supposed to have no will of their own, and to be unaware of what they produced.

Life in the tropics was depicted in this period as a burden, a punishment, a prison sentence for both masters and slaves. The discourse of the Church and the landowners held that arduous forced labour would discipline and civilize the slaves. There were even manuals – models for the application of exemplary punishments – that taught the plantation owners how to ensure that their slaves were submissive and to transform them into obedient workers. An example was the notorious 'slave-breaker', a punishment frequently used in Brazil to 'educate' newly arrived or newly acquired slaves, by means of a public whipping, to remind them that they had always to look down when in the presence of any authority.

According to Padre Jorge Benci, who visited the country at the end of the 1600s, the reason for submitting the slaves to these punishments was 'so that they would not become insolent, nor find cunning ways of avoiding submission to their master by becoming rebellious and uncontrollable'.[25] This, then, was the paternalistic and religious justification – with the promise of future redemption – for why the system could only operate through the use of force.

The repetitive, arduous, exhausting work on the plantations was in itself a form of violence. This forced labour, betokening as it did the authority of the master, instilled a constant feeling of dread, as well as terror of the collective punishments that were frequently applied.[26] Public chastizement in the stocks, the use of the whip as a form of punishment and humiliation, the iron collars studded with spikes to avoid escape, the iron masks that prevented the slaves from eating earth as a way of provoking a slow and painful death, the chains with which they were tied to the ground, created a world of violence in Brazil rooted in the figure of the master and his supreme power under the law, the marks of which were constantly registered on the bodies of his slaves. As for the Africans, the moment they set foot on Brazilian soil they had to learn the art of how to survive.

Any system like modern slavery can only be maintained through the continuous exercise of violence. On the part of the masters this was manifested in a frenzy of cruelty constantly inflicted on the slaves to cower them into submission and unquestioning obedience. On the part of the enslaved it ranged from persistent small acts of insubordination to large-scale revolts and the establishment of the *quilombos*.[27]

The marks left by slavery were so deep that even today customs and expressions from the time are commonplace in Brazilian society. If the *casa-grande* established the border between the family and the workers, the same symbolic architecture exists today in Brazil. Residential apartment blocks all have separate lifts, not just for cargo and deliveries, but for service providers and household employees whose skin colour is often consistent with the history of slavery in Brazil. Expressions from the time of slavery are still in use, although the original meaning has often been lost. The expression 'dry nurse' (*ama-seca*) was intended to distinguish the 'dry' from the 'wet nurses', slave women who were frequently unable to breastfeed their own children as they were required to nourish their masters' offspring. *Boçal* is still used to refer to a person whose reactions and thought processes are slow – a simpleton – just as *ladino* is still a synonym for 'clever' or 'smart'. In the original sense, *boçais* was the term used to distinguish newly arrived slaves who, unlike the second generation of *ladinos*, knew neither the language nor the countryside and thus had little chance of escape.

Some of the terms used at the time, however, have completely disappeared, for example the expression 'self-moving goods' (*bens semoventes*), which was indiscriminately used in inventories and wills to describe both slaves and livestock. But today Brazilian society is still marked by a division that is rarely mentioned: one that transforms a person's colour into an indicator of social difference. This is evidenced every day by the actions of the police, who stop and arrest many more blacks than whites. The practice is euphemistically referred to as 'interpellation'. There are many cases in which innocent individuals who are constantly harassed by the police begin to actually believe that they are somehow guilty. The anthropologist Didier Fassin calls this 'incorporated memory': the body remembers before the mind has time to reflect. During the time of slavery free blacks were stopped on the streets as 'suspected slaves'. Today they are detained in the same way for other alleged offences. This is racial profiling. Their real 'offence' is their ethnic origin.[28]

Although violence was generalized in the slave-based society, there was an internal hierarchy. The plantation slaves, who were many, were submitted to a gruelling work regime with rigorous controls, whereas the domestic slaves led quite a different sort of daily life. On the large *engenhos* there could be a hundred or more enslaved people working in the fields, many of whom the master hardly knew. Domestic slaves, on the other hand, were fewer and lived in close proximity to the family, working as cooks, nannies, pages and wet nurses – a body of servants who accompanied the family in its day-to-day routine.

However, apart from these relatively privileged few, there can be no doubt that all that awaited the vast majority of slaves was brutalizing work in the fields under the scorching sun of the northeast, at times for as many as twenty hours on end. The work in the grinding mills, the furnaces and the boilers could be even worse. From time to time an enslaved person would lose a hand or an arm in the sugarcane mills. There are several reports which mention that an axe was always kept close to the grinder so that if a slave's limb was trapped in the rollers it could be quickly severed, preventing damage to the sugar or the machinery.

The heat produced by the furnaces and boilers was unbearable; in addition to withstanding the sweltering conditions the slaves often suffered serious burns. The work was so arduous and dangerous that it was often reserved as a punishment for enslaved people who were considered 'insolent' or rebellious. There are also records of slaves being burnt on the cheek and on the chest, scorched with hot wax, tortured with red-hot irons, and of having their noses and ears cut off.

Suffering from the arbitrary abuse of the masters was daily routine. Women were frequently victims of their sadism. Their bodies were not only fit for labour; they were also an instrument of pleasure (and guilt) for the masters and an object of hatred for their jealous wives. It was in these secret, sexual rendezvous that the despot enjoyed the 'apparent' passivity of his female slave. She had in fact surrendered out of terror and fear of reprisal. Padre Antonil wrote that the slaves were treated with three Ps: 'pau, pão e pano' – cudgel, bread and cloth. The real explanation is that the white overlords knew they were in a minority and could only control their slaves by creating an atmosphere of premeditated fear.

There was always an excess of work, always a shortage of clothing and food. Travellers to the country noted that slaves in Brazil went hungry. They were required to plant food for their sustenance, but Sunday was the only day reserved for this activity. Virtually starving, they often caught rats that infested the plantations and cooked them in the senzala. Their basic diet was manioc flour with dried meat or fish – chicken and fresh meat were reserved for slaves who were ill. There is still a popular saying that goes 'when there's chicken to eat in a poor man's house, either the poor man's sick or the chicken is'. The foreign travellers also noted that in some regions of Brazil dried codfish (bacalhau) was referred to as 'negroes' food'. Ironically, the whip with thongs of twisted leather that was used to chastize the slaves was also called the 'bacalhau'.

That is why, from the start, the slave economy was accompanied by high mortality rates. The slaves brought to America died easily as they had no immunity to the diseases of the New World. They were also both physically and morally shattered after the Atlantic crossing and fell victim to opportunistic diseases. Thus their first year was the most precarious, in every sense. They not only had to get used to the gruelling work regime, but also to learn the language and adapt to a different climate. Child mortality was even more alarming: the insalubrious conditions, lack of medical attention and malnutrition led to high rates of stillborn babies and of children who died before the age of three.

The work regime was the greatest villain. It drained the women of their vigour and killed off the 'old' (slaves of over forty were considered old). According to the inventories of the *engenhos*, 6 per cent of the slaves died of 'fatigue' – exhaustion, total collapse of the body. On the Sergipe do Conde *engenho* in Bahia, between 1622 and 1653, five new slaves a year were purchased to replenish a group of seventy because of the constant deaths. Account books from *engenhos* in the northeast also register numerous cases of abortion and suicide – individual forms of rebellion by those who refused to accept their enslavement. The idea that Brazil had a more benevolent brand of slavery than the United States can only be refuted. Life expectancy for Brazilian slaves was even lower than in the United States – twenty-five as compared to thirty-five – although the same discrepancy also existed between the white populations of the two countries.

This regime of privations affected every part of the slaves' daily routine, including the clothes they were given, which were often little more than rags. Records from the time show that the slaves worked virtually naked and were thus very susceptible to changes in the weather. The men were normally bare-chested and wore thin baggy trousers that reached below the knee. To stop sweat from running into their eyes they tied a cloth or handkerchief around their heads. The women's attire was a little more complete – corsets, petticoats, blouses and skirts. It is sometimes mistakenly thought that these were reserved for festive occasions or for when the slaves were sold. In general these clothes were made from 'mountain cloth', a thick fabric woven from raw cotton thread that scratched the skin. Clothes were distributed twice a year: at harvesting time and when the cane was ready for grinding.

The domestic slaves were better dressed than those on the plantations. They were frequently seen in full dress, at times with top hats and an umbrella that they held open to protect their masters from the sun. In the cities, the average number of slaves per master was considerably lower. They spent much of their time away from the master's vigilance, hired out as newspaper sellers or to work in the streets. A daily or weekly rate was charged for their time, at the end of which they delivered the money they had earned to their masters. They worked in a wide range of occupations, as painters, bricklayers, carpenters, dockworkers, tailors, blacksmiths, dressmakers, coach drivers, cart drivers, barbers and shoemakers. The women worked as domestics, cooks, cleaners and nurses, as well as washing, ironing and starching clothes. They sold manioc pap, dried shrimps, sweets, cakes and delicacies from Africa. They walked around the streets offering their wares, often carrying their children on their backs, tied in a cloth that displayed their nation of origin called a 'Pano da Costa'. Some of them worked as messengers as they were always walking around the town and could thus transmit information and even news of rebellions. Enslaved females were also forced to work as prostitutes in the areas surrounding the port, selling their bodies and handing their earnings to the master.

In a slave-based society all work that required physical effort was considered degrading and was 'relegated' to the slaves. Colour became a demarcation line in Brazilian society, which associated black Africans with physical labour. 'Mulattoes', for example, many of whom were the illegitimate children of their masters, were generally chosen for household tasks. Although they made up only 7 per cent of the total slave population on the *engenhos*, they represented 20 per cent of domestic slaves.[29]

Brazilian slavery was unusual in that it offered an opening for an enslaved person to achieve her or his freedom, called *'alforria'*. Freedom was usually conferred for good behaviour, but could occasionally be purchased by slaves. They were allowed to make savings and a few of the mulattoes who had specialized skills could actually hope to be freed sometime in the future. Despite not being included in any Brazilian law, either civil or religious, the opportunity for release had always existed. Freedom could be granted in wills, as a recompense for loyalty, or out of personal affection. Women, children and those with special abilities accounted for the highest number of releases. In Bahia, 45 per cent of all the slaves granted freedom were mulattoes.

However, the number of releases was small – in the sixteenth and seventeenth centuries it never surpassed 1 per cent per year of the total slave population. Meanwhile, the likelihood of being re-enslaved was extremely high. All release documents could be revoked; their maintenance depended on the former slave's behaviour being considered 'appropriate'. 'Disloyalty' was considered sufficient reason for revocation of a slave's release. Former slaves who travelled were frequently arrested and had their documents invalidated.

In the absence of any authentic system of justice, violence and abuse became established customs. Throughout the colony there was contempt for laws that sought to control violence, facilitating the practice of illegal re-enslavement. The requirement for slaves to carry passes and written permission from their masters in order to travel was applied to any person whose physical features suggested that she or he may have once been a slave. It was very common for black people to be stopped and ordered to show their travel documents, proof of identity or passports. By this process, many men carrying documents that attested their freedom had these confiscated and were then taken prisoner and sold back into slavery.[30]

The scorching flames of the furnaces, combined with the sweltering heat of Brazil's northeast, the lack of food, the constant ill-treatment and the gruelling work regime, meant that labour on the *engenhos* was indeed a hell on earth. It was Padre Antonil, again, who defined the colony as 'a hell for blacks and a purgatory for whites'. The word 'hell' became a metaphor for work in the colony. However, despite the cruelty and sadism, it is clear that the violence of the system stemmed from economic considerations: to force the slaves to accept their condition and to produce as much as possible.

It was very hard to escape from slavery. The system was established throughout the colony, making Brazil the largest importer of forced labour that had ever been known. Slavery permeated every level of society: owning slaves was by no means a privilege reserved for the few. Priests, soldiers, civil servants, artisans, tavern owners, merchants, small farmers, poor people and even freed captives owned slaves. Thus slavery was more than just an economic system: it influenced behaviour, defined social inequalities, made race and colour the indicators of a fundamental difference, underpinned rules relating to command and obedience, and created a society that was conditioned by its paternalism and strict hierarchical structure.

And there is a further indicator that refutes the worn-out argument that slavery in Brazil was less violent than elsewhere. Of all colonial slaves, the Brazilians were among those who reacted most vigorously, killed their masters and overseers with more frequency, took refuge in *quilombos* more often, and orchestrated recurring revolts. There are a number of explanations for the extent of slave rebellion in Brazil: the fragility of institutions such as the police and the law, the lack of cohesion among the landowning classes – who were divided into small-, medium- and large-scale property owners scattered throughout the colony – and above all, the all too evident truth that violence generates violence.

After all, the enslaved were by no means inert – a fact that is often overlooked. Within the galling limitations of their condition, they fought to gain a little free time, to maintain their families, to recreate their customs and religious practices in a foreign land, and above all to protect and care for their children.[31] While appearing to be good Catholics and true converts to the faith, who attended Mass and worshipped the saints, they maintained a secret, parallel system that related each of these Catholic saints to an African orisha.

Through worship, Brazilians entered into a sort of religious dialogue. Many Africans who arrived in Brazil and were forcefully converted to Catholicism embraced both the religion and its saints; but they also altered the saints' names, features and significance. Thus they created a new pantheon that allowed them to discreetly worship their own kings and deities as they outwardly took part in religious festivals that venerated the Portuguese Crown and the Christian saints. The martial art called capoeira originated in a similar way. The name refers to the places where the sport was first practised, the plots of land cleared and burnt by the slaves where the grass had begun to grow back. Originally a fighting sport, it was presented as a recreational dance.[32] Faced with severe restrictions, the slaves constantly created false appearances – fights were disguised as dances, and orishas as saints. Slavery created a world of disguise and negotiation.

In fact, from the very beginning of the colony there was a sense of tit for tat. In reaction to their harsh lives the Africans sometimes escaped, and, whenever they could, they rebelled. As long as the slavery system lasted there were always *quilombos*. No form of slavery is better or worse than any other. All kinds of slavery have one thing in common: they generate sadism, the naturalization of violence and the perversion of society. What has remained, in all places that allowed the existence of slaves, is the ignominy of having assimilated such a system and perpetuated it for so long. The fight for freedom was always the greatest desire and only objective of the slaves. Although the masters generally manipulated the situation by ill-treatment and punishments of every conceivable kind, they did at times offer positive incentives, promising days off work and even freedom. The slaves too were obliged to negotiate. They made requests to be allowed to spend Fridays and Saturdays looking after their own affairs, demanded to choose their own overseers and be placed in charge of the plantation equipment. They wanted to care for their children and worship their gods alongside the saints they had discovered in the New World. There is a rare document in which the scrivener registers a petition by the slaves to be able to 'play, rest and sing' without asking permission. There was little hope and a lot of violence, but the workers who came from Africa did more than just survive. To escape from their condition as 'pawns' they sought any loophole in the system through which they could recreate their culture and aspirations as they dreamt of freedom and rebellion.

TIT FOR TAT: REBELLIONS, UPRISINGS AND ORGANIZED ACTION

The enslaved never relinquished their will to have agency and control over some aspects of their own lives. In the first place, they created ties of affection, religious associations and social networks. Travellers noted that at times they established affectionate relations with the wives and children of their masters, and close ties were maintained between *malungos* (fellow travellers during the crossing). They also showed their resistance to the gruelling work regime by bargaining with the overseers, refusing to execute certain tasks, or by simply not doing what their masters demanded.

But they also reacted with violence to the brutality of their daily routine. Escapes – both individual and en masse – were frequent, as were organized uprisings and the murder of masters and overseers. The slaves that fled took refuge in the *quilombos* and *mocambos* (the smaller settlements for escaped slaves) that began to appear in Portuguese America during the sixteenth century. The word *mocambo* means 'hiding place'; *quilombo* was a Kimbundu term used in Angola for a certain type of fortified military camp made up of warriors who underwent initiation rites, adopted strict discipline and practised magic.[33] The use of the word to designate groups of escaped enslaved people began after the establishment of Palmares – as we shall see, the most successful and persistent grouping of *quilombos* ever established in the country – but only became generalized in the eighteenth century. In an attempt to prevent their proliferation, the Portuguese authorities passed a law that no more than six slaves could gather in the same place at any time, except for when they were working.

From the middle of the sixteenth century, when the first news of the appearance of *quilombos* began to arrive in Salvador and rapidly reached Lisbon, to the mid-nineteenth century with the start of abolitionist writings, escaped enslaved people persistently sought to establish a place for themselves in a society that offered no alternatives.[34] Between the harsh reality of the slave-based society and the attempt to reinvent a viable reality, many enslaved people did not think twice: suicide was an extreme solution, and to venture off alone along roadways and through villages was too risky. The answer was to escape into the interior in groups and try to establish communities in the forests or the uninhabited, inhospitable *sertão* (the arid hinterland), outside the slave-based society. *Quilombos* were generally established in places that were difficult to reach, to protect them from the police who were based in the cities, far from the traffic along the highways and the intense vigilance of the plantations. Although ironically, there were *quilombos* that maintained trading relations with nearby settlements.

The proliferation of *mocambos* and *quilombos* throughout the colony was the result of complex characteristics and identities. They were not just transitory settlements for runaways with no viable future, the emblematic spurning of rules of a slave-based society, nor did they exist in complete isolation: many of them established commercial relations with nearby communities. They were a radically new element in the political landscape, combining resistance with negotiation, and rebellion with pragmatism.[35] For those who lived there, they were dangerous and, at times, spelled tragedy.

The *quilombos* provided a concrete alternative to slavery, and for this reason they became a very real concern, causing fear among the colonists and the authorities, who prepared to systematically confront them. However, because of the variety of connections they established, the *quilombos* also became a part of the society that sought to repress them. They established a wide variety of commercial links with neighbouring communities, built networks of varying degrees of complexity for obtaining information, and, as was inevitable, formed bonds of friendship (and love ties) with plantation workers and communities on the edge of the towns.

The population of the *quilombos* survived on food they found in the forest, on vegetables they planted (mostly corn, manioc, beans and sweet potatoes), by breeding chickens and by trading with nearby communities.[36] All the *quilombos* established some kind of friendly coexistence with their neighbours. Many, however, also created hostility because certain groups raided settlements on the outskirts of towns, sacking farms and carrying off the animals as well as assaulting travellers on the highways.

In the mid-eighteenth century, *Buraco do Tatu*,[37] a *quilombo* located in Itapuã,[38] dangerously close to the city of Salvador, maintained its economy by theft. It had loyal accomplices among the slaves and freemen of the city who brought supplies of livestock and munitions.[39] In one aspect all *quilombos* were the same: their chances of survival depended on the network of social connections they managed to establish with neighbouring communities. With their proliferation, scattered around the most productive captaincies of the colony, they soon formed an underground world – the *campo negro*, 'the black region'[40] – which allowed them to extend their area of influence and increase their degree of autonomy.

A remarkable variety of characters and social types gravitated around the *quilombos* with different degrees of complicity and commercial interests. By no means were all of these associates enslaved people and freemen. They included smugglers; slaves from the plantations who provided information and carried messages between the *quilombos*; peddlers who brought gunpowder, *cachaça*, clothing and salt, as well as the booty from sackings by roving *quilombo* residents.

Not even the *quilombo* residents who chose to live by theft and sackings were able to dispense with the complicity of this network of relations and interests. For their part, the authorities did what they could to neutralize these support systems. Sending the police from

Salvador was not enough to destroy a *quilombo* like the Buraco do Tatu; troops of Indians had to be mobilized and sent to attack them.

In the Lower Amazon region, in the extreme north of Portuguese America, the encampments of escaped slaves along the Curuá and Trombeta tributaries[41] were established 'in the midst of the turbulent waters' above the first rapids and waterfalls on the left bank of the vast river. This was dense forest near the frontier with present-day Suriname.[42] In order to survive there, physical fitness, courage and acute perception were not enough; it was crucial to know the forest. The *quilombolas* (inhabitants of the *quilombos*) adapted to forest life by establishing relations, at times friendly and at others hostile, with the local Indians, and with local animals. They adapted their diet, substituting flour for babassu coconut paste[43] and eating turtle meat when fish was in short supply. They also sculpted images of their deities using pulp they extracted from palm-tree trunks; and they discovered the economic value of nuts and the medicinal use of certain plants, such as caraíba oil and *salsaparrilha*.[44] In due course they became '*bichos do mato*' (forest creatures) – sons of the forest.

PALMARES: THE QUILOMBO REBELLION

Every *quilombo* has its own story, but Palmares – the largest and possibly the longest-lasting community of escaped slaves in Portuguese America – became a national symbol of the long tradition of bravery and resistance of Brazil's *quilombo* warriors. It is generally thought that the original nucleus of Palmares was made up of around forty slaves, all of whom were from the same *engenho* in Pernambuco. They escaped, climbing the Serra da Barriga in the *Zona da Mata*,[45] in what today is the state of Alagoas, probably around the year 1597.[46] The location, surrounded by mountains and completely unpopulated, provided a natural fortress from which the fugitives could ward off attack. Palm trees were abundant in the area, providing sustenance and comfort, including the *palmito* (hearts of palm), which they ate, and fronds for thatching houses, making clothes and laying traps. The palms were powerful symbols; it was only natural that the fugitives should settle in their midst, and baptize the place Palmares.

Palmares did not refer to one single *quilombo*, but to a confederation of communities of various sizes scattered around the region. They were interconnected by pacts, but they conducted their own business affairs, were autonomous, and chose their own leaders. They included the Acotirene *quilombo*, whose name was a tribute to the matriarch and counsellor of the *quilombola* leaders; the Dambrabanga *quilombo*, named after an outstanding military leader; the Zumbi *quilombo*, named after the community's religious and military leader; the Aqualtune and Andalaquituche *quilombos*, named respectively after Zumbi's mother and brother; the Subupira *quilombo*, which served as the military base for the *quilombolas*; and the *Cerca Real do Macaco*,[47] the largest and most important *quilombo* in the region. It was from here that the Palmares leader Ganga Zumba, the 'Great Chief', presided over the council of leaders and made decisions on vital questions of war and peace.

Although later, with its expansion, the *quilombola* confederation became a multi-ethnic society, many of the first inhabitants were from Angola and the Congo and the refuge was initially known as *Angola Janga* – 'Little Angola'. This attempt at the recreation of an African nation in Brazil demonstrates not only that the inhabitants saw themselves as foreigners, but also that they created a politically organized community with public administration, its own laws, form of government and military structure, as well as religious and cultural principles, all of which helped forge and strengthen a collective identity. The colonial authorities also recognized the existence of Palmares: in documents sent to Lisbon they referred to it as a 'republic', a term which at the time was used to refer to any area, whether in Portugal or overseas, that had its own administration, was regulated by a political system, and possessed a relative degree of autonomy.[48]

At its peak, Palmares had a population of around 20,000. Of these approximately 6,000 lived in the Cerca Real do Macaco. This was at a time (around 1660) when the population of Rio de Janeiro, including Indians and Africans, was estimated at 7,000.[49] The *quilombola* confederation maintained a thriving trade with neighbouring towns and villages. For more than a century it encouraged slaves to escape en masse, made innumerable attacks on *engenhos*, farms and hamlets, and repelled all the military expeditions that were sent to destroy it. The first Portuguese attack on Palmares was launched in 1612, and the last, during which the leader Zumbi (Ganga Zumba's successor) was killed, in 1695. Between 1644 and 1645, during the Dutch occupation of the sugar-producing region in the northeast – notably the captaincy of Pernambuco – the West Indies Company ordered two attacks on Palmares, both of which failed. The Dutch became the victims of forest guerrilla tactics that employed ambushes, skirmishes and surprise attacks.

Palmares took advantage of the crisis caused by the Dutch occupation, by expanding. This was to be a recurring feature of the slaves' resistance: they always acted at moments when the slave-based society was weakened or divided, whether due to war, foreign invasion or internal disputes. After 1670, as the threat posed by the *quilombolas* grew and the fame of Palmares spread throughout Portuguese America, the colonial authorities formulated a strategy of systematic destruction. This included annual attacks, reconnaissance missions, and the elimination of commercial links between the *quilombos* and neighbouring communities. Although Portugal's attempts to eliminate the *quilombos* continued to fail, it did finally reap the benefits of the eventual infighting between the *quilombo* leaders.

In 1678, Portuguese representatives met in Recife with a large group of rebels sent by Ganga Zumba to celebrate a peace treaty proposed by the colonial authorities. The agreement arranged for the return of all escaped slaves to the Crown, in other words all the *quilombolas* who had not been born in Palmares. The Portuguese plan was to put an end to the complicity between the *quilombolas* and the slaves on the *engenhos*. In exchange, Portugal guaranteed freedom, the donation of land and the status of subjects of the Crown for all those who had been born in Palmares. The Recife Agreement divided the *quilombolas*, pitted Ganga Zumba against Zumbi, and inaugurated the most violent period in the community's history. Ganga Zumba was poisoned after being declared a traitor and all his military leaders were beheaded. During the next fifteen years Zumbi led the war against the Portuguese authorities, maintained the autonomy of the *quilombo* and guaranteed the freedom of its inhabitants. The war only ended with the fall of the Cerca Real do Macaco after a siege of forty-two days, the defeat and execution of Zumbi, and the total destruction of Palmares.

Palmares was to serve as an example for both sides. The colonial authorities used it as evidence that ruthless repression and total destruction were the only response to slave resistance. But Palmares also became an emblem of resistance, and a clear refutation of the idea that Brazil's population of enslaved people and formerly enslaved people were merely passive victims. Instead, they had agency: they were unwilling to submit to a perverse regime like this.

In August 1870, nearly two hundred years later, the abolitionist poet Castro Alves[50] wrote 'Salute to Palmares', a harsh condemnation of the brutality of slavery and the degradation of human relations, and an exaltation of the *quilombos*.[51] The great poet was far ahead of his time: it was only later that this powerful federation of slave refugees was to become the subject of academic research and national curiosity. During the eighteenth and nineteenth centuries, while slavery still existed,[52] the *quilombos* were the cause of widespread fear. The greatest of them all was that the phenomenon of Palmares would be repeated. It was only during the twentieth century that there was a major shift in the way Palmares was viewed in historical writings, in intellectual discourse, and in the culture in general. It became not only a symbol of the struggle of the slaves and of all black people in Brazil, but an icon of how other moments and memories in Brazil's history can be constructed.[53]

THE MANY FORMS OF THE FIGHT FOR RESISTANCE

Not all slaves who escaped founded or joined *quilombos*. But escape was always an act of resistance, and the captives had many good reasons to do so: the extreme violence of the physical and moral punishments, the dividing up of families and loved ones, the arbitrary nature of the masters' power; escape might also bring bargaining power, reinforce demands to halt punishment and overwork. And it was, of course, a clamour for freedom. Throughout the seventeenth and eighteenth centuries '*tirar o cipó*' meant 'to head for the bush' – and to risk a myriad of dangers.

Whether by an individual or group, escape was always a challenge to the ruling class. A slave who escaped was an affront to the principle of property, a threat to the social order and a financial loss to his master. Brazilian society soon discovered that the punishments inflicted on recaptured slaves, however horrific, were not enough to deter escapes. It was essential to create mechanisms for the control and maintenance of slavery and to develop effective strategies of repression. The creation of this control apparatus was gradual, systematic, and had the backing of the law, which in turn had a broad scope of repressive tactics. There was a firm belief in the efficacy of public punishment, a theatrical exhibition of the force of the law. This public punishment took several forms. One was mutilating the offending slave's body so that all who saw him, at any time and under any circumstances, would see the marks and remember his 'crime'; another was public humiliation at the *pelourinho* (a pillory in the form of a stone column displaying the royal arms, erected in the main square of all the towns as a symbol of loyalty to the Crown), to which the slaves were chained and then whipped; another was the public display of the decapitated heads of captured fugitives and *quilombolas* whose refuges had been destroyed in the innumerable incursions.

But this was still not enough. The colonial authorities were convinced that trained professionals were needed, even if this meant the landowners had to pay. The solution was, to a certain degree, predictable: the development of a specialized force to chase down escaped slaves, a sort of professional body of highly militarized men with the authority to capture black fugitives on highways, in forests and in the *quilombos* – and with orders to kill, torch and destroy any persons or points of resistance. At the centre of this apparatus of repression the Portuguese established the position of the slave catcher, the *capitão do mato*.[54] Before the creation of this post in the mid-seventeenth century, the pursuit of escaped slaves had been sporadic, organized by the overseers, who were responsible for both managing the *engenhos* and punishing the slaves. But, starting in mid-century, with well-defined laws and permission to search villages to prevent escapes, the *capitães do mato* were recognized by society and were an integral part of the institution of slavery.[55]

From the seventeenth to the nineteenth centuries there were thousands of *capitães do mato* scattered throughout the colony. Many of them were former slaves who boasted about their inside knowledge of fugitive behaviour. Since within this slave-based society slaves and *quilombos* were associated with the worst images of hell – painful death, hiding in forests inhabited by demons, the practice of idolatry – it was decided to put these *capitães do mato* under the protection of a person of great substance, St Anthony of Padua. He was the most venerated saint in both the colony and the seat of the empire, where he was held to be the warrior saint who defended Portuguese America against invasions. Without his permission, for three centuries St Anthony lent his divine collaboration to the recapture of slaves and the destruction of the *quilombos*.[56]

The earthly *capitães do mato*, on the other hand, were hired and paid by the slave-owners, in accordance with services rendered. The amount depended on the distance between the location of the escape and the location of the capture: the greater the distance, the higher the pay. Payment was made on delivery, either of the slave himself or of his decapitated head, which the *capitão do mato* carried in a leather bag to show his employer and prove he had met the terms of their agreement.[57]

Escape was not the only form of resistance. Others included murdering or poisoning the master, suicide and abortion; the enslaved made demands and were steadfast in rejecting their situation. But the simplest act of disobedience was a threat to the master's authority, because in order to run his estate and ensure his profits the master needed the blind obedience of his workforce. The slaves knew all too well the risks they ran. The enemy had daunting forces at his command and, if they were captured, they had no protection under the law. Thus it was essential for all acts of resistance to be committed in secret, whether theft, assassination, suicide, abortion or mere insults – not to mention disobeying and manipulating employees or other small but disconcerting acts of disobedience.

Resistance required creativity, luck, collusion and cleverness. The strategy adopted was often indirect, often aimed at wearing the enemy down. Sabotage was a constant danger, and success could be achieved with very little effort. The smallest of actions could wreak destruction: a spark in the sugarcane fields, a piece of lemon dropped in one of the bronze cauldrons used for producing molasses, or a spoke broken on one of the giant wheels used for extracting sugarcane juice, propelled by water power or animal traction.[58] Any of these small interventions, however insignificant, affected the sugar production and, in more extreme cases, could cause the loss of the *engenho*'s entire production.

For enslaved Brazilians, an indispensable ingredient in developing resistance was the preservation and cultivation of memories of Africa, the traces of cultural roots. As the generations passed, these roots were modified, mixed together and recreated, and within the new reality of slavery. They became an important instrument for the construction of a religious life, forms of recreation, the development of a collective identity and group resistance.

On the coffee and sugar plantations, and in urban environments, slaves often faced up to their masters and bargained for the right to drum and to dance and sing in accordance with their religious rites, without permission from the overseer, and particularly without the intervention of the police. These activities usually took place in clearings in the woods, prepared with special care by the slaves, in areas near the *engenhos* and towns. They were called *terreiros*.[59] The rituals practised there incorporated a unique combination of cultural and religious elements. Music, dance, rhythm and movement were integrated to form a distinct spiritual language of worship, characterized by its connections to the oral transmission of African rituals and possession by the deities.[60]

This reconstruction of African rituals, based on the traditions of the Nagô peoples and culturally influenced by groups of Jejes, has been known as candomblé – the religion of the orishas – since the beginning of the nineteenth century.[61] From the outset, candomblé combined a number of cultural elements the slaves absorbed through contact with different groups of peoples brought from Africa. In many ways candomblé created itself: breaking down cultural barriers between the different groups, generating principles of symbolic importance for harmonious community life, and serving as a channel of communication with other segments of the slave-based society. It also incorporated the religious traditions of the Indians, so that even today *candomblé de caboclo* evokes the ancestors of the peoples who lived in Brazil long before the Europeans arrived.

The *quilombos* were privileged spaces meant to protect the autonomous spiritual and private activities of the slaves. At the end of the seventeenth century, the Brazilian poet Gregório de Matos,[62] nicknamed the 'Mouth of Hell' due to his scabrous satirical verses, made a passing reference to the religious rituals performed in the *quilombos*, to the beating of drums: 'There's no fallen lady/or bankrupt fop/who doesn't visit the *quilombo*/and dance till they drop.'[63] In this poem, called 'Precept 1',[64] de Matos was probably referring to the specific rhythm of *calundu*, a ritual in which a deity is invoked to foretell people's futures.

From the ritual transformation of *calundu* to the origins of samba, the community life of the African slaves and their descendants, despite the deprivation, was one of creativity.[65] If the relationship has always been asymmetrical, the reactions have never been cast in stone. It may be possible to try to turn people into property, but one cannot destroy their agency, creativity and resourcefulness. More than merely surviving, the enslaved Africans became Brazilians, foiling the designs of their tormentors and a perverted regime steeped in violence.

4

Gold!

THE CATAGUÁS SERTÃO

By the beginning of the eighteenth century, Portugal's finances had been seriously affected by the high cost of running the empire. The sugarcane industry was beginning to feel the impact of the competition from the Antilles, from where the Dutch, who had been expelled from Brazil, were transporting sugar to Europe, seriously affecting the plantations in the northeast of Brazil. Meanwhile, in Salvador, the governor-general of the colony, João de Lencastro, pondered over whether or not the discovery of gold in the *sertão* could be a lucrative business for the Portuguese Crown. In spite of the optimism coming out of Lisbon, the governor-general remained sceptical about the quantity of gold. He doubted that the small nuggets of gold found in streams located in what is today the central region of Minas Gerais would compensate for the enormous investment the Crown had made in the colonization of America, or inject new energy into its imperial enterprise.

'Cataguás' was the name of an indigenous group who lived in the southern, western and central regions of the territory of Minas Gerais – the first to face the colonizers. They were descendants of the Tremembé, a group who, in the sixteenth century, had migrated from the northeast coast of what is today the state of Ceará. They had actually called themselves 'Catu-auá'; 'Cataguá' was a Portuguese corruption of this original name. They are now extinct. Cataguás was also used generically by the people in the lowlands to designate the Indians who lived in the El Dorado of the mountainous regions of Minas Gerais, where amid the coarse sand of the riverbeds there glittered tiny specks of gold.

It had taken two centuries, but the Portuguese Crown had not given up – the search for precious metals had always been central to their obsession for immediate enrichment.[1] There was a prevailing sense of optimism among the authorities in Lisbon, who for some time had been predisposed to believe in the existence of immense treasures in America, just waiting to be discovered. The astonishing amounts of gold and silver the Spanish had found in their American colonies and taken to Seville in the first half of the sixteenth century had dazzled the courts of Europe. The Crown of Castile had accumulated a vast fortune, enough to be the source of any European monarch's envy, and certainly enough to keep the dream of American riches alive among the Portuguese.

In the mid-sixteenth century the news that the lucky Spanish had found an entire mountain of silver in the middle of the Andes – the Cerro Rico de Potosí, in what is today Bolivia – set the imagination of Europe alight and convinced Lisbon of two things: there must also be large deposits of precious metals in Brazil and the only way of finding them was to colonize the interior. Such journeys presented innumerable hardships, but those who undertook them were confident they would end in success. At the time mapmakers believed the American continent was so narrow that the Portuguese explorers were virtually neighbours of the fabulously wealthy mountains of Upper Peru. It was thought that if an expedition set out from the port of Santos the journey, by land or water, would take only twelve days.[2]

It was the duty of the colony's governor, who also held the military post of captain-general, to protect the colony against invasions from corsairs and pirates, and from rival European powers such as Holland and France, keen to establish their own imperial colonies and benefit from the profits of maritime trade. He was also required to promote the colonization of the interior in the search for precious metals. However, Governor-General João de Lencastro had good reason to be cautious about the news that gold had been found in the *sertão* of Cataguás. The small amounts of gold that had been discovered between 1560 and 1561 in the mountains that cut across the present-day states of São Paulo and Paraná, above all between Iguape, Paranaguá and Curitiba, did very little to satisfy the appetite of the Portuguese. In the opinion of Lisbon: 'What we wanted to find in Brazil was Peru, not Brazil.'[3] Their intention was to convert the Paranapiacaba Mountains (the indigenous name for the Serra do Mar)[4] into a replica of the Andes. They even planned to import two hundred llamas to transport the gold. But the amount of gold found there was negligible; the veins were not continuous and the production from the mines was very low.[5]

Like his contemporaries, for João de Lencastro economic growth meant the sugarcane industry, which had prospered since the 1570s, above all in the Recôncavo in Bahia, which became the economic centre of Portuguese America, and on the coast of Pernambuco. At the beginning of the eighteenth century, Padre Antonil also thought the authorities' obsession with finding gold was a risk for the colony. It was not difficult to understand why. Sugar constituted the wealth of Brazil and the *engenhos* were the centres for the missionary work of converting the slaves. All this could be destroyed if gold were discovered in Minas Gerais, with the consequent mass migration to the interior.[6]

As we have seen, the economic life of Portugal's South Atlantic Empire was based on the combination of sugar and slaves. This combination created the mercantile communities that gravitated around the wealth produced by the large estates. Salvador, the dynamic centre of the Portuguese administration, also served as the largest port for this rural society. A good governor-general, as João de Lencastro undoubtedly considered himself to be, had to be cautious about any new proposals surrounding the mining of gold. His first priority was to be responsive to the demands and interests of the existing mercantile elite and the masters of the *engenhos*.

In the middle of 1697 news of the discovery of gold arrived in Salvador. It had been found mixed in with the gravel on the bed of a small river in a valley covered with humid forest, surrounded by the steep escarpments of the Serra do Espinhaço. The local indigenous people called the river Tripuí ('dark beneath the waters').[7] The governor-general could have had no idea that Tripuí was just the beginning: the discovery of its *ouro preto*, 'black gold',[8] proved to be the first clue to finding a gigantic mass of the precious metal, extending as far as Carmo and Sabará, at the point where they were intercepted by the Guaicuí river (the original name of the Rio das Velhas).[9] The governor-general continued to believe that the discovery of gold in Minas Gerais was in fact a serious problem. In 1701 he wrote a long letter to Dom Pedro II[10] containing a number of suggestions. The first was to seal off the area where gold had been found by closing all the routes that gave access to the interior. The second was to concentrate all the trade that emanated from the mines in Salvador and to subject the whole mining region to the jurisdiction of the captaincy of Bahia.[11]

No one in Lisbon was impressed by João de Lencastro's wariness. Despite the innumerable expeditions that had failed, the Crown's obsession with mountains of gold and silver had by no means abated. The authorities also believed that among the inhabitants of São Paulo de Piratininga – the base from which the explorers set out on expeditions into the interior – there were people who knew exactly where most of the gold could be found. After all, they had been exploring the *sertão* long before the discovery of gold in the 1690s. What they had been seeking, however, was something else: 'red gold', a term coined by Padre Vieira during his struggle against Indian slavery and that referred to the blood of the Indians captured and enslaved by the settlers.[12]

These colonists travelled for months or even years on end, almost always on foot, walking in single file, barefooted like the Indians, with feet splayed out and ankles turned inwards to alleviate the fatigue and cover the ground more quickly. Throughout the seventeenth century innumerable expeditions to capture Indians penetrated the *sertões* that are now a part of Minas Gerais, making the inhabitants of São Paulo (*Paulistas*) famous throughout the colony. These people seemed to have been born on the Piratininga plateau with the sole purpose of exploring the unchartered interior, confronted at every turn by arrows, wild beasts and fevers,[13] and travelling further and further inland.

This exploring had begun with the town of São Paulo de Piratininga, which was surrounded by the Serra do Mar – a series of densely forested mountain peaks stretching towards the horizon. It was thus strategically located to protect its inhabitants from intervention by the imperial authorities in Rio de Janeiro. The town was built on the top of a hill and was guarded from a distance by the forts in the Cantareira Mountains. It was also surrounded by a providential network of rivers. These were later to be used by the explorers to travel by boat to the Paraná river, from where they entered the network of tributaries in the River Plate basin and made their way upstream into the southernmost part of the colony.[14]

The town of São Paulo developed around a college that had been built by the Jesuits of the Society of Jesus, the walls of which were made from a mixture of clay and sand. It had a small church and a large plot of land surrounded by Indian houses. It stood at the exact location of what today is the Pátio do Colégio, at the very heart of the city centre. The college was a cherished project of Manuel da Nóbrega, the leader of the Jesuits in Brazil: to gather the Indians of the region together and with them to build a new society of devoted Christians – a society that would be free of both the pagan customs of the natives and the bad habits and vices of the Europeans. The project was a dismal failure. The natives had no intention of abandoning their beliefs and the Portuguese colonists were equally reluctant to forgo their predatory behaviour. But the town remained, strategically located at the entrance to the hinterlands from where the settlers captured and enslaved the Indians, claiming, as they always did, that this was a 'righteous war'. The Indians were put to work in the fields, used for breeding cattle, for domestic tasks, and even as a means of transport.[15]

In the first half of the eighteenth century these expeditions began to be called *bandeiras*, a term that was adopted throughout the colony, although other names were also used, including *entradas, jornadas, empresas* or *conquistas* (intrusions, journeys, undertakings, conquests). The *bandeirantes* who set out from the Piratininga plateau began to assume the form of militarized hunting expeditions for the enslavement of Indians or the search for precious metals, producing a mode of life that some Brazilian historians in the late nineteenth and early twentieth centuries referred to as *bandeirantismo*.[16] The expeditions that set out from the town of São Paulo combed the interior of Minas Gerais and did all they could to hide the existence of gold from the representatives of the Crown. They had good reason for this: keeping the colonial administrators at a distance meant avoiding both the exorbitant taxes and the rigorous imperial laws that restricted the number of Indian slaves.

Negotiations between the Crown and the *Paulista*s who discovered the first deposits of gold began in the early 1690s. The agreement was directly authorized by the King of Portugal, Dom Pedro II, and guaranteed the discoverers titles, royal favours and the ownership of the mines they discovered. In addition, the Crown authorities granted the *bandeirantes* the power they most desired: to be allowed to 'manage' the Indians they captured in the interior and put them to work as slaves on the Piratininga plateau. Only then did the gold begin to appear.[17]

Further discoveries of gold in different areas of Minas Gerais occurred almost simultaneously, all of which lay along the line that connects the present-day cities of Ouro Preto and Diamantina, between the basins of the Rio Doce and the São Francisco river. There – in the centre of what is today the state of Minas Gerais – astonishing amounts of gold were found in the beds of the small rivers that flowed through the valleys and *chapadas*[18] surrounded by the steep slopes of the Espinhaço Mountains. The gold appeared in the form of tiny nuggets of various colours – off-white, yellow, grey, black or opaque and grimy. This last was nicknamed 'rotten gold'.[19] The black colour resulted from the mixture with the chemical element palladium and indicated a high concentration of gold. The white was a result of the mixture of gold and nickel and had a much lower value. However, whatever the colour, the gold was everywhere. Over a period of millions of years it had dropped from clefts in the rocks of the Espinhaço Mountains.

This was alluvial gold, completely different from the gold that the Spanish had extracted in huge quantities from the underground deposits of Mexico and Upper Peru. It was soon discovered that a long sequence of adjoining mines existed in the region; no matter what direction one looked or travelled there was gold to be found. Thus at the beginning of the 1720s the captaincy received the name of Minas Gerais (General Mines).[20] The area where the most important mines were located became known as the Gold District. Most of these were discovered at the source of the Rio das Velhas, in the present-day municipality of Ouro Preto (where the Cachoeira das Andorinhas[21] is located). Rapid migration to the area resulted in the creation of the first three towns in Minas Gerais, all founded in 1711: in January, the village of Nossa Senhora do Carmo[22] was granted the status of 'vila'; in June the mining centres of Ouro Preto, Antônio Dias, Padre Faria and Tripuí were joined into one and named Vila Rica; and in the same month the village of Sabarabuçu officially became the Vila of Nossa Senhora da Conceição[23] do Sabará. These are the modern-day cities, respectively, of Mariana, Ouro Preto and Sabará.[24]

Between the last decade of the seventeenth century and the first decade of the eighteenth, the inhabitants of the Piratininga plateau began to think they were being deceived. The Portuguese Crown had promised much more than it was prepared to deliver; it had no intention of granting the ownership of the gold mines to the discoverers. Between 1707 and 1709 discontent erupted into what became known as the War of the *Emboabas*. The enraged *bandeirantes* started a war against the *emboabas* for the control of Minas Gerais. The term *emboabas* originated from the Indian word for a breed of chicken whose feet were covered with feathers. When used to refer to 'outsiders' who wore marching boots, especially the Portuguese, as opposed to the inhabitants of Piratininga who went barefoot, it was taken as a grievous insult. Enemies were identified by their boots and the expletive *emboaba* was frequently hurled at them. Even today, on hearing a loud bang in the distance, a *Mineiro*[25] mutters 'either a dog or an *emboaba* just died'.

With the inhabitants of the region seething with anger, the Crown decided pragmatically to pardon the rebels. It did not, however, cede political ground: it nominated *emboabas* to all the important administrative posts in the newly created towns, thus putting an end to the aspiration of the *Paulistas* to gain political control of the area.[26] Finally expelled from Minas Gerais, they returned to their exploration of the hinterlands, where they made two further discoveries of major gold deposits. The first, in 1722, were the Sutil Mines in Mato Grosso, where the capital of the state, Cuiabá, is located today. The second, five years later, were the Vila Boa Mines, in the captaincy of Goiás. Thus, by the end of the 1720s, the three major areas of gold deposits in Portuguese America had finally been identified.

GOLD MINES THAT WERE 'GENERAL'

On the morning of 21 July 1674, Fernão Dias Pais Leme set out from the town of São Paulo de Piratininga on his last great adventure. At the head of four companies of men made up of a hundred Indians and forty whites – including his two sons, one legitimate, Garcia Rodrigues Pais, and the other mestizo, José Pais, as well as his son-in-law Manuel da Borba Gato – he made his way towards the *sertão*. He was around sixty years old at the time, the owner of a considerable fortune and veteran of numerous expeditions to capture Indians. He owned a vast estate near São Paulo, located in what is today the district of Pinheiros.[27] For two years he had been planning every detail of the mission, corresponding with both the governor-general and the Crown. In his pocket he carried a licence from the governor-general granting him authority over all the members of the expedition as well as any people who had already penetrated that part of the interior or who were to do so after the expedition had passed.

Fernão Dias was in search of the mythical mountains called

Sabarabuçu. According to the Indians, they shone so brightly they could be seen from afar, dazzling anyone who tried to get too near. In Tupi-Guarani they were known as the 'sun of the earth'.[28] A river over-flowing with sparkling emeralds and pieces of silver and gold was said to descend from the slopes. The Spanish explorer Felipe Guillén said that he had been told the Indians collected the stones and used them for making troughs – but only for pigs as they believed that the metal 'was the cause of diseases'.[29]

Before entering the territory of the Minas Gerais, Fernão Dias sent a group ahead to set up a supply base to ensure the expedition's survival. The camp, which occupied the villages of Santana and Sumidouro on the banks of the Rio das Velhas, was a combination of a military encampment and a rapidly expanding settlement, surrounded by exten-sive plantations of corn, sweet potatoes, pumpkins, beans and yams. The following year, 'at the end of the rains, at the start/of autumn when the land, parched with thirst/had drunk deeply of the waters of the season',[30] to quote from Olavo Bilac's beautiful poem[31] 'The Emer-ald Hunter', published in 1902,[32] the expedition penetrated the *sertão* in the direction of the northeast. Between 1675 and 1681 they followed the ragged outline of the Serra do Espinhaço, crossing the entire extent of Minas Gerais until finally reaching the region of the Jequitinhonha and Araçuaí rivers. There, at the extreme northeasterly point of Minas, the members of the expedition believed they had discovered the great lake of fabulous wealth of Indian mythology – Vapabuçu – the legend-ary source of the continent's rivers that connected Brazil with the Andes.[33]

Vapabuçu was the fruit of European as well as of Indian imagina-tion. The banks of the river where the expedition camped did indeed seem to glisten with emeralds. But it was an illusion – they were tour-malines, a semiprecious stone of little value. Already ill with malaria, Fernão Dias made his way back to the lake of Sumidouro – the mysteri-ous 'waters that disappeared' through a cavity in the forest and were constantly renewed by underground streams – where a few days later he died.

'And those emeralds/Mines that killed/with hope and fever/that never were found/and when found/were nature's delusion?'[34] in the words of Carlos Drummond de Andrade's poem about Fernão Dias, written two hundred years later.[35] The location of the mythical mountain had not been found and Dias's expedition had produced not a single piece of gold for the court in Lisbon. Nevertheless, the expedition was still an important accomplishment: the *bandeirantes* had acquired a survival strategy, ways of adapting to the conditions of the interior of Minas Gerais that allowed them to remain for long periods in this isolated region, surrounded by intractable natural conditions, wild beasts and hostile Indians. At the time, the conquest and appropriation of the region was at least as important to Lisbon as finding treasure, and this was what Fernão Dias had achieved. His expedition adopted the military strategy of clearing land in the bush to plant food for the sustenance of the troops during their forages into the interior, a strategy that was to prove decisive both in combating the Indians and in occupying the land.[36] Thus a path into Minas Gerais had been opened up, albeit one that still presented an enormous challenge to any who ventured along it. Fernão Dias's expedition had carved out a single route connecting the coast to the Serra da Mantiqueira,[37] passing the Rio das Velhas and continuing on to the northeast of Minas. This was the *Caminho Geral do Sertão*, also known as the *Caminho Velho* or *Caminho de São Paulo*;[38] the 'mouth of Minas' connecting São Paulo de Piratininga to São Sebastião do Rio de Janeiro, and from there to the recently discovered Ouro Preto and Nossa Senhora do Carmo on the banks of the Rio das Mortes and the Rio das Velhas.[39]

Crossing the Serra da Mantiqueira was particularly hard. The range had been named the 'weeping mountains' because of its profusion of streams and meandering rivers. At the point known as the *Serra do Facão*,[40] a razor-edged path crossed five of the highest peaks, 'preventing the weak from entering Minas' as was said at the time. This was only an undertaking for the fearless and the strong. The mountains were covered with a dark green blanket of humid forest that travellers entered after the first few days of their journey, after crossing the *Garganta do Embaú*[41] in the Paraíba Valley, at the point which today marks the division between the states of Rio de Janeiro and Minas Gerais. The mountains further tormented the travellers with clouds of poisonous insects and sudden downpours of rain. The crossing was particularly dangerous during the rainy season when the mountain peaks were covered in mist. The ice-cold water froze the travellers to the bone and dripped from their beards as they descended the slippery slopes that overturned mules and cargoes as the path became mud and clay beneath their feet.

News of the discovery of gold soon spread. In São Paulo, Rio de Janeiro and Salvador it was the talk of the town with many of the residents sending excited messages to relatives in Portugal. There was nothing that could be done. Neither the Crown's efforts to keep the location of the mines a secret – to prevent arousing the avarice of rival powers – nor the alarm of local authorities at the mass exit of inhabitants from towns along the coast, not even the prospect of crossing the Serra da Mantiqueira could control the hunger for gold or the frenzied masses that rushed to the region.

'Nothing like it had ever been seen before and nothing like it would be seen again until the California gold rush of 1849,' wrote the English historian Charles Boxer in 1962. In their anxiety to reach the gold, people of every kind jostled against each other along the paths. Amid the crowds there were those who were desperate to climb out of poverty, others who dreamt of rapid enrichment, and yet others who were fleeing from political or religious persecution. This last group included enemies of the king and of the monarchy, New Christians, groups of gypsies and heretics of various hues. Among them was Pedro de Rates Hanequim, a verbose millenarian who defended somewhat unorthodox theories in relation to Brazil. In one of these he argued that paradise on earth was concealed in the midst of a mountain chain in the centre of Portuguese America, at right angles to which stood the throne of God. In another he suggested crowning the King of Portugal Dom João V's brother, the Infante Emanuel, as Emperor of South America, under whom a 'Fifth Empire' would be created in the interior of Minas Gerais.[42]

The governor-general João de Lencastro referred to this multitude as 'worthless, ill-mannered rabble'.[43] The authorities in Lisbon finally echoed his sentiments: those who penetrated the interior of Minas Gerais were 'intruders, a rootless mob who had no love for a country where they had not been born'. They did in fact originate from many places. Some of them came from Portugal, leaving their wives and children behind. A large number came from the other captaincies, above all São Paulo, Bahia and Rio de Janeiro, having sold everything they owned and cast in their lot with the gold hunters. 'Where the paths end, the mines begin', *Paulistas* of the seventeenth century used to say. Those who managed to reach Minas Gerais knew all too well what they wanted: to get hold of as much gold as they could, as quickly as possible. Dazzled by the sheer quantities of the precious metal that gleamed from the rocks around them, in their frantic efforts to locate new veins the miners forgot the most basic fact of all: they could not eat gold.

It was a disaster. Between 1697 and 1698, 1700 and 1701, and again in 1713, having failed to plant enough manioc, beans, pumpkin and corn to provide sustenance for the multitudes that continued to arrive, the inhabitants of Minas Gerais, in the words of Padre Antonil, 'died of hunger with their hands full of gold'.[44] To avoid starvation the *Mineiros* ate anything they could get their hands on: dogs, cats, roots, insects, snakes and lizards. They even ate the *bicho de taquara*,[45] a poisonous white larva found inside the stems of bamboo.

For those who set out from the northeastern ports of Recife and Salvador there was only one path that led to Minas, the *Caminho Geral do Sertão* (also known as the Bahia Trail or the Trail of the São Francisco Corrals). Of the three 'mouths of Minas', this was the longest. Those who took it in the search for gold were mostly settlers from the plantation areas of Bahia and Pernambuco who, with the decline of the sugar industry, were losing their livelihood. The route was well known to the *Paulista bandeirantes,* who had used it since the beginning of the seventeenth century. It had a number of advantages: its forests were not as dense as those of the Serra da Mantiqueira, the trees were wider apart, interspersed with open spaces covered with vegetation and bushes. Most importantly, it was crossed by rivers that could be navigated by canoes.

'The *sertão* was another unchartered sea', as the twentieth-century historian Raimundo Faoro so fittingly described it in his book, *Os donos do poder*.[46] The journey between the peaks and chasms, the abyss of the unknown, was a long and lonely one. Many left the path before reaching the mines and settled in the interior: criminals pursued by the law, insolvent debtors, sons of small farmers whose land was too small to divide up any further, and poor workers who had no land. They stopped their journeys and claimed land in isolated places; beyond the reach of the law and dazzled by the prospects of captured Indians, golden lakes and mountains gleaming with precious gems, they continued the devastation of Minas Gerais. For people escaping from poverty, looking for land, avoiding prison or concealing the crime of sedition, it was the perfect refuge.

This generalized belief that the interior of Minas Gerais was beyond the reach of the law transformed the Caminho Geral do Sertão into the most popular smuggling route for gold. As Pedro Barbosa Leal, who knew the region well, explained to the authorities, the interior 'was full of "loopholes": deserted fields, virgin forests and unused paths which could be used for escape.'[47] And the smugglers knew the exact location of the 'loopholes'. With surprising audacity they risked travelling down the São Francisco river in canoes. This was the first stage of a long journey for the gold, either northward to Europe or southward to the River Plate. Casting anchor at clandestine wharfs in the dead of night, when the soldiers guarding the beaches could see nothing but blackness, they slipped past the ports of Jacobina and Rio das Contas – inspection posts where the king's taxes were levied – and with the gold safe and sound, they would set out on a journey of several weeks through the *sertão* to Pernambuco, Paraíba, Rio Grande do Norte or Ceará, where the gold was finally put on board the vessels that shipped it out of the colony. There was an alternative route, by land, which represented an even longer and more perilous journey for the smugglers. It followed along the banks of the São Francisco river as far as Parnaguá, in what is today the state of Piauí. From there it continued on to Maranhão from where the gold was smuggled to Europe.[48]

To the despair of the Crown, a substantial part of the gold found in Brazil slipped through the hands of its inspectors. Smuggling gold became a major illegal business – the profits of which were considered large enough to offset substantial perils and risks. The colonial authorities did everything they could to stop the smuggling: the routes into Minas were monitored by inspection posts manned by tax collectors as well as military guards. Padre Antonil's book was confiscated by the Crown in 1711 and banned for describing the route between Salvador and the gold-producing region. The Caminho Geral do Sertão was closed to travellers and the transport of merchandise – only cattle for the sustenance of the *Mineiros* was allowed to pass. But the measure was of little use. Gold continued to disappear. The audacious smugglers hid themselves among the cattle traders with their pouches of gold well concealed. They made maximum use of corruptible priests, who, exempt from searches at the control posts, managed to divert large quantities of gold from the royal coffers. Lisbon was furious and, in 1709, banned the presence of religious orders in Minas Gerais.

The Caminho Geral do Sertão entered the gold-producing district at Sabará, the first and at the time the largest town in Minas Gerais. It was there that cattle, leather, dried beef, pork and fish, rock salt and *rapadura* (a sweet made from sugarcane) first entered the region, all of it extremely expensive. In 1703, Padre Antonil noted that an *alqueire*[49] of flour cost 640 réis in São Paulo, whereas in Minas it cost 43,000 réis.[50] He went on to note the extraordinary discrepancy in prices: 'A pound of sugar, 120 rs. in São Paulo; in Minas 1200 rs. A chicken, 160 rs. in São Paulo; in Minas, 4000 rs. In São Paulo, an ox for slaughter 2000 rs; in Minas an identical beast 120,000 rs.'[51]

The last of the great famines occurred in Pitangui in 1730. The town had been founded by *bandeirantes* from São Paulo as a stopover on their way to Goiás at the end of the *Emboabas* War. The Pitangui mines were located near the entrance to the *sertão* and were protected by independently minded people whose anger with the Crown had not abated since the war. These people were famous throughout the eighteenth century for the straightforward way in which they resolved any political or property disputes – through the barrel of a gun, or in this case, a blunderbuss.[52] The scarcity of livestock in Pitangui all but ruined the town. Some of the inhabitants fled to attempt survival in the forest, all supplies disappeared, and food prices shot up to unbelievable heights. While people were starving, gold seemed to sprout from the soil beneath their feet. There was a particular knoll that earned the nickname 'Potato Hill' because the enormous pellets of gold that were found there were shaped like potatoes.[53]

Food supplies only improved with the opening up of a new route to the mines. The *Caminho Novo* was planned by the Governor of the Southern Department, Artur de Sá e Meneses. It created a network of trails for the transport of merchandise that connected the mining region to the country's two most important supply centres – the port of Rio de Janeiro and the town of São Paulo. This third and last 'mouth of the mines' began at the end of the Guanabara Bay, in the middle of the *Baixada Fluminense*[54] where the present-day city of Duque de Caxias is located. Before it started its climb into the Serra da Mantiqueira it crossed the *Caminho de São Paulo* at the town of Taubaté. This new route was to transform Rio de Janeiro into Minas Gerais's leading supplier, with an ever-increasing flow of travellers, merchandise, cattle and innumerable African slaves all passing through the city.

The *Caminho Novo* considerably shortened travel times – with luck it could take just twenty days to travel from Rio de Janeiro to Vila

Rica. But crossing the Serra da Mantiqueira was still an ordeal. Carts could only be manoeuvred along short stretches of the track. Men and animals floundered in the mire and spent the nights in filthy straw shelters, fighting off bats and a multitude of insects: ants, mosquitoes, ticks, fleas, cockroaches and spiders. A century and a half later the great English explorer Sir Richard Burton was to complain of similar woes assailing him on the *Caminho Novo*: nights passed without sleeping in shelters for muleteers, infested with mosquitoes and 'swarms of round, fat worms that crawled into my flesh and made their home beneath my nails'.[55]

By the time gold production reached its height, farms were already established along the frontier between the mines and the *sertão* and on the banks of the Rio das Velhas. These were enormous estates – all of them equipped with docks to receive the goods that came from Bahia down the São Francisco river and the Rio das Velhas. They included estates such as *Minhocas*, the *Macaúbas* and the *Jaguara*;[56] the last of these had the capacity to lodge up to 2,000 people. At the heart of the mining region, along the stretch of the route that climbs to the top of the Serra de Capanema (which today still links the town of Ouro Preto to Sabará) tiny settlements emerged where food was planted for immediate consumption: Santo Antônio do Leite, Amarantina, São Bartolomeu, Santo Antonio da Caza Branca (present-day Glaura) and Curral de Pedra. From the very beginning, as the existence of these villages show, a thriving internal market for agricultural production and cattle-raising grew in the region.

Until about 1750 there was still an abundant supply of gold. Throughout this period the traffic of people and merchandise along the Caminho Novo remained intense. The route supplied Vila Rica with sugar, *cachaça*, cattle, gunpowder, tobacco, olive oil, rice, salt, quince jelly and wine. With the expansion of towns and villages, Minas Gerais began to receive supplies of a large variety of products and knick-knacks: glass, mirrors, firearms, knives, lead, velvet, chinaware, buckles, furs, red damask breeches, hats adorned with ribbons of gold and silver thread, leather boots with laces for ladies and jackets lined with silk or fluffy wool.[57]

From one end of the Caminho Novo to the other, a new terror now threatened the travellers. It was no longer the fear of being ambushed by the Cataguá, Guaianá or Tupinambá. The danger now was of being attacked by the *quilombolas*, who were spreading panic throughout the region with their systematic assaults on travellers, farms and the outskirts of villages and towns. There were *quilombos* scattered all over Minas Gerais; it almost seemed as if they had sprung up spontaneously to complement the rugged terrain. Most of them were relatively small, but very dangerous due to their proximity to the towns. The *quilombo* of São Bartolomeu, for example, took its name from its strategic location at the top of the mountain range of that name. It sheltered enough highway robbers to torment the lives of travellers making their way to Vila Rica along the Caminho Novo and to seriously affect the communications between Vila Rica, Mariana and the village of Cachoeira do Campo.[58]

A complex social network of contacts developed between the *quilombos* and the urban centres. The black women who sold fresh produce on the streets were at the centre of this network. Inhabitants of the gold-producing region frequently complained that these women, who sold fruit and vegetables to the grocery shops as well as from their stands in the streets, maintained close ties with the *quilombolas*. Out of solidarity, they also acted as go-betweens, helping runaway slaves to take refuge in the *quilombos*, in addition to supplying these with livestock and information. It was this last that most exasperated the authorities: 'black thieves from the *quilombos* receive information about the whereabouts of people they can rob [. . .] and everything is facilitated by these black women who help them and give them shelter'.[59]

As the colonizers settled in Minas Gerais, an increasing number of *quilombos* emerged in the countryside surrounding the towns and villages. With this proximity, the food shops eventually became centres for the trade in contraband with the *quilombos*. To the irritation of the authorities, and even more of the inhabitants, who now lived in constant fear, there were no legal constraints preventing this trade: 'The shop owners offer escaped slaves protection for as long as they see fit, and the blacks from the forests offer them shelter in their so-called "houses" [. . .] They leave in the early hours of the morning. In this way every grocer's shop has become a *quilombo*.'[60] These shops became centres of resistance, expert in eluding the authorities: they were places for parties and lovers' trysts, shelters for escaped slaves and vagrants, where the environment was ideal for the exchange of smuggled goods with the *quilombos*.

In 1718, as the population of slaves increased, the governor of the captaincy, the Count of Assumar, a fierce adversary of escaped slaves, resigned to the fact that he could not 'change the way they think or their natural desire of freedom', advised the king that 'the adoption of more violent remedies is required as deserving punishment for these scoundrels'.[61] Among the 'remedies' he suggested was cutting the slaves' Achilles tendon to prevent them from escaping. The proposal was not considered unreasonable, so much so that twenty years later, in 1741, the authorities in Minas Gerais once again sent it to Lisbon for approval; and in 1755 the proposal was passed with acclaim by the Town Council of Mariana, which once again sent it to Lisbon. Meanwhile, the count informed the inhabitants of the captaincy of the measures he intended to implement for the recapture of slaves and *quilombolas*: 'Any person who offers them shelter, or knows where the said *quilombos* are located, and fails to inform the authorities will, if white, be whipped in public and banished to Benguela, and if black, be put to death.'[62]

The Count of Assumar could be excessively cruel, but he was by no means alone in this, nor did he act just on his own account. The colonial authorities produced an endless flow of proclamations, royal charters and letters patent in their attempt to maintain the stability of the slavery system by preventing escapes and suppressing resistance. A royal decree of 1741 determined that an escaped slave be branded on the shoulder with a red-hot iron, and, in the case of reoffending, have one of his ears cut off.[63]

In addition to the ferocity of the *quilombolas*, travellers were under constant threat of being assaulted by gangs of whites, free blacks, mestizos and mulattoes[64] – a wide variety of men and women who, for one reason or another, had not been absorbed into the mining, cattle-raising and agricultural economy and who existed at the periphery of Minas Gerais society.[65] The colonial authorities had designated this surprisingly varied group as 'loafers'. They were poor – with no social status, a very fluid group that was difficult to control or discipline. Evidently not all of them were highway robbers. Nevertheless, every traveller that set out faced a high risk of being attacked by one of these organized gangs and, if not murdered, at least of being stripped of all his possessions.

Some of these groups made history. The gang of Manuel Henriques, nicknamed 'Glove Hand' because he used a padded glove to replace a hand he had lost in a fight, operated in the region of Cachoeira do Macacu, on the far side of the Paraibuna river in the captaincy of Rio de Janeiro. His fame was so widespread it even reached Lisbon. His highly trained band had approximately two hundred men including whites, freed blacks and *pardos*, divided into groups led by trusted agents. They illegally prospected gold in the area and laid ambushes at the entrance to the Serra da Mantiqueira for the convoys that set out from the port of Estrela headed for Vila Rica.

The most notorious group in Minas Gerais was the 'Mantiqueira gang'. They assaulted travellers on the high ridges that led to Vila Rica, near the junction between the Caminho Novo and the town of São João del Rey. They were led by José Galvão, nicknamed 'Mountain'; a huge brown-skinned man with long hair and a bushy beard who was said to be of gypsy origin. The gang had a network of spies in the towns, all watching out for convoys transporting gold or traders with large baskets of merchandise – a sure sign that they were travelling with money. Galvão's men made a deep impression, due both to their violent methods and their audacity. Travellers were lucky if they did not end up murdered and buried, their bodies relieved of all possessions, documents and clothes, in the secluded heights of the mountains. As the news of these attacks began to spread among the settlers the atmosphere in the towns became increasingly tense, but in spite of constant appeals to the governor no effective measures were taken. Traffic along the routes began to diminish, and it was not uncommon for travellers to providently make their wills before setting out.

The gang was only routed, after a great deal of effort, in 1783, by the ensign Joaquim José da Silva Xavier, 'Tiradentes',[66] who was then the commander of the Caminho Novo detachment. To this day the inhabitants of Minas Gerais advise travellers against spending the night near the mountain peaks along the Caminho Novo, which are known for the appearance of mysterious lights on stormy nights, visions of the souls of murdered men hovering around the places where they were killed, white apparitions disturbing travellers' sleep, and the sound of phantom hooves cantering along the Mantiqueira mountain passes.

Minas Gerais was settled very quickly and in a short period of time. The production of gold started at the beginning of the 1690s and reached its height between 1730 and 1740. By 1750 it was already in decline. The techniques used were rudimentary and largely improvised. The pellets of gold glistened in the sun on the beds of rivers and streams. They were about the size of a pea and were easily spotted where they lay buried among the gravel. A gold panner needed good eyesight and had to be prepared to enter the freezing cold water of the mountain streams. He also needed the physical strength and the knowledge required to wield the tin or cedarwood basin used for washing and sieving the gold, separating it from the sand, gravel and clay. During the rainy season, when the floodwaters made panning impossible, they excavated the sand along the banks of the rivers or at the foot of the hills, where they chipped away at the gold encrusted in clefts in the rock.[67]

When the supplies of gold that could be panned began to fail, water was used to wash away the earth that covered the gold deposits. This task was only possible because of a large-scale workforce of black slaves, most of whom came from West Africa (Cameroon, Nigeria and Senegal) and Central Africa (Angola, Congo and Gabon), and, in lesser proportion, from East Africa (Mozambique). Since the opening of the first mines, large numbers of slaves had been brought to the region to meet the demand for gold. Between 1721 and 1722 it is estimated that there was already a population of 45,554 African slaves in Minas Gerais. By 1745 this number had grown to 95,366, and by 1786 had reached 174,000.[68] Enslaved people were also brought in from the sugar plantations. These men diverted waterways and made dams, dug the canals where the gold was separated from the gravel, and piled up blocks of stone cemented with mortar to drain off the mud.

The labour for deep mining was also provided by slaves. To reach the water table they dug wells up to fifteen metres deep and carved funnel-shaped tunnels into the rock. While the tunnels were being constructed, the earth often collapsed, killing the slave workers. They also operated the water wheels connected to a chain of open crates that were used to bring up the earth. The water provided the energy to push the inverted crates downwards and to rotate them as they dug out the mud from the bottom of the pits. The marks left by deep mining can still be seen in the countryside of Minas Gerais. In the seventeenth century a traveller knew by the signs that he had arrived in Minas: quarries in the hills, muddied rivers, devastated forests and the ubiquitous potholes.

Many people made their fortune from one day to the next, even though the cost of merchandise was the highest in Portuguese America and gold dust was the currency used. Padre Antonil was horrified by the eccentric and ostentatious behaviour of the wealthy *Mineiros*: 'accompanied by troops of musketeers, always at the ready to perpetrate acts of violence' and 'lavishing money on superfluous goods: a black slave acquired at a cost of a thousand cruzados [whose task it was to herald their master's arrival in public places by blowing a bugle] and a mulatta of ill repute (purchased at double the usual price) with whom they steadfastedly committed multiple scandalous sins'.[69]

Portugal knew very well what was happening in the interior of its colony. It had been waiting impatiently to find gold for more than a century. The dream had now come true in Minas Gerais, and Lisbon began to move in to take control. In 1700 a tax of one-fifth of the value of all gold discovered was imposed; it was called the *quinto* (fifth). The miners were required to take their gold to the forging house, where it was made into bars and the tax was deducted.

Unsurprisingly, very few miners paid the tax. But the Crown was determined to set up a taxation system that would squeeze every last drop of profit out of Minas Gerais. It created a Gold Commissariat, appointed tax collectors, set up customs posts at the exit points and installed forging houses throughout the region. Over the years it increased and diversified the taxes. A panning tax that affected all miners was instituted as well as a general annual tax charged from each of the four administrative districts – Rio das Velhas, Rio das Mortes, Vila Rica and Serro do Frio. A per capita tax was imposed on every single individual and each economic activity, including on all the slaves who worked in the captaincy. After 1751, Portugal increased the pressure even more: an annual minimum of a hundred arrobas (around 1,500 kilos) was established for all gold brought to the forging houses. Anyone who failed to reach the quota was obliged to pay tax on the difference.[70]

The gold left along the River Tagus for other countries in Europe almost as soon as it had arrived by that same waterway. England was the main destination, where it was used to pay for imported manufactured goods that were otherwise unavailable in the Portuguese domestic market. Despite the high levels of tax evasion and quantities of smuggled gold, vast amounts of the precious metal entered the port of Lisbon during the first half of the eighteenth century: a total of 196 kilos in 1713; 946 kilos in 1720; 3.4 tons in 1725; 4.2 tons in 1731; and 11.5 tons in 1741.

The peak of production was reached between 1737 and 1746. By the middle of the following decade it was already in decline. The situation was irreversible: during the 1760s the amount collected from the 'one-fifth' tax had fallen to around 209 kilos per year, and by 1771 to just 147 kilos.[71] The result was dramatic: the *Mineiros* were convinced that their diminishing income was not the result of a decline in production, but rather of the exorbitant taxes. Thus the seeds for revolt were sown. But the positive outcome of the gold rush was also irreversible: by the end of the eighteenth century, Minas Gerais was the only area in Portuguese America where the settlers had created a network of towns and cities. This was the origin of a unique society capable of developing a highly distinctive and sophisticated culture.

VILA RICA DO OURO PRETO

The traveller who dismounted his horse in Vila Rica during the last three decades of the eighteenth century would certainly have been surprised at the exuberance of that 'strange city surrounded by rocks, silence and shadows'[72] and also by the fact that Minas Gerais was no longer a world in the making. The population of the town at the time was about 80,000, out of a total of 320,000 scattered around the whole captaincy, excluding Indians.[73] The inhabitants of Vila Rica navigated steep, hilly streets lined with a wide variety of buildings: palaces built from stone and mortar, town houses with tiled roofs, low wooden buildings and thatched huts made from wattle and mud. At the bottom of the slopes there were wide streets and open squares where public notices were posted and the *pelourinho* was installed, from which narrow alleyways wound their way back up the hillsides.[74]

The neighbouring town of Mariana, where the bishop resided, was the seat of the diocese and thus responsible for guiding the faith of the inhabitants of Minas Gerais. Unlike Vila Rica, its streets were crowded with oratories, crucifixes and Stations of the Cross. But the architecture of Vila Rica, the administrative seat of the richest and most populated captaincy in the colony, was more imposing, as was appropriate for the seat of the Crown's authority. By 1780 the town already had a Governor's Palace, built of stone, erected on the hill of Santa Quitéria. It had four bastions and a curved ramp dotted with sentry boxes in the style of a military fortress. The magnificent town house of the contractor João Rodrigues de Macedo – probably the richest man in the region, in charge of collecting the taxes on all incoming merchandise – had also already been built. He had his residence, the Casa dos Contos,[75] built on a stone foundation; it had a monumental staircase lined with paintings, a large balcony and countless windows and doors – a sign of the owner's social status. It was the most admired stately home in all the captaincy.

The gold was still paying the bills. By the beginning of the 1780s Vila Rica had erected churches whose interiors were lined in gold. They were the wonder of every visitor to the town, and still are today: São Francisco de Assis, the Basilica of Pilar and Nossa Senhora da Conceição de Antônio Dias. The precarious wooden bridges were replaced with stone ones equipped with arches, parapets, pillars and seats, all cemented with fish oil and quicklime. Seven drinking fountains were erected, where people met to gossip as they collected the water. Made of richly decorated bronze or soapstone, they were set into walls around the city. The bridges and fountains were meeting places for slaves, washerwomen and muleteers, and became centres of rumour-mongering. People stood around the arches of the Ponte dos Contos or beside the gargoyles on the Gloria Fountain, listening attentively and exchanging the latest news.

At the end of the eighteenth century, Cláudio Manuel da Costa, Tomás Antônio Gonzaga and Alvarenga Peixoto, the three great poets of the captaincy, would describe these novel urban surroundings as a framework for their verses. In his poem 'Vila Rica', written in 1773 or thereabouts, Cláudio Manuel da Costa sings the praises of the town's façades; of the fountains and other sources of water; of the many bridges built to facilitate the transport of goods throughout the town; of the elegant clock tower, a beautiful example of Minas Gerais architecture; and of the splendid churches (whose magnificence he may have considered immoderate, as he comments 'they have exhausted our funds').[76]

Cláudio Manuel da Costa was the doyen, and possibly the main intellectual reference, of a group of scholars who were all members of the highest social class in Minas Gerais. They were the sons of wealthy landowners, gold-mine proprietors, civil servants, members of the clergy and high-ranking military officials. All of these young men had been educated at universities in Europe – at Coimbra or Montpellier.

The group was of crucial importance in generating information about Minas Gerais, including the production of cartographic records, studies about the mineralogical potential of the captaincy and the diversification of its economic production. This knowledge was to provide the fuel for the *Conjuração Mineira* (Minas Conspiracy), the most important anti-colonial plot in the history of Portuguese America, and the first with clearly republican leanings, as we will see in the next chapter. Furthermore, some members of that group created a form of poetry which was to be a turning point in Brazilian literature.

This group of poets in Minas Gerais created new standards for Brazilian literature. They considered themselves Arcadians with a direct connection to the fashionable poetry of eighteenth-century Western Europe; poetry that depicted gallant shepherds and gentle shepherdesses in scenes of idyllic pastoral life. They were all masters of the terms and style of the European Arcadians, but they were also cosmopolitan: they incorporated the natural surroundings, customs and aspirations of Minas Gerais into their verses. Furthermore, within the traditions of Arcadian pastoralism, they expressed the uniqueness of their position as privileged intellectuals, increasingly aware of the antagonism between the Portuguese colonial enterprise and the reality of day-to-day life in the towns of Minas Gerais; of the conflict between the interests of those settlers born in Portugal and those born in Brazil, and between their own aspiration for freedom of intellectual expression and the rigid censorship imposed in the colony.

And, obviously, many of the poems of these three great writers sang the praises of Vila Rica. *Cartas chilenas*,[77] for example, is a series of poems, dating from around 1787 and attributed to Tomás Antônio Gonzaga, but on which Cláudio Manuel da Costa and Alvarenga Peixoto may well have also collaborated. In this series of poems, the streets of Vila Rica are depicted as crowded with people going about their daily work. In the hustle and bustle, free blacks and mestizos wander along alleyways and steep streets, steering clear of the law's harsh repression – death sentences, prison and beatings. Innkeepers, shop workers and black women make their appearance in the poems, the latter marketing food either out of doors, or in the shops serving slaves and poor freemen miners, who dreamt of the gold once so easy to find. Shoemakers, tailors and muleteers also emerge – planning to improve their social status by entering the militia.

In *Cartas chilenas* the poet also describes the town's recreational activities: tournaments, processions, the Opera House. The new theatre was the pride of the captaincy's wealthy elite. It seated three hundred people and was equipped for every type of spectacle. Step by step, Gonzaga describes how the Town Hall was erected, with the slaves being driven on by the whip as every morning they struggled up the hillside of Rua Direita de Antônio Dias with their tools. It was a magnificent building inspired by Michelangelo's work on the Capitoline Hill. It also housed the gaol, including the dreaded 'secret' cells where prisoners were tortured and the 'oratory' cells where those condemned to be hanged spent their last hours awaiting the noose.[78]

Gonzaga was right. Society in Minas Gerais was mixed, with people of different races mingling in the streets and squares of the town. Masters and slaves could often be seen working side by side. Town life allowed for a greater degree of flexibility than the plantations; the slaves had more autonomy and could, with luck, work towards achieving their freedom. Urbanization and the increasing incidence of *alforria* – slaves freed by their masters, especially when the said freedom was purchased, either with a single payment or in instalments[79] – were to affect this gold-mining society in three important ways. The first was in the high number of mixed-race people in proportion to the number of whites. The second was the formation of the largest group of freed slaves in the colony. The third was the opportunities for *pardos* and free blacks to improve, if only a little, their social status. This was achieved by working in commerce, perhaps becoming the owner of a small rural property, officiating at Mass, joining the military or learning the skills to become an artist – an engraver, a painter, sculptor or musician.

But the social structure of Vila Rica was far less fluid than it may seem; in practice, it remained strictly hierarchical.[80] At the top were the owners of the land and the gold mines, the elite group of intellectuals, high-ranking Crown officials and powerful contractors. At the bottom were the slaves. Between the two the lower classes mingled noisily: miners, muleteers, shop workers, soldiers and artisans. At the very bottom, almost as if they did not exist, came the large population of vagrants.

The Baroque style was adopted wholeheartedly in Portuguese America, albeit a long time after its first appearance in Europe. It became the predominant form of artistic expression in this society, deeply associated with its religious, political and economic aspirations.[81] Although it had first appeared during the sugar cycle in Salvador and other towns in the northeast, it was in Minas Gerais that it seriously took root. It offered an appealing and effective means of religious communication through the theatrical beauty of its forms and images that could be adapted to different contexts, whether to altars in the churches or fountains and oratories in the streets. It flourished across all the art forms throughout the colonial world.

The Third Orders and lay fraternities that replaced the religious orders which had been expelled by the Crown in Minas Gerais financed the construction of the churches. Strategically located on the hilltops, with their monumental architecture, sumptuous decorations and altars painted in gold, they exemplified the splendour of Minas Gerais Baroque. Some of the lay fraternities, such as the Third Orders of the Carmelites and the Franciscans, were closely associated with the white economic and intellectual elite. Others, such as the Amparo and the Mercês fraternities, gave assistance to artisans, free mulattoes and *pardos*, while the Fraternidade de Nossa Senhora do Rosário[82] was exclusively for slaves. During religious processions and festivities, however, the hierarchy was broken down and all groups came together amid a stirring mass of saints, crosses and colourful flags.[83]

Whereas the churches were the Baroque scenic spaces *par excellence*, the processions and feasts represented the grandeur of its popular dimension. By definition an enrapturing, spectacular, theatrical style, the Baroque was visually mesmerizing, and seemingly horrified with the concept of empty spaces. The visual aspect of these festivities, their sumptuous trappings, enchanted the Vila Rica inhabitants. The atmosphere was one of festive and religious ecstasy: images of saints covered in a profusion of colours, liturgical vestments and precious gems, the solemn file past, the stately pace of the procession, the silk and damask cloths hung from the windows along the route, all permeated with the mystical smell of incense. The magical world of the Minas Gerais Baroque had to be seen to be believed.

The unique and expressive nature of this Baroque was the result of both the mining society's urban environment and the creativity of the local artists, who reinvented European Baroque. The work of Antônio Francisco Lisboa – Aleijadinho ('the little cripple') as he was nicknamed, due to a degenerative disease that deformed his body – represents the high point of this creativity. He was a master sculptor, engraver and architect. He was of Portuguese and African descent – his father Portuguese and his mother a slave. His work in stone and wood expresses not only his faith and spirituality, but the entire range of human emotions. Aleijadinho was the architect of the São Francisco de Assis church, the jewel in the crown of Minas Gerais Baroque, as well as the creator of its internal decorations – a perfect expression of harmony between architecture, sculpture and painting.

In the same church, Antônio Francisco Lisboa worked with another great master of the day: Manuel da Costa Ataíde, known as Mestre Ataíde. The brightly coloured, cheerful figures that appear almost to be moving, characteristic of Lisboa's work, found their match in the work of Mestre Ataíde; the two offset and complement each other. All of Aleijadinho's sculptures, whether on the altar, the pulpit or lining the walls, have energetic expressions and bright, sparkling eyes. According to his biographers, 'Antônio Francisco was a soft-spoken mulatto with a deep voice and a burning genius'.[84] Perhaps this is the reason why these figures, full of vigour and so mobile and alive that they seem to gesticulate, were so essential to his work. His partner, Mestre Ataíde, created stunning scenes on the ceiling, walls and throughout the architectural detailing of the São Francisco de Assis church. For the panel at the back of altar he used straw-coloured paint so that the glitter of the gold would not be eclipsed. His masterpiece was painted on the ceiling of the nave, with an illusionary perspective in which the columns appear to advance and the ceiling to open up towards the sky. A superb, chubby mulatta Nossa Senhora da Porciúncula floats upwards, wreathed in clouds, accompanied by a retinue of mestizo angels playing a concert on musical instruments that were typical of an orchestra of the time.

The deposits of gold 'always ended. They weren't eternal',[85] whereas the Baroque awoke a sense of the intangible, a world without frontiers. Minas Gerais at the end of the eighteenth century was a place where gold and the Baroque went hand in hand. With its mestizo saints – mulattoes with oriental eyes – the Baroque intuited and connected the two extremes of the Portuguese Empire, which began in Macau and ended in Vila Rica. Or vice versa.

5

Revolt, Conspiracy and Sedition in the Tropical Paradise

The Minas Conspiracy was the most significant anti-colonial movement in Portuguese America. It threatened the status quo of the colony and turned Minas Gerais into the centre of a plot that was clearly republican in nature. And – a startling fact that is often overlooked – it occurred *before* the outbreak of the French Revolution. Furthermore, the conspiracy was certainly not an isolated case of defiance in the colony. Very unlike the image often promoted by Brazil, both nationally and internationally, Brazilian history is a far cry from a fairy tale, exempt from wars, conflicts and routine violence.

In the first place, a society based on slavery from one end to the next presupposes the use of violence. And the currency of violence was by no means restricted to the relationship between masters and slaves. Other conflicts that erupted around the country showed the discontent to be both deep-rooted and long-lasting. It was clearly manifest in the resentment of the settlers over their isolation, at their submission to the Portuguese Crown – both in times of abundance and at times of crisis – and at the arbitrary behaviour of the local elites, who acted with complete autonomy due to the habitual negligence of the Crown when it came to passing laws for its vast and distant colony. The national myth of a human and natural paradise where harmony and peaceful coexistence prevailed does not stand up to a closer examination of the forced labour system and the daily routine of the colony. There was no 'happy ending' to be had.

'LONG LIVE THE PEOPLE' AND 'DEATH TO THE GOVERNOR'

In the early hours of 8 December 1660 a group of farmers decided that the time was long overdue for a revolt against the new taxes imposed by the governor of southern Brazil, Salvador Correia de Sá e Benevides, who needed to raise money for the defence of São Sebastião de Rio de Janeiro. The town was constantly threatened by foreign invasions – from the French, the implacable enemies of the Portuguese, and from the Dutch, who were at war with Spain – as well as the occasional forays by pirates and corsairs. The defiant settlers owned land in the region that was referred to as the *Banda d'Além*,[1] on the far side of Guanabara Bay, which began in the parish of São Gonçalo do Amarante and whose boundaries became less and less clearly defined as it spread towards the interior of the captaincy.

Everything was planned in utmost secrecy. The farmers waited cautiously, met, and finally decided. Guided by only a sliver of moonlight and enveloped in darkness, they set their boats in the water and crossed Guanabara Bay. They silently made their way around the enormous granite rock marking the entrance to the bay, which the Portuguese had baptized 'The Sugar Loaf' – a reference to the extremely valuable cone-shaped sugar blocks, shiny on top and darker toward the bottom, just waiting to be packaged and sent off to Europe. Before sunrise, they moored at Praia de Piaçaba at the edge of the Largo do Carmo (the square now called Praça XV).[2] These were the docks used by all travellers who disembarked in Rio de Janeiro during the second half of the seventeenth century.[3] Thus began the first settlers' revolt in the history of Portuguese America.

The date and the place had been carefully chosen. It was the feast day of Nossa Senhora da Conceição[4] when large crowds traditionally gathered in the Largo do Carmo, a central meeting place in the city. This public square was where the Municipal Council Chamber, responsible for the administration of the town, and the São José Church were located, as well as the *pelourinho*. Furthermore, Rio de Janeiro was temporarily without its leader: Governor Sá e Benevides had been called away to Paranaguá, the southernmost point of the vast Southern Department that comprised the captaincies of Espírito Santo, Rio de Janeiro and São Vicente, which the Crown had placed under his command. He was on a mission to verify the news that had arrived in Rio de Janeiro of the discovery of gold deposits on the border between São Paulo and Paraná.

It is not known whether the insurgents met any resistance from the city guard, which consisted of around 350 men who had not been paid for several months. It is known, however, that the rebels landed shouting 'Long live the people' and 'Death to the Governor'. People who were still asleep were woken up by the uproar and the devotees of Nossa Senhora da Conceição. They had arrived early for the festivities, and now rushed to join the insurgents. At five in the morning the crowd invaded the Municipal Council Chamber, removed its members from office, and deposed the governor.[5]

For the next five months the political and administrative life of Rio de Janeiro was controlled by the colonial insurgents, who attempted to install their own form of government. They called elections for the new members of the council, extending the right to vote to the entire area around the bay, including the Banda d'Além. Thus, the inhabitants and landowners in the rural areas of Rio de Janeiro were included in a process that had previously been restricted to those who were privileged enough to be established in the town. They also suspended taxes authorized by Sá e Benevides, and his allies were imprisoned in the Fortress of Santa Cruz.[6] His closest associates were expelled from the captaincy.

Nevertheless, loyalty to the Crown was demanded loudly and clearly. The Cachaça Revolt, as the episode became known, was not a revolt against the Portuguese king, but against the fiscal policies of the governor. And it was definitely against a very specific royal decree, which limited the production of *cachaça* and its exportation in order to protect the consumption of Portuguese wine in the colony. Former governors had turned a blind eye and not interfered with the clandestine production of *cachaça* by the inhabitants of the captaincy.

According to Frei Vicente do Salvador,[7] in 1620, out of a total of 230 sugar plantations in the colony (most of which were in the northeast), forty were located in Rio de Janeiro. The sugarcane cultivated around Guanabara Bay had a low content of sucrose and, when crushed, produced large quantities of watery juice. The quality of the sugar was consequently poorer than that produced in Pernambuco and Bahia. But this was of little importance for the distillation of *cachaça*, which, as we have mentioned, was a key by-product for the sugar-based economy. Whatever the quality of the sugar, *cachaça* exports were guaranteed due to the demand from the slave trade, especially in Angola and Guinea, where it was used in exchange for slaves.[8]

By the end of the sixteenth century, slave labour was indispensable for running the plantations in the colony, and two of the items most in demand for purchasing slaves, manioc flour and *cachaça*, were shipped directly from the port of Rio de Janeiro. Thus the *Carioca* settlers[9] became experts in the art of smuggling. Avoiding the insatiable tax inspectors, skirting the blockade that prevented trade between the various colonies of the empire, and using *cachaça* as a currency for barter, they managed to become active participants in the slave trade. Smuggling undoubtedly caused incalculable losses to the Crown, but it was one of the few colonial activities where the profits remained entirely in the hands of the settlers.

There was also a thriving domestic trade in *cachaça*. Considered 'a man's drink', it was mostly consumed by the poorer classes – slaves and free blacks, *cafuzos*,[10] poor whites and vagrants. Its high calorie content served as a dietary supplement for these segments of the population. It was always available for purchase, displayed in gourd shells alongside *rapadura* (lumps of unrefined sugar) and tobacco – 'the saintly herb', as it was then called. It was easily found in the shops in the towns and villages and along the routes that were opening up into the interior.[11]

Unfortunately for Rio de Janeiro's inhabitants, the finances of the captaincy were in a calamitous state and Governor Sá e Benevides was attempting to remedy the situation by raising taxes. The high mortality rate among slaves due to outbreaks of smallpox had seriously affected the production of sugar, leaving the city devoid of funds at a time when money was needed to fortify the entrance to the bay and guarantee the payment of the troops that garrisoned the city. In 1660 the outlook for the near future was one of unpayable debts: Rio de Janeiro was bankrupt.

Sá e Benevides was certainly a character: courageous, astute, vain, gallant with the ladies, sympathetic to the Indians, disinterested in the fate of the blacks and autocratic with the settlers.[12] His ambitions had never been moderate. On an island in Guanabara Bay where his family had established the first sugar plantation in the captaincy, he installed his own shipyard with the intention of building the largest galleon in the world. He built six in all, one of which, the *Padre Eterno*, weighed 2,000 tonnes, was 53 metres in length, and had 144 pieces of artillery mounted on its decks. It was indeed the largest ship to navigate the oceans at the time.[13] The *Cariocas* were so impressed with the *Padre*

Eterno that they baptized the island *Ilha do Governador* and the location of the shipyard *Ponta do Galeão*.[14]

It was not by chance that Sá e Benevides had been appointed governor: he was from one of the most illustrious families of the colony. He was the great-great-nephew of Mem de Sá, Brazil's third governor-general, who had expelled the French from Guanabara Bay, and a cousin (three times removed) of Estácio de Sá, Mem de Sá's nephew and the founder of Rio de Janeiro. As the fourth generation of his family to govern the captaincy, Sá e Benevides considered Rio de Janeiro as part of his property holdings, and his inheritance. It was this distorted view that permitted him to override the decisions of the Council, impose unpopular taxes, drain the city funds, and abuse the power invested in him by the king.[15]

The accusations of the insurgents may well have been justified, but they had underestimated Sá e Benevides. Not only was he a senior official of the Crown, he was also an exceptionally able military commander with an impressive history of service to the King of Portugal in the naval struggle against the United Netherlands, a formidable maritime power. His most memorable feats of valour included the reconquest of Angola, defeating the fleet led by Admiral Piet Heyn off the coast of the captaincy of Espírito Santo and setting fire to Dutch ships in the port of Salvador as they were finally expelled from Bahia.

The *Carioca* rebels had taken on more than they had bargained for. Instead of simply marching on the city, Sá e Benevides took up position on the Piratininga plateau and waited for the Portuguese ships that had sailed from Bahia to help him retake the city. When he received confirmation that they were approaching Rio de Janeiro, equipped with weapons, ammunition and reserves of food, he finally departed from São Paulo. In the early hours of 6 April 1661, as the Portuguese fleet entered Guanabara Bay, Sá e Benevides, in command of a small army of Tupi bowmen, faithful allies of his family since the times of Mem de Sá,[16] entered Rio de Janeiro. He defeated the sentries at the Fort of São Sebastião,[17] occupied the Council Chamber, invaded houses, confiscated weapons and arrested their owners. Before the day was over Rio de Janeiro had been retaken, the insurgents defeated, and their leader Jerônimo Barbalho Bezerra beheaded.[18]

THE SEMANTICS OF REVOLT

The Cachaça Revolt may have been the first insurgency, but it was by no means the last. There were to be many occasions on which exasperated, resentful settlers turned to rebellion as an instrument for applying pressure on the government to meet their demands, to counteract abuses by the local authorities, and to protest against the rigidity of the rules imposed by Lisbon. At their height, incessant protests throughout the colony posed a serious threat to the stability of Portugal's Atlantic Empire.[19]

To confront these manifestations of discontent Portugal adopted new forms of administrative discipline for the colony. It subdivided the protests into a number of categories: insurrection, sedition, revolt, uprising, rebellion, riot, tumult, and so on. Names are only invented when there is a reality to justify them, just as rules are established for circumvention. In this sense, Brazil was no exception: measures were disseminated for the control of the population, and organized according to these categories, which sought to classify the gravity of the threat.

In the vocabulary of the time, the word 'insurrection' was used to designate an angry group, at times joined by slaves, with immediate, concrete goals. 'Sedition' was used to refer to a gathering of ten or more armed colonists with the deliberate attempt to disturb public order. When such gatherings totalled thirty thousand or more they became a 'rebellion', an extremely dangerous event that could lead to anarchy or civil war. An 'assuada' meant a gathering of the colonists with the purpose of disrupting public order and enacting a specific offence to an authority. An 'uprising' was a gathering of a large amount of people venting all sorts of discontent. A 'tumult' was a revolt of the 'people', where the term 'people' referred either to the population as a whole or to the lowest levels of the social pyramid: the plebeians, the masses, the rabble. Although they went under different names, every one of these acts of insubordination was political in intent.

The increasing occurrence of civil disturbance revealed the extent to which political struggle involved questions of broad public concern. Uprisings of the least privileged classes were frequently joined by freed blacks and escaped slaves, with an escalation of violence that caused terror among the population. Obviously those involved were exposing themselves to enormous risks. As far as the Lisbon authorities were concerned the penalties for these crimes were prescribed in the Philippine Ordinances, Portugal's longest-lasting legal code, promulgated in 1603 by Dom Filipe I (Philip II of Spain), the first sovereign during the period of Iberian unification. Anyone who confronted one of the king's officials could be condemned for the crime of lèse-majesté, with punishments that ranged from being publicly whipped to having one's property confiscated, being sent to the galleys for life or being put to death.[20]

Nevertheless, rebellions against the colonial authorities continued to occur with alarming frequency. The motives behind the Cachaça Revolt were just the beginning of a long list of recriminations seen by the settlers as sufficient justification for protest, with the risk of being branded a rebel and putting one's life in jeopardy. Revolts would begin as an expression of discontent with the 'mismanagement of the colonies', the draconian introduction of interminable taxes with no prior consultation, the abuse of power on the part of crown officials in the colony, and the enormous distance that separated Brasil from Portugal, and the king, whose arbitration was required for the resolution of conflicts, from his colonial subjects.[21]

The frequency of these revolts left the imperial authorities in a state of constant alert. There was the perennial risk of armed assaults on crown officials, uprisings by disparate social groups, and the threat of the overthrow of local governments. The main danger was political contagion: as the uprisings increased in number, they spread throughout the territory. The motives may have differed, but every protest chipped away at the stability of the colony and caused further unease in Lisbon.

REVOLT OF THE VASSALS: POLITICAL DISCONTENT IN PERNAMBUCO, SERGIPE, MARANHÃO AND BAHIA

At the end of August 1666, five years after the Cachaça Revolt, the governor of Pernambuco, Jerônimo de Mendonça Furtado, was arrested in broad daylight while walking down Rua São Bento[22] in Olinda. The group of conspirators that arrested him was made up of members of the property-owning elite of the captaincy, who had won over popular support to confront the most powerful crown official in Pernambuco. And they had no intention of discussing the matter. Without further ado, they incarcerated the governor in the Brum Fortress in Recife and then packed him off to Lisbon.[23]

These were powerful men who had an extensive list of complaints against Mendonça Furtado. They accused him of illegally enforcing the payment of debts, confiscating property, openly protecting allies in debt to the National Treasury, failing to respect ecclesiastical immunity and arbitrarily arresting or releasing people – all in exchange for bribes. Rumours were rife in Olinda and Recife that the governor not only pocketed part of the revenues owed to the Crown, but also increased these revenues by minting coins in the palace. Mendonça Furtado was despised by the people, who nicknamed him *Xumbergas* – a derogatory term for a dissolute libertine, for a drunk person with odd manners.

Xumbergas was one of a succession of despotic local governors who made use of the powers invested in them by the Crown to get rich as quickly as possible through bribery and corruption. In Padre Vieira's fine words, there was no remedy for the greed that was putting Portugal's control of its colony at risk. The priest, who knew these governors well, proclaimed from the pulpit: 'This is the prime cause of the ills of Brazil: taking from others what is not theirs, greed, covetousness, underhanded dealings for personal gain, where the State is plundered and justice ignored.'[24] And he concluded, 'To put it simply, Brazil is doomed because of these ministers of His Majesty who come here not to promote our good, but to expropriate our goods.'[25]

In Pernambuco the reason for discontent was the corruption and inordinate power of the local authorities. When these were added to frustration over the burden of taxation it was a sure sign that a tempest was brewing, whether in Pernambuco or any other part of the colony. In 1671, for example, a rebellion erupted in the northern captaincy of Sergipe del Rei.[26] The settlers, with the support of the Municipal Council, decided to expel the *capitão-mor* Joaquim Antônio Monteiro Correia (the title of captain-major was conferred on the head of the administration and military forces of the captaincy until such time as a governor was appointed by Lisbon). The uprising was a serious concern for the administrators of the Northern Department, the long stretch of coastline that included the captaincies of Rio Grande, Paraíba, Itamaracá, Pernambuco and Bahia. Sergipe del Rei was of particular strategic importance to the Crown because it permitted communication by land between Bahia – where the capital of the colony, Salvador, was located – and Pernambuco, the nerve centre of the sugar industry.[27]

In 1684 the storm of rebellion broke over Maranhão. The brothers Manuel and Tomás Beckman, the former a sugar plantation owner and the latter a poet and lawyer, with a following of about eighty armed men including merchants and sugar planters, led the movement.[28] Their discontent had led to specific goals: to remove the governor and to put an end to the *Companhia de Comércio do Maranhão e Grão-Pará*,[29] which had been granted a monopoly on all exports by Lisbon in an attempt to avoid smuggling and tax evasion. And while they were at it, they had a mind to pay back the Jesuits, whom they blamed for the Crown's 1680 edict preventing them from enslaving the Indians. From the settlers' point of view this prohibition was disastrous for the economy of Maranhão, where labour for the sugar plantations was in short supply.

On the night of 24 February 1684 the men under the command of the Beckman brothers mingled among the crowd gathered in the centre of São Luís for the festivities in honour of Our Lord of the Via Crucis.[30] They then stormed the Monopoly Trade House, where the products the settlers were forced to sell to the *Companhia do Comércio do Maranhão e Grão-Pará* were stored. They proceeded to occupy the strategic points of the town, disarming the municipal guard and arresting the king's representatives.

The following day they established a government junta, based at the Municipal Council Chamber. Here, as they aired their longstanding resentment of the Jesuits, their indignation erupted. With cries of 'Kill! Kill the priests of the Society of Jesus'[31] the rebels took to the streets, knocking on doors and exhorting the townspeople to attack the Colégio Nossa Senhora da Luz where the Jesuits were installed. The crowd invaded the internal patio of the college and surrounded the church and its tall stone tower. But they arrived too late – the twenty-seven priests had already fled into the interior of the captaincy.

The Beckman brothers' revolt lasted a year, until a Portuguese fleet with a well-armed contingent of soldiers arrived with the new governor of the captaincy, Gomes Freire de Andrade, who retook the city and proceeded to arrest the rebels. He restored the privileges of the *Companhia do Comércio* and erected a gallows in the main square.[32] Manuel Beckman and Jorge de Sampaio e Carvalho, the two main leaders of the rebellion, were summarily condemned to death and hanged. Tomás Beckman, who had been sent by the rebels as an emissary to Lisbon in an attempt to convince the authorities of the justice of their cause, was arrested and forbidden to return to Maranhão, while the other participants in the revolt were condemned to be whipped in public.

In 1711 there was yet another rebellion, this time in Salvador. The revolt was led by the *baiano*[33] João de Figueiredo da Costa, nicknamed Maneta. He was a merchant as well as a smuggler, and astute enough to understand the workings of the political forces at the heart of the colony's administration, and to use them in his favour. The *Motins do Maneta* (Maneta Uprisings), as the revolt was known, had no pretentions to seizing power. The crowds it attracted were essentially impulsive, but with two specific demands. The first was for a reduction in the price of salt, a staple, essential for the conservation of meat and fish. The second was for an end to the new taxes on imported goods and on slaves that had been imposed to finance the refurbishing of the Portuguese fleet, in an attempt to prevent the frequent corsair attacks into the Bay of Salvador. The revolt reflected the generalized frustration at the Crown's establishment of yet another tax collection and inspection unit in Bahia, the Paço da Madeira, which taxed all seagoing vessels, as well as weapons, furniture, fruit, coal and cork.[34]

Excessive taxation was behind the Maneta revolt; but in reality, all sorts of people were inclined to rebel, including smugglers, *tumbeiros* (crews of smaller slave-trafficking vessels), slave traffickers, small tradesmen, open-air market tradesmen, innkeepers and clerks. As the taxes affected the lives of virtually all the inhabitants of Salvador, the indignation was general – it spread to the masses and even to the troops, where those of low military rank enthusiastically supported the rebellions. The only group that remained aloof from such movements were the powerful landowners and merchants of Bahia – men who possessed '*grossa fortuna*' in the expression used at the time.

An uprising only really begins when an angry crowd has formed. In the case of Salvador, this was sparked off by alarming rumours about new taxes, and the crowd was summoned by the furious chiming of the bell installed at the top of the Municipal Council Chamber (by whom, it is not known). As the size of the throng increased the rebels gained confidence. They occupied the slopes that divide the *Cidade Baixa* from the *Cidade Alta*[35] and advanced in the direction of the governor's palace. They stopped twice along the way. The first stop was outside the luxurious villa that belonged to Manuel Dias Filgueiras, the largest tithe collector[36] and salt contractor in the town. They invaded the house, threw the elegant furniture out of the windows, broke open the casks of imported wine and tipped the contents into the street, and then proceeded to destroy a deposit of salt they discovered behind the building. The second stop was outside the town house of Filguieras's business partner, Manuel Gomes Lisboa. There, the furniture thrown from the windows included small chests with padlocked drawers, from which, to the delight of the crowd, gold dust spilled all over the slope that led up to the house in Largo de São Francisco.

Terrified, the newly appointed governor, Pedro de Vasconcelos e Souza, appealed to Archbishop Sebastião Monteiro da Vide for help. His holiness did not hesitate. He immediately summoned the priests and the cannons and friars from the fraternities who, invoking the wrath of God, berated the insurgents. The bishop organized a procession that descended the steep slopes of the town, solemnly displaying the sacred symbols of the Eucharist to the turbulent throng, exhorting them to calm themselves. But to no avail. The crowds showed great respect as the procession went by, laying aside their weapons, baring their heads and kneeling in contrition. But as soon as it had passed they picked up where they had left off: taking up their weapons, they surrounded the palace and forced the governor to surrender. Governor Pedro de Vasconcelos e Souza had no choice but to give in to all their demands: he suspended the new taxes, reduced the price of salt, and promised a pardon to all those involved.

Uprisings are sudden explosions. They are essentially impulsive forms of political expression, with no clear strategy or even a short-term plan for holding power. Their aggressive energy rapidly dissipates, as if the rioters are suddenly overcome by exhaustion and disband.[37] No sooner had the crowd dispersed than Pedro de Vasconcelos, blithely abandoning his agreement with the rebels, had the leaders arrested and severely punished. But this was not the end of the story. Less than fifty days after the pact had been broken, furious crowds once again occupied the slopes of the city.

THE MINAS GERAIS REBELS

With the settlers' anger and resentment towards Lisbon ever growing, the risk of rebellion was always present. These undercurrents of discontent were both dangerous and contagious, emboldening people throughout the colony to plan revolt. Anti-government feelings were at their strongest in Minas Gerais. The authorities there were hard pressed to maintain the rule of the king, to ensure the settlers respected imperial law and to thwart their desire for self-government. Well aware of the crimes in the captaincy and convinced of the ungovernability of its population, Governor Pedro Miguel de Almeida e Portugal, the Count of Assumar, was famed for his discipline. He solemnly declared the people of Minas Gerais predestined to be a thorn in the side of the Crown. This famous declaration forms the part of his *Political and historical dissertation on the uprising in Minas that occurred in the year 1720*, the most important of all the documents he sent to the authorities in Lisbon:

> Of Minas and its inhabitants, sufficient be it to say [. . .] that these are intractable people [. . .] The earth appears to exude rebellion; the water to emanate tumult; the gold to provoke confrontation; the wind to disseminate revolt; insolence is vomited from the clouds; insurgencies are determined by the stars; the climate is a tomb for peace and a cradle of mutiny; nature is ill at ease with itself, replete with inner turmoil, as it is in hell.[38]

During the period in which he governed the captaincy (1717–21), Pedro Miguel de Almeida e Portugal became notorious for his implacable repression as he attempted to reaffirm the authority of the Crown. The *Dissertation* was written to the king by way of accounting for his ferocity in repressing the 'Vila Rica Sedition'. This was the third insurrection he had been forced to confront. Between 1717 and 1718 the inhabitants of the town of Catas Altas had revolted, and there was a revolt by the townspeople of Nossa Senhora da Piedade de Pitangui, which lasted from 1717 to 1720.[39]

The 'Vila Rica Sedition' of 1720 was the most important revolt in the captaincy prior to the Minas conspiracy. Once again the motive was the invasive practices of the Royal Treasury officials. The conspirators planned to force the Crown to suspend the installation of further Forging Houses (where the gold was made into bars and the 'one-fifth' tax deducted).[40] It was an audaciously open challenge to the Crown's authority. Urgent discussions were held between the governor, the Vila Rica *ouvidor*,[41] and representatives of the social and economic elite. Every evening a group of hooded men, armed to the teeth, would suddenly emerge from a hilltop behind the town[42] and descend towards the centre of Vila Rica to the sound of the beating of drums and cries of 'Long live the people and death to the emissaries of the king'. They would run through the streets, sacking and pillaging as they went. And the terrified inhabitants would in turn take cover in their homes. On one such occasion the town house of the *Ouvidor-Geral* was destroyed. Its owner, the most detested dignitary in the captaincy, barely escaped being lynched, and fled to Rio de Janeiro.

The reaction of the governor was ruthless. In three days he settled the score with the inhabitants of the captaincy who had not given him a moment's peace during the four years of his government. He sealed off all the entries to Vila Rica, arrested the rebels and packed them off to Rio de Janeiro; he also authorized the population to exterminate their hooded attackers, and ordered the Portuguese dragoons – the elite military force of the captaincy – to set fire to all the properties of Pascoal da Silva Guimarães, the most important leader of the revolt. The terror of the town's inhabitants had been so great that it still lives on in Minas Gerais mythology – legend has it that on dark nights the clatter of horses' hooves can be heard cantering through the streets. Even so, the governor still was not finished. He gathered the town citizenry in the Largo da Câmara, the main square where the Council Chamber was located, and ordered the immediate execution of Felipe dos Santo who, although not a part of the leadership that planned the revolt, had incited the people to rebel on numerous occasions during the 'Vila Rica Sedition'. The governor had spectacularly reaffirmed the power of the Crown and of the king's justice.

About ten years after these events, the interim governor of Minas Gerais, Martinho de Mendonça de Pina e de Proença, found himself facing another uprising, this time in the northeast of the captaincy. In 1736 the population that lived along the banks of the Rio das Velhas and the São Francisco river gave vent to their anger in what became known as the 'Revolts in the Backlands'. Once again, the cause was excessive taxation, particularly the requirement to pay the 'one-fifth' tax on all gold discovered, by any individual, including slaves, directly to the captaincy, which claimed ownership of all the land.[43] At the height of the rebellion, with secret nightly meetings at cattle farms and groups of insurgents roaming the streets, looking for the tax collector in order to cut him to pieces, Martinho de Mendonça still refused to see the revolt as a serious threat. He considered the claims of the rebels to be 'non-negotiable' and put them down to the 'poor quality' of the inhabitants of the colony.[44] But a few months later, with all the prisons overcrowded, he changed his mind and declared: 'This conspiracy was larger than it appeared . . .'[45]

WHEN SUBJECTS PLOT AGAINST THEIR KING

Whatever form they took, in one aspect all the settlers' revolts were remarkably similar: none of them questioned the authority of the Portuguese Crown.[46] Quite to the contrary, the language used by the rebels expressed their unswerving loyalty to the monarch, reaffirming the king's symbolic role, always ready to listen to the afflictions of his people. However, the slow pace of communication between the metropolis and the colony was a source of frustration and viewed as the reason for the mismanagement and excesses of His Majesty's representatives overseas. There was only one exception to this general rule of support for the monarchy: the uprising in Pernambuco in 1710 when, for the first time, the insurgents openly questioned the Crown's authority.[47]

The revolt of 1710, which nineteenth-century historians called the *Guerra dos Mascates*,[48] took place within the wider context of a breakdown of colonial order.[49] The trouble began when the sugar barons of Olinda (Pernambuco), who were regarded as conceited and decadent by the merchants in neighbouring Recife, reacted to pressure from the latter for the establishment of their own independent Municipal Council. Their anger was also directed at the crown authorities in the captaincy who controlled the production of sugar, still the colony's principal source of revenue.

During the rebellion, which lasted for less than a year, ample use was made of the rural militias. These were made up of troops at the service of the sugar barons who came from the poorest classes of the free population. When they marched on Recife, provoking the inevitable flight of the governor to Bahia, a large part of the captaincy fell into the hands of the insurgents. Far more serious, however, was the intention of the rebels to declare the independence of Pernambuco. The majority of them wanted to form a republic. They discussed how to raise the resources for prolonged armed resistance and planned a possible extension of the rebellion to Bahia and Rio de Janeiro. In the event of the conspiracy failing, they contemplated a French protectorate. 'Pernambuco would be better off as a republic,' suggested Bernardo Vieira, one of the leaders of the revolt. He went on to say: 'If for any reason [. . .] the war goes against us, it would be preferable to seek the support of the sophisticated French than to submit to the ill-mannered *mascates*.'[50]

The conspiracy ended in disaster for the sugar barons of Olinda. The following year the maligned *mascates* got even with a vengeance. They won back Recife, attacked the rebels in the interior of the captaincy, and received reinforcements from the Portuguese fleet, which arrived with a new governor, appointed by Lisbon to negotiate the terms of a royal pardon. The outcome of the conflict was the complete victory of Recife: the town was elevated to the status of 'vila', granted its own Municipal Council, and converted into the capital of the captaincy in the place of Olinda.

Although the rebellion of 1710 was restricted to Pernambuco, the ideas behind it spread well beyond the borders of the captaincy. The sugar barons of Olinda were the first conspirators in Portuguese America to plan self-government and independence; the first to state their preference for a republic over the monarchy. Approximately sixty years later the term 'self-government' was in general use in political circles throughout the colony. This was certainly not a good sign for the empire.

During the last three decades of the eighteenth century, a small group of Brazilians, especially in Minas Gerais and Bahia, definitively adopted the term *Conjuração* to refer to a new kind of revolt. *Conjuração* implied a particular kind of political conspiracy, in which the conspirators contested the power of the king and the authority of crown officials. Such conspirators were accused by Lisbon of *inconfidência* – a newly coined term for the crime of disloyalty to the monarch.

CONSPIRACIES AND DISLOYALTY: MINAS GERAIS, 1789

In December 1782 the poet Tomás Antônio Gonzaga arrived in Vila Rica, having been appointed to the post of *ouvidor-geral*. The journey on horseback from Rio de Janeiro had taken him fifteen days. His arrival completed the group of intellectuals[51] that a few years later was to form an alliance with the economic and administrative elite of Minas Gerais to contest Brazil's colonial status, plan an armed uprising against the Portuguese Crown, and disseminate the notion of a politically autonomous republic in Portuguese America.

It was an eclectic group. Its members included erudite priests, such as Luís Vieira da Silva, owner of an impressive bookstore and professor of philosophy at the seminary in Mariana. The group also included music-loving members of the clergy, such as Carlos Correia de Toledo, Vicar of São José del-Rei – today the town of Tiradentes – and three major poets: Tomás Antônio Gonzaga, Cláudio Manuel da Costa and Alvarenga Peixoto. Other intellectuals involved included the doctor and naturalist José Vieira Couto, the military engineer José Joaquim da Rocha, the philosopher, natural scientist and mineralogist José Álvares Maciel, and a young doctor recently graduated from Montpellier, Domingos Vidal de Barbosa Lage. There were also a number of commissioned officers in the group – the highest-ranking among them was lieutenant-colonel Francisco de Paula Freire de Andrade, commander of the dragoons – and a considerable number of the captaincy's economic elite: businessmen, farmers, merchants, money-lenders, contractors and powerful local magnates such as João Rodrigues de Macedo, owner of the magnificent town house in Vila Rica where the conspirators often met.[52]

The group had ties with the highest level of Minas Gerais society, whether through business, family or friendship, and were involved in a wide variety of activities connected to 'local interests' that were somewhat incommensurate with what the Portuguese authorities would have considered ideal for the colony and its obedient subjects. Padre

José da Silva e Oliveira Rolim,[53] for example, who was devoted to the conspirators' cause, had spent much of his life defrauding the Crown. He produced counterfeit money, bribed the authorities – including ecclesiastical officials – lent money with interest, and diverted diamonds from the Tejuco mines from the official route to Lisbon to a clandestine one that ended in Amsterdam.

He was, without doubt, an extravagant and somewhat explosive mixture of smuggler, loan shark, wild adventurer and incorrigible seducer; a fascinating character who was, however, by no means alone in these transgressions. Most of the conspirators were involved in some way or other with the smuggling of gold and diamonds, duping the inspectors and cocking a snook at the government. They maintained close links with clandestine gold prospectors and the go-betweens[54] who organized the illegal transport of precious stones to Europe. However, these conspirators also understood the diversity of the captaincy's economy and the feasibility of its becoming self-sufficient.[55]

Despite all this, for the time being at least, no one seemed inclined to start a rebellion. What transformed a group of intellectuals and landed subjects of the king, completely integrated into this world of royal absolutism, into the leaders of a political revolt such as the *Conjuração Mineira*, without precedent in Portuguese America? It was a combination of resentment and the realization that the captaincy could be economically self-sufficient. As the ensign Joaquim José da Silva Xavier – better known as 'Tiradentes' – was to remind Lieutenant-Colonel Francisco de Andrade, Minas Gerais 'was a country like no other; it contained every kind of wealth.'[56]

When the conspirators decided to act it was due to a combination of three distinct factors – political-administrative, economic and cultural – which to a varying degree affected every social class in the captaincy. In the first place, the rigorous laws imposed by Lisbon showed no understanding of the process of gold production nor any intention of considering alternatives for the exploration of Minas Gerais's economic potential. The other two factors were somewhat circumstantial: the political disaster of Governor Cunha Meneses' corrupt administration, coupled with the arrival of highly unpopular royal 'Instructions' drafted by Martinho de Melo e Castro, Trade Secretary of the Navy and Overseas Dominions, which had been sent to the new ruler of the captaincy, the Viscount of Barbacena. These so-called instructions instituted a new tax for the mining areas, which required that all inhabitants bring 100 arrobas of gold to the forging houses every year; those who failed to meet the quota were liable for tax on the difference. This was a double blow for Minas Gerais. Precisely when there was a recession due to the decline in gold production, Lisbon was imposing new taxes. Furthermore, all previously existing contracts were annulled and the access of the local elite to the royal inspection posts was restricted.[57]

There is no clear consensus as to precisely when the conspirators began to seriously outline their plans, but it was probably some time between 1781 – the year that students from the colony at the University of Coimbra swore an oath to the sovereignty of the colony – and 1788, when the idea of autonomy for Minas Gerais was first debated in local meetings. In the second half of the 1780s the idea developed into the concept of a *República Florente*, as Tiradentes liked to describe it[58] – *florente* meaning both 'prosperous' and 'flourishing'. A republic nourished by the natural wealth of Minas Gerais, allowing the people to be masters of their own destiny without having to share their sovereignty with the Portuguese Crown.

Tiradentes was the most active propagandist of the foundational ideas of the Minas conspiracy, transmitting them to a wide variety of social groups – a task that was greatly facilitated by his itinerant lifestyle. He frequently travelled the routes between Minas Gerais and Rio de Janeiro, where he made contact with people of every social class. He had previously been a muleteer, before being appointed as the commander of the Caminho Novo, the perilous path along the Mantiqueira Mountains that was infested with *quilombolas* and gangs of highway robbers.

One of the reasons for his journeys was his 'great ability [. . .] to remove and mend teeth'.[59] On his travels Tiradentes also cured illnesses, prescribing remedies based on his knowledge of medicinal plants. A companion on the journey to Rio de Janeiro, Captain José de Souza Coelho – a member of the Municipal Council of the town of Pitangui – said of him:

> He is a master of many skills: part surgeon, part dentist, knowledgeable of herbs that heal wounds and fevers; a master of paving, bridges, mills and drainage, who knows every peak and grotto like the palm of his hand and the names and nicknames of all their inhabitants.[60]

The republican ideas disseminated by Tiradentes spread throughout the captaincy. The three most important transmission centres were the districts of Vila Rica, Rio das Mortes and Serro do Frio. Sedition, economic self-sufficiency and political autonomy became subjects of debate in the lodging houses, inns and farms along the Caminho Novo. They were discussed in the apothecaries, in the barracks and outside churches in the surrounding villages; in the taverns and brothels scattered across Minas Gerais and by clandestine gold panners in the valleys of the Serro do Frio.

The conspiracy was intended to begin with an uprising in Vila Rica, in February, sparked off by the gold quota tax. If the conspirators were successful the whole of the captaincy would join the revolt. Their plan included the announcement of Minas Gerais's declaration of independence and the instruments by which the new Republic would be implemented. The conspirators carefully observed the progress in North America, where new institutions were being established as a result of the revolution. The Minas conspirators were seeking a structure for their republic that would reflect the principles defended by the North American colonies during their struggle against the British.

There is discernible evidence that the Minas Conspiracy included the constitutional innovation of a Confederate Republic – a community of independent states, each with legislative autonomy. The importance the conspirators gave to the Municipal Councils is further indication they were planning to establish a republic with political autonomy for the legislative bodies scattered around the captaincy. The North Americans' victory over the British was of fundamental importance for the military planning of the conspiracy: Portugal would be at a great strategic and logistic disadvantage. It would be fighting a war in Minas Gerais that it could not win. Portuguese troops would have to cross the Atlantic and then climb the mountain paths leading to the interior. The conspirators did not expect to win the war and expel Portuguese troops, but rather to wear the empire down, economically and militarily, until the Crown would be forced to negotiate.

But the Minas Gerais conspirators were alone in their endeavour. None of the other captaincies joined the conspiracy. Furthermore, the international context was particularly unfavourable for their plans for autonomy. The meeting between Thomas Jefferson and José Joaquim Maia e Barbalho[61] in Nîmes, France, was of little avail: the North

American Republic was seeking a trade agreement with Portugal – later signed by Jefferson in 1786 – and had little intention of risking the benefits to be gained by supporting an uncertain, if promising, future for Brazil. Meanwhile France, to which the majority of the conspirators looked for support, was entangled in political problems that left it impotent on the international stage.[62]

Probably on 18 May 1789, at dusk, a figure – it is not known whether a man or a woman – was seen climbing the steep alleyways of Vila Rica, making its way through the mists enveloping the town at that time of year. He or she was wearing a long black cloak with an enormous hat pulled over the eyes, and was walking swiftly and stealthily observing the surroundings. The 'hooded figure', Embuçado, as the character has come to be known, crossed Vila Rica looking for the conspirators to warn them the conspiracy had been uncovered and that they were at risk.[63] First the hooded figure went to Cláudio Manuel's house and warned him at the door. At Gonzaga's house, a message was left with his slave Antônia. In the rush, urgently wanting to get the message to Lieutenant-Colonel Domingos de Abreu Vieira, a colleague of Tiradentes, the Embuçado got the wrong house, found a door ajar and entered. Upon seeing the neighbour's wife at the top of the stairs and realizing the mistake, the figure rushed out of the house and disappeared into the mist, never to be seen again.

The Embuçado was right. The Viscount of Barbacena had received six denunciations of a conspiracy under way in Minas Gerais.[64] The first, and most important, was made by Joaquim Silvério dos Reis, who was one of the conspirators himself. He was a rich man, and also the conspirator who was most in debt to the Crown. His betrayal of the cause was motivated by the prospect of his debts being pardoned. He related everything in detail several times, and then in writing: the particulars of the conspiracy, the password, the names of the main conspirators, the political plan and the military strategy. After receiving this information, Barbacena still waited for two months. Then he suspended the quota tax, had the conspirators arrested, and opened a judicial inquiry. This last entailed the search for proof, interrogation of the culprits, and the examination of witnesses from which the Crown would build its case.

From the time of Silvério dos Reis's denunciation to the signing of their final sentences by Dona Maria I,[65] the Queen of Portugal, the accused passed three long years of torment and interrogation. The Count of Barbacena sent them to Rio de Janeiro where they were imprisoned in the *Cadeia da Relação*[66] and on the *Ilha das Cobras*.[67] At the end of the trials the punishments handed down to the conspirators found guilty of disloyalty included exile to Africa, life imprisonment in Portugal (for the ecclesiastical members), confiscation of property and death by hanging.

From the moment they were arrested in Vila Rica, the conspirators were made all too aware of the strength of royal authority and the horror of its punishments. On the morning of 4 July 1789 the poet Cláudio Manuel da Costa was found dead in a cubicle that had been transformed into a cell on the ground floor of João Rodrigues de Macedo's house.[68] This was the very house that had been the scene of many of the conspirators' meetings – today the *Casa dos Contos*[69] in Ouro Preto. It had been requisitioned by the governor because the *Cadeia Nova*[70] was under construction; it was being expanded because there was not enough space for so many prisoners. The official version was that Cláudio Manuel's death was suicide, by hanging. No one in Vila Rica believed it. Cláudio Manuel da Costa was not only a poet, but was also a lawyer of great prestige in the captaincy; it was generally believed he had been murdered on the orders of Barbacena because he knew too much about the involvement in the conspiracy of members of the economic elite and also about groups connected to gold smuggling, which included the governor and his most intimate circle.

To this day Cláudio Manuel's death is considered suspicious and is debated, not only among historians, but also among authors. Two hundred years after the event, the novelist Silviano Santiago questioned the cause of the poet's death in his fine novel *Em liberdade*, which is framed in the tension between history and fiction and underscores the importance of questioning official versions of a political prisoner's death by suicide: 'What force is it inside me that cannot accept that Cláudio took his own life in the Casa dos Contos?'[71]

Tiradentes was arrested in Rio de Janeiro in May 1789 during one of his journeys to convert more people to the cause. Although not the leader of the Minas Conspiracy, he was its foremost propagandist. He was a controversial figure, impetuous, gruff and wide-eyed; but he was gifted with an enormous talent for persuasion. He was well aware of this and worked hard to polish his rhetoric. During interrogation he admitted he had carefully chosen his words to attract new supporters, adapting them according to the characteristics and interests of each individual or group. His fellow conspirators reported that, according to his audience, Tiradentes would intersperse his calls to action with playing the guitar and singing *modinhas*,[72] which contributed to his success as he stopped by gathering places along the Caminho Novo: brothels, such as the *Casa das Pilatas*, lodging houses such as that of João da Costa Rodrigues, and taverns such as the one in the village of Matosinhos.

These were the reasons why the punishment he received from the Crown was exemplary and public – so the horror of it would be ingrained in the colonists' memory. Tiradentes was hanged on 21 April 1792, in the *Largo da Lampadosa*, and his body was drawn, quartered and salted.[73] His arms and legs were displayed at the most important points along the Caminho Novo. His head was impaled on a post in front of the governor's palace in the main square of Vila Rica until it rotted, at the spot where a memorial statue to him stands today. According to legend, after the first day someone removed the head during the night and buried it in the surrounding hills. The Minas Conspiracy had failed, but its legacy was to remain. It gave impetus to the many revolts that were to come.

SALVADOR, 1798

One day in early 1798 the citizens of Salvador awoke to find that the gallows beside the *pelourinho* in the central square had been burnt to the ground. As we have mentioned, the *pelourinho* was the symbol *par excellence* of the power of the Crown: it was here that royal decrees were posted and slaves were publicly whipped. The gesture spoke for itself – it was a challenge to Lisbon's political authority. The person responsible is not known, but whoever it was left no doubt as to his or her opinions, expressed in abusive satirical pamphlets left at the foot of the charred remains and at the city gates.[74] What precisely these pamphlets said is still unknown, nor whether or not they were read and circulated among the inhabitants. The Portuguese authorities could not yet imagine what was coming.

Some months later, on the morning of 12 August, much to their surprise, citizens of Salvador, including the authorities, awoke to find pamphlets scattered all over the town. They had been left in places where they were most likely to be found: along the seafront, outside shops and government buildings, and nailed to posts along the steep, narrow streets linking the Cidade Baixa to the Cidade Alta. Three more had been left in church sacristies in the heart of the city. On 22 August, again taking the authorities by surprise, two more pamphlets were found by the Carmelite priests in the Church of the Carmelite Convent, located on a slope near the Largo do Pelourinho.[75]

It is very likely that there were even more pamphlets circulating in Salvador in 1798. And their political significance was considerable: distribution in public places allowed for the dissemination of news, ideas and opinions that had previously only been spread through clandestine channels. Those that have survived reveal openly democratic and republican ideas; they thus represented the first example in the colony of an all-inclusive political discussion, and the propagation of the concept of political equality among the poor.[76]

These Bahia pamphlets were written by members of the most heterogeneous and numerous segments of the social hierarchy: mulatto tradesmen – whose skin colour acted as a further impediment to their social ascension – artisans and soldiers.[77] This was something new in Brazil: unlike the defamatory, pornographic or satirical pamphlets that had been in vogue since the end of the sixteenth century,[78] these pamphlets represented an important channel for the dissemination of news and radical propaganda. They were a public expression of the intent to break away from the Portuguese Empire.

The target of the pamphlets, with their abrupt, coarse, irascible style, was the 'people' of Bahia – in other words, the poor and mixed-race citizens of Salvador.[79] Presenting the 'people' as the source of the sovereignty of a republic in Portuguese America in this way was inflammatory and audacious. Above all, it was an indication of the influence of French ideas on the conspirators. These principles of freedom, originating with the French Revolution – particularly with the Jacobin government in Paris – were odious to the Portuguese authorities. The vocabulary of the pamphlets, with their warning tone and frequent use of imperatives – 'Order', 'Instruct', 'Forbid', 'Demand'[80] – leaves little doubt as to the writers' perception of the people as a powerful, ferocious force when provoked and agents of their own destiny.

In 1798 the tension in Salvador increased, as did enthusiasm for so-called 'French' ideas. Their popularity was reproduced both verbally and visually. The mulatto João de Deus Nascimento, for example, was a tailor[81] and corporal in the militia, up to his ears in the simmering conspiracy. He was well aware of the link between a person's politics and the way he dressed, so he walked the streets of Salvador dressed as a 'Frenchman'. He wore 'close-fitting breeches and long-pointed shoes that barely covered the ankle'. The public prosecutor Francisco Xavier de Almeida, who happened to pass him in the street, asked him the reason for this extraordinary attire, to which João de Deus retorted: 'Shut up! This is the way the French dress. You'll see, sir. Very soon everything will be French.'[82]

João de Deus Nascimento may have been insolent, but his words were meaningful: clothing distinguished a person and revealed quite a bit about his politics. And his behaviour proved to be contagious. The *baiano* conspirators could be easily recognized by the way they dressed. As José de Freitas Sacoto, a mulatto freeman, explained to the colonial authorities, the conspirators did not conceal their convictions: anyone who was seen in the street 'wearing an earring, with a beard covering half his cheeks and an Angolan *búzio*[83] on his watch chain, was "French" and belonged to the rebellion party.'[84]

Adornments and clothing were a part of establishing an identity – the use of cowrie shells, with their connection to practices of divination within the traditional African religions, such as candomblé, suggested ethnicity, religious practices and political ideas. They also attracted others to the cause. The Bahia conspirators had no intention of remaining anonymous; on the contrary, they made a point of displaying their 'colours', being easily identifiable by their clothing and adornments, reflecting their conception of freedom as something that must be public and visible to all. This idea was expressed on the conspirators' flag: a red five-pointed star against a white background with a globe between each of the points, under which there was an inscription, also in red: 'Show yourself. Do not hide.'[85]

This enthusiasm for 'French' principles encompassed a wide range of aspirations and interests and was embraced across many levels of eighteenth-century Bahia society, including slaves, former slaves and impoverished freemen – most of whom were creoles or mulattoes. These principles provided a framework for arguments that challenged the Portuguese Crown. Although there is no mention of an end to slavery in any of the extant pamphlets, one that has not survived, according to Antônio José de Mattos Ferreira e Lucena, a captain in the grenadiers, promised 'freedom for the slaves'.[86]

The Bahia Conspiracy radically changed the central discourse of the colony. Now men and women who suffered a double injustice – the daily struggle for survival and marginalization based on race – began to realize they had an equal right to citizenship, to be protected by law, and to conduct business in the captaincy. As Lucas Dantas, one of the leaders of the conspiracy, explained to João de Deus regarding attracting new conspirators: 'When you talk to them, say this: the people are planning a revolution to make this captaincy a democracy where we'll be happy. The only governors will be those who have the capacity for the task, whether white, mulatto or black; people of intelligence, which is better than being governed by fools. Say that and you will convince them.'[87]

But before the conspirators could put their plans into military action, the leaders were arrested during a meeting where they were carefully evaluating their rebel forces and when they could begin the revolt. Lucas Dantas, João de Deus, as well as Manuel Faustino and Luís Gonzaga das Virgens – all poor mulattoes – paid a very high price for the audacity of claiming the right to political visibility. The four were denounced by the crown authorities as the leaders of the rebellion and were hanged in Salvador on the morning of 8 November 1799. A fifth member, a goldsmith called Luís Pires, was also condemned to death, but managed to flee and was never found. The bodies of the four were drawn and quartered and displayed in public places around the city. The hands of Luís Gonzaga, who was accused of writing the pamphlets, were nailed to the gallows. It was an example of the enormous imbalance of power between the Crown and the colonists, of what happened to any citizen who dared to violate the law, and of the instruments of repression that the the Crown had at its command.[88]

As had been the case in Minas Gerais, the punishments inflicted by the Crown on the Bahia conspirators were based on a political calculation. In Bahia the weight of the Crown's wrath fell on anonymous, simple men – poor and mulatto – who had dared to adopt a 'public voice'. The Bahia Conspiracy was something radically new: it proposed the inclusion of distinct groups of people, of differing social and economic statuses and with diverging interests. Despite their achievements, the leaders of the conspiracy have been unjustly overlooked by Brazilian historians. Outside restricted academic and cultural circles in Salvador, they are virtually unknown.

The Crown's response crushed the Bahia Conspiracy. It did not, however, root out the seed from which a succession of future rebellions was to grow, setting in motion a process that would teach Brazilians a multitude of political lessons. To this day Brazil clings to the idea of a stunning tropical paradise, where the Portuguese colonizers lived in peace and harmony. But history tells a different story. Between the seventeenth and eighteenth centuries the settlers began to see life in the colony in another light: they claimed the right to engage in previously unthinkable debate and political negotiations, gradually preparing the way for a richer form of communication between the people and the governing powers. Not one of the conspiracies was successful. But they bequeathed a legacy to the nineteenth century: a set of political and intellectual tools that could be mobilized, adapted and applied to bring about change. It is true that revolts do not last forever. But they reveal the vulnerability of power and cast an eye towards the future.

6

Ship Ahoy! A Court at Sea[1]

Each era dreams of the next.

Jules Michelet

By the end of the eighteenth century, words like 'revolution', 'uprising', 'rebellion' and 'sedition' had established their place in everyday vocabulary. This was an era of change and upheaval; the invention of the train in 1804 is perhaps the best metaphor for this. In the paintings of J. M. W. Turner and Claude Monet locomotives emerge dramatically from the morning mists, like dark phantoms, in an allusion to the all-pervading confidence in what the future would bring. There was the belief that society had broken free from the stagnation of the past, had severed the shackles of backwardness. An example of this overriding self-confidence is an inscription on the back of a locomotive built in 1808 with the proud challenge: 'Catch me if you can!' This was the mentality prevailing in the countries that held sway over world affairs: nothing could stop the new inventions and structural transformations of the era.

Events were moving so fast it was indeed a challenge to keep up with them. In 1776 the thirteen British American colonies had won their independence from Great Britain during a revolutionary process which, for the first time, incorporated a list of citizens' rights, made republican values integral to political modernity, and proved that the status of the colony was not permanent. Straight after, around 1780, a broad industrial revolution erupted in England, involving large economic investments, new technologies and the unrestrained use of labour. To complete the scenario, in 1789, a new event of significant consequence was to occur: in France, the Revolution disrupted that which had seemingly been the natural order of the Universe. In 1793,

Louis XVI, stripped of his divine right by an increasingly radical regime, was sentenced to the guillotine. His death was a presage of many others, symbolic or not. The Revolution tore down a centuries-old system in which the monarch was an icon at the centre, where he had absolute rule over the state. Not to forget the Haitian Revolution (1791–1804), which turned the island of Santo Domingo upside down: slavery was abolished, and the first republic – outside of the African continent – by and for people of African descent came into being. Moreover, the event showed the world that societies founded on slavery were simply a perverse historical quirk and therefore changeable. The institution of slavery was not a product of nature nor was it the result of 'divine intervention'.

'Revolution' is a word typical of modern vocabulary: it describes an event that can take place in various facets and spaces of social life – customs, law, religion, politics, economy, states and even continents – and which implies transformation in earnest. The word designates the overthrow of what is seen as outdated, the condensation of time and the inauguration of a future – which is to be not only better, but heretofore unknown. In the case of the French Revolution, far from being localized and contextualized, it polarized international politics and the modern states of continental and Atlantic Europe: the logic of the socially stratified society – marked by rigid hierarchical structures based on birth – and the Old Regime which began to collapse.

The various European monarchies felt the coup in distinct ways, but no one was immune to it. The ruptures were so extreme they would eventually alter notions of time and space: the world would seem smaller as the nineteenth century progressed – the greater speed of travel by sea or by land had made it more accessible – and time seemed shorter now that news could travel from one country to another within a single day. The push towards modernity was happening, beginning in the late eighteenth century, driven by a rupture with the feudal past and a hunger for goods, products and wealth. In its anxiety to overthrow the past, new productive forces emerged that relied on a workforce that was supposedly free, but in reality was based on new forms of labour characterized by increasing alienation and exploitation. After the first wave of revolutions the western world was virtually unrecognizable. The speed of the Industrial Revolution permanently altered the landscape, transforming hierarchies and the relationship between the countryside and the cities. By the end of the nineteenth century the landscape would look like the aftermath of a scorched-earth policy. The world had definitely changed: daily routine had been turned on its head.

In the small and once opulent Portuguese court of the late eighteenth century, the atmosphere was one of unease. The situation resembled a chessboard with Britain and France as the knights and castles and Spain and Portugal as the pawns. While Britain and France vied for the position of the most powerful nation in Europe, Spain was struggling to keep what remained of its autonomy, and the once vast and powerful Portuguese Empire could no longer hide its vulnerability. The country was largely dependent on its American colony, much of whose wealth was squandered on inefficient administration and the construction of ostentatious monuments, notably churches. Faced by these disadvantages, Portugal did what it could to maintain its image of neutrality, adopting contradictory positions that aimed at pleasing everyone but in fact pleased no one. Dona Maria I, the Queen of Portugal, and later her son, Prince Regent João,[2] adopted a dubious diplomatic policy that oscillated between supporting France or Britain, based on the fear that favouring one would imply being seen as a foe by the other.[3]

These were uncertain times in which Portugal stood to lose everything: its colonial empire, its monarch and its traditional alliance with Britain. The healthy trade balance it had once enjoyed was now a thing of the past. These events led to closer cooperation between the two colonial powers of the Iberian Peninsula to resolve the problem of frontiers in their South America territories. In October 1777 they signed the Treaty of San Ildefonso in which Portugal, in return for territory in South America, ceded the Colônia do Sacramento to Spain and relinquished its control of the Islands of Fernando Pó and Ano Bom,[4] fundamental to the Spanish slave trade.[5] Next a double marriage was promoted to strengthen the ties between the two: the Infante João of Portugal was married off to the Spanish Infanta Carlota Joaquina, and the Spanish Infante Gabriel to the Infanta of Portugal, Mariana Vitória.

But the apparent calm was short-lived. The French Revolution put Portugal's alliance with Spain at risk and forced Portugal to take a firmer stand in its alliance with Britain. Portugal also needed to navigate its relationships with France and England, who were on opposite sides of the North American independence movement. Faced with this tense situation, Portugal tried to sustain its complicated policy of neutrality. The country had some experience, given that for many years, in moments of conflict, Portugal had managed to temper international relations with balanced doses of agreement and discretion. Above all, the Crown wanted to preserve its autonomy and guarantee its overseas territories.

The Revolution in France, however, would take unexpected paths: in January 1793, Louis XVI was executed. In Portugal the reaction was immediate: fifteen days of private mourning followed by a further fifteen days of public mourning,[6] during which the theatres were closed in tribute to the monarch who had been a friend and relation of the royal family.[7] Wild rumours spread terror among the inhabitants of Lisbon, especially among the elite. The superintendent of police in the capital, Pina Manique, was adamant in his defence of the rights of the monarchy: French ships were seized and republican soldiers forbidden from coming ashore; republican books were banned, intellectuals arrested, and all French residents expelled.[8] Only French citizens who supported Louis XVI and remained in the city as spies for the Portuguese Crown, seeking to obtain information from France,[9] were allowed to stay. Mistrust was everywhere, as a witness described:

> There are spies everywhere. They proliferate in every part of the city: in the squares, in the streets, in the cafes, in the theatres, at the Royal Exchange, at the National Assembly, in judges' chambers, in merchants' offices and even inside people's homes.[10]

Neutrality on the Iberian Peninsula was now little more than a fairy tale. The British government signed treaties with Portugal that contained specific clauses granting protection, and then did the same with Spain. Neither country was aware of the pacts the other had entered into. Cooperation between the two Crowns was swiftly being converted into confrontation.

It is worth taking a closer look at Lisbon and the reign of Dona Maria. Her firstborn and heir to the throne – Dom José, Príncipe do Brazil – died in 1788, at twenty-seven, without satisfying his royal duties. At the time, the queen showed the first signs of dementia and losing control of her government. If Dona Maria could no longer govern, her second son, Prince João, now the presumed heir, would only begin to rule from 1799. Weak, and without significant power to make decisions, the young prince was supported by his State Council when he took power as Regent. Meanwhile the political situation went from bad to worse: the Crown feared not only the imminent invasion of the peninsula, but also the loss of Brazil, which could be occupied by either of the litigant powers, France or England.

The pressure came from both sides. In Lisbon, the 'English Party' and the 'French Party' vied for Prince João's attention. There was no ideological difference between the two; both were made up of aristocrats who were loyal to the monarchy and eager to avoid a war. The only difference between them was the solution they envisaged. The French Party was represented by a diplomat, an intellectual named Antônio de Araújo de Azevedo, Count of Barca, who dominated the political scene between 1804 and 1807. His position was somewhat paradoxical: he supported closer ties with France because he feared and rejected the Revolution, but he believed in the benefits of its culture and civilization. The English Party was also led by a diplomat, the president of the Royal Treasury, Rodrigo de Sousa Coutinho. His priority was to defend the Atlantic for Portuguese ships and thus safeguard the country and its empire. To achieve this he advocated maintaining the traditional alliance with Britain. In both his personal and political convictions, Coutinho was a rationalist. He had great confidence in the achievements of Britain's Industrial Revolution and believed the alliance would further the progress of the empire.

The Prince Regent oscillated between the two like the pendulum of a clock. But he was under no illusion: Portugal's frontiers needed defending against both the old enemy and the new (Spain and France). As soon as he became Regent, Dom João turned his attention to defence, reinforcing the border with Spain. The chaplain of the Swedish Legacy was shocked by what he saw: 'Violent press gangs can be seen on the streets every day. I frequently see as many as twenty recruits pass by, tied together by ropes.'[11] The situation was exacerbated by the shortage of funds to meet these new expenses: this time the onus fell on the clergy, who were required to pay a 10 per cent tax on the value of their property.[12] And there was no lack of initiatives for raising an extra shilling or two, as a contemporary commentator discovered when he learned that the royal carriages were being hired out for the transport of corpses to the cemeteries.[13]

For a short time the new defences seemed to work. But in 1801 the roving eye of Napoleon, whose expansion policies were becoming increasingly aggressive, once again focused on Portugal. He now demanded the fulfilment of previous demands the Portuguese government had failed to meet – it had always been conveniently forgetful in this regard. Napoleon moved once again to block the English from landing on the continent and instructed his Spanish ally, Charles IV, to transmit his orders to Portugal. He made it clear that the possibility of an invasion was not a mere threat. Dom João tried to buy time. He mobilized his diplomatic corps and there followed a flurry of appeals to Paris, Madrid and London, none of which had any effect. Charles IV's minister, Manuel de Godoy, led an army from Galicia to Andalusia to confront the Portuguese troops at Trás-os-Montes in the Douro and in the Algarve. The Spanish dislodged their adversaries in one fell swoop.

The surrender was signed in Badajoz. Losing Olivença[14] was the least of Portugal's worries. What hurt the most was having to pay an indemnity of 20 million francs to the French, and being forced to comply with the terms of the treaty that demanded the closure of its ports to the British. However, due to its continued policy of dissimulation and the period of comparative calm that ensued, Portugal was able to stall yet again. It was a strategy of wait-and-see. Meanwhile, the ambassadors from Paris, General Lannes and General Junot, were ceremoniously received in Lisbon. They had come to strengthen the ties between the two nations with the aid of Antônio de Araújo de Azevedo, who was exerting increasing control over the government. Little is known about Junot's activities as ambassador. We do know, however, that Madame Lannes, with her uninhibited sense of fashion, made a great impression on the conservative inhabitants of Lisbon. French songs became popular and 'during the week before St Anthony's day the Marseillaise was played every evening in honour of the Saint'.[15] Peace was finally declared when France and Britain signed the Treaty of Amiens in 1802, in which the French conquests were recognized by the British. The treaty was followed by a brief period of truce.

But there was still little peace for Portugal. This time the problem came from inside the palace itself. In 1805 a conspiracy was hatched by Dom João's wife, Carlota Joaquina, who had previously embarrassed the Crown on numerous occasions by her support for policies that defended the interests of Spain. As a woman she was ahead of her time: she rode horses, knew how to fire a cannon and had extramarital affairs, which was most likely one of the greatest obstacles to her bland husband's peace of mind. She now prepared to depose him, alleging mental incapacity, and to replace him as Regent. Although the Prince Regent reacted quickly, banishing those involved, the incident highlighted the Crown's insecurity and the presence of an agent of Spain at the very heart of the royal family.[16]

Meanwhile Napoleon – Emperor of France since 1804 – yearning to reshape the map of Europe, was concerned with removing the only thorn that remained in his side: the British. In 1806 he decreed a continental blockade, forbidding all European nations from trading with Britain. The British reaction was proportional to the provocation: it declared all commerce and navigation from enemy ports to be illegal and claimed the legitimate right to seize any ship proceeding from these ports.[17] The following year, after being defeated in battle, both Russia and Prussia signed peace agreements with Napoleon. With these threats hanging over Portugal's head, the government began to draw up a provisional plan for transferring the Crown to the colonies.

The foundation of a grandiose empire in Brazil was by no means a new idea – it had been considered every time the royal family felt its sovereignty was under threat. As early as 1580, when Spain invaded Portugal during the War of Restoration, one of the claimants to the throne, the Prior of Crato, was advised to leave for Brazil.[18] Padre Vieira had also suggested Brazil as a refuge for Dom João IV– 'where a place for a palace would be found where he could reside in comfort during the four seasons of the year, and where he could found the fifth empire . . .'[19] In 1738, during the reign of Dom João V,[20] Luís da Cunha[21] offered the same advice. Luís da Cunha thought the transference of the royal family to Brazil would create a more balanced relationship between Portugal and its colony.[22] In 1762, fearing a Franco-Spanish invasion, the Marquis of Pombal was reported to have advised Dom José I:

> to take the necessary measures for his journey to Brazil; and for many months the ships could be seen anchored in front of the Royal Palace, in preparation for safely transporting the magnanimous sovereign to another part of his empire . . .[23]

It thus comes as no surprise that, with Europe in a state of turmoil, the Prince Regent's advisers should resuscitate the idea. As early as 1801 the Marquis of Alorna[24] had discreetly broached the subject: 'Your Royal Highness should arm all your ships as soon as possible [. . .] and put the princesses, your sons and your treasure onboard.'[25] At the time the Prince Regent was displeased with the suggestion and was said to have shown 'great repugnance'. As Portugal's Foreign Minister in the 1790s, Rodrigo de Sousa Coutinho (the head of the 'English' faction) had nurtured similar ambitions for the colony. In preparation for the transfer of the Crown, he made contact with the Brazilian elite, soliciting their opinions on how to improve the management of the mining business and the colony's administration.[26]

Meanwhile, the British government was insisting on the transfer of the royal family as quickly possible. In 1806 a British delegation went to Lisbon and informed the government of the imminent danger of an invasion, suggesting that, unless Portugal were determined to confront the French 'vigorously and efficiently', a move to Brazil would be the best alternative, for which they could count on British support.[27]

In July 1807, Napoleon's patience ran out. The Portuguese ambassador in Paris, Lourenço de Lima, was given the unenviable task of transmitting the emperor's instructions to Dom João. The message was short and to the point: the time had come for the Portuguese to declare war on the British. They must recall their ambassador from London and demand the withdrawal of the British ambassador from Lisbon, close the ports to British ships, arrest all British residents in Lisbon and confiscate their property. Furthermore, the emperor gave the Portuguese one month, until 1 September, for his demands to be met. Failure to meet the deadline would be considered a declaration of war against France and Spain (also a signatory to the letter). By this time Spain, whose geographical location was equally disadvantageous, had already submitted to the French. But this was not enough for Napoleon, who instructed General Junot, formerly his ambassador to Lisbon, to organize the formation of an armada in Bayonne, on the French–Spanish border.

During all this time Dom João was in poor health and had taken refuge in the palace of Mafra, thirty kilometres from Lisbon.[28] There, protected by the thick walls of the monastery, he tried to forget the war. On 12 August he received a visit from his minister Antônio de Araújo de Azevedo, the leader of the French Party, who brought him the news that Napoleon had issued an ultimatum. The caricatural game of neutrality was over. This time the Prince Regent had no choice: he would have to go to Brazil.

Between the receipt of the news and the departure of the court for Brazil, important decisions were taken in secret and the days were filled with frenetic activity, so much so that reports from the time contain contradictory accounts. Nevertheless, this was the start of a defining moment in the history of Portugal and Brazil. It is rare for monarchies to move; when they do, their baggage is heavy. Dom João was no exception. He lived in isolation in the vast palace of Mafra, surrounded by his ancient library and cared for by monks with the aid of bats, which consumed the hordes of insects that invaded the palace. But the Prince Regent was under no illusion: he was aware of the immensity of the task of transferring not only the royal family but also the institutions and the imperial court to Brazil.

It was by no means an easy decision. It was the first time in Western history that the seat of an empire was to be moved to a colony. The situation required the immediate convocation of the Council, whose members included Antônio de Araújo de Azevedo and Rodrigo de Sousa Coutinho.[29] The Prince Regent also consulted with his closest friends: José Egídio Álvares de Almeida, head of the Cabinet; João Diogo de Barros, secretary of the Infantado; Tomás Antônio Vilanova Portugal, official of the Treasury; Manuel Vieira da Silva, his physician; and Francisco José and Matias Antônio Sousa Lobato, who were in charge of the Royal Wardrobe. The Privy Council actually first met at the palace at Mafra on 19 August, when, in the heat of the moment, they drafted a document declaring that Portugal agreed to close its ports to the British, but refused to expel them from Lisbon, nor would they even consider confiscating their property.

One of the councillors at the meeting reminded those present of other monarchs who, as a result of the Napoleonic Wars (which by then had lasted for more than ten years), had 'temporarily absented themselves from their capitals and their states in order to safeguard their sovereignty and independence'. The roll call included:

The King of Spain, on French soil, begging for Napoleon's protection; the King of Prussia, a fugitive from his own capital, which was held by French troops; Stathouder, claimant to the throne of Holland, who had taken refuge in London; the King of the Two Sicilies living in exile from his beloved Naples; the royal families of Tuscany and Parma, adrift in Europe; the King of Piedmont banished to the court of Cagliari; the Doge of Venice and the Council of Ten reduced to pawns on the political chessboard; the Tsar of Russia ceremoniously receiving French allies and swearing friendship to safeguard his throne in St Petersburg; the Scandinavian countries on the verge of imploring Napoleon to appoint one of his marshals as king; and, from time to time, the Holy Roman Emperor and the Pope himself, forced to abandon their eternal, intangible thrones.[30]

He concluded by proposing that the British government be contacted immediately and requested to place its ships at Portugal's disposal.

A second meeting took place on 26 August, during which a further attempt to postpone a decision was obvious. An envoy of the British government, Lord Strangford, informed London that the Portuguese planned to gain time by feigning to prepare for war against Britain. The Portuguese knew it was no longer possible to escape from Bonaparte, so-called 'preparations' would be only for show. Another topic at the meeting was more controversial: whether or not to send the Prince Regent's eldest son, Pedro, Príncipe de Beira, to Brazil, as a way of preserving the monarchy. This course of action meant that if Portugal went to war, the House of Bragança and its principal colony would be safe.[31] There was no lack of opinions on this matter. Some argued that sending the Prince Regent's son Pedro would be better than sending the entire royal family, which was currently made up of 'a lunatic, her listless son and a load of children'.[32] Others were concerned that the sudden disappearance of the royal family would anger the people.[33]

Despite the urgency of the situation, three weeks were to pass before Dom João reconvoked the Council, on 23 September. Napoleon had repeated his demand for the closure of the ports and the seizure of British subjects and their property. Portugal insisted that it was only prepared to close its ports to the British. Faced with this deadlock, the French and Spanish representatives in Lisbon gave a final date for their ultimatum: 1 October.[34] Meanwhile the dialogue with the British continued and the flagships *Afonso de Albuquerque* and *Dom João de Castro*, the frigate *Urânia* and the brig *Voador* were made ready to set sail from the mouth of the Tagus river as soon as the Prince Regent commanded.[35]

As the month of September came to a close, the tension increased.

The French and Spanish ambassadors, fulfilling their threat, withdrew from Lisbon. Meanwhile, the Prince Regent finally conceded full powers to his ambassador in London, Domingos de Sousa Coutinho, Rodrigo's brother, to secretly negotiate the terms of an agreement with Britain. In September, instead of reconvening the Council, Dom João instructed the members to meet without him. Opinions on the departure of his son Pedro to Brazil were divided, with some in favour of an immediate alliance with the French and others of arming the royal fleet for the defence of the port or for a sudden departure of the entire royal family. The only thing that changed was the tone of the meeting, increasingly grave, and marked by anxious appeals for urgent action.

By this time the topic of the 'journey' to Brazil was no longer restricted to government circles. Rumours abounded and the hectic activity in the shipyards and at the port aroused speculation and anxiety among the people. Further suspicion was caused by royal instructions to the heads of the Church, in Lisbon and the provinces, requiring them to deposit their silver in specified locations for inventory. The public's response was to solicit divine intervention. Public prayers and Masses were held; the Cardinal celebrated the Eucharist with the *Collecta pro quacumque Tribulatione*[36] and on 18 October a grand procession left the Igreja da Graça and solemnly made its way through the streets of the city.[37]

British citizens were also seen going about their business in the streets; their objective, however, was rather more practical. They were selling their goods and preparing to board the ships that Britain had sent to rescue British subjects. They were also increasingly alarmed by the recurring attempts of the Portuguese government to ease the situation by making a show of its allegiance to France: a decree closing the ports to British ships was issued on 22 October. Nonetheless, what only a few people knew was that this was part of a double game. On the very same day a secret treaty was signed in London: Portugal would close its ports to British ships, but at the same time it would allow them to occupy the island of Madeira and would open one of the Brazilian ports for the importation of British goods with a reduction of taxes. In return, a British fleet would escort the royal family if it decided to leave for the colony, and would only recognize the legitimate heir of the House of Bragança as King of Portugal.[38] Thus the Portuguese government became embroiled in a situation of its own making: on the one hand publicly favouring the French, while on the other secretly holding talks with the British. A friar who lived on the banks of the Tagus, after being informed of the closure of the port to the British, wrote to the Prince Regent: 'The government's secrets are a mystery that cannot be understood by reason alone.'[39]

Let us calculate dates. The quickest route to send mail between Paris and Lisbon, by land, took ten to eleven days. Thus, between sending a letter and receiving the reply almost a month went by; whereas from London to Lisbon letters were sent by sea, a process that could take only a week.[40] Therefore, the delayed response between nations was also aggravated by the practical problem of messages getting through. And this was precisely what happened in early November. Although Portugal had declared its support for France on 22 October, it only learned about Napoleon's latest demands on 1 November, demands Napoleon had dispatched on 15 October: 'If Portugal does not do what I wish, the house of Bragança will no longer reign in Europe.' Furthermore, to put an end to the double game, the emperor sent an army under the command of General Junot, which was already crossing the Pyrenees.[41]

But the Portuguese still wanted to defer. From one side, the Viscount of Anadia,[42] arguing in favour of the policy of secrecy, suggested the property of the British might be confiscated and then 'secretly returned', and that the port should remain open so that 'individuals [. . .] may leave the country under the semblance of flight'.[43] On the other hand, an attempt was made to please the French emperor by sending an envoy to congratulate him on his conquests, bearing a splendid gift of diamonds.[44] Once again the delay in communication foiled these plans. France and Spain had already signed a treaty dividing Portugal into three parts: Entre-Douro and Minho would go to the Queen of Etruria – a kingdom Napoleon had created in Tuscany with Florence as the capital; the Alentejo and the Algarve would be given to Spain; and the largest part – Beira, Trás-os-Montes and Estremadura – would go to France. The Portuguese American colonies would be divided up between the successors of the new monarchs of Portugal.[45] Bonaparte was also playing a double game: while threatening on the one hand, he held out the offer of negotiations on the other, thus managing to retain the Prince Regent in Lisbon. It is possible that Dom João still had a few cards up his sleeve: although his planned departure for Brazil escorted by a British fleet had been confirmed, in absolute secrecy, he continued to flirt with Napoleon.

England grew tired of waiting. George Canning, the British Foreign Secretary, informed the Portuguese government that he would accept the closure of the ports but that any other measure taken against British subjects would be considered a declaration of war. And there was worse: if the Prince Regent decided against the move to Brazil, the British would start to bombard the capital. The atmosphere in Lisbon was now so tense it had begun to affect the inhabitants' daily routine. Everywhere military preparations were under way and a torrent of prayers and gossip engulfed the town. A devout churchgoer spread a rumour around the city: she had received a revelation that if the monarch left for Brazil, his ship would sink. When the premonition reached the ears of the Prince Regent it left him in a 'state of confusion'.[46] To add insult to injury, by this time food was becoming scarce in the markets: meat and wheat were in short supply and on 16 November a decree was issued rationing flour.[47]

The Portuguese government's representative in London, Domingos de Sousa Coutinho, was worried.[48] He wrote to the Prince Regent warning him that the squadron that had been sent to save him would turn its guns against Lisbon should he make an agreement with the French. Coutinho did not yet know that the Portuguese delegates in Spain and France had been ordered to leave. Nor had he been informed that the Marquis of Marialva[49] was on his way to Paris to pay his compliments to Bonaparte. Meanwhile, Dom João had no idea that France and Spain had already decided to carve up Portuguese territory through the Treaty of Fontainebleau.[50] What was more, the Prince Regent's counsellors could never have dreamt that in three days' time – on 11 November – Le Moniteur, the official journal of the French Empire, would make public the resolution to remove the House of Bragança from the throne. The Regent's future was now hanging in the balance: the solution to his predicament depended on the time it took to deliver the journal from Paris to Lisbon.

A few days later, Portugal recalled its ambassador to the Spanish court and the Spanish reciprocated by recalling theirs from Lisbon. On 16 November the British squadron appeared at the entrance of the port of Lisbon with an army of seven thousand men.[51] Meanwhile the court – which continued to ignore Napoleon's ultimatum – still favoured an understanding with France. What was not known in Lisbon was that Junot's troops had already arrived at the border and were stationed in Alcântara. The days that followed were tortuous. In consultations with Lord Strangford it was decided that the British fleet would be commanded by Admiral Sidney Smith. Smith had ample experience and proven ability as a naval officer. While still a lieutenant he had served with distinction at the British victory at the Battle of the Saintes, near Dominica, in April 1782 – starting thereby a history of his belligerent relations with France. He had acted as a marine official, and for his central role in the defeat of Russia he had received a commendation of Knight of the Order of the Sword, and the title of 'Sir' attributed by the British government.

Although Smith experienced many adventures during his career, let us recall just a few here: in Turkey he had acted as an amateur spy and proceeded to successfully attack the French on the coast of Brittany. Even so, Smith's escapades did not always work out: he was captured in 1796 and spent two years in The Temple (prison) in Paris. But by then he was a living legend and, once freed, was known on both sides of the Channel as the Lion of the Sea. After one such escapade, Smith was carried through the streets of London, whose citizens considered him a sort of redeemer of the British. His reputation was firmly established at the 1798 battle against the French in Egypt. He commanded troops including Turks, Albanian mercenaries, Syrians, Kurds, and British sailors and marines, managing to halt the advance of Napoleon's troops. The ships under Smith's command staged a two-month blockade; and after half of the French troops had been killed, Napoleon ordered the survivors to retreat.

Daring and independent, with vast experience of naval battles against the French, Smith was the ideal person to command the expedition that would escort the royal family to Brazil. He may have lacked experience of crossing the Atlantic in the company of royalty, but his reputation, bravery and strong personality ensured his capacity to defend his charges. Even Dom João, despite his stubbornness, was beginning to admit that there was no other option.

News in Lisbon that the French army had arrived on the frontier coincided with Smith's decision to order a blockade of the mouth of the Tagus river. The city was alive with rumours about the British army, the Spanish, and 'other spectres that haunted that time of tribulation'.[52]

The differences between the French and English factions now pushed them further and further apart. Rodrigo de Sousa Coutinho, the 'Anglophile', argued in favour of resistance and, if necessary, a rapid departure for Brazil. Antônio de Araújo de Azevedo, the 'Francophile', was still in favour of an understanding with France. Lord Strangford needed to exert all his powers of diplomacy. From Admiral Smith's ship he wrote to Dom João promising that all hostilities would be forgotten and British support guaranteed, as long as his departure were immediate:

> I've realised it is my duty to remove from His Majesty's mind all hopes of arranging affairs with the country's invaders, terrifying Your Majesty with sombre and lugubrious descriptions of the situation of the capital, which I left just a short time ago, and perhaps, in turn, entice Your Majesty with the brilliant prospects that lie ahead . . .[53]

As final proof of his argument, he handed the Prince Regent a copy of the inflammatory *Moniteur*. That was the last straw. On the night of 24 November 1807 the Regent summoned the Privy Council and informed them that the French troops had reached Abrantes. At a forced march they could arrive in the capital within three or four days. The preparations for departure began. A Government Junta of the Realm was appointed to govern in the sovereign's absence; its first action was to prepare an announcement to be made by the Prince Regent. In the early hours of 27 November, followed by the royal family, the Regent boarded the ship that was to take him to the New World. No sooner were they aboard than the stampede began: a seething mass of government officials, state councillors, civil servants, ministers' relations and members of the nobility with their families and friends, all desperate to find a place on-board one of the ships of the royal fleet. It was a scene from Dante's *Inferno*: wives separated from husbands, parents from children, brothers from sisters, overcrowded ships jam-packed with people – a panic-driven reign of chaos. The fleet sailed on the morning of Sunday, 29 November. Later that day Napoleon's troops entered Lisbon.

The Portuguese people were left with the last words of their monarch in a declaration he ordered to have printed and distributed once he was on-board. Even then the government was still attempting to avoid a rupture with France, by not using the word 'invasion'. The monarch referred to the French troops as a foreign army stationed on Portuguese soil and asked the people to receive them, so as to conserve 'the harmonious relations that must be established with the armies of other nations with which we share the continent'.[54] This was the last act in that theatrical show of neutrality.

MEN AT SEA, A COURT
ON THE ATLANTIC

Dom João had made his decision in the early hours of the morning of 25 November 1807. He could no longer postpone the immense task that lay ahead of him: to dismantle everything necessary for the survival and sustenance of the monarchy and its government, transfer it from land to the sea, and reassemble it in Rio de Janeiro. Time was short, the journey long, and the future unpredictable: for the first time in history a royal household was crossing the Atlantic and going to meet its destiny in a distant land. In contrast to the nation's intrepid discoverers, the Bragança dynasty was fleeing (according to its detractors) to avoid its dissolution (according to those who depended on its patronage), courageously escaping the humiliating treatment to which Napoleon had submitted the other royal houses of Europe (according to those who had a vested interest in the maintenance of the Portuguese Empire).

The plan was complex. It was not a case of a royal family travelling alone, with a few chosen favourites. They were joined by a host of others – the families of ministers, of counsellors, of the nobility, of the court, of civil servants – in other words, of all and sundry whose livelihoods depended on the Prince Regent. Nor was it a case of a few individuals making a hurried escape; this was the seat of the Portuguese State being transferred, along with its administrative and bureaucratic machine, its government offices, its secretariats, its law courts, its archives, its treasure and its employees. The Queen and the Prince Regent were accompanied by everything that represented the monarchy: its important figures, religion, institutions, trappings, etiquette, exchequer – the entire arsenal that was needed to sustain the dynasty and the business of the Portuguese government, and ensure their continuity. And thus, thousands of people arrived on the docks of Belém with cartloads of baggage and chests. In the words of José de Azevedo, the future Viscount of Rio Seco,[55] this was 'the host of people who had drained seven centuries of wealth to establish themselves in Lisbon'.

The Prince Regent immediately gave orders for all the ministers of state and the palace servants to travel with the royal family. He also made it clear that any of his subjects who wished to accompany the court were free to do so and that if no room were available they could follow the royal fleet in private vessels.[56] Even though it was midnight, José de Azevedo was summoned to the Palácio da Ajuda[57] and placed in charge of supervising the embarkation. He immediately set about organizing the transport of the royal treasure. He then directed his attention to the docks at Belém (on the Tagus river) where, armed with maps, he ordered that a tent be set up where he could 'distribute the number of families in accordance with the size of the ships and the accommodation available'. Even though no one could embark without a laissez-passer from the government, the confusion was such that it was almost impossible for the plan to run smoothly and many people were left behind.[58] The Royal Instructor of Equitation, Bernardo José Farto Pacheco, for example, who had embarkation papers from the Royal Equerry, the Royal Stable Master and from the Count of Belmonte, was unable to travel. Although he had the necessary papers, the commander of the frigate did not allow him on-board.

To add to the chaos, a gale blew in from the south bringing torrential rain that flooded the streets and filled them with mud. These conditions made it even harder for the carriages to reach the docks of Belém and to get the huge quantity of supplies on-board that would guarantee the crew's survival during the crossing.[59] A list of items that were still required on the eve of the departure gives some idea of the lack of organization:

Rainha de Portugal – 27 water casks empty. *Fragata Minerva* – has only 60 water casks. *Conde d. Henrique* – 21 water casks empty; needs livestock as it has none. *Golfinho* – 6 water casks empty; no livestock, chickens or firewood. *Urânia* – has no firewood. *Vingança* – has no water or firewood. *Príncipe Real* – needs livestock, chickens, rope, wax, 20 water casks, tar, cables and firewood. *Voador* – needs 3 water casks. *Príncipe do Brasil* – no olive oil, wax, rope, firewood; needs 30 water casks.[60]

At the height of the confusion, the papal ambassador to Lisbon, Lourenço de Caleppi, arrived at the Palácio da Ajuda to show his solidarity. He was a member of the court circle and the Prince Regent had invited him to accompany him on the journey. Despite his age, sixty-seven, the Nuncio accepted the invitation. He consulted the Minister of the Navy, Viscount Anadia, who offered him a place on either the *Martim de Freitas* or the *Medusa* where he and his secretary could be accommodated. But despite the Prince's personal invitation and the intervention of the naval minister, he was denied access to either ship on the grounds they were 'overloaded'. The Irish lieutenant Thomas O'Neill, who was on-board one of the British ships, noted down information confided to him by one of the Portuguese officers. Although the aim of his chronicles, at least in part, seems to be self-promotion, and some of them were probably invented, they nevertheless give a vivid depiction of the desperation that preceded the Prince Regent's departure: 'as soon as the Prince's intention of embarking for the Brazils became known, a dreadful scene of desperation and panic pervaded every rank; thousands of men, women and children, filed onto the beach, endeavouring to escape on-board. Many ladies of distinction waded into the water, in the hope of reaching the boats, with some even perishing in the attempt.'[61]

To make matters worse, country folk, in their fear and haste to get to Lisbon, and bewildered by the conflicting rumours, abandoned all of their belongings along the way.[62] The beaches and docks that lined the Tagus at Belém were littered with packages and trunks left behind at the last minute. Amid the chaos fourteen cartloads of silverware from the cathedral were left on the riverbank. Boxes of priceless books from the Royal Library were also left behind, much to the indignation of the city's booksellers, who yelled insults at royal officials in their disbelief at the sight of such negligence.[63] Luxury carriages, many of which had not been unloaded, were also abandoned. There were even those who embarked with no luggage, with only the clothes on their backs.[64] Too late, the Marquis of Vagos[65] realized the royal carriages with their saddles and harnesses had been left behind, and yelled orders from the deck 'in uncouth language' for an appropriate vessel to be hired to transport them to Brazil.[66]

The general atmosphere was emotional and highly charged:

Copious tears of sadness were shed on that occasion, some weeping the separation from parents, husbands, sons and loved ones, others criticizing the desertion of the Fatherland invaded by a foreign enemy, and reflecting on the evils they would suffer without protectors in the midst of the terrible French.[67]

The reaction of the inhabitants of Lisbon oscillated between alarm and disgust. Some of the fortunate few who accompanied the Prince Regent, as they made their way to the ships, were berated with 'insults and imprecations', and others were actually 'set upon'.[68] Joaquim José de Azevedo describes the reaction of the people:

Roaming [. . .] around the squares and streets, in disbelief, their tears and curses giving vent to the dolorous oppression that stifled their hearts amidst an effusion of sighs: the horror, the grief, the heartbreak, the noble nature of their suffering [. . .] well-nigh engulfing them in despair![69]

Descriptions of the Prince Regent's departure are as moving as they are contradictory. According to one version, he arrived on the docks disguised as a woman; in another, he left furtively during the night to avoid the people's anger. Yet another relates how he arrived at the port with no one to receive him, accompanied only by his nephew. Two policemen who were standing guard in the pouring rain allegedly placed wooden boards over the mud and helped the Prince Regent across before he was rowed out to the *Príncipe Real*.[70] Other versions ridicule his departure, mocking the attitude of the royal family by citing the only lucid words spoken by the queen, who by then had succumbed to dementia: 'Go slower! They'll think that we're running away.'[71] In reality, Dom João's departure was extremely discreet, totally lacking in pomp, and in no way recalling the all-powerful head of a once great empire.

All of the formalities had been concluded and everyone was on-board; now all that was needed was some good weather to begin the voyage. The morning of 29 November dawned bright and clear as the squadron set sail from the Tagus. When it reached the mouth it was greeted by a gun salute from the British fleet – the four ships that stood in readiness to escort the Portuguese squadron to Rio de Janeiro under the command of Sir Sidney Smith.[72] The admiral went aboard the *Príncipe Real* to pay his respects to the Prince Regent and received from the vice-admiral a list of the fifteen vessels that composed the royal fleet: eight ships of the line, four frigates, two brigs and one schooner.[73] In witness reports and in later studies the numbers vary, but they made an impressive sight nonetheless.

At least thirty private merchant ships followed in the wake of the royal fleet. There may have been many more. The British ship *Hibernia* sighted fifty-six vessels at nightfall on the first day of the journey. Sir Sidney Smith, although he did not count them, reported seeing 'a multitude of large merchant ships, fully equipped'.[74] At all events, the royal squadron formed a fighting unit that inspired respect: its eight warships each carried between sixty-four and eighty-four guns. Each of the frigates was armed with between thirty-two and forty-four guns, the brigs with twenty-two and the freight ship bringing supplies with twenty-six guns.[75] The royal family – the queen, Dona Maria, the Prince Regent with his wife, Carlota Joaquina, and eight children, the queen's sister, the widow of the Prince Regent's elder brother and Carlota Joaquina's Spanish nephew who had been raised at the Portuguese court – were distributed between the ships with the greatest capacity. Aboard the *Príncipe Real* were the queen, by then seventy-three; the Prince Regent, who was forty; the Infante Pedro, Príncipe de Beira, and his younger brother, the Infante Miguel, and the nephew, Don Pedro Carlos. Travelling on the *Afonso de Albuquerque* were the thirty-two-year-old Princesa Carlota Joaquina, with her daughters Maria Teresa, Princesa de Beira, and the infantas Maria Isabel, Maria da Assunção and Ana de Jesus Maria. And aboard the *Rainha de Portugal* travelled Dona Maria Benedita, the widow of Dom João's elder brother, Dona Maria Ana, the queen's sister, and the remaining daughters of Dom João and his wife: the infantas Maria Francisca de Assis and Isabel Maria.

According to Nuncio Caleppi's secretary, who viewed the entire exodus, 10,000 people travelled with the royal fleet. In his calculations the civil servant João Manuel Pereira da Silva[76] included the numerous merchants and landowners who had hired ships to follow the royal squadron: 'On that day around fifteen thousand people of all ages and sexes abandoned the lands of Portugal.' Five hundred and sixty-three passengers, including nobles, ministers of state, counsellors and court officials, were listed by name on the official register. However, comments beside the names reveal this number was, to say the least, imprecise: 'the Viscount of Barbacena with his family'; 'the Count of Belmonte, his wife and the Count, their son, with male and female servants'; 'José Egídio Alves de Almeida with his wife and family'; '[. . .] and more than sixty people, both men and women, not including the families that accompanied them [. . .]', and, vaguest of all, 'with others'.[77]

It was true that almost everyone on-board was accompanied by their families, close friends and servants. The Duke of Cadaval, for example, travelled with his French wife, their four children, a brother, eleven servants (one of whom was 'a coloured man who had been trained to sweep'), as well as a number of families attached to his household. The Marquis of Belas brought no fewer than twenty-four servants. The register also listed the employees of the royal household: the pantries alone employed twenty-three 'menservants' and the royal kitchens a further fourteen, all of whom brought their families. At the very last moment another register was opened with the intention of listing the names of everyone on-board. However, after mentioning a few aristocratic families, it ends rather abruptly with the words 'and another five thousand people'.[78]

But this number still does not include the crew and passengers on the merchant ships. According to historian Kenneth Light, it is probable that between 12,000 and 15,000 people embarked. He estimates the number of people on-board the *Príncipe Real* at 1,054, adding that the task of weighing anchor alone, tying it to the prow and storing the cable, occupied 385 men.[79] A veritable horde of people travelled aboard each of the ships. And there is controversy about the number of people who arrived in the colony. The historian Nireu Oliveira Cavalcanti, for example, calculated the number of crew members at 7,262.[80] It is thought that many of these remained in Brazil – some out of fear of the French invasion, others preferring to stay with the monarchy, others simply marooned. According to these estimates the total number of emigrants must have been more than 10,000.[81]

There can be no doubt that the food supplies were insufficient for the number of people on-board. The list for the frigate *Minerva* gives a total of 741 crew, similar to the number that sailed on the *Martins Freitas*. The *Minerva*, which had not been prepared in advance, presented problems from the time it set sail. On 26 November the captain had reported that his ship was at the mercy of fate 'because there hadn't been time to prepare her'. Even though there were only supplies of 'biscuits and gruel' on-board, and despite the 'woeful conditions at the Royal Arsenal, with confusion and lack of attendants in every department', the frigate set out with the fleet on 29 November. However, due to the 'need in which the ship found itself', on 5 December it received orders from the vice-admiral to separate from the fleet and sail to Bahia. When it docked in the city, on 10 January 1808, the *Minerva* had completely run out of supplies.[82] The warship *Medusa*, severely damaged, also docked on the coast of Brazil's northeast, ahead of the royal family. Despite all the hazards a journey of this kind entailed, there were no reports of deaths or serious accidents. But the hurried departure had caused a series of problems: families divided between the ships, belongings either lost or abandoned on the docks, overcrowding, lack of hygiene, and rationing of water and food – all of which would have to be borne throughout the two-month journey across the high seas.

At the very beginning of the journey the fleet ran into a storm. They escaped with little damage, but the second storm that erupted, in mid-December, as they passed the island of Madeira, separated some of the ships from the main body of the fleet, forcing a change of plan. Although part of the squadron was already headed for Rio de Janeiro, the *Príncipe Real* and the ships that accompanied her changed route and set sail for Bahia.[83] Apart from these hazardous moments, the journey went smoothly, at least as far as nature's moods and the state of the ships were concerned, every one of which – despite the inevitable damage suffered during the crossing – reached its destination.

But the excess of passengers caused a great many problems: 'there were no beds to sleep in, no chairs or benches to sit on; people sat down in the open, on the bare boards of the decks, with no plates to eat off, squabbling over the filthy little bowls of food that came from the kitchens.' The crew was too small for so many tasks. Water was reserved for drinking, and 'even the ships that conducted the Prince Regent, the queen and the princes, were disgraceful and stank like pigsties'. The ladies' hair became infested by fleas, obliging them to shave their heads. Thus the journey dragged on, monotonous, interminable. Apart from the distractions of watching the sails being hoisted, and of singing to guitars at sunset and on moonlit nights, there was nothing to do but play cards: *faraó*, *espenifre*, *pacau* and *chincalhão*.[84]

MEANWHILE, BACK IN PORTUGAL . . .

While the court was making its way across the Atlantic, free from the perils of war, those who remained behind faced a large-scale military invasion. On the turbulent day of 29 November 1807, no sooner had the royal squadron disappeared over the horizon than the first lines of French troops appeared on the edges of Lisbon.[85] A declaration by the French general was posted around the city, warning the inhabitants of the entry of his army and ensuring them of his protection: 'Inhabitants of Lisbon, live at peace in your homes: fear nothing from my army, or from me: only our enemies, and the wicked, need fear us. The great Napoleon, my commander, has sent me to protect you, and protect you I will.'[86]

On 30 November, Junot made his triumphant entry into Lisbon, with an entourage of officers filing past the Rossio,[87] followed by around six thousand soldiers, little more than half the number of the original contingent. Thousands had perished from an epidemic of fever and dysentery, and hundreds more had been murdered or wounded in the Portuguese countryside. The troops were a pitiful sight as they staggered into the town – ragged, barefooted, exhausted and starving.[88]

These men – as well as the Spanish troops who arrived in the following days – fanned out across the city, 'not even sparing the churches and chapels whose saints and altars were used as hat-racks for hanging their weapons and backpacks'.[89] A large contingent of troops was quartered in the Palace of Mafra. Junot established his headquarters in the town house of the Baron of Quintela, from where he gave orders for the confiscation of the property of the royal household and the nobility, seizing the entire fleet of royal horses and carriages as well as the goods and property of those who had fled. The French general immediately issued his first proclamation affirming that the occupation was an act of support for Dom João, who had declared war on England. He had come to save the kingdom from their mutual enemy: 'Fear not, peaceful inhabitants. My powerful army has both valour and discipline . . .' As paradoxical as it may seem, the general was corroborating the words of the Prince Regent himself who, on the eve of his flight, had instructed his representatives in Lisbon to receive the troops 'as if they were guests whom one wishes to please by acts of respect and kindness'.[90]

The pretence of friendship did not last for long. By December, Napoleon's agent was implementing a policy of increasing repression. Weapons were banned and all fishing was strictly controlled to prevent the inhabitants from escaping and making contact with the British fleet stationed off the coast at the mouth of the Tagus. A new tax was created, officially termed a 'contribution', which imposed a total payment of 40 million cruzados on the city's inhabitants. All gatherings that could lead to disorder – including playing music and ringing the Angelus – were banned. Cannon were fired every morning to signal when people could leave their homes, and at night to signal when they must return. Christmas 1807 was a sad time in Lisbon: there were no services since all the churches were closed. But worse was yet to come. On 1 February, while on the other side of the ocean Dom João was ceremoniously welcomed by the government of Bahia, in Portugal he was being formally dethroned by the French. Napoleon had finally received confirmation of the royal family's flight and angrily informed his new subjects: 'By abandoning Portugal, the Prince of Brazil has renounced all his rights to the Sovereignty of this Kingdom. The House of Bragança no longer reigns in Portugal . . .'[91]

Although popular discontent was evident, the time was not ripe for an organized reaction. The royal servants who had stayed behind found themselves in a delicate situation. In the absence of the sovereign, conflicts arose, some of which ended in bloodshed. This was the case of the friars at Mafra. Before he left, Dom João had limited the number of monks who could remain there. This led to fights breaking out; in one such skirmish several of the friars were stabbed.[92] The servants who remained in the royal palaces were left with neither food nor remuneration. On 7 December 1807 the warden of the Paço de Queluz[93] requested that urgent measures be taken as provisions for the forty-one servants at the palace had almost run out. The stocks in the larder had been reduced to 'thirty arrobas of bacon, 120 arrobas of codfish, fifty arrobas of garlic, 48 pitchers of olive oil, 25 crocks of vinegar, eight arrobas of sugar, eight barrels of butter and three barrels of lard'. On 30 December his tone became more desperate: he requested instructions about what to do next, as the pantry at the palace was now empty.[94]

Many managed to escape from Portugal, normally by evading French restrictions on movement and managing to board one of the ships in the British squadron. In May 1808 the diplomat Domingos de Sousa Coutinho, who had remained in London, wrote to the Prince Regent about the large number of Portuguese refugees who had come to England and wanted to embark for Brazil: 'People from every rank have come, and in such numbers that I know not how to help them. Indeed most of them have arrived with nothing, virtually naked.'[95]

For those who had remained in the country, the time for reaction soon came. In June 1808, after an uprising in Porto, the French were routed during the restoration of the Portuguese monarchy. The French tried to invade on two further occasions, in March 1809 and in the summer of 1810, before leaving the country for good in 1811. On both occasions the Portuguese with the British fought tooth and nail against the aggressors, forcing them back across the border. By this time, with Portuguese society torn asunder by years of war and foreign domination, their determination to fight back was indomitable. It was a fight between good and evil. The innumerable pamphlets that circulated at the time were apolitical in tone, but all shared a single vision: the sacred homeland that had been defiled must be returned to its people. History was crossed with myth, and reality with metaphor. France and Portugal created conflicting legends. For the French, Junot was the ingenious conquering hero; for the Portuguese, after years of humiliation, he was the mediocre usurper. In the eyes of the Portuguese, France and its Revolution stood for nothing but plots, betrayals and unfulfilled promises. But there was a second legend. Napoleon was the Antichrist ruling over an Empire of Shadows; freemasons and Jacobins alike were his agents of sedition, manifestations of the evil of all that was French. That was the Portuguese version of the Revolution.[96]

The departure of the royal court, the essential instrument for the operation of the *ancien régime*, deprived Portugal of its political stability and created a positive environment for the creation of ambivalent myths. An alchemical process was set in motion, in which feelings of abandonment and a mystical vision of salvation were transmuted into a new form of national consciousness. The ordinary people of Portugal clung to the symbolic image of the monarchy; when they rose up against their oppressors the conflict became a new crusade. The French had become the archetype of the infidel Moor whilst the banner of the Holy Cross had traversed Atlantic and been re-erected in Brazil.

In this context, religious feeling dominated, rather than any rational discussion of citizenship that the French Revolution had introduced years before. Even so, from this stalemate, the Portuguese monarchy was to emerge even stronger, albeit symbolically. The Prince Regent was no longer the monarch who had absented himself; he was the monarch who was present but 'hidden', like Dom Sebastian,[97] who had disappeared in the sands of the desert while fighting in the Crusades, but whose mythical presence remained. His departure had created a void (which included the period of the Iberian Union) but it also created hope: a mythological belief in a future king who would protect the future of this kingdom so cruelly humiliated and belittled.

This then was how Portugal first teetered onto the path towards modernity. It was a tortuous process, shaped by religious feeling and lingering traditional beliefs in every way shape and form. People began to await the great return of the monarch, who was to redeem the kingdom. The only problem was, the myth did not really fit the person, Dom João. In this romanticized version, although he still occupied the throne, he could not occupy the myth.

Meanwhile, after fifty-four days at sea, the *Príncipe Real*, with the Prince Regent and his retinue on-board, docked in Salvador on 22 January 1808. After spending a month in the capital of the colony, Dom João sailed on to Rio de Janeiro where he arrived on 8 March. The rest of the ships came behind him and arrived at the docks one by one. To commemorate this momentous arrival, his subjects greeted their prince with a special gift: the brig *Três Corações* sailed out to meet the *Príncipe Real* loaded with supplies of food and tropical fruit. Amid cashews and coconuts the American colony opened its doors to receive its Portuguese Prince. For the first time in history an empire would be governed from its colony below the equator. The world had turned upside down and its politics inside out.

7

Dom João and His Court in the Tropics[1]

On 22 January 1808, Dom João and part of his court arrived at his overseas colony. Coincidence or not, the Prince Regent was forced to make a transitory stop in Salvador, which had been the capital and largest city in the colony until 1763. The city could not have been more beautiful. As seen from the ocean, it stood out on top of a tall steep cliff that emerged dramatically from the bay. The 'City of Salvador' as it was known at the time – or the 'City of Bahia', as it was called in official correspondence, but also by its citizens – was lush with tropical vegetation and red soil that matched the colour of the tiles on the roofs. Against this backdrop was the incessant coming and going of ships in the bay.[2] Luís dos Santos Vilhena, a visitor to the city at the beginning of the nineteenth century, noted in 1802, that '[. . .] at its broadest [. . .] the city measured between 400 and 500 *braços*[3] across'.[4] A century earlier the British explorer William Dampier had reported the existence of two thousand houses, with paved streets and public promenades and gardens. He also described the superb churches and beautiful two- to three-storey town houses, like those in the Alfama district of Lisbon.[5]

The initial enthusiasm, however, may have cooled a little at the timid reception awaiting the travellers. As soon as the governor of Bahia, Saldanha da Gama, received the news that for the first time in history a European royal family would set foot on American soil, he did what he could in the limited time he had. Planning a royal reception with no prior warning was an enormous challenge, and along with the Prince Regent's ship there were three others, one of which was from the British fleet.

The day after their arrival, the royal family and the Portuguese nobles who accompanied them – with the exception of the queen, Dona Maria, who was in a 'great state of nerves' – disembarked beneath the scalding sun of the tropical summer. There were immediate impressions on both sides. Local people thought the royal party dressed for the oncoming winter in Europe was an extraordinary sight. The court, on the other hand, must have found the dirty, badly paved streets of Salvador equally strange. They were crowded with people selling everything from fruit and candies to smoked sausages and fried fish, all of whom threw their refuse into the open gutters where herds of domestic animals came to forage for food.[6]

Although the urban landscape was similar to Lisbon, everything else was strikingly different. The almond blossoms flowering in autumn in the streets of Portugal were replaced by an exuberant landscape of palm trees laden with fruit and a profusion of vibrant colours. The salty tang of the sea spray intermingled with the exotic aroma of palm oil as food was prepared in the streets.[7] However, accounts of the time are unanimous that the slaves made by far the greatest impression on the new arrivals. The brutality of the treatment of the Africans shocked even people acquainted with the appalling conditions of captivity in Europe. Slaves were commonly seen being whipped in the streets or almost crushed beneath the weight of their burdens. Among their many tasks, they also carried the sedan chairs and litters wherein travelled white-skinned ladies seated behind fine linen curtains. The multitude of slaves, selling their wares, preparing food, performing their religious rites from Africa, dominated the streets of Salvador.

Since the sixteenth century Salvador had been the centre for imported merchandise and, above all, the lucrative commerce of slaves. At the beginning of the nineteenth century, although their entry into Portugal had been banned since 1767, African slaves continued to supply the work-force for the colony and arrived in vast numbers at the port. To a large extent Portugal's trade with Africa was conducted via the ports of Bahia, Rio de Janeiro and Recife. 'There were commercial exchanges between the regions, Africa received and Africanized the hammock, the manioc and the corn, while Brazil [. . .] incorporated the use of dendê oil and chilli peppers and the custom of building granaries along the coast.' In the words of ethnographer and photographer Pierre Verger, between 'the Africans of Brazil and [the] Brazilians of Africa' there was 'an unforeseen consequence of the flux and return flow of the traffic of slaves'.[8]

There could be no doubt in the minds of the new arrivals that this was a distinctly New World. Anxious to rectify the initial bad impression, while the court remained in Salvador the government did its best to make up for lost time. Religious ceremonies were held for the royal party in the capital's churches, with their splendid gilded interiors and jacaranda furnishings, and visits were organized to the city's most eminent citizens.

It was in Salvador that, on 28 January 1808, without the presence of his most important ministers and counsellors, Dom João signed the law that opened Brazilian ports to friendly nations. It was the first measure to be adopted from the new seat of the Portuguese Empire. With the signing of that decree, 'All agricultural and other colonial produce' could then be transported not only by Portuguese ships, but also 'by foreign ships from all countries friendly to the Empire'. Under the new decree the import tariff on wet goods (wine, aguardente and olive oil) was doubled, and dry goods (all other types of merchandise) were taxed at 24 per cent of their value. Foreigners could export all colonial goods and products with the exception of brazilwood and other Crown monopolies.[9] The significance of the decree was enormous. It put an end to the Portuguese monopoly of trade with Brazil that had existed since the beginning of the colony. The transport of merchandise to and from Portuguese America was no longer restricted to Portuguese ships or to countries with whom commercial partnerships had been signed. Merchandise could now be imported directly from other countries; Brazilian ships could dock at foreign ports, except for in France and Spain, which were still at war with Portugal.

The opening of the ports was not so much an act of benevolence as a necessary and inevitable outcome of events in Europe. With Portugal under French occupation, the supplies needed in Brazil – where virtually everything was imported – were no longer arriving, nor was Brazil able to export anything produced there. Furthermore, one country was particularly interested in the decree – in fact, its greatest beneficiary and, at the time, Portugal's greatest friend: Great Britain. With access to Britain's traditional markets cut off since 1806 by Napoleon's continental blockade, there could hardly be a more propitious moment for the Brazilian market to open up.

The immediate result was that Britain began to export vast quantities of merchandise to Brazil, far more than the country could absorb. Most of the products were hardly commensurate with the colony's needs. Some, in fact, were virtually unusable. This last category included ice skates, ladies' shark-fin corsets, copper (bed) warming pans, thick woollen blankets and mathematical instruments. The British also sent an ample supply of wallets to a country where there was no paper currency and where men of property never carried money, a duty that fell to their slaves.[10] The Brazilians showed considerable creativity: the warming pans, once they had been punctured, were used for skimming boiled sugar in the mills; the blankets were used as sieves by the gold panners; and the ice skates were made into door latches. But this ingenuity was still not enough to exhaust the supply. The excess had to be disposed of at public auctions and special sales.

The immediate result of the royal decree was that trade relations between Britain and Brazil were consolidated; and even more so with the signing of a Commerce and Navigation Treaty in February 1810. This treaty reduced import tariffs on British products, making them more competitive than those from other countries, including Portugal. In sum, the treaty – which imposed a 15 per cent import duty on British goods entering the country, while Portuguese goods were taxed at 16 per cent and those from other countries at 24 per cent – was the price the colony paid for Britain's assistance to the royal family during its flight. Its 'reciprocity' clauses did not alter the fact that products that came from Portugal were taxed at a higher rate than those that came from Britain; although the difference was only 1 per cent, it was highly symbolic. The 1810 commercial treaty was complemented by a further agreement, the Treaty of Peace and Friendship, which granted Britain special purchasing rights and permission to acquire and operate timber mills in Brazil. The treaty also banned the Inquisition from visiting the colony and stipulated the gradual abolition of the slave trade.[11]

While still in Salvador the Prince Regent began organizing the colony as the new seat of the imperial government. In addition to decorating prominent local figures and taking routine administrative measures, Dom João implemented groundbreaking initiatives, previously unknown in a Portuguese colony. In 1808, for example, he granted the licences for a School of Surgery to be set up in Salvador's São José hospital and for a Medical School of Anatomy and Surgery to be established in the Military and Naval Hospital of Rio de Janeiro. These were the forebears of Brazil's medical schools. However, with the continuation of the Crown's policy to restrict educational institutions to Portugal, there was a chronic shortage of specialists in the colony. The lack of doctors encouraged the activities of apothecaries, barber surgeons, shamans and 'herbalists', which often clashed with the scientific knowledge brought into the country by medical students, mainly from the university in Coimbra.

Lisbon had prohibited schools of higher education in its colonies, unlike Spain, whose cultural policies encouraged higher education institutions in its colonies. Until the arrival of the Prince Regent only artillery and military architecture had been taught in Brazil, apart from occasional courses in the 'courtly sciences' of philosophy, Latin, rhetoric and mathematics. All other education was conducted by the religious orders in convents and seminaries. The opening of the ports was the beginning of a radical about-turn in Portugal's previous policy for the colony. As a further indication of this liberalization the Prince Regent licensed the production of glass and gunpowder in Bahia, as well as the installation of wheat mills.

Despite his hosts' insistent efforts to persuade him to stay – above all those of the governor, who never lost hope that his city would be restored to its old status as the colony's capital – on 26 February the royal squadron weighed anchor and sailed out of the bay. Promising that he would order a luxury palace to be built in the city, the Prince Regent kept to his plan and, resisting the now famous Bahia hospitality, set sail for the final port of call on his journey.

RIO DE JANEIRO: THE TROPICAL SEAT OF THE EMPIRE

History is only predictable with hindsight; at close-up, everything is uncertain. This was certainly true for the Viceroy of Brazil, Dom Marcos de Noronha e Brito, Conde dos Arcos. In October 1807, while still trying to maintain a policy of neutrality, Dom João had decided to close the ports to the British, causing immediate concern over possible retaliation against the colony. Instructions were sent from Lisbon for Pernambuco, Bahia and Rio de Janeiro to prepare to defend their territories against a possible attack. On 11 January 1808 the count published an edict containing the measures that had to be taken to protect the capital from an attempted invasion.[12] Just three days later all his expectations were turned on their head: the brig *Voador* arrived in the city with the news that the French had invaded Portugal and that the royal family, with the support of the British, had decided to retreat to the colony, from where the empire would be governed. From one day to the next, not only had the enemy changed, but also all the measures that had to be taken. The count was now able to turn his thoughts to more peaceful concerns, but ones that were no less urgent: to prepare the unsophisticated city of São Sebastião do Rio de Janeiro to receive the court and to become the seat of the Portuguese Empire.

It was no small task. At the beginning of the nineteenth century, Rio de Janeiro was an emerging town whose centre was constricted by four hills: Castelo, São Bento, Santo Antônio and Conceição. The city centre was at the foot of Morro do Castelo (Castelo Hill), where its defences had been installed since the time of its foundation, and from where it spread out into the four urban parishes: Sé,[13] Candelária, São José and Santa Rita. The town had forty-six streets, four bystreets, six alleys and nineteen public squares, all of which were of beaten earth, full of potholes, puddles, marshes, and littered with rubbish.[14] In fact, most of the terrain was swampland since the chief preoccupation of the city's authorities in urban expansion had been to stave off flooding.

However, not far from the Morro do Castelo was the main square, facing the ocean – the Largo do Paço, where the government of the colony had been established. Here the town assumed a more imposing appearance. The square was first called *terreiro do Ó* (Ó yard), then *terreiro do Polé*. And finally, Largo do Carmo when the Carmelite Order built its church and convent in the area. In the 1740s the Royal Treasury and the Council Chamber (which also housed the prison) were erected and, shortly afterwards, the Royal Mint and Royal Storage House. These last two had been joined together and expanded to serve as the seat of the government of the captaincy and, after 1763, of the viceroyalty. During the government of Viceroy Dom Luís de Vasconcelos the square was paved and a fountain installed, based on the designs sent to Rio de Janeiro executed by Charles Mardel, the most important architect at the court in Lisbon. In 1789 the original fountain was replaced by a new one: the work of the Brazilian sculptor and engraver Valentim da Fonseca e Silva, known as Mestre Valentim.

Nevertheless, as the capital of the colony, Rio de Janeiro left much to be desired. The power of a monarchy can be measured by the magnificence of its palaces and monuments, and, in this respect, the new capital of the Portuguese Empire had very little to offer.[15] There was, however, one exception: the group of imposing buildings formed by the church and hospital of the Carmelite Order, which had been built in the 1700s. These were beautiful buildings, and although they could not officially be called a 'palace' – a prerogative reserved for royal residences – they nonetheless became known as the Paço dos Governadores (Governors' Palace), and later when the capital was transferred to Rio, the Paço dos Vice-Reis (Viceroy's Palace). Next to the palace, a carved stone quay had been constructed with three stone steps and a ramp that led down to the sea. The street that ran through the square was called Rua Direita – Straight Street – (present-day 1º de Março), 'the largest, busiest and most beautiful street in the town [. . .] irregular and crooked despite the name'.[16] The street was the centre of commerce, which, like in every small town, closed for a long siesta after lunch. Rio de Janeiro was in fact a sleepy village. The arrival of the court woke it up.

The count had a lot of work ahead of him. He began the preparations on 14 January by moving out of the Viceroy's Palace and having it made ready for the royal family. The Council Chamber and prison also underwent remodelling: the bars were removed and doors were widened to allow for the entrance of carriages. A new gallery was built connecting the palace to the Council Chamber, so that the royal family would not get their footwear dirty in the muddy streets. A Decree for the Distribution of Lodgings was issued, instructing the owners of the most suitable houses in the immediate surroundings to vacate their properties, which would be used for housing the aristocrats, military officers, merchants and civil servants who had arrived with the Prince Regent. Two letters were written in chalk on the street wall of the houses selected: PR. They officially stood for 'Príncipe Real', but in popular jargon they soon acquired a new meaning: *'ponha-se na rua'* ('put out in the street'), or *'prédio roubado'* ('stolen building').

The count was equally preoccupied with providing food for the illustrious visitors. He solicited help from the governors of São Paulo and Minas Gerais, both of whom sent supplies. Although scarcity of food was one of the largest problems in the town, he managed to provide a bill of fare that contained foods well known to Europeans, with the addition of one or two novelties: beef, pork, mutton, fowl, manioc, sweet potatoes, beans and corn, as well as grapes, peaches, guavas and bananas. But physical nourishment was not enough. Divine protection also had to be invoked, and a space for the feast provided. An ample programme of religious and civil festivities was decreed, which included the illumination of the city for eight consecutive days, dances and popular entertainment. The streets were adorned and decorations hung from the windows in preparation for the royal procession, in which the Prince Regent and his retinue would be conducted from the docks to the cathedral where a Te Deum would be sung to celebrate his arrival. There would be bullfights, horse races, firework displays, music, dances and theatrical presentations.[17] The greatest novelty would be the royal receptions, which included the ritual of kissing the monarch's hand.[18] It was traditional for these ceremonies to be conducted by the viceroy in front of a portrait of the Prince that symbolized the royal presence and the legitimacy of his representative. Much to everyone's excitement, they would now be conducted by the Prince Regent himself.

It was a struggle. On the morning of 20 January – before he had managed to complete the preparations – he received a semaphore communication from the fortress on the Morro do Pico at the entrance to Guanabara Bay: the royal squadron was approaching the city. There was great excitement in the streets. In their curiosity, people ran to the Praia de Dom Manuel in the area around the port, or climbed to the top of the Morros do Castelo and de São Bento to watch as the fleet arrived. At the end of the afternoon, seven Portuguese ships accompanied by three British vessels dropped anchor in the bay. To the tremendous disappointment of the public – and, to a certain extent, to the relief of the viceroy – only two of the queen's sisters, Dona Maria Benedita and Dona Maria Ana, and two of the infantas, Maria Francisca de Assis and Isabel Maria, were on-board. Their ships had been separated by the storm and had made their way directly to Rio de Janeiro. They knew nothing of the other ships' whereabouts. Although they were invited to disembark, the princesses did not accept: they would not set foot in the colony before the Queen and the Prince Regent arrived. They were only to come ashore a month later, on 22 February, after receiving the news that their relatives were safe in Bahia, and would shortly join them in Rio.

Finally, on 7 March 1808, the *crème de la crème* of the imperial court arrived in Guanabara Bay. The city came to a halt; not a soul remained indoors. Houses, shops, government departments – all were completely deserted. As soon as the royal squadron was sighted on the horizon the signal was given for the tributes to begin: the church bells pealed and fireworks were set off in the streets. All the ships in the port and the fortresses around the bay were decked out with banners and ensigns. The sound of cannon salutes followed by rounds of rifle fire was simply deafening. It would not have been surprising had the honorees become terrified, fearing the war had now broken out in the tropics! But the noise was not war, it was celebration. No sooner had the fleet docked than the tributes to Dom João and his wife Dona Carlota Joaquina began. Even happier were the Portuguese aristocrats whose ships had been separated from the fleet, and now re-encountered the families and friends whom, for all they knew, had been left behind amid the chaos on the docks in Lisbon. The priest Luís Gonçalves dos Santos – nicknamed Padre Perereca (tree frog) due to his frail build and bulging eyes – was among the observers, and commented with his usual enthusiasm on the royal family's arrival.[19]

The royal family, however, did not come ashore that day. The solemnities the Council had been preparing since 16 January had to wait until the following morning, when the travellers had recovered from the long journey. At around four o'clock in the afternoon on 8 March the royal family – with the exception of the queen, Dona Maria – entered the boats that were to take them to the dock. For the people of Rio, to whom the Prince Regent had thus far been little more than a figurehead on coins, pamphlets and engravings, this was an historic occasion. The members of the court were received by the Senate, the clergy and the nobility of the land, wearing their finest clothes and powdered wigs. However, if anyone expected to see a pair of regal figures in purple mantles lined with ermine, they were sorely disappointed. Dom João was short, had a long face, large forehead, a glazed expression in his eyes, meaty lips, low chin ending in double chin, protruding belly, large legs and a shy look. His wife Dona Carlota Joaquina was also short, but unlike her husband, she was angular and bony, and she had a limp. Her face, remarkable for its thin lips, prominent jaw and warts, also revealed the signs of an incipient moustache.[20]

The disappointment, however, had to be set aside, as the ceremonial could not wait. At an altar in front of the docks, especially set up for the occasion, holy water was sprinkled on the royal family, incense was lit and the Holy Cross presented to the Prince Regent for him to kiss. A line was formed to pay homage to the royal couple, composed of government officials, civilians, military officers and clerics from the various Orders, which followed the Prince and the Princess in a solemn procession to the city cathedral (Igreja do Rosário). The route had been strewn with white sand and aromatic leaves. Quilts of damask and silk hung from windows and verandas from where people threw flowers onto the cortège. In the Rua do Rosário, where a large bandstand had been erected, hymns were sung in praise of the Prince Regent, who was rapidly becoming Brazilian royalty. Meanwhile the chanting of excited crowds could be heard from the streets: 'Long live our Prince. Long live the Emperor of Brazil.'

When the religious ceremony was over, the Prince Regent and his family left the cathedral for what was now the Paço Real.[21] The square was adorned with a display of allegorical figures carved out of wood beneath a balustrade inscribed with verses from Virgil. At the centre of the piece, the coat of arms of the Senate of Rio de Janeiro was mounted on an orb that displayed the royal crest of Portugal: the mother nation united with her American Empire. A portrait of Dom João, adorned with a wreath of roses, was framed by symbolic figures representing the virtues attributed to the Prince: religion, justice, prudence, strength and magnanimity. Before him, between two allegorical figures – on the one side Africa, on the other Portugal, weeping for the absence of her sovereign – knelt an Indian who represented Brazil. Wearing a mantle and leather boots, with his feathered headband resting on the ground, in his outstretched hand he offered the sovereign gold and diamonds: the riches of the land.

To complete the tribute was a painting of the Prince Regent's ship, entering Guanabara Bay to the sound of cannon fire from the fortresses, and heralded by the words:

> For the greater glory of America,
> A bounteous heaven sends us John the Sixth.[22]

Above the ship was painted a serene sky filled with clouds – a metaphor for a peaceful future – and verses by Manuel Inácio da Silva Alvarenga, the Arcadian poet from Minas Gerais:

> From afar black clouds exhale
> Havoc, poison, pain and death,
> Whilst here at home with every breath,
> Tranquillity and peace prevail.[23]

Silva Alvarenga was one of the leaders of the Minas Conspiracy who had been arrested ten years earlier for his part in the plot to found a republic. He was still alive and must have been infuriated that his verses had been purloined to salute a monarch.

It had been a long day. After the Prince Regent and his retinue had retired to the Royal Palace the people continued to celebrate far into the night. There were fireworks, music, poetry recitals and speeches in honour of the Prince Regent, all of which were observed by the Prince from a window in the palace. It had been a good pretext for a fine reception, but also for the symbolic affirmation of the new government. Across the colony, from Recife to São Paulo and Santa Catarina, there were spontaneous demonstrations of support. After all, as far as the people knew, the monarchy had come to stay. Until 1820, that date, 7 March, was decreed a public holiday in Brazil, celebrated as a new discovery.

TIME TO SET UP HOUSE

As soon as he set foot in Rio de Janeiro, the Prince Regent must have realized the amount of work it would take to transform the new capital into the seat of the royal court. He was used to the splendour of Mafra, his favourite palace, and of Queluz, where his mother the queen had resided. The palace now placed at his disposal was a far more modest affair. But if the town could not adapt to the monarch, the monarch would have to adapt to the town. With his wife and children he moved into what had previously been the Viceroy's Palace in the Largo do Carmo, annexing the Council Chamber and Royal Prison next door as a residence for the palace servants. However, since there was still no room to accommodate the queen, the Carmelite convent was requisitioned as a residence for her, and the friars were transferred to the Order's seminary in Lapa. It was not long before the Prince Regent found a new palace to live in, however – and one that was at a convenient distance from his wife, with whom his relations had been strained for some time. A rich Portuguese merchant, Elias Antônio Lopes, ceded his country house in São Cristóvão,[24] on the outskirts of the town, for the monarch's use. Although he insisted he had no other motive than 'His Majesty's well-being', years later he would be generously remunerated for his 'gift'.

Meanwhile the government continued to requisition houses for members of the nobility, civil servants and military officers who had nowhere to live. Some of the local property owners managed to defend themselves against this 'invasion of aristocrats' by 'simulating or even effecting renovations that were entirely unnecessary. Renovations that lasted forever . . .'[25] Others simply ignored the government's demands. Instead of directing their anger at the Prince Regent himself, citizens turned against members of the royal entourage. They were seen as remorseless 'liberty takers'.[26] As more and more of the royal retinue landed, more and more of the local elite were forced to renounce their houses.

The merchants who already lived in Rio de Janeiro, the majority of whom were Portuguese, did not take kindly to the presence of their fellow countrymen who, with the acquiescence of the Crown, were gradually taking their places. The government soon realized it needed to appease the local people, and to restore itself to the good graces of the aggrieved merchants and local landowners. And what better means of achieving this than by conferring a title of nobility or some other distinction? To this end a General Register of Grace and Favour was established and, in 1810, the Noble Corporation of the Heraldic Kings – as the means for the creation of a nobility in Portuguese America. By the time he returned to Portugal in 1821, Dom João had bestowed no fewer than 254 titles, including eleven dukes, thirty-eight marquises, ninety-one viscounts and thirty-one barons.[27] He also created the Order of the Sword and the titles of Knight and Commander of the Grand Cross.[28] As Prince Regent and, after 1816, as king, Don João created 2,630 Knights and Commanders of the Grand Cross of the Order of Christ: 1,422 of the Order of St Benedict of Avis and 590 of the Order of Santiago.[29] Alongside the titled aristocracy in Portugal, a new nobility was emerging in Brazil, avid to display the new symbols of its distinction.

The Prince Regent now turned his attention to an effective administration for the new seat of government. Since his arrival in Rio de Janeiro, Dom João had made it clear he would govern the empire from the colony, a decision that he had taken before leaving Lisbon.[30] From Brazil he would now send instructions out to all the Portuguese dominions. Dom Rodrigo de Sousa Coutinho was appointed Minister of War and Overseas Affairs; João Rodrigues de Sá e Meneses, Viscount Anadia, Secretary for the Navy and Overseas Dominions (the post he had held in Portugal); and Fernando José de Portugal, Viceroy of Rio de Janeiro from 1801 to 1806, Minister of Internal Affairs.

This triumvirate of ministers soon became the target of popular sarcasm. They were known as the 'three clocks': the one that was always fast (Dom Rodrigo); the one that was always slow (Dom Fernando Portugal), and the one that had stopped altogether (Viscount Anadia). And the hands of all three moved prince-wise.[31] Meanwhile the number of civil servants continued to grow, clogging up the machine of government and inflating its cost: positions were created with the sole purpose of accommodating the new arrivals, who expected the court to provide them with a means of survival. The hordes of hangers-on – ranging from monsignors, judges, legislators, doctors, royal household servants, the king's personal servants and favourites of the royal household – behaved like a 'gang of parasites'. 'They were vagrants and scroungers [. . .] who continued the profession they'd pursued in Lisbon in the colony's capital: living at the state's expense and doing nothing for the good of the nation.'[32] In order to fund this increasingly bloated administrative machine, new taxes were imposed on activities all over Brazil. The people's anger at such unbridled corruption was expressed in ironic verses:

> Pinch a roast chicken
> And jail's your reward
> But plunder the coffers?
> They'll make you a Lord![33]

The government of the colony was based on the strictly hierarchical structure of institutions in Portugal. The Municipal Chambers were subordinate to the governments of the captaincies, which were in turn subordinate to the government-general of the colony, which was subordinate to the Palace in Lisbon where all power was centralized. The plan now was to create a new seat of the empire that would be a mirror image of the old, with the transference of Portugal's institutions, lock stock and barrel, to the colony: 'Organizing the empire from Brazil [. . .] meant reproducing the structure in Lisbon and using it to provide jobs for the unemployed.'[34] The most strategic government functions were the first to be transferred: the military, the courts, the police and the exchequer. As Brazil had been governed in accordance with the Philippine Ordinances – the legal code that had been in force in

Portugal since the seventeenth century – some of Portugal's key institutions were already established in the colony. The transference of the others was thus a process of superimposing, merging and adapting them to those that already existed. These institutions were the safeguard of the sovereign's power, in keeping with the tenets of the Ordinances: 'The king is the law incarnate on earth. He can make the law and revoke it as he deems fit.'[35] The High Court[36] was already established in Brazil, under the jurisdiction of the Supreme Court of the Portuguese Realm,[37] based in Lisbon.[38] Now the Supreme Court itself was brought to the colony along with other ancient Portuguese courts that came as part of the package: the Royal Dispatches[39] – the highest court in the land – and the Royal Council of Conscience,[40] which had jurisdiction over the Archdiocese of Brazil.[41]

The absolute power of the sovereign was, however, by no means unanimously accepted in his American colony. Whereas in Europe the danger came from the example of the French Revolution, in America it came from the republican ideals of the United States. Thus on its arrival in Rio de Janeiro, the Portuguese Crown took immediate steps to reinforce its policy of centralization. On 5 April 1808 the Court Police Commissariat for the Brazilian State (which had existed in Portugal since 1760) was established by royal decree. Almost everything became the responsibility of the Court Police: guarding the king, organizing his schedule, installing military barracks, conducting municipal works, inspecting the theatres, cataloguing carriages and seagoing vessels, registering foreigners, issuing passports, controlling public festivities, detaining escaped slaves, and pursuing and imprisoning those who opposed the government. This new structure for the defence of the colony included the foundation of the Military Archive for the creation and storage of charts and maps of Brazil and the other Overseas Dominions, and, in 1810, of the Military Academy, for teaching the sciences of mathematics, physics, chemistry, natural history, fortifications and defence.[42]

Thus, although a number of Portuguese institutions were already established in Brazil, with the arrival of the royal court their number and the scope of their activities grew beyond all recognition. One of the indirect effects of such far-reaching changes was that business activities in the colony acquired a far greater degree of autonomy. A significant example of this was the creation of the Banco do Brasil in 1808. Its official task was to facilitate trade and meet the needs of the market, but the consequences of its activities were soon to go beyond the reach of state control.

'A VENEER OF CIVILIZATION'

The process was completely new. For the first time in history a colony was being turned into the capital of an empire. This inversion of roles required the production of vast quantities of documents: treaties, decrees, legislation and registers of the acts of the various departments of government. And all this vast amount of material needed to be printed, with the one small obstacle that printing presses were forbidden in the colony. The solution was the creation of the Royal Press, on 13 May 1808, the Prince Regent's birthday.[43] In addition to official documents, the Royal Press was allowed to print other works, and books. All the new publications, however, were subjected to restrictions. The directors were required to examine everything sent for publication and to exclude all documents and books whose content contradicted the government, religion or public morality. Thus, from the outset there was censorship to protect the fragile stability of the Portuguese Crown.[44]

The Royal Press was behind schedule from the day it was founded. To give an idea of the amount it had to process, by 1822, the year of Brazil's Independence, it had published no fewer than 1,427 official documents[45] and 720 titles – pamphlets, brochures, sermons, prospectuses, scientific works, literary works, translations of French and English texts on agriculture, political economy and philosophy, plays, operas, novels, poetry, children's literature – a little of everything, with the only condition that it had first been examined by the censors. In addition, at every anniversary, funeral or royal birthday, reams of obsequious commentaries were produced.

The Royal Press published Brazil's first periodical: the *Gazeta do Rio de Janeiro*, which was launched on Saturday, 10 September 1808.[46] From then on, there were two weekly editions, on Sundays and Wednesdays. As an official government publication, the journal was edited by friar Tibúrcio José da Rocha, an employee of the Ministry for War and Overseas Affairs, and never disguised its role as 'propaganda for the state'. It was used to describe the activities of the monarchy and promote its image. Content was restricted to reporting official undertakings, praising the royal family, and reproducing articles from European newspapers. By 1814 the *Gazeta do Rio de Janeiro* was commenting on the war in Europe, with special attention to the victories over Napoleon. Such articles, first published abroad, referred to the French as 'the plague that assailed Europe' and to Dom João's departure as 'the wisest measure taken'.[47]

Among those who most objected to the periodical's submissive editorial policy was the journalist Hipólito José da Costa Pereira Furtado, who commented acidly: 'the fine-quality paper used on such poor material would be better employed for wrapping butter'. Hipólito, who was Brazilian and had been the director of the Royal Press in Lisbon, had become an enemy of the Portuguese government after being accused of being a Mason and imprisoned by the Inquisition between 1802 and 1804. He then escaped to London where he set up his own newspaper, the *Correio Braziliense*, three months before the first edition of the *Gazeta* was published in Rio de Janeiro. The *Correio*, which he published until 1822, was well informed, hard-hitting and free from censorship. In it Hipólito published news, analytical commentaries and criticism of the political events of the time. Although the periodical was banned from entering Brazil, copies were smuggled in and secretly read in the captaincies.

Between 1808 and 1810 the government concentrated on administrative measures. This also involved bringing 'civilization' to the colony, a project that began to accelerate after 1811. The first of such measures had been the establishment of Rio de Janeiro's Botanical Garden in 1808, modelled on that of the Paço da Ajuda in Lisbon where samples were collected and botanical experiments conducted. Its Brazilian counterpart, located in the public park on the Lagoa Rodrigo de Freitas,[48] was created the same year. The area was designated by the Crown for the acclimatization and display of spices and plants 'of exotic origin'. These included black pepper, red pepper, cloves, camphor, cinnamon and nutmeg, as well as fruits including breadfruit, sugar apples, mangoes, jackfruit, rose apples[49] and star fruit.[50] The first Royal Palm (*Oreodoxa oleracea*) was imported from the Antilles and planted by the Prince Regent himself. The colony's first tea plantation was established in the gardens in 1810 with plants brought from Macau, accompanied by a group of two hundred Chinese to administer their cultivation. In 1819 the park on the Lagoa Rodrigo de Freitas was annexed to the Royal Museum, which had been founded on 6 June 1808, and was opened to the public under the name of the Royal Botanical Gardens.[51]

In 1816 the Royal School of Sciences and Arts was inaugurated at the Royal Museum with the objective of 'promoting botanical and zoological studies at the location'.[52] Since the museum had no collection, Dom João donated some of his personal possessions, including paintings, engravings, stones, indigenous artefacts and stuffed animals, all of which gave the place the appearance of 'an old curiosity shop'. Perhaps the most significant of all these measures was the creation of the Royal Library. It had taken three journeys to transport the priceless personal library of the Bragança family – abandoned in the streets of Lisbon during the chaos of the departure – to Rio de Janeiro. It was opened to the public in 1814.[53]

In order to sustain the presence of the court apparatus, with the government departments and civil servants in tow, the inhabitants of the colony paid a heavy price. Half of the money circulating in Portugal and the 80 million cruzados in gold and diamonds loaded into the royal chests in Lisbon were just a drop in the ocean. The Banco do Brasil alone funded almost all the expenses of the royal family, the law courts, the payroll and the pensions.[54] As the taxes became more onerous, resentment in the colony grew. Nor did the royal household trouble to disguise how it squandered its wealth. The royal larders became symbolic of royal dissipation. An example is the daily consumption of the nursery of the Infante Dom Sebastião, Dom João's grandson: three chickens, 10 lbs of beef, half a pound of ham, 2 lbs of sausages, 6 lbs of pork, 5 lbs of bread, half a pound of butter, two bottles of wine, a pound of candles, as well as sugar, coffee, pastry, fruit, vegetables, olive oil and other seasonings.[55] Throughout the year of 1818 records show that 620 fowl per day were consumed in the Royal Palace.[56]

Although the presence of the court brought undoubted political benefits to Brazil, the price it had to pay was extremely high. As the government machine acquired increasingly gigantic proportions, so did the taxes needed to maintain it.[57] Although the measures the Portuguese monarchy took while based in Rio de Janeiro were largely self-serving, those were years of political and administrative growth that set the course for the colony. It was a course that was both unpredictable and irreversible. And while neither entirely European nor exactly an empire, Portuguese America was gradually abandoning the status of a colony.

A KING IN BRAZIL

It had been six years since Dom João had arrived in the tropics. The colony had freed him of his gout and distanced him from the complex game of European politics, which, even with the defeat of Napoleon, was still plagued by confrontations and territorial disputes. This was the period of the Holy Alliance when, between 1814 and 1815, Russia, Austria and Prussia came together at the Congress of Vienna. During these great diplomatic meetings, which took place after Napoleon's defeat, the restoration of the pre-revolutionary monarchies and the collective restructuring of Europe were negotiated. Despite the prospects for pacification and the return of the *ancien régime* states, Dom João remained hesitant. To his credit, however, the decision to maintain the court in Brazil permanently altered the face of Rio de Janeiro. The tropical city was no longer recognizable, no longer the 'bogus Lisbon, vulgar and lawless'[58] that had welcomed the Prince Regent and his entourage. The population of Rio de Janeiro had grown by 50 per cent, from around 60,000 inhabitants to 90,000,[59] and 'people of every race, colour and conceivable culture' now filled its streets.[60]

To the foreign visitor, however, the capital of Brazil was still mean and shabby. John Luccock[61] described it as 'one of the dirtiest congregations of human beings under the sun'. Despite the presence of the royal court, the routine of a sleepy provincial town continued. And life at the Royal Palace was no exception: after lunch, the Prince Regent would retire to the cool of the drawing room, where the peace and quiet was only broken by the squealing infantes teasing the caged monkeys, and otherwise annoying the dogs, parrots, macaws and cockatoos.[62]

There is a probably exaggerated story that is often told about Dom João. After being bitten by a tick he started to bathe in the sea on his doctor's orders, but as the swelling increased and made it difficult for him to walk, he began to travel short distances in a chair, carried by his slaves on their shoulders.[63] Overnight this new mode of transport became all the rage in the 'elegant' streets near the Paço – the Rua Direita and the Rua do Ouvidor. More practically, for short distances, mule or ox-drawn carts with curtains were the most frequently used form of transport, guided by a slave on foot; for longer journeys, carriages drawn by one or two pairs of horses.[64] It was also possible ('with all decency') to hire slaves to drive the vehicles. But all of these means of transport were expensive and the quality was deplorable. In 1819 the Prussian Theodor von Leithold[65] compared them to 'market carts'.[66]

The city offered almost no recreational facilities nor even the most basic requirements for an urban society. The Passeio Público, the public gardens built in the district of Lapa between 1779 and 1783, were for many years one of the only attractions in the city. Bullfighting was also a popular form of entertainment. Von Leithold attended one of the fights that took place in the Campo de Santana:[67] 'The Portuguese, Brazilians, mulattoes and blacks booed all the way through; the mangey bull, whose wrath a few costumed figures sought to provoke with their red capes, remained calm.'[68] The Real Teatro de São João, founded in 1813, offered further entertainment, and for ten years remained the only theatre in the city. As for music, Dom João was clever at combining local talent with artists visiting from abroad. He surrounded himself with professional artists such as the mestizo composer José Maurício,[69] who until 1810 was in charge of all sacred and profane music at the court, where – entirely without competition – he was affectionately known as the 'Brazilian Mozart'.[70] In 1811, however, he was overshadowed by the arrival of the composer Marcos Antônio Portugal,[71] a musician accustomed to the tastes of the court. Marcos Antônio Portugal had studied in Italy and been the conductor at the São Carlos opera house in Lisbon. The position grew: by 1815, the Royal Chapel boasted fifty singers, both domestic and international.

The Fazenda Santa Cruz,[72] owned by the monarchy, was sixty kilometres outside the city, and as famous for its 'production' of musicians, all of whom were of African descent, as it was for its agricultural produce. The enslaved on this estate, in addition to working in the fields, were taught to sing and play musical instruments. As their fame increased, the estate became known as the Conservatório de Santa Cruz (Santa Cruz Conservatory). Although the estate had been in decline since the expulsion of the Jesuits, the music teachers[73] had continued their work, paving the way for the transformation the school was to undergo with the arrival of the royal court.

In 1817 the building was remodelled, and the chapel was redecorated to accommodate orchestral and choir performances. And then the Palace of Santa Cruz officially became the royal summer residence, with all the solemnities befitting its new status. The enslaved musicians spent much time studying music theory and practising on their instruments, under the supervision of none other than José Maurício himself. The Prince Regent began the custom of incorporating musicians from Santa Cruz into the military band, the orchestra at the Palace of São Cristóvão, and into the choir of the Royal Chapel. The instruments included strings (violins, violas and cellos), woodwind (clarinets, oboes, flutes and bassoons), brass (trumpets and trombones), as well as drums, soprano clarinets and ebony piccolos. They performed patriotic marches, *modinhas*, waltzes and quadrilles. They also presented operas. Dom João, who was a great lover of music, appeared at the theatre for gala performances, where he would fall asleep in the royal box. When he woke with a start he would turn to the faithful chamberlain at his side and ask: 'Have the rascals got married yet?'[74]

The new capital presented a number of very original problems. Insects were a constant topic among travellers, who described the annoyances of those 'little monsters' with long legs: 'Because of them, anyone who lives in Brazil calls the country the land of the slaps. Because in order to defend ourselves against the mosquitoes at night, we have to continually slap ourselves left and right.' It was not just the mosquitoes they complained about. Rats, burrowers, cockroaches, vermin that crawled into the skin between the toes, and dogs that barked throughout the night, all of them were the dread of foreigners.

Other 'problems' specific to Brazil were those generated by the presence of Brazilians of African descent and the still numerous indigenous groups spread throughout the colony. For example, on 13 May 1808 the Prince Regent signed a royal decree ordering the governor of Minas Gerais to attack a cannibal group of Indians, the Botocudo.[75] The decree referred to the Indians as barbarians and cannibals who committed atrocious acts, 'not infrequently murdering Portuguese and peaceable Indians, wounding them and then sucking the blood from the wounds, often tearing up the bodies and eating the dreadful remains'. Dom João ordered the summary elimination of the group in the name of 'civilization', to protect a society that was 'meek' and 'peaceable'. There was also a great deal of fear regarding possible slave rebellions, a phenomenon that became known as 'Haitisim' in reference to the successful slave revolution in Haiti. This was a source of terror (among the elites) and of hope (among the enslaved). It is no wonder the elites vilified the Africans and their customs merely to justify holding them captive. The Marquis of Borba left a revealing statement, expressing the general opinion of the court: 'There is nothing so terrible as these blacks [. . .] This [town] is an infamous Babylon . . .'[76]

In the eyes of the racially prejudiced newcomers, the black population garnered significant attention: they were fundamental to the local economy, and thus were incorporated into every aspect of daily life in the colony. At the time slavery was still a powerful institution in both North and South America, still potentially growing as a system and politically sustainable. It was so common, it pervaded every public space, including the printed page, especially in the classified advertisements for sales and rentals. A typical communication in the *Gazeta do Rio de Janeiro*, of a type found nearly every day, ran thus:

Manoel Fernandes Guimarães, mulatto slave, escaped in 1804, thirty years old, known as Joaquim. Bought in the Captaincy of Espírito Santo by padre Antônio Gomes, can be recognized by the following signs: tailor and barber by trade, of average height, tightly knit hair, thick lips (the upper as thick as two) and pockmarked skin. Anyone with news of him wishing to denounce him should go to the house of Manoel Gomes Fernandes, Rua Direita no 26, where he will receive the reward of 40$000 rs.[77] [6/6/1810][78]

The enslaved people reacted by planning escapes, rebellions and assassinations – or else fighting back with irony, as in these verses directed against white corruption:

White master steals too
We black men steal chicken
Steal bags of beans
When white master steals
It's silver and coins
When we black men steal
It's prison for certain
White master when he steals
Ends up a baron.[79]

Africans and slaves worked in every kind of activity in Rio de Janeiro. They sold fruits and *angu* (a dish made of manioc flour boiled with water and salt), made delicacies, carried weight and litters – in the case of the latter, often fitted out in flamboyant livery – ran errands, sold newspapers, caught lice, worked as carpenters, or were hired out. This last constituted the largest group: slaves could be hired out for a day, a week or a month. They provided a variety of services: selling merchandise, carrying water and wood, transporting litters – all activities that were regulated by a code from the Senate.[80] The figures show how deeply rooted this type of labour was: in the 1820s the court owned around 38,000 slaves, at a time when the total population of Rio de Janeiro was only 90,000, a figure that did not include the free blacks, who were everywhere present throughout the public spaces of the city.

It was the largest concentration of slaves since ancient Rome, with the difference that, in Rio de Janeiro, their number equalled the number of inhabitants of European descent. In fact the balance tended to tip in favour of the enslaved: with the waves of captives brought in by the traffickers, the city became increasingly African in appearance. Near the Paço the concentration was such that the area became known as Little Africa. And there was no doubt that 'Rio de Janeiro looked like an African coastal town',[81] with different groups of Africans proudly displaying the distinct scars and markings of their nations on their faces and bodies. Paradoxically, the arrival of the royal family and the opening of the ports, rather than restricting the traffic, increased it.[82] The elites became so worried by the sheer number of Africans that policies were implemented 'to support the white population'. Couples were brought in from the Azores and given a monthly allowance, housing, tools, ox-drawn carts and everything else they required.[83]

The court also adapted to the city's routine of festivities, which were equally heterogeneous. There were seven main religious processions that shook up the city annually: St Sebastian, the patron saint of the city, on 28 January, eight days after his name day; St Anthony, on Ash Wednesday; Our Lord of the Via Crucis, on the second Thursday of Lent; the Triumph, on the Friday before Palm Sunday; the Burial on Good Friday; Corpus Christi in June and the Visitation on 2 July.[84] On these occasions the court and leading figures joined the parades in embroidered uniforms, accompanied by processions of soldiers, religious banners and singers from the Royal Chapel. There were also firework displays, public auctions, drum beating, fandangos, horse races, the burning of Judas on Holy Saturday, the feast of the Emperor of the Holy Spirit, royal birthdays, church holidays – anything that would interrupt the apparent calm of the city's routine.

This love of festivities was not a local invention. It was both a Portuguese and an African custom, in their countries of origin, to participate in royal and religious processions. Nevertheless, in this distant American colony, such festivities played an even more strategic and symbolic role. In his public appearances – whether in royal processions or in religious ones – the Prince Regent represented the Portuguese Empire itself, spread throughout the four corners of the globe and now governed from the colony.

Now the celebrations of the monarchy itself were added to the already busy calendar of festivities. On 16 December 1815, on the eve of the commemoration of Queen Dona Maria's eighty-first birthday, Dom João elevated Brazil to the title of the United Kingdom of Portugal, Brazil and the Southern Territories, transforming the colony into the seat of the Portuguese Empire. The measure was a tribute to the country in which he had lived for seven years. However, it was also motivated by political, economic and diplomatic considerations: it eased trade relations, met British demands, and was clearly aimed at preventing revolutions like those in British America and the neighbouring Spanish colonies. In other words, it was a move meant to protect Brazil from the process of independence, the creation of a republic, and from the ever-present danger of fragmentation.

Even with the decisions of the Congress of Vienna, revolutionary movements were brewing in Europe, revealing a fragile political order. Poland was going through a revolution; Russia was facing reforms; Prussia and Austria were still battling for Germanic hegemony; Sweden and Denmark were at odds over Norway; Belgium and Holland could not manage to remain united and, while Naples had become an experiment in liberalism, Spain was the seat of the extremists.

Europe abounded with instability – and this was grounds enough to dissuade Dom João from leaving the colony. In fact, the elevation of Brazil to a kingdom both defended the country's territorial integrity and provided a logical response to a series of problems. On the one hand, it was clear that some degree of autonomy was essential, since all negotiations were now conducted from the colony. On the other hand, Portugal's coalition partners received Dom João's measure with apprehension. They requested that the Prince Regent, once general peace had been established, restore the status of Portugal and its empire to a greater degree of 'normality'.

Thus, ruling the empire only looked easy from afar. When Brazil could find the time between festivities, the country was gradually breaking away from the restrictions of its imperial past. And it was no small feat. As a result of the Treaty of 1810, Rio de Janeiro had been transformed into an immense Brazilian trading post with an enormous quantity of products entering and leaving the port: textiles, metals, industrialized foods and even Spanish wine shipped from Britain; luxury items, trinkets, furniture, books, prints, butter, silk, candles and liqueurs from France; beer, glass, linen and gin from Holland; from Austria (including northern Italy and southern Germany), clocks, pianos, linen, silk and velvet fabrics, tools and chemical products; from the other German states, Bohemian glass, toys from Nuremberg, and brass and iron kitchenware; from Russia and Sweden, tools, copper, leather and tar; from the coast of Africa, specifically from Angola and Mozambique, powdered gold, ivory, pepper, ebony, wax (many kilos of which were consumed by the churches), dendê oil, gum arabic and – still, disturbingly – African slaves. Nonetheless, the trade was not one-sided anymore. For one thing, Brazil had begun to replace Lisbon in trade with Portugal's African colonies; and for another, products from India and China also stopped in Rio de Janeiro from where they were re-exported to Lisbon and other European ports, and to the rest of America. The main exports from the port of Rio de Janeiro included sugar, coffee, cotton and tobacco.[85]

Furthermore, Dom João's political situation was soon significantly altered. On 20 March 1816, after many years of mental illness, Dona Maria I died. Every day she had been taken around Rio de Janeiro in her litter, unable to recognize anything. The slaves who carried her had become used to her visions – she frequently insisted on getting out of the vehicle because there was a devil blocking the way.[86] Her death was the occasion for a full display of royal mourning.[87] The churches were wreathed in purple and decorated with Corinthian capitals, black velvet domes, and gold and silver cordons. A year's mourning was declared while the country waited impatiently for the acclamation of the king.[88]

The following year, 1817, brought on another round of mourning. In June, Antônio de Araújo de Azevedo (Count of Barca) – the politician who had so vehemently represented the interests and customs of France in the Portuguese government – also died. French cultural influences had steadily been revived and, since 1814, French fashions were now taking Brazil by storm. In the newspapers French immigrants offered their services as teachers of the language, promising miracles to anyone able to learn the language spoken at the Bourbon court, and French fashion designers dressed the young ladies of the tropical elite as if they resided in a calm, temperate climate. A constant flow of lace, gold and silver embroidery, plumes, fans, perfumes, jewels, hats, silk boots and shoes arrived from Paris. The Royal Press printed academic treatises in French as well as the first French novels to arrive in Portuguese America: *Le Diable Boiteux* (*The Devil on Two Sticks*) by Alain-René Lesage, translated in 1809, and *Paul et Virginie* by Bernardin de Saint Pierre, translated in 1811.[89] Nonetheless, it was only in 1815 with Napoleon's defeat that French literature became the predominant influence in Brazil, from hugely popular novels to the high culture of Voltaire's epic poem *La Henriade* and Racine's *Phèdre*. The presence of French works in Rio de Janeiro bookshops was radical, and included books on religion, philosophy, arts and sciences, geography and history, as well as novels, dictionaries and joke books.[90] As soon as diplomatic relations were re-established between the two countries, French products – elegant, but in some cases of curious usage – began to appear in the shops along the Rua do Ouvidor: wall clocks, crystal chandeliers, mahogany four-poster beds, sewing tables, tea tables, glasses, china, paper, fabrics and Chinese lacquer screens.

This taste for French literature and products increased in part because of yet another initiative during Antônio de Araújo's time at court. In 1816 he was responsible – if not for the invitation – for the warm welcome and housing of a group of French artists. In 1815 the Marquis of Marialva, who had been appointed as Portugal's new Trade Secretary to France, supported the idea that a number of famous artists within his circle should emigrate to Brazil. These were artists who had lost their jobs as a result of the fall of Napoleon and were afraid of possible political reprisals. In fact, the idea had come from the artists themselves, led by Joachim Lebreton, who had been Secretary of the Academy of Fine Arts. The government in Rio de Janeiro saw the request as an opportunity to bring artists to the colony and a means of improving its image in Europe; they thus helped to finance the group. The expectations of the French were high. They saw this not only as an opportunity to escape from a continent ruined by war but also to earn good money at the court and in a society where no formal artistic education existed. The undertaking was not without risk, however. The colony was remote and unknown and its ruler had declared war on Napoleon, who had previously been their greatest patron.[91]

They could not have foretold that Antônio de Araújo de Azevedo, the group's greatest supporter and its principal Maecenas, was to die soon after their arrival, causing their plans to create an Academy of Fine Arts on the French model to flounder. Without his presence the group faced both an indifferent reception and hostility from Brazilian and Portuguese artists who were furious at being passed over by a group of 'unemployed *Bonapartistes*'. There remained, however, plenty of opportunities. With the death of the queen and the preparations for the acclamation of the new sovereign, two events of fundamental importance in a monarchical state, the artists were soon to find employment constructing grandiose stage sets for the immigrant court.

Joachim Lebreton led the French Artistic Mission in Brazil, a group that included the painter Nicolas-Antoine Taunay and his brother, the sculptor Auguste-Marie Taunay, the painter of historical scenes Jean-Baptiste Debret, the architect Grandjean de Montigny and the engraver Simon Pradier. Apart from the wide range of specializations of its members, the group was also distinguished by the high quality of its artistic production.[92]

The group intended to establish a 'new artistic culture' in Brazil, free from the influence of the Church. Although there were plenty of artists and apprentices in the colony, there were no art schools. Since the eighteenth century, Brazilian art had been dominated by the Baroque, as exemplified by the churches in Rio de Janeiro, Recife, Salvador and, above all, Ouro Preto and Sabará. The exception was the mining town of Diamantina in the north of Minas Gerais, where the main example of Rococo architecture in Brazil could be found. Works of art were almost exclusively commissioned by the government or ecclesiastical authorities and had to comply with their requirements. Portugal itself lacked artists. Although there were academies, priority was not given to artistic activities, and there were very few artists who dedicated themselves to painting. This may have been the reason the court made the artists so welcome. They were seen as a kind of European vanguard, or, at the very least, talented and well trained in academic schools. Furthermore, they had been educated in the neoclassical style, which had been used in France to portray the Revolution for posterity.

Now the government of the newly formed kingdom planned to commission works from these artists to consolidate the image of the monarchy. It was a perfect fit. As the royal family was the sole patron of arts in the colony, the French group had no choice but to place themselves under their protection and execute work that they commissioned. The funeral ceremonies for the queen were followed by preparations for the celebrations of the arrival of the future Empress of Brazil, Caroline ('Maria') Josepha Leopoldine von Habsburg-Lothringen, in 1817, and the acclamation of Dom João in 1818. The artists also worked on major buildings and monuments, as well as temporary exhibitions for the commemoration of state events.

The first member of the group to receive a commission was the architect Montigny – who was to design the new Fine Arts Academy, a venture that in fact was constantly postponed. The most regular commissions were for work related to the public festivities, which the artists undertook with relative success. On the one hand, they had brought the neoclassical style from Europe, with grandiose works drawn from Antiquity. But on the other hand, despite the government's intention to recreate the metropolis in the new seat of the empire, it was by no means an easy task for the group to fit its classical forms into the context of a colonial port with a slave-based economy.[93] This was in late 1816, when it seemed the group of émigré artists were somewhat unlucky in their endeavours. And there were further difficulties ahead. The two celebrations planned for the beginning of 1817 – the acclamation of Dom João and the commemoration of the arrival of Princess Leopoldina (as she became known), the future wife of his son Dom Pedro – had to be abruptly postponed due to the revolution that broke out in Pernambuco on 6 March the same year. The temporary triumphal arches, the fragile stage sets and mock verandas would have to wait until peace was restored in Portugal's tropical domain.

AGITATION APPROACHING: MAY THE CORONATION BE DELAYED

If up to that time Dom João had considered his stay in his tropical colony as ideal, from 1817 a new reality was to interrupt his peaceful daily life. In addition to the obstacles caused by the revolutionary movements in Pernambuco, two additional conflicts disrupted the Prince Regent's foreign policy: the question of Cisplatina and the recurrent issue of abolishing the slave trade.

The transference of the seat of the Portuguese monarchy to Brazil opened another chapter in diplomatic relations. One of Dom João's first foreign-policy decisions in the colony was the official declaration of war against France. Subsequently, he sent an expedition to occupy Cayenne (present-day French Guiana), as a demonstration of his more offensive new posture. It is not known whether the new behaviour was a result of the royal family's transference to tropical lands; whether it was a consequence of discovering the movements of Junot's army; or whether it was part of the alliance with England. Nevertheless, motivated by the now formal belligerency, Dom João's government obtained a surrender from the French colony on 12 January 1809. The situation was maintained until the Congress of Vienna, when it was determined that Portugal was to return the annexed territory to France. Nonetheless, the restitution only took place two years later, in 1815.

Yet diplomatic problems were not limited to the local sphere. In Europe, Napoleon removed Carlos IV from the Spanish throne and stripped his heir, Fernando VII, of his rights. This led to the upheaval in America that precipitated the separation movements. In Brazil, Fernando VII's sister, Carlota Joaquina, had her eye on the Spanish colonies on the River Plate, of which she now saw herself as the rightful ruler. But her plans were thwarted because her husband, Dom João, had little reason to trust her. In 1811, when Cisplatina (today's Uruguay) began the process of independence, Dom João, under the pretext of supporting the province and blocking potential invasion, put the Portuguese troops on alert. Then, on 9 July 1816, when the United Provinces of the Rio de la Plata declared independence, the conflict intensified. These provinces had previously been held by the Spanish Viceroyalty with the capital in Buenos Aires. Once again the Portuguese government intervened: ostensibly to prevent invasions, the non-explicit intention was, however, to annex the so-called *Banda Oriental* to Brazil. The *Banda Oriental* was the portion of the Spanish Empire located on the east bank of the Uruguay river (where today Uruguay and Rio Grande do Sul, Brazil's southernmost state, are located). What was at stake was the control of the estuary, where all the commerce of the extreme south was concentrated. While Dom João was contemplating a sort of internal imperialism in the region under Portuguese control, Carlota Joaquina focused on the rights of the Spanish Crown.

Dom João took a pragmatic approach to foreign policy, generally falling back on a 'wait and see' approach, a maxim that was not easy to adopt when the question concerned the slave trade. Although abolished in Brazil in 1810 by the Peace and Friendship Treaty with Britain, such commerce was to be the topic of debate and campaigns for nearly half a century. According to Article 10 of that treaty, the Prince Regent declared himself 'convinced of the injustice and bad policy of the slave trade' and committed to adhering to the British policy of prohibiting slave-trafficking by Portuguese subjects outside of Portuguese domains in Africa. If this were not yet enough to satisfy Britain, which had abolished slave-trafficking within the British Empire and intended to do the same throughout its domains – thus favouring mercantile commerce – at the very least, it was now illegal to engage in the trade of black people. Thus, when slave traffic was conducted outside of the Portuguese domain, those ships could be legally confiscated. Yet no matter how well equipped the British navy was, it was impossible to capture all of the ships engaged in slave-trafficking, especially when it came to laissez-faire lusophone policies: everything was done just for show, only 'for the English to see'.

The question was complex, and Dom João's lack of resolve was apparent. In 1815 the topic of abolition once more came to the forefront. During the Congress of Vienna a clause abolishing the slave trade throughout the northern hemisphere was passed. Portugal thereby lost one of its main sources of slaves: the African countries north of the equator. Not only did the Prince Regent agree to abolish slave-trafficking north of the equator, he also introduced new laws regulating the treatment of the enslaved population in Brazil. However, in a society so permeated with the institution of slavery, such regulations were largely ignored. Between the legal statute and the reality there was an immense abysm, which was impossible to close solely through decrees. Furthermore, Dom João's attitude was always to placate all sides, as if to gain time in that increasingly lost cause. But the heat was on. Even the King of France, in a letter of 24 November 1818, urged 'your good brother and cousin' to abolish the slave traffic altogether. Some time later, after the Congress of Aix-La-Chapelle, where the suppression of the international slave trade was broached, other European nations were to apply similar pressure.

These measures not only affected the slave traffic, but the entire institution of slavery so integral to the running of the empire. For the first time the violence associated with the system was publicly denounced. The appalling conditions of the crossings were condemned, as well as the inhuman treatment of the slaves upon their arrival in Rio de Janeiro at the Valongo dock, less than a kilometre from the Royal Palace. In 1817 there were at least twenty 'depots' in the Valongo district where over a thousand captives, the majority of whom were boys and men between the ages of six and twenty-four, were simultaneously put on display.[94] But the authorities seemed little disposed to take any serious measures against such a degrading exhibition. The same year, in a new victory for the abolitionists, Britain began to inspect any ship suspected of transporting slaves on the high seas. The measures were valid for fifteen years, and Portugal agreed to cease their slave-trafficking operations with immediate effect. It was at once momentous and momentously insufficient.

The Prince Regent also suffered troubles on the domestic front with increasing dissatisfaction from several sources. A revolution broke out in Pernambuco in 1817, which rapidly became a thorn in the government's side. Up to that point, Dom João's empire had been largely united. Now the north was in revolt against the 'heavy taxes and excessive conscription' that came in the wake of the conquest of the Banda Oriental 'in which the Brazilian people have no part and which they judge to be contrary to their interests', in the words of Hipólito da Costa, who expressed the dissatisfaction throughout the colony from the offices of the *Correio* in London.[95] Expanding the empire to the south was sure to come at great cost. It led to both higher taxes and greater regional inequality. In the remoter parts of the colony people believed the arrival of the royal court had simply transferred domination by one distant city – Lisbon – to yet another, Rio de Janeiro. The captaincy of Pernambuco particularly was also suffering from the effects of the fall in sugar and cotton prices combined with a steady increase in the price of slaves. The situation was further exacerbated by the unpopularity of the governor, Caetano Pinto Montenegro, who was accused of cowardice and treachery.[96] He was lampooned in verse and prose: 'Caetano in name, Pinto in his lack of courage, Monte in height, and Black in actions.' Some blamed the unrest on the 'abominable French ideas' that circulated in Recife, inspiring a 'readers' revolution' based on authors like Raynal, Rousseau and Voltaire.[97] The rebels were also inspired by the ideas of the founding fathers of the United States; Cabugá (Gonçalves da Cruz), one of the rebel leaders, travelled there seeking support.[98]

Regardless of ideology, the movement was a reaction to the gravity of the crisis that afflicted the captaincy. That same year a general recession provoked in part by the fluctuation in prices of export crops led to increasing dissatisfaction. Further aggravation resulted from a drop in commodity prices – mainly sugar and cotton – on the London markets, coupled with a severe drought that destroyed the already inadequate subsistence crops. Local people blamed all their woes on the court's extravagant spending and excessive taxation. Thus, with no lack of motive, an insurrection united diverse groups, merchants and landowners, members of the clergy and the military, judges and artisans, as well as receiving widespread popular support from freemen and other members of the poorer classes. The rebels seized the city of Recife on 6 March and established a provisional government for the new Republic of Pernambuco, proclaiming equal rights and religious tolerance, but without touching on the tricky issue of slavery.

But while the city was adjusting, the Count of Arcos, who had been Viceroy of Brazil until Dom João's arrival, planned the government reaction. He acted quickly to crush the uprising, sending a force of more than 8,000 men from Rio de Janeiro to reinforce the local troops who were blockading the capital and adjacent ports. Faced with the prospect of overwhelming defeat, the rebels succumbed to bickering and discouragement. The internal conflicts soon led to an unsustainable situation. Meanwhile, the Prince Regent had been forced to postpone his acclamation and responded with all the force at his disposal.

On 19 May the Portuguese troops disembarked in Pernambuco, finding the capital city abandoned and with no leadership. As had occurred after the Minas Conspiracy in 1789 and the Conspiracy of Bahia in 1798, the monarchy provided a brutal demonstration of its political and symbolic power. Again, their repression was indescribable, exemplified by their violent enforcement of law and order. In Recife, Salvador and Paraíba the rebels were publicly executed and displayed in a grotesque manner intended to set an example: 'When they are dead their hands and heads shall be cut off and nailed to posts and the remains of their bodies tied to horses' tails and dragged to the cemetery.'[99] Once again the government of Portugal used an exaggerated ritual of repression to show the extent of its power. Nonetheless, the Pernambuco revolt was deeply rooted. There had been rebellion as far back as 1710. Such unrest was building an anti-colonial mindset against which the monarchy's theatrical display of brute force no longer had the effect it had achieved in the past.

ACCLAMATION AND MARRIAGE: A WEDDING AT THE COURT

With the defeat of the revolution in Pernambuco the Crown was confident that less turbulent, more stable times lay ahead. The plans for the acclamation of the new king could finally come to fruition. Dom João wanted to be certain the ceremony would leave nothing to be desired, including a solemn entry into the Royal Palace, the ceremonial kissing of the royal hand, and all the great festivities marking the occasion. Celebratory events took place as far north as Bahia, where the streets were decorated with lanterns, the church bells pealed, and cannons fired in salute of the Prince Regent's victory, acclaiming him king. On 6 February 1818 a decree was issued terminating the investigations into the rebellions in Pernambuco, finally putting an end to the conflict and reaffirming the magnanimity of the sovereign. Harmony had been restored between the monarch and his vassals. Or so it was hoped. Let the people celebrate – it was from them that the monarch's power derived.

The *Gazeta do Rio de Janeiro*, ever ready to extol the achievements of the monarchy, dedicated a special edition to the event.[100] On 10 February its commemorative edition hailed 'the glorious act of the Acclamation of Dom João VI, our August Sovereign and Model of Monarchs of the Universe'.[101] Torches, treats and beverages, fireworks, pictures of the royal family, and emblems of both America and Asia, all contributed to the festive atmosphere. By a convenient manipulation of the calendar, the sacred date of the Five Wounds of Christ was made to coincide with the date of the acclamation,[102] thereby dividing it between saints and kings. The contributions of the French artists further glorified the occasion. Grandjean de Montigny erected three neoclassical monuments evoking antiquity: a Greek temple to Minerva, an Egyptian obelisk and a Roman triumphal arch.[103] He was assisted in creating these grandiose settings in faux marble, granite and bronze by Auguste-Marie Taunay, Debret, and Marc and Zéphryn Ferrez.[104] The decorations were doubly symbolic: whereas the allegories and evocations of the classical world supplied a tradition the celebrations lacked, the materials from which they were made in fact reflected the ephemeral nature of the political moment.

People anxiously awaited the evening of 13 May 1818, when *Hymen*, a four-act allegory in praise of the Portuguese monarchy, was to be performed, and *Historical Ball*, an epic canvas by Jean-Baptiste Debret, was to be unveiled. The painting combined gods from classical mythology with members of the royal family. A regally attired Dom João was supported by allegorical figures representing the three nations – Portugal, Brazil and the Southern Territories – below which knelt Hymen and Amor, holding portraits of the prince and princess. Brazilian art had never known such pomp: Debret and Montigny spared no effort to confer the grandeur of classical antiquity on this empire adrift.

It was the first time that such a celebration had been seen in the New World. The Largo do Paço (Palace Square) was carefully prepared and crimson damask quilts were hung from the windows of the buildings along Rua Direita, together with other decorations. Every care was taken for the king to be in clear view to as many people as possible. The prince, now formally Dom João VI, finally presented himself as king. There he was, for his people to see, all decked out in the royal mantle of crimson velvet covered in gold, embroidery, and displaying the insignia of all his orders. At his side walked the heir to the throne Dom Pedro and his younger brother, the Infante Dom Miguel. The procession made its way to the Royal Chapel where a Te Deum was sung.[105]

Four towers had been erected in the Campo de Santana, a large park near the Praça da Republica. Each had twenty-four rooms, all of which were lit up, with groups of musicians playing symphonic music. At the centre of the gardens there was a square formed by sixteen statues and an artificial waterfall that fell in a cascade into a large tank full of exotic shells. To illuminate the scene, 60,000 lights had been installed: 102 aglets, 64 lanterns, a Chinese pavilion, pyramids with 400 candles and a theatre lit by 400 more.[106] The monarch's special guests were offered dessert, in a hall lined with damask, in sumptuous gold and silver bowls, while for the multitudes gathered outside there was an endless supply of sweets and drinks. Meanwhile, in the Teatro de São João, which had become the city's main venue for political manifestations, people waved handkerchiefs and sang hymns in tribute to the sovereign.

With the revolution in Pernambuco behind it, the monarchy once again turned to its plans for the arrival of Dom Pedro's wife.[107] The archduchess Caroline ('Maria') Josepha Leopoldine, niece of Marie Antoinette, guillotined in the French Revolution, arrived in the colony shortly before the acclamation. The marriage of the heir to the Bragança empire had involved negotiations at the highest diplomatic level on American soil. The Marquis of Marialva's mission in Vienna to find a wife for Dom Pedro had been successful[108] and all impediments to the union had been swiftly resolved. The prince's virtues were hard to ignore: his good looks, the nobility of his origin, the vast wealth and geographical extent of the Portuguese Empire, and his position as one of the few members of Europe's royal elite who was available to take a wife. Princess Leopoldina, on the other hand, despite her supposed lack of physical charms,[109] was well known for her intelligence, education and easygoing manner, but also for her determination. To show her commitment, as soon as the marriage contract had been signed, the future Princess of Brazil dedicated herself to the study of Portuguese as well as to the history, geography and economy of her future kingdom. She was particularly interested in mineralogy and botany. In her luggage she brought specimens of new plants to be acclimatized in Brazil.

The expenses of the Portuguese Embassy in the Austrian capital had included the distribution of jewels and gold bars to members of the court and and the Ministry of Overseas Affairs, and the hosting of a lavish party at the Augarten Imperial Gardens where the Marquis of Marialva had a dining room erected and gave a supper for four hundred guests. The wedding of the royal couple was celebrated on Dom João's birthday, without of course the presence of the bridegroom. On 13 June the group arrived in Florence to await the arrival of the Portuguese squadron that was to take the bride to Brazil. But there were a series of delays. In addition to the revolution in Pernambuco in 1817, Emperor Francis was concerned about his daughter's safety and refused to allow her to embark. He preferred to send her directly to Lisbon where she could join the royal family of which she was the latest member. Meanwhile the Austrian Foreign Minister, Metternich, strove to ward off pressure from the British, guaranteeing that the archduchess would fulfil the marriage agreement.

In Brazil, in the meantime, preparations had started again. The news of the royal wedding was celebrated with Masses and greeted with the pealing of bells, artillery salutes and prayers of thanksgiving. Tomás Antônio de Vilanova Portugal, the Business Secretary of the Kingdom, was placed in charge of organizing the event, which he proceeded to treat as a matter of utmost strategic importance to the government – which indeed it was. The Senate published a decree ordering the decoration of houses and windows and the cleaning of all the streets along which the procession would pass.[110] Montigny constructed a new triumphal arch bedecked with garlands of flowers and medallions on which the attributes of the princess were engraved.

With these festivities, the nation was symbolically founded. As the engineering of the ritual was perfected, it was the representation that created the reality – not the other way round. The policing of the streets was redoubled, pavilions were erected and ornaments were hung in the streets along which the procession was to pass. From the São Bento hillside to the Royal Chapel sand, aromatic herbs and petals were strewn along the ground and the houses adorned with flowers. Leopoldina came ashore at the Navy Arsenal and after greeting the royal family Dom Pedro took her by the hand. The royal procession was watched with great enthusiasm; everyone wanted to see the new princess. It was thirty degrees when, at three o'clock, the couple arrived at the main entrance to the Royal Chapel. The wedding ceremony lasted an hour. The court then left for the Palace.[111] Night was falling as the city was lit up and there was even a serenade sung to the princess. Dom Pedro, his sisters Princess Maria Teresa and the Infanta Maria Isabel took it in turns to sing an aria, and the musicians of the Royal Chamber joined with those of the Royal Chapel in performing a dramatic piece that lasted until two o'clock in the morning.

Despite the heat and the mosquitoes, Leopoldina adapted quickly to life in the colony. Very soon, to the general joy, it was discovered that she was with child. It was the first time that a royal heir was going to be born on Brazilian soil, a promising sign for the future stability of the distant and fragile kingdom in the Americas.

8

The Father Leaves, the Son Remains

The tide carried off what the tide brought in.

Oliveira Lima, 1945[1]

THE PORTO REBELLION: LIBERAL FOR PORTUGAL, CONSERVATIVE FOR BRAZIL

In 1814, after Napoleon's defeat by the allied forces, the political situation in Europe seemed to have finally settled down. Everything pointed to the return of the 'old order' with the strengthening of the power of the monarchies under the political command of the Holy Alliance, mainly in the European territories. Nonetheless, Dom João's decision to prolong his sojourn in the New World was seen as an indication that he was gradually putting down roots in his American colony. The king's 'transformation into a Brazilian' was under way: in 1808 he established the open-ports policy; in 1815 he elevated the colony to the status of 'United Kingdom'; and in 1816 he was preparing himself to be consecrated as Dom João VI, King of Portugal, Brazil and the Algarves. All of this took place in this tropical colony.

However, in a short period the situation was to change dramatically. In Brazil the insurrections of Minas Gerais in 1789, of Bahia in 1798 and of Pernambuco in 1817 had made it clear that emancipation movements were now a major force in political experiments and local utopias. By then, the British Americas had become virtually independent, with the exception of the islands of the Caribbean, Equatorial Guiana and the cold domain of Canada. In the Spanish Americas, except for the Antilles, the prospect of independence was becoming increasingly real. 'Abominable French ideas' and American republican principles were spreading throughout the colonies, upsetting long-held certainties and ingrained beliefs.

Meanwhile the same revolutionary breeze was beginning to blow in Lisbon. At the beginning of the French invasion, in 1807, and particularly after Dom João declared war against Napoleon on 1 May 1808, there had been popular demonstrations in support of the Bragança dynasty. Two further Napoleonic invasions, in 1809 and 1810, intensified the widespread hostility towards the French. It almost seemed as if, in spite of the uprisings, Napoleon's troops were unwilling to accept defeat, could not resist the attempt to control the now kingless metropolis. Meanwhile, the Anglo-Portuguese forces' final expulsion of the French towards the end of 1810 fundamentally modified the situation: with the re-establishment of Portuguese sovereignty, there was no longer any justification for the king to remain in Brazil. Faced with King João's apparent inertia with regard to returning to Lisbon, the last demonstrations of blind loyalty to the monarch from the Portuguese population gave away to general indignation.

To make matters worse, a crisis now engulfed the Portuguese state. Crops failed, coins became scarce, paper currency lost its value, and the credit offered by other European countries vanished. According to the Portuguese elites, to re-establish Portugal's wealth and stability Brazil's increasing autonomy would have to be reined in. Not only did they attribute the growing financial disasters to Brazil, they also accused their 'Brazilian brothers' of neglect: 'From Brazil they sent us neither troops, nor money, nor meat, nor flour, nor sugar, nor rice [. . .] nor indeed anything at all.'[2] Deprived of the resources of its overseas dominions, without profits from colonial trade and humiliated by its dependence on Britain, Portugal had been relegated to a secondary position within its own imperial system. Even the king seemed oblivious to the plight of its citizens. The crisis was economic, political and symbolic. The Portuguese elite believed that in order to avoid irreversible, radical consequences a gesture of great symbolic importance was now essential: the return of the king.

Within this context the 1820 Liberal Revolution of Porto broke out. The revolution represented two different aspirations. On the one side were the constitutionalists, who proposed that the constitution delineate the fundamental laws of the state, a general system of government, and the regulation of the rights and duties of citizens. Their slogan was *'Cortes e Constituição'* ('Courts and Constitution'). On the other side were the monarchists, who defended a sovereign national monarchy – which, in this case, meant the immediate return to Portugal of Dom João VI or, even better, of the whole royal family. These opposing factions in Portugal developed within a broader divide. One faction defended the ideal of political 'Regeneration', a shaking-up of Portuguese despotism. Supporters of this movement promoted freedom, constitutionalism and constitutional liberalism. The other faction demanded 'realistic restoration', the return and strengthening of monarchic regimes as proposed by France and the coalition formed by Russia, Austria and Prussia. Representatives of these countries, better known as the Holy Alliance, met at the Congress of Vienna between 1814 and 1815.

This polarization was the background from which a liberal, nationalist, constitutionalist movement now emerged. Their goal was clear: to restore the Portuguese-Brazilian Empire, based on a constitution, and to ensure that Portugal maintained its political and economic control at all costs. It goes without saying that these ideas were not well received in Brazil. They indicated that Lisbon was still unable to see beyond the traditional colonial structure and was only concerned with guaranteeing its own interests. The dream of a Luso-Brazilian Empire had almost come to an end.

It is hard to see how the Portuguese Revolution of 1820 could have been anything but a paradox. It was late in coming: participants in the Congress of Vienna were already imposing conservative measures across the continent of Europe. Nevertheless, new ideas and social practices were introduced: the intention of the revolutionaries was to establish a constitutional monarchy that would put an end to the *ancien régime*, although they viewed the king, rather than the nation, as the central force in this new society. Lastly, but no less importantly, they preferred the concept of 'regeneration' to that of 'revolution'.[3]

With the arrival of Reason and Light on the political scene, a new political language emerged. In Portugal, the term 'liberal' had been adopted after the *Cortes de Cádiz* – the assembly of Spain's *Cortes Generales* that had met in exile in Cádiz in 1810 and proposed the abolition of the *ancien régime*. In this context a 'liberal' was a person who defended the 'good of the Fatherland' in everything he did – a proponent of law and order, a believer in the freedom of expression and influential in public administration. This new political agenda included concepts such as the social contract, the importance of the constitution, and the autonomy and sovereignty of Parliament. In the Portuguese context, liberalism allowed for the recognition of the rights of others and a constitutional political system, which stood in contrast to the *ancien régime* model.

The works written by the 'fatal' encyclopedists – the group of eighteenth-century French Enlightenment intellectuals, including Rousseau, Montesquieu and Diderot – circulated within the kingdom despite systematic repression: books were burnt, banned from circulation or confiscated and locked away inside public libraries. The Portuguese press published abroad also did much to regenerate revolutionary ideas in Portugal. Chief among these publications was the *Correio Braziliense*, published in London by Hipólito José da Costa between 1808 and 1822, and banned in Portugal between 1811 and 1817. But there were several others, including the *Investigador Português em Inglaterra*, founded in 1812 in opposition to the *Correio*, but which changed its position in 1814; *O Português ou Mercúrio Político, Comercial e Literário* (the most contentious, and for this reason the most censored); and the *Campeão português* (the most doctrinaire of the journals, banned in 1819). These periodicals all actively sought to disseminate liberal ideas. A taste of their rhetoric can be seen in this example published in *O Português* on 30 April 1814:

> While great revolutions spread across Europe, only the Portuguese government [. . .] sleeps deeply, on the edge of the abyss [. . .] erecting an impenetrable wall to block out the lights that come from our neighbours, as though they were contraband.[4]

Despite their differences, the various periodicals embarked on a campaign of enlightenment, uniting in their demand for a Portuguese constitution. It is no coincidence that, in June 1820, a month before the revolution occurred, *O Campeão* appealed to the king: 'Awake, father, and hurry; if you don't hurry, there may be no one left to save.'[5]

Dom João, however, remained immune to such appeals, preferring to remain in his palace in São Cristóvão in Rio de Janeiro, even if the price to pay was the adoption of a constitutional regime in Portugal.[6] However, with the climate as it was in Europe, decisions could no longer depend entirely on the wishes of the king. On the one hand, the movements in favour of 'regeneration' sought to establish a liberal constitutional monarchy as the best solution for Portugal – in which the role of the king would be limited and the actual control of the government would be the responsibility of Constitutional Courts.[7] On the other hand, more radical groups were already openly discussing a change in the dynasty or even in the political regime. Nevertheless, 'freedom' was still a rare word in Portugal, where newspapers were censored and secret societies persecuted.

However, it was precisely in these clandestine meetings, especially societies associated with the Masonic lodges, that the revolution was hatched. In Porto, on 22 January 1818, a group of nobles and property owners, many of whom were lawyers, formed a secret society that they called the Sanhedrin.[8] Although the movement expanded during the next few years, it had no clearly defined revolutionary goals.[9] The profile of its members was sufficient explanation for their moderation. Furthermore, the society never questioned the legitimacy of the House of Bragança. The members of the military who joined the insurgents in 1820 were equally cautious, and for the same reason. But the radicalization of the movement was unstoppable and on the morning of 24 August 1820 revolutionary troops seized the Campo de Santo Ovídio, Porto's main plaza and barracks. After the formation of a provisional government, the Constitutional Courts were convened for the first time since 1698 and given the task of preparing a new constitution. The House of Bragança was to be spared but the royal family's immediate return to Portugal was demanded as a question of national honour. An outdoor Mass was held, soldiers and citizens applauded the speeches and cannon salutes were fired. And thus began the Liberal Revolution of 1820.

The Courts appointed a Constitutional Assembly made up of members of the nobility and the bourgeoisie, including members of the clergy and military officers, all of whom were drawn from the ranks of the Sanhedrin society. But new converts to the cause were needed, and it was not difficult to find them. Naturally there was disagreement between the 'revolutionaries' and 'realists'. Nonetheless, the movement continued to gather momentum and, on 15 September 1820, Lisbon joined the revolution. On 1 October the Provisional Constitutional Assembly decreed its first measures, which changed censorship laws and established elections of the deputies who were to write the new Imperial Constitution. The Courts were then established as the principal representatives of the nation, and elections were to be regulated. Throughout 1821 and 1822 the Constitutional Courts consolidated the clauses of the new constitution, while upholding the fundamental role of the monarchy.

The elected deputies began by establishing the internal procedures of the Courts, appointing commissions and establishing a new regency government. The work began on 26 January 1821 with a full agenda, including freedom of the press, new civil and criminal codes, the abolition of the Inquisition, a reduction in the number of religious orders and amnesty for political prisoners. Since the Middle Ages the Courts had been an institution for consultation. Now, faced with the responsibility of reconstructing the country, they acted as an executive body. The plan was to get the political support of the entire Portuguese Empire for the proposed Regeneration. In the north of Brazil the captaincies of Pará and Bahia immediately joined the Portuguese cause. As King João continued to postpone a decision, the opinions of his advisers and ministers were divided. Some thought either he or his son should depart for Lisbon immediately. Others believed he should remain, arguing that it was better to be a complete monarch in Brazil than half a monarch under a constitutional monarchy in Portugal. And there were still others who realized that a liberal revolution in Portugal would lead to greater freedoms for the colony as well.

The national debate occurred even among men close to the king. The Count of Palmela,[10] for example, upon his return to Rio de Janeiro in December 1820, suggested that the king's son, Dom Pedro, should be sent back to Portugal instead of the king himself. The Count of Palmela believed King João's absence would have disastrous consequences for the colony. Tómas Antônio de Vila Nova Portugal, the king's closest adviser, thought the monarch should impose his authority by simply remaining where he was and demanding obedience and submission from Portugal. The Count of Arcos, Minister of the Navy, was more pragmatic; he had little doubt that the king's days in the colony were numbered.

There was also disagreement among the various political factions. The 'Portuguese party' in Rio de Janeiro was in favour of the king's return to Lisbon. The members were high-ranking military officers, merchants and bureaucrats, whose interests were best served by a return to the old colonial system with the subordination of Brazil to Lisbon. The 'Brazilian party', on the other hand, wanted the king to stay in Brazil. This faction was made up of owners of rural estates in the captaincies surrounding Rio de Janeiro, bankers, military officers and members of the government and the judiciary who had been born in Brazil. They began to draw up plans for a 'government independent from Portugal'. The third group was known as the 'democratic party'. Its members included most of the clergy and the civil service whose goal was to establish 'independent provincial governments'.[11]

These were not exactly 'parties', at least not in the modern sense of the word, but rather associations of people with similar opinions and interests that positioned themselves in favour of or against certain political practices. The word 'party' had a negative connotation at the time because it was linked to the notion of political factions and groups that promoted public disorder. As a matter of fact, throughout 1821–2 the term 'parties' was used to describe various groups expressing their discontent. The newspapers referred to the complaints of the *Paulista* party', the 'ultra party', the 'European party', the 'colonial oppression party' and the party of 'demagogues and anarchists'. In general, these so-called parties could be divided into two broad categories. The first, predominant in Rio de Janeiro, was made up of Portuguese military officers and merchants loyal to the Courts in Lisbon. The second adopted a more independent stance and looked to the king's son, Dom Pedro, for leadership. The role of the Masonic lodges became increasingly important for the latter group, serving as its political voice and a catalyst for discontent.[12]

For his part, King Dom João was still in doubt. He was neither prepared to return to Portugal nor to send his son – an alternative plan, incidentally, that was known to everyone except the prince himself. Married and with children of his own, Dom Pedro was kept completely in the dark. During this period, a pamphlet, written in French, began to circulate in the court, entitled 'In the present circumstances, should the King and the Bragança family return to Portugal or remain in Brazil?'[13] The ideas in the pamphlet were based on those of Tomás Antônio de Vila Nova Portugal who, as mentioned above, was opposed to the king and his family's return to Portugal. The pamphlet's argument went as follows: 1) Portugal needed Brazil more than the other way round; 2) the departure of the royal family would be a catalyst for independence; 3) Dom João could consolidate his authority in Brazil, from where he could found an empire with worldwide political influence; 4) in Lisbon, Dom João would be a hostage of the rebels; 5) he could better control the prosperous Portuguese Empire from Brazil; and 6) he could implement the changes currently being demanded at some future date. The authorship of the document was attributed to the French emigré Lieutenant-Colonel Francisco Cailhé de Geines. However, within court circles it was known that it had been written on the instructions of Tomás Antônio de Vila Nova Portugal, with the acquiescence of the king.[14]

At that time, pamphlets – both printed and in manuscript – were one of the few available means for disseminating political opinions and information on controversial topics.[15] Those circulating throughout 1821 and 1822 revealed an emerging population of engaged citizens, and they adopted a new political vocabulary. Pamphlets could be written to undermine the legitimacy of royal authority as well as to support it, to question the ties between Brazil and Portugal, or to promote the permanence of the Portuguese Brazilian Empire. Most of these documents were written in Bahia and Rio de Janeiro to encourage citizens to become involved, arguing that it was no longer possible to remain on the margins of these debates. The positions of the two captaincies were radically different. Initially, Bahia, whose trade was almost entirely carried out directly with Portugal and Africa, was against British 'interference'[16] and in favour of the Courts. Rio de Janeiro, on the other hand, which had been the greatest beneficiary of Dom João VI's government, placed all its bets on Dom Pedro remaining in the colony.

At the beginning of 1821 it was deemed fit to at last inform Dom Pedro that his departure for Lisbon was virtually certain. Despite the fact that his wife, Princess Leopoldina, was eight months pregnant and the two would have to be separated, the prince was delighted with the idea. He saw it as a chance to make his triumphal entry into the political scene. But he did not depart, not at that time. The idea seems to have been a manoeuvre to give Dom João yet another excuse to procrastinate; nevertheless, he made haste to comfort his daughter-in-law, fearing that the idea of her husband's departure could affect the birth of his future grandson. The situation rapidly came to a head. In February 1821, Dom João found himself obliged to swear fealty to the new constitution, his final official act in Brazil. With the prospect of the weakening of his royal authority, the monarch was assailed by another attack of chronic indecision. Then on 7 March the Courts in Lisbon issued decrees determining the return of the king to Portugal, with his son Dom Pedro to remain in Brazil as regent; furthermore, rules were set in place for the election of the Brazilian deputies who would represent the colony in Lisbon.

The situation, which was already serious, became explosive. On 21 April 1821, in one of Rio de Janeiro's main civic buildings, located on the Praça do Comércio, a meeting of the electorate was abruptly interrupted with shouts of 'Let the People rule Brazil!' and 'Revolution!' The crowds demanded that Dom João VI sign the Spanish Constitution of Cádiz of 1812, and remain in the country. While the king hesitated and was inclined to agree, his son ordered the demonstration to be crushed. Maria Graham, the princes' tutor, described the attack, lamenting the thirty deaths and many wounded.[17] The next day the words 'Bragança Butcher' appeared scrawled across the building's façade.

When the court finally departed on 26 April 1821 there was one person who seemed delighted to leave: Queen Carlota Joaquina, who had never concealed her dislike of court life in Rio de Janeiro. Only Dom Pedro remained behind as the monarchy's arm in Brazil. A retinue of ministers, court officials, diplomats and their families, estimated at four thousand people, left along with the king. The Brazilian deputies followed a few months later. 'To go or not to go, to stay or not to stay' – that was the tropical 'Shakespearean' dilemma the king had to face.

Dom Pedro, who now took on the hopes and ambitions for the future of Brazil, was twenty-two. In his last documented conversation with his father the king, it was clear as they parted that their lack of intimacy was surpassed only by the distance between them. There they were, face to face, the hesitant King Dom João VI and the wilful regent, Dom Pedro. It was on 24 April and in two days 'el-rei' would finally embark with the rest of the family back to Portugal. The regent was then summoned to his father's room, where the famous discussion of very few words took place. Our only source for what the king said on the occasion is a letter written by the prince to the king the following year: 'I still recall and will always recall what Your Majesty said to me in your room two days before your departure: Pedro, if Brazil breaks away, better it be by your hand, with the respect you have for me, than by the hand of one of these adventurers.' It is impossible to say whether these words, endlessly repeated in the official version of Brazilian history books, were actually spoken. Memory is always tricky, and whether or not Dom João said that to Dom Pedro, and whether or not Dom Pedro later recalled the conversation, is open to debate. What we do know is that in his decree of 22 April 1821, King Dom João VI uses the word '*saudade*' – 'longing' – a sentimental word of many meanings in the Portuguese language: 'It has become indispensable in order to provide for the government and administration of this Kingdom of Brazil, which I leave with such strong feelings of *saudade*, that I return to Portugal . . .'[18]

It is said that when he left, on 26 April 1821, Dom João was overcome with such a jolt of sadness that, slumped in his bergère, the poor man barely spoke. He proposed a short stop in Salvador on the pretext of giving the order that the new government must be obeyed. But this time, even the king's adviser, the Count of Palmela, thought enough was enough. It was better to clean out the public coffers and carefully transport the treasury arks and the safes from the Banco do Brasil. The king alone carried with him over 60 million cruzados in minted gold and in bars. Not to mention the diamonds stored in the fortified houses of the Banco do Brasil. In the streets, the people, who once again followed the exodus of the Portuguese court, came up with satirical poems: '*With eyes a-sparkle/and steps so light/we board the ship/with wealth in sight.*'

DOM PEDRO'S RETURN

While Dom João VI and his retinue travelled back to Portugal, the new constitutional assembly in Lisbon debated the articles pertaining to the monarchy. An indication of the importance of the king's return was their order to resuscitate the *Regimento de Entradas em Lisboa*, the historical ceremony devised to celebrate the return of Dom Manuel I on 30 August 1502. The Courts intended to invest the monarchy once again with the aura of the kings from the era of the Great Discoveries. As part of the ceremony, King Dom João VI was handed the keys to the city.

Although the king was received with pomp and circumstance, he was in no doubt as to where real power now lay. Before disembarking on 4 July, he received delegations from the regency and the Courts. In a display of strength, the latter forbade the arrival of eleven of the king's advisers, who were considered 'dangerous'. These included the Count of Palmela, the minister Tomás de Vilanova Portugal and Joaquim José de Azevedo, the Viscount of Rio Seco, all of whom were sent back to Brazil. In this ongoing tug of war it was the *vintistas*,[19] as the Portuguese revolutionaries were known, who won. On the very same day, the king was obliged to appoint a new Cabinet, which replaced the regency; and to become a constitutional monarch, which changed his political status. But if anyone believed the symbolism of the monarchy could be diminished, they were mistaken. The entrance of the sovereign into Lisbon, accompanied by the queen and the Infante Dom Miguel, was heralded as a triumphal event and on 5 July, although hostage to circumstances, the monarch was received in Lisbon as the greatest trophy of Portugal's victory.

Although Dom João VI accepted the new situation, Carlota Joaquina did not. She was radically opposed to the revolution and the attack on royal prerogative. She was the only member of the royal family who refused to swear an oath of loyalty to the new Constitution in 1822. She was confined to the Palácio do Ramalhão in Sintra,[20] but never lost her nerve. She wrote to her husband from the palace, decrying those who 'surrounded and tricked' him. Meanwhile, although he remained at a distance in Brazil, Dom Pedro was not his father's puppet. He had his own desires. Thus, at first he became an easy target for the local elites, who, fearful of the progress of the revolution in Portugal, were trying to preserve their societal advantages.[21]

But the new regent soon rolled up his shirtsleeves and got down to work, transitioning from the wings to centre stage. In its first proclamation, which seems to have been written by the Conde dos Arcos, the interim government approved a series of reforms in education, agriculture and commerce, and warned that it expected 'strict adherence to the laws' and 'constant vigilance'. The practical effect of the measures may have been small, but they achieved what the new regent intended: to make his presence felt. It was a time of caution; no one yet knew what the consequences of the events in Portugal would be. The Courts in Lisbon now proposed replacing the concept of two autonomous kingdoms governed by one monarch with that of a single kingdom, divided into two parts: European and American.

The Courts were in a hurry to see their plans implemented and requested that a Brazilian delegation be sent to Portugal. The first reaction came as a pleasant surprise. Not only did Rio de Janeiro and Bahia – the former capitals of the viceroyalty – enthusiastically support constitutionalism, but even the northern province of Pará, which was administered separately from the rest of the colony, followed suit. The Liberal Revolution was initially welcomed in Brazil as part of the struggle for freedom against the despotism of the *ancien régime*. Brazilians were not yet aware of the strength of the movement to recolonize the country – the Portuguese elites were only in favour of constitutionalism in Brazil if it were to be subordinated to their own.

But at the outset the colony's reaction was positive and Brazil began the process of electing its deputies to the Courts. Instructions issued on 22 November of the previous year were clear: all citizens of the empire were considered eligible with the exception of state counsellors and employees of the royal court. There was to be one deputy for every 30,000 inhabitants. In the case of Brazil, governing assemblies loyal to the revolution were to be installed in the various captaincies, which were from then on to be known as provinces.[22] Population figures were based on the numbers for 1808, the year of the court's arrival, when it was estimated at 2,323,386 inhabitants. Thus, the country had the right to elect seventy-seven deputies (although in fact only forty-six attended the sessions). Portugal had the right to one hundred deputies, Madeira and the Azores to nine, and the African and Asian possessions to seven (Cape Verde, Bissau and Cacheu; Angola and Benguela; São Tomé and Príncipe; Mozambique; Goa; Macau, Timor and Solor).[23]

The deputies from Pernambuco were the first arrive in Lisbon, on 29 August 1821. Among them were Muniz Tavares[24] and Araújo Lima.[25] The delegations from Rio de Janeiro and Bahia also included important Brazilian figures – in the former the future Marquis of Paranaguá,[26] and in the latter Cipriano Barata de Almeida[27] and Francisco Agostinho Gomes.[28] Members of the São Paulo[29] delegation, however, were the only ones to have done their homework. They brought a list of explicit instructions, which bore the hallmark of José Bonifácio[30] and the subjects that concerned him most: the abolition of slavery and the catechization of the Indians. The São Paulo delegates included Antônio

Carlos Ribeiro de Andrada Machado e Silva (perhaps the most talented of José Bonifácio's brothers). The Andrada Machado e Silva brothers were the sons of a rich and well-connected merchant from Santos. José Bonifácio was a well-known intellectual and statesman. He had spent many years in Portugal where he had studied and been a professor at Coimbra, and he had held important administrative posts. The document the São Paulo delegation brought with them also stipulated that the two kingdoms be represented by the same number of deputies and that the seat of the monarchy alternate between the two. But it received little attention. The Courts had been in session since January 1821 and one of their first measures had been the subordination of local governments to Lisbon and the revocation of the trade agreements signed during King Dom João VI's reign. The lack of agreement between Portugal and Brazil was all too clear from the outset, and the rift between the two was only to be widened by the intransigence of the Courts. Those who had travelled to Portugal in the hope of participating in a debate about principles of equality before the law and the rights of Brazil were frustrated: for many of the Portuguese deputies the colony was nothing more than 'a land of monkeys, bananas and little Negroes harvested from the coast of Africa'.[31]

In Brazil the situation was equally unstable. Whereas in Pernambuco and Bahia the groups in power supported Portugal's policy, in Rio de Janeiro they were divided into two – the Conservatives, linked to José Bonifácio, and the radicals, who were led by Joaquim Gonçalves Ledo.[32] Dom Pedro, now the new Prince Regent, oscillated between attending to local concerns and loyalty to his father. In a display of filial devotion, he sent letters to the king in which he expressed affection and concealed his doubts: 'My daughter asks after her grandfather every day, she's already walking; my son is now holding his head up and is larger and stronger.'[33] Dom Pedro faced many difficulties, not least finding ways of solving the financial difficulties he had inherited. The problem had been caused by the hurried departure of the royal family and was further aggravated by the appalling situation of the Banco do Brasil, once again on the verge of bankruptcy.

Dom Pedro's notoriety as a seducer also dates from this time. In less prudent letters to his father he mentioned his extramarital indiscretions in the palace and how his behaviour had set the servants' tongues wagging. The prince was equally romantic about his political participation, and was anxious for an important role in imperial politics. Perhaps this is the reason why he was infected by the nationalist fever that began to take hold of most of the Brazilian deputies in Portugal, a fever that had made its way back to Brazil. This change in attitude had been provoked by the Portuguese Courts: on 13 July 1821 they established the provisional assemblies that proceeded to revoke the laws of King João's reign, including that which appointed his son Dom Pedro as head of the 'general government and entire administration of the Kingdom of Brazil'. Between late September and October 1821 a number of measures issued by the Portuguese Courts made their real intentions clear: to transfer Brazil's main government departments to Lisbon. New contingents of troops were sent to Rio de Janeiro, and finally, on 29 September, a decree was signed demanding the Prince Regent's return to Portugal. Initially Dom Pedro replied that he would respect the order and that he 'no longer wanted to influence events in Brazil'.[34] But the Courts' decrees came as a shock to Brazilian politicians and Dom Pedro was not to keep to his word.

The Courts also determined that Brazil's provinces be transformed into Portuguese overseas provinces, thus Rio de Janeiro would no longer be at the centre of a unified Brazil. Any requirement for the Prince Regent to remain in Brazil was nullified. On 14 December 1821, Don Pedro wrote to his father: 'the publication of the decrees caused great shock among Brazilians to the point that they have taken to the streets saying: if the constitution is doing us harm then it can go to the devil.' The prince hurriedly added that he would unquestioningly respect the decrees but, at the same time, would remain 'sensible' if he were 'obliged by the people not to entirely fulfil such sovereign instructions'.[35] There was pressure from every side. If he left, Brazil would declare independence; if he stayed, it would remain united, but would no longer accept orders from the Portuguese Courts. In the last of his letters to his father in 1821, Dom Pedro wrote, 'before the opinion [in favour of independence] was not general, but now it is very deep-rooted'.

The year 1822 began with few certainties and many doubts. The Brazilian party was doing everything it could to make sure the prince remained in Brazil, as were the radical groups, some of which started publishing periodicals whose entire focus was to persuade him to stay. Although previously there had been conflict, for the prince to remain in Brazil was now the unanimous position of all parties. But as communications took two months to arrive from Lisbon, Dom Pedro remained cautious. He too suffered from the Bragança family's infamous indecisiveness. His wife, Princess Leopoldina, decided to add to the pressure; she found him 'not as positively decided as I would wish'.[36]

With time, the princess was to become one of the great influences favouring Brazil's emancipation from Portugal and Dom Pedro's disobedience to the Courts; she seemed apprehensive of Portuguese constitutionalism and the corrosion of monarchical power. The Brazilian party needed to sway Dom Pedro with a symbolic act, the natural procedure of any person or group preparing an historical event. The *Clube da Resistência* (Resistance Club) was founded in Rio de Janeiro, São Paulo and Minas Gerais on 9 December 1821 following the arrival of the decrees from Portugal ordering Dom Pedro to return to Lisbon immediately. The leader of the Brazilian party, Gonçalves Ledo, suggested that the president of the Senate, José Clemente Pereira, sound out Dom Pedro as to how he would react to a formal request to stay. Then, on 1 January 1822, José Bonifácio sent the regent a letter formally petitioning him to remain and not to 'become the slave of a small number of destroyers'.[37] José Bonifácio, who had been vice-president of the Provisional Junta of São Paulo since June 1821, was exerting increasing influence over the regent.

On 9 January, at a reception for the Senate held at the Royal Palace, Dom Pedro was handed a formal petition with over eight thousand signatures asking him not to leave for Portugal. The objective was clear: to guarantee the presence of the heir to the throne in Brazil, in an attempt to attenuate the wave of colonialist sentiment enveloping Portugal. It was on this occasion that Dom Pedro allegedly uttered his famous words, 'Tell the people I will stay.'[38] Whether he actually spoke them or not is in doubt. A second declaration was annexed to the minutes. According to the first rendering, the prince in fact replied: 'Convinced that the presence of my person in Brazil is in the interest of the good of the entire Portuguese nation, and knowing that it is the wish of some of the provinces, I shall postpone my departure until the Courts and my August Father and Lord deliberate in this regard, in full knowledge of the circumstances that have occurred'. In a postscript, however, the document states that these were not the regent's exact words, and that they should be replaced with the following: 'As it is for the good of all and for the general happiness of the nation, I am ready.

Tell the people I *will stay*.'[39] Whether these last words were spoken or not, the prince then proceeded to the palace balcony and declared: 'And now, all I can recommend is union and tranquillity.' Interestingly enough, it is precisely the phrase 'I will stay' that does not appear in the Senate records for the next day, 10 January, which state that on the previous day pronouncements had been published 'with considerable alterations to the words', motivated by the 'joy that took hold of all those in the audience room'.[40] Politics often is subject to different versions of events – in this particular case, the most resonating phrase has remained. At any rate, let us stick with the second declaration, since Dom Pedro's 16 February letter to the Portuguese Courts declared his intention to stay put, and that Brazil wanted 'to be treated as a brother, not as a son; a sovereign with Portugal, not a subject; independent [. . .] as she is, and nothing less.'

Despite the uncompromising terms of the letter, it is important to remember that the majority of the Brazilian elite still wanted to stay with Portugal, as long as Brazil could preserve the autonomy it had achieved. This was the position of the conservative administration surrounding José Bonifácio, which was seeking a moderate solution. These conservatives were opposed by radical groups in favour of a new form of representation, perhaps even republican. Despite the differences between the factions, the new direction was self-evident: the old order would not return. It was, however, a two-way process, resulting from events both inside Brazil and abroad: on the one hand the intransigence of the Portuguese Courts and on the other the growing awareness in Brazil that independence was now the only available course. Some even think that, at this point, Portugal actually wanted to be rid of Brazil and its provocations. The fact of the matter is that incidents flared up on both sides of the Atlantic in the short period between Dom Pedro's symbolic promise to stay and his famous declaration of independence on 7 September on the banks of the Ipiranga river.

INDEPENDENT, *SORT OF*

It is possible to speculate that, without the policies of the Courts, pro-independence sentiment would have taken much longer to emerge in Brazil. Bahia had still not forgiven Rio de Janeiro for taking its place

as capital of the viceroyalty and, while the northern provinces continued to clamour for a capital in the region, in the south there was a
faction demanding that it be transferred to São Paulo. Nonetheless,
there is nothing like a common enemy from the outside to bring adversaries together. Dom Pedro, ever more conscious of his role, declared he
was 'tired of the insolence',[41] and public opinion had begun to assimi-
late the notion of independence. The Brazilian Army – called *Exército
de 1a Linha* (1st Line Army) – was established in response to the Portuguese troops having refused to swear loyalty to Dom Pedro. A new
ministry was also formed. Among the decrees issued by the new
government was one that forbade the expedition led by Francisco Max-
imiliano e Sousa to disembark in Rio de Janeiro on 9 March. He had
been sent by Portugal to take Dom Pedro back to Lisbon, to be escorted
by a squadron like the one that had sailed with his father.

In the meantime, the Courts were hearing various reports on the
prince's stance. For the first time, they sent a more conciliatory missive:
it behoved them to tighten the reins, not to sever them. Nonetheless,
the atmosphere was one of tension. Soon the temperature rose again:
the Portuguese, in their fury over Dom Pedro's attitude, referred to José
Bonifácio and his Cabinet colleagues – whom they believed were influ-
encing the prince – as 'depraved thieves'. Events now developed quickly.
By February 1822 the Southern Region of Brazil had formed a single
political bloc, with the provinces of Rio de Janeiro, São Paulo, Santa
Catarina and even Minas Gerais agreeing to the plan for independence
with the Prince Regent as its head. José Bonifácio believed the only way
to avoid separatism, or even more liberal popular revolutions, was to
centre the movement around a monarch; and his opinion was gaining
ground. Independence was in the air. Despite the provinces' significantly conflicting interests, in theory they were united around the idea
of independence.

There was no less tension at the Courts in Portugal. The proposals
put forth by the Brazilian deputies were constantly blocked. As one of
the deputies wrote in a letter to the *Correio do Rio de Janeiro*: 'The
rivalry has turned to hatred, not only between the Portuguese and the
Brazilian deputies but also among the people.'[42] Several Brazilian deputies would neither swear by nor sign the Portuguese Constitution.
When it became increasingly clear their goals had been thwarted, some
of them fled surreptitiously to London.[43] Among those who left were

Diogo Antônio Feijó,[44] José da Costa Aguiar de Andrada and Antônio Manoel da Silva Bueno – all from São Paulo – and the deputies Cipriano Barata, Francisco Agostinho Gomes and José Lino Coutinho, all from Bahia.[45]

Meanwhile back in Brazil, Dom Pedro, with his tendency to romanticize, was drawing closer to the Masons. They had been a major influence behind his famous 'I'll stay' moment. And they became even more important when, on 13 May 1822, during King João VI's birthday celebrations, Dom Pedro received the title of 'constant defender of Brazil' from none other than José Bonifácio de Andrada e Silva, the Grand Master of the Masonic Lodge of Brazil. There were, however, other important members of the Lodge who disagreed with José Bonifácio's stance. Although he was opposed to slavery, José Bonifácio did not conceal his conservative political position on independence: he defended greater autonomy but was against any kind of radical separation from Portugal.

Within Masonry itself opinions were divided between the most conservative groups, who wanted a constitutional monarchy with limited representation, and the more radical groups, who envisaged a republic with popular political rights. Nowhere was this division more evident than in the discussion about whether or not to elect a Constituent Assembly in Brazil. José Bonifácio and his group were against the convocation, whereas Gonçalves Ledo (part of the most radical faction) and Martim Francisco (José Bonifácio's youngest brother), among others, were in favour. The radical factions came up with a petition demanding the convocation of a Representative General Assembly. The document, which had more than six thousand signatures, was delivered to Dom Pedro in May 1822.[46] In response to this pressure, Dom Pedro summoned a Constituent Assembly on 3 June. After all, while Brazilian voices were stifled at the Courts of Lisbon, the country had no representation, no legitimate administration and, gravest of all, no protection against recolonization. Leaders like Gonçalves Ledo and Januário da Cunha Barbosa reacted with inflammatory speeches, and newspapers poured fuel on the fire with their ardent campaign against the Courts. Although Gonçalves Ledo wanted direct elections, whereas less radical groups wanted indirect elections, the urgency to find a solution brought the two sides together.[47]

This was the situation when the Brazilian Constituent Assembly was convocated on 3 June. The final text was the work of José Bonifácio, but most of the ideas were those of Gonçalves Ledo. The central theme, which had been included in Dom Pedro's proclamation of the previous day, was 'independence moderated by national union'. The decree also established the criteria for the election of deputies: Minas Gerais would have twenty representatives; Mato Grosso, Santa Catarina, Rio Grande do Norte, Piauí and Rio de Janeiro would have one each; São Paulo would be represented by nine; and Bahia and Pernambuco by thirteen.[48] An additional act, signed by the Prince Regent on 4 May 1822, required that all laws, orders and resolutions, which continued to flow from the Portuguese Courts, be approved by the Brazilian Cabinet. Once again, the legislation was in reaction to the increasing hostility from Lisbon. Each and every ship brought disastrous news: the formation of new army regiments, the creation of a special council to oversee Brazil, the revocation of Dom Pedro's title of 'defender', and the refusal to allow the Kingdom of Brazil to be either united or independent.

Following his investiture, Dom Pedro was invited to become a member of the Masonic Lodge, where he was given the name Guatimozim ('initiate into the mysteries') and immediately elevated to the position of Grandmaster of the Lodge of Brazil. The rituals of Masonry appealed to the imagination of the young Prince Regent who, in the atmosphere of secrecy, allied himself with the more conservative sectors of the group. At the same time, with his wilful nature, he increasingly rebelled against the instructions from the Courts whose members, still unaware of his power in Brazil, continued to provoke him, referring to him as that 'youngster' or 'miserable wretch'.

A litigious divorce had became inevitable. The separation was finally declared in the manifesto of 1 August 1822 drawn up by Gonçalves Ledo, but attributed to Dom Pedro: 'Brazilians! It is time to stop deceiving the people [. . .] The southern provinces of Brazil, now united, will take the majestic stance of a people that recognizes its right to freedom and happiness, a people that now turns to me, your friend and the Son of your King . . .'[49] By way of Gonçalves Ledo's quill, Dom Pedro was seemingly the narrator, and took strength in his own actions, in the certainty they had been provoked by 'the villainy of the Portuguese'.

By this time, the liberal faction led by Gonçalves Ledo had suffered a significant setback, which weakened their position. On 19 June their motion for direct elections to the Constituent Assembly had been defeated. Brazilian independence, born of the country's refusal to accept further interference from the Portuguese Courts, represented a victory for José Bonifácio and his supporters – conservative, monarchist and only mildly constitutionalist. The conservative group had absorbed Gonçalves Ledo's Brazilian party. By this time José Bonifácio's, Masonic adherents, rural property owners and wealthy merchants controlled the workings of the government.[50] Another manifesto, issued on 6 August, was also José Bonifácio's work.[51] Despite proclaiming, 'If the monarchy goes, Brazil is lost', the document was largely antagonistic towards Portugal. That same month the Prince Regent declared all Portuguese troops enemies; and provincial governors in Brazil were ordered not to allow officials appointed by the Courts in Lisbon to take office. A new surge of decrees made it clear the colony had become autonomous. All that was lacking was the formal ceremony.

'FROM THE PLACID MARGINS OF THE IPIRANGA'[52]

The consecration finally took place in São Paulo. Not even the Andradas – José Bonifácio and his brothers, so often accused of favouring their home province – could have dreamt of such an outcome. After visiting the provinces of Rio de Janeiro and Minas Gerais to resolve local conflicts, Dom Pedro left for São Paulo on 14 August 1822, accompanied by a small group of close advisers: Luís de Saldanha da Gama (later the Marquis of Taubaté), his principal official, valet and political secretary; Francisco de Castro Canto e Melo, Gentleman of the Imperial Chamber, and brother of the future Marquesa de Santos, a favourite of the Prince Regent;[53] Francisco Gomes da Silva (nicknamed *Chalaça*), his companion, secretary and – according to gossip – the man who orchestrated the comings and goings of the royal bedchamber; João Carlota, a personal servant; and João Carvalho, Gentleman of the Wardrobe, equerry and Superintendent of the Royal Gardens. The group was later joined by Lieutenant-Colonel Joaquim Aranha Barreto de Camargo and the priest Belchior Pinheiro de Oliveira, the prince's confidant and mentor. In Rio de Janeiro, Princess Leopoldina was appointed regent, responsible for presiding over the Council of Ministers and for giving public audiences in place of her husband – accompanied by the head of the Cabinet, José Bonifácio. The small party took their time, ten days to cover the 470 kilometres between Rio de Janeiro and São Paulo. They spent the nights in farms, in Areias, Lorena, Taubaté and Águas Brancas, where they received support but also heard criticism from opponents of the Andrada brothers. Before they reached São Paulo they were joined by the Honour Guard, wearing dragoons' helmets and boots à l'écuyère,[54] and a group of officers in the service of the prince. They entered São Paulo on 25 August 1822. At the time the small city, of no more than 6,920 residents, was made up of narrow, curving streets. On 1 September the prince left São Paulo for Santos, from where he was only to depart on the fateful morning of 7 September.

Dom Pedro's objective in São Paulo was to resolve the conflicts that had erupted during the uprising known as Francisco Inácio's bernarda. The origin of the term came from St Bernard and the alleged ignorance with which the Benedictine monks had reacted to his reforms. The term had become synonymous with 'stupidity', as used by Tomás Antonio Vilanova Portugal to describe the 1820 constitutional revolution of Porto. His use of the word bernarda was widely commented on in newspapers, and was eventually employed colloquially as a synonym for 'mutiny' and 'popular uprising'. The ins and outs of the terminology do not matter; what is important is that the Prince Regent interpreted Francisco Inácio's bernarda revolt against the power of the Andrada family as a personal affront, to which he reacted by appointing José Bonifácio's brother, Martim Francisco, as his Finance Minister. He decided to visit São Paulo in person to make his support of the Andrada brothers clear.

Dom Pedro's journey to Santos had political motives; but there was nothing to prevent him, while he was there, from breaking the sixth commandment. His fame as a seducer preceded him, and it was said he was never without an attractive, willing female companion, whether from the nobility, the court, or among his slaves. One famous case occurred in Santos, when the prince saw an enslaved girl who was so beautiful he insisted on acquiring her then and there. But the most notorious case, which was to eclipse all the other gossip associated with Brazil's independence, was yet to take place. It involved Domitila de

Castro Canto e Melo, the daughter of Colonel João de Castro Canto e Melo and his wife Escolástica de Oliveira Toledo Ribas.

Domitila had been born in São Paulo and was almost a year older than Dom Pedro. She was a mature woman, graced with a great deal of beauty – and was suffering both from an unhappy marriage and, in her own words, 'the limitations of provincial life'. Although she may not have been a good mother to her children, whose father she judged to be inferior, it would be a mistake to rush to judgement: Domitila herself could never have imagined the role she was to play during that trip. On the contrary, at the time she was having difficulties with her husband, who had accused her of adultery and thus claimed the guardianship of their three children. It is not known whether she planned to request Dom Pedro's intervention through her brother, a member of his inner circle, or whether their meeting was a matter of chance. Little does it matter. The story circulating in the 1820s was that Dom Pedro was returning from a distant neighbourhood of Santos when he passed a beautiful woman in a litter carried by two slaves. The prince dismounted gallantly to greet the stranger, praising her beauty.

After this brief exchange, he lifted the litter. 'How strong you are, your Majesty!' she is said to have murmured, to which he replied, 'Never again shall you be attended by little negroes like these.'[55] Although the tale may well have been embellished over time – despite the prince's terrible choice of words – their meeting does seem to have been by chance. To this day, though, it is still unknown what exactly Domitila's brother – Francisco de Castro Canto e Melo – did in the prince's entourage. Whether this meeting was due to a brother's intervention, to destiny or to a premeditated encounter, it is impossible to know. What is known is that their meeting marked the beginning of the most famous love story in Brazilian history. The affair relied on the complicity of Domitila's entire family: her brother, her father, her uncles and her cousins, all of whom received privileges, honours and distinctions from the emperor. The date of the meeting was probably between 29 and 31 August 1822. From that time on the relationship between the two was only to grow closer.

At any rate, it was time for Dom Pedro to get back to Rio de Janeiro. The return attracted very little attention, mainly because the Prince Regent's special guard of thirty young soldiers had been dismissed; his visit had become increasingly unofficial. By this time the decision to separate from Portugal had already been made; only the formal announcement was yet to come. As soon as the prince had left Rio de Janeiro, on 14 August, José Bonifácio issued a circular to the diplomatic corps in which he declared the emancipation of Brazil.

All that remained was to catapult Dom Pedro to centre stage. The occasion arose soon enough: on 28 August the brig *Três Corações* arrived in Rio de Janeiro bringing the customary bad news from Lisbon: the Courts ordered the immediate return of the prince, revoked a number of measures they considered privileges, and accused Dom Pedro's ministers of treason.

José Bonifácio summoned the Council of Ministers in Rio de Janeiro and they came to a swift decision: the time had come. The urgency was such that José Bonifácio requested the courier, Paulo Bregaro, to gather as many horses as he required. The messengers, however, found the prince in circumstances less than noble. He had climbed the mountains to Cubatão, the town at the top of the *Serra do Mar* separating Santos from São Paulo, on a ragged nag and wearing a plain military uniform. To make matters worse, on that morning of 7 September, Dom Pedro was in a sorry state, which, although not serious, was undoubtedly uncomfortable. Perhaps from a change in diet or possibly from impure drinking water, the prince had woken with an upset stomach. So it was that, from time to time, suffering severe cramps, he had to absent himself from the travelling party, causing the march to come to a halt. One of his companions on the journey, Colonel Manuel Marcondes de Oliveira Melo, euphemistically described the situation by saying the prince was frequently obliged to dismount so that he could 'attend to himself'.[56] It was hardly the time for a grandiose statement, but it was the moment destiny had chosen.

As soon as the first messengers arrived at the village of Moinhos, Francisco de Castro Canto e Melo informed Dom Pedro of the news from Portugal. Later, Domitila's brother was to write a glorified version of the events of 7 September, giving great importance to the roles played both by himself and by the prince.[57] True to his tempestuous personality, Dom Pedro immediately galloped off enthusiastically towards São Paulo. But José Bonifácio's messengers met him halfway at 'the top of a hill near the Ipiranga stream'.[58] At the crest of this slope, with the small town of São Paulo seen in the distance, at about four o'clock in the afternoon, Dom Pedro received the correspondence from Major Antônio Ramos Cordeiro.

There were several letters: administrative acts from the Courts, letters from José Bonifácio, Antônio Carlos and Princess Leopoldina (one dated 28 August, the other 29 August). After reading the correspondence, Dom Pedro informed his exhausted entourage that the Portuguese Courts were planning to 'massacre' Brazil. He read aloud the documents that demanded he dissolve his ministry and convoke a new council. The most emphatic letter was from José Bonifácio: 'May your Majesty decide as soon as possible, because lack of resolution and mere warm measures [. . .] will serve for nothing and a moment lost could bring catastrophe.'[59] Along with the letters it was rumoured that Dom Pedro had been replaced as heir to the throne of Portugal by his brother Dom Miguel. So he took action: independence was declared.

That is the version of the story commonly narrated in history books, but it is high time to rewrite those somewhat theatrical events. At half past four in the afternoon, mounted on his horse, overcome with intermittent attacks of diarrhoea and exhausted from the journey, Dom Pedro made the formal declaration of what was already a reality. He tore the blue and white ribbon (the constitutional colours of Portugal) from his hat, threw it on the ground, and drawing his sword shouted loudly and clearly: 'The time has come!. . . Independence or death! [. . .] We have separated from Portugal . . .' According to Canto e Melo, all those present then swore 'an oath of honour binding them to fulfil the grandiose idea of freedom'.[60] Years later Domitila's brother created an imaginative account, saying it was thronged with people, despite the fact that it is known to have taken place in an isolated, secluded spot.

There is yet another version told by the prince's good friend, the priest Belchior Pinheiro, who claimed to have read the letters aloud to Dom Pedro, who in turn trembled with rage, tore the letters from the priest's hand and stomped on them. Then, on the priest's advice, Dom Pedro supposedly composed himself and, buttoning up his uniform, asked him, 'What now, Father Belchior?' To which the priest replied: 'If your Majesty doesn't make himself King of Brazil, he will be taken prisoner by the Courts and probably be disinherited. There is no other path except for independence and separation.' According to Father Belchior the prince then said: 'If this is what they want, this is what they'll get. The Courts are persecuting me, they refer to me with contempt as a wretched boy and a Brazilian ... Well, they will see what this wretched boy can do.' And he continued: 'Friends, the Courts [. . .]

wish to enslave and persecute us. From today on our relations are terminated. There are no longer any ties between us!' He then allegedly shouted 'Long live the independence and separation of Brazil', and concluded: 'By my blood, by my honour, by my God, I swear to make Brazil free.'

As can be seen, the words differ according to the narrator, who always seems to cast himself in the main supporting role. What has been passed down through history is Dom Pedro's cry of 'Independence or Death!' – present in both Belchior's and Canto e Melo's versions – which has come to symbolize the occasion. The cry was repeated by the troops, bestowing on that remote spot the solemnity called for by the occasion. Even if events – witnessed by only thirty-eight people – did not take place precisely as recounted, they immediately became history. The slogan 'Independence or Death!' was repeated in triumphal expressions of support as soon as the news arrived in São Paulo and Rio de Janeiro.

Dom Pedro received an effusive homecoming in Rio de Janeiro. The periodical *O Espelho* reveals how the news gained momentum. On 17 September the periodical informed the public in a simple note that the prince had returned to Rio de Janeiro from his brief five-day trip to São Paulo. However, on 20 September it declared in blazing colours: 'Independence or Death! This is the cry that unites all Brazilians . . . Brazil has awoken from its lethargy [. . .] and has resolved, with dignity, to shake off the weight that oppressed her [. . .] Thus the Perpetual Defender of Brazil responds to the outcry of his faithful people who prefer a declared enemy to a treacherous friend . . .'[61]

Dom Pedro's return to Rio de Janeiro had been much faster than usual. Perhaps galvanized by the developments, in just five days he had made a journey that usually took messengers up to nine, arriving at São Cristóvão Palace at dawn on 14 September. The Prince Regent entered soaking wet from the rain, but wearing a green ribbon on his arm (the colour of the Bragança dynasty) above a gold-plated metal plaque engraved with the words 'Independence or Death'. The blue and white ribbon the Courts had adapted as the new symbol of Portugal had been replaced with a green and yellow one, the new national colours. Whether the yellow represented the yellow flower Domitila had given Dom Pedro, or the House of Habsburg, the reader may choose. The new ribbon became the fashion, as shown in the advertisements in the periodical *Volantim*, offering yellow and green ribbons and other 'independence ornaments': 'For sale: gold-coloured ribbons with the inscription Independence or Death, available for 12 vinténs at each of the haberdashery stores in the Rua da Quitanda (n° 40, n° 84, n° 58 and n° 10 behind the Asylum) and in the Rua da Cadeia, n° 58.'[62] The new colours were incorporated into the national flag and Brazil's coat of arms. They were displayed in the houses of the nobility, on the arms of the elite, and on objects – cups, jugs, mugs, clocks, fans – that were found in every home.[63]

The celebrations for the acclamation of Brazil's first emperor, which took place on 12 October, were reminiscent of the festivities that had greeted his father, Dom João, in 1808. Despite the rain, silk quilts were displayed from the windows and the streets were strewn with aromatic leaves. The Campo de Santana, where the ceremony took place, was subsequently renamed the Campo da Aclamação. The festivities included parades, the appearance of the emperor on the palace balcony, a Te Deum at the Imperial Chapel and the hand-kissing ritual, followed by a special performance at the theatre. Popular entertainment included bullfights, dances, drinks, banquets, horse races and pantomimes. Far from insignificant, these activities were political rituals meant to engage people with both the reality of the separation from Portugal, and with Dom Pedro's new role as emperor. The goal was to make it a memorable occasion, one that would solidify his position.

That times had changed was made abundantly clear by Dom Pedro in the first letter to his father after the declaration of independence on 7 September. Without questioning his father's role, the prince challenged the authority of the Courts: 'Rio de Janeiro, September 22, 1822. My father and Lord: I had the honour to receive a letter from Your Majesty dated August 3, in which your Majesty reprehended me for the manner in which I write and speak of the Portuguese-Spanish faction . . .' The letter continues in increasingly exalted terms:

> We shall reply with two words: We do not want (this) [*Não queremos*]. If the people of Portugal had the right to a constitutional revolution, it is clear the people of Brazil have twice the right [. . .] Standing by these unassailable principles, I declare [. . .] to this bloodthirsty caliphate that I, as Prince Regent of the Kingdom of Brazil and its Perpetual Defender, declare null and void all the decrees and all else that has been imposed

on Brazil by these factious, abhorrent, Machiavellian, chaotic, depraved and pernicious Courts [. . .] From Portugal we want nothing, absolutely nothing [. . .] They are no more than a gang of villainous anti-monarchists and murderers who are holding Your Majesty in the most ignominious captivity. Brazilian independence triumphs and will triumph, or we will die defending it [. . .] First of all they will learn more about the 'wretched boy' and his capability, despite not having attended the foreign Courts. [. . .] I remain, with all respect, your Majesty's loving son and subject who greatly venerates you. – Pedro.[64]

This was the letter, with its grammatical errors and exalted terms, in which the 'rascal' declared his revenge.

And thus, emancipation was complete. An emancipation that was unique among independence in the Americas, which had given birth to republics, not monarchies. The fact is that this emancipation came without radical changes, although it produced rich political commentary – in the form of pamphlets – which is evidence that independence was a question of great interest to society as a whole and that people from all walks of life took part in the debate. The emancipation had placed at the very centre of power not a president, but a king: a Portuguese monarch from the House of Bragança. Perhaps for this reason a sort of 'Independence legend' was created, which retells an epic through a series of events profiled and sewn together: the arrival of the royal party, the opening of the ports, Brazil's status of United Kingdom, the 'I Stay', the 'Abide by', and finally the declaration of Independence, in 1822. It is a sequence that seems to lead to a foregone conclusion, a series of occurrences flowing inevitably toward the establishment of the Brazilian Empire.

It should be said, however, that this conservative solution was by no means the only possibility. The plan for the empire had triumphed over other more radical projects, including that of a republic. In fact, support from the provinces for the Brazilian Empire did not come as easily as is often told in history books. The process of emancipation was not limited to the years between 1820 and 1822; the foundation of the empire based on the concept of the construction of a single state was a version of events publicized by those involved to express the point of view of the *Carioca* elite. It is worth mentioning that independence was a by-product of José Bonifácio's beliefs, either because he meant to curb the popularity of the radical liberals (in other words republicans), or because in his opinion the existence of Brazil pre-dated the provinces, thus Portuguese America was predestined to become a massive empire. In Pernambuco, for example, public opinion had always opposed the idea of a single state, which was seen as unfairly beneficial to Rio de Janeiro.[65] Bahia basically waged civil war from late 1822 to mid-June 1823, only joining the union on 2 July of that year, accordingly still celebrated as the date marking the emancipation of the state.

Nevertheless, 7 September is a symbolic date that brought to a culmination the long process of rupture, beginning with the arrival of the Portuguese Court and finally ending with the establishment of a monarchy right in the middle of the Americas. Surrounded by republics, Brazil placed an emperor at the centre of power, to the shock and distrust of its Latin American neighbours. Emancipation was by no means the exclusive work of the quixotic Dom Pedro. It was, rather, the outcome of a series of tensions and arrangements arising from the colonial system and the absolute monarchy, so characteristic of the end of the modern era. As the *ancien régime* disintegrated, so too did the foundations of mercantile colonialism.

Brazil's emancipation managed to be both unique and banal. Although liberal, in that it broke with colonial domination, it was also conservative in its maintenance of the monarchy, slavery, and the dominance of the landowning classes. What is more, though the process of emancipation began with the arrival of the royal court in 1808, the final result was shaped by pressures from both abroad and inside Brazil – not the least of which resulted from transferring the capital from the northeast to the southeast of the country.[66] Furthermore, despite the establishment of a new political order, the notion of citizenship remained extremely limited, with the exclusion from all political activity of the vast majority of the population and the equally vast contingent of slaves. As a result, the political institutions were only minimally representative: independence had created a state but not a nation. To develop a culture, to build a society, to engender a sense of nationalism would be left to the First Reign, and especially to the Second.

9

Independence *Habemus*: Instability in the First Empire

AN EARTHLY EMPIRE: MYSTICAL AND HYBRID SYMBOLS

Brazilian independence gradually became a reality with no turning back, despite the fact that many still questioned the decision to found an empire in the Americas. The maintenance of the monarchy seemed a contradiction in terms. It was hard to imagine a process of emancipation in the region without the establishment of a republic. The decision to create a country with a representative constitutional monarchy had been one choice among many. The chief aim was to avoid the disintegration of the former colony with the unfortunate precedent of Spanish American territory, where four viceroyalties had splintered into fourteen different countries. It also confirmed the domination of the Brazilian elites, most of whom had been educated at Coimbra during the reign of Dom João VI.[1]

Empire involved the juxtaposition of new and old elements.[2] Dom Pedro had the example of two exceptional yet distinct emperors to follow: Napoleon I and Francis II. The first, a French general and self-appointed emperor; the second, Pedro's powerful father-in-law, who had become the head of the Habsburg Empire. And there was another example in the Americas. The same year, 1822, the Mexican elite, in their struggle to deter Spanish attempts at recolonization and to suppress the republican nationalist movement in the country, had proclaimed a general called Iturbide emperor, with the title of Augustín I. It was a short-lived experiment, but it meant that Brazil was not the only case of a monarchical regime on the republican continent.

All history is multifaceted. For some a 'Brazilian Empire' represented a continuation of the centuries-old desire of the Portuguese to increase their dominions, which had started with the reconquest of their Iberian territories from the Muslims. The Reconquest had lasted for seven centuries; from the ninth century onwards it acquired an aura of mysticism and was regarded as a holy war. The wars came to an end in 1492 with the conquest of the last Muslim kingdom. This was immediately followed by the beginning of Portugal's spectacular imperial expansion which, at its height, stretched from Asia to America.

But Portugal's progress had also suffered setbacks. One of the most notable cases was that of Dom Sebastião I, the seventh king of the Avis dynasty, who, with the aim of recreating the glories of the past, set out for Morocco on a holy crusade. His defeat at the battle of Alcácer-Quibir in 1578 and subsequent disappearance led to a succession crisis and the creation of the myth surrounding him, called *Sebastianismo*. He had ruled for only three years, but nonetheless became known as the Hidden or Sleeping King. Later, people associated the political, economic and social decline of the Portuguese Empire with the disappearance of Dom Sebastião, who, it was speculated, would return in the future to redeem the country. Years later, in the seventeenth century, Padre Vieira in his 'History of the Future' announced that the Portuguese Empire should be situated in Brazil: a palace could be situated there, where the fifth empire could take advantage of all four seasons of the year.

Thus the notion of empire had many shades of meaning, more or less strategic, more or less ancient or miraculous. At all events, the empire created in the nineteenth century represented the unmistakable arrival of a new era, foreseen in verse and prose since the times of Dom Sebastião, when Portuguese power was at its height, but the shadow of decline was already perceptible. There are other conceptions associated with the idea of empire. 'Empire' signified the expansion of a cause, with a notably political connotation. In Brazil the notion of empire[3] was associated with a large extension of land within a single territory.[4] José Bonifácio saw further associations: a statesman and one of the most important agents of Brazilian independence, he claimed that, in Brazil, use of the word stemmed from the Festival of the Holy Spirit, during which, even today, an emperor – generally a young boy – is chosen by the public.

Drawing on this potent combination of various mythologies, 'empire' was the most convincing political expression for a country of continental proportions – and monarchy emerged as the best (available) means to prevent political and territorial fragmentation. In the view of the local elites, only the figure of a king could unite this gigantic country with its deep internal divisions. But the new monarch was still Portuguese, and the symbols of the monarchy were still those of the fatherland. The royal family's colours and coat of arms remained on the Brazilian flag, and the wyvern that represented the power of the Braganças was still depicted on the sceptre. Against a backdrop of caution and distrust – both internal and from abroad – great importance was given to the ceremonial aspects of the new Brazilian court after the declaration of independence in 1822. Dom Pedro was acclaimed emperor on 12 October the same year – a date that was initially held to be more important than 7 September. There is a Portuguese expression that says 'A rainy wedding, a happy marriage', and the wedding of the emperor to the Brazilian nation, to judge from the pouring rain that nearly ruined the acclamation ceremony, was a case in point.

To mark the date and the continuity of the royal dynasty, in an act laden with symbolism, as soon as the storm passed, Dom Pedro and Dona Leopoldina came onto the balcony of the stately house in the Campo de Santana – the scene of so many celebrations during the reign of Dom João VI – and held up their baby daughter Dona Maria da Glória for the crowd to see, symbolizing the continuity of the empire and of the Bragança dynasty. For the people, who were unaccustomed to such rituals, a gallant prince, with his heir to the throne and his princess at his side, ignited the imagination more than any political theory could.

Changes quickly followed, above all in emblems and symbols: a sort of new calling card for a new regime. On 10 November the diplomatic corps were informed that a new green and yellow national flag had been adopted in Brazil. The green background represented the House of Bragança, while the yellow diamond superimposed on the green symbolized the Lorena House, used by the Austrian imperial family. The diamond shape was a barely hidden and awkward tribute to Napoleon, although the monarchic coat of arms in the middle of the diamond emerged from an array of Brazilian plants. This reconstruction was typical of the cultural process in Brazil: the traditional elements of European heraldry coupled with a precise tribute to the monarchs of the young nation represented the new national reality.

The coronation took place on 1 December, the anniversary of the start of the Portuguese revolution of 1640, which led to the end of the Iberian Union and the beginning of the reign of the House of Bragança. Once again the ceremony linked the new independent monarchy to the deposed one, which was now observing events from Portugal. The ritual had to be memorable, and to this end it combined elements of Napoleon's coronation in Notre Dame and the coronation of the emperors of the Holy Roman Empire in Frankfurt, in a unique marriage of the traditional and the modern. It also incorporated an element from royal coronations in Hungary, swiping the air with a sword, in an allusion to Dom Pedro's title of 'Perpetual Defender of Brazil' – his first popular investiture, which had now become a reality. To further enthrall the public, the emperor wore a green silk tunic, riding boots and spurs, and was swathed in a mantle made of green velvet, lined with yellow silk and embroidered with stars and gold braid. The symbolism was evident, combining traditional elements with the new symbols of the land. This attention to detail was also apparent in the imperial cloak, which was made of toucan feathers, the work of indigenous craftsmen and supposedly a tribute to Indian chiefs.

To complete the ceremony the new emperor received the sacred anointment legitimizing him as king in the eyes of the sovereigns of Europe as well as in the eyes of his people. With his desire to break from Portuguese tradition, on the one hand, and influenced by Napoleon's coronation in 1804 on the other, Dom Pedro personally oversaw the arrangements for the religious ceremony, which was based on the first book of the ancient Roman Pontifical.[5] This document established that the sovereign should be anointed and consecrated with holy oil during the performance of Mass, a custom that had been long abolished in Portugal. From then on the imperial culture was created based on two aspects of the fledgling nation: the monarchical state, determined to civilize the nation; and the vast territorial extension the state claimed as its own.[6]

One of the best examples of this imperial culture is a project undertaken by the French artist Jean-Baptiste Debret. He had arrived from France in 1816 and was now virtually an official court artist. During the reign of Dom João he had been responsible for most of the official depictions of the court. In 1822 he was instructed to create an allegory for the stage curtain in the royal theatre – the Teatro São João – where Dom Pedro I would give his inauguration speech and then watch a presentation commemorating his coronation as the first emperor of Brazil. Debret was a neoclassical artist and a relative of Jacques-Louis David, with whom he had worked in his Paris atelier. David had been the artist of the Revolution and had gone on to work for Napoleon as his principal painter. In Brazil, Debret may have found it difficult to transfer the civic virtues of revolutionary France to the slave-based economy and monarchical system of Brazil.

But in this case Debret surpassed himself. The allegory was intended to be the first symbol of Brazilian royalty, to seduce the new subjects. The Empire of Brazil was to be depicted in all of its singular pomp. Debret recorded his meeting with the theatre director, who wanted to replace the existing stage curtain depicting the Kingdom of Portugal surrounded by kneeling figures. After all, it was hardly appropriate for the declaration of independence to be celebrated against a backdrop of servitude to the Portuguese Empire. Debret redesigned it to represent 'the fidelity of the Brazilian population to an allegorical figure representing the imperial government, depicted seated on a throne covered with a rich tapestry supported by palm trees'.[7] While the tapestry was reminiscent of Europe, the palm trees were symbols of the *sui generis* empire in the tropics. The imperial government was represented by a woman in a cloak with a green lining – the colour of the Brazilian forests – and embroidered with gold in an allusion to the wealth of the land. In her left hand she held a shield with the emperor's coat of arms, and in her right the Brazilian Constitution. Once again a combination of contrasting symbols was presented. In the foreground 'fruits of the country' were tipped onto the steps of the throne from a horn-shaped vessel. On the left a boat loaded with sacks of coffee and crates of sugarcane represented the basis of the new empire's economy.

But the most interesting aspect of the stage curtain was the depiction of the country's mixed-race population. On one side, the artist portrays a black family's loyalty to the emerging empire: a boy carrying an agricultural tool accompanies his mother who in her right hand holds an axe for felling trees, and in her left a gun belonging to her husband, who has been called up and is leaving to join the army. In Debret's words, far from questioning slavery, this African woman is armed in preparation to defend the new monarchy. Dividing the curtain, a 'white Indian woman' kneels at the foot of the throne, holding a pair of newborn twins – symbolizing the promise of a peaceful future guaranteed by 'the assistance of the government'. In the background armed Indians show their support for the new state. Opposite them there are loyal naval officers and one of the founding fathers of São Paulo, and in front of these are *Paulistas* and *Mineiros*, 'equally dedicated and enthusiastic' holding sabres. Lastly, '*caboclos* kneel in an attitude of respect'. As a last decorative touch the waves of the sea break at the foot of the throne, a reminder of the empire's unique geographical location.[8]

Debret's allegory and accompanying text, reproduced in his book *Voyage pittoresque et historique au Brésil*, provides perhaps the clearest descriptions of the new state's aspirations. The various groups that made up the nation would be submitted to the power of the imperial throne, to which they would offer their loyalty. They would in turn be the beneficiaries of 'civilization' as introduced by their sovereign into the distant tropics. There is no 'sign' of any conflict, neither civil nor political; only union. This would be a unique form of royalty, ruling over its multiracial subjects. The throne, at the centre of the scene, directs the eye towards the allegorical figure representing the emperor, with the letter P and the crown directly above her head, and in her arms a copy of the constitution, the symbol of the western state. The whole stage curtain was conceived to describe a new nation, founded in the tropics, whose essential characteristic was its difference.

With all its exuberance of detail, Debret's stage curtain was no more than a formal presentation of a situation that did not actually exist. The monarchy was by no means stable and the atmosphere in the country was far from calm. In the first place there was the evident contradiction between a monarchy acting as a civilizing force and the deeply rooted regime of slavery throughout the territory. It was a sort of legalized, 'moral' violence, a system not only official, but accepted as natural throughout the country. In 1808 the total population of Portuguese America was 2,424,463, of which 31.1 per cent were slaves.[9] In Salvador, for which there are no precise figures, it is estimated that in 1807 blacks and mestizos, both slaves and freemen, accounted for 80 per cent of the approximately 51,000 inhabitants of the town. In 1835 this figure had grown to 72 per cent of the population estimated at 65,500.[10] In Rio de Janeiro in the same year the total population had grown to 79,321, of which 45.6 per cent were slaves.[11] These people, by definition, had no rights and could not even be considered citizens. The slave-owners still feared the example of the Haitian revolution in the late eighteenth century. They lived in a situation where there were 'six slaves for every master and where, consequently, those who desired vengeance were in a majority of 6 to 1'.[12]

At the beginning of the nineteenth century, when periodicals were rare but gossip was plentiful, Haiti was frequently in the headlines and the subject of discussion in the pharmacies – the location of choice for hearing the latest news. There was talk about the slave rebellions that ravaged the island, leading to a general loss of control, or conversely, to the Africans gaining control, which, in the language of the time, implied the lack of many essentials: rules, government and rationalism. With no access to objective news from the island, fear prevailed. Information was vaguely understood: the wealthiest French colony – the Pearl of the Antilles, as that part of the island was called – was in a state of upheaval. In the eighteenth century, Haiti had been Brazil's competitor in the sugar trade, in which it had held a considerable advantage. The colony was also known for the remarkable ratio of slaves to whites. In 1754 there were 465,000 slaves to just 5,000 whites, an even greater disproportion than existed in Brazil at the time. Even so, the situation in Haiti cast a shadow over the fearful Brazilian elites.

The first slave revolt in Haiti had occurred in 1754; though rapidly repressed by the French, they were unable to quell the clamour for independence. The second revolt was sparked off by the outbreak of the French Revolution and spread throughout the entire island after the Jacobins' 1791 declaration abolishing slavery in the French colonies. The revolutionary process lasted for twenty-three years, during which there were many setbacks. But what made the greatest impression on the Brazilian elite was in 1804 when Jean-Jacques Dessalines – a freed slave – expelled the French from Haiti and declared himself 'emperor'. European countries and their Caribbean colonies immediately imposed a blockade on Haiti that was to last more than sixty years, the consequences of which are still in evidence today. As for those in power in Brazil, they feared Haiti like the Devil himself. Repercussions of the 1804 revolutionary events in Haiti were felt throughout the country, as several restrictive measures were taken, among them the increasing centralization of power in post-independent Brazil. The country reinvented itself as staunchly anti-Haiti: in contrast to the island governed by Africans, Brazil was white, Christian and civilized.

This was in part a reaction to the unstable situation in Brazil. Not all of the provinces immediately embraced the independence movement centred in Rio de Janeiro. Minas Gerais and the southern provinces declared they were in favour of consultation regarding the acclamation of Dom Pedro. Pernambuco swore its allegiance in December 1822, although it had taken the precaution in September that year of electing its own deputies. Since the territory was so vast and communications difficult, Goiás and Mato Grosso only declared their allegiance in January 1823. Rio Grande do Norte, Sergipe and Alagoas, in the northeast, then followed suit. However, the four provinces in the north – Pará, Maranhão, Piauí and Ceará – together with Cisplatina in the extreme south and, as mentioned, Bahia, remained faithful to the Courts in Lisbon.[13]

Foreign nations were equally divided. Brazil's Latin American neighbours initially refused to accept the new situation, suspicious of a country that had maintained the monarchy rather than follow in the footsteps of the new republics; and, what was more, it had enthroned a Portuguese emperor as the head of the new state. However, the United States, already exerting hegemonic influence over the American continent, recognized Brazilian emancipation from Portugal in 1824. Meanwhile, troops loyal to Lisbon resisted in the province of Cisplatina, but were finally expelled from the country in November 1823. Their departure was followed by the beginning of the war for Uruguayan independence, which lasted until 1825, in which the enemy was no longer Portugal, but Brazil.

Portugal, the Motherland, demurred, finally accepting its colony's independence in 1825. It should come as no surprise that the British offered their services to mediate the negotiations. To this end, they sent a special representative, Sir Charles Stuart, to Portugal with the task of negotiating the terms of Brazil's independence. A series of conferences were organized in Lisbon where the matters discussed included the royal succession, mutual support in the form of ships and soldiers, financial restitution – both to the Portuguese government and to private citizens – and the negotiation of a trade agreement. It was decided that there would be reciprocity in the treatment of citizens between the two nations, hostilities would cease, Portugal would be compensated for advance payments, and trade relations would follow the basic principle of a 15 per cent tax on imports. But the question of financial restitution remained. Portugal demanded payment for all the objects that had been left in Rio de Janeiro. The total amount equalled half the Brazilian public debt to Britain in 1807, or the *'bagatelle'* of 12,899:856$276 réis. The document entitled 'List of the objects which Portugal has the right to claim from Brazil', drawn up at the fourth conference in Lisbon, on 15 April 1825, included furniture, silverware, warships, military officers' salaries, freight charges for the transportation of troops, military divisions, weapons, artillery and the notorious Royal Library, which alone was evaluated at 800:000$000 réis.[14] [15]

Once the negotiations had been concluded and the bill was paid, the British turned their attention to curbing Brazilian presence on the African continent and to thwarting the plan for an independent Angola, which could then be incorporated into the empire.[16] The Portuguese colonies in Africa reacted in different ways to Brazil's emancipation. In Guinea, Angola and Mozambique groups of slave traders joined ranks with rebels from Rio de Janeiro. It is no coincidence that the Kingdom of Dahomey was the first country to recognize the Brazilian Empire. In Angola, a pamphlet produced in Brazil invited Benguela to join the 'Brazilian cause'.[17]

But Great Britain was determined to suppress the slave trade. It had abolished human trafficking in its empire in 1807, and now began to take action against the countries that still practised it. Without a doubt Brazil was the largest market. The activities of the British Navy were to change the fundamental structure of Brazil's social hierarchy and work practices, which were still based on the continued importation of African slaves. Vast sums of money had been accumulated from this transatlantic traffic and from the sale of slaves on the domestic market. This commerce created a direct link between Brazil and Africa and was dominated on the American side of the Atlantic by Brazilian and Portuguese merchants in major ports such as Salvador, Rio de Janeiro and Recife.[18]

It should not be forgotten that at the beginning of the nineteenth century the slave trade was one of the most profitable businesses in the colony, with the slave traders themselves forming a part of the country's elite.[19] Between the mid-sixteenth and the mid-nineteenth centuries, Brazil imported approximately four million slaves, 40 per cent of the total number transported across the Atlantic between the sixteenth and nineteenth centuries. Of this total, 80 per cent entered the country in the eighteenth and nineteenth centuries, the majority coming from outposts in Angola, the Congo, the Gold Coast, the Bay of Benin and Cape Verde. The system was deeply rooted in Brazilian society, consolidating social hierarchies, the wealth of elites and systems of political power.

Great Britain meant to charge dearly in return for its protection of the royal family on their 1808 journey to Brazil, and this included the question of slave-trafficking, which was broached in the first treaty between the two nations. Britain's campaign for abolition arose from a combination of economic, political and humanitarian interests. Both Portugal, and later Brazil, did all they could to evade the pressure. In the treaty of 1810, as has been seen, Dom João had accepted the gradual elimination of the slave trade in principle but, in fact, had done nothing. Five years later the Congress of Vienna gave its support to the abolitionist campaign. But it was only in July 1817 that the suppression of the traffic was formalized, with judicial commissions established on both sides of the Atlantic to evaluate the seizing of ships and to set free the Africans encountered on-board. The Portuguese-British commission based in Rio de Janeiro only prosecuted one ship, in 1821: the schooner *Emília* bringing slaves from the Gold Coast. The 352 Africans were declared free, registered, and given letters of emancipation. Housing was provided for them in public and private institutions. This was, however, an isolated case, perhaps not surprisingly given that the superintendent of police at the time, Paulo Fernandes Viana, was notorious for his association with wealthy slave traders.

Between 1825 and 1826 a new treaty was signed as part of the negotiations for Great Britain's recognition of Brazilian independence. The new constitution drawn up by the Constituent Assembly in 1823 included José Bonifácio's recommendation that slavery should be eliminated in the medium term. However, the article (number 254) that foresaw 'the gradual emancipation of the African slaves' was removed from the 1824 Constitution, in which no mention of slavery was made. Yet another treaty, drawn up between 1826 and 1827, determined that ships transporting slaves be treated as pirate vessels. But this was merely for appearances: between 1826 and 1830 there was a dramatic increase in slave-trafficking, a result of the fear of imminent abolition. Whereas in the first half of the decade approximately 40,000 slaves had been transported, between 1826 and 1829 the figure rose to more than 60,000 a year. Nothing had changed. There were innumerable ways to circumvent the laws. Scandalous impunity of the traffickers continued to prevail.[20]

This open and insidious attitude opposing the prohibition of slave-trafficking contributed to the precarious nature of slave *alforria* (or freedom), to collusion with the illegal enslavement of African newcomers, and to freed men and men of colour having no guarantee they would not once again be forced into slavery. The onus of proving their freedom fell upon them, in a country where freedom itself was becoming an increasingly rare 'good', and difficult to sustain. In any case, the policy of defending the slave trade and maintaining the system of slavery was at the heart of the formation of the new Brazilian state. Thus, the founders of the empire engaged in a discourse of 'gradual abolition', all the while preserving the state apparatus of slavery. The most important consideration, at the outset, was to guarantee the continuity of trade relations with the United States and Europe, all the while maintaining the traffic in slaves. Thus the Brazilian government remained intimately connected with the infamous trade, an issue that, in spite of the pressure from Britain, was to take many years to resolve. The new nation, in this crucial formative phase, excluded large sectors of society from citizenship – Indians, slaves and women – and postponed the prospect of abolition to an indeterminate date in the future.

With so many weaknesses, the Brazilian Empire was born trying to hide structural problems. The situation is best summed up by the character Tancredi in Giuseppe di Lampedusa's novel *The Leopard*: 'If we want everything to stay the same, everything must change.' Slavery remained untouched, as did the monoculture of sugarcane and the vast estates owned by the elite. Above all, nothing had been done to reconcile internal political differences or to deal with the fundamental question of the distribution of power between the national authority in Rio de Janeiro and the regions.

DOMESTIC CRISIS: AN EMPIRE DIVIDED

The country still remained politically divided. Although the final form of Brazilian independence represented a victory for the conservative Coimbra group led by José Bonifácio and his brothers, divisions immediately became apparent. There was no agreement, for example, about the basic structures on which the new state should be built. During the first two years – between 1822 and 1824 – this debate was centred around Brazil's first constitution. The process for the election of the deputies was set in motion and the Constituent Assembly first met in May 1823.

At the Constituent Assembly, groups with very different positions confronted each other. The 'moderate liberals' wanted to limit reforms granting greater political and civil freedoms: to consolidate the achievements of independence without compromising the existing social order and status quo. This group was composed of rural landowners and merchants from Minas Gerais who had ties to the court and were associated with politicians and military officers of the bourgeoisie.[21] They mainly wanted political and institutional reforms aimed at limiting the powers of the emperor. They defended the constitutional monarchy, subject to a division of powers, with greater authority for the Chamber of Deputies and an independent judiciary. They had no interest in democracy, nor in general enfranchisement.

The 'exalted liberals' wanted more far-reaching reforms, including social and political changes. Although there were divisions within the group, broadly speaking, members wanted a federal system, the separation of Church and State, incentives for Brazilian industry, universal suffrage, the gradual emancipation of the slaves and, in some cases, the establishment of a democratic republic.[22] They were behind various alternative political projects, generally advocating greater citizens' rights and the reduction of social inequalities.

Both groups, however – the moderate and the exalted liberals – were united against the 'Portuguese party' made up of Portuguese and a few Brazilians who supported an absolute monarchy and wanted absolute powers for Dom Pedro I. The 'moderate' and 'exalted' liberals together formed the Brazilian party because both groups wanted the monarch to be answerable to the parliament. There was one more group, the 'Bonifácios', led by José Bonifácio, whose followers defended a strong, centralized constitutional monarchy and the gradual abolition of slavery.

It was within this context of divided opinions that the work of the Constituent Assembly began in 1823. The meeting resulted in a bill limiting the right to vote or to stand for election to those whose income was equivalent to the price of the manioc flour produced from 150 *alqueires*[23] of land, so people called the bill 'Manioc'. The measure demonstrated the influence of the agricultural elite, who, having guaranteed full rein to Dom Pedro I during the emancipation process, now wanted to clip his wings. Antônio Carlos de Andrada had outlined the bill, using the French and Norwegian constitutions as models. It had then been sent to the Constituent Assembly for debate and approval.

Delegates from the Brazilian party proposed three powers, along the lines of Montesquieu's classical division, with the Executive composed of the emperor and six ministers of state. The Legislature was to consist of a General Assembly composed of deputies (four-year terms) and senators (lifetime terms). And finally, the Judiciary, made up of judges and the courts. The most daring component of the project was the supremacy of the Legislature over the Executive. The measure irritated Dom Pedro I and the Portuguese party, neither of whom concealed their desire for an absolute monarchy. The Portuguese were even more irritated by another measure, one forbidding foreigners from participating in Brazilian politics, whether as deputies or senators.

But the divisions in the Assembly went even deeper. For different reasons both the 'exalted liberals' and the Portuguese party opposed José Bonifácio, turning the Andrada brothers into a common enemy. And Dom Pedro I, realizing the Brazilian party intended to turn him into a puppet head of state, began to side with the Portuguese party.

The atmosphere was one of unease, with intensifying xenophobia. The proposals became increasingly aggressive. The emperor had no intention of seeing his powers dwindle away. On 12 November 1823 he ordered his troops to surround the Constituent Assembly building. Despite the presence of the army, which remained loyal to the emperor, the deputies remained in session until the early hours of the morning and declared Dom Pedro an 'outlaw'. The emperor then issued a decree dissolving the Constituent Assembly. The episode became known as the 'Night of Agony' due to the resistance of the deputies who refused to leave the building. Despite declaring they would only leave prodded by 'an imperial bayonet', most of them were allowed to go home peacefully. However, six of them were deported to France, among them the three Andrada brothers.

It is somewhat ironic that, not only did Brazilian independence establish a monarchy instead of a republic, but the country's first constitution was vetoed and never became law! Actually, in 1824, Dom Pedro I presented another constitution to, or rather imposed one on, the country. The nickname stuck, and to this day the first Brazilian constitution is known as the *Outorgada*: 'the imposed one'. There is no denying that the beginning of the country's political life as an independent nation was, to say the least, complex and turbulent.

THE 1824 CONSTITUTION: THE PUPPET CUTS THE STRINGS

To avoid any further risks, this time the emperor met behind closed doors with ten people whom he trusted unconditionally to draw up the new constitution. All of them had been born in Brazil, were legal scholars who had studied at Coimbra, and were members of the Council of State that had been created in 1823.[24] The text of the constitution was drawn up in fifteen days, based on the 'Manioc project'.[25] The copyist was Luís Joaquim de Santos Marrocos, archivist of the Royal Library and notorious for his dislike of the natives of the former colony. He had arrived in Brazil with the books from the Royal Library, immediately after the prince Dom João, and not a day had gone by without his complaining about the climate, the mosquitoes and the absence of social life. Nevertheless he had never left the country: he both married and met his maker in Brazil.[26]

The text was then sent to the various Chambers, where, according to the official version, very few comments were made; it was then rapidly confirmed during a ceremony in the Imperial Cathedral on 25 March 1824. The document followed the liberal French model of a representative system based on the theory of national sovereignty. The form of government was monarchical, hereditary, constitutional and representative, with the country divided into provinces. The constitution showed the influence of Benjamin Constant, the Swiss-French liberal political philosopher.[27] The novelty was the introduction of not just three powers – executive, legislature and judiciary – but four, following and adapting Benjamin Constant's proposal, which was for five: the monarchy represented the continuity, had the representation of opinion, the power of the judiciary, and had veto power over the others. Benjamin Constant had been educated at the University of Edinburgh, and had spent time in France, Switzerland, Germany and Great Britain. As a renowned intellectual, he was influential in French politics during the second half of the Revolution – between 1815 and 1830 – when he was the leader of the opposition group known as the 'independents', a left-wing liberal movement. In 1819 he published *La liberté des anciens est des modernes* in which he discussed the role of the individual in relation to the state. He praised the British model of constitutional monarchy but he also defended slavery; he believed the system of slavery allowed citizens to participate in civic activities. He also published a tract entitled *Cours de politique constitutionnelle*, which included the concept of the 'Moderating Power', subsequently introduced into the text of Brazil's constitution.

The Moderating Power afforded the emperor full powers and exclusive rights, including the use of coercive force, the right to appoint and dismiss ministers of state, lifelong members of the Council of State, presidents of the provinces, ecclesiastical authorities, lifelong senators, magistrates and judges, as well as to appoint and dismiss ministers of the Executive. The emperor was also above the law and could not be prosecuted for his actions. Whereas in the 1823 Constitution the head of the Executive only had the power of veto, he now had the last word. According to the text, the Moderating Power was intended to ensure harmony and balance for the state. As per the definition of the time, it was a 'neutral power'.

The rest of the constitution was generally accepted. It granted freedom of religion although, according to the law, all temples, synagogues and churches were already permitted. Elections continued to be indirect and very limited, in two rounds. In the first round, voting delegates were chosen, in the proportion of one delegate to every one hundred households. In the second round, the delegates elected the deputies and senators. Initially three senators would be elected; but only one would serve, according to the emperor's final choice.

The Church was subject to the state, since the emperor had the right to make appointments to the Catholic Church. The General Assembly was made up of two Chambers – the Chamber of Deputies and the Chamber of Senators. As previously mentioned, the deputies were elected for a temporary mandate and the senators, elected by the provinces, for life. The Council of State was maintained with lifelong members appointed by the emperor.

The 1824 Constitution, albeit imposed, was advanced for its time: all men over twenty-five with a minimum annual income of 100 *mil-réis* were allowed to vote. Freemen could vote in the primary elections and the requirement for a minimum income did not exclude the poor, since the majority of workers earned more than 100 *mil-réis* per year. Illiterate people were also allowed to vote. The 1824 Constitution remained in effect until the end of the monarchy. A comparison of the data is noteworthy: before 1881, 50 per cent of the adult male population in Brazil voted, the equivalent of 13 per cent of the total population. In Great Britain, around 1870, 7 per cent voted; in Italy 2 per cent; in Portugal 9 per cent; in Holland 2.5 per cent; and in the United States 18 per cent. Universal male suffrage only existed in France and Switzerland.[28]

Nevertheless, for all its liberal pretensions, the 1824 Constitution concentrated power to a large degree in the hands of the emperor, maintaining an absolute monarchy through the mechanism of the Moderating Power, and it ignored the question of slavery. This was a reaction against the bill of 1823, which had sought to curtail the powers of the monarch. The constitution was imposed on the citizens of Brazil from above, and the country's wilful emperor personally oversaw every detail. Two years later, when he also succeeded to the throne of Portugal as Pedro IV, the emperor was to repeat this performance in relation to the Portuguese 1826 Constitution, this time provoking a national crisis. This was a personal style that was soon to become a national problem.

THE CONFEDERATION OF THE EQUATOR, 1831

Dom Pedro I's dissolution of the Constituent Assembly and imposition of a new constitution made waves. Furthermore, his new inner circle of bureaucrats and merchants were either Portuguese or had strong ties to Lisbon. In Pernambuco, for instance, a province known for its revolutionary disposition and republican and federalist leanings, there were new voices of protest, among them Friar Joaquim do Amor Divino, better known as Frei Caneca. With a humble background, and having been educated at the seminary in Olinda, he became a well-regarded intellectual and strong political activist. In 1824 a rebellion broke out in Pernambuco called the 'Confederation of the Equator'. It was initially set off by the appointment of an unwanted governor, but the movement also produced the first reaction to the absolutist and centralized politics of the government of Dom Pedro I. Those involved were striving for a republic based on Colombia's constitution, which at that time in South America most closely resembled that of the United States. The Confederation of the Equator had deep roots, dating back to the eighteenth century, to the *Guerra dos Mascates* of 1710–11, and to the Pernambucan revolution of 1817, both republican in nature. There were also internal divisions between the north of Pernambuco, where there was a concentration of sugar and cotton cultivation and populous villages, and the monocultures more typical of the south, a virtually exclusive sugar basin where settlements were no more than annexes of the estates.

Pernambuco had accepted the monarchy in the belief that the province's autonomy would be protected. However, the promulgation of the 1824 Constitution, with its excessive centralization, led to great frustration. Pernambuco was divided into two factions, one monarchist and the other liberal republican. The province was governed by the leader of the monarchist faction, Pais Barreto, who had been appointed by Dom Pedro I. Pais Barreto resigned under pressure from the liberals; and the republican Manuel Pais de Andrade, one of the important leaders of the revolt, was elected. The conflict, however, was not limited to the two men. When Dom Pedro I found out, he ordered that his appointee, Pais Barreto, be returned to the governership, a demand that was ignored. To demonstrate his power, Dom Pedro then sent warships to Recife, the capital of the province, to impose his rule. But the liberals remained steadfast in their support of Manuel Pais de Andrade and the revolt erupted. Dom Pedro tried to negotiate by appointing a different governor, but it was too late. On 2 July 1824 the revolutionaries proclaimed the independence of Pernambuco and invited the other provinces of the north and northeast to join them in the foundation of the 'Confederation of the Equator'. The hope was that the new independent federalist state would include the provinces of Piauí, Ceará, Rio Grande do Norte, Alagoas, Sergipe, Paraíba and Pernambuco. In fact, only a few towns in Paraíba, Rio Grande do Norte and especially Ceará joined the rebels in Pernambuco.

The confederate revolutionaries advocated the 'American system', which they considered 'the Enlightenment of the century', rather than that of 'old man Europe'. They emphasized federalism, characteristic of North American republicanism. Their revolutionary flag featured not only the two products of the region – cotton and sugarcane – but also representations of a republic and of federalism. The emperor condemned the rebels in a royal decree issued on 25 July 1824, and ordered their arrest. But the revolution continued.

On 12 September, Recife was attacked by land forces under the command of Pais Barreto, and the rebels were defeated. Some of the leaders were killed while others, including Frei Caneca, were arrested. The rebels in Paraíba met the same fate. Judicial proceedings to investigate the accused began in October 1824 and continued until April the following year. Of the hundreds of people who had taken part in the revolt in the three provinces, fifteen were condemned to death, including Frei Caneca. Although the executions put an end to the movement, they left a deep impression in Pernambuco, where the frustration was unabated. The people hoped the first constitution of the empire would be federalist, with administrative autonomy in the provinces. All the other provinces involved were pardoned by the emperor on 7 March 1825. This gesture, however, did nothing to conceal divisions, nor decrease resentment.

PROBLEMS IN THE PUBLIC AND PRIVATE LIFE OF THE EMPIRE

Meanwhile the emperor's private life was equally turbulent. In the lives of kings the separation between the public and private spheres is often tenuous. After all, royal births, weddings and deaths are all matters of state. Dom Pedro I was no exception. On 2 December 1825, Dona Leopoldina, the increasingly isolated wife of the emperor (ever since his trip to São Paulo he only had eyes for Domitila), gave birth to a son, the heir to the yearned continuity of the empire – the future monarch, Dom Pedro II.

The new prince held everyone's high hopes. On his father's side he was descended from a line of illustrious ancestors, immortalized in Portuguese literature. He was the nineteenth Duke of Bragança, a family closely related to the Capetians of France. On his mother's side he was related to Emperor Francis I of Germany, Austria, Hungary and Bohemia, and his wife Empress Maria Theresa. Francis I was the son of Leopold II, the emperor of Germany and brother of Marie Antoinette, Louis XVI's wife. Dom Pedro II's family tree stretched back to St Stephen, King of Hungary; to Philip II and Phillip IV; to the kings of Castile and Aragon; and to the kings of France. As a descendant of the royal houses of Bourbon, Habsburg and Bragança, his baptism was surrounded by an aura of exceptional mysticism. The ghosts of these kings, saints and madmen, emperors and adventurers, melancholy, romantic and illustrious princes, were to haunt the prince for the rest of his life.

Three months after the prince's birth, on 10 March 1826, his grandfather King Dom João VI died, aged fifty-nine, at the Palace of Queluz, allegedly from indigestion after a large supper. Dona Carlota Joaquina preferred not to be at her dying husband's side and, professing illness, left the palace and travelled to Lisbon. Before she left she made it quite clear that she favoured her second son, Dom Miguel I, as her husband's successor. Dom João VI had always wanted to be succeeded by Dom Pedro I, despite the fact that, as Emperor of Brazil, he was now officially considered a foreigner. However, true to his indecisive nature, before he died Dom João VI appointed his daughter Dona Isabel Maria as regent until such time as the 'legitimate heir' assumed the throne, but failed to mention who that legitimate heir was to be. Dona Isabel Maria immediately sent a committee to Brazil to greet Dom Pedro, who received the title Dom Pedro IV as the new King of Portugal. But the impasse continued because the Portuguese Constitution did not allow Dom Pedro to ascend the two thrones. The solution was to have Dom Pedro's daughter, Dona Maria da Glória, marry his brother Dom Miguel I. Whereas his mother, Dona Carlota Joaquina, was disliked in Portugal, Dom Miguel I had become increasingly popular since his return to Lisbon. Dom Pedro I, on the other hand, after declaring the independence of Brazil, was now virtually persona non grata in Portuguese territory.[29]

With the Portuguese succession still undecided, the emperor received another unexpected blow. On 11 December 1826 his wife, Dona Maria Leopoldina, died after a complicated birth. Her passing was accompanied by rumours that the emperor himself, because of his brutal treatment of her, had caused her death. Dom Pedro I's private problems now became extremely public. Maria Leopoldina's death led to much talk about the 'barbarous' prince – as she referred to him in letters to her sister Maria Luisa (who had been married to Napoleon) and to her father, the powerful Emperor Francis of Austria.

Contrary to popular belief, the princess's life had been anything but a fairy tale. She had played an important part in the independence process in 1822, but was then completely isolated at court. She began to write letters complaining about her husband and what she called 'this dreadful America'. She defended the people and stressed her sacrifice, but in the end the impression that remains is one of a melancholy princess without friends and no husband at her side. In her last letter, dated 8 December 1826, and addressed to Maria Luísa, she refers to her husband as a 'monstrous seducer' and no longer hides her resentment: 'He has just given me the latest proof of his negligence toward me, mistreating me in the presence of the very person who is the cause of all my afflictions.' She was referring to Domitila, the Marquesa de Santos, who now occupied all the young monarch's time. On 23 May 1824, Domitila had born Dom Pedro I a child, Isabel Maria, who was officially recognized as the emperor's daughter two years later and granted the title of Duquesa de Goiás.

NEW INDEPENDENCE, 1831

Meanwhile public life resumed in Brazil with elections to the Chambers taking place in late 1824 and the first meeting of the deputies in 1826. Although the sessions were initially hesitant, the opposition soon began to rally and press for social change. When new opposition newspapers were published, the emperor's reaction was to respond personally to specific articles. He also used his Moderating Power, dismissing ministers for the slightest slip or merely on a whim. His temperamental nature was more in evidence than ever as he continued to allow his private affairs to interfere directly in the affairs of state.

In foreign policy the monarch maintained his father's expansionist approach. The intention was to extend Brazil's southern frontiers to the banks of the River Plate. Brazil continued to wage war with Argentina for the control of Cisplatina. However, the emerging independence movement in the province was finally victorious, and the new nation of Uruguay was founded in 1825. Brazil and Argentina lost the war, resulting in very considerable financial losses for both.

Meanwhile the emperor's turbulent private life continued. After Leopoldina died, Dom Pedro I was then unfaithful to Domitila. By 1827 he had decided to remarry, to choose a new wife from one of the courts of Europe. The love affair with Domitila dragged on for another three years, but the emperor was firmly decided. His search for a new empress, however, proved to be harder than he had thought because his reputation as a temperamental husband was by now common knowledge in Europe. After three years of searching he finally married Amelia of Leuchtenberg, Princess of Bavaria. She was seventeen years old and her beauty, it was said, greatly improved the emperor's temper.

It became increasingly clear to local politicians that the emperor's interests were limited to his private life and political developments in Portugal. He constantly attempted to interfere in Portuguese affairs, sending dispatches to Lisbon signed as 'Dom Pedro IV'. He made no distinction between Brazilian finances and those of Portugal and his main concern appeared to be the question of the Portuguese succession. In 1827, when Dom Miguel I turned twenty-five, the legal age for assuming the regency, Dom Pedro I suggested his brother ascend the throne as provisional monarch to rule temporarily in his place. Dom Miguel, who had spent a long period in Austria, returned to Portugal in 1828, to the delight of his mother, Dona Carlota Joaquina, who saw in his return an opportunity to avenge past opponents. He was crowned king and his repressive reign began, during which many politicians were put to death and others fled the country.

By 1830 the situation in Brazil was reaching a critical point. Tension in Rio de Janeiro was exacerbated by a series of conflicts. From one side, the 1830 revolutions in Europe, which led to the fall of Charles X in France and the crowning of Louis-Philippe – the Citizen King who openly declared his sympathy for some of the ideas of the French Revolution – encouraged the Brazilian liberals to mobilize against the absolutist character of Dom Pedro I's government. From the other side, the murder of the journalist Libero Badaró in São Paulo, on 20 November, led to further anger on the part of the public and, above all, the press. Libero Badaró was an Italian who had settled in Brazil and become the owner of the opposition newspaper O *Observador Constitucional*, which argued that the imperial government was exercising a type of negligent authoritarianism. Articles exhorted Brazilians to break all links with any Portuguese monarch, including Dom Pedro himself. The rumour quickly spread that the man who had ordered the crime, a High Court judge named Cândido Japiaçu, had done so in collusion with the emperor. The liberal majority in the Chamber of Deputies confronted the government head-on, concluding the last session on 30 November with demands for constitutional reform.[30]

This was the mood of the country when Dom Pedro decided to visit Minas Gerais in an attempt to control the pro-federalist disturbances that had broken out there. Rumours were spreading that he was preparing an absolutist *coup d'état* and planning to shut down the Congress. On his return to Rio de Janeiro, on 11 March 1831, Dom Pedro received a mixed welcome. The Portuguese merchants organized festivities including bonfires, fireworks and flags flying the national colours. The liberals saw these celebrations as an affront to national dignity. Rioting broke out, known as the 'Night of Bottles', with the opponents hurling bottles at each other. The chaos in the streets – fighting, shouting insults, the destruction of property – lasted until the night of 16 March. While groups of liberals shouted 'Long live the constitution, the Assembly and freedom of the press', their opponents called on the emperor to become an absolute monarch. Historical documents include descriptions of Africans and Afro-Brazilians wearing jackets and hats with national ribbons. Order was restored on 17 March, but not for long.

The same day twenty-three deputies and one senator, Campos Vergueiro, drew up a formal document demanding that the emperor punish the Portuguese aggressors. The tension was such that Dom Pedro I's appointment of a new Cabinet composed only of Brazilians and his nomination of a new superintendent of police had virtually no effect. The atmosphere at court and in the provinces was 'electric', in the words of John Armitage,[31] with the newspapers pouring fuel on the fire. Even the moderates, who had previously attempted to calm things down, now joined in the general discontent. Putting their differences aside for the time being, the 'moderate' and 'exalted' liberals joined forces to overthrow the emperor. People in the streets took to using the same green and yellow ribbons that had been worn by the supporters of independence, while exalted liberals and republicans alike sported straw hats with a *sempre-viva*[32] in their buttonholes.

On 25 March, the anniversary of the constitution, rebellion broke out in the streets of Rio de Janeiro. Dom Pedro I, who was watching a military parade in the Campo da Aclamação, was confronted by people shouting 'Long live the constitutional emperor'. Public protests and tumult in the streets became a daily occurrence. But the straw that broke the camel's back came on 5 April when Dom Pedro dismissed his Brazilian ministers for failing to control the riots and appointed new ones from his inner circle of supporters. The next day a crowd of over four thousand men gathered in the Campo da Aclamação – which was rapidly becoming the most popular location for public unrest – and proceeded to spread throughout the city streets. They were protesting the dismissal of the Cabinet and the appointment of a new one, whose members' only qualification was their proximity to the emperor. There were shouts of 'Long live the constitution' and 'Long live Brazilian independence', as if these declarations were in fundamental opposition to the emperor. Rumours were rife. There were claims that constitutional guarantees had been suspended, that senators had been arrested, and even that some of the deputies had been killed. It was also rumoured that Dom Pedro I himself was planning a *coup d'état*, which only increased the tension and calls for a final break with the emperor.

In an effort to control the situation Dom Pedro I sent a manifesto to be read aloud in public, in which he declared himself to be a 'devoted constitutionalist' and gave his imperial word that nothing sinister had taken place. However, before the justice of the peace who was reading the declaration had finished, it was torn from his hands by protesters shouting 'Death to the Emperor' and 'Long Live the Federation and the Republic'. The Brazilian politicians now made a further attempt to calm the situation: three justices of the peace were sent to the palace of São Cristóvão to request the deposed ministers' reintegration. The sovereign refused, claiming his constitutional right. When they returned with the news of his refusal, the judges were greeted with shouts of 'Death to the traitor!' and 'Citizens to arms!'[33]

Pressure became so intense that the emperor decided to play his last card: he abdicated in favour of his son. It was in fact the only way of quelling the revolt while guaranteeing the continuity of the monarchy in Brazil. At 3 o'clock in the morning on 7 April the emperor's abdication was read out in public. The news was greeted ecstatically. Patriotic songs and civic hymns were sung amid cries of 'Pedro II, constitutional emperor of Brazil!' Dom Pedro I's last act was to appoint a tutor for his children who would remain in Brazil. Paradoxical as it may seem, he chose his old friend José Bonifácio, whom he had once exiled to France.

It turned out that Dom Pedro I was better at abdication than at ruling. Supercilious, he declared the situation was irrevocable: 'Everything is over between me and Brazil. Forever.' He returned to Portugal with his wife, assuming his previous title with the added words 'perpetual defender of Brazil'. He now put all his energies into fighting for the right of his daughter, Dona Maria da Glória, to succeed to the Portuguese throne.

In Brazil the atmosphere was one of euphoria. The abdication was seen as foundational, as an inauguration. Many considered it an exemplary revolution, because there had been no bloodshed. Others called it 'the regeneration of Brazil'. An entire historical memory was fabricated regarding the abdication, as if it represented a new era: one of real independence.[34] The date of 7 April became more symbolically important than that of 7 September, in terms of consecrating the public as actors in the political arena and the group of 'exalted liberals' who had managed – through informal means – to give voice to the country's citizens.

Nonetheless, once again the seeds had been sown for future discord. The new monarch was not yet six years old and the years to come were to see a series of regencies. Other people would have to govern in young Dom Pedro II's name, until he reached 'adulthood'. Further attempts at a citizens' federation were to be made and further uprisings were to occur. But now the noise was like an echo: the echo of voices from the other provinces of Brazil.

10

Regencies, or the Sound of Silence

It is said that the sound of silence can be deafening. The period of the regencies, which began in Brazil with the abdication of Pedro I in 1831, is a case in point. Brazil is an enormous country with vast, disparate regions that were virtually unknown to the court. From a distance they appeared settled and peaceful, and the impression was that this was how they would always remain. The political emancipation of 1822 was consolidated around the court in Rio de Janeiro, through the symbol of the monarchy and the idea of national unity. But the desire for autonomy in the provinces was strong. After the break with Lisbon, the unity imposed during the colonial period weakened. Two incompatible movements emerged: the centralizing impulse of the court and the desire for self-government in the provinces.[1]

The question was where the centre of sovereignty would be: in the provinces (and this would require a new constitutional pact) or in Rio de Janeiro. Many of the provinces rejected the centralization integral to independence; acceptance was not peaceful and unanimous. Pernambuco and Bahia, for example, were fully prepared to govern themselves. Although independence had established national unity around the figure of the emperor – 'that majestic fundament of social architecture, from the River Plate to the River Amazon' in the words of José Bonifácio – the struggle for federation would shake the country during the period of the regencies. After Dom Pedro I's abdication the instability increased. The situation was even more complicated because at the time of Dom Pedro's abdication, his son, Prince Pedro II, was just five years and four months old. Because he was so young, it was decided that he should live isolated in the palace of São Cristóvão, along with his two sisters – Francisca (Chica) and Januária. The new Prince Regent would only be able to take over the government when he reached the age of eighteen. That is why the 'depository of the hopes and aspirations of the nation' was to be carefully guarded. Thus a political vacuum was created that was to have serious consequences. On the one hand, the immediate practical and bureaucratic problem was solved by appointing Brazilian politicians to govern as regents in a succession of four regencies. Two of these were composed of a council of three (known as the 'triple regencies') and the other two of just one (known as the 'single regencies'). But, on the other hand, with no emperor ruling the country, the question of succession inflamed the provinces, which began to contest the legitimacy of the regents whose governments were seen as giving too much priority to Rio de Janeiro and the court. And the provinces made themselves heard, loud and clear.

First there was a general debate over the excessive political and administrative centralization imposed by Rio de Janeiro. Ideas of forming a federation and a republic were aired. And the debate was not restricted to parliament. A series of rebellions occurred in the provinces that, despite their different characteristics, had one thing in common: the demand for autonomy. Isolated from the centre of power and rejecting the direction Brazil had taken under Dom Pedro I, new leaders appeared with a fresh agenda for the country. Revolts like the *Cabanagem* in Pará, the *Balaiada* in Maranhão, the *Sabinada* in Bahia and the *Guerra dos Farrapos* in Rio Grande do Sul, as we shall see, revealed the potential danger, should the rebels unite behind a single cause.

Almost none of these uprisings were intended to overthrow the monarchy. In general they expressed impatience for the new emperor, Pedro II, to be crowned. But while the young prince was growing up, demands for autonomy from the provinces also grew. The new regents were under pressure to develop a political structure representing provincial interests, without endangering territorial unity or the centralized monarchy. With so much at stake, the period of the regencies was the most dynamic of the empire in terms of new political projects, proposals and forms of government. One wonders whether the palace, with its child monarch, had seemingly decreased in size, or whether the expansive four corners of the country had become increasingly distant. At any rate, Joaquim Nabuco[2] was later to comment: 'In Brazil the regency was, in fact, the republic. A provisional republic.'

THE CHILD EMPEROR AND
THE REGENCIES

As an institution, the regency was foreseen in the constitution and was thus the most legitimate means of maintaining continuity in light of the abrupt departure of the emperor, whose reign had lasted for fewer than ten years. Thus, when the Senate received the official news of Dom Pedro I's abdication they immediately elected a provisional regency made up of three senators: Francisco de Lima e Silva (a military officer with a long political career); Nicolau Pereira de Campos Vergueiro (a lawyer who had studied at Coimbra, a member of the *Paulista* group connected to the Andrada family, and now an influential politician); and José Joaquim Carneiro de Campos (the Marquis of Caravelas, who had also studied at Coimbra and was one of the signatories of the 1824 Constitution; he had succeeded José Bonifácio as Minister of Foreign Trade). The regents held opposing opinions, both in relation to groups they supported and in terms of politics: Francisco de Lima e Silva was considered a liberal, in favour of federalism; José Joaquim Carneiro de Campos and Nicolau Pereira de Campos Vergueiro were conservative, the latter considered a diehard centralist.

The government needed to take strong measures to appease the provinces as soon as possible. The regents acted fast, restoring the ministers dismissed by Dom Pedro I to their posts, summoning a Legislative Assembly to write a new body of laws, granting amnesty to all political prisoners and dismissing foreigners from the army, those deemed 'suspect and unruly'. To guarantee peace and demonstrate their goodwill, the regents drew up a manifesto calling for order and laying out new political and administrative measures. Even so, in Rio de Janeiro and some of the provinces, notably Bahia and Pernambuco, there were demonstrations against the Portuguese restoration party, which by then was advocating the return of the monarch.

Meanwhile, to promote the symbolic force of the young emperor, the Legislative Assembly acclaimed him Emperor of Brazil on April 9, just two days after the abdication. Once again the French artist Jean-Baptiste Debret was summoned to 'immortalize' the occasion, which was in reality no more than political expediency. The child was so small that when he was introduced from the balcony of the palace he had to stand on a chair so the crowd could see him waving his handkerchief. The political elite had now resorted to displaying the country's future stability incarnate in the form of the child monarch.

In appointing José Bonifácio de Andrada e Silva as young Pedro II's tutor, Dom Pedro I recognized the political maturity and intellectual qualities of his one-time friend, who had dared to confront Dom Pedro I during the 1823 Constituent Assembly. It was a dramatic moment and the former monarch knew he might never see his children again. To ensure their privacy and protect them from prevailing political unrest, the three royal children – the last members of the royal family remaining in Brazil – were taken to the São Cristóvão palace in Boa Vista, to keep them at a safe distance from the bustling capital centre. At the palace, the children's days were tedious, strictly scheduled with very few visitors allowed, and many lessons to be studied and learned. The future emperor's education was an absolute priority. He had to be kept in a calm environment, while outside the city was in a state of turmoil. There was even a suggestion that the young monarch should be taken to São Paulo, but it was rejected on the grounds that if he travelled he would attract unwanted attention.[3]

Dom Pedro I finally left Brazil on 13 April 1831, and his departure – 'the fall of the tyrant' – was celebrated in the streets. Meanwhile, although the young prince's authority was seriously endangered by the general unrest – uprisings and revolts throughout the country – he was nonetheless used as the mainstay of the regency's rule. The first announcements of the 'bloodless revolution' – the term used to refer to the abdication – referred to a constitutional monarch who would free the country from the authoritarianism of Portugal: 'Citizens! We now have a homeland; we have a monarch who is the symbol of our union, of the integrity of the empire who, taught by us, is receiving, almost from the cradle, the first lessons in American freedom, and learning to love Brazil, the country that gave him birth . . .'[4]

The political atmosphere was complex, with the main newspapers completely divided. In 1833 a journal called *Dom Pedro I* was founded, which defended the restoration, and a few months later another, called *Dom Pedro II*, which advocated the union of all parties against the return of the Portuguese monarch. The young emperor's name was already being used to defend a cause about which he understood nothing.

Little is known about the childhood of Brazil's second emperor. We have just a few portraits, and descriptions by his mediocre teachers of the monotonous daily routine of the boy and his sisters. In a letter of 8 May 1833 he wrote to his sister Dona Maria da Glória, now Queen of Portugal:

> Dear beloved sister. I am taking the opportunity of the visit to Paris of the brother of our Tutor, Sr. Antônio Carlos d'Andrada, to send you this letter and to give you news. It has been a long time since we have received news from you or from our dear mother . . . Here we make every effort to follow your example: Writing, Arithmetic, Geography, Drawing, French, English, Music and Dance divide our time; we work constantly to acquire knowledge and it is only these efforts that mitigate how sorely we miss you during our separation . . .[5]

Away from the family, all he had were studies, which, like the diligent heir that he was, he took very seriously.

FROM PROVISIONAL TO PERMANENT

The peaceful atmosphere did not extend beyond the palace walls. The provisional regency needed to take immediate action; simple decrees would no longer suffice. In Pernambuco, Bahia and Minas Gerais, Portuguese citizens were being attacked by Brazilian activists in a new wave of xenophobia. Elections for a new Assembly were held on 3 May 1831, with the objective of establishing the regency system. On 17 June the permanent triple regency was elected, made up of deputies José da Costa Carvalho, João Bráulio Muniz and Senator Francisco de Lima e Silva. José da Costa Carvalho was the Marquis of Monte Alegre. He had studied law at Coimbra and on his return had been elected deputy for the province of Bahia. He was also the founder of the journal O Farol Paulistano, the first periodical to be printed and published in São Paulo. João Bráulio Muniz was from Maranhão and had been a classmate of José da Costa Carvalho at Coimbra. They also worked together at the Farol Paulistano. Senator Francisco de Lima e Silva, Baron of Barra Grande, president of the province of Pernambuco between 1824 and 1825 and then senator of the empire, had fought in the brigade that suppressed the Confederation of the Equator.

This was a regency made up of moderate politicians, two of whom were from the Chamber of Deputies. They were members of the political elite in the service of the emperor; this was a government marked by its capacity for organizing the country's political structure and controlling unrest through negotiation. As we have seen, the three members of the regency had all been well educated and had long track records of public service. For them, the strengthening of the state and national union fulfilled not only their political goals but also their concrete objectives.[6] The composition of the regency was an attempt to centralize power and to balance opposing parties: members of the triumvirate represented states from the north (Maranhão), the northeast (Bahia) and the southwest (São Paulo).

Like its predecessor, the new regency had to act quickly. It started with less controversial measures, reforming the schools of medicine and surgery in Rio de Janeiro and in Salvador, converting them into universities and granting them greater autonomy. The prevalent spirit of nationalism led to broad support of this type of measure, since intellectual autonomy highlighted the country's independence. Measures aiming at a similar effect were to follow: the reorganization of the Judiciary and the establishment of trial by jury. The reform of the Legislature, limiting the Moderating Power of the regency and giving more power to senators and deputies over the Executive, was perhaps the one that had the most effect.[7]

The triple regency had yet more surprises in store, among them the creation of a National Guard to suppress uprisings and demonstrations. The guards were recruited from the provinces and were under the authority of the Ministry of Justice. The new institution was based on the French model in which enlistment was compulsory. All citizens between twenty-one and sixty who had the right to vote – an annual income of over 200 mil-réis for city dwellers and over 100 mil-réis for voters in rural areas, excluding, obviously, slaves – were obliged to enlist. However, because it was made up of relatively privileged members of society, the National Guard, rather than being a citizens' army, quickly became an instrument for maintaining order and suppressing local revolts. Furthermore, the political elites from the provinces chose the colonels and majors. The National Guard was so conservative and so active that it remained in service until the First Republic, mainly in rural areas of the country. Furthermore, because the National Guard was made of members of the elite, they did not mix with the general population as had occurred in the rebellions prior to independence and in the unrest in the provinces preceding the emperor's abdication. The National Guard (rather than the military) was considered a reliable repressive force, largely because of the background of its members.

But neither decrees nor new nominations could control the financial crises and uprisings threatening national unity. The three political parties confronted one another: the moderate party (or *chimangos*),[8] the exalted party (or *jurujubas*[9] and *farroupilhas*[10]) and the restoration party (or *caramurus*).[11] The restoration party, led by José Bonifácio, advocated Dom Pedro I's return from Portugal. During this time Padre Diogo Antônio Feijó – the man most associated with the regency period – began his political ascent. He was a deputy who had been nominated Minister of Justice, and was an arch-enemy of José Bonifácio and the *caramurus*. He accused them of trying to destabilize the regency in order to force Dom Pedro I's return to Brazil. In the midst of these accusations a revolt broke out in Rio de Janeiro on 3 April 1832, which José Bonifácio was accused of instigating. With the support of the Senate he maintained his post, but José Bonifácio's days were now numbered. He was accused of plotting against the regency, arrested, and sent to the island of Paquetá,[12] where he was confined to his summerhouse. Although he was absolved, he never managed to recover his political position and was to die a few years later in Niterói.[13]

Padre Diogo Antônio Feijó emerged all the stronger after his confrontation with José Bonifácio, yet with a series of problems. He too ended up losing his post as Minister of Justice. Furthermore, the revolt, which had started in Rio de Janeiro, began spreading to the provinces. There were uprisings all over the country and the old fear of Portuguese America becoming divided came back to haunt the government.

In 1832 the *cabanada* revolt broke out in Pernambuco, a province with a long history of rebellion. The revolt brought together Indians, escaped slaves, squatters and landowners, all prepared to fight against the 'Jacobins' and in favour of Dom Pedro I's return. The *cabanos* expressed very diverse interests and resisted bravely for four years: they formed a uniformed army and attacked to the sound of cornets, flutes and drums. By 1832 they were already considered masters of the woodlands in Pernambuco. They concentrated their efforts along the frontier with Alagoas. It was mainly the less well-off who expressed their bewilderment and dissatisfaction over Dom Pedro I's abdication.

Once again the symbolic power of the monarchy was manifest. However, rather than a real monarchy, the longing was for a mythical one, very distant from day-to-day reality. The return of the emperor may well have been a utopian dream, given the situation, but for the rebels it had concrete significance. The *cabanos* came from a wide variety of groups, all of whose interests had been affected by the abdication: military officers who wanted to maintain their posts; rural landowners who wanted to increase their power; bureaucrats who needed to keep their jobs in order to make a living; and the elite of Alagoas who had had more autonomy under the Crown. Above all, though, they came from the scrublands and the poverty-stricken interior, enslaved Indians and Africans who felt threatened by the new government. For all of them, restoration meant hope for the future and a return to the recent past.

The revolt was ruthlessly supressed in 1835 by Manuel de Carvalho Pais de Andrade, the same man who had proclaimed the Confederation of the Equator and now presided over the province. But the *cabanos* still resisted. The president organized a political alliance with neighbouring provinces and implemented a scorched-earth policy. The region controlled by the rebels was demarcated and anyone within its borders was automatically considered an enemy. Between March and May of that year it is estimated that 1,072 *cabanos* were arrested and 2,326 were killed. Luck turned, as did the hand of the clock, marking the countdown to the revolts.

THE AMENDMENT ACT OF 1834 AND THE FEIJÓ REGENCY

With uprisings occurring simultaneously in Rio de Janeiro, Pernambuco and Maranhão, the government had no choice but to change the rules of the game, at least at the legislative level. An amendment to the constitution was passed in 1834, aimed at limiting the powers of the central government. As early as 1831 radical changes, such as eliminating the Moderating Power and establishing a federal monarchy, had been considered. The final text of the 1834 amendment was less ambitious. It was based on the North American model, although not quite as bold. In addition to establishing a single regency, the 1834 amendment to the constitution dissolved the Council of State, created Legislative Assemblies in the provinces, made the court a neutral municipality (separate from Rio de Janeiro province), and maintained the lifetime term of senators.

The amendment, which was the result of protracted negotiations, was contradictory in that it concentrated power in the hands of a single regent, elected for a four-year mandate, while giving greater autonomy to the provinces through the new Assemblies. It also conceded greater powers to the presidents of the provinces, who were appointed by the regent on behalf of the emperor without a fixed term of office. In fact, they could be replaced at any time. The amendment was a faithful reflection of the state of the government, supporting neither side with conviction.

This was the situation when the first election for a single regent took place. Padre Diogo Antônio Feijó was elected. He was from São Paulo and a member of the moderate party. His regency began on 12 October 1835, and he was to remain in the post until 19 September 1837. Considering the fragile political situation, it was a reasonable term of office. Regent Feijó faced innumerable challenges. He had many political enemies, including the Church, because he did not support celibacy among the clergy. It was said at the time that few ministers could put up with his bad temper for long and there were constant changes of Cabinet. Instability seemed to have become the system of government, with the regent moving a small group of ministers from one post to another. But what really marked the first single regency was the outbreak of two serious conflicts in extreme parts of the country – the *cabanagem* in Pará and the *farroupilha* revolution in Rio Grande do Sul.

REVOLTS ON ALL SIDES: CABANOS IN THE DISTANT PROVINCE OF GRÃO-PARÁ

There can be no analysis of the regencies without discussing the series of rebellions that marked the period. Historians used to see them as 'nativist' – isolated events that reflected local discontent – but they have since come to be seen as a national phenomenon reflecting the deep divisions between the union and federalist parties. Anger at the centralization of power in Rio de Janeiro had been the cause of much of the political turbulence during the First Reign and had been responsible for Pedro I's abdication.

There were many minor uprisings of short duration, but there were a few with far more serious impact, creating panic among the regency elite barricaded in Rio de Janeiro. The first of these major rebellions was the *Cabanagem* in the distant northern province of Grão-Pará. The province had been one of the last to approve the declaration of independence, only doing so on 15 August 1823, and even then only under pressure.

The whole history of Grão-Pará was one of independence from the rest of the country. The region was first occupied at the beginning of the sixteenth century by Dutch and English settlers seeking spices, particularly *urucum*,[14] *guaraná*[15] and pepper seeds. The Portuguese only arrived in 1616, when they erected the Forte do Presépio, the first building in the city of Belém, at the time known as Santa Maria do Belém do Grão-Pará. In 1621 the captaincy of Grão-Pará and Maranhão (with the capital in São Luís do Maranhão) was created as a response to confrontations between the different European groups settled in the region and their difficulties in getting along with the local indigenous people. The government of the new captaincy was independent from the Brazilian state. The new captaincy was founded in order to create a direct link between the region and Portugal, which was interested in medicinal plants and the cultivation of sugarcane, cotton and cocoa.

In 1755 the powerful Portuguese statesman Marquis of Pombal founded the *Companhia Geral do Comércio do Grão-Pará e Maranhão*. It was created to develop and control commercial activity, including trade in African slaves, given the prohibition of enslaving the indigenous peoples of the region. Among other privileges the company was granted a monopoly of the slave trade and of the naval transport of all merchandise to the region for a period of twenty years. The company employees were officially considered to be in his majesty's service and were answerable directly to Lisbon. An additional advantage for the government was that its control of the company gave it the means to suppress the widespread practice of smuggling and tax evasion.

In accumulating so many privileges, the company also created resentment among the local elites, which was ignored by the Marquis of Pombal who wanted to protect his financial interests in the region.

With all of the company's activities, trade with Portugal, previously minimal, began to flourish. Ships of the *Companhia Geral do Comércio do Grão-Pará e Maranhão* left Belém weighed down with rice, cotton, cocoa, ginger, wood and medicinal plants; and this without including the slave-trafficking. Whereas in 1755 it was estimated that there were 3,000 African slaves in the region, between 1755 and 1777 the population of African slaves grew to 12,000, all of whom had been bought with company funds. They had been taken from their homes in Cacheu, Bissau and Angola.[16]

With the death of the King of Portugal, Dom José,[17] and the fall of his powerful minister the Marquis of Pombal, the period known as the 'turnabout' – a *Viradeira* – began. Dom José's daughter, Dona Maria I,[18] was opposed to all of the Marquis of Pombal's policies. In 1778 the queen not only cancelled the monopoly but closed the company itself. Grão Pará had already been separated from Maranhão four years earlier in 1774. Nevertheless, despite a few crises, trade between the region and Portugal continued to flourish from 1800 to 1817. Between 1796 and 1799, Pará and Maranhão combined were responsible for 13.6 per cent of the products exported to Portugal from all the regions that make up present-day Brazil. Between 1804 and 1807 this percentage rose to 19 per cent with the two captaincies occupying fourth place in the volume of exports.[19] In contrast to the areas of the country dominated by monoculture, the northern region offered an exotic variety of products to the European market including cocoa, coffee, rice, cotton, leather, cloves, cinnamon, *sarsaparilla*, *puxiri*,[20] indigo,[21] *urucum*, Brazil nuts and every imaginable variety of wood.[22]

During the independence period, as we have seen, the region Grão-Pará had a very different history from the rest of Brazil and was not inclined to accept the new political regime. A network of powerful families working in business and agriculture dominated the region. Furthermore, there was a large concentration of foreign immigrants and migrants from other parts of Brazil, creating a mixture of people, languages and cultures.[23] And, finally, the direct trade links to Portugal continued and there was little motivation to demonstrate loyalty to a government that had until then ruled a separate country. There was a great deal of resentment in Grão-Pará over its political exclusion from the decisions of the central government, which nevertheless imposed heavy taxes on the region's medicinal produce.

Like the revolt of 1832 in Pernambuco, the *Cabanagem* in Grão-Pará brought together distinct social groups, each of which had their own demands. The names of the two uprisings – *Cabanada* in Pernambuco and *Cabanagem* in Pará – both stem from the word *cabana*, the mud-and-wattle shacks that served as homes for the indigenous peoples, mestizos and Africans. But, unlike what had occurred in Pernambuco, in Pará these groups confronted the local elites directly.

The revolt began with a bang. On 7 January 1835, under the leadership of Antônio Vinagre, the rebels – who included groups of *cabanos*, *tapuios*,[24] indigenous peoples and Africans – attacked the army barracks and the governor's palace in Belém, assassinating the governor of the province and seizing a large amount of weaponry. They then appointed a new governor – Félix Antônio Clemente Malcher – who at the time was a political prisoner because of his stance against the regime. But he was not to last long in the post. With the increasing radicalization of the revolt, Malcher, a sugar plantation owner, ended up betraying his allies, ordering them to lay down their arms, return to work, and swear allegiance to the regency. He was deposed on 19 February the same year. After this, tempers gradually cooled off and the *cabanos* retreated, leaving Belém in July.

But there was another outbreak in August when Mariana de Almeida, a Portuguese woman, was murdered. She was the seventy-year-old widow of a Portuguese merchant. It was said that her body was dragged through the streets and exposed to public abuse over her loyalty to Pedro I. The revolt was one of the most violent in Brazilian history. The leaders were accused of being insubordinate, evil anarchists. It cannot be denied that the *cabanos* committed some extreme acts. Slaves tied their former masters to tree trunks and whipped them; Indians who had been press-ganged killed their commanding officers and took their military ranks (they were all lieutenant-colonels) and then proceeded to destroy the district of Nazaré.

As the movement became more radical, the Africans and indigenous peoples acquired greater autonomy and the role of the African leaders increased. The slaves made all the difference during the *Cabanagem*. Their participation led to the *cabanos* being referred to as 'evil', and also to the recurrent fear that an event similar to the Haitian revolution could occur in Brazil. There was nothing 'naturally evil' about the *cabanos*; in fact, they were fighting against what they saw as a lack of religion on the part of the Portuguese usurpers of Belém, whom they accused of following orders from the court in Rio de Janeiro. They also saw the president of the province as a foreigner and accused him of being a Mason.

The movement spread like wildfire across what are today the states of Pará and Amazonas. The government's reaction to such 'audacity' was to dispatch four warships to Belém in February 1836 with instructions to take the city. On 13 May the imperial troops regained control of the area. This did not, however, stop the revolt. Between 1836 and 1840 the rebels penetrated the interior of the province and their demands became more radical: the end of slavery and the establishment of local autonomy. They also reaffirmed their hatred of the Portuguese and all other foreigners. During the next ten months the local elite lived in terror of the *cabanos* gaining control. Hidden in the forests, the rebels fought on until 1840, at which point they were entirely exterminated. The loss of life was appalling, estimated at between 30 per cent and 40 per cent of the population, at the time numbering 100,000. Thousands were also taken prisoner and loaded into the imperial navy's corvettes – especially the *Denfensora* – which were transformed into prison ships.

Although a few of the *cabanos*, strange as it may seem, maintained a mysterious loyalty to the young emperor, Pedro II, the vast majority demanded a political alternative to the centralized Brazilian Empire. Although they called themselves 'patriots', the term referred neither to being Brazilian nor to the government's political and national plans. The indigenous peoples, the African slaves and mestizos, all of whom came from very different cultures, created new forms of identity that had little or nothing in common with the European model of the government in Rio de Janeiro.[25] In fact, the conflict reflected an extreme situation of cross purposes: a combination of attitudes from the colonial past and the empire between 1822 and 1840 attempting to efface the enormous differences that existed in that region. Euclides da Cunha,[26] a very influential Brazilian thinker, defined the Amazon as a region 'on the margins of history' and the *cabanos* ('shack dwellers') as representing the 'increasingly wider gap between the inhabitants of the interior and those of the coast'.[27] Perhaps this was an alternative history, in conflict with that of the Brazilian Empire. In this case, the relationship seemed more like a litigious separation.

FROM FEIJÓ TO PEDRO DE ARAÚJO LIMA: A NEW AGENDA FOR THE REVOLTS

By 1837 the regent was finding himself increasingly isolated in Rio de Janeiro. His political support was so precarious that on 19 September he was forced to return to his home in São Paulo and resign, allegedly due to illness. His fall was the result of increasing pressure from the conservative opposition and of the revolts in the provinces. The regency passed to his political opponent Pedro de Araújo, the Marquis of Olinda, who had been minister for the empire since September 1837. The elections the following year confirmed Pedro de Araújo – whose temperament was the very opposite of that of the explosive Padre Diogo Antônio Feijó – as regent. Before he was confirmed in the post, Pedro de Araújo had founded the Colégio Pedro II, a school in Rio de Janeiro, which was soon to become the model for Brazilian education. Araújo Lima had also founded the Instituto Histórico e Geográfico Brasileiro in 1838, another institute that was to become a key element in the imperial policy of Dom Pedro II, and the Escola Militar in 1839. Nevertheless, at the time, the measures were not appreciated. It seemed superficial to give priority to such matters while there was the danger of the provinces in the extreme north and south of the country seceding from the Union.

Pedro de Araújo's most significant measure was to put an end to the liberal policies of the previous regencies. The criminal prosecution code, which had conceded judicial autonomy to the provinces, was eliminated. And another constitutional amendment was drawn up, that of 12 May 1840. The objective was clear: to put an end to the autonomy of the provinces and municipalities and maintain the regents' control, especially of the Judiciary. They wanted to halt the nationwide revolts once and for all. These were the 'backward-looking' measures of Pedro Araújo Lima's government. But it was by no means easy to suppress the revolts that were breaking out, sprouting like mushrooms in the north, northeast and south of the country.

POLITICAL MOVEMENTS HAVE COLOUR: THE REVOLT OF THE MALÊS AND THE SABINADA

Although the 1824 Constitution declared all free men equal, including freed slaves, in practice the descendants of slaves were systematically excluded from all the benefits of society. Not by coincidence, during this period people of African descent began to take to the streets demanding to be included in the emerging new nation.

The turbulence began in Bahia – a province that traditionally aspired to political autonomy – with great popular support. In 1798, as has been seen, the Bahia conspiracy had contested the hegemony of the Portuguese Crown. The province had only recognized Brazil's independence on 2 July 1823, almost a year after independence had been declared in Rio de Janeiro. Between 1820 and 1830 a series of revolts broke out. During the first half of the nineteenth century, the establishment of *quilombos* and the practice of *candomblé* became widespread and intertwined. In 1826, on the outskirts of Salvador, a group of slaves who had taken refuge in the Urubu *quilombo* started an uprising that provoked an outburst of violence. The aim was nothing less than to invade the town, murder the white population and free all the slaves. Government troops were quick to react, besieging the *quilombo*. The inhabitants resisted ferociously under the leadership of a woman, Zeferina, who confronted the invaders armed with a bow and a quiver of arrows. In the document, which registered the destruction of the Urubu *quilombo*, the word '*candomblé*' appears for the first time. It was used by the Count of Ponte in his reference to the refuge of the rebel slaves.[28] The revolt had been suppressed, but the governor of the province was left in no doubt about one thing: henceforth, in Bahia, religion would be a fundamental element of the political organization of the slave and former slave population.

What in other provinces – such as Minas Gerais – was merely a rumour became a reality in Bahia, with the slave revolt spreading terror throughout the province. The turbulence lasted throughout the first half of the nineteenth century. Between 1820 and 1840 the province was witness to military revolts, anti-Portuguese uprisings, rebellions demanding a federation, and crowds going on the rampage, with the destruction of public and private property. Poor people and slaves took a major part in them all, both in Salvador and in the towns of the Recôncavo. Between 1807 and 1835 the province's slaves were responsible for an extraordinary sequence of large-scale revolts in the *engenhos*, on the plantations and in the fish markets, both in the capital and in the Recôncavo. These revolts had certain characteristics typical of slave struggles in Bahia: cooperation between rural and urban slaves; the concentration of large numbers of Africans from the same ethnic group, with a shared cultural and religious identity; and the involvement of the *quilombos*, whose number was rapidly increasing in the suburbs of Salvador, providing refuge for escaped slaves and vibrant centres for the practice of the African religions.[29]

In May 1807 a group of slaves sparked off a cycle of revolts in Bahia that were instigated by a concentration of rebels from a specific ethnic group – which may or may not have been joined by other groups – with a strong religious bond, Islam. The slaves that planned the 1807 uprising were Africans from the north of what is today Nigeria, a region occupied mainly by Hausa. They were prepared to take their revolt beyond the captaincy's borders. The revolt began on 28 May, during the celebrations of Corpus Christi, when the slaves set fire to the customs house where the slaves imported from Africa were received, and to a church in the district of Nazaré. The idea was to distract the troops' attention. The slaves would then invade the town from the *quilombos* on the outskirts of Salvador. But that was not all. The plan was to mobilize blacks and mulattoes, poison the white population, burn statues of saints in the public squares, and then proceed to Pernambuco to liberate the slaves of the Hausa ethnic group. The struggle would continue until all the whites were dead and an Islamic kingdom had been established in the interior of the region.[30]

However, before the revolt began the plans were denounced to the governor. The punishments were harsh: the leaders were arrested, the slaves were sentenced to be whipped at the pillory, all African gatherings and festivities were outlawed, and the freedom of movement of freed slaves in Salvador and the Recôncavo region was forbidden. But a precedent had been established and the Hausa were well organized. After their defeat, large numbers escaped to *quilombos*, which were ever increasing in the forested areas around the city, where they bided their time until a new opportunity arose.

In 1814 the Hausa attacked again. During the second revolt they launched a series of attacks between February and April that grew more and more violent. The assaults were commanded from the *quilombos*, both in the Recôncavo and in the villages surrounding Salvador. In May the governor received another denunciation: the Hausa were planning to carry out the same plan that had failed in 1807. But this time they were better organized.[31] They had supplied their arsenal with gunpowder, cane for making bows, and iron arrowheads, all concealed in the woods. Furthermore, unprecedented numbers of Africans from other ethnicities had joined the movement, including mulattoes and *crioulos*.[32]

Although the Hausa were defeated once again in 1814, the government's victory could not conceal the fragility of the slave regime in Bahia. The slaves continued to rise up against their owners and the number of attacks increased, especially in the *engenhos* in the Recôncavo. In 1816, Santo Amaro, in the heart of Bahia's Recôncavo region, was terrorized by a new revolt: for four days the town was attacked, *engenhos* were burned, and whites, and any blacks who refused to join the movement, were put to death. The uprising was rapidly suppressed but the terror it put into the hearts of the landowners was not so easily subdued.

In 1835, more than two decades after the first rebellion, the largest of the slave revolts broke out in Salvador.[33] This time the attack came from inside the city, and it was terrifying. In the early hours of 25 January, groups of slaves and freemen armed with clubs, knives and working tools, fought soldiers and civilians in the streets for over three hours. Once again religion was an inextricable part of the revolt. Many of the rebels fought wearing *abadás*, the white tunics worn for prayer by African Muslims, and amulets inscribed with verses from the Koran and prayers for their protection.

The rebellion was led by the *Sociedade dos Malês* (Society of Malês) – the name by which the African Muslims in Salvador were known. Their motivation was both religious and political. Islam was exclusively an African religion in Brazil. It was not restricted to any ethnic group and thus had the potential to bring together slaves and freemen of different origins in the fight against slavery. It was a key factor in the mobilization and integration of the rebels due to its capacity to provide a common language and minimize the ethnic and cultural differences within the African community.

The Malê uprising was aimed at establishing Bahia for Africans and was meant to shake up the city of Salvador. The plan was not to occupy the city, but rather to create chaos with lightning attacks against army barracks, churches and government buildings. It observed the Islamic rules for military actions: the rebels did not invade private residences, kill slave-owners or set fire to the city. They only fought against the military forces that were sent against them. The Malês had high hopes for the revolt. They planned to descend on the Recôncavo region, where the majority of slaves were concentrated, and mobilize the captives on the sugar plantations.

The Malê uprising was not only the largest slave rebellion in Bahia, but the largest in Brazil. It was also the last. The rebels considered the 1835 revolt a slave rebellion; nonetheless, it turned into a conflict between religions and ethnicities, and between slaves, coopted by their owners, and rebels. Seventy rebels died during the confrontations and after their defeat around five hundred were punished with death, whipping or deportation.[34] There were several reasons for the failure of the revolt: once again there were denunciations, the secret escaped, and the revolt was forced to begin before the established date. It was also weakened by the lack of unity between *crioulos*, *pardos* and Africans. But the decisive factor was the unity of their enemies. The entire free population of Bahia – white and mulatto, rich and poor – either through common interests or through fear, opposed the insurrection. But although the rebellion was suppressed, the idea that freedom from the condition of slavery was within their grasp lived on among the captives of Bahia.

The turbulence in Bahia continued, with the participation of the middle classes, the military and the poor urban population. Anti-Portuguese sentiment was strong due to the Portuguese monopoly on trade and on the highest posts in the government and in the army. The situation had become more critical with the 1834 amendment that limited the autonomy of the provinces and then again with Padre Diogo Antônio Feijó's resignation from the regency in 1837.

With discontent at fever pitch, all that was needed was an event to trigger people's anger. The poor were demanding greater participation in society, the military an increase in wages, and the middle classes greater control of commerce. The discontent brought together government employees, artisans, tradesmen, officers and soldiers, as well as freed slaves. They shared a common hatred of the Portuguese and common access to the urban space that was shared by rich and poor, whites and Africans, *pardos* and *crioulos*. The governor of the province was well aware of the climate and wrote to the newspapers warning that a 'Tumult Party'[35] which sympathized with the revolts in Pará and Rio Grande do Sul was being formed. But he assured the public there was no need for concern, as everything possible was being done to make sure the 'Hydra didn't raise its head'.[36]

But the Hydra did raise its head. On the evening of 6 November 1837, officials from the artillery corps – fearing the introduction of compulsory enlistment to fight against the separatist movement in the south (the *farroupilhas*) – left the São Pedro fort and occupied the surrounding areas. They were joined by civilians, including Francisco Sabino Vieira and João Carneiro da Silva Rego. The next day, having taken control of the city, they convened a special session of the Municipal Chamber where they passed an act legalizing the movement. This was the start of the *Sabinada* revolt, which took its name from one of its leaders, Francisco Sabino. A document was drawn up with 105 signatures, declaring the province 'entirely and perfectly disconnected from the central government in Rio de Janeiro' and henceforth 'a free and independent state'. The convening of a Constituent Assembly was planned and the lawyer Inocêncio da Rocha Galvão was appointed president with Francisco Sabino as his first secretary. But since Inocêncio da Rocha Galvão was living in exile in the United Sates, Francisco Sabino became the de facto head of the province.

It is interesting to note that, a few days later, a new document – an amendment – was signed, this time by just twenty-nine people. It stated that independence of the province was only to last until the new emperor came of age. (Some people called the amendment 'a slip of the pen'.) Thus, despite the declaration of autonomy, the movement was loyal to the monarchy and the future emperor. The movement highlighted two important aspects of the regency period: the deep-rooted desire in Bahia for autonomy and the support still felt for the mystique that surrounded the prince and the monarchy, even during times of crisis.

Meanwhile, Francisco de Souza Paraíso, the deposed president of the province, and his commander-at-arms, Luís da França Pinto Garcez, took refuge in the Recôncavo region, from where they began to mobilize troops, mainly from the National Guard. In March 1838 the imperial government ordered them to besiege the capital. Under siege, Salvador first suffered from lack of livestock, and then from the damage caused by a fire that broke out in the city. Demoralized by the lack of food, the rebel leaders declared a truce in return for impunity. Their petition fell on deaf ears. The repression that followed was severe, including the suspension of all the prisoners' rights and many of the rebels being sent into exile. Francisco Sabino was captured on 22 March in the residence of the French consul.

The official reaction was, as always, exemplary. According to official data, 1,258 rebels and 594 soldiers died in combat, and a further 2,989 rebels were captured, most of whom were imprisoned on-board ships belonging to the imperial navy. A total of 1,520 men were deported to Rio de Janeiro and Rio Grande do Sul to await judgement, and all the freed slaves were deported to Africa.[37] But a different destiny awaited Francisco Sabino. An imperial decree signed on 22 August 1840 declared an amnesty, and he was sent to Goiás where he became involved in local politics. He was later deported to Mato Grosso, where he died in 1846.[38]

It is not easy to understand a separatist revolt that brought together military officers, tradesmen, liberal professionals, slaves and freemen, and that was also loyal to the monarchy. Francisco Sabino himself was *mulatto*, a descendent of enslaved Africans, and that is why they made an example of him. Between 1798, the year of the Bahia conspiracy, and 1838, the year of the *Sabinada*, there had been forty years of revolts, slave uprisings, sackings and lootings in Bahia. The participation of slaves, blacks, *pardos* and free mulattoes in a province dominated by slavery shows that the revolts against the authorities were also a question of origin and colour.

THE GUERRA DOS FARRAPOS: A LONG AND PERSISTENT REVOLT ON THE COUNTRY'S SOUTHERN FRONTIER

Even with the end of the Sabinada rebellion, the regent could not sleep well: a new revolution in the south of Brazil had become a serious issue. The motives were the same; only the places had changed. There was condemnation for the concentration of power in the court, and there was support for the re-establishment of the autonomy of the provinces. The uprising is known as the war of the *Farrapos* – the ragamuffin war – or the *Farroupilha* revolution, because fighting first broke out between Brazilians loyal to the government and poverty-stricken rebels labelled *farrapos* ('ragamuffins') due to their sparse, threadbare clothing. In fact the movement was not just made up of the peasants who worked on the ranches. It included landowners and cattle-breeders and people from across the entire social spectrum.[39]

The *Farroupilha* rebellion is yet another demonstration that Brazil has many different histories. The extreme south had been incorporated into the colony relatively late and shared a border with a territory that was strategically essential and changed hands many times: the region that gave access to the River Plate basin. The territory had been initially occupied in 1626 by Jesuits from Paraguay who claimed it for Spain and set about establishing missions and villages for the indigenous peoples. With the arrival of the bandeirantes, the Jesuits left, leaving behind them a special breed of cattle known as *chimarrão*. In 1680 the Portuguese Crown took over the territory and founded the colony of Sacramento in what was later to become the independent state of Uruguay.

The Spanish frequently invaded the area, only for the Portuguese to take it back. After all, they considered it an extension of their territory in the south. At the end of the seventeenth century the Jesuits returned, took over the area once again, and founded the Missions of the Seven Peoples.[40] But the Jesuits and the Guarani Indians were defeated by Portuguese and Spanish troops in the *Guerra Guaranítica*, which was waged between 1753 and 1756 after the Jesuits and Guarani refused to be relocated to Spanish territory on the western side of the Uruguay river. An agreement was then signed granting the Missions of the Seven Peoples to Portugal and the colony of Sacramento to Spain. Meanwhile, many of the treaty's articles were annulled, leading to frequent skirmishes and direct conflicts between the two countries over the ownership of cattle and land. The Portuguese Crown officially incorporated the territory into its domains due to the vital importance of the River Plate for Brazilian commerce, the need to prevent the smuggling of silver from Potosí and, above all, for its strategic military importance.

The discovery of gold in Minas Gerais in the seventeenth and eighteenth centuries had created a considerable demand for draft-animals and beef. As a result the situation in the south began to change with the arrival of muleteers and cattle dealers who drove herds of cattle and mules back to Minas Gerais. Many of the muleteers settled in the south and became cattle breeders, petitioning the Crown to be granted ownership of the land. It was in the Crown's interest to settle farmers in the region along Brazil's southern border. In 1737 the government officially established the Southern Department due to the need to stave off the frequent attacks from the Spanish on the colony of Sacramento. The Crown also granted land to military officers, as well as distributing *sesmarias*[41] to the cattle breeders, providing incentive for the creation of large ranches, which acted as a further deterrent to the Spanish.

At the end of the eighteenth century the region began to produce jerked beef – salted and dried meat – which soon became the national diet for slaves. As has been seen, in 1820, with the help of the ranchers, Dom João VI defeated the Spanish and incorporated the eastern region – the *Banda Oriental* – into Portuguese America, naming it the Province of Cisplatina. Due to its distance from the capital and its strategic military importance, the province enjoyed a relative degree of autonomy.

But things changed after independence and the concentration of power in the hands of the *Carioca* elite. The landowners in the south resented the high taxes levied on cattle, on land and, above all, on dried meat.[42] On the other hand, the loss of the province of Cisplatina, in 1828, after the creation of the independent state of Uruguay, came as a severe blow. When General Bento Gonçalves complained that 'they have transformed Rio Grande into a hostelry for the empire', he was expressing the general resentment of a people who felt their role had been reduced to supplying meat for the empire and defending its southern borders.

Farroupilhas (or *farrapos*) was the name of the groups from Rio Grande who rebelled against the imperial government. The term had been used pejoratively for at least ten years in reference to supporters of the Rio Grande liberal party, which opposed the central government. The nickname caught on and became a badge of pride, so much so that in 1832 the *farroupilha* party was founded whose manifesto declared its opposition to all the Portuguese who held high ranks in government and in the army. Many believed the only way of achieving autonomy was to create an independent state. The movement drew in a wide range of the population, including ranch-owners, military officers, abolitionists and even slaves, who saw in it a chance for their liberation. At the beginning not all the *farroupilhas* were republicans and federalists, but the chain of events eventually made them set their differences aside and adopt those views. Many of the leaders of the movement were Masons, including Bento Gonçalves, who adopted the improbable codename 'Sucre'.[43]

The general feeling in the extreme south of the country was one of impotence and injured pride. The time had come to take up arms again, and this time against the imperial government. The long war against the central government to create a separate republic in the south began on 20 September 1835, and was to last for almost ten years, until 1 March 1845, five years into the reign of Dom Pedro II. The movement was so important that it influenced liberal movements in São Paulo, as well as the Sabinada, in Bahia. It was an integral part of the history of the Brazilian Empire.

'The Centre exploits the South' became the slogan of the *farroupilhas*. And while preparing to go to war with the rest of Brazil, relations with the neighbouring newly created state of Uruguay oscillated between friendly and hostile. There were close family links between the inhabitants of the two regions. Bento Gonçalves, for example, was married to a Uruguayan. At times friendly overtures were made in an attempt to increase trade; at others, hostility towards the Spanish reigned. After all, the Spaniards had never ceased in their efforts to change the frontiers in the region.[44]

The contradictions were such that when the revolt broke out in September, Bento Gonçalves made a declaration to the periodical *Recopilador Liberal*[45] explaining that the war was to defend the province's freedoms, which were under threat. At the same time, he reaffirmed his loyalty to the monarchy, to the 'maintenance of the throne of our young emperor and the integrity of the empire'.[46]

During the ten-year war, the *farroupilhas* won and lost innumerable battles. On 11 September 1836 they proclaimed the foundation of the Rio-Grandense Republic. The act was ratified by the Municipal Chamber of Piratini,[47] which declared the independence of the province of Rio Grande do Sul and appointed Bento Gonçalves as president. Piratini would be the new capital. The government was to be republican, with federative ties to all other Brazilian states, which would in turn commit to the same form of government. This was a dramatic about-turn for the movement, which had until then declared its loyalty to the Crown. Nevertheless, the newly created state maintained two fundamental features of the empire: restricted franchise and slave labour.

During this long war a few participants acquired near mythical status. One of them was Bento Gonçalves, who on two occasions made spectacular attempts to escape from jail. In one of them, he dug a tunnel from the cell with the other prisoners, but when his fellow-fighter Pedro Boticário proved to be too fat to get through, he stayed behind in solidarity. On another occasion, when he was imprisoned in the Forte do Mar, in Bahia, he escaped by sea, swimming out to a boat where his comrades were waiting for him. Another legendary revolutionary was the Italian Giuseppe Garibaldi – later one of the heroes of Italian unification – who, during the conquest of Santa Catarina (the province to the north of Rio Grande), managed to transport two ships overland, drawn by oxen, all the way to the estuary of the Capivari river. It was there that he met the beautiful – and equally legendary – Anita, his partner in love and war.

But the war dragged on for too long and the cost in energy, money and men was very high. Towards the end of the conflict slaves were enlisted to fight on the battlefields alongside their owners, in exchange for their freedom. By 1840 the imperial government had managed to contain all the other rebellions that had broken out in the country, and was now able to concentrate its forces on fighting against the *farroupilhas*, although peace was still a long time coming. The Baron of Caxias finally put an end to the war. He was to become a central figure during Pedro II's reign, when he became known by the well-earned but somewhat ironic soubriquet 'the Pacifier'. The ceasefire was declared on 28 February 1845, with the signing of the treaty of Poncho Verde. The revolutionaries in the south called the treaty an 'honourable peace' as it met a number of their demands: the debt accumulated by the province during the conflict would be paid by the empire; the officers of the *farroupilha* army were incorporated into the imperial army, maintaining their rank; the slaves who had fought in the war were granted their freedom; the safety of individuals and their property was guaranteed; all prisoners of war were released; and, above all, the rebels were allowed to freely elect the president of the province.

The *farroupilha* was the last of the revolts to be suppressed during the regency period. The war and its leaders were to become fundamental elements in the construction of the identity of Brazil's southern provinces and, later on, states.[48] But the regency period was to witness yet another revolt, which started after the *farroupilha* revolution had begun. This time the revolt broke out in the extreme north of the country, in the distant province of Maranhão, which had once been a part of the state of Grão-Pará. The *Balaiada* rebellion began in 1838 and, once again, galvanized the lower rungs of the socioeconomic hierarchy.

THE *BALAIADA*: THE MARGINALIZED OF THE NORTH UNITE AGAINST THE CENTRAL GOVERNMENT

In the past Maranhão had had a direct link to Portugal. This special relationship was to significantly influence its politics and its relationship with the rest of the empire. During the entire colonial period, with the exception of the years 1652–4, Maranhão, along with the captaincies of Ceará, Grão-Pará and Amazonas, had formed the colonial state of Maranhão and Grão-Pará, which had its own administration.[49] The seat of government was in São Luís do Maranhão and all administrative, financial and political questions were broached directly with Lisbon. Although the region had much in common with the rest of Brazil, this vast area maintained its own identity. They shared the official language, had large estates run on slave labour (mostly located along the coast), and were considered Roman Catholic – along with widespread practice of other religions among the slaves and indigenous populations – but their loyalty was to only one sovereign: the King of Portugal. The region had much closer ties to Africa and Europe than it did to the other Brazilian captaincies.

During the reign of Dom José I (1750–77), the Marquis of Pombal introduced major changes. The 1750 Treaty of Madrid redrew the borders between the Spanish and Portuguese colonies. In the south, Uruguay was incorporated into Castile, and in the north, the whole of what is today the Brazilian Amazon was given to Portugal. The capital of the state was moved from São Luís to Belém and the state itself was renamed Grão-Pará e Maranhão. After the Marquis of Pombal's government outlawed the enslavement of 'natives', the region became a centre for the Atlantic slave traffic. At the height of its wealth in the nineteenth century, Belém would be the capital of the whole region, which stretched from the west of Brazil's northeast to the Amazon basin.

Between 1772 and 1774 the state was divided into two states, but continued to be subordinate to the court in Lisbon.[50] They were the state of Grão-Pará and Rio Negro[51] in the extreme north and the state of Maranhão and Piauí in the mid-north. The two states were only integrated into Brazil in 1811. It was no coincidence, then, that the provinces of Pará and Maranhão were the last to accept independence and the new Brazilian Empire, which they only did in 1823. They had no desire to become 'Brazilians'.

To complicate matters even further, after Brazilian independence in 1822, Maranhão began to suffer from the same ailment that plagued the other provinces in the country: heavy taxation from the court in Rio de Janeiro with very little return. However, the revolt had its own characteristics: most of the participants were peasants protesting against the owners of local estates. The province was undergoing a period of crisis, since the price of its main product, cotton, had fallen due to increasing competition on the international market. Still, there was no reduction in the taxes levied by the central government and the poverty was becoming unsustainable.

The group that suffered most were the workers – farmhands, cowherds and slaves – and they were the first to mobilize in protest against the injustices that plagued the region. But they were not the only segment of the social hierarchy that was dissatisfied. The liberal professionals began to demand changes in the rules for local elections. To this end they founded a newspaper – the *Bem-te-vi*[52] – to broadcast republican and federative principles. Mutual dissatisfaction brought the urban middle classes and rural labourers together in a common cause.[53]

The revolt, which began in 1838 with neither a large amount of followers nor any clearly established goals, took its name from its leader: Manuel Francisco dos Anjos Ferreira, who was nicknamed *Balaio* (basket). He was a basket-maker and had been a victim of police brutality. Local police had raped two of his daughters and had gone unpunished. He reacted by gathering a small group of men and began to take his vengeance, terrorizing the interior of Maranhão.

But what sparked off the revolt was the arrest of José Egito, a local politician with ties to the *cabanos* in Pará. On 13 December 1838 his brother, Raimundo Gomes, stormed the prison where José Egito was held, the Vila de Manga, and set him free. Raimundo Gomes then asked Balaio for his support, which he readily gave, and the rebels set about destroying and sacking estates. In 1839 they seized the city of Caxias.[54] They proceeded to organize a provisional government and adopt two emergency measures: the deactivation of the National Guard, which was seen as representing the military arm of the rural landowners, and the expulsion of all Portuguese residents from the city. From then on the movement became more radical. Cosme Bento, who was the head of a local *quilombo* and had a following of three thousand Africans, was the new leader.

To confront the rebels the regency government sent Colonel Luís Alves de Lima e Silva[55] to Maranhão. The colonel had considerable experience; he had fought in the war of independence in Bahia, in 1823, and in the war in Cisplatina, between 1825 and 1828. Many middle-class people who had supported the rebels were now frightened at the radical direction the revolt was taking. They began to support the imperial forces. The insurrection was finally suppressed in 1841, with an appalling death toll: 12,000 rural peasants and slaves were killed in combat. The young emperor granted amnesty for the prisoners of war and Luís Alves de Lima e Silva was awarded with the title of Baron of Caxias in recognition of his victory.

Although shaken to its very foundations by the revolts occurring all over the country, the empire did not fall. But the fear of further insurrections and separatist movements loomed like a spectre. None of Brazil's former neighbours – the Spanish viceroyalties of New Spain, New Granada, Peru and Rio da Plata – had survived the popular uprisings of the early nineteenth century. They had been split into a number of different countries, none of which could now be compared in size to Brazil.

During the regency, the vacant throne created an atmosphere of uncertainty in many cities of the empire. This was the fertile backdrop against which new political societies and protests for civil rights emerged. One of the best known of these was the Society for the Defence of Freedom and Independence of the Nation, founded on 10 May 1831. It was formed by politicians who were opposed to Dom Pedro I, the so-called exalted liberals, military officers from the moderate liberal party, and by a few of the former monarch's collaborators, including José Bonifácio de Andrada. The Defence of Freedom Society stood for the maintenance of the social hierarchy and status quo. Although they professed to defend the public interest, their first activities were aimed at controlling the 'rabble'. They were also interested in creating a 'high Society' in Rio de Janeiro, to which end they organized parties and civic events. Another political movement that emerged was the short-lived Federal Society, which was founded on 31 December 1831 and whose aim was to put pressure on the Senate to pass constitutional reforms. A conservative party also emerged – the Society for the Conservation of the Brazilian Constitution – which defended the emperor and was made up of military officers faithful to the monarchy.[56]

In the words of the anthropologist Gilberto Freyre, the regency was 'a period of such frequent social and cultural conflicts between groups of the population – conflicts that were complex but appeared to be simply political – that the whole period was characterized by restlessness and trepidation'.[57] In addition to the revolts that have been described in this chapter, there were an additional seven that occurred in 1831 alone – five in Rio de Janeiro, one in Ceará and one in Pernambuco – as well as a number of conflicts of lesser proportions in other provinces. The revolts reflected how large and diverse the country was and how the government's policy of centralization was unconvincing.

It was no coincidence that during Araújo Lima's second government the political disputes in the Congress increased. Opinions were bitterly divided, except on one important point. There was consensus that the only possible solution to the unrest was to anticipate young Pedro II's ascension to the throne. He was fourteen years old. A king's age does not count, or if it does, it is disguised by the ritual of his position. In the eyes of the politicians, it was only by crowning the boy as Emperor Pedro II, the first monarch to be born in Brazil, that the fragile unity of the country could be guaranteed. Although most of the rebellions had been suppressed, there was nothing to suggest that new ones would not occur. So the stage was prepared, the emperor's age manipulated, and he was crowned at the greatest public ceremony that Brazil had ever seen.

II

The Second Reign: At Last, a Nation in the Tropics

The idea of crowning Dom Pedro II in 1843, before he came of age (eighteen years old, according to the constitution), was by now an open secret. After all, the elites had been urging his ascension to the throne since 1835. But the process gathered momentum from 1840 when the liberal deputies opposed to Araújo Lima's regency – the majority Club – confronted the Senate, demanding that young Pedro II assume the throne. Strange to think that after all the rebellions during the regency period, all the revolts in favour of a republic and the general atmosphere of radicalization, the solution – incredible as it may seem – was to strengthen the monarchy and reaffirm the centralization of power in Rio de Janeiro.

Meanwhile the young prince was kept in the palace, unaware of the government's plans and with little understanding of the urgency of the political situation. In a report dated March 1840, Pedro Araújo Lima related one of his conversations with the young monarch. According to the regent, when Dom Pedro was consulted about the possibility of announcing his majority, he answered: 'Actually I haven't thought about it.'[1] The official version of the conversation was rather different: when consulted the young monarch allegedly replied 'Let it be at once!', revealing an emotional maturity that is hard to credit. Thus began the process of constructing an image for the emperor that was to last until his death: a monarch who was always calm, who chose his words with caution and was decisive on political issues, supposedly above politics, and who had come to redeem the nation. According to reports of the time, with the possible exception of his build – he had long, slender legs – and his strident voice, he represented the incarnation of a European king. Physically he resembled the Habsburgs – pronounced chin, very blue eyes, white skin and straight blonde hair – in contrast to the subjects of his kingdom, the majority of whom were black, mulatto or mestizo.

Newspapers and pamphlets distributed in Rio unceasingly praised the prodigious qualities of the young Pedro: his education, intelligence, culture, the classical and modern languages he spoke, and his skill at riding and fencing. Thus Brazil's second monarch – the longest-reigning and most popular – took the throne in the midst of a theatrical promotion of his precocious maturity. His adult clothes, his fame as a multilingual philosopher and his equanimity all contributed to his projected image as a great monarch: the mirror opposite of his father. Everything was thus ready for the ritualistic consecration and coronation of Dom Pedro II.

A SPECTACLE WORTHY OF GREAT KINGS

The day fixed for the festivities was 16 July 1841 and Rio de Janeiro woke up once again ready to celebrate. Dressed *de rigueur*, the entire court waited for the ritual to begin. A pamphlet specially printed for the occasion – *Arrangements for the Coronation of His Majesty the Emperor* – gave the details of the ceremony with which the state intended to display all the grandiosity of the empire and mark the beginning of a new era. The booklet of ten pages, distributed all around the town, gave a description of the three parts of the ceremony – the procession, the coronation and the reception, including the rules of etiquette for the banquet. The ritual began at midday, involving hundreds of people, each of whom joined the procession at a given moment with a specific role, each one having his moment of glory. Officers from the cavalry, carriages and archers filed by, to the occasional roar of cannon salutes. It was all flawlessly planned to be both seductive and intimidating.

The calendar of events was carefully laid out: the order of proceedings for the coronation, the day for receiving tributes, the night for the city to be illuminated, the visit to the São Pedro de Alcântara theatre and, finally, the grand ball. The public coffers were ransacked to pay for it all. The whole town became a massive depository for wood, cloth, glass, paint and tools, while the streets teemed with carpenters,

painters, firework-makers, fashion designers, artists and their apprentices. Manuel de Araújo Porto-Alegre, an architect and painter, was
commissioned to design a special building – the famous Veranda – from
where Dom Pedro II would wave to the people after his coronation.
Following tradition, the monument was to be an expression of the excellence of the regime, of the authority of the governor, and of the mutual
trust between the prince and his subjects.

Marc Ferrez, one of the artists who had come from France during
the reign of Dom João VI, was commissioned to make the sculptures
for the occasion. Chandeliers, candleholders, orbs, lamps, inscriptions,
engravings, wallpaper, gold-plated ornaments, gold and silver goblets,
embroidery, lace, velvet, damask and silks, and tapestries. These are
some of the items included in the document describing the Veranda.[2]
The building was so large it occupied the entire space between the
Royal Palace and the Imperial Chapel. It was decorated with allegories
representing the hopes and expectations for the new reign. The area at
the centre of the building where Dom Pedro II was to take his seat after
the coronation was called the 'temple', lending the event the aura of a
religious ritual with a divine presence. Inscribed over the two pavilions
on either side were the words 'Amazonas' and 'Prata'[3] in tribute to the
two rivers marking the northern and southern frontiers of the country,
each represented by a colossal statue. Two lions – symbolizing Strength
and Power – stood at the foot of the staircase that led from the Prata
Pavilion down to the Imperial Chapel. On the upper floor all the images
were taken from Antiquity: chariots, a triumphal carriage, statues of
Justice and Wisdom, and an inscription that read 'God protect the
Emperor of Brazil'. The throne room was inside the temple. In the middle of the ceiling, in plasterwork, the Emperor Dom Pedro I – with a
halo of stars symbolizing his immortality – was depicted handing the
crowns of Portugal[4] and Brazil to his two children.[5]

There was much more. In the allegory representing Brazil, the country's coat of arms was depicted in gold, and at the feet of Portugal lay
the laurels of her past glory. The provinces of the empire were represented by stars against a blue background, where the signs of the zodiac
through which the sun was passing on the date of the prince's birth and
of his accession to the throne – Sagittarius and Cancer – were also
depicted. Large medallions representing Charlemagne, Francis I, Napoleon and Peter the Great, all of whom had founded empires, stood as

symbols for the destiny of Brazil's new emperor. Beside them the coats of arms of Portugal and Austria were displayed side by side, the cradles of the Brazilian imperial dynasty. Above the throne there were portraits of Pedro I and João VI and on the wall there was an apocalyptic depiction of what was at stake: on the one side the emperor, governing within his constitutional rights, and on the other the calamities and crimes that had torn the country apart during the 'anarchical state of the country during the minority'. Here the figures are seen fleeing in terror back to hell, from where they had emerged, making way for the wisdom and virtue of the new regime.

The ideological meaning was clear. The regencies represented devilishness and anarchy, whereas revitalized imperial rule promised stability and prosperity. The regencies were characterized by vanity; the empire by wisdom, science and civic virtue. The republican experiments during the regencies represented acts of barbarity that were now being buried along with the past. History was being manipulated to display coherence and continuity between the past and the future. The galleries and pavilions were decorated with carefully chosen tributes to illustrious national figures and events – including Dom Pedro I's declaration that he would stay and the declaration of independence. Only the moments when the monarchy had achieved approval and popular support were portrayed. The image of the emperor reverberated simultaneously around the city and in the imagination of its people.

Meanwhile, the poor boy could hardly conceal how overwhelmed he was by the voluminous robes, the heavy crown, the long sceptre and the cloak trailing behind him along the ground. There was a veritable battle over these images. The first that appeared in Brazil and abroad showed the boy ill at ease with ceremonial vestments that were far too big for him. But in the official pictures he appeared as a Bourbon or Habsburg king. Ever since the disappearance of Dom Sebastião during his crusade in Morocco and the birth of the myth that he would return, the Bragança monarchs had not been actually crowned, but only acclaimed. But in Brazil the emperor was acclaimed, crowned and consecrated, in an effort to offset the political fragility of the moment by restoring the ancient tradition.

New elements were also introduced into the ritual. Pedro de Alcântara was invested as 'Dom Pedro II, by the grace of God and unanimous acclamation of the peoples, Constitutional Emperor and Perpetual

Defender of Brazil'. This was a combination of the old and the new: the consecration was maintained, but at the same time the new emperor, like his contemporaries, was a constitutional monarch. He represented both continuity and a new beginning. This was reflected in the insignia: the sword, the sceptre, the cloak and the crown. The cloak of the founder of the new empire, was made of green velvet with an embroidered band, decorated with gold stars, dragons and orbs, and lined with yellow silk. It signified a tribute to the new world and its poncho shape was a reference to the traditional clothes of the region. The sword, which had belonged to Dom Pedro I, displayed the Portuguese coat of arms on the blade. Beside it, on a salver, was a copy of the imperial constitution, wrapped in a green velvet cover and sealed with a ribbon of the imperial order of the cross. The imperial orb, a symbol central to the consecration ritual, was a silver armillary sphere with nineteen gold stars arranged around the cross of the order of Christ. The ring, worn on the fourth finger of the right hand, encrusted with diamonds, depicted two dragons tied together at the tail. The monarch's silk gloves displayed the imperial arms. The solid gold sceptre, which was 1.76 metres long, displayed the symbol of the Braganças – a wyvern, a kind of serpent with wings and diamond eyes. Immediately after the coronation Marc Ferrez made a plaster cast of the emperor's right hand, which was given the name of the 'hand of Justice' and distributed to grandees of the court. The crown measured sixteen inches across, too large for the emperor's head. The base was decorated with diamonds and pearls, some of which had been taken from Dom Pedro I's crown, possibly due to lack of time and funds.[6] The new elements symbolizing Brazil included the Southern Cross and other constellations of the southern hemisphere. The plume of toucan feathers and the russet-coloured shoulder pads (made from feathers of the *galo-da-serra*)[7] were an idealized reference to the indigenous peoples.

The ritual was planned to enchant the public. The cortège alone was made up of more than fifty people. There were soldiers and honour guards, a band, a herald, ushers, court officials, the emperor's confessor, and various carriages transporting aristocrats and members of the imperial family.[8] Members of the court had gathered at the Imperial Chapel for the ceremony of kissing the monarch's hand.[9] It was said that since French hairdressers were in short supply many ladies had to have their hair styled the day before, and spent the night already dressed for the occasion and propped up with pillows. Everything was done so that the event resembled a European coronation.

The most notable difference was the new emperor's dark-skinned subjects and the rustic surroundings, which the official painters had tried to disguise. The bells pealed, the canons discharged, and the crowds saluted the monarch. With the heavy crown on his head, the train of his cloak dragging along the ground, and his mantle of feathers giving him the exotic look of a boy emperor during the Festival of the Holy Spirit, Dom Pedro II walked up the steps to the throne and looked down at the crowds. He was so small that he looked like an allegorical figure. But it was the logic of the spectacle that mattered. The monarch's age, the haste with which the ceremony had been organized, the artificial character of much of the spectacle – all these were forgotten. It seemed that all the political disturbances of the regencies had been banished by ritual consecration.

CONSTRUCTING A NATION AND SCULPTING ITS EMPEROR

The period between 1841 and 1864 was an important phase for the consolidation of the monarchy in Brazil. The rebellions in Bahia, Pará and Maranhão had been suppressed with the help of the Baron of Caxias, who by then had become something of a local hero. The Majority Cabinet declared amnesty for all rebels who handed themselves over to the authorities and the end of the rebellions was celebrated by conservatives and liberals alike.

Dom Pedro II's civic education was handled with the utmost importance: he was aided by his steward Paulo Barbosa, who undertook to train him in the exercise of power.[10] In a note dated 1842 the young emperor asked him: 'What is the royal herald's name? What is the name of the master of ceremonies? How many gentlemen of the bedchamber are there and what are their names? I don't know exactly how much is spent on maintaining the stables . . .'[11] Although the monarch had not yet become a political figure, the politicians around him were already acting in his name. His picture began to appear in government departments, in national and foreign newspapers, and his likeness on neckerchiefs and coins.

According to royal tradition, as he approached eighteen it was important to arrange a marriage for him so that it would be clear to one and all that he was an adult and had truly come of age. This was no easy task. Brazil was a distant, exotic empire, its reputation still clouded by the notoriety of Pedro's father. What was more, Pedro II was shy, and blushed at the very idea of marriage. Pedro Araújo Lima wrote to Paulo Barbosa, commenting on the young monarch's reaction to the idea of matrimony:

> I asked him whether he would authorize me to initiate negotiations which I could not contemplate beginning without his consent, as it was a business that intimately involved his person and would influence his domestic happiness. He was kind enough to say that I should do what I thought best [. . .] Afterwards I explained that it would be fitting for the marriage to take place as soon as possible, so that he would be equipped to begin to exercise power.

The account reveals the interests of several parties and the various strategies of the wedding. It was not actually a question of Pedro II's 'domestic happiness'; instead, it was a question of public demands: after all, marriage would sanction his majority. With the emperor's formal approval the negotiations got under way, aimed at organizing three marriages simultaneously: that of Dom Pedro II and those of his two sisters who had remained in Brazil, Dona Januária and Dona Francisca. Obviously the most strategically significant of the three was the emperor's. A bride was found, and on 23 July 1843, along with the marriage contract, a small portrait of Teresa Maria Cristina, Princess of the Kingdom of the Two Sicilies, arrived. Teresa was descended from the Bourbons through three of her grandparents, and from the Habsburgs through the fourth. Her branch of the family was not, however, wealthy, and her dowry was small. Furthermore she was almost four years older than her future husband and was descended from a less important family line than he was. She was, nevertheless, a niece of Maria Amélia, Queen of the French and sister of Ferdinand II, King of Naples. She was also said to be a good singer. Abandoning his usual shyness, the young Pedro said that he liked the portrait – which, it must be said, emphasized the appealing qualities of the future empress while concealing her defects. The marriage took place by proxy, in Naples, and immediately after the ceremony Teresa Cristina set out on the long journey to Brazil. The expenses were by no means negligible. The government spent 3:555$000 réis[12] on the emperor's portrait, the wedding gift for the future empress, and gold bars, as proof of the wealth of the empire.

Eighty days later the princess arrived in Rio de Janeiro: on 3 September 1843 the frigate *Constituição* docked in Guanabara Bay. Everything was prepared for the ceremony. His majesty, in his admiral's uniform, boarded the royal launch, which was decorated with the winged dragon of the Braganças and rowed by twenty-four oarsmen with armbands displaying the colours of the Two Sicilies. After saluting the crew he made his way to the empress's rooms. There he was met by the Count of Áquila, his future brother-in-law, who was to marry his sister Dona Januária. At eleven o'clock the imperial couple disembarked and rode in the royal carriage to the Imperial Chapel, where a Te Deum was sung, followed by the ritual of kissing the emperor's hand. The carefully planned festivities that followed included public spectacles, a gala dinner in the palace, and balls in the parishes where the slaves 'were authorized to display their dances in tribute to Her Imperial Majesty, mother of the Brazilian people'.

Despite the festivities, the young Dom Pedro had experienced an unpleasant surprise. None of the information he had received about the princess's virtues had revealed the fact that Teresa Cristina was short, overweight and slightly lame. It was said that the young bridegroom managed to conceal his disappointment but afterwards wept in the arms of the Countess of Belmonte, his nurse, and on the shoulder of Paulo Barbosa, who said to him: 'Remember the dignity of your position. Do your duty my child!' His sisters were more fortunate. The two travelled to the courts of Europe where Dona Francisca, 'the beautiful Chica', married the Prince of Joinville, son of Louis-Philippe of France, in 1843. Dona Januária married the Count of Áquila, Teresa Cristina's brother, the same year. Marriages of state were a political business, and, somehow or other, the imperial marriage was consummated. The couple's first son, Dom Afonso, was born in 1845. He died when he was one year old, on 11 June 1847. In 1846, Teresa Cristina gave birth to her first daughter, Isabel, and the following year to her second, Leopoldina. The couple's fourth child, Dom Pedro Afonso, also died when he was one year old, on 10 January 1850, at the Fazenda de Santa Cruz. This, it was commented at the time, seemed to be the fate of the male heirs of the Bragança dynasty: they never prospered.

Nevertheless, the emperor's virility was taken as a sign of his maturity, and from this point on he began to become more and more involved in affairs of state. In Europe the year 1848 was marked by a wave of revolutions that began in Paris with the Second Republic on 24 February, and spread to Germany, Bavaria, Austria, Hungary, Milan, and finally to Sicily. Pedro's two sisters were both directly affected. Dona Francisca, who was married to the son of Louis-Philippe, the now deposed King of France, was obliged to go into exile in Britain and Dona Januária, married to the son of the King of the Two Sicilies, had a miraculous escape. In contrast, Dom Pedro II's empire appeared to be heading in the opposite direction: it seemed like an island of tranquillity.

GOOD AND BAD WINDS

Far from the storms in Europe, the young king started to face a series of new challenges and surprises, some better than others. The ministry that had been in power in Brazil since 1848 was ideologically conservative: Araújo Lima (the Marquis of Olinda), Eusébio de Queirós, Paulino José Soares de Sousa and Joaquim José Rodrigues Torres. Of the seats in the Chamber of Deputies, 110 were held by conservatives, and only one by a liberal. Nevertheless, the ministers, who tended to suffer from inertia, were obliged to confront a number of questions of radical importance: the problem of landownership, incentives for immigration, and the thorny issue of the slave traffic.

First, the recurrent pressure for the end of the 'infamous trade' was ever greater, with England at the helm. Between 1839 and 1842 the number of seizures of ships carrying slaves progressively increased and by 1850 the situation had become unsustainable. The issue was an embarrassment: despite collusion with the traffic, the Brazilian government knew prohibition was essential if political autonomy were to be maintained. Furthermore, for Brazil to be among the 'barbarous nations' still engaging in slave-trafficking was in direct contrast to the civilized image the country sought. To make matters more complex, the interior provinces were entirely dependent on slave labour and not in favour of making any changes. Between 1841 and 1850, 83 per cent of all the Africans transported to the Americas came to Brazil; 12 per cent went to Cuba and the rest were divided between Puerto Rico and the United

States.[13] These statistics only scratch the surface; dealers reaped enormous profits from both the slave trade and the commerce affiliated with it.[14]

The issue of slave-trafficking had become so important that it permeated other government legislation. In 1850, in response largely to British pressure, Brazil adopted the Eusébio de Queiróz Act that prohibited the maritime trade in slaves. The question was of such importance that it began to affect other domestic issues in the empire. For example, the 1850 Land Law, which had first been presented in 1843, was aimed at reorganizing the agricultural system in Brazil with an eye to the end of slave labour.[15] It passed only a few days after slave-trafficking had been interrupted. This was the beginning of a struggle that was to last until the end of the empire. The aim of the land law was to discourage subsistence farmers and prevent future immigrants from owning land. A further measure taken at this time was the centralization of the National Guard, to strengthen the federal government in the event of a conflict with landowners from the interior. These landowners were against both the prohibition of slave-trafficking and the regulation of landownership. The same year a new commercial code was passed into law, made necessary by the vast number of new businesses that had emerged funded by capital previously invested in the slave trade.

Every cause has many effects, and the end of the slave trade in 1850 is no exception. Since a great deal of the slave traffic had been conducted illegally, large amounts of profit had been concealed from the official state accounts. Thus, with the end of slave-trafficking, vast quantities of resources appeared, virtually overnight, as if by magic. The government's response was to invest in the country's infrastructure, above all railways. Between 1854 and 1858 the first railways were constructed, the first telegraph lines erected, navigation routes were established, gas lighting was introduced in the cities, and the number of schools and educational institutions began to increase. Investment in trafficking was transferred to other sectors of the economy, and imports grew by 57.2 per cent in a period of two years: a pleasant surprise for a government that was basically sustained by import tariffs.[16]

A little bit of luck goes a long way, and it so happened that the prohibition of the slave traffic occurred simultaneously with the rise in the international price of coffee. Between 1840 and 1844, Brazil's coffee trade had been making a net loss, but after 1845 it became extremely profitable. Between 1850 and 1851 sales rose by 23 per cent and optimism began to pervade the empire. The financial situation was indeed encouraging: for the fiscal year of 1831 to 1832, immediately after Pedro I's abdication, the government's total receipts had been 11 171:520$000.[17] For 1840–1, after the new emperor's majority, this figure rose to 16 310:571$000. For the fiscal year of 1862–3 it tripled to 48 343:182$000. This period of economic growth became known as the 'Mauá Era' – the name of the Brazilian entrepreneur[18] who owned seventeen different companies. His sphere of business extended as far as Uruguay and Argentina, with investments in the financial and industrial segments – a very fortunate circumstance since between 1854 and 1889, 10,000 kilometres of railroads were constructed in the country.

The empire's foreign policy was also successful. Brazilian troops defeated the Uruguayan leader Manuel Oribe, thus putting an end (at least temporarily) to the complicated political dispute over the region of the River Plate, a dispute that, among other factors, had led to Pedro I's abdication. At the same time, in the wake of the new land law and the prohibition of the slave traffic, the government launched a policy to attract European immigrants. Brazil had little to offer them compared to the United States, which offered greater facilities for the acquisition of land, had a more developed transport system and, in much of its territory, no slave labour to compete with. Nevertheless, from 1850 onwards, immigrant workers began to arrive from Europe and the East. Since the prohibition of the slave traffic, the price of a slave had doubled on the domestic market, and the policy of attracting immigrants had been planned to replace them.

But the policy of importing farm labourers, financed by landowners, created a series of problems. A model emerged that was no more than a form of slavery through the accumulation of debt. The immigrants had to pay the landowners back for all their expenses, including travel, housing, use of the land and farming tools. Having been tricked with the promise of plots of land of their own, many left for the towns. Revolts followed, the most famous of which occurred on the estates of Senador Vergueiro in 1856. Three years later the Prussian government banned all emigration of its nationals to Brazil.[19]

At the end of the 1860s the government decided to finance immigration. One of the aims was the 'whitening' of the population, which, according to the scientific theories of the time, would be beneficial for the country. There was concern over the 'future of a country of mixed races'[20] and, with slaves still a majority, the old fears of a Haitian-style revolution had not been laid to rest. In 1849 there were 110,000 slaves living in Rio de Janeiro, and 266,000 white people.[21] The district around the palace was known as 'Little Africa', a name that could appropriately be applied to the city itself.

The long, difficult decade ended in tragedy. In 1859, Rio de Janeiro succumbed to its first major epidemic of yellow fever, with thousands of deaths, including one of Pedro II's young sons.[22]

LIFE AT COURT[23]

But even with good and bad moments, the decade of the 1850s would be remembered for its financial stability and for the domestic peace the country was to experience from then on. In Rio de Janeiro the impact of the end of the slave traffic was greatest. In fact, the city was undergoing an enormous transformation. The urbanization was meant to transform the city into a bourgeois Paris, although the reality oscillated between elegant residential districts and working-class neighbourhoods, where slaves and freemen predominated.

Urban slavery was present throughout, in all the town houses, large or small. All that varied were the particular characteristics of any given town and the wealth of its inhabitants. In larger houses a hierarchy of enslaved pages, message boys, nurses and domestic servants, well dressed and neatly turned out, were a symbol of the status of their owners. In the smaller houses belonging to single women and widows or to the lower rungs of government employees, male and female slaves toiled alongside their owners, and above all their wives, creating bonds of friendship. These, however, did not lessen the violence that always lay beneath the surface of urban slavery. Some of these household slaves were emblematic, like the wet nurses, whose photos appeared alongside the family in picture albums and on *carte de visite* photos which, when taken to Europe, offered the exotic, romantic and peaceful image of slavery that Brazil was eager to export. But the tension – albeit latent – was always there. The young masters were identified by their Christian names and surnames, while the wet nurses remained anonymous.

The streets were filled with all kinds of characters. Slaves who were hired out, the so-called *escravos de ganho*, who earned daily wages, bustled about either looking for work or executing tasks. They carried enormous loads – barrels, crates, pianos – and stood out with their burdens, singing in syncopated rhythms. Similarly, female street vendors and snack sellers stood out for their independence in their trades and social contacts. Many of those women managed to save enough money to buy their freedom. They sometimes formed families of their own by purchasing young slaves, who were later granted their freedom as well. In the world of urban slavery, where vigilance was not so strict, many ways of practising a profession and of moving about freely were invented. Slaves and freemen joined together with the poor and through ties of solidarity and mutual help created an invisible world, alongside the brilliance of the court, which now shone brighter than ever.[24]

This so-called modern urban world was meant to reflect the aspirations and mores of a white society along traditional European lines. Perhaps this is the reason that, practically from one day to the next, palaces, public gardens and wide avenues were built. The court accomplished several other significant improvements. They contracted the planting of trees (from 1820), cobblestone pavements (1853), gas street lighting (1854), a sewage network (1862), donkey-drawn trams (1868) and piped water (1874). The traditional streets for commerce also began to change. The once elegant Rua Direita – where both high fashion and haberdashery and dry goods were sold – no longer seemed sufficient. The narrow city streets teeming with slaves, with the smell of sewage and the damp sea breeze, all seemed to contribute to an aura of decay.

This was the beginning of the golden age of the Rua do Ouvidor, where French fashion stores, florists, jewellers, hairdressers, tobacconists and even ice-cream shops were opening every day. In contrast to former times, being out and about town became fashionable: evening walks, and teas in elegant cafés, with passers-by decked out in elegant suits tailored in British fabric, and the latest fashions recreated after Paris couture. It was no accident that Rua do Ouvidor became the symbol of this new urban sophistication – the European boulevard in the heart of the tropics. This exaggerated aspiration did not escape the pen of the great author Machado de Assis,[25] whose short story 'Fulano' features a character, Fulano Beltrão.[26] In the short narrative, Mr Beltrão's social and political ascension led him to stroll along Rua do Ouvidor.

When his wife died, 'he ordered the construction of a magnificent mausoleum in Italy', which was then brought to Brazil and 'displayed in the Rua do Ouvidor for almost a month'.[27] Not only was Rua do Ouvidor the very heart of social life, the street was also the centre for political debate and the meeting place for journalists, writers, poets and artists.

As 'high society' became more established, Rio de Janeiro became both the centre of comings and goings, and the place where social customs and manner of speech were established for the rest of the country. It was not by chance that while 'marriageable young women' dreamt of life at court, wealthy landowners wanted their sons to experience the pleasures of the 'Babylonian court'.[28] These large landowners took pride in their coffee plantations and manors, more than adequate for balls and perhaps even a visit from the emperor himself – the ultimate trophy. But it was in the big cities that social life was becoming established amid a fever of concerts, parties and balls.

And then there were the theatres, where people went to see and be seen. The most important stages in Rio de Janeiro included the São João theatre and the Lírico Fluminense theatre, located in the Campo da Aclamação. In the latter, Carlos Gomes[29] presented his first opera, *A Noite do Castelo*, and his most famous work, *Il Guarani*, was first performed there on 2 December 1870, in honour of the emperor's birthday. In addition to actors from abroad, these theatres featured Brazilian artists, such as the playwright Martins Pena,[30] known for having introduced the comedy of manners to Brazilian theatre. In one of his plays, *O caixeiro da taverna*[31] the character Francisco complains: 'All you see in this town are French tailors, American dentists, English engineers, German doctors, Swiss watchmakers, French hairdressers, foreigners from the four corners of the earth . . .'[32] In Martins Pena's plays Englishmen are addressed as *'senhor mister'*, but he saves most of his satire for the Brazilian fixation on the French.

The most popular pastimes, however, were the balls and the soirées. Here lectures were given, jokes told, waltzes danced, arias sung, poetry was declaimed and women courted.[33] The balls were at the height of their popularity and importance at this time; both political and social, opponents argued and rifts were healed at the balls. 'One cannot talk politics without croquettes,' the Baron of Cotegipe[34] used to say, referring to soirées accompanied by Donizetti, Rossini and Verdi arias. The women were dressed elegantly with, of course, fillers and corsets that miraculously transformed their figures. Bouquets for the ladies, cigars for the men, the casino balls were filled with silks, bonnets, golden bracelets, plumes, Belgian lace, and fans made of ivory, mother-of-pearl, tortoiseshell or sandalwood – the balls at the casinos displayed all the luxury of life at court, the dream of living in Brazil as people lived in France, despite the heat of the tropics.

But it would be a mistake to believe that Rio de Janeiro was Paris or that Recife was London. The two cities were islands surrounded by plantations where slave labour was omnipresent. In his bitter short story 'Pai contra mãe',[35] Machado de Assis comments that 'slavery creates its own professions and its own tools': the steel mask, the iron ring around the neck, the profession of capturing slaves whose escapes were advertised every day in the press. In the same short story, Cândido Neves, a capturer of escaped slaves, is proud of his job. On the verge of being forced to hand over his own son because he is so in need, he captures a pregnant mulatta who aborts as he is chasing her. 'Not all children prosper' is Neves's only comment.[36]

While the court attempted to maintain a system of slave labour alongside paid workers as silently as it could, the contrast with its pretensions to civilization was all too obvious. The density of the slave population was in evidence everywhere. During the nineteenth century the number of slaves fluctuated between half and two-fifths of the population of Rio de Janeiro. According to the Almanak Laemmert,[37] in 1849 the city was home to the largest number of slaves since the end of the Roman Empire, 110,000 in a population of 266,000 residents. In the eight parishes that formed the rest of the city – Sacramento, Engenho Velho, São José, Candelária, Santa Rita, Santana, Glória, Lagoa – the proportion of slaves was lower, but their impact was greater. These centrally located parishes were the centre of government activity, with government buildings, public squares and the bustling trade. Of the total of 206,000 inhabitants who lived in those regions, 75,000 (38 per cent) were slaves.[38] The area around the palace was known as the Kingdom of Obá or, as mentioned above, Little Africa. The inhabitants were mainly Africans and crioulos, both slaves and freemen. In fact, according to the 1849 census, one in every three residents was African. The proportion of slaves was even greater in other Brazilian cities. In Niterói, four-fifths of the population were slaves in 1833, and in Campos,[39] 59 per cent were slaves. Salvador, with its smaller population (around 81,000 inhabitants in 1855), also had a greater proportion of slaves as residents than Rio de Janeiro.

But it was not only slavery that eclipsed the empire's aspirations to civilization. There was an enormous imbalance between the population of the cities and that of the rural areas. In 1823 the population of the provincial capitals represented 8.49 per cent of the country's total population; in 1872, 10.41 per cent and in 1890, 9.54 per cent.[40] The situation was further complicated by the fact that approximately 50 per cent of the city dwellers were concentrated in just three capitals – Rio de Janeiro, Salvador and Recife: 59 per cent in 1832; 48 per cent in 1872; and 58 per cent in 1890.[41] It is clear, then, that while the court was the centre of society and fashion, it was also the exception. The fashionable world was for the few. Slavery and the abandonment of the rural workers were, and would remain, the great contradictions of Dom Pedro II's purportedly civilized reign: a quasi-European empire.

POLITICS IN THE SECOND REIGN: MORE OF THE SAME

The world of politics was also only for the few. After Pedro I's death in 1834, his supporters joined the monarchist party – then known as the conservatives – who won the elections of 1836 and governed from 1837 to 1840. That year, the liberals – the other major party – in alliance with a few conservatives, won the elections and governed until 1841. The two parties continued to take turns: 1841–4 the conservatives; 1844–8 the liberals; 1848–53 the conservatives, until in 1853 a 'national conciliation' government took power, with representatives from both parties. The union lasted for five years, during which time the fragility of both parties became evident, as well as the potential of the monarchy to intervene in politics. Brazil had no bourgeois class to regulate social relations through market forces, and thus it fell to the state to consolidate the nation and enact policies of economic protectionism.[42] It helped that the governing elite was homogeneous in terms of social background, ideology and training. During this process of increased state involvement in the economy, the bureaucratic sector, which had previously been run by magistrates and military offices, was gradually taken over by liberal professionals and lawyers – the so-called *bacharéis*.

The white elite viewed the court as a sort of club for privileged members, independent of political factions. And in a sense, it was true. Members of both parties – the conservatives referred to as *saquaremas* and the liberals as *luzias* – came from the same social class, had been educated at Coimbra, had followed careers as doctors or lawyers, had titles and moved in the same circles.[43] Although they were divided on the issue of the degree of government centralization, they closed ranks when it came to slavery or the structure of the state. The Brazilian elite of the time could be described as 'an island of literati in a sea of illiterates'.[44] Education was what distinguished them from the rest of the country. The census of 1872 showed that just 16 per cent of the population knew how to read, 23.43 per cent of the men and 13.43 per cent of the women. Among the slave population, illiteracy was 99.9 per cent. Before independence the majority of the country's elite had studied law at Coimbra. After 1828 there were two colleges for studying law in Brazil: one in São Paulo and the other in Olinda (later transferred to Recife). Even early education was predictable. Wealthier families hired private tutors, who prepared young members of the elite for entry into the lyceums, especially the Colégio Dom Pedro II. The school was founded in 1837 and guaranteed a *bacharel* in literature, as well as the best chance of getting a place at one of the law colleges. This was followed by a 'gap year' in Europe and then entry into one of the country's two law schools, or two medical schools, which were in Rio de Janeiro and Salvador.[45] It was not only legal scholars and lawyers who graduated from the law schools, but future deputies, senators and diplomats: in other words, the entire state civil service.

However, the excessive number of people studying to compete for government jobs encouraged the growth of political patronage among civil servants and in government circles in general. Thus the term *bacharel* came to have a broader application. In theory the word referred to a graduate in law, but in practice young people with degrees in mathematics or literature – and at times without a degree at all, but with the right contacts – also used the title in order to acquire a desirable post as a government bureaucrat. These people are treated ironically by the renowned legal scholar Silvio Romero[46] in his book *Doutrina contra doutrina*.[47] He describes them as always in dress coats, going from door to door looking for a job, preferably a sinecure requiring no personal effort. They were lawyers without clients, doctors without clinics, writers without readers, magistrates with no one to judge, who used their diplomas as a means of gaining social distinction and ensuring a stable income.[48]

But these bureaucrats were not powerful. Important decisions on national policy were made by members of the Executive and the Legislature, state advisers, ministers, senators and deputies.[49] At the top of the pyramid was the Council of State, 'the brain of the monarchy'. It was first established in 1823, and then abolished during the 1834 reforms. In 1841 it was reinstated as the New Council of State and remained active through the end of the empire. These were the men who were closest to the emperor, with a lifelong mandate, which could, however, be suspended by the monarch for an indefinite period. The ministers represented the Executive, of which the emperor was the titular head; he was therefore at liberty to appoint and dismiss them at will.[50] The emperor's power to intervene, and his power of veto, combined with the *sui generis* way in which the government was structured, meant that in general the Cabinets were short-lived. Between 1841 and 1861 there were eleven ministries, and between 1861 and 1889, the last year of the empire, a further twenty-three.

Next in the hierarchy of power came the senators. As mentioned above, they were chosen by the emperor from a list of three elected names. A senator was required to be at least forty years old and have a minimum annual income of 800$000 réis.[51] The senators had a mandate for life, and hence their power. Some remained in their posts for as long as thirty years. Below the senators came the deputies. They were the 'most numerous but least powerful group',[52] although the post was an important stepping stone for ascending within the hierarchy. Deputies were required to be at least twenty-five years old and have a minimum annual income of 400$000 réis.

With the combination of his Moderating Power, which gave him the right of veto in various instances, and being surrounded by an elite group from the same social class – even though divided between two parties – Dom Pedro II began increasingly to really 'govern' as well as 'reign'. In the middle of the century it was generally commented that there was nothing more like a *saquarema* than a *luzia* in power. The term *saquarema* referred to the conservatives because it was the name of the home county of one of their leaders, the Viscount of Itaboraí. The term *luzia* was a reference to the liberals, and was the name of the city of Santa Luzia in Minas Gerais, where they had suffered their worst defeat. The politician Afonso Celso[53]commented: 'Liberals and conservatives alternated in power without leaving any trace distinguishing one party from the other. Changes in government were hardly noticed. The driving force behind the political struggle was "Now you leave, because it's my turn." '[54] In one of his short stories, the 'Teoria do medalhão' (1882),[55] Machado de Assis imagines the advice a father might give his son on the vicissitudes of a career in politics: 'You can belong to any party, liberal or conservative, republican or ultramontanist,[56] as long as you don't associate any specific ideas with these names . . .'[57]

But apart from the scandalous similarities, there were a few significant differences. Between the end of the regencies in 1841 and the suppression of the rebellion in Pernambuco that lasted from 1845 until 1848 – known as the *movimento praieiro*[58] – the *luzias* introduced policies aimed at greater autonomy for the provinces. But the policies were restricted to political discussions and parliamentary debates, with neither party producing an official programme. The names of the two parties were increasingly associated with specific circumstances – for the *luzias*, military defeat, and for the *saquaremas* their pressure for more centralized government during the liberal regime of 1844 to 1848. This may be the reason the term *saquarema* took hold during the imperial period, since it was associated with conservatives in Rio de Janeiro. *Saquarema* also had negative connotations of political protectionism, or even of looting since the verb *saquear* may have that meaning in Portuguese. And there were further differences between the two: the Conservative Party was formed by an alliance between government bureaucrats and the country's leading tradesmen and exporters of agricultural produce, whereas the Liberal Party was mostly composed of urban liberal professionals with links to agriculture in the domestic market and to the newly colonized areas.[59]

However, in some aspects the proximity between the two parties was such that it caused generalized mockery: of the lack of political programmes, of the art of fawning on the emperor, and of the theatrical display of politics. The members of the Chamber of Deputies were masters at posturing and courting the adulation of the press, which published their speeches – preferably two hours long – full of digressions, quotations and other artifices of oratory. But life for the deputies was also 'fun'. They left their wives in the provinces so that they could enjoy a 'bachelor life' in the capital.[60]

The fact remains that this temporary reconciliation between the two parties led to the strengthening of the empire and of the emperor himself. The so-called Conciliation Cabinet was created thanks to Honório Carneiro Leão, the Marquis of Paraná,[61] with both liberal and conservative members. In practical terms this Cabinet represented a period of political stability not seen since independence. The conciliation united the interests of the elites who controlled the nation's political life and maintained a centralized structure around the emperor.

During this period Pedro II began to take a decisive role in national culture. In his notes in the margins of his copy of the epic poem *Confederação dos Tamoios*, especially commissioned by the state in 1856, he scribbled that he had two major tasks: 'to morally organize the nationality and form an elite'. In constructing a Brazilian culture and unifying its territory, the importance of sponsoring and creating a romantic nationalism was immense. But the challenges were enormous. Most of the population was excluded from the political process, while the country's image abroad projected a very different reality: a country organized on the European model, with a constitutional monarchy, a young king who was famed as a scholar, an elected Congress and stable political parties. How could he transform the diverse provinces and realities into a nation? How to render a population into a cohesive political community when they were scattered all over the enormous territory, barely united in their loyalty to their provinces, and conditioned by an economy based on slave labour? How could he instil a sense of nationality? The answer, along with developing modernization programmes, was to invest in a 'tropical culture' entirely detached from the system of slavery.

AT LAST A PARTICULAR AND ORIGINAL STATE: A TROPICAL MONARCHY

The nineteenth century became known as the 'era of nationalism'. Nations were imagined through their heroes, their sense of history and their customs.[62] The creation of monuments to national culture, the use of national anthems and flags, the celebration of national dishes and traditional costume, all of these were characteristic of the era.[63] Romanticism tended to exalt precisely that which was unique to each nation, more so than what they had in common.

In the case of Brazil, things were somewhat different. Romantic nationalism did emerge locally, in relatively small regions that were linguistically and culturally homogeneous. But it was hard to create this type of national sentiment in a country of continental proportions with such a heterogeneous population. The solution was to ignore slavery and idealize the indigenous peoples, who had been systematically killed in the forests and now reappeared in official or semi-official novels and paintings. Representations of this indigenous (and masculine) country created an image of a Brazil that was American as well as monarchical and Portuguese. Whereas in European countries, national romanticism was often a means for one country to assert itself against another, in Brazil romanticism was sumptuous and financed by the monarchy, which led to its conservative nature.[64] Thus, although Brazilian nationalism did not reach every corner of the empire, it was historically significant. It allowed the country to form an identity, distinct from that of Lisbon, based on local characteristics – the tropical climate and native inhabitants. At the same time, Brazil maintained cultural ties to the Old World; after all, the country still had the most traditional of monarchies, descended from the Braganças, the Bourbons and the Habsburgs.[65]

In order to understand the importance of the monarchy in Brazilian romanticism, one must consider the institutions and intellectuals surrounding the emperor. During this time, Pedro II began attending meetings at the Historical and Geographical Institute and the Imperial Academy of Arts. He wanted to form a group of artists and writers – as young as he was. This was the era of Romantic Indianism, of the huge neoclassical paintings from the Imperial Academy of Arts and the exams at the school named after Pedro II. Nature was transformed into both a cultural landscape and an emblem of wealth and progress. In this construction of a national identity, the historian Francisco Adolfo de Varnhagen[66] contrasted Brazil's constitutional monarchy with the country's republican neighbours, which, according to him, were characterized by chronic instability, lack of freedom and civil wars. Before the rest of the world, Brazil wanted to be identified as the only civilized nation in the Americas. But within the country there remained the seemingly irresolvable contradiction of maintaining the Bragança dynasty on a continent filled with republican governments.

This American monarchy was viewed with suspicion by Brazil's neighbours, making it all the more important to foster culture and memory – an identity that would consolidate the monarchy and a sense of nationhood. In this context, an institute dedicated to Brazilian Letters was founded in 1838: the Instituto Histórico e Geográfico Brasileiro or IHGB (the Brazilian Institute of History and Geography), based on the French Institut Historique, created in Paris in 1834. Intellectuals believed it was important that Brazil had its own cultural institutions, separate from Portugal. The Brazilian version brought together Rio de Janeiro's economic and literary elite. In the 1840s the IHGB was the meeting place for writers of the Romantic school, and the emperor took a personal interest in its activities, frequently visiting the establishment.

From this time on, the Brazilian Institute of History and Geography became a leading educational establishment, promoting literary research, stimulating intellectual life, and operating as a link between intellectuals and government entities. It was probably the institution that made the greatest contribution to the forging of Brazil's national identity. The association between the palace and the IHGB became increasingly close: in 1838 Dom Pedro II was invited to be the 'protector' of the institute; in 1839 he offered one of the palace rooms for institute meetings; in 1840, on the monarch's birthday, a medal was minted on which were inscribed the words: *Auspice Petro Secundo. Pacifica Scientiae Occupatio*; in 1842 the emperor became a member of the French Institute, and lastly, between 1842 and 1844, the monarch introduced prizes for the best work written by a member of the Brazilian Institute of History and Geography.

The members of the Institute were mainly drawn from the court elite. They met on Sundays to debate previously selected topics with intellectuals. Their overriding aim was to construct a national history by selecting carefully chosen events and persons that could be converted into national heroics and heroes. The ties to the government were significant, the institute received three-quarters of the funding from the Crown. Thus through the financing of poets, musicians, painters and scientists, a process began that was not only aimed at strengthening the monarchy and the state but also at building nationhood through cultural unification. This was how Dom Pedro II earned his reputation as a patron of the arts: a 'wise emperor of the tropics'. Following the example of Louis XIV, Pedro II carefully selected a group of historians to forge a national memory, painters to create an exalted image of the country, and writers to create a national type.

This was a judiciously moderate group. Manuel de Araújo Porto Alegre,[67] well known for his activities in the Academia de Belas Artes, the writers Joaquim Norberto de Sousa e Silva,[68] Joaquim Manuel de Macedo,[69] Gonçalves Dias (1823–1864) and the historian Francisco Adolfo de Varnhagen (1816–1878) began to frequent the IHGB in 1840. The Institute's magazine was ideal for disseminating their ideas. Furthermore, its royal associations guaranteed that its members' works would be well received. On the other hand, the close relations they had with the government and with Dom Pedro II prevented more radical artists from coming to the fore. It was ironic that at the same time that the indigenous peoples of Brazil were glorified in epic poems describing heroic chiefs and tragic love affairs, politically these native Brazilians were being completely ignored. At the time dictionaries of indigenous languages became best-sellers, and the emperor himself began to study Tupi and Guarani. Meanwhile there was no official policy to protect these groups.

All of this contributed to consolidate the image of a 'wise emperor'. Dom Pedro II personally financed historical research programmes that delved into Brazilian archives and libraries, and the resulting studies were published at home and abroad. He also took an interest in American ethnography and linguistics. He funded the work of notable scientists such as the German botanist and explorer Carl Friedrich Philipp von Martius,[70] the great naturalist Peter Wilhelm Lund[71] and the mineralogist Claude-Henri Gorceix. He supported a swathe of others – the naturalists Louis Couty[72] and Émil August Goeldi,[73] the geologists Orville Derby[74] and Charles Frederick Hartt,[75] the botanist Auguste François Marie Glaziou,[76] the linguist and philologist Christian Friedrich Seybold. He also financed professionals in other areas, including lawyers, agronomists, architects, primary and secondary-school teachers, engineers, pharmacists, doctors, military officers, musicians and painters. This private funding was known at the time as 'grants from the emperor' and helped Dom Pedro II to promote his image as a Louis XIV of the tropics. The emperor liked to declare, whether those present were interested or not: 'La science, c'est moi.'[77]

THE INDIAN DIES SO THAT THE NATION CAN LIVE[78]

While historians created a new pantheon of national heroes, it was the novelists and poets who gave life to this 'new national identity', again as part of the state's literary policy. The first great work to demonstrate the 'national validity of the indigenous theme'[79] was the epic poem written in 1856 by Gonçalves de Magalhães, the *Confederação dos Tamoios* (*Tamoyo Confederation*). Returning to the theme of the 'noble savage', Gonçalves de Magalhães wrote what was the country's greatest national epic, centred around the courage and sacrifice of the heroic Indians. In an attempt to merge 'the eccentricities of romanticism with historical research', the author believed it was possible to overcome regional differences and create a foundational myth of a new national identity.[80]

Inspired by an 1834 article by Baltasar da Silva Lisboa,[81] the poem is a saga of the Tamoyo nation fighting for their freedom against the Portuguese – characterized as barbarous adventurers. Both groups were subdivided. The whites were made up of boorish Portuguese colonizers (who enslaved a free people) and Jesuit priests (whose virtues were linked to the future empire). The Indians in turn were either savage forest dwellers (innocents converted to Catholicism) or indomitable natives living freely amid the glories of nature. In this battle of dualities, the pure are always made noble: the Portuguese of the future empire, who personified national unity and the Christian faith, and the Indians who had not been defiled by civilization. In a significant passage, Tibiriçá, a converted Guaianá Indian, tries to convince his rebel nephew, Jagoanharo, of the advantages of the European world. Thus the poem introduced the trope of the Indian as a noble savage defeated by the emergence of a new empire. Jagoanharo was both hero and victim. Born free, he dies free in the cause of a new freedom. This poem, like other works of the period, forged national unity through the representation of the (noble) Indian, the very Indian who was in fact one of the empire's greatest victims.

The poet Antônio Gonçalves Dias[82] also caught the emperor's eye. Considered a great Brazilian Romantic poet, he introduced Indianism to his poetry. Based on historical documents and his own ethnography,

Gonçalves Dias wrote poems that depicted the early years of the colony. The central theme of his most famous poem, *I-Juca-Pirama* – 'He that must die' in Tupi – is the bravery of the warrior hero and the practice of cannibalism. The poem tells the story of a Tupi warrior taken prisoner by the Timbira, who, while awaiting his death, tells of his fears for his father who is old, weak and blind, and from whom he became separated in the woods. When the father is also captured, the son weeps. Seeing his weakness, the Timbira let him go because, according to their belief that they incorporated the qualities of the victims they ate, they would not eat a coward. The old man is appalled at his son's weakness and curses him. The young man suddenly decides to confront the Timbira warriors alone, and thus earns the right to be sacrificed and reconciled with his father.[83] Thus the Indian, despite his sacrifice, emerges as an idealized model of purity and honour, an example to be followed. In such work, the dividing line between literature and reality, between fiction and nonfiction, was blurred to say the least. History was at the service of a mythical form of literature, which in turn was at the service of creating a national identity.

In 1865, José de Alencar[84] published *Iracema*, a novel that ignited the public imagination and revolutionized Brazilian literature by breaking with traditional Portuguese literary form. The book is not only set in the breathtaking natural surroundings that were central to the genre, but its title is also an anagram for America, as well as meaning 'honey lips'. Set in an idealized seventeenth century, the work is an allegory of the birth of Brazil, via a depiction of the sacrifice of the Indians. The central couple – Iracema, a Tupi Indian maiden, and Martim, a Portuguese settler – symbolize the first inhabitants of the country, their union producing a predestined race. At the end of the book Iracema dies so that their son Moacir ('the child of suffering') can live. The book broaches themes including hybrid language, syncretic religion and a nation of mestizos. Once again, in a Brazil far removed from the realities of the nineteenth century, its white and Indian heroes intermix in a setting of untamed nature, behaving with honour and dignity.

Iracema was not José de Alencar's first book with an indigenous theme. He had previously written a much longer novel, *O Guarani*, which was first published in instalments in the *Diário do Rio de Janeiro* between January and April 1857, and was published in book form later that year. The story is also set in the seventeenth century and its central character is the Indian Peri, who falls in love with the blonde, white-skinned Ceci, daughter of a Portuguese nobleman. At the end of the novel Peri tries to rescue the 'blonde virgin' and the story closes with their declaration of an almost platonic love, carried away by the torrential waters of the river – a metaphor for the idea of purification. The composer Carlos Gomes based the Italian libretto for his opera *Il Guarany* on José de Alencar's book. The first performance was given at La Scala in Milan in 1870. Carlos Gomes's work was also financed by Pedro II, and was conventionally European, with some original touches taken from Brazilian culture. Romantic music was composed, but with an indigenous foundation, as if affirming an identity at once universal and singular.

These and many other examples show how Romanticism in Brazil was not restricted to aesthetics. It was both cultural and political, with deep connections to nationalism, to the monarchy, and to cultural independence. Although they were attacked by historians such as Varnhagen, who called them 'caboclo patriots', the Romantic Indianists were successful in establishing a romanticized picture of the Indian as a national symbol. It is interesting to note the answer that Gonçalves Magalhães published in the press, defending his book. 'The fatherland is a concept, represented by the land where we were born.'[85]

The idealized portrayal of the Indian not only resurrected what was 'authentic and noble', but also helped to construct an image of an 'honourable past'. Contrary to the Africans, who were an ever-present reminder of the shameful institution of slavery, the Indian provided an origin for the country that was both mythical and aesthetically malleable. The country's luxurious natural resources had a parallel function: Brazil may not have mediaeval castles or Renaissance churches, but it had the largest rivers and the most beautiful vegetation. The monarch, the state and the nation were depicted surrounded by palm trees, pineapples and exotic birds, displaying the country's unequalled natural exuberance.

The Imperial Academy of Fine Arts – which had been created in 1826 but only began to operate on a regular basis during the reign of Pedro II – was also a fertile field for Romanticism. During this time a major transformation occurred with the rejection of the Baroque in favour of neoclassicism, above all at the court and in some of the provincial capitals. The change had first come about with the arrival of the group of French artists on 26 March 1816, but now became more firmly established, financed by both the state and the monarchy. The emperor adopted a similar policy with the Imperial Academy of Fine Arts that he had introduced at the IHGB, with the distribution of prizes, medals and scholarships to study abroad. He also participated enthusiastically in the annual General Exhibition of Fine Art, and awarded the most outstanding artists with the Order of Christ and the Order of the Rose. In 1845 the emperor inaugurated the annual Travel Fellowship, which funded the winner's studies and living costs abroad for three years. And there was more: Dom Pedro II commissioned artists to paint official portraits, which were distributed around the country and taken with him on his travels, first within Brazil and later overseas. Some of these artists – such as Simplício Rodrigues de Sá[86] and Félix-Émile Taunay[87] – taught the emperor and his sisters the art of painting or became the official court painters. The exaltation of the exotic, the wonders of nature and romanticized Indians all became characteristic of the paintings produced at the Academy.

As the producer of the official images of the empire, the Academy would impose not only styles but also themes: the noble motif, the portrait, the landscape and the historical indigenism would become à la mode. Most such images were produced abroad and represented an idealized picture of Brazil's landscapes and people, as is to be expected from one observing from afar. This is the case of Victor Meirelles de Lima,[88] the painter of iconic works such as *A primeira missa no Brasil* (1860)[89] and *Moema* (1866), and of José Maria Medeiros's *Iracema* (1881).[90] Paintings such as these were part of the Romantic Indianist movement in vogue in the 1860s. In these works, idealized and passive Indians are depicted against the background of a tropical landscape as if they were almost an element of nature. In these large canvases the colonization process is not portrayed as an invasion, but rather as a harmonious, consensual meeting between two peoples.

Brazilian Romanticism was widely disseminated, and the main symbol was the native Brazilian. Ironically, while the monarch and Brazilian culture became more and more tropical, the indigenous peoples had never been so 'white'. The African slave population and even the early colonizers were overlooked as the role as a 'legitimate representative of the nation' was left to the idealized Indian. Pure, honest and courageous, the native Brazilian was depicted as a king of the exuberant forests, where he lived in harmony with nature. The early travellers, chroniclers and historians – names such as Gabriel Soares de Sousa,[91] Sebastião da Rocha Pita[92] and Manuel da Nóbrega – are mere footnotes in the narratives on which the paintings were based. History and myth went hand in hand but also had a didactic purpose: the 'noble Indian' was part of a remote past and could thus become a mythical figure, the inspiration of the Romantic dramas produced at court. Native Brazilians were seen in the grandiose canvases and the beautiful operas that presented the European public with a picture of an exotic and noble empire in the tropics. The 'noble Indian' made it possible for the young nation to make peace with its past and foresee a future filled with promise.

Dom Pedro II's patronage of the arts went even further. He was a great admirer of opera and in 1857 had gone as far as commissioning an opera for Rio de Janeiro from Richard Wagner. Although the composer respectfully declined the offer, the emperor was present in Bayreuth at the first presentation of the composer's *Der Ring des Nibelungen* in 1876, where he sat beside the German Emperor and other nobles. Dom Pedro II made a point of explaining that he was 'an historical Wagnerian' and not, unlike so many of the others in the audience, experiencing this revolutionary music for the first time. In 1857 he had created the Imperial Academy of National Music and Opera, whose objectives were to train Brazilian musicians and popularize opera.

The emperor was equally interested in medicine, financing the research of Brazilian professionals and investing his own resources in the city's asylum, which was named after him in 1850. He was also the patron of the first Scientific Exploration Committee (1859) – nicknamed the Butterfly Commission by its opponents – which collected species in the north of the country.

So Brazil became a 'tropical empire' and, at the same time, a (somewhat distorted) mirror image of Europe. During a period of political tranquillity, Dom Pedro II was used to epitomizing Brazilian nationality, appearing crowned as a Roman Caesar amid coconut palms and cotton plants, coffee trees and tobacco leaves, with books arranged on his lap to display his erudition and wisdom.

But in 1865 the disastrous Paraguay War, which marked both the high point of the Brazilian monarchy and the beginning of its decline, broke out. The war ended five years later, in 1870, with an appalling death toll, casting a shadow over the empire for its part in the massacre. The Republican Party was founded the same year, and the abolitionist movement gained an impetus that was irreversible. The idea that the tropics were a natural, eternal paradise where people coexisted in peace and harmony was no more than a figment of the imagination.

12

The End of the Monarchy in Brazil

THE PARTY IS OVER: THE LONG, DISASTROUS WAR IN PARAGUAY

As the 1870s approached a radical change took place in what, until then, had been the placid routine of Dom Pedro II's reign. In 1865 the most notorious international war in which Brazil had been involved broke out: the Paraguayan War. Unlike what the monarch, his ministers and generals – and even the country's allies Argentina and Uruguay – had assumed, the war was neither easy nor short. And it demanded so much of the government's time and capital that little was left over for domestic reforms. The cost of the war was enormous: 614,000 *contos de réis*, eleven times the government budget for 1864, creating a deficit that was to persist until the end of the monarchy.[1]

Tensions in international relations had been rising in the run-up to the war. In 1862, while the country was preparing to participate in the Universal Exhibition in London – where it was to display the wealth of its agricultural produce – the diplomatic incident known as the Christie Affair occurred. William Douglas Christie had been the British representative at the Brazilian court since 1860 and was known for his confrontational behaviour. Things came to a head when three drunken British officers wandering around the streets of Rio de Janeiro were arrested for disorderly conduct. Christie reacted immediately to what he considered an unacceptable affront to his country. He had the British squadron stationed in Rio de Janeiro blockade the port. Five Brazilian merchant ships were apprehended by the British navy outside Guanabara Bay, causing a serious international incident that could even have led to a declaration of war. The politicians at the time generally treated Christie's confrontational behaviour with irony. 'He learnt diplomacy in the land of the Mosquito,' commented the Baron of Penedo.[2] 'These are the follies of Mr. Christie,' declared the minister Zacarias.[3] But the greatest of the British representative's follies was still to come. On 2 December 1862 he failed to attend the emperor's birthday celebrations, to which the diplomatic corps had been summoned. This time Dom Pedro II decided to force Christie to back down and broke off diplomatic relations with the British government. Leopold I of Belgium, who was asked to arbitrate, decided that Brazil had been wronged and Britain offered a formal apology. Even so, diplomatic relations between the two countries remained suspended for two years.

But this was by no means the worst of the government's problems. The 1860s saw an upsurge in the abolitionist movement. With the prohibition of the slave traffic in 1850 the question of slavery had become a major political issue. In 1865, with the end of the Civil War, the United States passed the thirteenth amendment to their constitution, abolishing slavery in North America. There was fear among the local and government elites that Brazil would soon follow suit. Apart from Brazil, Cuba was the only other country where slavery was still legal. International pressure was increasing.

Yet, the crisis in the River Plate region put the question of abolition on hold. The Paraguayan War, also known as the War of the Triple Alliance, evolved into a national problem so enormous that all political differences were put aside. At the beginning of the 1860s the region was in a state of fragile peace. Four countries, with conflicting interests, had frontiers between the Uruguay and Paraguay rivers: Brazil, Uruguay, Argentina and Paraguay. Shipping access in the River Plate basin, and which country should control the area, was a fraught question. The region was so volatile that a long list of conflicts had occurred long before the beginning of the Paraguayan War. The ambitions of the Argentinean dictator, Dom Juan Manuel Rosas, had led to a serious incident in 1849. Rosas wanted to revert to the former viceroyalty established in the region by Spain. He had already conquered Uruguay and now threatened Brazil's southern border in the province of Rio Grande do Sul. The Brazilian government was aware of Dom Juan Manuel Rosa's intentions, but thought it best to avoid a conflict, a decision that led to the fall of the ministry and the appointment of a new President of the Council: Eusébio de Queirós.[4] The government was under pressure from many directions: increasingly aggressive attacks in the region of the River Plate and the prospect of a gradual end to slavery. There was generalized unease at the high concentration of slaves in the southeast due to the expansion of the coffee plantations there in the 1830s and 1840s.[5] In a political move the government conducted a new census and introduced civil registration, to evaluate the number of slaves and the imminent risk of rebellion. But the elite rejected the idea: the landowners, as was their wont, preferred not to know what the proportion of either slaves or freemen really was.[6]

But from 1851 the 'business of the Plate' took centre stage in Brazilian politics. Although the first confrontation ended quickly, with Brazil entering the war in 1851 and Dom Juan Manuel Rosas' surrender in February 1852, the volatility of the region caused increasing concern. In 1863 a civil war broke out in Uruguay. On the one side were the supporters of the moderate Colorado Party, led by General Venancio Flores, and on the other those of the conservative Blanco Party, led by the divided country's president, Atanasio Aguirre. Brazil and Argentina supported General Flores, as both countries were afraid of the expansionist plans of the Blanco Party.[7] But this particular conflict soon subsided. On 15 February 1865, Aguirre capitulated and signed a peace agreement with Brazil.

Still, trouble in the region was soon to start again, only this time with a different enemy: Paraguay. The state of play was changing: in Argentina the federalists were defeated when Bartolomé Mitre won the presidency and implemented a centralization process. In Brazil, after fourteen years of conservative rule, the Liberal Party came to power. In Paraguay, President Carlos Antonio López died in 1862, and was replaced by his son, Francisco Solano López, who lost no time in entering into confrontation with Brazil. The Brazilian government did not appreciate his attempt – failed, by the way – to arbitrate in the conflict between Brazil and Uruguay. Furthermore, Paraguay vied with Brazil to be the main supplier of maté[8] to the Latin American market, and had aspirations to take over Montevideo as an outlet for its exports, demanding that the borders be redrawn. The Argentinean federalists had the same aspiration, for very similar reasons. Thus two unofficial blocs were formed: on the one hand the Argentinean federalists, the Uruguayan Blancos and Paraguay; and on the other the Brazilian Empire, the Colorado Party and the Argentinean government.

The whole region was undergoing a period of political reconstruction following independence. In addition to the discord over the River

Plate basin, there were internal divisions as well, due to the conflicting ambitions of the governments involved. The countries were also separated by their cultural differences and political regimes. Brazil liked to see itself as a stable regime surrounded by unstable republics; an example of civilization compared to aggressive expansionism, and led by an emperor rather than a dictator.

War was in the air; all it needed was an event to spark it off. That event occurred in 1864, in Uruguay. The Brazilian government issued an ultimatum demanding that rapid measures be taken against alleged abuses of Brazilian residents in Uruguay. Cattle-breeders in Rio Grande do Sul, on the Brazilian side of the border, were also subject to attack and Brazil would have none of it. When the Uruguayans ignored the ultimatum, Brazil invaded the country. Meanwhile, there were confrontations between the other countries in the region. Perhaps the most serious of all stemmed from President Solano's determination that Paraguay gain access to the sea. War broke out when, on 12 November, the Paraguayan authorities seized the Brazilian steamship *Marquês de Olinda*. Then in December, President Solano invaded Mato Grosso. Four months later, in April 1865, he invaded Argentina, attacking Corrientes and Entre Rios, two provinces that had previously been his allies. From then on the Paraguayan leader found himself isolated in a very dangerous game.

Meanwhile, Pedro II, encouraged by the successful resolution of the Christie Affair, headed for Brazil's southern border on 7 July 1865. He was to be 'the army's first volunteer'. The march ended in Uruguaiana, the city on the eastern bank of the Uruguay river,[9] where the emperor met with the Brazilian military chiefs and his allies in the war: President Mitre of Argentina and President Flores of Uruguay. He was soon to learn that, although it is relatively easy to enter a war, it is much harder to withdraw, or to calculate the consequences. In addition, the complexity of a conflict with so many contenders would inevitably lead to altercations even among the allies. There was even disagreement within Brazil as to the origin of the war. On the one hand, some blamed President Solano's aggressive expansionism and his authoritarian style. Pedro II had a particular dislike of his fraudulent politics and the fact that he had set himself up as a dictator. On the other hand, some saw the war as a result of Great Britain's imperialist policy. In order to maintain financial influence in the area, the country had allegedly played a double game, setting one party against the other. According to this interpretation, Francisco Solano López was an anti-imperialist hero, the defender of South American independence and victim of an international conspiracy. There is a third interpretation based on analyses of the domestic situations of the countries involved. Brazil had to maintain access to the Paraná and Paraguay rivers, which were the western province of Mato Grosso's crucial routes to the rest of the country. Furthermore, Brazil wanted to control the flow of commerce in the River Plate basin. As for Argentina, whose expansionist aspirations had been temporarily checked, they still wanted to annex neighbouring territories and generally increase their influence in the area. As far as President Solano was concerned, once Paraguayan autonomy had been secured and Argentina's attempts at expansionism checked, disputes with his neighbours over the navigation of the rivers and the negotiation of frontiers became the major issue. These South American Republics that had cast off imperial repression also eyed the vast Brazilian Empire and its slavery system with considerable suspicion. Thus, even without the intermittent provocations by one party or the other, the region was at best like a massive simmering cauldron, ready to boil over at any time.

On 1 May 1865, in Buenos Aires, the secret Treaty of the Triple Alliance was signed between Brazil, Argentina and Uruguay. The treaty determined that peace would only be negotiated once President Solano had been deposed. New frontiers were established for the countries involved in the dispute and it was agreed that Paraguay, the aggressor, would be forced to pay reparations for the war. The arrogance of these terms reflected the allies' confidence and their belief – entirely mistaken as it turned out – that the war would soon be over due to their obvious military advantage. The three countries combined had a total of 11 million inhabitants (of which 9.1 million were Brazilian), while Paraguay had just 318,144 soldiers at its disposal. The annual exports of the three allies totalled £36 million, whereas those of Paraguay were worth less than half a million.[10] Paraguay thus entered the war at a great disadvantage, especially since it had lost its previous allies: the Argentinean President Atanasio Aguirre had been defeated and in Uruguay General Flores had been elected. Furthermore, President Solano's invasion of Argentina had alienated the governors of Corrientes and Entre Rios.

It should be borne in mind that, until the outbreak of the war, the

Brazilian Empire had a small, poorly trained army. The most significant military-type body was the National Guard (created in 1831 and reorganized in 1850), basically made up of (and depending on) the owners of large estates. This was the first time the country had formed a professional army, with compulsory conscription. After the first year of the war, when joining the army had been seen as an act of patriotism, there were too few volunteers to make up the army.[11] At the beginning of the war a wide variety of motives led young men to join the war effort. In his novel *Iaiá Garcia*, Machado de Assis tells the story of Jorge, 'one of the leading dandies of the Rua do Ouvidor', who signed up to impress Estela. In the eyes of Machado de Assis's character, the war was nothing more than a pretext for making a romantic declaration of love, and upon his departure Jorge's main concern was 'the crease on his uniform trousers and the shine on his boots'.[12] At court, fervent patriotism prevailed and every victory was celebrated. Another of Machado de Assis's characters, Fulano Beltrão (the one who displayed his wife's mausoleum in the Rua do Ouvidor), celebrated Brazil's victory at the Battle of Riachuelo[13] with a sumptuous ball, where he displayed 'naval weapons and flags in a Hall of Honour, in front of a picture of the Emperor'.[14]

Brazil's growing military strength was cause for optimism. The navy was re-equipped, with its number of warships increasing from forty-five in 1865 to ninety-four by the end of the war in 1870. In 1865, Argentina meanwhile had six thousand well-trained soldiers and Uruguay had four thousand. The enthusiasm in Buenos Aires was such that General Mitre declared the alliance's troops would control 'the barracks in 24 hours, Corrientes in three weeks, and, in three months, Asunción'. However, contrary to everyone's hopes, after Uruguaiana surrendered, ending the first phase of the war, the conflict continued. It turned into a five-year war, with terrible sacrifices and loss of life, which threatened the unity of the alliance and became increasingly unpopular at home.

To make matters worse, there were also internal disagreements within the Brazilian armed forces. Admiral Tamandaré,[15] commander of the naval forces, was nearly sixty years old and past his prime. General Caxias, on the other hand, who was now a senator for the Conservative Party, was held in high esteem for his suppression of the rebellions during the regencies. His entry into the war marked a turning point: as the second phase of the conflict began he undertook a thorough reorganization of the army. When he arrived in Paraguay, in November 1866, he found an army short on troops and low in morale. The region was insalubrious and the troops, completely ill-prepared and ill-equipped. Furthermore, by this time, the government had begun to resort to compulsory conscription. Public opinion had turned against the war, with the *Correio Mercantil* of 9 November 1866 referring to it as the 'Paraguayan slaughterhouse'.

Many Brazilian slave-owners began sending their slaves to fight in their place, to exempt themselves from 'the punishment of war'. In the 1866 Council of State meetings opinions were divided: some favoured slave conscription, whereas others objected to the presence of freed slaves in the ranks of the army. Deputy Pimenta Bueno,[16] who was in favour of giving slaves their freedom (with no compensation for their owners) in return for fighting in the war, argued that it was 'preferable to spare the more civilized, moral class, rather than the other, which is less civilized and potentially dangerous. It behoves us to choose the lesser of two evils.' Senator Nabuco de Araújo,[17] on the other hand, thought the practice would create problems for the future, and said that it should only be continued if 'after fighting as soldiers, [the African Brazilians were] returned to slavery'. But he also thought there was a possibility that if 'the slaves were freed and became citizens before becoming soldiers, they would make disciplined soldiers because they were accustomed to obeying orders'.[18] However, Counsellor José Maria da Silva Paranhos, the future Viscount of Rio Branco,[19] warned that 'a large army of freed slaves [. . .] would be a danger, because their recruitment could lead the slaves within the empire to revolt, not only of their own volition, but also through incitement by secret groups'.[20] Even General Caxias himself complained that 'the introduction of slaves into the ranks is already producing detrimental results due to the immoral example and lack of discipline of these men who do not understand the meaning of country, society or family'.[21] In Brazil, whenever any subject under discussion touched on abolition, there was widespread disagreement. The change in the 'colour' of the Brazilian Army did not go unnoticed by the Paraguayan press, who began to refer to the country's soldiers as *los macaquitos* ('little monkeys'). The *Cabichuí*, a periodical directly linked to President Solano, produced a series of cartoons depicting the Brazilian troops, as well as the emperor and empress, as monkeys.

In the meantime, in Rio de Janeiro the government tried to play down the gravity of the war by discouraging the propagation of detailed accounts. But luck was against them. In 1867, precisely when the city was fighting a cholera epidemic, the battles on the country's southern borders had become veritable slaughters. With so much going wrong, the public began to blame the government for the prolonged war and for the blind determination of the army's high command to keep fighting until President Solano was deposed. In 1868, when the empire achieved its greatest victories at the battles of Itororó,[22] Avaí,[23] Lomas Valentinas[24] and Humaitá,[25] even General Caxias proposed a cessation of hostilities. It was only the following year, however, that the Brazilian troops finally took Asunción – with no resistance. With the occupation of the Paraguayan capital, Caxias considered the war over and withdrew from the conflict, despite the emperor's protests. When he arrived back from the battlefields, the general was not greeted with the celebrations he had expected. Even so, he was awarded the *Grão-Colar da Ordem de Dom Pedro I* – the first person to receive the honour since its creation at the beginning of the empire – along with the title of Duke.

However, there was another returning general who was acclaimed as a popular hero: General Osório.[26] Whereas General Caxias was known as a great military strategist, General Osório became a kind of national icon for bravery. His courageous feats impressed both the allies and their Paraguayan foes; among the troops he had become a mythical figure. People would say he had *o corpo fechado*[27] and that, after battles, he would 'shake his poncho and the bullets would fall out'.[28] Even without the generals Caxias and Osório, the pursuit of President Solano continued, this time under the command of Princess Isabel's husband, the Count of Eu, who took command of the troops on 22 March 1869. Ignoring the appeals of his wife, who wanted to see her husband safe in the palace, he now found himself in charge of 26,000 exhausted men, most of whom were desperate to desert. But on 12 August, 700 Paraguayans were killed and 1,100 men taken prisoner. On 16 August, 2,000 Paraguayan soldiers died and 2,300 were taken prisoner at the Battle of Campo Grande.[29] The pursuit of President Solano only came to an end when he was surrounded by Brazilian troops at Cerro-Corá and was killed along with his adolescent son. The consequences of the war for Paraguay not only included the removal of the head of state, but the destruction of the state itself.

There is disagreement over the number of Paraguayan lives lost: estimates vary between 800,000 and 1.3 million.

There are similar discrepancies in Brazil's statistics, starting with the number of men who were sent, which ranges between 100,000 and 140,000. The official numbers released by the imperial government in 1870 were 4,332 killed, 18,597 wounded and 988 missing, making a total of 23,917.[30] Brazil's victory was overshadowed by the numbers of deaths and the emergence of the details of the horrors of the war. The emperor's image suffered greatly. From a peace-loving monarch and supporter of the arts with little interest in politics, he had become the leader of a terrible war.

The 'triple disgrace' as the alliance became known had erred gravely in its calculations. A war they thought would be over in a few months lasted for five years, taking on vast proportions. With the end of the war, the status of the empire was radically altered, both within and beyond its borders. Perhaps most importantly the war had consolidated the army as an institution. Whereas in 1865 there were no more than 18,000 men in the army, only a year later this number fluctuated between 38,000 and 78,000. By the end of the war a new army had been formed, separate from the National Guard. After the army's victory a military career became a means of bettering oneself. The institution of the military assumed an important role in society, something that had previously been unimaginable. An elite was formed within the army that was both socially and intellectually antagonistic to the civilian elite, dissatisfied with the situation of the country and with their position in the hierarchy of power. After fighting side by side with black soldiers, the army also began to reject its former role of pursuing escaped slaves. Thus it became a source of discontent within the empire and from amid its ranks republicans and abolitionists began to emerge.

It is important to understand that there are no such things as slave soldiers. When the former owners decided to send them to the army, in order to avoid sending their own sons, the slaves were immediately considered free. This meant that when the hostilities were over they were in a strong position to negotiate a permanent end to slavery. According to *The Times* newspaper of 23 June 1869, 7,979 freed slaves had served in the Brazilian Army.[31] Thus military conscription and the thorny question of abolition became intrinsically linked, creating one of the most serious political crises of Pedro II's reign. Whereas the generals Osório and Caxias returned from the war as heroes – immortalized in public monuments and articles in the press – the black soldiers, although they had been freed, were confronted with the system of slavery that still prevailed. Many of them could still be forced to return to work as slaves because their newly won freedom could easily be revoked. Angelo Agostini – a declared abolitionist – drew a cartoon entitled 'Return from Paraguay', which was published in 1870.[32] The drawing shows a black soldier, with military decorations on his chest, returning from the war to find his mother being whipped at the pillory. The caption read: 'Full of glory, covered with laurels, after having spilled his blood in the defence of his country and freed a people from being enslaved, the volunteer returns home to find his mother tied to the pillory! Hideous reality . . .'

Brazil had spent 600,000 *contos de réis* on the war, making the country even more financially dependent on Britain; thousands of soldiers had been lost in battle and the image of Brazil as a peace-loving nation had been destroyed. On the other hand, for the first time the notion of a fatherland began to spread, most notably at the beginning of the war, when there had been victorious battles and huge numbers of volunteers. The national flag was hoisted on a regular basis, the emperor became the leader of the nation, responsible for mediating between the two political parties, and new national heroes were created: the Duke of Caxias, General Osório and Admiral Barroso.[33]

In addition, artists such as Pedro Américo[34] and Victor Meirelles produced grandiose canvases depicting battle scenes and glorifying the fatherland. Victor Meirelles painted the Battle of Guararapes in the 1640s,[35] linking the Paraguayan War with the creation of a fatherland. Pedro Américo depicted the carnage of the Battle of Avaí as the struggle of civilization (Brazilians) against barbarianism (Paraguayans). The North American composer Louis Moreau Gottschalk[36] composed a virtuoso work for piano, the 'Grand Fantasy on the Brazilian National Anthem', which he played before an enthusiastic audience in Rio de Janeiro, and the Romantic poet Bernardo Guimarães[37] wrote 'The Volunteer's Farewell'.[38] But the internal wounds were hard to heal. There were no facilities for returning veterans, with most of the former combatants, above all those of African descent, being left to their own resources. Freedom in Brazil was a kind of trophy, difficult to win and nearly impossible to keep.[39]

THE ABOLITIONIST CAMPAIGN: FREEDOM MUST BE GRADUAL

With the end of the Paraguayan War the campaigns for a republic and the abolition of slavery came to the forefront once again. At the beginning of the 1870s the Republican Party, the Society for Freedom and the Society for the Emancipation of Slavery were founded in Rio de Janeiro. On 28 September 1871 the *Lei do Ventre Livre* (Law of Free Birth) was passed. This law freed the offspring of all slaves born after the date of its promulgation, but not their mothers. It stipulated that the children would remain with their mothers until the age of eight, at which time their owners could choose between receiving compensation (60,000 réis) or continuing to use their services until they were twenty-one. Despite its limitations and gradual approach, it was at least a step towards abolition. But in such a heated political climate, the opposition saw it merely as a cynical government manoeuvre to placate them. It also earned the suspicion of the slave-owners, who began to mistrust the monarch.

Although the law was moderate, it sparked all kinds of reactions. Regional differences account in part for the discrepancies in response to the law. The provinces of the northeast accepted it far more readily than those of the southeast. The figures of the 1872 census go a long way towards explaining this: in the northeast 37 per cent of the population were slaves, whereas in the four coffee-producing provinces of the southeast (including Rio de Janeiro) this figure was 59 per cent, and in the other provinces (in the south and the midwest) just 7.3 per cent.[40] These differing positions created conflict between the coalition of land-owners in the northeast and the coffee planters of the southeast, which called the government's legitimacy into question. As Joaquim Nabuco – who was becoming a symbol of the abolitionist movement – commented at the time, the situation expressed the 'dialectic of ambiguity': while the state was the cornerstone of slavery, it was also the only entity that could eliminate it.

There was another aspect of the law that alienated the plantation owners in the southeast and increased their hostility towards the monarchy: it formally recognized the existence of slave families. Slave registries for emancipation were established, and these were based on slave families rather than individual slaves. This also meant that the traditional process was reversed: whereas previously 'free men of colour' had been required to prove their freedom, this now became the responsibility of the slave-owner, who had to produce the slave's certificate. Without such proof, any 'person of colour' was considered legally free. So the *ventre livres* (those born after the law took effect) were free, despite the clause in the law requiring them to work for their mothers' masters until they were twenty-one. They were also citizens. The question remained controversial until the *Lei Áurea* – 'the Golden Law' – was passed, finally abolishing slavery in 1888. When it came to laws regarding 'people of colour' the government's main concern was to act gradually, maintaining mechanisms of control. Gradualism, tutelage, dependency and policies of control were part of the state's strategy in order to deal with freed slaves. In addition, there was a general understanding that both the state and society were entitled to compensation for the loss of workers. The truth was, the prevailing view was to delay the prohibition of the private ownership of slaves. Furthermore, the state's position of official mediator in all such matters put the government in a direct conflict of interest with the rural elite. Meanwhile, with the new law, abolitionists could pursue the issue in the courts of São Paulo and Rio de Janeiro.[41]

But the 1871 law also had the effect of cooling things down and putting the abolitionist campaign on hold. By acting first the government had maintained its control of the slavery issue. Unlike the United States, the Brazilian government had avoided a civil war, and it had also avoided a slave revolution like the one that had occurred in Haiti. It had been essential to postpone any measures until after the end of the Paraguayan War in order to maintain the number of troops that could be conscripted. The motto of the conservative elite was 'do little to avoid the worst'.

Even the emperor muddled along with piecemeal gestures without touching on the crucial questions of imperial policy. In 1870 he renounced the title of sovereign, as sovereignty belonged to the people. In 1871, on his return from his first visit to Europe, he put an end to the tradition of kissing the monarch's hand, 'o beija-mão', and began to refuse further titles or monuments. The royal vestments were now only used on official occasions, such as the opening of Congress and speeches from the throne. On all other occasions Dom Pedro II preferred to be seen as a 'modern monarch', surrounded by books, globes, pens and other symbols of his erudition. Notwithstanding his attempt to stay out of this difficult public debate, he was part of it. Although he declared he was against slavery, he never used his power to hasten abolition.

THE REPUBLICAN PARTY: FEDERALISM IS FINE, BUT DO NOT MENTION ABOLITION

Meanwhile new opposition factions were emerging and among them, for the first time, were political groups with no connection to the monarchy. The first edition of the newspaper *A República* was published on 3 December 1870. It contained the 'Brazilian Republican Manifesto', which was to provide the basis for the foundation of the Republican Party on 17 January 1872. The new party, which was mostly made up of liberal professionals from São Paulo, organized its first Congress in July 1873, when it was joined by influential new supporters: *Paulista* landowners, unhappy with what they considered interventionist policies on the part of the government, decided to join the opposition.

Another important aspect to consider is that although São Paulo was the largest coffee producer and was becoming the richest province, it was represented by very few senators: three in 1859, the same number as Pará, but fewer than Pernambuco, Bahia, Minas Gerais and Rio de Janeiro. Even in 1889, São Paulo had the same number of representatives in the Chamber of Deputies as did Ceará, and fewer than Pernambuco, Bahia, Minas Gerais and Rio de Janeiro. The situation in the Council of State and in the Cabinet was no different.[42] Meanwhile, in the last three decades of the nineteenth century, São Paulo's coffee plantations expanded throughout the west of the province, and during the 1880s its production overtook that of the province of Rio de Janeiro.

Thus, although this was not the first time the idea of a republic had been contemplated, from 1870 onwards it became a more viable alternative. In 1873 there was a split in the Liberal Party; a faction became the São Paulo Republican Party. This group was highly critical of the over-centralized power of both the Crown and the administration of the empire. Their proposal was for a peaceful transition to a federal republic. In the previously mentioned 1870 manifesto published in *A Republica*, the republicans had claimed that centralization was comparable to disintegration, and decentralization would lead to unity: 'centralization – dismemberment; decentralization – unity'. Their preferred from of government was to be 'American and for America'.[43] When the manifesto was published it had attracted further supporters from São Paulo, Minas Gerais and Pernambuco. But there were other provinces where the idea was not so enthusiastically received. In Bahia, for example, which had influential monarchist groups, the manifesto made little impact. In Paraíba the Republican Party did not even exist, and in Ceará, the first state to propose abolition, the party was only founded in 1887. But in São Paulo the Republican Party was strong, counting among its members doctors, engineers, lawyers, journalists, merchants and a large contingent of coffee planters from the west of the province. This group, representing 50 per cent of the delegates, met at the Itu convention present on 18 April 1873.[44] It was the first republican convention ever held in Brazil.

Although the emergence of republican parties occurred at the same time as the abolition campaign, the two groups did not work together. The republicans avoided the issue of slavery so as not to risk their alliance with the farmers from the west of São Paulo. It was, to say the least, an opportunist approach. Many of the members of the Republican Party were also slave-owners themselves. The new republicans were concerned with the maintenance of order and developed policies for gradual emancipation based on compensation for the owners. Out of fear of a civil war they kept silent on the question of abolition.

AT THE HEIGHT OF THE CRISIS THE MONARCH TOURS THE WORLD

By the end of the 1870s there were three main factions that opposed the empire: the republicans, the abolitionists and the army. Meanwhile Pedro II was withdrawing more and more from politics. The vogue for caricatures of the emperor dates from this period. He was mocked for how he dealt with state affairs and for his indecision (which was becoming increasingly apparent). He began to be called nicknames including *Pedro Banana*, *Pedro Caju* and *Emperrador* (Banana Pedro, Cashew Pedro – a reference to the long format of his head – and *Emperrador* means 'someone who holds things up' from the verb *emperrar*). The Brazilian press had been free since 1850 and the emperor was often the target of its jibes. Illustrated journals were popular, especially those carrying the work of three European cartoonists: Angelo Agostini and Luigi Borgomainerio – both Italian and who drew for the *Revista Ilustrada* and *Le Figaro* respectively – and Rafael Bordalo Pinheiro, a friend of the great Portuguese novelist Eça de Queirós, who had recently arrived from Portugal and founded the periodical *O Mosquito*. There were more than twenty periodicals of this kind, of which the best known was the *Revista Ilustrada*, founded in 1876. The emperor's studiousness, his thin legs, strident voice and lack of interest in politics provided these satirical magazines with ample material. The image of the emperor as an old monarch, a patron of the arts with a long white beard, was widely lampooned. He was depicted falling asleep during meetings of the IHGB, while overseeing the examinations at the Colégio Dom Pedro II or presiding at Congress. He was also shown either dozing or looking like a puppet as he gave speeches from the throne, oblivious to the issues at hand. But the most controversial decision he made at this time was to travel the world, which led to a spate of sharp, bitter comments. The relentless periodicals began to mock what they called his 'motomania': the 'sickness' that drove the monarch to travel. Nonetheless, the emperor set off travelling both inside and outside Brazil, but mostly to Europe. During 1871, 1876 and 1887 he barely set foot in the country.

In 1871, in the throes of political upheaval, a seemingly bored Dom Pedro II was preparing to visit a world he only knew through books. His departure led to all sorts of partisan controversy. It is interesting to note that, despite the public character of the trips, his personal motives always underpinned the official justifications. In this first case, the pretext was the death of his daughter, Princess Leopoldina of Saxe-Coburg and Gotha, who lived in France and left heirs under his tutelage. After declaring an official mourning period, the emperor left on 25 May 1871 for Europe and the Middle East. The sovereign enjoyed travelling. He returned only in March 1872, and he was so thrilled with the experience that he soon planned another trip.

The official reason given for the second journey was again of a private nature: the fragile state of the empress's health. Dona Teresa Cristina left the entourage upon their arrival in Europe and went to take the waters at Gastein, in Austria. After the first stop the emperor continued his journey, with a retinue of two hundred people, to the United States and Canada, then on to Asia and parts of Africa. He then returned to Europe where he visited Germany, Denmark, Sweden, Norway, Russia, Turkey, Greece, Austria, Holland, Belgium, Switzerland and Portugal, in addition to spending six weeks in Paris. Dom Pedro II had turned his trip into a marathon. The monarch, who had never wanted to leave the tropics, now appeared to be in no hurry to return.

Apart from his visit to the East, Dom Pedro II's second journey was mostly remembered because it was the first time a ruling monarch had set foot in North America, and to visit a republic at that! Dom Pedro II, along with US president Ulysses Grant, opened the 1876 Centennial Exhibition (World's Fair) in Philadelphia. The emperor was then received with great interest in New York. And as for him, he vowed, 'the crown would hold its head high', adding that, after all, he was 'the only sovereign in the Americas'.[45] Perpetually dressed in his formal black coat – 'the monarch in tails' as the Portuguese author Eça de Queirós ironically referred to him – and forgoing his honorary title of 'Dom', the emperor's routine was a busy one. He had meetings with intellectuals, inspected pavilions at the exhibition, and visited industries, road-building projects, research institutes and museums.

In his conversations with Alexander Graham Bell, who allowed him to test his most recent invention – the telephone – as well as in his visits to historical monuments, the emperor sought to recover his image as an enlightened, liberal monarch. One of the highlights of his travels was his meeting with Victor Hugo, the great propagandist of the French Republic. During his stay in Paris, Dom Pedro II invited the writer to call on him in his hotel; but as his offer was refused, the monarch decided to abandon protocol and went to visit Victor Hugo at his home. That is where the following dialogue allegedly took place: when the writer's daughter introduced the visitor as 'His Majesty from Brazil', the emperor is said to have replied: 'My dear, there is only one Majesty here: Victor Hugo.' After the meeting they exchanged photographs. The visit was, no doubt, a boon to Brazilian republicans, but the monarch's triumph would not last long. On his return he found the mood very different from when he had left.

SCANDALS ON THE HORIZON

It is said that the efficacy of a ruler is directly related to his or her capacity to remain untouched by scandal. The 1870s brought on a deliberate campaign in the press to denounce the exaggerated expenses of the court. The expenses were listed, the country's finances verified, and transparency in the submission of accounts demanded. In 1873 the *Carioca* newspapers printed controversial details of the emperor's expenses when he had stayed at the Hotel do Porto, in Portugal, the previous year. Public opinion was divided between those who wanted to preserve the emperor and those who wanted to raise questions about his behaviour as a citizen; in other words, between those who wanted to keep the information secret and those who wanted to secure the constitutional right of freedom of the press. Whether for or against, the monarch's public image had been compromised.

The greatest scandal of the period was known as 'the theft of the crown jewels'. Although the episode in itself was of little importance, the repercussions were an evident sign of the mistrust that now surrounded the monarchy. In the early hours of 18 March 1882 some rare jewels belonging to the empress disappeared from the Palace of São Cristóvão. The chief of police, Trigo de Loureiro, quickly realized it was an inside job, a crime committed by someone who knew the palace well. Manuel Paiva and his brother Pedro de Paiva – long-standing servants at the palace – became the principal suspects, a fact that the press accused the emperor of covering up. When the two were arrested and confessed their crime, neither was prosecuted. Even after the jewels, thought to be worth 'a fortune', were found in Manuel Paiva's house, hidden in cans of butter, the two were let go without punishment.[46] The public reaction was one of indignation. The *Jornal do Commercio* declared: 'The restitution of the stolen goods may be enough for the proprietor, but it does not meet the moral requirements of society.' In *A Gazetinha*, Raul Pompéia[47] went as far as accusing the emperor of having raped Paiva's daughter and having released Manuel Paiva out of fear of retaliation. The *Gazeta da Tarde* attacked the emperor's 'weakness', while the *Revista Ilustrada* published a satirical article demanding that justice be done. News of the scandal was even transmitted by telegraph to papers abroad. It was evidently a deliberate attempt to systematically attack the emperor, and his image was seriously compromised.

Although Dom Pedro II did what he could, his traditional policy of dissimulation was hard to sustain. He had always had lovers, but now his infidelities were commented on in public. The court had always had an ample budget, but it was only now that someone remembered to produce the accounts. Later, Gilberto Freyre would point out that by 'exchanging the crown for a top hat' the monarchy had put itself at risk. He called Dom Pedro II 'a grey emperor in a land of tropical sun' and saw an incompatibility between the people's expectations and the new image the emperor had adopted.[48] After his return from Europe it seemed he had distanced himself from the local imagery, as if he were the king of another people. During the 1883 carnival one of the floats displayed an image of the emperor, sitting alone, with the inscription: 'They've stolen everything from him'. Another float satirically referred to his interest in the passage of the planet Venus, mocking his interest in astronomy. Perhaps the most pertinent comment came from a cartoon by Agostini: 'From staring at the sky so much, the emperor will lose his way on earth'.

CRISIS AT HOME – THE EMPEROR TRAVELS TO EUROPE

By the beginning of the 1880s the emperor was besieged with problems. In 1880 the Brazilian Society Against Slavery was founded, and in 1883 the Abolitionist Confederation. The same year the Romantic poet Castro Alves published his poem 'The Slaves' ('Os escravos') and Joaquim Nabuco published his book on abolition (*O abolicionismo*). Both were to become highly influential, the first in the field of literature, the second in political science. The times were changing and new voices were needed to correct the injustices of the times. Castro Alves wanted to transform the world. His poetry reached 'the clouds of humanity's tears' and became 'the herald of freedom'. It was described as 'lightning's brother' and 'the tempest's son'. He wrote his poetry to be recited in public and to penetrate the souls of the audience. As his work suggests, he dedicated most of his life to the fight against slavery.[49]

In 1884 slavery was officially abolished in the provinces of Ceará and Amazonas, and on 28 September 1885 the Saraiva-Cotegipe Law, also known as the *Lei dos Sexagenários* (Sexagenarian Law), was passed. The law granted all slaves over sixty their freedom, although it required them to work for a further three years after its promulgation. The conservative nature of the measure led to an immediate reaction. Between the passing of the *Lei do Ventre Livre* and the *Lei dos Sexagenários* the origin and distribution of slaves had radically altered. According to the *Report of 1886*, due to death and release from slavery the number of slaves in the country had been reduced by 412,468. Estimates for 1886 assessed the slave population at 1,133,228, and the number of officially registered slaves in 1887 was 723,419. Furthermore the distribution of slaves around the country was changing: slaves were being transferred from the north to the south, and many more of them were being granted their freedom in the former than in the latter.

Another blow fell in 1885, when a cholera outbreak decimated the population of Rio de Janeiro. Nevertheless, the emperor – who had made a loan of £50,000 to the Knowler Foster Bank in London – kept to his plan to return to Europe, setting off on 30 June 1887. This third trip received a great deal of criticism from the press. Some newspapers alleged that Dom Pedro II was travelling to get away from the urgent political questions. Others put it down to his failing health. At sixty-two years old, the emperor did indeed appear tired and old, with deep wrinkles on his forehead, a glazed look in his eyes, and an immense white beard.

A small committee travelled with the emperor and his wife aboard the *Gironde*. Among them were the emperor's grandson, Pedro Augusto, the Count of Carapebus, the emperor's doctor Count Mota Maia, the Viscount of Saboia, and José Maria da Silva Paranhos, the Viscount of Rio Branco. The emperor had fallen ill in 1887 and again at the beginning of 1888. It was said that if his first journey had been motivated by the desire to see the world, and the second by the empress's illness, the third was an attempt to conceal the fact that Pedro II himself was ill. On many occasions during the journey, which lasted several months, Princess Isabel, along with her husband the Count of Eu, stood in for her father. The Count of Eu was becoming an increasingly unpopular figure, with rumours circulating about his alleged greed and certain shady deals. He owned the 'government boarding houses'. On 3 August 1889 the *Diário* accused him of being a 'slum landlord' and a 'wandering usurer', increasing general concern about the power the Frenchman would wield if his wife were to succeed to the throne.

While the rumours were running wild at home, the emperor's journey went smoothly. On 19 July the royal party arrived in Portugal, and by 22 July they had reached Paris. But Dom Pedro II was a changed man. His 'Romantic era', with his interest in Victor Hugo and Wagner, was something of the past. Even so, he did what he could to keep his image as patron of the arts alive. He visited intellectuals such as Louis Pasteur and Ernest Renan and translated texts and wrote poetry, which he sent to friends and relatives. He managed to rest for six months; but this was hardly enough to prepare him for the turbulence that was to greet him when he arrived home.

MEANWHILE . . . ABOLITION

On 10 June 1887 the Countess of Barral wrote to Princess Isabel: 'I cannot congratulate you on the regency that you now have to exercise, but trusting in your good judgement and the advice of your husband, I pray to God that everything will go well during his majesty's absence.'[50] In her letter the countess, who was the princess's mentor and an intimate friend of Dom Pedro II, seems to have had a premonition that all might not go well with her protégée's government. Perhaps it was her knowledge of France; be that as it may, the political situation in Brazil was truly fragile. The Republican Party was gaining ground and the army's dissatisfaction was on the rise. Nonetheless, the most urgent issue, by far, was the question of abolition. By the 1880s the abolitionist movement was divided between the moderates, who looked to Joaquim Nabuco for guidance, and the radicals, among whose leaders were Silva Jardim,[51] Luís Gama,[52] José do Patrocínio[53] and Antônio Bento.[54] Abolition was the most discussed subject in the streets and the favourite topic of newspapers,[55] pamphlets and satirical magazines.

At this time it was common for the population of Rio de Janeiro to participate in processions, rituals and ceremonies of the court, and to see Romantic plays put on at the Royal theatres. Public protests against slavery were also common, and yet had become increasingly ineffective.[56] No matter how hard the government tried to show its 'reforming zeal', by passing legislation such as the sexagenarian law, the measures seemed to backfire. Attacks came from every quarter, not to mention the slave uprisings all over the country. An atmosphere of fear and uncertainty pervaded: on the one hand, freemen feared they would be re-enslaved, and on the other, people were terrified of the ever present violence. Not only were there slave uprisings, the entire system became more violent as it came to an end. Slave-owners, faced with the inevitable – and disproportionately invested in slaves – began to demand more exacting labour and longer working hours. This resulted in constant escapes, murders and attacks on farmers and overseers. There were widespread protests from emancipated slaves and from the population at large about the increasing cruelty of the punishments. Aware that slavery was losing its legitimacy and the support of the country, groups of slaves became better organized and more daring, planning uprisings, escaping, committing crimes, and demanding autonomy and better living conditions. In areas where the concentration of slaves was high, the rebellions took on alarming proportions. In an attempt to control the panic the government took the side of the slave-owners, arresting slaves, ignoring denunciations of cruelty, and repressing the activities of the abolitionists. But the disobedience of the slaves spread from plantation to plantation and their crimes became increasingly violent, thus reversing one of the basic rules of a slave-based society, where the slave-owners have a monopoly on corporal punishment and violence.[57] The almost impossible task of keeping the repression strictly within the law began to raise the question of governability. Slaves revolted and fled during the night, abandoning the coffee plantations in groups that were often led by sympathetic abolitionists. It was not unusual to see bands of slaves on the roads at night, invading the towns.

In the late nineteenth century, with the support of abolitionists, several refuges for escaped slaves were developed on the outskirts of Rio de Janeiro: the Camorim *quilombo* in the rural area of Jacarepaguá; the Raimundo *quilombo* in Engenho Novo; the Miguel Dias *quilombo* in Catumbi; the Padre Ricardo *quilombo* in Penha; and the Clapp *quilombo* on São Domingos beach, not far from the centre of the city of Niterói. Another popular escape route was through the valley of the Paraíba river in São Paulo, which ended in the famous Jabaquara complex of *quilombos* on the outskirts of the port of Santos. At the end of the nineteenth century there were three independently run *quilombos* in the complex: that of Pai Filipe, Garrafão and the Jabaquara *quilombo* itself.[58] At the Jabaquara complex, escaped slaves from São Paulo plantations received help from the legendary Caiafases group. Under the leadership of the lawyer Antônio Bento de Sousa e Castro, who had become the leader of the *Paulista* abolitionists after the death of the poet Luís Gama, the Caiafases provoked the fury of the slave-owners. From 1884 onwards the group transferred as many slaves as possible to Ceará, a province that was of little interest to the central government, and where, along with the province of Amazonas, slavery had been abolished four years before the rest of the country was to follow suit.[59]

The *quilombo* of Leblon, although smaller than the Jabaquara complex, was another important settlement in Brazilian history. The refuge was established in the garden of a Rio de Janeiro estate that belonged to José de Seixas Magalhães, a capable Portuguese businessman with money in his pocket and advanced ideas. He manufactured and sold leather goods, both in Brazil and abroad, using steam-driven equipment. The Seixas e Cia store was located in a large warehouse in Rua Gonçalves Dias in the heart of the city and was a meeting place for leading abolitionists: the poet Olavo Bilac,[60] journalist José do Patrocínio, jurist Rui Barbosa, writer Coelho Neto,[61] and other renowned intellectuals including André Rebouças,[62] Paula Nei[63] and Joaquim Nabuco, almost all of whom were in favour of immediate abolition without compensation.[64]

Seixas Magalhães was an active member of the Abolitionist Confederation, which had been founded in Rio de Janeiro. The confederation was an amalgamation of thirty anti-slavery clubs and associations, located in virtually every province of the empire. Their work was to encourage slaves to escape, to provide fugitives with shelter, to write pamphlets and organize conferences. The confederation supported the fugitives in Leblon, organizing and maintaining the slave refuge that José de Seixas Magalhães had established on his estate.

The *quilombo* in Leblon became famous because the slaves who had taken refuge there grew flowers commercially, above all white camellias. The abolitionist movement adopted the flower as its symbol. At the time camellias were extremely rare in Brazil and the abolitionists saw in the flower's fragility a symbol of the slaves' aspiration to freedom. The camellia needed special care to thrive and had to be cultivated by the hands of free workers and not by slave labour, which was now seen as obsolete, criminal and condemned to extinction. From then on, those who wore a camellia in their buttonhole or grew them in their gardens were making an open statement of their engagement with the abolitionist cause. The fashion caught on: in São Paulo, the Caiafases sent escaped slaves to Rio de Janeiro by train, with the assurance that they would be met at the station by a man with a white camellia in his buttonhole, whom they should look out for on the platform at the city's Central Station. The abolitionists in Recife also adopted the symbolism of the flower, naming the barge that took escaped slaves to Ceará the *Camellia*. Public support for the legitimacy of the abolitionist cause now led, for the first time in the country's history, to the development of a political strategy within government to emancipate the slaves.

At the same time the links between different groups of slaves were strengthening, whether through acts of solidarity, blood ties, marriage and adoption, or through the black fraternities that began to proliferate. As the authorities were by now clearly losing control, they opted for negotiation: contracts between masters and former slaves, promises of wages and autonomy. Everything was still aimed at making the process a gradual one, in an effort to postpone the inevitable. Yet, abolition was actually already becoming a reality, due to both private initiatives and those of the slaves themselves. New heroes of the movement emerged, among them José do Patrocínio, a republican and democrat whose mother had been a slave. Vast crowds gathered to listen to his inflammatory speeches. The struggle for abolition took three major forms: the fight of the abolitionists, the actions of the slaves themselves, and the political struggle at the national level. Brazilians flocked to join the new great cause.

It was becoming harder and harder to resist. Perhaps it was for this reason that the *Lei Áurea* was so succinct: 'As from the date of this law, slavery in Brazil is abolished. All dispositions to the contrary are revoked.' The law, signed on 13 May 1888, emancipated 700,000 slaves, which by this time represented a small proportion of the total population of Brazil, estimated at 15 million people.

This belated freedom for the slaves meant the last strong tie to the monarchy had been broken. The coffee planters had lost all hope that they would receive some sort of financial compensation, which resulted in legal action against the Crown. Celebrated abroad as a victory for Dom Pedro II's government, the law of 13 May also brought joy and optimism to most Brazilians. It was certainly for them the most popular measure of Dom Pedro II's reign. On 23 May 1888, Joaquim Nabuco – now known as the prince of abolition – wrote: 'Abolition has been achieved! No one expected that such a great feat would be achieved so soon, and no national event has ever been commemorated with such enthusiasm. For twenty days the city has been in a state of delirium [. . .]. The monarchy is more popular than ever . . .'[65] The famous politician was both right and wrong. Some people believed the emperor had travelled to Europe intentionally to allow his daughter Isabel to sign the popular legislation, thus paving the way for her succession to the throne.

Certainly the princess's public image changed dramatically after the law – she became known as 'the Redeemer of the blacks'. But the way that abolition was officially enacted – as if it were a gift rather than a conquered right – ignored the part that the slaves themselves had played in the struggle. The strategy was to pretend that slavery had been 're-evaluated' by the government. The idea was that, upon receiving the 'gift' of their freedom, former slaves should be grateful and continue to work as dependents of their new employers. Once again, in the interpretation of the law, the long-standing idea of a gradual process towards emancipation was evident. The government was planning to restructure the former relations of servitude, and to engage in complex processes of the exchange of favours and the maintenance of traditional forms of submission.

The law was to have far-reaching consequences. Abolition led not only to material losses for the plantation owners, but to the loss of their prestige. This small but powerful group that had had such close links to the Crown now rapidly abandoned their previous ally and joined the republicans. Despite the attempt of the monarchy to compensate them with titles and baronetcies, the lack of financial indemnity led to a permanent break between the coffee planters and the state. Furthermore, the fears surrounding a possible regime with Princess Isabel as empress led to an increasing number of plots and intrigues against her husband, the Count of Eu. He was presented as a 'Frenchman' and a foreigner, and compared to the 'Austrian' Marie Antoinette, whom the French had never forgiven.[66] Despite Isabel being known as 'the Redeemer', and the climate of euphoria that the government did its best to capitalize on by issuing commemorative coins and decorations, there could be little doubt that the theatre of the monarchy was coming to an end.

Ten days later, when he received the news of abolition, the emperor was in Milan. When she considered that his health had recovered sufficiently, the empress read him the telegram which had been sent by his daughter Princess Isabel on 13 May. Most reports say that his response was 'serene' and that all he said was 'Thank God'. This has a certain appearance of political propaganda, coming from a man who had done nothing to abolish slavery for at least fifty years. The royal party set out on their return to Brazil, a country that for the first time in almost four centuries no longer had any slaves.

However, contrary to predictions, the emperor's reception was heart-warming. On the top of the Sugarloaf an enormous flag had been hoisted with the single word *Salve*.[67] It was now the emperor who needed attention: he was ill. Dom Pedro II was in fact no more than a ghost of his former self – and the same was true of the monarchy.

THE MONARCHY STUMBLES – AND FALLS

To all appearances the year 1889 started well. On 28 February the French writer and geographer Pierre Émile Levasseur informed the government that he had completed his long article on the Brazilian Empire, which would be published in the *Grande Encyclopédie*. With the aid of the statesman, the future Baron of Rio Branco,[68] it had been extended from the original fifteen pages to fifty-one. Only one country – Germany – was allocated more space in the encyclopedia than Brazil. The same year the Grand Rabbi of Avignon, Benjamim Mossé, wrote a biography praising the emperor. It was generally suspected that this tribute to Dom Pedro II was also really the work of Rio Branco. In 1889, Brazil participated in the Universal Exhibition in Paris, constructing a grandiose pavilion in the style of a fantasy castle. The building had a glass dome and a majestic tower 40 metres high. There was a kiosk where coffee was sold, and the halls were decorated with enormous paintings of tropical fruits by the black artist Estevão da

Silva. Six colossal statues represented the rivers of Brazil, and a *Victoria amazonica* lily floated in a vast basin of water.[69]

Overseas, everything seemed to be going well for the empire; however, at home the picture was very different. While the country paid tribute to the centenary of the French Revolution, the republican movement was gaining strength, and it was becoming increasingly radical. During the liberal government led by the prime minister, the Viscount of Ouro Preto, a Black Guard was created to protect the monarchy, as a kind of parallel force to the army.

The situation was complex and paradoxical. Many former slaves supported the monarchy and opposed the republicans (who were referred to as 'the *Paulistas*') as if they had been their oppressors. Given the very real possibility of a return of slavery, they preferred to support the devil they knew: it was the monarchy that had abolished slavery and deserved their loyalty. Many Brazilians were suspicious of the Black Guard. Rui Barbosa,[70] for example, called it 'a band of ragamuffins chanting Long Live the Monarchy and the Liberal Party'. He also called it 'legalized capoeira'.

The atmosphere was already tense when, on 15 June, as the imperial family were leaving the Teatro Sant'Ana after attending a concert by Giulietta Dionesi, a shout of 'Long live the Republic' came from the middle of the crowd. The emperor seemed unperturbed and told the officer in charge to 'leave those people in peace. Let everyone do as they please.'[71] A few minutes later, however, after the monarch had entered his carriage, a shot was fired at him. The police arrested the culprit: Adriano do Vale, a twenty-year-old Portuguese immigrant who had recently lost his job in a shop. The next day the event was dramatized in the press, with many newspapers displaying the picture of the 'regicide' on the front page. In the tense atmosphere of 1889 this relatively insignificant event acquired a significance it hardly deserved. It was seen by some as symbolic of the fragility of the monarchy, and by others as clear evidence that the monarchy's enemies were preparing to act.

The reaction came swiftly: the chief of police, José Basson de Miranda Osório, threatened to prosecute anyone who shouted 'Long live the Republic' or 'Death to the Monarchy' in a public place, under article 90 of the criminal code. Meanwhile the culprit was locked up in a cubicle on the Ilha das Cobras while the jury considered its decision.[72] During the second half of the year hardly a day went by without some incident indicative of the restless mood. On the occasion of Princess Isabel's silver wedding anniversary, on 15 October, 1,500 members of the Black Guard lined the streets. The newspapers added fuel to the fire with sensationalist stories about a wave of anarchy and Dom Pedro II's plans to abdicate in favour of his daughter. At the same time the army began to demand greater representation in government.

On 6 June 1888 the Cabinet headed by João Alfredo[73] had fallen and was replaced by another, this time led by the Viscount of Ouro Preto. He planned to take the wind out of the sails of the rapidly growing republican movement. His political platform was freedom of religion, greater autonomy for the provinces and municipalities, freedom of education, reform of the State Council and a reduction in export rights. Opinion was divided: for some the programme was too radical, but for others it did not go far enough. When the conservatives, who had a majority in the Chamber of Deputies, rejected the Viscount of Ouro Preto's plan, he decided to dissolve the body. The incident was not only a clear indication of the ferocious struggle between conservatives and liberals, but also that the issue of centralized monarchy was becoming a side issue. The more radical idea of ending the monarchy and establishing a republic began to be openly discussed.

The greatest fear was that the situation would get out of control. Members of the *Paulista* Republican Party began to create ties with the military and draw up plans for a counter-revolution. Meanwhile, the *Baile da Ilha Fiscal* (Ball on Fiscal Island), which has become the symbol of the fall of the monarchy, took place on 9 November 1889.[74] Dom Pedro II had come down from the peace and quiet of his winter palace in the mountain town of Petropolis to inaugurate the São Sebastião hospital in Caju. After presiding at the meeting of the Council of Ministers the emperor attended a ball being held by the government to welcome the Chilean navy. The event caused a great stir. The ostentation and luxurious setting were seen as provocative given the political situation; it was said that the armed forces had intentionally been excluded from the guest list, and it was rumoured that orgies had taken place. In his novel *Esaú e Jacó*, Machado de Assis recalls: 'Seen from the docks or from the sea, inside and outside, it was like a Venetian dream; all those people from *Carioca* society living a few hours of splendour, new to some, memories of the past for others.'

The ball was held in an oblong hall, decorated with the flags of the two countries. Of the imperial family, only Pedro Augusto waltzed. Their Imperial Majesties, the Count of Eu and Princess Isabel left early, at one in the morning. The luxury of the occasion was intentional. The island was located opposite the palace, just a short distance by boat. It provided the perfect stage on which to demonstrate the grandeur of the empire. The ball on Fiscal Island was the first ever hosted by a government of the empire. Three thousand invitations were distributed and the main hall was lit up with thousands of candles. Putting their differences aside for the occasion, liberals and conservatives, members of the royal household and the aristocracy, even the first lieutenant of the navy, José Augusto Vinhais – who a few days later was to play a key role in the overthrow of the monarchy – all joined the party.

Although the people of Rio de Janeiro were excluded from the celebrations, entertainment was provided for them in the palace square, including fandangos, singing, and a police band in gala uniform.[75] When he came ashore, helped by his ever-faithful doctor Mota Maia, the emperor stumbled. Without losing his presence of mind he said: 'The monarchy stumbles, but it doesn't fall.' Little did he know, it would not be standing for long.

Meanwhile the conspiracy began and things started to move very quickly. On 10 November, Marshal Deodoro da Fonseca,[76] Benjamin Constant,[77] Sólon Ribeiro,[78] Rui Barbosa and the leaders of the Republican Party, Quintino Bocaiúva,[79] Francisco Glicério[80] and Aristides Lobo,[81] met at the marshal's house. The elderly general needed a good deal of persuading because he preferred to wait until the emperor died. In order to convince him, his companions bombarded him with rumours and denunciations of what the court was planning for the army. There were just four days to go before the overthrow of the monarchy.

As conspiracies proliferated, the monarchy was becoming more and more isolated. In 1874 a serious rift had occurred between the Church and the State. The trouble began with the arrest of two bishops – Dom Vital and Dom Macedo Costa – who had tried to restrict the role of the Masonic lodges in Brazil. But the real reason went deeper – the bishops were frustrated at the government's hegemony and autonomy. The government, in turn, had reacted harshly with the arrests, and the release of the bishops in September 1875 had done little to heal the rift.

But the army was the deepest source of discontent, and among their ranks were some of the main supporters of positivism and republican government. Since the end of the Paraguayan War, military leaders had been protesting over the ban on officers from making political statements in the press. The tension had been increasing since 1884 when members of the armed forces had supported the movement of the *jangadeiros*[82] – led by Francisco do Nascimento, nicknamed the 'Dragon of the Sea'. In Ceará, Francisco do Nascimento had refused to transport slaves to the ships that were to take them to the southeast, to the coffee planters and landowners who had bought them. In 1886, in a further demonstration of the army's independence, Deodoro da Fonseca refused to punish a group of officers for insubordination, and was dismissed from his post. When he arrived back in Rio de Janeiro in January 1887, instead of repudiation, the military student cadets gave him a hero's welcome.

Under pressure from the *Paulista* republicans and the increasing unrest in the army, Marshal Deodoro da Fonseca was forced to act before he was ready. Upon hearing the rampant rumour that Major Sólon had been arrested, he mounted his horse and rode to army headquarters, where he somewhat confusedly presented himself with the words: 'Long live His Majesty the Emperor, the Imperial family and the Army.' He then made his way to the court where he deposed the Viscount of Ouro Preto and said that he would personally form a new government for the emperor. There is controversy as to whether this was how it actually happened. It appears more likely that Marshal Deodoro da Fonseca and Benjamin Constant met at the army headquarters where they were joined by a contingent of around a thousand men, in addition to members of the navy. But the atmosphere was still one of uncertainty. It is unlikely that there was any public proclamation of the Republic at that point.

Between the dismissal of the Viscount of Ouro Preto and the proclamation of the Republic there was a lapse. The emperor waited in the palace for Marshal Deodoro da Fonseca's visit, but the general never came, probably because he felt he could not face the old monarch. The hesitation of the conspirators was obvious. In the end, the youngest member of the Municipal Chamber, José do Patrocínio, announced the proclamation of the Republic in their meeting. The next day, the first edition of the *Diário Oficial da República dos Estados Unidos do Brasil* published the proclamation of the provisional government – announcing the extinction of the monarchy. But no one had yet informed the emperor. Such was the embarrassment that instead of sending a committee of high-ranking officers or senior politicians and diplomats, a delegation of subaltern officers was sent, at three in the morning on 16 November, to inform Dom Pedro II that the imperial family had been banished.

Before the imperial couple had come down to the city of Rio de Janeiro from their winter palace in the hills of Petrópolis, the empress had expressed her dismay that all was lost, to which the emperor had replied: 'Nonsense dear lady! As soon as we get back all this will be over.'[83] But his confidence was soon shaken. The provisional government gave the imperial family a period of twenty-four hours to leave Brazil. Ever theatrical, in his official response the emperor of the tropics, Dom Pedro II, paraphrased Napoleon, affirming that he would now leave the country 'that was so dear to his heart'.[84]

It had been decided that Dom Pedro II would depart the afternoon of 17 November, after eleven o'clock Mass at the Carmelite church. However, anxious that pro-monarchy protesters would clash with republican students, the provisional government resolved to have the imperial family depart immediately. And so it was that Dom Pedro II and his family embarked before dawn. As the story goes, this was the only time the emperor engaged in a tense exchange. Dom Pedro II is said to have asked Marshal Deodoro da Fonseca if he was 'mixed up with this', and on receiving an affirmative reply, retorted: 'I'm not an escaped slave. I will not leave in the middle of the night.' Then, lashing out against the republicans, he yelled, 'All of you are mad!' Later in the day the provisional government published the following announcement: 'Fellow citizens: the people, the army and the national armada, in perfect communion with the feelings of our fellow citizens in the provinces, have decreed the deposition of the imperial dynasty ...' The terms were changing, and they were announcing new times. As the emperor boarded the *Parnaíba*, he was surrounded by others who were either leaving of their own volition or had been exiled. With their departure, the fate of the monarchy was sealed. But as yet the new Republic was far from being established.

The republican project – despite the initial hesitation – was a legitimate solution to the collapse of the empire. It was more than an institutional change; instead, it was a response to increased public participation throughout the 1880s. Politics were no longer restricted to the parliament. With incidents such as the corruption surrounding the 'theft of the crown jewels', the monarchy had begun to lose its legitimacy. Intellectual trends were also influential insofar as learned people were using new language, were unafraid of controversy, and were undermining the three pillars of the empire: the monarchy, religion and romanticism in the arts. The intellectuals transformed the theories of evolution, materialism and positivism into action. Progress and modernization were associated with the word 'republic'. New concepts – public space, learning and intellectual thought – created a new political culture and new symbols. The new Republic was under way.

But even so, *uncertainty* – the steady companion of even the best-laid plans – reigned. In his novel *Esaú e Jacó*, Machado de Assis recounts the hilarous story of a certain Mr Custódio who owned a shop called 'The Imperial Bakery'. Coincidentally, on the day of the proclamation of the Republic, Mr Custódio had sent his bakery sign out to be touched up. When he learned about the proclamation, he tried to catch the sign painter in time, so he could have him stop the work. It was too late, the sign was finished. In desperation, Mr Custódio consulted the good Counsellor Aires, who advised him to change the name to 'The Republican Bakery'. But then the two of them, worried about future political changes, had second thoughts – what if the Republic fell? Counsellor Aires suggested another new name, 'The Government Bakery'. Next, they realized every government faces opposition, and someone might even destroy that sign. It then occurred to Counsellor Aires that the name 'Imperial Bakery' could be maintained, with a simple addition – 'founded in 1860' – just to avoid problems. They soon realized that name sounded old-fashioned – definitely not a good idea in such modern times! They finally agreed the shop should be named after the owner, 'Custódio's Bakery', and the problem was solved. The narrator concludes the anecdote with the comment: 'He had to spend a bit of money to have the word "Imperial" changed to "Custódio's", but revolutions always entail expense.'[85]

13

The First Republic: The People
Take to the Streets

A NEW ERA AND A BATTLE
OF SYMBOLS

On 17 November 1889, a Sunday, the imperial family departed at three
in the morning, with a few of their supporters who had chosen to accompany them into exile. It is said that those in charge thought it best the
family leave before the sun came up, to avoid a public outcry. The former emperor, refusing to bow before defeat, let it be known he would
take nothing with him except a first edition of Camões's *The Lusiads*,
'that was all he needed'. In so doing, he maintained the perspective that
'kings are never exiled, they decide to take their leave'. Of course, that
is not what actually happened: as soon as Dom Pedro II arrived in Portugal, the Brazilian government formally decreed his banishment. The
decree of 23 December 1889 also provided financial assistance of 5,000
contos de réis for him to establish himself and his family in Europe. But
the former monarch refused to accept the money. His attitude irritated
the provisional government and in an amendment written by Cabinet
minister Rui Barbosa the donation was eliminated; and that was the end
of the matter. The time had come to turn that page of Brazilian history
and to open a new one: the era of the Republic.

To prove the Republic had come to stay, place names and national
symbols were changed as quickly as possible to give a public face to the
new regime. The name of the Largo do Paço (the main palace square)
was changed to Praça XV de Novembro; the Pedro II Railway Station to
Central do Brasil; the Colégio Pedro II to the Colégio Nacional, and the
Vila Ouro Preto, a development of elegant town houses, was renamed
Vila Rui Barbosa. The images on the banknotes were also, of course,
changed: Pedro II and the monarchy were replaced with symbols of the

new Republic of the United States of Brazil. Newly born children were named after historical figures from North America, such as Jefferson, Franklin and Washington.[1] The name of Rio de Janeiro was changed by decree, from 'The Court' to the 'Federal Capital', although for a long time the *Cariocas* continued to refer to it by its old name. The national celebrations previously listed in the *Almanack Laemmert* were also altered: 1 January became 'universal fraternity' day; 13 May, 'Brazilian fraternity'; 14 July, 'the republic', and 21 April, 'precursors' day'. This last was in tribute to Tiradentes, the only participant in the Minas conspiracy who had been condemned to death (in 1789). Since no one knew anything about his physical appearance, he was increasingly depicted like the figure of Christ: a candid look, white garments with a crucifix on the chest, and long hair coming down to his shoulders.[2] From that moment on, the image of the new hero would triumph in Brazil's political iconography, which presented Tiradentes not only as a revolutionary symbol but also as the martyr who sacrificed himself for the Republic.

On 20 January 1890 a public contest was organized for a new national anthem. The winning submission was a composition by Leopoldo Miguez[3] and José Joaquim de Campos de Medeiros e Albuquerque, and yet the old anthem was maintained, even though it had not even been in the contest. Apparently Marshal Deodoro da Fonseca said he 'preferred the old one'; this, despite the rumour Pedro I had helped to compose it! Even the new national flag maintained the colours green and yellow, representing the colours of the Houses of Bragança and Habsburg, not Brazil's forests and mineral wealth, a concept attached to the flag later on. The new flag maintained the diamond; the only difference was that the imperial coat of arms therein was replaced with the positivist slogan 'Order and Progress'.[4] Despite all these efforts the images of the monarchy continued to be deeply rooted in the popular imagination, as they continue to be today, not only in political rhetoric, but also in Brazil's fascination with honorary orders and rituals of consecration.

Nonetheless some changes had come to stay. The symbol of the Indian to represent the empire was now replaced by that of a heroic woman, who came to represent the Republic in newspaper advertisments and even in official documents. This association dated back to classical Rome, and more recently had been popularized in France in the period preceding the Third Republic. But whereas in France the image of Marianne was popular, with her bare breasts, mantle and Phrygian bonnet – representing the ideals of liberty, happiness and maternal fertility – the allegory failed in Brazil, even in its positivist form. In Brazil, women stayed at home, with their breasts and virtually every other part of their body clothed – and without the right to participate in politics.

THE 'COFFEE WITH MILK' REPUBLIC[5]

The 1891 Constitution defined the new regime – a presidential, federalist and bicameral system.[6] The separation of Church and State was established, as was a national register of births, marriages and deaths. The new federalist government was no longer centralized, in part to establish a clear break with the monarchical system. Former provinces – now known as states – were given greater autonomy and powers of fiscal control. The idea that a monarchy was necessary for the sake of national cohesion was put to rest.

The centralizing mechanism during the empire – the Moderating Power – was replaced by a system of balance of powers between the Executive, Legislature and Judiciary. Freedom of religion was guaranteed, life mandates for senators were abolished, and suffrage was extended. The right to vote remained as restricted as it had been under the empire: only adult male Brazilians who could read and write were enfranchised. Those who were not enfranchised included women, beggars, soldiers, sergeants, and members of religious orders that imposed restrictions on individual liberty.

Long-standing policies of the empire were also held in place. Indeed, one of these was the oligarchical structure of the nation: new electoral laws perpetuated the limitations on voters and on citizens eligible for public office. In 1874 only about 10 per cent of the population voted. During the Republic, instead of the sharp increase in the number of voters that could have been expected, the restrictive suffrage criteria were extended. In 1910 only 67,000 were entitled to vote out of a population of 22 million. In 1920 the percentage was between 2.3 and 3.4 per cent of the total population.

The role of the army in the new regime was of prime importance. It should not be forgotten that the Republic resulted from actions taken by a group of officers who were both socially and intellectually opposed to the civilian elite of the empire. They were dissatisfied not only with the situation of the country, but also with their own political status.[7] But there were internal divisions within this group as well: they disagreed as to the significance of republicanism and the objectives of the institutions of the new regime. They were also divided by personal ambitions and rivalries, and by their ideas for the future of the army and the country itself. Furthermore, the prestige the Republic conferred on the military encouraged the political ambitions of the officers, which also exacerbated internal disputes. On top of this, the civilian elites were uneasy and divided on the subject of the role the army should play in the new regime.

At the outset the republican regime was maintained by force. Until 1894, the country had been governed by the military: Marshal Deodoro da Fonseca, leader of the *coup d'état* of 15 November 1889, became the Republic's first president, followed by his vice-president, Marshal Floriano Peixoto. Deodoro da Fonseca's presidency was far from easy. In 1891 the first 'revolt of the Armada' broke out. The spark that ignited the revolt was when President Deodoro da Fonseca, in flagrant violation of the constitution, closed the Congress in an attempt at a second coup d'état. His action was largely a response to his inability to deal with the opposition. His detractors were frustrated with the economic chaos that marked the first years of the Republic, the rampant speculation, fraud and inflation. Under the command of Admiral Custódio de Mello most of the fleet anchored in Guanabara Bay revolted. The armada – as the navy was called at the time – threatened to bombard the city if the Congress was not reopened. Faced with a choice between defeat and a civil war, President Deodoro da Fonseca resigned on 23 November 1891.

Instead of calling new elections as established by the constitution, the vice-president, Marshal Floriano Peixoto, simply claimed the presidency. Under his rule a new element was introduced into Brazilian politics, a form of Jacobinism that became known as *florianismo*. The popular movement reached its height in Rio de Janeiro between 1893 and 1897.[8] It was the first spontaneous political movement of the Republic, under the leadership of a president who galvanized the urban middle classes and the population in general by proposing an egalitarian regime, albeit one that could only be sustained by President Floriano Peixoto's authoritarian military regime.

But the discontent in the navy had not abated and in September 1893 the second armada revolt broke out, commanded by officers demanding new elections. Considering the battles they had fought defending the empire, the navy and its officers resented being marginalized from the new government. Admiral Custódio de Mello promoted a naval uprising against President Floriano Peixoto to restore the prestige the navy had once enjoyed. For his part, the president was already dealing with the federalist revolution in the south, and he now had to defeat the armada. He managed to do this by 1894, although it left an open wound.[9] President Floriano Peixoto was essentially governing under a state of siege, and had been nicknamed the 'Iron Marshal'. Meanwhile, the federalist revolution became a bloody civil war that lasted from 1893 to 1895. The gaucho[10] positivists of the Rio-Grandense Republican Party, who supported a state dictatorship, were pitted against the Federalist Party, whose members defended the 1891 Constitution, municipal autonomy and a centralized federal government.

New elections were called in 1894. The winning candidate was Prudente de Morais, of the *Paulista* Republican Party. His was the first civilian government of the Republic. The party was moderate and pragmatic: the objectives were to pacify the country and guarantee the interests of the São Paulo coffee planters, transforming the Jacobin republic into an oligarchic republic. Prudente de Morais managed to get his chosen successor, Campos Sales, elected, in 1898. From this point on, control of the federal government alternated between the states of São Paulo and Minas Gerais. In 1898, Campos implemented the 'governors' policy' – or 'states' policy' as he referred to it. This system established complete autonomy for regional elites, facilitated their manipulation of state deputy elections, and opened the federal coffers to meet their needs. In return, the central government required the states to support all federal decisions – political conflicts were to remain at the local level.[11]

The federal government was, from then on, controlled by Minas Gerais and São Paulo. The distribution of power in the Republic was regulated according to each state's position in the federal hierarchy. The political strength of a state was determined by the size of its electorate and consequent representation in parliament. Furthermore, stability of the Republic depended principally on three elements: the state governors' confining of political conflicts to their region; the federal government's recognition of complete state sovereignty; and the maintenance of an electoral system characterized by fraud, despite measures to control local disputes. Fraud occurred in every phase of the electoral process – from the selection of the voters to the recognition of the winners. Some of the methods were notorious. The 'stroke of the pen' win dated back to the empire, and consisted of forging signatures and altering names on voting forms. The 'decapitation' technique was simply the refusal of the verification committee within the Chamber of Deputies to recognize the candidate, thus eliminating adversaries by annulling their election. The 'tame vote' – 'voto de cabresto' – became a culturally embedded political practice whereby loyal voters cast their ballot for the local chief. Lastly, the 'corral electorate' referred to an improvised building where voters were kept under watch and given a good meal, and only released upon the casting of their ballot, which was handed to them in a sealed envelope.[12]

The vote was seen as a currency of exchange and relationships of power began at municipal level. This was the origin of the phenomenon known as *coronelismo*.[13] Colonel was the highest post in the hierarchy of the National Guard. With the founding of the Republic, the National Guard lost its military status, but the colonels maintained their political power in their municipalities. From this time on, *coronelismo* was the term used to refer to a complex system of negotiation between these local leaders (or bosses) and the state governors, who, in turn, negotiated with the president of the Republic. *Coronelismo* became one of the cornerstones of the traditional oligarchic structure based on the power of local individuals, generally the owners of farms and large estates.[14]

Thus the 'colonel' was a fundamental part of the oligarchic system. He gave his support to the government in the form of votes. In exchange, the government guaranteed his power over his dependents and rivals. This was accomplished mainly through the granting of public posts, which ranged from chief of police to primary-school teacher. Thus, the early twentieth-century Brazilian Republic was based on the exchange of favours and loans, favouritism, repression and negotiation. Seen from this angle, as the satirical magazines of the time pointed out, the country was little more than a large *fazenda* (plantation).

A BRAZIL OF IMMIGRANTS, A BABEL OF LANGUAGES[15]

With the abolition of slavery and the consequent upheaval in the labour system, the government embarked on a series of initiatives to attract immigrants, above all from Europe. Similar policies had been implemented during the empire, but the scope was now much wider. Faced with competition from countries such as Argentina, Cuba, Mexico and the United States, it was by no means easy for the Brazilian government to sell the idea of an 'earthly paradise'. The large majority of immigrants were supposed to work in the fields; official colonies were established in the southern states and, above all, in the coffee-producing regions of the southeast. However, most of the immigrants ended up settling in the bustling towns, which were growing and where they would find a greater diversity of employment and services.

Enticed by the government's propaganda, waves of immigrants – Poles, Germans, Spaniards, Italians and Portuguese (and, from the late 1910s, Japanese) – emigrated to Brazil. The poor and oppressed of Europe were drawn by the mythical abundance of the tropics. With the growth in the world population and the modernization of transport, large numbers of unemployed peasants were looking for work.[16] It is estimated that more than 50 million Europeans abandoned their continent in the search for 'freedom' in the form of property and employment.

Although most of these emigrated to North America, 22 per cent of them – around 11 million – came to Latin America, of whom 38 per cent were Italian, 28 per cent Spanish, 11 per cent Portuguese and 3 per cent French and German. Of these, 46 per cent went to Argentina; 33 per cent to Brazil; 14 per cent to Cuba; and the rest were divided between Uruguay, Mexico and Chile.[17] Between 1877 and 1903 around 71,000 immigrants came to Brazil, of which 58.5 per cent were from Italy. Between 1904 and 1930 this number increased to 79,000, with Portuguese immigrants accounting for 37 per cent of the total. In 1908 the first wave of Japanese immigrants arrived, adding to the diversity of cultures spreading across Brazil. And if the origins were different, all of them had in common the same desire: 'to make it in America'.

From the outset the immigration process had distinctive characteristics. There were large areas of unoccupied land in the south of the country, so immigrants were offered small plots for farming. Whether the project was run by the government or by private enterprise, plots of between twenty and twenty-five hectares were sold in instalments, usually laid out along the waterways. But these colonies were extremely isolated, and the new settlers were subjected to innumerable adversities: attacks by Indians, hostility from the local population, and difficulty in selling their produce.

On the coffee plantations, however, especially in the state of São Paulo, the government or private landowners hired the immigrants directly to work on the land. Thus very few of the settlements in Espírito Santo, Rio Grande do Sul, Santa Catarina (the states where coffee was not grown) or Paraná prospered, whereas the number of immigrant workers on the coffee plantations increased. After pressure from the farmers, which began in the 1890s, the central government began to finance the influx of immigrants according to the increasing demands of the local economy. By 1900, the federal government had financed between 63 per cent and 80 per cent of immigrant arrivals. It was only after the turn of the century, with an increase in the Portuguese and Spanish populations in São Paulo, that the private sector took on this role. This was possible because urban-industrial activities intensified.

The immigrants' financial difficulties began on the journey; they were exploited by intermediaries who overcharged them for the tickets. Crammed together in rundown ships, their cultural differences soon surfaced – and these became even more pronounced when they arrived in their new home. The immigrants were not only from different regions of the same country, but also came from rival countries with very different customs. Thus, their close proximity gave rise to constant conflicts: northern Germans fought with southern Germans; Japanese fought with Italians, Poles with Germans, and all of them with the Brazilians. They spoke different languages and dialects; all of them had difficulty adjusting to the local diet of beans, rice and coarse flour, as well as to the living quarters: rows of thatched houses built from mud bricks. Far from a homogeneous group, the newly arrived settlers stuck to their various customs. Some, like those from the northern regions of Italy, were used to living in towns. Others, like those from the Veneto region, simply readjusted the rural lifestyle of their homeland to Brazil. They substituted rice for polenta, learned about new fruits and vegetables, and waited patiently, breeding the animals they needed to make sausages and bacon, which they hung out to dry from the beams of their huts.

The Poles and the Italians, who were devout Catholics, did not take easily to the casual religious practices of their religion in Brazil. They reaffirmed their faith by decorating their houses with images of saints and patriotic symbols. Ideas about personal hygiene also differed between the groups. The Italians bathed once a week, merely scrubbing their hands and sweatiest parts of their body on a daily basis. They thought it odd that locals, with the abundance of water in Brazil, bathed in the rivers or washed in tubs every day; and equally unusual, the Japanese custom of bathing in groups, in *ofuros*. And that was not the only aspect of Japanese customs the others considered exotic. The Japanese seemingly cared solely about whether or not the rice was growing. They were not interested in soaking dried meat to make it soft and apparently did not realize that dried cod, too, needed soaking to remove the salt. Nor did they eat the beans or coarse flour. Unlike most of the Europeans, they generally did not prioritize improving their houses; they did not tend to decorate them. All of their money was saved for relatives or for a much dreamed-of return to Japan.[18]

Despite all the difficulties, the majority of the immigrants ended up adapting to life in Brazil. Certain aspects of their different faiths were shared. Herbalists and faith healers went from farm to farm, filling the void that was left by the lack of doctors and medicines. There were three 'remedies' for a host of ills: cod liver oil for purification; Epsom salts for gas and constipation; and castor oil was an effective purgative. From Rio Grande do Sul to the farms in São Paulo there was demand for these miraculous medicinal products, and when nothing worked, the solution was to delve further into prayers and the healers. In Bahia these tasks were performed by the *ifás* – the intermediaries of the Orishas – using herbs from Africa. The same was the case in the north, where Amerindian traditions lived on, including the generalized use of hallucinogenic plants. The combinations of all these traditions produced a whole medicine cabinet of mestizo prescriptions.

Nevertheless, by the beginning of the 1930s, transatlantic immigration had reduced considerably. In 1927, for example, immigration to Europe was much greater than immigration to anywhere else. Even so, a number of governments began to restrict immigration: first the United States, and shortly thereafter, Brazil. Between 1917 and 1924 the United Sates limited the number of immigrants; President Getúlio Vargas adopted the same policy in December 1930. The Brazilian president's motive was to control what historian Sérgio Buarque de Holanda called the 'disorganized mass of foreigners' who were thought to be responsible for unemployment among Brazilians.[19]

But the mixture of peoples in Brazil had changed forever. In São Paulo today you might eat pizza on a Sunday night, enjoy a pasta lunch on Saturday, followed by an evening meal of kebabs and tabbouleh, or maybe chop suey. *Paulistas* buy their bread from the Portuguese bakery on the corner and season their salad with Spanish olive oil. Perhaps it was the writer, poet and engineer Juó Bananère (pen name for Alexandre Marcondes Machado, a *Paulista* with no Italian ancestry) who best expressed this uncommon mixture. He wrote his works using the patois spoken by the Italian colony in São Paulo. In his parodic *La divina increnca* (*The Divine Confusion*), published in 1915, he referred to himself in dialect as a *'Gandidato à Gademia Baolista de Letras'*. In standard Portuguese the reference would have been to a *Candidato à Academia Paulista de Letras* – that is, a candidate to the *Paulista* Academy of Letters.

A NEW LANDSCAPE: CITIES AND THEIR INDUSTRIES

Between 1880 and the 1930s there was a dynamic transformation in Brazilian society. The new configuration was the direct result of increased population and Brazil's aggressive policy to attract foreign immigrants prior to President Getúlio Vargas's restrictions. In addition, Brazil's First World War policy of import substitution, combined with the crisis in agriculture, stimulated the growth of Brazil's cities and industry.

The population of Brazil grew by an average rate of 2.5 per cent per year. The population of towns with 50,000 inhabitants or more rose by 3.7 per cent; and of those with 100,000 or more, by 3.1 per cent. Specifically, during the first decade of the Republic the rural population fell by 2.2 per cent and the urban population rose by 6.8 per cent. Urbanization was a reality that had come to stay and it was rapidly changing the face of Brazil. Nevertheless, the country's economy was still overwhelmingly agricultural. According to the 1920 census, of the 9.1 million people in the work force, 6.3 million (69.7 per cent) worked in agriculture; 1.2 million (13.8 per cent) in industry; and 1.5 million (16.5 per cent) in other services.

There were only a few large cities.[20] These included Rio de Janeiro (the 'heart' of the Republic), São Paulo (its 'head') and, a few years later, Brazil's first planned city, Belo Horizonte, 'created in the Republic's own image'.[21] These three cities controlled the country's resources and established beyond doubt the economic predominance of the southeast. Although the initial aim of the immigration policy had been to provide rural labour, with the crisis in agriculture and the growth of the towns many immigrants moved to urban areas. The new opportunities and specialized professions attracted them. Apart from farm labourers, immigrants worked as bricklayers, bakers, shoemakers and shopkeepers, diversifying the number of services offered in the towns.

There was also large-scale internal migration as a result of the gradual dismantling of the slavery system. Between 1872 and 1900 the population in the northeast decreased. This was because slaves were transferred from the sugar and cotton plantations there to coffee plantations in the southeast. The droughts of the 1870s led to a further wave of migrants from the northeast to Rio de Janeiro, which was like a magnet due to the ample offer of employment in federal and state government institutions.

The three southern states, Paraná, Santa Catarina and Rio Grande do Sul, also attracted many migrants, as did specific regions in the north due to the booming rubber trade in the Amazon. With new developments in transport, latex was in high demand; hordes of workers escaped the poverty of the northeast and penetrated the forests throughout the vast Amazon region in search of rubber to extract. The 'rubber era' was short-lived, ending in the 1910s, but it left its mark on the capital, Manaus. The city was transformed into the most important metropolis of the north with elegant avenues, theatres and bourgeois customs. The wealth of the state seemingly appeared from one day to the next.

The government now set about modernizing and improving the cities to represent the new Republic: refurbished public buildings, newly created suburbs for the poor, public transport and new state buildings.[22] During the period known as the 'regeneration', President Rodrigues Alves (1902–6), hoping to civilize the city, appointed a team of technicians to transform Rio de Janeiro into a modern showpiece for the new Republic. The team was given unlimited powers and they came up with a three-pronged strategy: the modernizing of the port, entrusted to the engineer Lauro Müller; improved public health and sanitation, under the leadership of Dr Oswaldo Cruz; and urban reform. The engineer Pereira Passos, who was familiar with Baron Haussmann's project for the remodelling of Paris, was put in charge of this last initiative. A parallel and complementary measure was to expel the poor population from the central region, to rid the city of slums. The black writer Lima Barreto, himself an inhabitant of the *Carioca* suburbs and an important critic of the events of that time, referred to the period as the dictatorship of the '*bota-abaixo*' (tear down). And in fact, houses, tenements and cheap hotels ('*zungas*'[23] or '*caixotins humanos*'[24]) were all demolished.[25]

From the 1870s onward the city of São Paulo underwent a socioeconomic, urbanizing, physical and demographic transformation. Due to the prosperity of the coffee plantations and the gradual abolition of slavery, it became an important commercial and financial centre: the 'coffee metropolis'. Public electric lighting was installed, a public tram system was built, and the famous Butantã Institute, which produced serums from snake poison, was founded. New avenues were constructed, old avenues extended, squares and public gardens refurbished and opened. São Paulo's 'high society' adopted new habits: shopping at fashionable stores, going to horse races, and spending the evenings at balls or at the theatre. It should be recalled though that the São Paulo urbanization process meant both the 'embellishment' of the city and the expulsion of poverty. If the city infrastructure altered with the opening of new districts and elegant streets, such as the Avenida Paulista, modest houses and slums were destroyed in order to extend and expand new streets, avenues and squares.

The development of the city of Belo Horizonte, the new capital of Minas Gerais, is also emblematic.[26] Local republican politicians built the city in an attempt to unify, politically and culturally, a state whose economy was in decline. Furthermore, state politics were bogged down by infighting between the different factions within the oligarchies that governed from the old state capital, Ouro Preto. The development of Belo Horizante was both authoritarian and violent. The existing village of Curral del Rey was completely destroyed and its impoverished residents were exiled to the new suburbs. The new capital itself was planned and built by the most modernizing and republican of the regional elite, who dreamt of progress and technology. Thus the new town was curiously modern, with wide avenues allowing for a better flow of traffic, an abundance of public squares, and the strict observance of a sort of urban hierarchy. Services, including the railway, the hospital and the shops were established on one side of the city; and on the other side, the theatre, schools and the State Assembly. The layout was planned for maximum dramatic effect. At the highest point of the city there was a rectangular plaza surrounded by imposing government buildings, including the governor's palace – and in the centre, a statue representing Liberty. The plaza was named the *Praça da Liberdade* and the palace the *Palácio da Liberdade*. After all, this was the land of the Republic and of Tiradentes, the hero of the 1789 Minas conspiracy.

These three cities were forerunners of what was to occur in other Brazilian towns. The royal court in Rio de Janeiro was reinvented as the federal district of the Republic. São Paulo was restructured as the political and economic hub of the wealthy coffee region, and Belo Horizonte was planned and built to be the new capital of Minas Gerais. Those in the republican government were bound and determined to forge a modern alternative to the empire. And yet there was no getting around the fact that Brazil's economy was still sustained by agricultural exports. It was not just a simple question of the Republic versus the monarchy – progress versus backwardness. It was a time when the past coexisted with the present, social inclusion with social exclusion, and modern technology with political and social repression. Furthermore, although there was an increase in opportunities for employment, the movable professions experienced the most growth – street sellers, small businesses, carpenters, shoemakers and coach drivers. Two completely different worlds existed side by side, yet were unexpectedly interconnected.

And it was not long before another aspect of modernity emerged. The marginalized rural population – banished to the darkest corners of the interior – began making headlines in the newspapers. But it was from the cities, not the countryside, that the first signs of revolt were to come.

RUMBLINGS FROM THE CITIES

Between 10 and 16 November 1904 the people of Rio de Janeiro revolted against measures enacted to eradicate yellow fever. The most serious uprising was in the suburbs, where the poorer classes reacted against the compulsory smallpox vaccination ordered by Oswaldo Cruz.[27] The uprising was mainly the result of misinformation, aggravated by the different origins and customs of the immigrants. The situation led to chaos. Trams and public buildings were destroyed and the sanitary agents were attacked. The government reacted harshly: a state of siege was declared, constitutional rights were suspended, and the leaders of the movement were deported to the south of the Amazon, in what is the present-day state of Acre. The revolt was finally controlled and small-pox eradicated from the city of Rio de Janeiro; but the cost had been 30 deaths and 110 wounded.

From the government's side, the plan for the eradication of disease was objective and rational. Public health had become a priority. The question had increasingly concerned Brazilian intellectuals and politicians since the 1880s. Travellers, journalists, doctors, social scientists and the literati were all aware of the high incidence of tropical diseases and illnesses transmitted by African slaves and immigrants, both in the cities and in the rural areas.[28] Above all, miscegenation was considered a terrible problem, almost a local plight. Racial theories based on social Darwinism and the criminal anthropology of Cesare Lombroso, who penned his theory in the middle of the nineteenth century in Italy, were greatly in vogue in the country.[29] It was thought that humanity was divided into natural hierarchies and each race had distinct and unalterable potentials, with the white Caucasians at the top of the social evolutionary pyramid and the black Africans at the bottom. According to these theories the mixed races were considered the worst of all, with a propensity for every kind of 'hereditary degeneration'. According to Brazilian professionals such as Dr Raimundo Nina Rodrigues (1862–1909) of the medical school in Bahia, people of mixed race were more likely to be criminals and suffer from madness as well as other racial 'stigmas'. Given the doctor's beliefs, it is no coincidence he published a book entitled *The Human Races and Penal Responsibility in Brazil* (1894) wherein he proposed two different penal codes, one for whites and the other for blacks, adapted according to the 'evolutionary stage of each group'.

While fallacious theories must be questioned, it is true that there were a series of epidemics in Brazil. In October 1916, Dr Miguel Pereira commented, 'Brazil is still an immense hospital.' The phrase became a metaphor for the country, almost an epitaph. Medical statistics of the time reveal a terrifying list of contagious diseases. Some epidemics were considered 'imported', such as cholera, one of the main causes of fatalities at the time. Others were seen as 'domestic'; among these were yellow fever, smallpox and the bubonic plague. Specialists believed the improvised huts where most people lived only worsened the situation. They were made of clay, the natural habitat of the insect known as the 'kissing bug',[30] the transmitter of the recently discovered Chagas disease. It was also thought that these dwellings contributed to the prevalence of malaria and intestinal infections. And the immigrants were blamed for introducing trachoma, a dangerous form of infectious conjunctivitis. All these epidemics were a stain on the country's already fragile reputation and the republican government's urban reforms were aimed at eradicating them. They were in large part successful.

The Oswaldo Cruz Institute sent scientists into the interior of the country to introduce the same health measures that were being implemented along the coast. Between 1907 and 1913 they travelled to regions in the interior of São Paulo, Minas Gerais, Bahia and the São Francisco and Tocantins basins, reaching as far as the Amazon.[31] In addition to the diseases mentioned above, many people died from leprosy, syphilis and tuberculosis. Although these 'Brazilian pathologies' affected the population as a whole, including agricultural workers in the interior, it was the formerly enslaved people, the immigrants, slum dwellers, workers and those who lived in the countryside who suffered most.

Of all these 'dangerous groups' of Brazilians, the sailors in the navy took pride of place. In November 1910, in Rio de Janeiro's Guanabara Bay, these sailors rebelled in what became known as the *Revolta da Chibata* (Revolt of the Whip).[32] The seamen, most of whom were African Brazilians or mestizos, were brutally controlled by a system of corporal punishment, especially flogging. The revolt exposed the violence against the poor population, as well as the racism and cruelty that prevailed within the armed forces. Whipping was a tradition inherited from the Portuguese navy, but in Brazil it carried deeper significance due to its association with slavery. Although slavery had been abolished in 1888, flogging continued in the navy, supported by a law that permitted officers to 'break the will' of rebellious sailors.

The revolt broke out on 16 November 1910, when a number of Brazilian and foreign ships anchored in Guanabara Bay for the investiture of the new president, Marshall Hermes da Fonseca. Rui Barbosa had been the favourite to win the election, which for the first time had excited widespread popular interest. Marshall Hermes da Fonseca's victory – despite the fact that he had been supported by Pinheiro Machado from the republican Conservative Party – represented the return of the military to power. Rui Barbosa, in contrast, was in favour of republican institutions and a civilian government.

While the president's investiture was celebrated on land, at sea the situation was entirely different. On-board the largest and most powerful of the navy's battleships, the *Minas Gerais*, which was anchored in the bay, the crew, standing at attention, were forced to witness the flogging of the sailor Marcelino Rodrigues Menezes. After 250 lashes, he was taken straight to prison without any medical treatment. For some time the sailors had been planning to revolt against such brutal punishments, and this was the last straw. In the evening of 16 November, while Hermes da Fonseca was attending a reception in honour of his victory, the sailors seized control of the battleships *Minas Gerais*, *São Paulo* and *Bahia* – as well as the patrol ship *Deodoro* – and proceeded to fire warning cannon shots at the city. They demanded that corporal punishment be abolished within the navy, or the city would be bombarded. The National Congress accepted their demands and gave amnesty to the rebels, who returned the battleships to their officers. A few days later, however, on 4 December, the government took revenge. Twenty-two sailors were arrested on the Ilha das Cobras and charged with conspiracy. They were tortured so brutally that only two of them survived. One of the survivors was the leader of the revolt, João Cândido – dubbed the 'Black Admiral' by the press – who, to the fury of the navy, became a popular hero.

The 'Revolt of the Whip' had serious consequences. Until the end of the First Republic, in 1930, the navy was virtually excluded from politics. But the sailors' uprising was a far from isolated event among the military. The same period saw the 'revolt of the military academy', the 'revolt of the sergeants' and the 'bloody spring', all of which exposed dissatisfaction at the heart of the Republic. These rebellions reveal two important aspects of the way the military interacted with the government. The first is that much of the significant political action in the country took place outside the realm of institutions or political parties. The second is that the military's intention was to bring about government reform. The participants saw themselves as the instrument of the will of the people and, to some extent, reflected the concept of the 'citizen soldier'.[33]

In general, however, the 'regeneration of the cities' – as the urban reforms were called at the time – went along with the conviction, based on scientific determinism prevalent at the time, that the poor and mestizo populations were somehow 'degenerate'. With an economy based on services and agricultural exports and limited by emerging industrialization, urban life was precarious. There were periods when supplies were insufficient, and food prices constantly rose, as did the cost of rents and transport. Inflation made conditions even worse for the poor and increased the uncertainty. In the ironic words of writer Mário de Andrade,[34] in the new cities 'there were as many shacks as coconut trees'.[35] On the other hand, sometimes less is more. After all, there were many occasions when people took to the streets to protest the shortages, rent increases, and everything else that made their lives unstable.

ANOTHER COUNTRY WHERE 'THE OTHERS' LIVE

Unrest was not restricted to the towns. In various regions of the country social movements erupted that combined issues of agrarian reform and the struggle for landownership with a strong element of religion. These conflicts – Contestado, Juazeiro, Caldeirão, Pau-de-Colher and Canudos – combined mysticism and revolt. They were the result of the modernization that excluded the population at large. Abandoned by a republic that used rural property to bolster the power of the local oligarchs, groups of poor farmers from the interior began to demand the right to own land. Most interestingly, they made an unexpected mystical link between history and millenarianism, with visions of living in a community that would be harmonious and just.

In 1896 an armed conflict began in the *sertão* (backlands) of the northeast that was to garner much attention in the early years of the Republic. The conflict became a national scapegoat, a 'monarchist canker' according to the elite gathered almost two thousand kilometres away in Rio de Janeiro. The enemy of the newly founded republic was the poverty-stricken population of a village called Canudos in the arid interior of Bahia. In 1897 journalist Euclides da Cunha was sent to cover the conflict by the newspaper the *Estado de São Paulo*. He was appalled by what he saw.[36] A fervent republican, he had disembarked in

Bahia with the conviction that the government forces were about to defeat a horde of ragged fanatics – accused of being 'monarchists' – holding out in a primitive village. He was amazed to discover, there in the Bahia *sertão*, a long and mysterious war, an enormously brave and determined adversary, a sacred refuge, an organized community and unknown lands. The impact of his discovery radically changed Euclides da Cunha's point of view. He began to write down everything that he saw – and the book that resulted from those notes turned him into one of Brazil's greatest writers. *Os Sertões*[37] went far beyond a report on the war. It became a denunciation. The book reveals the devastating effect of the droughts and wildfires on the arid landscape of the northeast. Euclides da Cunha was able to inscribe the natural surroundings with fear, isolation and abandonment. In the *sertão* of the northeast he saw Brazil's centuries-old collective abandonment of its people.

Os Sertões was published in 1902 and gives a far more detailed analysis of the war than Euclides da Cunha's original articles for the *Estado de São Paulo*.[38] But it maintains his accusations. He blames the Church, the Republic, the state government of Bahia and, above all, the army for the massacre of the inhabitants of Canudos. He denounces the war against the poverty-stricken backlanders as fratricide. After his detailed description of the local terrain he constructs his account of the Canudos tragedy as though it had emerged from the local topography, with images of the ravages of war, the decapitation of prisoners, and the courage of those who resisted, decimated by hunger, thirst, disease and the heavy weaponry of the army. Euclides da Cunha's book is a monument to the memory of Canudos.

Above all, the Canudos campaign (1896–7) made a great impression on the collective imagination of the country.[39] The socio-religious war was led by Antônio Conselheiro. The region was home to a myriad of rundown estates, a consequence of the severe droughts and chronic unemployment. Thousands of men, women and children wandered those arid backlands. In May 1893, Antônio Conselheiro and his followers arrived at the village of Bom Conselho, in the interior of Bahia. They soon learned about a drastic tax increase on the produce they had brought to sell at the local market, a new tax imposed by the Republic. In front of everyone gathered at the market, Antônio Conselheiro tore down the proclamations nailed to the walls and burned them. In response, the governor of Bahia, Rodrigues Lima, sent the military police to arrest the holy man and disperse the group. But the backlanders fought back and put the soldiers to flight. After the conflict, Antônio Conselheiro decided to stop travelling around the region. He withdrew, along with his followers, to the abandoned Canudos estate. From the day of his arrival to the end of the war the number of his followers grew from 230 to around 24,000, making it one of the most densely populated areas in Bahia. They renamed the village Belo Monte.

The republican government and the landowners of the region viewed Canudos as a significant threat. The new way of life in the arid *sertão* that Antônio Conselheiro promoted did not include submission to those in power. On the other hand, life in the village was not an experiment in egalitarianism. The design of the urban community, the social relationships and distribution of tasks all indicated that social hierarchies had not been eliminated. Nonetheless, it is equally true that it was a social and political experiment. Life in the village was very different from that of the central republican government: work was based on the principle of collective ownership and use of the land and the distribution of what it produced. Everyone who arrived there received a plot of land to cultivate and a place to live. The villagers planted crops, bred cattle and mules, and fabricated tanned leather. The result of all production was divided between the worker and the community. What is more, Antônio Conselheiro's religious authority did not depend on recognition by the Catholic Church. Canudos was controlled neither by the local estates nor by the region's political leaders. It was a subversive experiment in a society that heretofore had been run by the landowners.

The Republic sent four increasingly large military expeditions to Canudos. In March 1897, Colonel Moreira César, commanding 1,300 soldiers, led the third expedition to attack the villagers, submitting them to machine-gun fire for hours on end. Nevertheless, the villagers managed to defeat the government troops. Colonel Moreira César was shot and killed. As the surviving government soldiers fled they were ambushed and attacked by the backlanders and hundreds of them died. The repercussions of the defeat were tremendous. In Rio de Janeiro, the capital of the Republic, the newspapers declared that Canudos was a stronghold of primitive and reactionary monarchists that had to be destroyed. The people of the village were steadfast in their resistance, even when faced with the violent attacks of the fourth expedition, which comprised 421 officers and 6,160 soldiers, all armed to the teeth. In October 1897 the army guaranteed that the lives of all those who surrendered would be spared. Unfortunately, they were not true to their word and many of the men, women and children who surrendered were decapitated. On 5 October the army set light to the village with kerosene and then dynamited the remains.

The republican government tried to make Canudos into a great example: the fight of barbarism against civilization; of backwardness against modernization. Antônio Conselheiro's cranium was part of this state performance. It was brought to Rio de Janeiro where it was dissected by Dr Nina Rodrigues with the intention of corroborating his theory about the link between madness and the mixture of races. But the Canudos campaign had revealed the abyss between the different regions of the country, and it was a warning to the intellectual and political elites that they could no longer ignore the interior. The divide between the government and its people is perhaps most eloquently expressed by Euclides da Cunha in the closing words of Os Sertões: 'And so this story ends [. . .] We will always remember this page of our history as profoundly moving and tragic; we end its narration hesitantly and without pride. We have watched like one who stands at the top of a very high mountain. And the view from above has left us dizzy.'[40]

More important than analysing every single revolt of this period – and there were many – is to consider that they were motivated by the same causes: the demand to own land, the desire for justice, and religious fanaticism. They were fuelled by a powerful combination of mysticism and protest. All of them reveal the persistence of polarized power structures, such as those between priests and the faithful; colonels and their soldiers; holy men and their followers; saints and their devotees; brigands and the armed bands that followed them.[41] It is no coincidence that during this period armed bands, roaming the backlands and far beyond, gained notoriety. Armed bandits and their gangs, such as Antônio Silvino, Lampião and Antônio Dó, were ambiguous characters. Their form of power represented an alternative to that of the landowners. However, although they could be romanticized as creating a more just and egalitarian way of life, everything they did was based on the traditional model of arbitrary violence. Ignoring all models of citizenship and any idea of equal justice for all, these heroes, or villains of the backlands, are essential to an understanding of the early years of the Republic.

THEM AND US: THE WORKERS GO ON STRIKE

In the 1910s the workers in the country's incipient industrial sector also began to show their dissatisfaction. Although they were not exclusively responsible for the growing popularity of anarchism among the workers, the immigrants newly arrived from Europe had brought the movement into Brazil, beginning in the 1890s. The political movement was joined by Italians, Spaniards, Portuguese and many Brazilians, and was to be the basis for the political organization and mobilization of workers for more than thirty years.

The industrialization process in Brazil began in the 1840s, bringing with it the demand for labour, especially in civil construction and the building of railways.[42] From the 1860s, when the first textile factories were opened, Brazilian industry was increasingly concentrated in the central and southern regions of the country. In the 1880s industrialization developed rapidly, accompanied by an increased demand for labour. Between 1880 and 1884, 150 new factories were opened; by 1907 this number had increased to 3,410, and by 1929 there were 3,336 new establishments employing a total of 275,512 workers.[43] This labour force was made up of migrants from all over the country – and from the 1860s, especially in the states of São Paulo and Rio de Janeiro, of immigrants, mostly Italians. São Paulo during this period became the country's major industrial centre, above all for textiles, and a centre for immigrant labour. In 1912, 60 per cent of the textile workers in the state were Italian, most of whom were from Naples, the Veneto region, Sicily and Calabria.

The immigration from Italy helps explain the association of the workers' movement in Brazil with anarchism – at least in São Paulo.[44] After all, it was the tenet of workers' organizations in Italy. And, in accordance with the age-old revolutionary tradition, when an Italian anarchist immigrated, it was his mission to propagate libertarian ideas. This thinking was also spread by Spanish and Portuguese immigrants, who took a leading role in the workers' movement in Rio de Janeiro and Minas Gerais. The objective of anarchists is to create a stateless society made up of self-governing communities whose daily routine is governed by the principles of freedom, experimentation, solidarity and fraternity. In Brazil the anarchists created associations whose aim was to improve workers' living standards and to provide them with access to education. They founded a number of newspapers – O *Amigo do Povo*, *A Voz do Trabalhador*, *A Terra Livre*, *A Plebe*, *A Lanterna*[45] – and their main form of mobilization was through strikes. They were divided into two main groups. The anarchist trade unionists predominated in São Paulo, where their associations engaged mainly in politics. The anarchist communists, on the other hand, believed in insurrection as the best form of revolutionary action. However, on one point they were all agreed: only through workers' direct and autonomous initiatives would it be possible to abolish capitalism and establish a system of anarchy.

Not by coincidence, between 1906 and 1908 the number of strikes increased. The working class were reacting to the appalling working conditions. There were no restrictions on child labour nor on the number of hours in a working day. They also had to fight for better wages and for the creation of trade unions and political parties to represent them. Children worked in the factories starting at the age of five – and boys and girls under the age of eighteen accounted for half of the total workforce. The industrial census of 1919 also reveals the large number of women employed. The presence of women and children working in the factories led to lower average wages, and the situation became even worse during the years of the First World War.

The workers became an important component of public life of Brazil. They began to establish trade unions, then federations of trade unions, as well as other kinds of organizations. By 1906 they had founded a trade union centre with anarchist sympathies – the Brazilian Workers' Confederation (COB). Between 1900 and 1920 approximately four hundred strikes were organized in the fight for better working and living conditions (salary increase, workers' protection, decreased hours, right to organize). Other strikes were explicitly political in nature: against the First World War and in solidarity with the struggle of international workers. In 1902 the first major strike took place in Rio de Janeiro, in a shoe factory. The next year the city was witness to the country's first general strike, which included painters, typesetters, hat makers and other sectors. It was suppressed by the police. In 1904 there was another major strike, coordinated by employees of the Santos Docks Company and supported by typesetters in São Paulo and dockworkers in Rio de Janeiro. In 1906 one of the largest railway strikes in Brazil took place in São Paulo, motivated by the constant abuse of local workers and a reduction in their wages. In 1907 the first general strike in São Paulo took place, demanding an eight-hour working day. The movement soon spread to other cities in the state of São Paulo, including Santos, Ribeirão Preto and Campinas. Workers in the food industry and the metallurgy factories had started the strike. Shoemakers and typesetters eventually joined. Finally, there were as many as two thousand workers taking part. However, despite the great surge of activity, in a country where the system was based on political patronage and there was little interest in political representation for the majority, strikes continued to be the target of police repression. A number of immigrants were expelled from the country for being 'anarchists and troublemakers', and many Brazilian workers were arrested and beaten under the same pretext.

The strength of the anarchist movement can be explained by a series of factors: the crises of 1910 and 1913, unemployment and longer working hours. In 1917 between 50,000 and 70,000 workers in Rio de Janeiro went on strike and in São Paulo almost the entire working population walked out. Although there were few concrete results at the time, the activity helped workers to mobilize and form trade unions later on.[46] And the movement did not lose its momentum: between 1919 and 1920 there were sixty-four strikes in the city of São Paulo alone, and a further fourteen in the interior of the state. On 1 May 1919 between 50,000 and 60,000 people joined in a protest in Rio de Janeiro, including industrial workers, anarchists and communists. Similar numbers turned out in São Paulo, including bakers, textile workers, shoemakers, typesetters and industrial labourers.

Beginning in the 1920s, the violent repression of workers by the police reduced the number of strikes and weakened the power of the trade unions. In 1922, with the creation of the Communist Party, founded mainly by former anarchists, the leadership of the workers' movement gradually passed to the communists. The internal divisions between the anarchists and communists decreased their ability to mobilize. The first two strikes of the 1920s – the textile workers in São Paulo and the railway workers in Rio de Janeiro – were a failure. But the workers' movement had come to stay. It grew and become increasingly organized and complex in the following decades.

In fact, country life and city life now had more drawing them together than they had separating them. Perhaps the best illustration of this phenomenon is the relation between the war at Canudos and the *favelas* (shantytowns) that had begun to develop on the outskirts of the cities. The first shantytown in Rio de Janeiro, near the port, on the *Morro da Providência* (Providence Hill), was built by soldiers returning from the Canudos war. It is said that the former soldiers, whose wives prepared meals for the entire regiment, camped outside the War Ministry with their families, demanding to be provided with homes. These campsites, which began as temporary lodgings, became permanent. A similar process occurred in the other *favelas* that were beginning to be built on the hillsides around the city. *Favela* was the name of a hill at the centre of the battlefield in Canudos – the *Morro da Favela* – which in turn had been named after a plant that grew abundantly in the scrublands. The word has since become synonymous with 'shantytown'. It is ironic that a word originating from the location of a war between the elite and the poverty-stricken inhabitants of the interior, should now be used throughout the country to refer to the communities that are the greatest symbol of the divisions in Brazilian society.[47]

ANTHROPOPHAGITES UNITE: MODERNISM AND A NEW WAY OF BEING BRAZILIAN

The dissatisfaction was generalized and not limited to any one group. The 1920s marked a turning point in Brazil with the emergence of new customs and attitudes that were to influence future generations. But along with the widespread disappointment with the Republic, there was also hope for the creation of a modern Brazil. Intellectuals and artists began to question the country's cultural traditions and to confront republican institutions. They began to increasingly challenge the status quo. These new voices firmly believed that all citizens had the right to participate in society.[48]

The pivotal year in this process was 1922, when two major and contrasting events took place. The first was the celebration of the centenary of Brazil's independence; the second was the *Semana de Arte Moderna* (Modern Art Week), which took place in São Paulo. This event was of fundamental importance in understanding a generation that made a radical break with the established culture, which was essentially academic. Until 1922, cultural standards had been determined by the *Academia Brasileira de Letras* (ABL – Brazilian Academy of Letters). Founded in 1897, the Academy was the brainchild of a group of intellectuals and public figures, the most important of whom were Machado de Assis, Graça Aranha, Oliveira Lima, Rui Barbosa and Joaquim Nabuco. The Academy was based on the French model, the *Académie Française*. The Brazilian Academy had forty members, all of whom were well-known intellectuals, considered a kind of 'intellectual, moral and political framework' for the nation.[49] But with the passage of time this group became stultified and increasingly out of touch with the vanguard, the symbolists and modernists, and, above all, with the bohemians who met in bars and bookshops in Rio de Janeiro.

Various forms of modernist art began to appear simultaneously, revealing novel forms of artistic expression and a new outlook. The 1922 *Semana de Arte Moderna* acted as a catalyst for this movement, a forum for new ideas that challenged the status quo. This symbolic event took place between 11 and 18 February 1922, in São Paulo's beautiful neoclassical *Theatro Municipal* (the opera house). It was organized by intellectuals, including authors Mário de Andrade and Oswald de Andrade; painters Tarsila do Amaral, Di Cavalcanti, Anita Malfatti and Victor Brecheret; and the composer Heitor Villa-Lobos. Graça Aranha, who was a member of the Academy, was also one of the organizers of the event. Paulo Prado, an intellectual and coffee planter, helped to finance the event. A very important aspect of the *Semana de Arte Moderna* was the rejection of the imported artistic movements and theories and their influence on Brazilian art. These artists and intellectuals believed it was high time that Brazil created its own national art forms. The intention was to overhaul the artistic and cultural status quo and adopt a Brazilianized form of the European vanguard: Italian futurism, cubism and expressionism.

Although the *Semana de Arte Moderna* had very few immediate consequences – on the contrary, it was highly criticized – over time it became very significant and famous, especially insofar as it has been associated with the Brazilian avant-garde and with modernism. In 1924, Oswald de Andrade published *Poesia Pau-Brasil*,[50] a book advocating a uniquely Brazilian form of poetry. Then, in 1928, he published his *Manifesto Antropófago* (*Anthropophagic Manifesto*) in the first edition of the *Revista de Antropofagia*.[51] Oswald de Andrade was a cosmopolitan figure who came from a wealthy family. On his visits to France he had been impressed by the experimentation of the avant-garde. He became familiar with African and Polynesian art, read about psychoanalysis, and made contact with the local intellectuals. The *Manifesto Antropófago* was foundational for the Brazilian modernist movement and the key work for an entire generation of artists. The book is a mixture of lively references to Rousseau, Montaigne, Picabia and Freud, and exposes the contradiction between two distinct contemporary cultures: the primitive (Amerindian and African) and the Latin (European). Contrary to the Romantic Indianism of the nineteenth century, the idea was not to present a process of peaceful assimilation, but one of conflict, stemming from the tension inherent in the confrontation between the two. This opposition would lead to one swallowing the other, as expressed in the ironic aphorisms 'Tupi or not tupi, that is the question' and 'I'm only interested in what isn't mine.' In other words, this was the antithesis of the artistic movements of the empire.

'Anthropophagy' was now the key word, and the aim was to produce a new literary language that 'had not been catechized'. Oswald de Andrade developed the concept to show how, in Brazil, the practice of cultural anthropophagy would lead to the 'swallowing' of other cultural traditions and the emergence of new ones. Foreign influence would be 'devoured and vomited out', thus creating a truly national culture. This process included a return to the traditions of Amerindian and African art.

One of the finest examples is the 1928 novel *Macunaíma* by Mário de Andrade. In it he narrates the story of a hero 'with no character' who travels all over Brazil searching for an amulet– the *muiraquitã* – that brings good luck. The central character jumps from one location in Brazil to the other, making geographical reality illusory. The book became a classic upon publication with its description of the misadventures of its Brazilian hero. This impish hero rejects all universally accepted norms of behaviour: he lies, wheels and deals, and causes harm to others; but at the same time he is lovable, and sensitive to the point of shedding tears. In a central metaphor, this Brazilian hero, who was a 'jet-black' man, turns into a white man, one of his brothers is transformed into an Indian, and the other brother becomes a black man (although the palms of his hands and the soles of his feet are white). As the author concludes: 'And there in the cave, sheltered from the sweltering sun, the three brothers made a very beautiful sight, one blonde, one red and the other black, standing tall and naked.'[52]

Thus *Macunaíma* represents a fertile period of reassessment of Brazilian culture.[53] The novel incorporates Indians, hillbillies, backlanders, blacks, mulattoes and whites, many of whom had previously been ignored in the arts. Mário de Andrade, who lived in São Paulo and never went abroad, was, without doubt, the most significant figure in this process of 'Brazilianizing Brazil'.[54] This is not to say he was xenophobic or averse to foreign values. Rather, his aim was to create a unique language in which to represent the history and culture of his country. The author and his novel were icons of this new movement in which Brazilians began to reflect on Brazil and capture it in art. Not only did the novel deny the defeatist, previously held prevalent views on race, it transformed the presence of mixed races and of African Brazilians into a fundamental characteristic of the country – and its great good fortune.

Although São Paulo was undoubtedly at the centre of the movement, it is important to put the city's role in perspective. Senador Saldanha Marinho came up with the catchphrase of a whole generation who adopted modernism as a means of expressing their cynicism: 'This is not the republic of my dreams.' He was a founding member of the Republican Party, a signatory of the manifesto of 1870, and one of the group who drew up the 1891 Constitution. The sentence expresses the cynical viewpoint of the intellectuals, especially in Rio de Janeiro. They would meet in bars and cafés and considered the city their stage, all the while developing their satirical, hilarious style of writing. It was a bohemian group, shabbily dressed and adept at drinking and arguing away the evening in the bars of Rio de Janeiro. In contrast to 'good boys' of the Brazilian Academy of Letters and the clean-cut intellectuals of São Paulo, this group of liberal professionals set out to shock the public. Not only that, they also associated with dubious crowds, such as those that used to meet at the house of *Tia Ciata*.[55]

Born in the town of Santo Amaro da Purificação, in Bahia, Tia Ciata (Aunt Ciata) was the leader of a group of Bahian blacks who lived in the *Carioca* district of Saúde, near the docks. The *tias* were older Bahian women who took the leading role in communities. Hilária Batista de Almeida (Tia Ciata) was the most well known among them. She made Baiano delicacies and her stall was the most famous in the city. She also made dresses for the *baianas* of the carnival clubs and walked through the streets of Rio de Janeiro dressed in those flowing, white Baiana dresses. At the weekends, groups gathered at her house to sing and dance. According to João da Baiana, an assiduous member of the group, there was dancing in the living room, samba in the back rooms, and drumming in the yard behind the house.

These parties put Tia Ciata in contact with other personalities of the city. Composers, intellectuals, artists, journalists and publicists, as well as a fair number of rogues, all attended her gatherings. Tia Ciata was an important figure in the candomblé centre run by João de Alabá because she was a daughter of Oxum,[56] having been initiated in candomblé in Salvador. She was also a herbalist and faith healer. The first samba recording took place at Tia Ciata's house. It was called *Pelo telefone*[57] – and a man by the name of Donga, a composer, registered it in his name at the National Library in Rio de Janeiro. In so doing, he secured the rights of a work that was almost certainly a collective composition. Donga's presumption caused considerable irritation among the group, who protested throughout the city through – among other means – poetry: 'Oh chutzpah/To claim all around/That this composition is yours!/It is by the good Hilário/And by old Ciata/That's what you wrote, sir'.

This irreverent atmosphere provided fertile ground for the development of *Carioca* samba – whose leading lights included Pixinguinha,[58] Heitor dos Prazeres,[59] Caninha, China, João da Baiana and Sinhô. The mood was also welcoming to the re-emergence of Afro-Brazilian culture, including the *Carioca* modernists who frequented the same social circle. The frontiers of what had previously been a limited group were now extended to include the poor, mulattoes and blacks, as well as intellectuals and the children of the bourgeoisie.

A fine example of this was the invitation from President Hermes da Fonseca's wife to the popular singer Chiquinha Gonzaga to sing *Corta-Jaca*[60] during an official reception at the Catete Palace.[61] If we were to compare the different modernist groups, the *Cariocas* were perhaps the most informal and far reaching. In addition to Tia Ciata and Chiquinha Gonzaga, the group included Suzana – the pseudonym of Tina Tati, the owner of a cabaret who had been an activist in the abolitionist movement – and Maria Bragança de Mello, a defender of nudism and student of the occult.

The group was very influenced by artists of the previous generation such as Paula Nei, Pardal Mallet and José do Patrocínio. But it also included important artists like the writer Lima Barreto, the critic Gonzaga Duque, the cartoonist Raul Pederneiras, the poet Emílio de Menezes and Bastos Tigre,[62] who earned the sobriquet *Don Quixote* due to his acidic commentaries. They called themselves the *confraria humorística*[63] and adopted the Café Papagaio[64] as their headquarters.[65] Organizing performances, finding forums for simulating debates, giving improvised speeches and engaging in general mockery were among the many specialties of this bohemian group. At the Café Papagaio even the parrot – nicknamed Bocage[66] – was ill-mannered, squawking obscenities and reciting indecent verses.[67] Collectively their notoriety was such that it was said even the parrot had run-ins with the law. If the group made the most of life and had much *joie de vivre*, they also wrote, and a lot: articles for magazines and journals, novels and works of poetry. After all, modernism is a collective concept, and true to that idea, various parallel projects were taking form.

The modernist movement took different form in different regions. In São Paulo, for example, due to its new role on the national scene, there was much insistence on 'their particular modernity'. For example, the *Bandeirantes* were no longer seen as mere wild adventurers, capturing slaves and Indians. Instead, they were transformed into the 'heroes of a race', symbols of the *Paulista* entrepreneurial spirit. In Minas Gerais, the modernists established the early eighteenth- and nineteenth-century baroque churches as the 'cradle of Brazilian culture'. The idea was to exclude the imperial past, considered 'artificial and imitative' and embrace a mixed race country.

The 1933 publication of *Casa-Grande e Senzala* is equally iconic of the period. The over 600-page tome by sociologist, anthropologist Gilberto Freyre established a new sociological approach to Brazil's society. Taking on the subject of the relation of 'the three races', Gilberto Freyre, a Pernambucan intellectual, portrays the private experience of the *casa-grandes* of the northeast, which he transforms into a collective identity. The work introduced a new model for Brazil's multiracial society. The author inverted the old fears of miscegenation and racial conflict through new cultural analyses. The 'melting pot' was written as an optimistic myth about the coexistence of the three races in Brazil. In Mr Freyre's words, 'All Brazilians, even the blond-haired whites, carry in their soul – and more often than not, in their body and soul – the image or the complexion of the Indian and the African.'[68] And he thus transformed the mestizo culture into an integral part of Brazilian society.

In part, because of this well-known book, miscegenation between different social groups – often violent – become a distinguishing trait of Brazilian society, a sort of model of socialization. Not that Mr Freyre's book ignores the horrors of the past; but he idealized a new civilization based on the model of the *casa-grandes* of the northeast. In contrast to the urban modernism of São Paulo and Rio de Janeiro, Gilberto Freyre conjures up the colonial sugar plantations of days gone by to describe a national identity founded on coexistence. Social exclusion and social inclusion are opposing forces that balance each other out: the patriarchal master and the faithful slave.[69] In his book Mr Freyre leaves the concepts of hierarchy based on racial criteria untouched, while at the same time acknowledging the violence and sadism characteristic of slavery. The novelty of *Casa-Grande e Senzala* is that it emphasizes the intimacy of the home, tones down the harshness of labour on the plantations, and transforms everything into a cause for optimism, as if a 'good form' of slavery were not a contradiction in terms.

THE 'DAY AFTER': BLACK POPULATIONS AFTER ABOLITION

As soon as the euphoria following the 1888 *lei áurea* had died down, the shortcomings of the measure emerged. Although the law ended slavery, it did not address the social inclusion of freed slaves and their descendants, who had little chance of competing for jobs with other groups, above all with the white population, be they Brazilians or immigrants. The idea, according to Rio Branco, the Minister of Foreign Affairs – in an unfortunate double entendre – was to erase the 'black past'. There was a verse in the 1890 republican anthem that went as follows: 'We can't believe that in the past there were slaves in such a noble land . . .' 'The past' was just a year and a half prior, but no one seemed to remember.

Although in reality, in the early years of the Republic, there was a real fear that new forms of slavery and/or other racist policies could be introduced. The newly freed slaves had to live with the heavy burden of the racially deterministic past. There was a reversal in expectations, since new criteria determined legal and social justice norms. These included race, religion, ethnicity and gender. According to opinion at the time, the lack of professional and social success of black and mestizo Brazilians was a biological problem, inherent to race, and not rooted in history or the recent past. Henrique Roxo, a doctor at the national asylum, stated in a speech given at the Second Latin American Medical Congress (1904) that blacks and *pardos* should be seen as a species 'that had not evolved' and had 'remained backward'. According to Dr Roxo, although every race carried a 'hereditary burden', in the case of these groups it was 'exceptionally heavy', leading to idleness, alcoholism and mental illness. He also included social issues in his argument, blaming the 'hurried transition' and the disorderly growth of the cities.

The fact was that Brazil maintained its image as a mixed-race giant which seemingly required care. Brazil was the only Latin American country to participate in the First International Congress of Races, in July 1911. The director of the National Museum in Rio de Janeiro, João Batista de Lacerda, was sent to London to represent the country. A scientist, he presented an article at the Congress entitled '*Sur les métis au Brésil*', in which he drew curious conclusions: 'It is logical to suppose that by the beginning of the next century the mestizos will have disappeared, an event that will coincide with the parallel extinction of the black race from among us.'[70] The text argued that the future would be white and peaceful, with blacks and mestizos disappearing to make way for a structured civilization that was increasingly white. But his thesis was greeted with pessimism in Brazil, and not for the reasons one might expect. On the contrary, it was thought that a century was far too long to wait for Brazil to become definitively white.

The anthropologist Roquette Pinto, president of the first Brazilian Congress of Eugenics (1929), also foresaw a country that would be increasingly white: by 2012 the Brazilian population would be 80 per cent white and 20 per cent mixed race; there would be no blacks or Indians. The predominance of such arguments diverted the post-abolition debate away from the legal question of equality and access to citizenship. Instead, discussions were based on biology. Science accommodated history and transformed social hierarchies into immutable data. There were two parallel processes at work: an emphasis on the so-called inferiority of the blacks and mestizos, and an attempt to eliminate the country's history of slavery and its legacy. Thus a class of 'sub-citizens' was created, which included the inhabitants of the interior as well as the slum dwellers in the cities. The life in these slums was brilliantly depicted in the 1890 novel *O cortiço* (*The Slum*) by Aluísio de Azevedo.[71] The writer portrays these communities as a bomb ready to explode, not only due to the mixture of the inhabitants – Portuguese, Spaniards, former slaves, and free negroes and mulattoes – but also due to the upheavals caused by the rapid urbanization and the hurried expulsion of the poor from their homes.

The newly freed slaves faced prejudice against both their race and their history as slaves. Lima Barreto wrote in his diary, 'In Brazil the mental capacity of blacks is discussed *a priori*, and that of the whites *posteriori*', and he concluded with frustration, 'It's wretched not to be white.'[72] After abolition, black people were treated with a kind of silent and perverse prejudice that had a considerable impact on their lives, based as it was on a hierarchy constructed according to gradations of colour.[73] Non-whites were thought to be lazy, immoral and socially disorganized.[74]

'Freedom was black, but equality was white.' While white elites enjoyed equality and citizenship and were allowed to vote, former slaves were supposed to be content with the mere right to come and go. A good example was their keenness to acquire goods forbidden to them during captivity. The traveller Louis-Albert Gaffre narrated how, immediately after abolition, black men and women used their modest savings to buy shoes, an accessory that would have been impossible for them to own while slaves. Although the demand for these items was large, the customers were disappointed with the results. As slaves they had gone barefoot, with calloused feet in direct contact with the ground. That made it hard for them to adapt to 'such a modern custom'. Witnesses related how in the city streets and in the fields they saw black people carrying pairs of shoes: not worn on their feet, but carried over their shoulders, as a

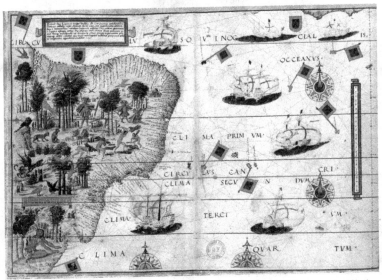

1. Johann Freschauer's coloured engraving from 1505 reflects the earliest period of European contact with Brazil, when the collective imagination ran wild, with the inhabitants shown as warriors and barbarians eating human flesh. In the background, Portuguese ships bring 'civilization'.

2. The Portuguese cartographer and cosmographer Lopo Homem travelled the world under royal warrant to help demarcate the Treaty of Tordesillas. In this map he draws Portuguese ships, compasses, parrots and indigenous peoples at war in the recently discovered territory. He also includes the brazilwood trees, used by the native peoples in craftwork and for decorative dyes, which were of great interest to Lisbon.

3. A colour engraving of 1662 by Johannes Blaeu. The discovery of the New
World flooded the European imagination; visions were split between Eden
and hell. Since Native Americans did not leave written records, the only
representations we have are European, reflecting Western conventions.
America was the ideal place on which to project stereotypes of
decadent, yet at the same time idyllic, indigenous peoples.

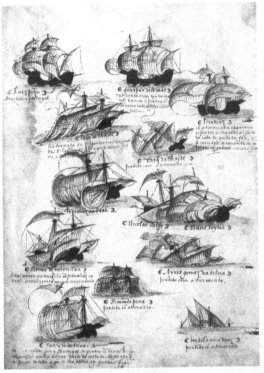

4. Despite the triumphant discourse of the Portuguese regarding their great voyages, their success was the result of a long process of trial and error, involving substantial losses and shipwrecks. These probably sixteenth-century images from the *Book of the Armadas of India* show a variety of disasters.

5. BELOW: The first sugar plantations (*engenhos*) began to spread throughout Pernambuco around 1535. Initially, the term *engenho* was used in reference to just the sugar mill. With time, the term came to mean the entire sugar production complex: the land, buildings, and crops. In this seventeenth-century painting, Frans Post's depiction is strangely idyllic.

6–7. Albert Eckhout (1618–66) lived in the captaincy of Pernambuco during Dutch rule. His illustrations reflect what his clients wanted to see: the exotic practices of those peoples. The painter depicts the Tapuia woman with a slain enemy's hand and foot in an allusion to cannibalism, of which Eckhout had no first-hand knowledge.
The couple are part of a series that includes other groupings: 'Brasilianen', Africans, mulattoes and *mamelucos*.

8. The slave market of Pernambuco, painted by Zacharias Wagener (1614–68) while he worked as a soldier with the Dutch West India Company. The Dutch colony was supplied with African slaves from Angola and Guinea.

9. The majority of slaves who disembarked in Brazil during the sixteenth and seventeenth centuries worked in the sugar mills. The work was exhausting. In this drawing by Frans Post, a man of small stature (right), fully clothed and with a hat and sword, inspects the process.

10. Part of a group of thirty-eight watercolours attributed to Joaquim José de Miranda and painted between 1771 and 1773, this drawing depicts the final confrontation in Paraná, which took place between the expedition under the command of Lieutenant Colonel Afonso Botelho de Sampaio e Sousa and the Kaingang Indians. Due to the Kaingangs' supposed 'indomitable disposition', a policy of virtual genocide was adopted. This image shows a rare Indian success.

11. Tiradentes was a faceless hero. Although extremely famous for his participation in the Minas Conspiracy, all the images we have of him are imaginary. His image therefore was free to become Christ-like – the beard and long hair and the clothing. In this painting by Antônio Parreiras (Niterói, 1860–1937), Tiradentes is immortalized as a hero of the Republic.

12. Many different peoples came from the African continent, including Balantas, Manjacos, Bijagós, Mandingas and Jalofos. They brought with them diverse religious traditions that took on new meanings as these mixed with Catholicism. Carlos Julião (1740–1811) was a Portuguese-Italian artist who worked in Brazil as an inspector of forts. He painted rare images of African life in Brazil.

13. Dom Pedro I's coronation ceremony on 1 December 1822 combined traditional European elements with idealized characteristics of Brazil, a mixture of Old World costumes and new symbols. Jean-Baptiste Debret's painting did the same thing, copying an original done for an Austrian monarch and altering the shape and size of the church where the ceremony was held.

14. The African slave trade was still a cornerstone of the local economy in the nineteenth century. This slave market in Rio de Janeiro scandalized foreign visitors, including Jean-Baptiste Debret. He painted the practically naked, skeletal slaves and the children with their distended stomachs. Note the contrast with the trader, with his big belly and aura of disdain, and with the standing man with his symbols of power: an arrogant posture, boots, hat and cane.

15. External pressure to end the slave trade increased and, between 1839 and 1842, the British led the movement by intensifying the seizure of slave ships. In 1845 the British sloop *Albatross* captured the Brazilian ship *Albanez* with 750 slaves on board, depicted in this painting by the navy officer Francis Maynell.

16. Commissioned by the Brazilian monarchy, the *Battle of Avay*, by Pedro Américo, was completed seven years after the Paraguayan War ended. The public's reaction to the painting was divided at the time: some appreciated the wealth of detail, while others condemned the bloodbath. The panoramic view denotes the grandeur of the event, but the violence conspicuously depicted is clearly in criticism of the empire.

17. By the end of the 1870s, the Romantic Indianism movement, which had already dominated literature, had reached painting. The native hero was appropriated to represent the origins of Brazil and to foment nationalism. In *Iracema*, José M. Medeiros (1849–1925) depicted José de Alencar's protagonist from the very popular eponymous novel, published in 1865. Her representation was fitting for the times: a passive figure destined to die for the life of the nation.

18. On the morning of 15 November 1889, pro-republican conspirators in the army headed to the Campo de Santana in Rio de Janeiro. There were no heroic acts and the population at large was oblivious to the plans. Pedro II was informed of the coup and the founding of the Republic. This painting depicts masses of people, who were never there, cheering Marshal Deodoro da Fonseca.

19. RIGHT: The triumphant Republic (a woman in a Phrygian cap, dressed like a Roman) stands on a winged chariot, galloping through the sky. Frederico Steckel's allegory is a wall painting done in 1898 for the old Secretary of the Interior of Minas Gerais building, now the Minas Memorial.

20. In 1888, four days after the law abolishing slavery in Brazil was signed, a multitude of nearly twenty thousand people, among them whites, blacks and mulattoes, filled the Campo de Santana in Rio de Janeiro for the ceremony celebrating the act. The royal family is to the left, with Princess Isabel seated strategically in the middle of the tent, which had been specially made for her.

21. The Republic was going through dizzying modernization: Avenida Central in Rio de Janeiro (*above*) was an icon of the times, with electric streetlights and Art Nouveau façades; the Theatro Municipal of São Paulo (*left*) in 1911 revealed how the travellers' old 'clay city' had been transformed into a European-inspired coffee metropolis; meanwhile, construction in Belo Horizonte evoked a republican utopia: straight streets, imposing avenues, and an enormous park – the Praça da Liberdade (*bottom*), whose English-style gardens and lakes were geometrically positioned throughout.

22. On 5 July 1922, twenty-eight rebel lieutenants participating in the Copacabana Fort revolt refused to surrender. They chopped up the Brazilian flag, divided it amongst themselves and left the fort, heading toward the Leme district, where they faced four thousand legalist soldiers. On Avenida Atlântica, ten gave up. The remaining eighteen, including one civilian who had joined the movement, continued their walk. Only two men survived the ensuing shootout. The lieutenants' march divided the officer class and brought on a cycle of military revolts that would eventually topple the First Republic.

23. RIGHT: In 1937, the *integralistas* paraded through Rio de Janeiro to launch the presidential candidacy of their supreme leader, Plínio Salgado, in elections scheduled for the following year.

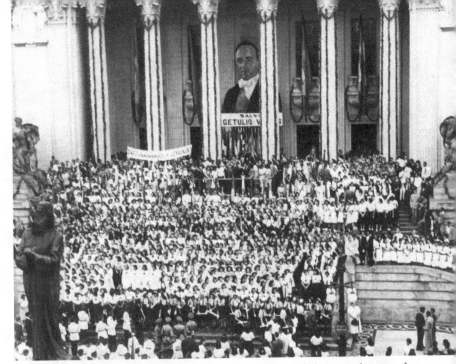

24. For ten years, the Youth Parade united young people between the ages of eleven and eighteen. The proliferation of civic demonstrations during the *Estado Novo* was meant to give the impression of a united nation supporting one leader, Getúlio Vargas. In this photograph, the monumental columns in front of the gigantic image of Vargas evoke fascist propaganda.

25. In 1951 the reporter Arlindo Silva, accompanied by the photographer José Medeiros, visited the candomblé *terreiros* (worship sites) in Salvador. The photographs, in the magazine *O Cruzeiro*, were controversial because they showed secret sacred locations unseen by the non-practising public. As a result of this article, the Banto candomblé site was closed. This image is of an Iaô, a novice in a state of worship going through the initiation ritual.

26. A large crowd accompanies President Vargas's body to Santos Dumont Airport in Rio de Janeiro; from there it went to Rio Grande do Sul for burial. But once the aeroplane had taken off, people realized that they were right in front of the general headquarters of the Third Air Zone. The air force took up their arms, with soldiers and officers firing at the furious, unarmed civilians.

27. As President Kubitschek liked to say, he 'flew in any weather and landed on any field'. The Targets Plan advanced, Brasília was under construction and he wanted to see Brazil 'progress fifty years in five'. He was very good at marketing. In official photos, he was always surrounded by achievements: in this case in an automobile made in a factory with 50 per cent Brazilian parts.

28. Highway construction in many ways was a rebirth of the 'westward march' mentality. It was a broad programme of territorial expansion announced by Getúlio Vargas. This photograph depicts the start of the BR-364 highway construction. The highway set out to challenge the Amazon rainforest by connecting the cities of Cuiabá (Mato Grosso), Porto Velho (Rondônia) and Rio Branco (Acre).

29. The composition of this photograph is probably the result of professional experience and a great deal of luck on the part of Orlando Brito. The classic image of the triumphant ruler has been inverted: the most imperial of generals to have ever governed Brazil, Ernesto Geisel, has become a mere detail before the colossal Brazilian flag. A fluke in lighting, however, lends the flag an aura of mourning that, for just an instant, captures the mood in Brazil.

30. The great metalworker strikes of 1978, 1979 and 1980, which took place in the ABC region, gave rise to the organization of unions that not only opposed the dictatorship but also strove to organize workers at the grassroots level, on factory floors. The workers, led by Luiz Inácio Lula da Silva, voted in enormous assemblies.

31. Street culture – hip-hop – became popular in the mid-1980s in central São Paulo. Groups of young people, most of them from peripheral zones, would meet at the São Bento metro station. Later, rappers and graffiti artists joined these groups. By the end of the decade, the cultural language of the streets became highly visible in Brazil's public spaces.

shoulder bag or a trophy. Freedom, in any case, meant the possibility to buy and use what one wanted, and to have a name and identity.

As it was, there was more continuity than disruption of customs established prior to abolition. Above all, in the rural areas freed slaves joined the ranks of the poor – a situation that was in no way new. What was new was the nomadic lifestyle that much of this segment of the population adopted. This vast group, made up of hillbillies, backlanders and *caboclos*, established temporary plantations and then moved on, working as cattle herdsmen, muleteers, horse trainers and newspaper deliverers in the south or raising cattle in the northeast. This explains their parsimonious lifestyle. They owned few personal items and generally did not raise livestock.[75] Black workers mixed with the peasant population, adopted the lifestyle of the hillbillies and *caboclos* in the state of São Paulo, worked on farms in Minas Gerais and on sugar and cotton plantations in the northeast. They preferred not to settle down and lived with the 'minimum essentials'. Their production of food and trade goods was geared towards a small surplus.[76] And their social life was restricted to rural neighbourhood and village gatherings.

Whereas some commentators harped on what they considered mestizo apathy and depravity, as if they were emblematic of an ailing country, there were also chroniclers who praised what they saw as a 'pure rural lifestyle'. In 1914, in an article entitled 'Urupês' in the *Estado de São Paulo*, its author Monteiro Lobato[77] created the character Jeca Tatu, who supposedly came from the hillbilly prototype of the Paraíba Valley. Juca Tatu became one of the best-known caricatures of the poor in the Brazilian imaginary. In spite of many obstacles and setbacks – his adoption as a child, political upheavals, widespread drought and famine – the *caboclo* was ever resilient. In one of his speeches Rui Barbosa used Jeca Tatu as an example. 'Who, after all, are the Brazilian people?' he asked. That squatting *caboclo*, whose vote could be bought for a drink in the bar or a roll of tobacco, or that gentleman who reads books in French, smokes cigarettes and frequents the theatres and the Italian operas?[78]

Political debates were filled with this type of question in the final years of the First Republic, which ended in 1930. The government's projects to modernize Brazil were one side of the coin, and the other side was very different. The poor populations of Brazil lived in wattle-and-daub huts in Minas Gerais; cavern homes in the Chapada

Diamantina; slave-built refuges in the northeast; and huts on stilts along riverbanks. In these places the rules of society were '*caboclo*', characterized by rites of respect, but also by violence. They planted their own food: manioc, corn and beans. On special occasions they ate chicken or dried meat with coarse flour, *pirão, angu* and *paçoca*.[79] They practised a very Brazilian kind of religion, a generous dose of Catholicism combined with Afro-Brazilian practices and immigrant traditions: a mixture of spells, witchcraft and prayers. This, then, was the other side of the coin.

INDIGENOUS PEOPLE AND AMERINDIANS: THE 'BARBARIANS' (STILL) AMONG US

Among the groups ignored by the Republic were the Indians: they were systematically excluded from all government plans and policies. During the empire the interest in the indigenous peoples had been more rhetorical than pragmatic, with the Indians featuring as heroes in Romantic novels rather than being the subject of any practical policy. In the Republic their exclusion was even more complete.[80] An example of this was the massacre of the Kaingang to make way for the Brazilian North-Western Railway. At the time, the director of the Paulista Museum, Hermann von Ihering, argued in the press that these groups should be exterminated.

The process of the demarcation of Indian lands – for the Guarani, Xavante and Kaingang tribes – began in the west of São Paulo in 1880. Although the first two groups were 'integrated', at the price of being culturally decimated, the Kaingang tribe resisted invasion of their lands. The confrontation reached its height in 1905 when the construction of the railroad began. The Indians resisted for a long time, forming what at the time was called the 'Kaingang wall'. The situation was only brought under control in 1911 after the government had virtually annihilated the group, and with the intervention of the Indian Protection Service (SPI). The man at the head of this institution was Cândido Mariano Rondon, a military officer who, among other activities, constructed telegraph lines between Mato Grosso and Goiás. The federal government was worried about the isolation and vulnerability of the borders. Cândido Mariano Rondon was responsible for incorporating the Amazon region into the country, not only through telegraph lines running from the central west to the south of Brazil, but also by mapping the area and venturing into unknown territory to make contact for the first time with the Indians.

Demarcation policies for Indian lands varied according to region. Some regions were considered new – like Amazonia, rediscovered because of the demand for rubber. Other regions had been colonized long before. By the time the Republic was founded, the situation of the indigenous peoples was no longer linked to labour. It had become a matter of landownership. In regions settled during the colonial period, the order was to secure village borders, whereas in the newly claimed territories and along the waterways, despite the use of Indian labour, the objective was to conquer new land. The government's justification was concern with the 'settlers' safety'. These policies per se were not new, but they had never been implemented with the explicit collusion of the government. The instructions were clear: either exterminate the 'savage' Indians, or 'civilize them and incorporate them into society'.[81] Despite the provisions of the republican constitution, it was to take a long time before a practical policy of protection and inclusion would be put in place.

CRISIS IN THE LAND OF FAVOURS

During the First World War a series of events had a considerable impact on the country. The first of these was the economic crisis caused by the reduction of agricultural exports due to constant droughts and fluctuations in the price of coffee. The second was the arrival of more immigrants – a rapidly increasing number following the war – and the consequent growth of the cities. The combination of these factors led to the emergence of a powerful new group of liberal, urban professionals. Furthermore, the process of 'import substitution', implemented during the war years, resulted in an increased number of small shops and industries run by minor retailers, artisans and industrialists.

On the other hand, increasing state intervention meant there were more people employed in the government administration. Government workers abounded. The authors Machado de Assis and Lima

Barreto – both civil servants themselves – described them satirically. Lima Barreto was highly critical of such sinecures:

> On my first day of work at the ministry, I realized that all of us had been born to be civil servants [. . .] I adapted so quickly that I thought myself destined to work for the State, with my limited grammar and terrible writing, in its mission to administer the progress and activities of the nation . . .[82]

It is significant that during the First Republic the agricultural export economy was not affected by the growth of the cities. On the contrary, the connection of the government with the system of *coronelismo* and the so-called 'cattle vote' (the rural population who voted according to instructions from the local *coronel*) neutralized the political voice of the new urban classes and allowed the government to continue to control the elections. It was difficult to be autonomous in this land of favours, of give and take. The system was far from liberal, there was no sense of collectivity even – perhaps especially – with regard to abolition. And certainly the idea that the Republic had been born of the citizenry was nonexistent. Political action was still highly dependent on the relationships between those in power. It was a system that can only be referred to as cronyism.

However, even prior to the First World War, autonomous groups, with no connection to agricultural interests, began to organize. There were several middle-class movements expressing discontent: *florianismo*, the 1909 *campanha civilista* (civilian campaign), protests against shortages, which spread from town to town, and the 1920s lieutenants' uprisings, which took place all over Brazil. These revolts further destabilized the already fragile First Republic. In 1920 most army officers were of lower rank – 65.1 per cent were first lieutenants or second lieutenants and 21.3 per cent were captains.[83] They had one foot in the army and one foot in society. The lieutenants, as they came to be known, believed Brazil needed a strong central government to intervene in the economy in order to develop natural resources, promote industry, and protect the country from foreign exploitation. They saw regionalism and corruption as the root of all the country's ills. They were liberal on social issues, but authoritarian in politics. And in public, they behaved like military men, prepared to protect the country and destroy the power of the regional oligarchies. They also wanted to reduce social inequality and end illiteracy – but they did not know how to achieve their goals, nor how to create the country of their dreams.

And so they set out, virtually alone, to confront the government. The actions known as the 'Copacabana fort eighteen revolt' broke out in Rio de Janeiro on 5 July 1922. It was the lieutenants' first uprising. And there were some dramatic moments: at the end of the rebellion in the fort,[84] twenty-eight officers continued the revolt and, in hopes of immortalizing their protest, they marched along Avenida Atlântica to confront the government troops. This great avenue runs along Copacabana beach to this day. Ten of them abandoned the group along the way, leaving just the eighteen, who continued marching towards the gunfire. Only two rebel lieutenants survived – Siqueira Campos and Eduardo Gomes. The second revolt, the 1924 *Paulista* revolution, was the largest military confrontation that São Paulo had ever seen. Beginning on 5 July (the second anniversary of the 'Copacabana fort eighteen revolt'), the military rebels occupied the city for twenty-one days.

In 1924 the revolt known as the Manaus commune broke out and spread as far as the region of Óbidos in the state of Pará. The region was destabilized as a result of a fall in the price of rubber, and there were widespread accusations of corruption in the administration. In an attempt to solve the crisis, the federal government offered more credit, which only increased the general level of indebtedness. The troops from the garrison in Manaus organized an uprising in the capital against the 'constituted powers of the republic'. Like the other lieutenants, they saw themselves as the legitimate leaders of the people and demanded a reversal of the political and economic situation.

However, the lieutenants' uprising with the greatest repercussion by far was the *Coluna Prestes/Miguel Costa* (Column of Luís Carlos Prestes/Miguel Costa), which swept the country between 1925 and 1927.[85] Although the initial goal was to overthrow President Arthur Bernardes's government, the movement had more far-reaching demands. Members of the movement demanded secret ballots, state school reform, compulsory primary education and the moralization of politics. They also denounced the exploitation and the wretched living conditions of the poor. The column was the union between the group of *Paulista* lieutenants (linked to Miguel Costa) and the mutinous troops from Rio Grande do Sul, under the command of Luís Carlos Prestes. Lieutenant Prestes symbolized the spirit of change that incentivized the lieutenants. He galvanized the support of the urban middle classes and became known as the Knight of Hope. Volunteers from all over the country flocked to join the ranks of the column. Over the course of two years and five months the column travelled 25,000 kilometres, crossing twelve Brazilian states. It had a fixed nucleus of around 200 men that grew to as many as 1,500 at certain points of the journey. In the cities where the column stopped, the reaction was mixed. While some people greeted them and saw them as saviours, others resented their arbitrary practices such as seizing horses and cattle without the owners' consent and confiscating medicines, bandages and food in the small towns and villages.

The column avoided any confrontation with government troops by moving quickly. This was indeed its purpose: to maintain the movement as a kind of armed protest that appeared invincible. And the strategy was a success: they crossed the country from Mato Grosso to Maranhão and then returned by the same path, taking refuge in Bolivia in 1927. In the army, admiration for the rebels began to grow among the officers and the troops. Years later General Dutra[86] recalled how the troops who were sent to combat the column would say to each other, 'Let them through'.

THE REPUBLIC THAT WASN'T 'OLD'

By the end of the 1920s, the First Republic was fragile and its achievements were mixed. On the one hand it would be remembered as the time of a boom in urban growth, industrialization and immigration. The first steps towards creating republican institutions were taken and the struggle for better working conditions began. On the other hand, it was a period of repression, of every kind of political fraud, of racist measures, and of the expulsion of the poor to the outskirts of the cities. With so many ambiguities, the Republic had become the scene of endless conflicts; cities were now considered centres for the activities of the 'dangerous classes' and for uprisings of the 'lower orders'.[87]

The positive went along with the negative. These were the circumstances in the early phases of the institutionalization of the republican state and the struggle for better working conditions. Furthermore, to emphasize solely the process of social exclusion, which certainly occurred, would be merely to mirror the vision of the governing elites of the time. They considered anyone involved in rebellious behaviour as 'anarchic hordes'. In fact, there were associations of very different types, frequently acting in an orderly fashion, collecting signatures and mounting public campaigns and organized protests. Perhaps this is the reason why the period is referred to as the Old Republic, a pejorative term created after the 1930 revolution. There are actually many reasons for the soubriquet and why it is still in use today.

The many political and social shortcomings of the regime partly caused the name to stick. But it is equally true that a process of democratization of Brazilian customs and institutions had begun to take shape. During the First Republic, various governing powers emerged, new electoral processes were developed, and early plans for full citizen participation in government were discussed. Thus, although the period was witness to many conflicts, to authoritarian governments that maintained their power by force, to states of siege and racial policies based on eugenics, it was also the period that inaugurated the transformation of the cities into spaces where citizens could protest and debate.

This was by no means the first time that politicians and intellectuals of a new movement have claimed all the merits of the new system and relegated the old regime to backward anonymity. New movements tend to suffer from myopia when looking at the past, selectively choosing one point of view: their own. This was certainly the case of the 1930 revolution, and of the state that was immediately designated as 'new': the *Estado Novo*. According to this point of view, the true *res publica* was yet to come, as was a genuinely modern, moral and political society.

Although the country had welcomed the Republic as the harbinger of modernity, by the end of the 1920s many were disappointed, longing to discover true 'Brazilian-ness', to examine the country's past and forge a new future. The literary critic Roberto Schwarz has commented that in Brazil everything seems to 'start again from zero' and that the nation is constructed by a process of subtraction.[88] In other words, each context creates new ways of envisioning the country and attempts to eliminate those that existed before. The time had now come to discover what precisely defined Brazil, to search for models of national identity and to sow new seeds. And certainly the country's attitude towards the mixed-race population needed to shift from a biological to a cultural perspective. The Brazil that emerged from early twentieth-century modernist projects was an ambivalent place. The past coexisted with the present; popular songs with classical music; folk literature with academic literature; modern methods of transport with donkey-drawn carts; an urbanized country with the vastness of the interior; social exclusion with the first moves towards social inclusion; cronyism with hitherto unknown processes for the creation of political and social institutions. Indeed, the men of the first generation of the Republic, who were born between the end of the nineteenth and the beginning of the twentieth centuries, began to rediscover the Brazil of the interior. Musicologists such as Mário de Andrade and Villa-Lobos, Indianists like Cândido Rondon, essayists, sociologists and historians like Sérgio Buarque de Holanda, sanitarians such as Carlos Chagas and Belisário Pena, soldiers like the lieutenants in the *Coluna Prestes*, all formed part of a movement that questioned and transformed attitudes, concepts and political behaviour. There was a movement built around the idea of 'incorporating the *sertões*'. This meant embracing the Brazilians of the interior – so frequently represented as isolated, abandoned, ill, nomadic, backward, resistant to change, without any land of their own, but who are at the heart of the constant rediscovery of Brazil.

The anthropologist Claude Lévi-Strauss, in his book *La Penseé sauvage*, affirms that man is a classifying animal. First he classifies a phenomenon and then gives it a meaning and finds a use for it. 'Old Republic' was the name that stuck. It reveals how the *Estado Novo* politicians saw themselves in relation to their predecessors. Like Narcissus, they thought everything they could not see in the mirror was ugly. They did not see that this period, albeit controversial and ambiguous, was a positive experience insofar as there were struggles for rights, a new distinction between public and private spheres, and progress towards the recognition of citizenship. The street came to the fore in a bustling display of fashion, social life, newspaper boys, striking workers, political protests and manifestations of popular culture. First Republic is a more appropriate name than Old Republic. 'First' because, for better or worse, the Republic preceded the new state. And 'First' because, for the first time, exercising rights to citizenship came to the fore.

14

Samba, Malandragem,[1] Authoritarianism: The Birth of Modern Brazil

THROUGH THE VOTE, OR THROUGH ARMED CONFRONTATION: THE FIRST REPUBLIC WILL COME TO AN END

On 1 March 1930, on a carnival weekend, those Brazilians who could read and write went out to elect the next president of the Republic and the new federal deputies. This was to be the twelfth presidential election of the Brazilian Republic. The small number of voters – they were required to be adult, male and literate, amounting to just 5.6 per cent of the population – did not prevent the election from being as gripping and closely run as when Rui Barbosa had run against Hermes da Fonseca in 1910, twenty years earlier.[2] Although Brazil had changed a great deal in the interim, and the candidates were new, the 1930 elections were in some ways reminiscent of that earlier dispute. The campaign took to the streets, spread throughout the states, and mobilized the country at political rallies – or 'meetings' as they were referred to at the time, in English. The popular engagement had brought two major issues to the fore: the rules and procedures for presidential succession and the policies of the republican government regarding social equality and citizens' rights.

The elections of 1930 had all the feeling of the end of an era. The last president of the First Republic, Washington Luís, had abandoned the 'governors' policy', endangering the tacit agreement between regional elites and the federal government. But no one expected him to interrupt the alternation of power between Minas Gerais and São Paulo by choosing the president of São Paulo, Júlio Prestes, as his successor.[3] Washington Luís did not believe a republic was really governed by elections and votes; he thought governing required strict control of regional political forces. Until Júlio Prestes's candidacy was launched in 1929, it had been business as usual: the regional elites controlled the state executives and, at federal level, power was distributed between the federal government and the states.

Washington Luís's presidency had been uneventful, especially when compared to that of his predecessor, Artur Bernardes, who had governed for four years under a state of siege. The strong-armed tactics employed by the police against urban workers throughout the 1920s had reduced the number of strikes and weakened the trade unions. The ferocious opposition from the *tenentes* also seemed to have lost steam after 1927, when the last remaining participants in the *Coluna Prestes/ Miguel Costa*, after crisscrossing almost the entire country, took refuge from the Brazilian troops in Bolivia and Paraguay.[4]

Washington Luís delayed the announcement of the official candidate for as long as he could. Throughout the First Republic, the unspoken agreement between the Union and the states meant that the winner of the presidential elections was a foregone conclusion: the president of the Republic nominated the official candidate, who received the full backing of the oligarchies throughout the country, making an electoral defeat all but impossible.

The presidential succession had become a ritual for the transference of power. It included a degree of political instability, but only while necessary adjustments were negotiated between Minas Gerais and São Paulo. The wheelings and dealings between these two states took place every four years amid a good deal of intrigue and tension. Yet it was precisely this arrangement that guaranteed stability. Between 1894 and 1906 the *Paulistas* had controlled the government, and between 1906 and 1918 the *Mineiros* had taken charge. Between 1919 and 1929 power alternated between the two states. In 1926, due to the instability during Artur Bernardes's presidency, the *Mineiros* duly nominated Washington Luís to succeed to the presidency. Although born in Rio de Janeiro, he was a legitimate representative of the interests of São Paulo. And, just to be on the safe side, they appointed one of their own, *Mineiro* Fernando de Melo Viana, as candidate for vice-president.[5] In 1929 the *Mineiros* awaited the return of the favour, meanwhile preparing to occupy the Palácio do Catete once again.[6]

Historians still debate why Washington Luís decided to risk everything by confronting the state of Minas Gerais. The president was a typical product of the system he helped to destroy. He was authoritarian, vain and averse to negotiation. He believed politics should be left to the restricted elite that controlled the electoral system and ran the country. 'Listen? That was something he never did', former deputy Gilberto Amado[7] wrote in his memoirs. And he continued: 'He had a complete lack of consideration for the effect of his words and actions on others. It never occurred to him that those he repelled and rejected could be hurt, resentful, or react.'[8]

Although Washington Luís was undoubtedly arrogant, he may have had the best interests of the country in mind. He probably believed Júlio Prestes was the right man to carry out the plans for economic stability he had implemented during his government. The two main goals of the plan were to stabilize the exchange rate with the pound – at the time the standard reference for the international market – and to protect Brazil's most essential commodity – coffee from São Paulo – from being constantly affected by fluctuations.

Washington Luis's second consideration may well have been that, because São Paulo had become the richest state in the confederation, it should rule the country. He had a great deal of confidence in the dynamic economics of *Paulista* coffee production, as well as in the control of the *Paulista* coffee producers over state politics. And there was a third consideration: the potential conflict between the *Mineiro* and *Paulista* coffee producers over the policy for increasing the commodity's value.[9] Taking all of these factors into consideration, coupled with his having built a career as a statesman in São Paulo, Washington Luís may well have believed he could dispense with the agreement between the two states. After all, by then coffee production in Minas Gerais was on a much smaller scale than in São Paulo, where there had been significant economic growth. It no longer seemed reasonable to submit the interests of São Paulo, for a period of four years, to the wishes of an elite from a state that was more fragile, both economically and politically.

In May 1928 the president of Minas Gerais, Antônio Carlos Ribeiro de Andrada, immaculately turned out in top hat and tails, arrived for the inauguration ceremony of the Rio de Janeiro–São Paulo highway, a high point for the Washington Luís administration. He mounted the platform and took his seat beside the president of the Republic. The president's inaugural speech left him aghast: with a complete lack of tact, Washington Luís welcomed Júlio Prestes (then president of São Paulo) as the 'future president of the Republic'. Antônio Carlos Ribeiro de Andrada saw himself as an aristocrat, his family had fought for independence against the Portuguese, he was a direct descendant of José Bonifácio – and his reaction was typically *Mineiro*. He had understood everything, and said nothing. He returned to Belo Horizonte and began to conspire.[10] A year later, when Washington Luís officially announced Júlio Prestes's candidacy, Antônio Carlos Ribeiro de Andrada sent him a message informing him the *Mineiros* were already committed to another candidate – from the opposition.

After endless discussion, Antônio Carlos Ribeiro de Andrada did his part: he agreed to renounce his own candidacy in order to build a broad-based alignment of regional forces not associated with the coffee sector, including dissident groups like the *tenentes* who had revolted during the 1920s. The elites of the two states that had joined forces with Minas Gerais in putting forward an opposition candidate – Paraíba and Rio Grande do Sul – did not agree that coffee exportation was the most important issue in Brazil. Instead, they tended to prioritize the domestic market. By the late 1920s the regional elites in Minas Gerias, Rio Grande do Sul and Paraíba had undergone a considerable transformation: their political leaders were younger and better educated, and eager to implement plans for reform in a society bursting with political, social and cultural progress.

After the 1923 federalist revolt, the opposing political forces in Rio Grande do Sul – the liberals (also known as *chimangos*) and the federalists (*maragatos*) – both had representatives in the state administration. For twenty years the two parties had been nurturing resentment against the unequal distribution of power among the states. In the eyes of the federal government, Rio Grande de Sul would never put a man in the presidency. After all, the state economy was restricted to the domestic market and the electorate was insignificant compared to those of São Paulo and Minas Gerais. Meanwhile, members of an emerging elite in Paraíba (a small state in the northeast) had been gradually curtailing the power of the huge plantation owners – the *coronéis*. They had big dreams and looked far into the future: their plan was to politically isolate their neighbouring state, Pernambuco, and lead a group of northeastern states onto the central stage of national politics.[11]

The opposition candidate for president was Getúlio Vargas, from

Rio Grande do Sul, and the candidate for vice-president was João Pessoa, from Paraíba. Getúlio Vargas came from a cattle-breeding family in the town of São Borja, in the extreme west of the state. His politics were consistent with those of the gaucho positivists, who were the power behind the republican dictatorship in Rio Grande do Sul. Getúlio Vargas had risen rapidly in public life: he had been a state deputy, a federal deputy, leader of his state's representatives in the National Congress and Washington Luís's Finance Minister between 1926 and 1927. João Pessoa was considered an efficient, honest administrator. His family had controlled politics in Paraíba for years – his uncle, Epitácio Pessoa, had been president of the Republic from 1919 to 1922.[12]

Ever prudent, Antônio Carlos Ribeiro de Andrada kept a watchful eye on the *Mineiros* while he schemed. The association of opposition forces – called the 'liberal alliance' – had all the necessary elements to take power. The alliance members represented a wide range of backgrounds and opinions. They thus formed a viable alternative axis of power and were able to garner the support of large segments of society with their refreshing approach to politics.

The name 'liberal alliance' became popular, a household word. It suggested not only dissident forces, but also a new political agenda. Members of the alliance used the term 'liberal' to underscore their conception of Brazil's potential, their intention to modernize the country. In this context, the 'liberal' agenda included support for industry, for the political rights of hitherto excluded social groups, and for social rights – specifically the eight-hour working day, holidays, a minimum wage, protection for women in the workplace and child labour restrictions.[13]

By the second half of 1929 the liberal alliance was ready to win the hearts and minds of the Brazilian electorate by taking to the streets, literally. The *Caravanas Liberais*[14] – a complete novelty – were made up of young militants who, with considerable success, reached out to Brazilians in public forums in several of the country's largest cities. They strategically began with some of the most popular issues: amnesty for the rebel lieutenants and soldiers from the 1922 and 1927 uprisings, workers' rights, the secret ballot, diversification of the economy and drought policy for the northeast.[15]

In early January 1930 the candidate for the presidency himself, Getúlio Vargas, disembarked in Rio de Janeiro. He was the star of the liberal alliance and was there to present its platform at a rally.[16] Up until that time, political campaigns had been tepid and dull. Candidates would present the electoral programme to a roomful of guests, with a banquet to follow. The idea of breaking with this tradition and mobilizing people in a public square was entirely unheard of, and caused a minor scandal. The rally took place on 2 January in the centre of Rio de Janeiro and attracted a huge crowd. On the platform, alongside the main alliance leaders, stood other popular members of the opposition, including attorney Evaristo de Morais[17] and Deputy Maurício de Lacerda,[18] an independent-minded journalist who was popularly known as the People's Tribune. Despite the drizzle, the crowd – estimated at over 100,000 – listened enthusiastically, spellbound as Getúlio Vargas read out the opposition's complete manifesto: thirty-one pages read by a dull-looking, short, pot-bellied candidate in a continuous, deadpan drone.

Nevertheless, the opposition had no realistic chance of winning the election. Julio Prestes was openly supported by Washington Luís and the powerful coffee planters in São Paulo. In addition, the president had garnered support for his candidate from seventeen state presidents, each of whom were free to use their own particular methods for obtaining votes. As usual, both sides resorted to fraud, bribery and electoral coercion in all the states, including those that supported the opposition candidate. Sinhô, one of the most popular singers of the day and an enthusiastic supporter of Júlio Prestes, whom he had met at a party given by Oswald de Andrade and Tarsila do Amaral, satirically commented on the political system, a closed contest with the result of the election a foregone conclusion.[19] Everyone conformed, as he sang in a very popular 1930s carnaval song, 'I hear that/for our own good/Jesus has chosen/Julinho (Prestes) to lead.' And Sinhô knew what he was singing about. When the votes were counted, Júlio Prestes was declared the winner with 1,091,709 votes, against 742,794 for Getúlio Vargas. In São Paulo the result was scandalous: 350,000 votes for the government candidate, as against 30,000 for the opposition. In Minas Gerais, where the liberal alliance expected good results due to the large electorate, Antônio Carlo Ribeira de Andrada had promised he would deliver 350,000 votes, but only managed 280,000. In Paraíba, where the electorate was small, the opposition led by 20,000 votes, but it made little difference. In Pernambuco, where the oligarchies were determined to put an end to Paraíba's plans to make an alliance with other states of the northeast, Júlio Prestes received 61,000 votes, as opposed to 9,000 for the liberal alliance. Getúlio Vargas was only victorious in his home state of Rio Grande do Sul, where he received 295,000 votes as against a mere 1,000 for Júlio Prestes.[20]

Once the winner had been declared, there was little the opposition could do beyond complaining about the electoral fraud, which in most cases was impossible to prove. The victory of Júlio Prestes meant the end of the opposition's adventure and the regional elites' return to traditional politics. Even Getúlio Vargas acknowledged his opponent's victory, returned to Rio Grande do Sul, re-established contact with the new administration, and considered the episode closed.

But the impression that things would go smoothly was an illusion. The liberal alliance was a broad coalition representing the interests of a variety of politicians, ideologies, and at least two generations of regional leaders, many of whom did not think along the same lines as Getúlio Vargas. Among these younger leaders, including Virgílio de Melo Franco and Francisco Campos from Minas Gerais and João Neves da Fontoura and Oswaldo Aranha from Rio Grande do Sul, there was still enthusiasm for the opposition programme. They were also eager to carve out political careers for themselves, from under the shadow of the old generation of leaders. They refused to accept their defeat in the elections and were determined to continue the fight. Júlio Prestes may have won in the ballot box, they muttered, but Getúlio Vargas would win in battle.

The alternative of an armed conflict was not a mere pipe dream of the young civilian leaders – it had the unwavering support of the *tenentes*. This group of low-ranking officers who had survived the uprisings of the 1920s felt they had been badly treated. They longed for the power they had been denied since the proclamation of the Republic. This time they were not prepared to let it slip through their fingers without a fight. The *tenentes* were idealists, highly admired by the troops and with the sympathy of the urban middle and working classes. They had military experience and were politically restless. There was also a small group of officers who acted as go-betweens between the three dissident states and key figures inside the army. These were Juarez Távora, Siqueira Campos, Eduardo Gomes, João Alberto, Miguel Costa, Agildo Barata and Juracy Magalhães.

The close ties between young officers and the civilian leaders of the opposition were to prove a catastrophe for Washington Luís's government, even though the most prestigious of all the *tenentes* – Luís Carlos Prestes – had turned down the invitation to take military command of the liberal alliance. In 1930, Lieutenant Prestes already had mythical status. He had been the leader of the last column of military guerrillas in the 1920s, had assumed the somewhat messianic role of awakening political awareness among the poor in the depths of the interior, and he had played a cat-and-mouse game in the *sertão*, evading government troops sent out to capture him. During the time he spent in exile in Bolivia, Argentina and Uruguay, his popularity was phenomenal. For the liberal alliance leaders, he was the military commander of their dreams. But in 1930, Lieutenant Prestes surprised everyone. Rejecting both the *tenentist* movement and the liberal alliance programme, he founded an organization to fight the government – the league for revolutionary action – and he began to sympathize with the communists.[21] This was the beginning of a long political career that would first take him to Moscow and would eventually lead to his joining the Brazilian Communist Party, which he did in 1934.

Despite the adherence of almost all the lieutenants and the political will of so many civilian leaders to join an armed struggle, coordination was lacking. Still, there were conspiracies everywhere: in Porto Alegre, Belo Horizonte, Montevideo and Buenos Aires it was rumoured that there would be a *coup d'état* to prevent Júlio Prestes from taking power. *Tenentes* in exile regularly crossed the border into Rio Grande do Sul to hold meetings with young opposition leaders, and arms and ammunition were smuggled into the country from Argentina. But the main leaders of the liberal alliance remained hesitant. Getúlio Vargas, ever the opportunist, watched and bided his time. Meanwhile Antônio Carlos Ribeiro de Andrada, nearing the end of his term, expressed uncertainty regarding support for the rebels in other states. He was soon to pass on the presidency of Minas Gerais to his successor, Olegário Maciel. So, while the conspiracy was kept alive, the military offensive was put on hold. The liberal alliance needed some external pressure to restore their motivation and to serve as the spark to ignite the rebellion.

That event came in the afternoon of 26 July, when the former vice-presidential candidate João Pessoa was murdered with three point-blank shots while in the company of fellow politicians in Recife's elegant *Confeitaria Glória*.[22] It was not a rival contracted murder – as commonly referred to, even today, in the northeast. The murderer was a lawyer called João Dantas, who was arrested at the scene and confessed he had committed the crime for personal reasons. A few weeks prior, the Paraíba police had searched his office, confiscated documents and, with João Pessoa's consent, given the material to the local press. The newspaper *A União*, the official voice of the state government, had published all of it on the front page. The material included erotic love letters exchanged between João Dantas and his lover Anayde Beiriz. Ms Anayde was twenty-five years old, single and an independent-minded teacher – she was a poet, a feminist and smoked cigarettes. She was devastated by the scandal and ended up taking her own life.

But João Pessoa's murder was also political. João Dantas was an ally of Colonel José Pereira, the powerful chief of the hinterland municipality of Princesa, on the border between Paraíba and Pernambuco. Colonel Pereira had led an armed revolt against measures adopted by João Pessoa to restrict the autonomy of the powerful *coronéis* (oligarchs).[23] The Princesa Revolt, as it became known, began in February 1930 – five months before João Pessoa was murdered – and attracted a large following. Under Colonel Pereira's command, the rebels occupied the whole area and declared independence from Paraíba. They repelled repeated attacks by the public force – as the military police was called at the time – sent by the state president to suppress the revolt, and José Pereira appointed himself governor of the 'Free Territory of Princesa'.

Not only did the rebels occupy the *sertão*, they also received outside support. Financial backing, weapons and information flowed into Princesa from Pernambuco, Rio Grande do Norte and, most significantly, from São Paulo where there was great interest in destabilizing João Pessoa's government. Washington Luís observed these events carefully, waiting for the ideal moment to decree federal intervention in the state and send government troops to crush the liberal alliance base in the northeast. At the same time groups in Belo Horizonte and Porto Alegre were planning to intervene on João Pessoa's behalf. Both Minas Gerais and Rio Grande do Sul found ways to send ammunition to strengthen the public force troops in Paraíba: thousands of cartridges were hidden inside cans of prunes and peaches, barrels of suet and packages of beef jerky. Antônio Carlos Ribeiro de Andrada even went as far as to send the single-engine plane *Garoto*, which belonged to the Minaws Gerais public force of Minas Gerais, to drop homemade bombs on Princesa, along with pamphlets urging the rebels to surrender.

With João Pessoa's murder, the regional crisis suddenly took on national importance. The liberal alliance seized the opportunity to accuse the federal government of inciting the rebellion as an excuse to intervene in Paraíba. They claimed that, out of revenge, Washington Luís had planned the murder from afar. João Pessoa's murder shocked the country and his death left the state virtually ungovernable – a situation the opposition immediately realized could be used to further their cause. João Pessoa's body was displayed in Paraíba adorned with the state presidential sash and then taken by ship to Rio de Janeiro, where dozens of members of the liberal alliance lined up to pay their last respects, in a direct affront to Washington Luís. Before the funeral cortege set off, Deputy Maurício de Lacerda jumped onto a cart beside the coffin and, seizing a megaphone, addressed the excited crowd: 'In the coffin you see before you, lies not the body of a great citizen, but the corpse of a nation! [. . .] *Gaúchos*, *Mineiros*, the time has come to fulfil your promise. The people are ready to die for freedom!'[24]

The civil and military revolt began on 3 October 1930. The military campaign was launched simultaneously in Minas Gerais and Rio Grande do Sul, followed a few hours later by Paraíba. The campaign was commanded by Lieutenant-Colonel Pedro Aurélio de Góes Monteiro, an officer highly respected within the military. Among his colleagues, he was considered a competent leader, but he was little known to the public at large. The first phase of his plan was to neutralize the federal troops – by winning them over to his side or by attacking their garrisons.[25] His strategy was simple: take barracks loyal to the federal government by surprise and, with widespread support among the subaltern officers, win over the sergeants – who controlled the troops. It worked: from captain downwards, the majority of the army supported the liberal alliance. But the greatest military support for the alliance came from the powerful state public forces. These were small but very well-equipped autonomous armies that took orders from the state presidents. And they were soon joined by battalions of armed civilian volunteers.

In Minas Gerais, all of the army garrisons resisted the rebels. In Belo Horizante, from 3 to 8 October, the twelfth infantry regiment was the state stronghold and was bombarded, day and night, by 4,000 public force men. They finally surrendered in the afternoon of 8 October, the confrontation having spread panic throughout the city. With the strategic position of the barracks, the constant firing from the trenches and the explosion of hand grenades, rumours began to circulate that the twelfth regiment had the artillery power to bombard the city. Panic increased when the São Paulo public force dropped two bombs from a military plane aimed at the seat of the Minas Gerais state government, the Palácio da Liberdade. Both missed their target. The first fell into a washtub in a house adjoining the palace, and the second, into the main square, the Praça da Liberdade, just opposite the police secretariat (Secretaria de Segurança). To the relief of the townspeople, neither bomb exploded.[26]

From its base in Paraíba, the liberal alliance launched attacks on the other states in the northeast. The commander of military operations in the region was Juarez Távora, who had participated in the *tenente* revolts in the 1920s. In March 1930 he had made a spectacular escape from the Fort of Santa Cruz in Guanabara Bay, where he had been imprisoned. In the middle of the night, accompanied by two other officers, he had descended the fortress walls using an improvised rope, swum out to a boat anchored offshore and disappeared out to sea. He reappeared two months later at the head of a group of rebel soldiers in a series of successful surprise attacks on public buildings in Recife.[27] In three weeks the rebels managed to take control of the states of Pernambuco, Alagoas, Ceará, Piauí, Maranhão and Rio Grande do Norte. The only state that still adhered to the federal government was Bahia, even though Salvador was under siege by the forces of the alliance.

In Rio Grande do Sul it took the rebels just over a week to gain military control. After neutralizing the government troops, General Góes Monteiro put his troops onto trains headed to São Paulo. The chances of success were high, and this time Getúlio Vargas openly joined the liberal alliance and, dressed in a khaki uniform, took the civilian command of the rebellion, joining the troops aboard the train. The most serious confrontation between the two sides was expected to occur in Itararé, on the border between Paraná and São Paulo. The city, in the interior of the state of São Paulo, had crucial railway lines leading to both Rio de Janeiro and the city of São Paulo. The location was of great strategic importance.

The country held its breath and all eyes were on Itararé as the newspapers announced 'the greatest battle of Latin America'. The government boasted that its forces were unbeatable: it had six thousand troops from the São Paulo public force and the army was entrenched with orders to block the rebels' progress at any cost. But the battle never happened. After establishing their lines of defence and exchanging a few shots, both sides decided to wait for an end to the torrential rains and a better definition of the political situation. It may have been a sensible decision, but with the prevailing climate in the country the public felt betrayed.

Washington Luís was slow to react. It was only on 10 October that he informed the country of the revolt.[28] He was also slow to accept that the size and extent of the rebellion were larger than he had thought. He was facing three problems simultaneously: he needed to contain the speed with which the rebel forces were approaching Rio, dispel the hesitancy of the government troops, and deal with the economic crisis of 1929, which had brought inflation, unemployment and currency devaluation. It was a grim picture, and the measures Washington Luís adopted, although tough, proved to be inadequate. He had established a state of siege, censorship of the press, and an extended public holiday (until 21 October) – to avoid a run on the banks. He had also instigated a campaign to repress the rumours and had called up the military reserves. The number of troops at the government's command was falling rapidly and both the army and the navy were reconsidering where their loyalties lay. Without decisive action from the military commanders, either the troops would be defeated by the rebels or the number of desertions to the liberal alliance would lead to a collapse in the hierarchy.

Washington Luís may have lost everything, but he would not give in. The president's official residence, the Palácio Guanabara, was surrounded by barbed wire and in constant danger of being bombarded; the cannons of the forts of Copacabana, Leme and São João regularly fired warning shots demanding his resignation; his generals had given him their last ultimatum and the whole city was threatening to revolt – but he did not waver. 'I won't resign! I'll only leave here in pieces!' he yelled at his ministers.[29] But no such sacrifice was required of him. He was deposed at seven in the morning on 24 October, less than thirty days before the end of his mandate. He was arrested and taken to the Copacabana Fort, from where, a month later, he went into exile in Europe.

On 3 November the provisional junta, formed of two generals – Augusto Tasso Fragoso and João de Deus Mena Barreto – and a rear admiral – José Isaías de Noronha – handed the keys of government to Getúlio Vargas. The First Republic was over. The Revolution of 1930 is seen by historians as a pivotal event in the history of Brazil[30] – less for the rebellion itself than for the results it produced: in the economy, in politics, in culture and in the society as a whole, it radically changed Brazil.

THE PROVISIONAL GOVERNMENT

Getúlio Vargas put away his military uniform, put on a suit and, adjusting his tie, walked up the steps of the Palácio do Catete to take office as the head of the provisional government. But the transformation was far greater than a mere change of clothing: with Getúlio Vargas in office all power passed to the Executive, which could now radically intervene in the political system. The National Congress, the State Legislative Assemblies and the Municipal Chambers were dissolved, the politicians elected during the First Republic lost their posts, the presidents of the states were replaced by *interventores* (appointed governors), and the opposition newspapers were censored. For the first time since the 1824 Constitution, all government posts were held by unelected civilians or military officials.[31] In a state of euphoria after the alliance's victory in the northeast, Juarez Távora arrived in Rio de Janeiro and declared that, from then on, Brazil's government would be neither democratic nor liberal: 'I support a dictatorship, with all its implications.' His enthusiasm knew no bounds: 'Dictatorship without limits, until everyone can verify, by acts and not by deeds, the regeneration and rehabilitation of our political and administrative customs.'[32]

Getúlio Vargas had no intention of risking the loss of what he had conquered. He knew that if he called elections the regional elites, who had maintained their power in the states, would win. In order to institutionalize the new order the political system had to be transformed. That meant a far-reaching programme of social, economic and administrative reforms needed to be carried out. It was an ambitious project that could not be implemented overnight, but not even Juarez Távora could have imagined in 1930 that the dictatorship he embraced was to last for a full fifteen years, with a brief respite between 1934 and 1937. However that may be, in his inaugural speech Getúlio Vargas presented a radical programme, which included almost everything the liberal alliance supported. A stream of decrees brought the changes about: amnesty for the *tenentes*, restructuring of the army, the creation of the Ministries of Labour, of Industry and Trade, and of Education and Public Health. There were also changes made to the teaching profession and the public education system.

Getúlio Vargas's greatest priority was the new labour policy.[33] In this area he revealed the two sides of his political self. First, he created worker protection laws: an eight-hour working day; female and child labour protection; holidays; worker registration documents; sick leave; and retirement pensions. Then he repressed any attempt by workers to create organizations outside government control and was especially aggressive when it came to dealing with any communist activities. He dissolved all autonomous trade unions. Unions from then on had to be subordinate to the state. And last but not least, he excluded rural workers from the benefits of the new labour legislation.

Although the government was provisional, President Vargas steered well away from two issues: the summoning of a Constituent Assembly and the date for new presidential elections. Under the new regime, none of the representatives, neither in the Executive nor the Legislature, were elected. However, as a demonstration of the government's good intentions, in 1932 a new, modern and democratic electoral law was introduced – but its implementation was continually put off. The new law created an Electoral Court to oversee elections and guarantee the secrecy of the vote. It thus put an end to the idea – popular with republicans of the seventeenth and eighteenth centuries – that voters were required to make their choices public.[34]

With these two measures, electoral fraud practices frequently used during the First Republic were not only illegal, but were virtually impossible. The secret ballot protected voters from being coerced by regional elites during state elections; professional judges of the Electoral Court inspected the election process; they oversaw the counting of the votes and declared the winners. The law also represented a tremendous victory for women: they earned the right to vote and to stand for election. The 1930 revolution had been supported by female battalions who were active in the rearguard of the military offensive. One such example was the João Pessoa female battalion, founded by Elvira Komel, a twenty-three-year-old lawyer from Minas Gerais, in which there were approximately 8,000 women from fifty-two cities enrolled.[35]

Despite this legislation, there was very little faith in democracy in the Brazil envisioned by Getúlio Vargas. The liberal alliance had promised to refound the Republic and kept its promise by implementing a far-reaching programme of reforms. But the major political actors representing the alliance were not a product of democracy, nor was it their vocation. They believed the democratic system laid down by the 1891 Constitution had failed because of the 'governors' policy', and they now opted for a strong, centralized government. The coalition that took power in 1930 was heterogeneous. The members disagreed on virtually everything – except for who their adversaries were. From the first days of the provisional government, they struggled with the dilemma of how to reform the Republic without destroying its foundations.

The proposal of the *tenentes* was to control the state police forces, re-equip the armed forces and prioritize industry, especially steel. They joined the middle classes and urban workers, who swelled the ranks of the liberal alliance, in favour of labour-market regulation and of social legislation. But they were against the idea of expanding democracy and openly favoured a state-controlled society. The young civilian leaders were mostly motivated by the chance to make a political career. Meanwhile the elites who had joined the alliance (from Minas Gerais, Rio Grande do Sul and Paraíba) wanted to increase their power in the federal government, while maintaining their regional power bases – in other words, to maintain Brazil's agrarian structure. All of the groups wanted to become the most powerful within the coalition and thus take control of the government.[36]

As for Getúlio Vargas, he did not show his cards. He planned to remain exactly where he was, in power, and to achieve this he conducted politics in the way he would have run a business. He followed his own rules, making unexpected political alliances when he thought they would serve his purpose. He resorted to distributing favours and compensations. And he would postpone final decisions until the time was ripe for him to arbitrate the disputes between the coalition forces that sustained his government.

FOR SÃO PAULO AND AGAINST BRAZIL:
THE CIVIL WAR OF 1932

In 1932, however, Getúlio Vargas's political astuteness seems to have deserted him. Increasingly suspicious, he planned to prolong the provisional government so long that it would become permanent; the liberal alliance, above all in Minas Gerais and Rio Grande do Sul, joined forces with the opposition and insisted that elections be held immediately. The newly formed 'leagues for a constituent assembly' organized protests in all the main cities. The atmosphere in Brazil became increasingly tense. However, Getúlio Vargas's main adversary was the state of São Paulo.[37] The rebels' 1930 victory had removed the *Paulistas* from power and turned the richest state in Brazil into a formidable enemy. Their anger increased as the list of what was seen as Getúlio Vargas's provocations grew longer. They were frustrated over São Paulo's loss of control of Brazil's coffee policy – which had been taken away from the Coffee Institute of the State of São Paulo and given to the National Coffee Council, an institution created by the federal government to confront the international economic crisis. And they were furious the state had lost autonomy due to the appointment of the *interventores*. The *interventores* were appointed governors, from different regions of the country and seen as intruders and puppets controlled by the federal government. To make matters worse, the *interventor* in São Paulo was João Alberto Lins de Barros, who was from the northeast and had been handpicked from among the *tenentes*.

Between October 1930 and the first few months of 1932, Getúlio Vargas had been obliged to appoint a succession of four *interventores* for São Paulo; the *Paulistas* were determined to show him that they were ungovernable. But the situation was to go from bad to worse. In 1932 powerful state politicians agreed to adopt a new programme. In a clear move to antagonize the federal government, they waved the constitutionalist flag, demanding the immediate summoning of a Constituent Assembly. They wanted revenge. Resentment and feelings of regional loyalty ran high. 'São Paulo is the locomotive that pulls the decaying old wagons of the federation!'[38] boasted Oswald de Andrade. And the protesters in the streets went further: 'For São Paulo with Brazil, if possible. For São Paulo against Brazil, if we must!'[39]

Not all *Paulistas* were in favour of secession, but they agreed that Getúlio Vargas's strong, centralized government, which had taken away the state's political and economic autonomy, must be confronted. The demand for a Constituent Assembly meant there would have to be new elections. If that were to transpire, São Paulo would recover political control of the Republic. This combination of wanting to summon a Constituent Assembly and to overthrow the government led to a movement that became known as the 1932 constitutionalist revolution. On 9 July 1932 around 20,000 soldiers – from the federal garrisons and the state public forces – took up arms against the Vargas government. The population of São Paulo, above all in the capital, joined the fight: thousands of civilians, including students from the law school (located in the Largo de São Francisco), enlisted in the volunteer battalions; factories adapted their production lines to make weapons; Italian and Syrian immigrants cared for the wounded and the Catholic clergy gave its blessings to the fighters. The 'Paulista cause' was defended with a fervour that had never been seen in the state before. Thousands of women, rich and poor, gave their jewellery to the campaign called Gold for the Good of São Paulo, which was set up to help fund the cost of the war. Between July and September approximately 90,000 wedding rings were handed over to the state for melting down.

Only the factory workers did not join the revolt.[40] In the state where the largest number of industries in the country was concentrated, the workers did not 'run to the rescue'. They did not believe this uprising would help their cause; and the regional elite was afraid that if the workers rose up the situation could get out of control. Throughout the conflict the industrialists kept a close watch on their factories to prevent a workers' revolt, and kept as many of their leaders as possible locked up.

São Paulo only had one chance of victory: to mount a military attack of major proportions against Rio de Janeiro before Getúlio Vargas had time to organize his forces.[41] But the *Paulista* troops moved slowly: they were waiting for backup from Minas Gerais and Rio Grande do Sul, where discontent with the federal government had also reached boiling point. They were also convinced the military barracks and garrisons in Rio de Janeiro would rise up against Getúlio Vargas. The war started well for the *Paulistas*: the rebels controlled the whole of the state, cutting off access to the Paraíba valley; they attacked the federal forces in Minas Gerais and blocked the railway tunnel on the line that crossed the Mantiqueira mountains. In a scene that could have been taken from a film, agents of the São Paulo government secretly purchased ten combat planes in Chile. They then hired North American pilots who managed to land them without being observed in Mato Grosso, and, after a series of mishaps, delivered them to the rebels.

But their luck was not to last. While the leaders of Minas Gerais and Rio Grande do Sul were furious with the centralizing policy of the provisional government, they were not prepared to run the risk of overthrowing a government that they themselves had put in power. They remained loyal to President Vargas and were later to send troops to invade São Paulo. Getúlio Vargas left the military strategy to General Góes Monteiro, who began the preparations for the attack. He planned the defence of Rio de Janeiro, where he suppressed an attempted *coup d'état*, and sent 80,000 men from the army and the navy, mostly brought in from the north and the northeast, against the 70,000 rebels. The state of São Paulo was surrounded by troops, the port of Santos was blocked and government planes fired on the rebel trenches. From north to south, the attention of the whole country was on the '*Paulista* war'.

São Paulo surrendered on 1 October 1932. Characteristically, Getúlio Vargas was quick to act. He arrested the rebels, expelled the army officers, revoked the civil rights of the leading protagonists, exiled the state political and military leaders and reorganized the public force, reducing its status from a military to a police organization. The *Paulista* elite had been defeated. Getúlio Vargas took the opportunity to consolidate his alliance with the military: in the mid-term he promised to re-equip the army, and in the long term to create a national weapons industry. He then negotiated with the state of São Paulo: he nominated a *Paulista* civilian to be the *interventor*, instructed the Banco do Brasil to take over the war bonds that had been issued by the São Paulo banks, and confirmed the summoning of a Constituent Assembly for 3 May 1933.[42]

A SHORT-LIVED DEMOCRACY

Since there were no national political parties and the opposition – the regional elites – was no longer in a position to manipulate votes, the elections for the Constituent Assembly brought a series of novelties. It became easier for authorities to circulate; there were several new parties with far-reaching, regional membership; it seemed like there had been a rebirth in politics.[43] The Constituent Assembly had a little bit of everything. The opening session was on 15 November 1933, in Palácio Tiradentes, the seat of the National Congress. There were a number of new deputies, elected mainly through the new system, which allowed for independent candidates (no party affiliation). There was also a large bloc of deputies who supported the government, mostly due to the work of the state *interventores* appointed by Getúlio Vargas. São Paulo politicians joined forces to elect a considerable number of deputies opposed to the government. The Catholic Church managed to elect a fair-sized group to represent its interests, and there was one, solitary female deputy – Doctor Carlota Pereira de Queirós. The Constituent Assembly worked for eight months, promulgating the new constitution on 16 July 1934. The next day they elected Getúlio Vargas as president of the Republic, by indirect vote.

Although the constitution granted Getúlio Vargas a new presidential term and approved everything that had been done by the provisional government, President Vargas was furious at some of its clauses, which he told his most intimate circle were 'monstrous'.[44] They were not; but they eliminated his power to act unilaterally. The new text submitted the Executive to Legislative oversight, revoked the right of the provisional government leader to bypass Congress, and granted complete independence to the Federal Court of Auditors. And, to enrage President Vargas even further, the deputies limited the presidential term of office to four years, with no possibility of re-election.

The majority of the newly elected deputies were in favour of a more modern, democratic system of government. To this end, the new constitution provided for the rationalization of authority, federalism, strong political institutions, and the inclusion of new social sectors in the electoral process. But it also exposed the limitations of this new republic that had remained in place after 1930: it altered nothing in the country's agrarian structure and maintained the exclusion of rural workers from labour benefits. The illiterate remained disenfranchised and immigrants' rights were restricted. The government could expel any foreigners considered a danger to public order or to the national interest. The text also implicitly granted the state unlimited powers by legalizing the right to declare a state of siege, as the government deemed necessary. Furthermore, the government could exercise censorship for all types of publication at will. Nevertheless, the 1934 Constitution broke new ground by increasing opportunities for civic participation. And yet, it was only to last for less than two years. In Brazil, like in other countries all around the world, the further the decade of the 1930s advanced, the more sombre the atmosphere became. A radical change was under way that was shifting priorities. Democracy was no longer at the top of the list of preferred political systems.

The aftermath of the 1929 New York stock exchange crash, which seemingly proved capitalism could only work with state intervention, was a period of crisis. There were other circumstances, though, that led to the proliferation of dictatorships. A far more threatening storm was on the horizon. On 30 January 1933, President Hindenburg of Germany appointed Adolf Hitler as chancellor, and barbarity came to power under the guise of modernity.[45] The Nazi Party was intolerant of opposition, militaristic, authoritarian, and had a penchant for genocide. On 27 February the German parliament (the Reichstag) went up in flames, and along with it, the hopes for Germany's democratic future. In addition to the Nazis, terrifying new forms of totalitarian government emerged in Europe – Stalinism in the Soviet Union and fascism in Italy. There was a collapse of the old, autocratic empires, which were plagued by civil war and economic crises.

In Brazil the fascist movement was called *Integralismo*, and the Brazilian Fascist Party, the *Ação Integralista Brasileira* (AIB, Brazilian Integralist Action), was founded in 1932.[46] It was the first party in Brazil whose aim was to stir up support among the masses. The AIB achieved this through inclusive national politics, belief in the party, in cooperation among special interest groups, and in state dominance. The party vigorously espoused anti-Semitism, which was already common among Brazilians. Support for the *integralistas* came from the urban middle classes, above all from civil servants, the clergy, liberal professionals, merchants, industrialists and even poets, and from regions colonized by German and Italian settlers. The Italian Embassy offered guidance and financial aid. And there was a group of intellectuals willing and able to produce a Brazilianized form of fascist ideology – Plínio Salgado,[47] Miguel Reale[48] and Gustavo Barroso among them. When all was said and done, the *integralista* party had militancy on their side.

In October 1934, in the city of São Paulo, a single march commanded by the AIB brought together around 40,000 *integralistas*, who marched in military formation, stomping their boots. The astonished *Paulistas* gathered to watch them go by. The procession was impeccable, minutely choreographed, with the men in closed ranks and arms extended, dressed in green shirts with armbands bearing the party insignia – the Greek letter sigma showing that *integralismo* represented the 'sum total' of all the Brazilian people – and with their banners unfurled in the sunlight. At the height of its popularity in 1937, the AIB had between 100,000 and 200,000 followers nationwide, out of a total population of 40 million. It was the public face of fascism. Less visible, however, were the closer ties with fascism among members of the government and the armed forces.[49] General Góes Monteiro, for example, the most prestigious military leader at that time, was convinced the Italian fascist model was the best alternative for Brazil.

On this point President Vargas was in complete agreement with the general. Getúlio Vargas considered *integralismo* a natural form of government, with its exaltation of nationalist values, emphasis on class collaboration, and belief in the socio-political organization of society by major interest groups – all of which appealed to his authoritarian convictions. But that was as far as his support for the *integralistas* went. While General Góes Monteiro believed the army should have full monopoly of weaponry and rejected any form of paramilitary outfits, President Vargas had no interest in supporting a party whose intention was to govern Brazil in his place – and the sooner the better. The *integralistas* confirmed his suspicions by organizing a hierarchical structure parallel to his government, which included the creation of paramilitary militias, the use of modern technology for propaganda – photography, radio and cinema – as well as populist welfare programmes in certain states and municipalities. By this time President Vargas realized the *integralista* party could not be ignored. Characteristically, he planned to use the fascist machine to his own advantage, to transform the *integralista* movement into a tactical ally against the new opposition groups – in particular the *Aliança Nacional Libertadora* or ANL (National Alliance for Freedom) and the communists.

The National Alliance for Freedom was created by a minority faction among the *tenentes* who either had not joined Getúlio Vargas or who were disenchanted with his government, or both.[50] The group, which included Miguel Costa,[51] Herculino Cascardo, Roberto Sisson,

João Cabanas, Carlos Leite, André Trifino and Agildo Barata, was small, but all of its members had participated in the 1920s uprisings, continued to be politically active, and were in favour of social reform. They wanted to change the direction the Republic had taken after the 1930 victory of the liberal alliance.

The *tenentes* followed these political developments attentively, and realized the fight against fascism was the only realistic option. They saw the emergence of the *integralistas* as an extension of European fascism and were concerned about the government's sympathy for the movement. They wanted to build a broad coalition that would unite the opposition in a reformist and anti-fascist movement. The idea was to reinforce and make additions to the liberal alliance platform: suspension of payment on the public debt; nationalization of public services; agrarian reform; wage increases; guarantee of individual rights – including religious freedom – and eradication of racism.

In early 1935 the leaders of the National Alliance for Freedom planned a special inauguration event. It took place in downtown Rio de Janeiro at the João Caetano Theatre, which had been built for Dom João VI and was the oldest and largest theatre in the city. The *tenentes* chose it for being such a symbolic forum – Brazil's first constitution had been signed there in in 1824. In spite of the importance of the venue and the carefully laid plans, the leading figures of the party were still taken aback at the astounding turnout. They had positioned themselves on the stage and, when the heavy red velvet curtains were opened, they were momentarily aghast. Around 10,000 people had come to hear the proposals of the National Alliance for Freedom: there were people standing between the rows of seats, crowded into the boxes, sitting on the steps and hanging from the balustrades. At the end of the ceremony Carlos Lacerda jumped onto the stage and brazenly put forward the name of Luís Carlos Prestes to be the honorary president of the National Alliance for Freedom. The crowd went wild and started to cheer and applaud. Carlo Lacerda, son of the populist leader Maurício Lacerda, was at the time a student, a member of the communist youth and already a gifted orator.

The communists had planned the whole thing, knowing full well the position did not even exist. They were equally confident the proposal would be impossible to turn down. Luís Carlos Prestes was the most prestigious political leader in the country, a popular hero, and a man with enormous charisma. He was charming, affable, and was highly convincing in any debate; furthermore, his shining eyes seemed to prove his sincerity. He was also authoritarian, vain and intolerant – but these characteristics were only known to a few. At that time he was seemingly invincible. The communists were following the lead from Moscow: the communist parties around the world were supposed to support all popular fronts against fascism, the Nazi threat and the danger of war. The strategy was a success, with popular front governments being elected in Chile, France and Spain. Through the nomination of Luís Carlos Prestes, the Communist Party had managed to join the National Alliance for Freedom.

The National Alliance for Freedom was a coalition for the masses. It acted constitutionally, with four hundred offices spread around the country. The movement had the infrastructure to support major campaigns in favour of citizens' rights and rallies that attracted thousands of people. The Communist Party, on the other hand, was a tiny, clandestine organization, with very little public support, but which planned to turn the popular fronts into a vehicle for revolt.[52] At the time the climate in the country favoured political protests. Workers in Rio de Janeiro and São Paulo frequently went on strike, there was dissatisfaction within the armed forces, insurrections in the states, and fierce confrontations in the streets between the National Alliance for Freedom and the *integralistas*. Meanwhile President Vargas was worried about the political unrest and astonished by the rapid growth of the National Alliance for Freedom – so he bided his time and waited for the right moment to intervene.

In 1935, on 5 July, the anniversary of the 1922 and 1924 *tenente* uprisings, the National Alliance for Freedom met for the last time at its headquarters in Largo da Carioca, in Rio de Janeiro. Political rallies had just been banned. The government's excuse for the ban was an inflammatory manifesto read at the National Alliance for Freedom's most recent rally. The manifesto, written by Luís Carlos Prestes, had been read aloud by none other than Carlos Lacerda: 'Brazilians! You, who have nothing to lose, but the immense wealth of Brazil to gain! Tear Brazil from the grip of imperialism and its lackeys! Everyone – join the fight for Brazil's liberation! Down with fascism! Down with Vargas's odious government! Long live the revolutionary government of the people! All power to the National Alliance for Freedom!'[53] This summons from Luís Carlos Prestes for the people to take up arms against the government was all that President Vargas needed to hear. The following day the National Alliance for Freedom was declared illegal and shut down by presidential decree.

Miguel Costa was furious, and he replied to Luís Carlos Prestes's manifesto with a very critical letter: 'You [. . .] perhaps because you were misinformed [. . .] launched your manifesto with the slogan "All power to the National Alliance for Freedom" [. . .] You should never have made this statement when the government still had the power to react.'[54] He was right. The text manifesto promised easy victory, oblivious to the actual political situation. It was contemptuous regarding President Vargas's ability to react, compromised the National Alliance of Freedom, and sorely overestimated the military capacity for the planned uprising. But the manifesto was not the result of Luís Carlos Prestes's ineptitude in assessing the conditions of the time; it was a directive from the Communist International in Moscow, the Soviet agency that instructed communist parties around the world on how to prepare for revolution. The directors of the Communist International knew very little about South America and even less about Brazil, whose situation they saw as being identical to that of China – an immense semi-colonial country with a central government ill-equipped to control the whole of its territory and thus susceptible to regional uprisings.[55] The Soviets were confident in Luís Carlos Prestes, who had lived in Moscow since 1931, because of his military experience and popular prestige. They had probably begun developing their plans for Latin America in 1933, with Luís Carlos Prestes at the centre. He was meant to lead the insurrection in Brazil. Between the end of 1934 and the first months of 1935 the Communist International sent personnel to Brazil, including specialists in explosives, sabotage and street protests. They also sent technicians to teach the Brazilians how to code and decode messages and radio transmissions, as well as an agent responsible for financing the Brazilian operation.

In March 1935 the organization transferred its Latin American office from Buenos Aires to Rio de Janeiro under the direction of Arthur Ewert. Mr Ewert had been a deputy in the German parliament in the 1920s and had worked for the international communist movement for years. In April 1935, Luís Carlos Prestes clandestinely returned to Brazil accompanied by Olga Benário, who was later to become his common-law wife. Ms Benário had been recruited by the IV Department of the Red

Army Joint Chiefs of Staff – the Soviet military secret service – and was sent with Luís Carlos Prestes to guarantee his safety. In November 1935 armed uprisings broke out at three different locations in Brazil. It was the first time in the history of the country that the communists had taken up arms to fight for their revolution.

The first uprising began on 23 November in the twenty-first gunners' battalion barracks in Natal, the capital city of Rio Grande do Norte state. The rebellion spread with surprising speed. With popular support and very little resistance, the communists managed to occupy the city for four days. In Pernambuco the twenty-ninth gunners' battalion, stationed in the town of Jaboatão dos Guararapes, revolted in the early hours of 24 November and marched on Recife under the command of two officers and an extraordinary communist leader: the then sergeant Gregório Bezerra. Throughout three days of fighting, Sergeant Bezerra coordinated the rebels and went from garrison to garrison in search of weapons and support, until he was forced to withdraw from combat after being shot while trying to capture, near singlehandedly, the headquarters of the seventh military zone. But in both Recife, where the threat of air bombardment terrified everyone, and Natal, the rebels acted alone. There were not enough of them to confront the government army troops deployed from Bahia, Ceará and Paraíba. By 27 November the rebels were on the run and the uprising in the northeast was over.[56]

The third and last uprising took place in Rio de Janeiro, in the early hours of 27 November, in two units of the military elite – the military aviation school, located at Campo dos Afonsos, and the third infantry regiment.[57] The rebels' plan was to steal and take off in aviation school planes, but they did not have the resources to protect the airport and were overcome by government troops. The strategy at the third infantry regiment was even more daring: the plan was to take over the barracks and then proceed to Guanabara Palace and arrest the president. But the plan failed. The third infantry regiment was located at the foot of the Sugar Loaf, occupying a narrow stretch of land between the sea and the hills, with only one point of entry. It was like walking into an ambush. The rebels took longer than planned to occupy the barracks, and in the early hours of the morning they found themselves surrounded by government troops. Besieged and under heavy artillery fire, after eighteen hours of resistance they realized that all was lost.

During the uprisings in Natal and Recife in November, President Vargas had managed to convince Congress to approve a state of siege. In December he increased the pressure: the government created the Committee for the Repression of Communism, General Góes Monteiro proposed the suspension of individual rights, and the deputies agreed to decree a state of war for ninety days – a measure that was renewed repeatedly until July 1937. The government could now act unfettered and implemented its brutal, large-scale programme of searches and arrests, which led to the imprisonment of thousands of people – members of the National Alliance for Freedom, communists, their sympathizers and anyone who the police considered suspect, including the popular mayor of Rio de Janeiro, Pedro Ernesto.[58]

The prisons were overcrowded and Brazilian navy warships were transformed into floating jails. Trials were brief, there were virtually no defence lawyers, and those found guilty were sent to the government penitentiaries on Ilha Grande and Fernando de Noronha. The writer Graciliano Ramos,[59] one of the numerous sympathizers of the Communist Party, was arrested in Maceió in March 1936 and taken to Rio de Janeiro, confined to the ship's hold. From there he was sent to the correctional colony on Ilha Grande, where he was detained without being charged until January 1937. After his release, he wrote Memórias do Cárcere,[60] which denounced the immensurable violence of the Vargas regime. The book, published posthumously in 1953, rescues his fellow prisoners from anonymity, relates the difficulties of an intellectual adapting to life in a Brazilian jail, and denounces the degradation of the prison system. The head warden of the Ilha Grande penitentiary used to yell at the prisoners: 'Here there are no rights. Listen carefully. No rights. [. . .] You're not here to be rehabilitated. No one will be rehabilitated: you have all come here to die.'[61]

President Vargas knew about the torture and the police violence; he was well acquainted with the ferocity of his government's repression. He was also regularly informed in advance of the communists' plans to spark revolts in distant parts of the country. One of the men sent by Moscow, Johnny (or Johann) de Graaf, who was in charge of teaching the rebels fighting techniques, was a double agent. He passed on information to Alfred Hutt, a director of the electricity company Light, in Rio de Janeiro, who was an agent of MI6, the British secret service. Alfred Hutt passed the information to the British ambassador; it was then examined in London and sent to President Vargas's Foreign Minister, Oswaldo Aranha, who in turn informed the president.[62] Between December 1935 and March 1936 the police, using the information supplied by Johnny de Graaf, managed to penetrate the Communist International, and finally discovered Luís Carlos Prestes's hiding place. Everyone found there was arrested. The body of Victor Baron, the soviet agent in charge of clandestine radio transmissions, was thrown out of a police headquarters window in Rio de Janeiro to simulate a suicide. He had been tortured to death. After long sessions of interrogations and torture, Arthur Ewert went insane – he died in a hospital in East Berlin in 1959. Luís Carlos Prestes was imprisoned for nine years, much of it in solitary confinement. Olga Benário, who was Jewish and communist, was deported to Nazi Germany. Although she was pregnant, she was turned over to the Gestapo and died in a gas chamber at the Bernburg concentration camp.

Now that President Vargas had eliminated the National Alliance for Freedom and jailed the communists, he set about liquidating what remained of the left-wing opposition to his government. His plan was simple: to put an end to the democratic regime established by the 1934 Constitution. In 1937, on the eve of the presidential elections, Getúlio Vargas imposed an additional eight years of dictatorship on the Brazilian people. And he did so with virtually no resistance. His cool head and tremendous capacity for political calculation – one step back, then another two steps forward – made this possible. He manipulated the deputies in Congress and the presidents of the states – notably Flores da Cunha, president of Rio Grande do Sul and a former ally who was now in exile. He also controlled every detail of his potential successors' political campaigns, chose his battles carefully and took advantage of the fragility of Brazil's democracy.[63] Rather than a series of sweeping victories, President Vargas built alliances one by one, above all with the army. He had the support of two generals: the head of the joint chiefs of staff, General Góes Monteiro, and General Eurico Gaspar Dutra, who had close ties to the *integralistas* and had been appointed Minister of War in 1936. The generals wanted a modern army and a weapons industry, in exchange for which they were prepared to support the *coup d'état* and sustain the dictatorship. The last important preparatory step was to convince the public that, after the 1935 uprisings, catastrophe was looming. In his radio address at midnight on 31 December, Getúlio

Vargas warned the country that 'Communism constitutes the most dangerous enemy of Christian civilization.'[64]

The combination of censorship, repression and propaganda produced an ideological tornado that demonized the communists, struck terror into the hearts of Roman Catholics, the bourgeoisie and the upper classes, and engraved an anti-communist image on the collective imagination that was to be a constant presence in Brazil's political life for the next fifty years. The 1935 uprisings became officially known as the *Intentona Comunista* – '*intentona*' meaning an 'insane or senseless project' – and the rebels were accused of innumerable crimes: the communist officers had supposedly murdered their pro-government comrades in cold blood as they slept in the third infantry regiment barracks, and there was allegedly looting, plundering and rape during the Natal uprising.

To justify his attacks, President Vargas forged accusations. On 30 September 1937 the country awoke to terrifying newspaper headlines: Moscow was planning another communist uprising in Brazil. The story was based on the discovery by the army of a secret plan for taking power – the Cohen Plan – which listed instructions for burning down public buildings, looting, and the summary execution of civilians.[65] The document, including the Jewish name, 'Cohen', was a fabrication. It had been written by Colonel Olímpio Mourão Filho, the *integralista* paramilitary militia leader and head of the organization's secret service. Colonel Mourão Filho worked in the intelligence sector of the army chiefs of staff. The fraudulent document he wrote was given to General Góes Monteiro, who treated it as authentic. He passed it on to President Vargas who in turn made it public.

Copies began to circulate in the barracks, newspapers rekindled fears over the dangers of communism, radios blared out their anti-communist message, and people were terrified. Pleased with the result, President Vargas waited for two months, then on 10 November 1937 he had Congress surrounded and sent all the deputies home. He announced he was implementing emergency powers, put the police on the streets, and imposed a new constitution. He baptized his new dictatorial regime the *Estado Novo* (New State). Hardly a shot had been fired. And thus began the long years of the *Estado Novo* dictatorship.

OUR TINY LITTLE TUPINAMBÁ FASCISM

The maintenance and operation of the *Estado Novo* were centred entirely around Getúlio Vargas. He was the sole commander of a civilian dictatorship, backed by the armed forces, and sustained by populist policies. The new regime drew on concepts from conservative political thinkers, such as Alberto Torres,[66] who believed that it was the task of the state to organize society, design policies and implement all changes. There were also fascist overtones. *Estado Novo* was the name of the Salazar regime in Portugal, which had begun in 1932. The Brazilian regime had many things in common with European fascism: the emphasis on Executive power personified by a single leader; the representation of interest groups and social classes in a form of corporatism, such as the political collaboration between an entrepreneur and his employees, with state oversight. There was also great faith in the idea that technology could be harnessed in the interest of government efficiency, accompanied by repression and the suppression of dissent.[67]

But despite this, President Vargas's *Estado Novo* was neither a reproduction of European fascism nor could it even be considered a true fascist state – like those in Italy, Portugal or Spain. It was an authoritarian, modernizing and pragmatic regime, sarcastically defined by Graciliano Ramos as 'our tiny little Tupinambá fascism'.[68] A society controlled by an authoritarian state – and not just by the masses – required repressive mechanisms to prevent any form of opposition. But the feasibility of the *Estado Novo* also depended on Getúlio Vargas's ability to restrict decision-making to a tightly knit few, while expanding his base of support to the fullest extent possible. This required a political apparatus equipped to recruit supporters and neutralize conflicts.

The elements of *Estado Novo* police repression had been put in place before the 1937 coup. The government by then had begun to ignore the 1934 Constitution.[69] In 1935 a new national security law that delineated crimes against the political and social order was passed, and in 1936 the National Security Court was created to summarily judge political opponents and send them to prison. Even before this, in 1933, President Vargas had created his political police force in the capital. The exclusive task of the special police for political and social safety (Desp) was political repression. The special police heard denunciations;

they also investigated, arrested and imprisoned any person whose activities were considered suspect – with no requirement to produce any evidence. Getúlio Vargas appointed Captain Filinto Müller, chief of the civil police,[70] to command Desp. As head of the unit, Captain Müller had no compunction in ordering the death or torture of anyone suspected of being an adversary of the state, or in letting them rot in one of Desp's prisons. A Nazi supporter, he maintained contact – with the collusion of the Brazilian government – with the Gestapo, which included the exchange of information and interrogation techniques.[71] Captain Müller was an army officer in active service; he was simply temporarily transferred to a post outside the regular chain of command and later returned to army duty in 1942. He never received any kind of formal censure from the high command for his actions while working for the *Estado Novo*. It goes without saying that he had Getúlio Vargas's unconditional support for everything he did.[72]

Like any government imposed by force, the *Estado Novo* depended on the consent of the majority of the population. No previous Brazilian government had exerted so much time and effort in constructing its own apparatus to prove its legitimacy and enforce its political ideology.[73] A great deal of time and energy was spent on censorship, a fundamental government instrument for suppressing dissent. The most essential part of this system – the element that guaranteed its efficacy – was conceived by Getúlio Vargas in 1939: a gigantic agency with the power to interfere in any area of communication, namely, the press and propaganda department (DIP). Directly subordinate to the presidency, it had affiliated bodies throughout the country and was run by the journalist Lourival Fontes, a loyal follower of Getúlio Vargas and an admirer of Italian fascism. The DIP was a complex organization. It was divided into six sections – propaganda, radio broadcasts, theatre and cinema, tourism and press – to promote and defend the *Estado Novo*. The agency intervened in every aspect of Brazilian culture, censoring all forms of artistic and cultural activities. The agency had in-house composers, journalists, writers and artists, who were trained in a variety of working methods. One of these was to exploit the potential of the press, which led to the creation of two magazines – *Cultura Política* and *Ciência Política*. Another was to gain control of every aspect of popular music – the most efficient means of spreading ideas in Brazil since it was accessible to the whole population.

During the 1930s, popular music (as opposed to classical or opera) was widely heard and became an important cultural component of daily life. Musical compositions prioritized the specific language of samba – a distinctive Brazilian form of musical expression. Two important new institutions gave voice to this genre: carnival became Brazil's most important popular festival; and the radio, which became the first vehicle of mass communication. These were the golden years of Brazilian urban samba, with composers including Ary Barroso, Wilson Batista, Ataulfo Alves, Assis Valente, Dorival Caymmi, Nelson Cavaquinho and Geraldo Pereira. And, of course, Noel Rosa, who wrote around three hundred songs in just seven years of activity, between 1930 and 1937.[74] Noel Rosa gave samba the form that we know today: the distinctive language based on everyday expressions, the relationship between words and melody, the poetical inventiveness and flexible musical treatment – at times speeding up, approaching a carnival march, at others slowing down and concentrating on the melody, with voice inflections that originated with the serestas[75] and modinhas. His sambas reflected the modernization of the period – the telephone, the talking movies, factory whistles, photography and the baratinha, a two-seater convertible sports car.

Noel Rosa died in May 1937 – he did not live to compose during the dictatorship. Nor did he live to witness the work of the DIP in the area of popular music. He would have been appalled: in 1942 alone the department banned 373 songs and 108 radio programmes. There was no area in which it did not intervene.[76] It instituted the date of 3 January as Brazilian popular music day, organized the Rio de Janeiro carnival (during which the samba schools were obliged to choose Brazilian themes, preferably historical), and cultivated samba as a symbol of national identity.[77]

The press and propaganda department proved to be highly effective in the use of new technology – radio and cinema – to promote government actions and initiatives. Radio was already a phenomenon of mass communication: it met the demand for entertainment from a growing audience and was a hugely successful vehicle for advertising. In 1939 the press and propaganda department began to transmit government propaganda via a nationwide network for an hour a day. The programme was called Hora do Brasil (Brazilian Hour), and President Vargas's voice became known all over the country. He gave short, simple speeches, communicating directly with the people. In 1942 the agency extended the programme, following the president's speeches with musicals and comedies. The agency promoted the phenomenally successful 'auditorium programmes' called *Rádio Nacional*, which became a sort of theatre that entered all Brazilian homes, including those of the poor. There were also fan clubs where people would listen to the popular singers of the moment.

Maintaining the legitimacy of the dictatorship of the *Estado Novo* depended on the ability of various government leaders to convince the public that President Vargas and the state were one and the same. This was achieved by associating the president's image with that of Brazil. One of the most important vehicles for government propaganda, the Ministry of Education and Health, was at the heart of this policy of embedding *Estado Novo* deeply into every aspect of Brazilian culture. The ministry was directed by Gustavo Capanema, a *Mineiro* who had wanted the post of federal *interventor* in Minas Gerais in 1933 but did not get it, and whom Getúlio Vargas brought to Rio de Janeiro the following year. The ministry is perhaps the best example of the ambivalence of political practices during the *Estado Novo*.[78]

Gustavo Capanema made the most of his appointment. He created the Institute for National Heritage and the Arts and appointed Heitor Villa-Lobos – Brazil's greatest classical composer – as superintendent of musical education. Mr Villa-Lobos trained large student choruses to sing at the mass events organized by the regime. Gustavo Capanema was responsible for the ministry's new seat in Rio de Janeiro, a modernist construction without precedence in Brazil. The architect and urban planner Lúcio Costa had been inspired by the new architectural language of Le Corbusier. Oscar Niemeyer collaborated on the project and the walls were covered with a mural of hand-painted tiles by Candido Portinari.[79] The building is still a wonderful sight, although rather rundown. In seemingly contradictory policies that perhaps best capture the *Estado Novo*, while Gustavo Capanema's ministry promoted the modernists and other vanguard groups, it remained silent with regard to the arbitrary arrests and the imprisonment of artists and teachers; it did nothing to prevent the persecution of communists and was also responsible for closing down the University of the Federal District.

Culture was seen as a matter for the state, used by the dictatorship to create closer ties with writers, journalists and artists. Between Gustavo Capanema's ministry on the one side, and the press and propaganda department on the other, a market for intellectuals opened up, offering government posts particularly attractive to those anxious to gain access to the decision-making nucleus of the government. Although there were some who refused to follow the party line, a large number of Brazilian intellectuals, on both the right and the left of the political spectrum, accepted the limitations imposed by the agents of the *Estado Novo*: poets including Carlos Drummond de Andrade, Mário de Andrade, Cassiano Ricardo, Rosário Fusco and Menotti Del Picchia; intellectuals including Gilberto Freyre, Alceu Amoroso Lima and Nelson Werneck Sodré; and novelists such as Graciliano Ramos. In fact, a transformation was taking place in Brazilian culture. A nationwide aesthetic and a collective vision that were no longer the product of regional traditions had come to the fore. The *Estado Novo* provided the ruler and compass for the construction of this triumphant national identity. On the one hand, there developed a belief in the authenticity of popular culture; and on the other, there was a heterogeneous mixture of cultural elements drawn from different regions. Here an African turban from Bahia or a tambourine from a *Carioca favela*, there some capoeira movements and the mellow sound of mulatto singing – the voice of all Brazilians. South of the equator nothing is pure, everything is a mixture.[80] In the victorious 1930s representation of the country, the Brazilian people were born alongside the mestizos. Being of mixed race was no longer seen as a disadvantage, but rather to be celebrated. A number of regional traditions – in cookery, dance, music and religion – were becoming 'de-africanized' and the source of national pride. To this day they are considered important symbols of Brazilian culture.

As is *feijoada*. Originally 'slaves' food, the combination of black beans cooked with chunks of pork and bacon and served with rice, manioc flour, orange slices and diced kale, which has become the national dish, also serves as a symbolic representation of Brazil. The black beans and white rice, once mixed, become a metaphor for the harmonious mixture of cultures and races; the green kale becomes a metaphor for the country's forests and the yellowish colour of the oranges for its gold. Using a somewhat exotic, aesthetic argument, a complete *feijoada*, when everything is mixed together, becomes a kind of portrait of Brazil. This process of absorbing previously rejected cultural traditions became increasingly widespread. Until the end of the nineteenth century, capoeira was suppressed by the police; it was listed as a crime in the 1890 penal code. However, in 1937, the *Estado Novo* decided to promote it, but no longer just for Africans. It became what was referred to in the early twentieth century as 'mixed capoeira' and the participants were mestizos, a mixture of the three races, Portuguese, Black and Indian. During Getúlio Vargas's government capoeira became an official national sport. Candomblé underwent a similar process.

The celebration of racial and cultural diversity allowed Brazil to offset the importation of European and North American culture by exporting its own. In 1939 the singer Carmen Miranda – Brazil's most internationally successful representative – went to the United States. She was already a great star in Brazil who recorded albums and sang in casinos and theatres. The public adored her. She was invited to New York by a group of American producers to appear in the musical revue *Streets of Paris*.[81] It is said that she took just six minutes to conquer Broadway, and with her first film, *Down Argentine Way*[82], she became world famous. Her ascent was as rapid as it was extraordinary – and possibly exaggerated: within a short time she was the highest-paid female star in Hollywood. She appeared on magazine covers, in advertisements and in shop windows, her records sold in the many thousands, and nightclubs vied with each other for the privilege of her presence – preferably accompanied by her Brazilian band, the Bando da Lua. Although she always told journalists that she had no voice at all – 'what I have is *bossa*'[83] – Carmen Miranda had genuine talent.[84] Despite her Portuguese origin, she was a gift for the *Estado Novo* in its promotion of a mixed-race society and culture. Her repertoire and inimitable style included lyrics that were virtually unintelligible, choreography that mixed elements of samba with exuberant gestures, and a comical musical side – rhythmic and accelerated – all against a backdrop of tropical scenery of, to say the least, dubious taste.

Improbable as it may seem, this mixture *did* have '*bossa*'; in other words, it revealed talent, coherence and style. Carmen Miranda dressed exaggeratedly as a woman from Bahia (*baiana*), with an immense rainbow-coloured turban that could accommodate one or two baskets decorated with pearls and coloured stones – and overflowing with bananas and other tropical fruits made of wax. She wore huge gold earrings, countless bracelets and necklaces and, as if that were not enough, extremely high platform sandals – essential for someone who was only 1.52 metres tall. She was almost engulfed by her bead chokers and large charm bracelets and necklaces – amulets originally used for requesting grace from the saints. By the end of each presentation Carmen had reinvented Brazil. A Brazil of blacks, whites and Indians that was hybrid, harmonious and happy.

In the early 1940s the tables turned, and the United States began to take a great interest in Brazil. Between 1933 and 1945 – the years of Franklin Roosevelt's presidency – the United States adopted a carefully calculated foreign policy. It used a combination of pressure and caution in the face of developments in Germany and the other countries of the Axis. This policy involved a radical change in the North American strategy in relation to Latin America. The United States government was looking for potential export markets to help the country recover from the catastrophic 1929 crash. Furthermore, policymakers were anxious to block the influence of Germany and Italy. President Roosevelt was determined that the United States be the main partner of Latin America and, instead of making impositions, began to negotiate. The practice of interventionism on the continent was replaced by the rhetoric of solidarity – Pan-Americanism – along with the offer of economic, technological and military cooperation. A project for closer cultural ties was also included in what Roosevelt ambitiously called his Good Neighbor Policy.[85] The project invested heavily in cinema, with films promoting pan-Americanism. Not all of them worked. *Down Argentine Way*, for example, caused outrage in Argentina. Not only was there no tango, but Buenos Aires was apparently full of crooks. The reaction to *Week-End in Havana* was even worse: the Cubans were indignant at the way they were depicted as little con men and Havana, their beautiful capital, as a casino surrounded by sugar plantations.

Then, in 1941, Disney Studios entered the business. In May of that year, Walt Disney himself flew to Mexico with a team of musicians, screenwriters and cartoonists, and then continued his journey to Brazil and Argentina. When he returned to the United States he brought with him the research and drafts for the future cartoons that were to transform the Good Neighbour Policy into an immense success: *Saludos Amigos (Alô amigos)*, which was first shown in 1943, and *The Three Caballeros (Você já foi à Bahia?)*, first shown in 1945. *Saludos Amigos* used Ary Barroso's 'Aquarela do Brasil'[86] as its theme song. The song – a samba – represents Brazilian identity, and has become a sort of alternative national anthem. *The Three Caballeros* also used compositions by Ary Barroso, sung by Carmen Miranda's sister, Aurora Miranda. The movie used sensational technological innovation, already employed by Disney Studies in *Fantasia* (1940). While singing, Aurora Miranda, dressed as a Baiana, appeared on screen alongside cartoon characters. In both films, Brazil was presented to North American audiences via the cartoon character Zé (Joe) Carioca, a livid green, dandyish parrot.[87] The character was inspired by the innumerable stories about parrots that the Disney team had heard in Rio de Janeiro. Zé Carioca was conceived of in a Copacabana Palace hotel room, temporarily converted into a studio. The parrot's features were vaguely similar to those of the popular songwriter Herivelto Martins. Probably unknown to the Americans, the association was an old one: the parrot was the bird used to symbolize Brazil in the accounts of sixteenth-century travellers – when the country was referred to as the Land of Parrots. Zé Carioca was a rare species – a 'parrot on the sidelines of capitalism'.[88] His success was instantaneous and long-lasting. He combined diverse cultural elements by becoming a seductive *Carioca malandro*, but without any malice – creating a synthesis representative of the Brazilian people. Zé Carioca was mestizo, lived off odd jobs, had no money and was lazy, always waiting for something to come up – the national characteristics that Brazilians today still identify with the *malandro*.

But he was also irresistible: free, happy, talkative, warm-hearted, easygoing, full of *bossa*, a great footballer, a great samba dancer and a bit of a rogue – it took him no time to pick up the tricks for reeling in tourists. From his first appearance Zé Carioca projected a positive image of Brazil abroad, and enchanted Brazilians, especially President Vargas's family. The president considered the film a North American tribute to his country and to his people and sponsored the first screening of *Saludos Amigos* in Rio de Janeiro. Also, the interest of the *Estado Novo* for all things Brazilian was wide and varied enough to include the choice for the country's patron saint. The Lady of the Apparition was caught by fishermen in the Paraíba river, battered by the waters, and was just as mestizo as the Brazilians.

This process of forging a national identity depended upon high levels of denial: the misery of the interior, the poverty of most town dwellers, and the extraordinary lack of commitment to any institutionalized form of public welfare. These too are 'coisas nossas' (our things), Noel Rosa commented in a song he wrote in 1932.[89] And he went on to list them: the *malandros* who drank but did not eat, the straw-covered shacks in the countryside, the moneylenders and the con men, the trams that looked like carts – all things that define a country that can joke about its own poverty. And, as the composer continued, all things that were as utterly Brazilian as the *mulatta*, the tambourine[90] or the guitar. Contrary to Noel Rosa's ironic verses, however, the country was beginning to reject the racial argument, to prioritize cultural traits, and to put the mixed-race characteristic of the population at the forefront in its dealings with the rest of the world.

This was the perfect context for the 1933 publication of Gilberto Freyre's *Casa-Grande & Senzala*. The book was an immediate success. Mr Freyre had an innovative interpretation of Brazil's multiracial society, arguing that the country was the surprising and original result of Portuguese efforts to adapt a European civilization to the tropics. The book presents a view of Brazil as a unique new society, benefiting from and enriched by its mixture of races.[91] It celebrated the contribution of Africans in the formation of Brazil and lauded the racial mixing that had previously caused so much anxiety, according to prevalent discourses about racial hierarchy and the dangers of degeneration. But Gilberto Freyre was not the only one to present a new interpretation of Brazil. In 1936, responding to Mr Freyre's book and to Getúlio Vargas's modernization programme, Sérgio Buarque de Holanda published *Raízes do Brasil*,[92] which contained a very different argument. He foresaw potential conflicts in Brazil and issued a warning. His book harshly criticizes the authoritarianism systematically adopted throughout Brazil's history, discusses the main historical figures responsible for the formation of Brazilian society, and predicts various future scenarios. It also criticizes the social tensions brought about by the modernization programmes.[93]

In 1942 a third iconic book was published: Caio Prado Jr's *Formação do Brasil contemporâneo*, which introduces yet another interpretation of the country.[94] For Caio Prado, Brazil's specific characteristics were not the result of its roots, nor of its being a mixed-race society: they resulted from the country's failure to make a clean break with its political and economic past and from patterns established during the colonial period. Because there had been no radical break, Caio Prado argued, there was no way of overcoming the country's poverty, subordination and dependence. He reinforces his argument by saying that any society that undergoes reform without a drastic shakeup will fail to eradicate the causes of its backwardness and poverty. These and other authors, including Oliveira Viana, Paulo Prado, Cassiano Ricardo, Alceu Amoroso Lima and Guerreiro Ramos, were responsible for the vogue of great interpretative essays, which ceased to consider the country as a fragmented reality and sought to understand the contradictions rooted in Brazilian society. For the first time, Brazilian intellectuals were analysing the country through different lenses, institutions and disciplines.

If intellectual critiques on all sides were increasingly sharp, so too did President Vargas continue his manoeuvres in the realm of culture and in the labour force, where his goal was to mobilize workers. State interference in labour relations always favoured the workers, recognized labour and social rights and increased the workers' power vis-à-vis their employers.[95] Between 1930 and 1945, President Vargas's government created the foundations for Brazil's labour laws, trade unions and social benefits, which are still largely in place today. But, as with every political strategy, there was a downside: the price to pay was the restriction of political freedom. The workers had to accept participation in a state-controlled system. Otherwise, they could risk forming their own clandestine organizations; either that, or their last resort: join the underworld of outlaws. That was the marginalized community – foreigners, anarchists, communists, beggars and *malandros* – forever denigrated in the press and pursued by the police. But *malandragem* was also a political choice, characterized by a disdain for the world of work.[96] The *malandro* was by no means a new phenomenon in Brazilian society. The word had been used in the nineteenth century to define a person who lived on the borderline between legality and illegality: he worked as little as possible and made his living from gambling, women and swindles.

President Vargas was persistent in his fight against *malandragem*. He realized it signified a rejection of the political system. Those, like composer Wilson Batista, perhaps the most expressive representative of a generation of sambistas who adopted *malandragem* as part of their Bohemian identity, knew it was almost impossible to escape the mythology of work that the dictatorship defended. Managing to dupe the censors, Wilson Batista, along with Ataulfo Alves, composed a hit song for the 1941 Carnival, 'O bonde de São Januário' ('The Saint Januário

Tram'). Sick and tired of the censorship – and to the delight of the public – he cleverly changed the word *operário* (worker) to *otário* (gullible fool). 'Those who work are right/I say it and I have no fear/The Saint Januário tram/Carries one more worker (fool)/It is me, going to work.' The composition was a huge hit as sung by Cyro Monteiro and established him in his career.[97] After getting past the press and propaganda department, the song circulated from mouth to mouth, but the song narrative changed when the composer made that slight – yet decisive – alteration. Little imagination was required to understand who was supposed to be the fool. To expose the discourse of power and reveal the deceit inherent in wordplay is the strategy of the *malandro*. It means to draw from both sides of the fence – the worker and the law – to use both to one's own advantage. This was the strategy Getúlio Vargas could not forgive.

FAREWELL, *ESTADO NOVO*

The Second World War was decisive for the *Estado Novo*: while it strengthened the regime's modernization programme, it also signalled an end to authoritarianism.[98] In its foreign policy, the Brazilian government did all it could to maintain the country's neutrality during the years leading up to the war. But, with the Japanese attack on Pearl Harbor on 7 December 1941, President Vargas came under increasing pressure to take a stand. Nonetheless, it took until 28 January 1942, at the last meeting of the chancellors of the American republics in Rio de Janeiro, for Brazil to sever diplomatic relations with the Axis powers – Germany, Italy and Japan. The reaction was swift: German submarines torpedoed Brazilian merchant ships in Brazil's territorial waters. People took to the streets, organizing the first major protests since the beginning of the dictatorship, demanding that Brazil enter the war immediately, on the side of the Allies.

While Brazil had remained neutral, President Vargas had sought to make the best he could of the situation without exposing himself too much. He had renewed commercial agreements with Nazi Germany, thereby consolidating Brazil's position as the Reich's main trading partner in the Americas. He had acquired submarines from Mussolini's Italy in exchange for exporting meat and raw materials. To offset these measures, he also investigated closer trade relations with the Allies, in addition to authorizing the purchase of destroyers from the United States and weaponry from Britain to equip the Brazilian navy. At a time when it was unclear who would win the war, when the Nazis had triumphantly invaded France, Getúlio Vargas believed Brazil's neutrality would allow the country to take full advantage of the circumstances. He traded with both sides, to the exasperation of his ministers, some of whom supported the Allies – like Chancellor Oswaldo Aranha and his own son-in-law, Ernâni do Amaral Peixoto, governor of Rio de Janeiro – and others who were frankly in favour of the Germans, including General Góes Monteiro and General Dutra.

The ideological sympathies of the *Estado Novo* tended towards fascism: a month before the fall of Madrid and the defeat of the republicans in the Spanish Civil War, Getúlio Vargas put caution aside and officially recognized the fascist government of General Franco. However, he maintained good relations with President Roosevelt, and did all he could to increase trade between the two countries. After all, Brazil's modernization programme depended on United States support in order to establish an industrial base. But President Vargas also applied pressure: he instructed Itamaraty, the Brazilian Foreign Office, to inform the Americans that he was not prepared to wait for them to support his industrialization project, insinuating that otherwise he might collaborate with Germany. He went so far as to send Adolf Hitler a telegram, including the words 'I wish you all personal happiness and prosperity for the German nation.'[99]

After 1942, with Brazil's entry into the war, an air and naval base near Natal was ceded to the United States to help protect the routes to North Africa. Brazil's collaboration with the Roosevelt administration changed dramatically, and President Vargas's industrialization programme was increasingly successful. The question of steel, which was at the heart of the project, had been a key element of the liberal alliance's plans back in 1930, and was part of the president's commitment to the armed forces, in exchange for their support of the 1937 coup. In 1942, with long-term loans from the Export-Import Bank, the *Estado Novo* created a mining company, Companhia Vale do Rio Doce, for the exploitation of iron ore. The government also built an enormous steelworks in Volta Redonda, a planned industrial town near Rio de Janeiro, which became a symbol of the self-sufficient economy that

President Vargas had planned for Brazil. He then also created the National Steel Company to control the plant, a joint-stock company of which the state was the majority shareholder. The project then expanded to iron ore, alkali processing, and the production of engines for planes and trucks. A policy was also outlined for the government's approach to oil exploitation. And, although Getúlio Vargas did not construct the planned state refineries, he laid the groundwork for the creation of Petrobras, the Brazilian state-owned oil company, a decade later.

By 1943 it had become clear to President Vargas that the war was approaching its final stage and that the Axis powers would be defeated. He also realized that the *Estado Novo* would not survive an Allied victory, even though Brazil had entered the war on the side of the probable winners. In August that same year, in a move that enraged General Dutra and General Góes Monteiro – who had absolutely refused to accept Brazil's entry into the war on the side of the Allies – Getúlio Vargas created the Brazilian Expeditionary Force, which was sent to fight in Italy in 1944. Approximately 25,000 men were sent to risk their lives, despite the intense cold and very inadequate training. The end of the war was a victory for democracy. The Brazilian people could now no longer deny the contradiction between fighting against fascism abroad and maintaining an authoritarian government at home.

In October 1942 the *Manifesto Mineiro* was signed by ninety-two public figures from the state of Minas Gerais. It called for the return to a democratic regime and opened the way for opposition forces to join the political struggle. President Vargas may not have thought much of the new opposition, but he realized circumstances had changed. He decided to pave the way for the transition to a constitutional regime. The transition was supported by large segments of the population that had benefited from the Vargas government's social and labour legislation. The strategy was a good one, but unfortunately the execution did not go quite as smoothly as planned.

15
Yes, We Have Democracy!

'WE WANT GETÚLIO!'

Brazil emerged from the *Estado Novo* with a profoundly mixed-race sense of beliefs and customs. But this sat right alongside ill-disguised internalized racism and a rigid social hierarchy based on friendship and blood ties. The country had also discovered a national rhythm in the beat of the *Carioca* samba, and had adopted a number of national symbols. By that time, Brazil had modern labour legislation and had laid the foundations of a rapidly expanding modernization and industrialization project. There were high aspirations and President Vargas was increasingly popular. But the political situation was becoming ever more turbulent. Opposition voices managed to find loopholes in censorship laws. The protests were getting out of control in a process that was now irreversible: Brazilians were demanding freedom of expression, a democratically elected president and a new constitution.

President Vargas had no doubt that the repressive apparatus of the *Estado Novo* was no longer efficient. He realized a change in the political system was inevitable. His first problem was how to proceed with the democratic transition and adapt the structure of the government so that he could remain in power. His second problem was when to initiate the transition. By early 1945 he knew time was running out. On 28 February he signed an amendment to the 1937 Constitution, which established that the date for elections would be defined within three months – both for the president of the Republic and for the National Congress.[1] A few days earlier the opposition forces had pre-empted President Vargas's plans by launching Brigadier Eduardo Gomes, commander of the Brazilian Air Force, as a candidate for president.

For Getúlio Vargas, politics had always been a question of

calculation and opportunity. In March he formally declared he would not be a candidate for the presidency, and – with remarkably little enthusiasm – announced the government's support for the candidacy of the War Minister, General Eurico Gaspar Dutra. Although the government's support appeared to be half-hearted, in reality General Dutra's candidacy suited the political strategy. The idea was to divide the armed forces, reducing the support for Eduardo Gomes, and divert attention away from any government moves to maintain President Vargas in power. Eduardo Gomes, or simply 'the Brigadier', as he was known, had fought in the uprisings of the *tenentes* – he was one of the survivors of the Copacabana fort eighteen revolt. He was extremely self-confident, with an heroic demeanour, and had solid democratic credentials. Some of Brazil's women voters were especially enthusiastic, and bandied the slogan: 'Vote for the Brigadier. He's handsome and he's single.'[2] General Dutra, on the other hand, was short, dull and utterly predictable. He had been a member of Getúlio Vargas's inner circle since the days when they were both cadets at the war college in Porto Alegre and had a reputation for being a legalist. He had been close to the *integralistas* and a notorious admirer of Nazi Germany.[3]

Both General Dutra and Brigadier Eduardo Gomes were devout Catholics – which was (and still is) a great help in getting elected – as well as being pompous, pretentious, and total disasters as candidates, above all when it came to asking for votes. On one occasion General Dutra attended a rally at the transport federation in Rio de Janeiro, where he gave an interminable speech on the great figures of Brazilian military history and left without having made a single mention of the workers who had come to hear him. Eduardo Gomes was little better. He managed the feat of bringing together all the main trade union directors of Rio de Janeiro purportedly to explain his electoral platform, and then uttered just four words: 'a pleasure' and 'thank you'.[4]

Neither of the candidates behaved like politicians, but like serving military officers. With the public focusing on each of their personal attributes – or lack of them – an important fact went virtually unnoticed: for the first time an air force brigadier and an army general were competing for the presidency. This was a novelty that did not bode well for Brazilian democracy. The armed forces, especially the army, were no longer playing a subordinate role.[5] On the contrary, the army had been President Vargas's most reliable ally throughout the dictatorship, as well as his main instrument of control. By 1945 the armed forces – especially the army – had become a dynamic element of the state, operating as a kind of executive power. The army no longer considered itself subordinate to civilian power, nor as an instrument of the will of the people. This was a different vision from that of the founders of the Republic in 1889, and of the *tenentes* in the 1920s revolts. Getúlio Vargas opened the door and the generals came right in. In 1945 the army was not only a modern institution, with weapons, equipment and troops; it had been transformed into an institution that was qualitatively different and, in political terms, far more lethal than before. It had become an autonomous, interventionist force, whose members were convinced the army was the only institution capable of forming a well-trained elite, with a national vision and prepared to lead the country. And, over the course of the next forty years of Brazilian republican history, the military were to act on this conviction. General Góes Monteiro, a competent officer who had worked with General Dutra on the modernization of the army, was very proud of his accomplishments and had an incorrigibly loose tongue. He would tell anyone who cared to listen that he 'had put an end to politics[6] in the army, so the military was now free to conduct army policy'.[7]

President Vargas was quick to discover what kind of politics the brigadiers and generals intended to practice: he was removed from power by the armed forces in October 1945, in the first coup conducted by all three military institutions – the army, the navy and the air force. This was the embryo of what was later to become more formally the joint chiefs of staffs of the armed forces (Emfa). It had been necessary for the three institutions to join forces in order to carry out the coup.[8] At the beginning of the same year, however, the situation had been very different. President Vargas was still convinced the brigadiers and generals were legalists, government supporters. He believed in his alliance with General Dutra and, above all, in his own capacity to exploit the internal divisions in the armed forces and to control the troops to protect his own political interests. He would simply manipulate the generals by using the ambitions of one group against another. In reality, he underestimated the scale of change in the institution that he himself had helped create. His plan to keep himself in power had concentrated on the political class and the urban workers. He had ignored the changes that had come about within the army – an error that was now too late to remedy.

The next important step was to grant amnesty to the hundreds of political prisoners who had been arrested during the *Estado Novo*. This included the communist leader Luís Carlos Prestes, who by this time had become a near mythical figure in Brazilian politics, surrounded with the mystical aura of half-martyr, half-hero, and whose personal popularity was at times far greater than that of his party. People paraded through the streets to celebrate the amnesty. The press hailed the release of the political prisoners and all over the country thousands of people signed manifestos calling for the return of the exiles. The public also clamoured for the right to organize political parties – including the Communist Party (PC).[9] On 18 April 1945, after the amnesty had been signed, a huge crowd gathered to greet Luís Carlos Prestes in front of the main entrance of the central penitentiary, located in Rio de Janeiro, on Rua Frei Caneca. Of the eighteen years between the end of his long march with his legendary column and the end of the war, he had spent eight in exile and nine in prison. When he appeared he was rapidly put into a car and driven away. But the public had got a glimpse of his thin pallor. He had aged a great deal. He knew very little about what had happened to his common-law wife Olga Benário and had never met their daughter, Anita, whose grandmother, thanks to a formidable international campaign, had rescued her from a Nazi prison when she was fourteen months old. At the time, Anita lived with her aunts in Moscow.

But Luís Carlos Prestes was anxious to renew his political career. A month after he left prison he addressed a rally organized by the communists in Rio de Janeiro, where he received an unforgettable ovation. Around 10,000 people squeezed into the São Januário stadium in the drizzle to hear him speak. No effort was too great to see and hear Luís Carlos Prestes, to wonder at the gigantic portrait of him planted on the grass, illuminated in neon lights beneath six gigantic letters that spelt the word 'Brazil', and to see the Brazilian and Soviet flags flying side by side in the centre of the stadium.[10] To everyone's surprise, Luís Carlos Prestes announced a complete reversal of the communist position: he declared unconditional support for the Vargas government, called for the convocation of a Constituent Assembly, and defended the deferral of the presidential elections. In theory, he could have been following instructions from Moscow, which recommended that the communists make alliances with their national governments, as long as these had fought in the war on the same side as the USSR, which was the case of Brazil. But by supporting a dictator who had extradited his wife to Nazi Germany, Luís Carlos Prestes had abandoned his principles. His intended alliance with Getúlio Vargas was excessively pragmatic and highly opportunistic: the communists were few, the party had been implacably repressed during the *Estado Novo*, its political force was close to zero, and its members still acted clandestinely. On the other hand, supporting Getúlio Vargas brought enormous advantages. Luís Carlos Prestes would have access to the trade union movement, be able to bring the party closer to the workers, ensure the democratic legitimacy of the communists – and become a candidate in the presidential elections.

Luís Carlos Prestes's reversal of policy did not convince some of the militants, such as the historian Caio Prado Jr, who wanted the communists to maintain a coherent platform. Yet, it was a highly successful move in terms of promoting the party's image. In May 1945, at the time of the São Januário rally, the party's leaders calculated there were around 6,800 party members in Brazil; two years later this number was somewhere between 180,000 and 220,000.[11] There were also large numbers of sympathizers who followed the directives of the party's central committee, and a group of prestigious artists and intellectuals who helped the party develop an alternative programme for the modernization of Brazilian society. Several of these artists were to abandon their political militancy, as was the case of the poet Carlos Drummond de Andrade, whereas others, like the writer Jorge Amado, were to remain committed for many years. Be that as it may, in 1945 a cast of stars gravitated to the communists: painters, including Candido Portinari, Carlos Scliar, Di Cavalcanti and José Pancetti; musicians like the famous conductor and composer Francisco Mignone; talented architects like Vilanova Artigas and Oscar Niemeyer; leading writers such as Graciliano Ramos and Monteiro Lobato; young filmmakers like Nelson Pereira dos Santos; songwriters, including Dorival Caymmi, Mário Lago and Wilson Batista; and popular singers like Nora Ney and Jorge Goulart.

For Getúlio Vargas, communist support, particularly that of Luís Carlo Prestes – the only political leader who could rival his popularity – was a triumph, but it was by no means the most important political card he held. As always, President Vargas kept his views to himself, and no one knew whether he was actually preparing the transition to democracy or whether he was manoeuvring to stay in power. But about one thing there could be no doubt: Getúlio Vargas had not arrived at the Catete presidential palace to be caught unawares. While the *Estado Novo* was disintegrating, he invested heavily in gaining the support of an unexpected group of people – the urban workers.

As was to be expected, the wind began to change direction in São Paulo. In early March 1945 members of the *Centro Acadêmico Onze de Agosto* – the oldest university student organization in the country – decided, at their own risk, to organize workers to fight for democracy and for the overthrow of the *Estado Novo*.[12] These students supported the candidacy of Eduardo Gomes and had close ties with São Paulo's Largo de São Francisco School of Law. President Vargas may have defeated the *Paulistas* in 1932, but they had never accepted it; nor did they let any opportunity for revenge pass them by. On this occasion the students organized the protest march, which made its way to the Praça da Sé,[13] at the heart of the city centre. They occupied the cathedral steps, improvised a political rally during rush hour when the number of pedestrians was at its height and, with microphone in hand, started to criticize President Vargas. But no one was prepared for what happened next. Suddenly, groups of workers meandering peacefully through the square reacted. They advanced on the speakers furiously, beating tins, brandishing pieces of wood, and grabbing anything they could find to throw at the people on the steps. In no time the infuriated crowd had the students on the run. They began to shout 'Long live Getúlio!', 'Long live the workers!', and 'We want Getúlio!', while smashing everything they saw around them, including the windows of the law school. Two days later the episode was repeated in Recife, causing the death of a student, and two further episodes were to follow, the first in Belo Horizonte and the second in Rio de Janeiro. The opposition was astonished. The *Estado Novo* had been overthrown, and yet President Vargas's prestige and popularity were greater than ever.[14] The urban poor and the urban workers supported Getúlio Vargas and wanted him to stay in power.

What started in São Paulo rapidly turned into a major protest movement, nicknamed *queremismo*, after the slogan 'Nós queremos Getúlio' ('We want Getúlio'). This type of participation was new for the Republic. Up until then, people had been kept at a safe distance from the mechanisms of power.[15] The movement's almost obsessive demand to keep Getúlio Vargas as president was clearly political: the workers wanted to guarantee the social and labour rights that they had obtained since the 1930s. When they realized the *Estado Novo* was drawing towards an end, and that Getúlio Vargas's days as president were numbered, they took to the streets. Without him, the workers suspected they would lose their recently earned rights.

True to his style of saying one thing, insinuating another, and finally doing a third, completely different, Getúlio Vargas insisted he was not running for a renewed term as president. He claimed he would preside over the elections and then withdraw from public life – to the peace and quiet of his home, he would add with a modest smile.[16] His real intentions were only revealed by his increasingly open support of the *queremismo* movement. He authorized the live transmission of their rallies and protests on national radio, granted them the discreet support of the press and propaganda department and the labour ministry, and facilitated access to private funding from his supporters among the entrepreneurs. By the second half of 1945 the *queremismo* movement had dozens of committees in towns throughout Brazil and *queremismo* militants were involved in feverish political activity: collecting signatures, publishing pamphlets, declaring support and solidarity, and promoting rallies. The movement grew and became increasingly organized. It was eventually joined by the communists and Luís Carlos Prestes – with his ever-opportunistic eye to which way the wind was blowing. When the *queremistas* realized President Vargas had not left office in time to be eligible to stand as a candidate for his own succession, they changed their demand and invented a new slogan: 'Constituent Assembly with Getúlio!'

The *queremismo* movement was a novelty not easily understood. It emerged as part of the transition to democracy, an authentically popular movement that took to the streets – and an important demonstration of Getúlio Vargas's continued popularity. But this movement alone, with its limited ideological scope, was not capable of taking over the country. It was no more than the spontaneous organization of people who had only recently gained access to the political process. In October 1945, however, to the astonishment of the opposition, President Vargas showed his hand, revealing a little more of his way of doing politics. Taking advantage of an event that attracted a great deal of public attention – the inauguration of the electricity network for the suburban trains in Rio de Janeiro – he mounted the stage and summoned the workers to join the recently created Brazilian Labour Party (PTB). He claimed the party would guarantee the workers a share in the administration of public businesses, and would prevent them from becoming 'a mass manipulated by politicians, of all times and ideologies, who, after getting elected by the workers, forgot their promises'. It was an affirmation perhaps difficult to prove, but then again, it was even harder to refute. 'The workers should go to the ballot box and choose the representatives who dwell in their hearts and understand their aspirations,'[17] he concluded.

It had been eight years since all legislative assemblies had been shut down, and associations, groups and popular fronts extinguished. Brazilians had finally recovered their right to form associations based on a wide variety of ideas, interests and values, to participate in the electoral process, and to propose their own laws. The same amendment to the 1937 Constitution that fixed the date for the elections also established new rules for the organization of political parties. Two of these, however, restricted the full exercise of democracy. The first, a nationwide requirement, prevented the resurgence of regional organizations such as those that had characterized the First Republic. The total number of political parties in the country was restricted to twenty – a figure that was maintained between 1945 and 1964 – a considerable improvement on the dozens of regional associations that participated in the legislative elections of 1933 and 1934. The second restriction gave power to the judges of the Supreme Electoral Court to interpret the difference between freedom of expression and the activities of any political association whose programme 'counters the democratic regime, based on the plurality of parties and the guarantee of the fundamental rights of man'.[18]

The transition was under way, and once again political parties were essential for the process. Opposition forces had been working since 1943 to create an anti-Vargas coalition. There were several different ways to be a part of the opposition: fight against the *Estado Novo*, plead the democratic cause, or simply espouse liberal beliefs. Opposition politicians made themselves especially significant when they attempted to remove people and institutions related to President Vargas from Brazilian public life. This ferocious *anti-getulismo* brought together politicians of widely differing interests in parties such as the

National Democratic Union (UDN) – or the 'Brigadier's party' as it was called at the time. Founded in April 1945 with a broad base of support,[19] it provided a political vehicle for the remainder of the regional elites, rich entrepreneurs, industrialists and coffee planters from São Paulo. Its members were from the middle-class establishment, previous supporters of the liberal alliance and the *Estado Novo*, but who had been asked to leave or had become disillusioned. The National Democratic Union also included democratic socialists and dissidents from the Communist Party. This last group was the first to break away. In 1947 they abandoned the anti-Vargas coalition, focusing their energies instead on publishing the newspaper *Orientação Socialista*, which advocated the return of a National Constituent Assembly in order to put an end to the *Estado Novo*. The following year, the socialists broke off and founded their own party – the Brazilian Socialist Party (PSB) – which supported a left-wing democratic programme.

This left the hardliners in the National Democratic Union to establish the party profile: conservative, moralist, anti-democratic, and with a vocation for plotting coups. The National Democratic Union claimed they were pro-democracy, but meanwhile they were planning a *coup d'état*. The members' political vision was restricted to morality in public life, with a rigid focus on the behaviour of those in power. The party had a number of competent orators who were radical and who worked closely together – this group was dubbed the Musical Band. They never let a day go by without tormenting their adversaries: Adauto Lúcio Cardoso, Oscar Dias Correia, Afonso Arinos, Bilac Pinto and Aliomar Baleeiro. The head of the National Democratic Union was Carlos Lacerda,[20] the same student who, ten years earlier, had so courageously (and impulsively) nominated Luís Carlos Prestes as the honorary president of the National Alliance for Freedom. He had renounced the Communist Party, become a devoted Roman Catholic and an ultra-conservative. Despite this, he was as daring and opportunistic as ever. He had verve, erudition, exceptional intelligence, and was extremely competent. Carlos Lacerda knew how to choose his words and was an unbeatable master in the art of political intrigue. He would systematically surprise his adversaries with suspicions, accuse them with or without proof, ridicule them and scoff at them. As Afonso Arinos, a fellow member of the party, used to say – revealing both fear and admiration – Carlos Lacerda was a crisis creator, who was particularly dangerous during crises he himself had provoked, precisely because he melded his own destiny with that of the republican institutions.[21]

Getúlio Vargas was the *éminence grise* behind the creation of two political parties. The first, the Social Democratic Party (PSD),[22] was founded in 1945 to take advantage of his fifteen-year control of every single state in Brazil through the *interventores* whom he had appointed. The idea was to use the state administrative machine to get the votes from the municipalities throughout each state. The Social Democratic Party nominated General Dutra as candidate for president and maintained stability in Brazil until the 1964 *coup d'état*. The members of the Social Democratic Party were professional politicians who loved power and, to keep it, combined meticulous vote-counting with a carefully calculated distribution of government posts and resources. In terms of reading material, as Tancredo Neves (one of the great party leaders) humorously described them, 'Given the choice between the Bible and *Das Kapital*, Social Democratic Party members opt for the *Official Gazette*.'[23] The party had the support of voters, regional prestige, and they understood that the mayors were essential for guaranteeing governors' power. They never questioned election results and were masterful in the art of building alliances. The party was 'to the left of the right and to the right of the left',[24] as Ernâni do Amaral Peixoto, Getúlio Vargas's son-in-law and founder of the PSD, used to say. The great *pessedistas*[25] were masters of political conspiracy: Tancredo Neves, Juscelino Kubitschek (JK), Amaral Peixoto, José Maria Alkmin and Ulysses Guimarães. But the Social Democratic Party also represented the old style of politics, based on the exchange of favours. The cunning regional leaders, sustained by the local '*coronéis*', used their power to control their deputies: Vitorino Freire in Maranhão; Benedito Valadares in Minas Gerais; and Pedro Ludovico in Goiás.

However, it was the second party – the Brazilian Labour Party (PTB), also founded in 1945 – in which the fundamentals of President Vargas's project for the country were enshrined.[26] The party's base was made up of the trade unions affiliated to the *Estado Novo* and from the bureaucrats who worked in the Ministry of Labour. This was a novelty in the sense that the Brazilian Labour Party was not conceived to be a party *of* the workers, but a party *for* the workers.

The biggest novelty of all, however, was the party's political project. The labour movement considered the situation of the working masses as the most important social question. They understood it could not be solved without government intervention, and believed the 1930s social legislation provided an ample programme of reforms for the legal protection for the workers.[27] Getúlio Vargas personified the party programme: his capacity to recognize the workers' lot and his government's concern with the welfare of the Brazilian people. He had always supported wage earners and the poorest segments of the population. And the political militants of *queremismo*, who by then were spread all over the country, provided additional support for the Brazilian Labour Party. Although Getúlio Vargas remained a mythical figure throughout the party's existence, by the early 1960s party leaders had expanded the labour movement beyond its initial dependence on his legacy. They cultivated nationalism, developed a programme of reform, and reached out to various social sectors, especially rural workers.[28]

Between 1945 and 1964 the Brazilian Labour Party espoused democratic socialism and combated, wherever possible, communist influence in the labour movement. With these policies the number of the party's deputies in the National Congress increased to the point where it rivalled the Social Democratic Party (PSD) as the country's largest political party. It had started out with 22 federal deputies in 1945, then increased that number to 51 in 1950, 56 in 1954, 66 in 1958 and 116 in 1962.[29] Among the party leaders, two were especially adept in promoting the socialist cause: João Goulart, President Vargas's chosen successor, and Leonel Brizola, the populist leader who inherited and radicalized Getúlio Vargas's legacy. Both were to play a major role in Brazilian politics in the years to come.

President Vargas had got it right once again. The alliance between the Social Democratic Party and the Brazilian Labour Party proved unbeatable. In a period of just nineteen years they elected three presidents of Brazil, and maintained democratic administrations. However, by the end of 1945, it seemed the situation could hardly get worse. People believed Getúlio Vargas's famed political ability had finally abandoned him. Many viewed the victory of Brigadier Eduardo Gomes as a foregone conclusion. On 29 October, President Vargas was deposed by his military ministers – with General Dutra's consent. General Dutra had been the Minister of War until he left the position in order to run in the elections. Less than forty-eight hours later the former dictator was packed off to his family ranch in São Borja, in Rio Grande do Sul, leaving him no time to organize a resistance movement. With Getúlio Vargas out of the arena, and just prior to the presidential elections set for 2 December, the Brazilian Labour Party seemed to have lost direction, and the Social Democratic Party had little confidence they would be able to elect the prosaic General Dutra unaided. The National Democratic Union (UDN), on the other hand, considered its victory a certainty. Their confidence, however, was to be short lived. In mid-November, Brigadier Eduardo Gomes gave a speech in Rio de Janeiro's imposing opera house, before an invited audience. Overconfident, he unwisely declared he did not need the votes of Getúlio Vargas's supporters, whom he disdainfully referred to as a 'rabble of loiterers'.[30] After almost a year of campaigning the Brigadier still did not seem to realize that for a candidate every vote counts. The *queremista* leaders seized the opportunity and bombarded shortwave radio stations across the country with the message that, for Eduardo Gomes, the workers were 'a rabble'.

To clarify whose votes Brigadier Eduardo Gomes considered expendable, the *queremistas* made it plain: the vote of the poor worker, who gets up at dawn in the suburbs, commutes great distances to work all day, makes very little money, and carries a *marmita* (lunch box) packed with rice, beans and a fried egg. Thousands of people related to this figure, and assumed proudly the identity of '*marmiteiros*' (lunch-box carriers). They enthusiastically wanted to bring down a candidate who disdained the poor, even during elections. So they flocked en masse to the last Brazilian Labour Party rallies, banging furiously on their *marmitas*, pots and pans, and proclaiming themselves enemies of the 'posh', that is, of the elite who were voting for Brigadeiro Eduardo Gomes. Unfortunately for the National Democratic Union, there were a lot of people toting *marmitas* – voters, one and all.

The workers turned against Brigadier Eduardo Gomes and the campaign concluded with Getúlio Vargas calling on the workers to vote for the Social Democratic Party's candidate, General Dutra. Just half an hour before the end of the last Social Democratic Party political rally in Rio de Janeiro, an emissary arrived with a message from Getúlio Vargas's farm, São Borja. His message went some way towards healing the resentment within the Social Democratic Party at his failure to support his own candidate, General Dutra. The message emphasized that a victory for the National Democratic Union (UDN) would mean the dismantling of his political project, and he finally declared his formal support for General Dutra: 'The candidate of the PSD, in innumerable speeches, and in his latest declarations, has clearly identified himself with the ideas of the Labour movement [. . .] He thus deserves our votes!' But he had not forgotten how General Dutra had betrayed him, and sent him a warning: 'If the promises of the campaign are not kept, I will be at the side of the people against the president.'

During the five days of the campaign that remained, militants from the Brazilian Labour Party (PTB) and the Social Democratic Party (PSD) flooded the country with photos of Getúlio Vargas, below which appeared a message that was simple and direct: 'He said: Vote for Dutra!' The photograph was hardly necessary; everyone knew who the 'he', with a capital H, referred to. On 2 December, 6,200,000 Brazilians – 13.4 per cent of the population – joined the queues outside the voting booths to vote for the first time after eight years of dictatorship. The Electoral Tribunal had to struggle to control the process and count the votes. But victory was secured, with General Dutra winning in every state except Ceará, Piauí and the Federal District, receiving 52.39 per cent of the votes cast, as against 34.74 per cent for Eduardo Gomes. General Dutra also won by a comfortable margin in the country's three most influential states: São Paulo, Minas Gerais and Rio Grande do Sul.[31] Even though the alliance between the PSD and the PTB had to be renegotiated at every election, the team had shown its political muscle.

But, as the country was soon to discover, although it had been possible to overthrow the dictator, removing the political strategist and his legacy was quite another matter. In the words of a popular song of the time, if it had depended on the will of the Brazilian people, the portrait of the Old Man would be back on the wall, at the same place.

HE WILL RETURN!

Combined, the Social Democratic Party (PSD) and the Brazilian Labour Party (PTB) formed a majority in Congress. The PSD received 42 per cent of the votes and the PTB 10 per cent. The National Democratic Union (UDN) received 26 per cent, and the recently legalized Communist Party (PC), 9 per cent – the remaining 13 per cent were distributed between candidates from smaller parties. The new deputies took office in January 1946, when the Congress assumed its parallel role of Constituent Assembly. Eight months later, on 18 September 1946, the members delivered the new constitution.

The new 1946 Constitution maintained all the social advances that had been achieved since the 1930s and restored democracy and political rights as irrevocable.[32] The text included democratic procedures for the republican institutions, with direct elections for Executive and Legislative posts in all three spheres of the Federation: the federal, state and municipal governments. It also guaranteed freedom of the press and opinion, recognized the importance of political parties, and moved towards universal suffrage, granting the vote to more than a quarter of the population aged over eighteen years. For the next twenty years the 1946 Constitution provided the basis for the return to democracy in Brazil. The constitution established Parliament as a key political player – above all in moments of serious institutional crisis – consolidated the role of political parties, strengthened the independence of the trade unions, and guaranteed regular elections, whose outcomes were only marginally affected by fraud.

Even so, there is still controversy surrounding the 1946 Constitution. Despite its unequivocal support for democracy, it did not reach traditionally excluded segments of the population. For example, illiterate people – a very high proportion of the adults – were still denied the vote. The right to strike was restricted and rural workers did not have the same rights to labour benefits as did the urban workers. Yet another cause of concern was the increasing interference of the military in government affairs. Nevertheless, even with these limitations, respect for democratic institutions and procedures during this period was as solid as it would ever be. There is a simple reason for this: no political regime is entirely democratic.[33] In the case of Brazil, the democratic procedures established by the 1946 Constitution became increasingly evident toward the late 1950s and early 1960s, as the rural workers became a more independent political force, and with the ever-growing popular pressure for a more inclusive society.

While Brazil was becoming more democratic, in the post-war world many countries were becoming more intolerant and polarized. The years following the Second World War tore down empires, redrew the map of the world, and introduced the Cold War.[34] During the Cold

War, geographical location was an all-important factor, and the United States saw the republics of Latin America as uncomfortably close to their terrain. From the perspective of the Pentagon, any political change in one of these countries could substantially alter the balance of power between the two superpowers, and leave the United States more vulnerable to attack by the Soviets. As the largest country in Latin America, Brazil attracted by far the greatest interest. The United States' worst fear was that a government would come into power in Brazil that might potentially facilitate the rise of the communists. They did not want to see Brazil transformed into a 'satellite of Moscow' – an expression used in both Washington and Rio de Janeiro.

Once installed in the presidential palace, the Catete, President Dutra did all he could to pacify the White House: he adopted a policy that was subservient to the North Americans, broke off diplomatic ties with the Soviet Union, and made a priority of pursuing the communists. Jokes went around mocking the president's subservience to the Americans. It was said that when he met President Truman his host greeted him with the words 'How do you do, Dutra?', to which he supposedly replied 'How tru you tru, Truman?' But the situation was not a joke. The Brazilian Communist Party (PC) was the largest and strongest in Latin America; it had seventeen deputies and one senator in Congress, forty-six deputies in fifteen state Legislative Assemblies, and a majority in the Municipal Chamber of the Federal District.[35] Whatever its ideological stance, the party was already an established political force. Enthusiastically sharing the radically anti-communist views that had spread among the armed forces after the 1935 uprising of the *tenentes* – views that had been exacerbated by the Cold War – President Dutra decided to act as quickly as he could, preferably upon taking office.

At the beginning of 1946, a wave of bank strikes started in São Paulo and rapidly spread to other states, including Minas Gerais, Rio de Janeiro, Espírito Santo, Santa Catarina, Bahia and Pará. The strike served as a pretext for President Dutra to implement his policy of repression of the communists and of workers in general. The Brazilian Workers' Confederation was outlawed, the Ministry of Labour ordered government intervention in 143 trade unions – out of a total of 944 – and the president issued a decree regulating the right to strike, aimed at preventing a complete paralysis of the country. After a thorough reading of the new decree, Antônio Ferreira Cesarino, a well-known legal expert, protested: 'With this decree, only perfume sellers can go on strike.'[36]

In March 1946, Luís Carlos Prestes gave President Dutra the pretext he needed to unleash his anti-communist campaign and send the party back underground. In a debate in Rio de Janeiro, Luís Carlos Prestes was asked what his position would be if Brazil went to war with the Soviet Union. His reply was immediate. In his professorial tone, he explained that the Brazilian government would be committing a criminal act, this would be an imperialist war, and the Brazilian communists would stand against it. A childish question and a stupid answer, but it was more than enough for President Dutra.[37] In May 1947, by a margin of three votes to two, the judges of the Supreme Electoral Court annulled the registration of the Communist Party. The court gave two reasons for its decision: it accused the Communist Party of not being a Brazilian party, but rather a section of the Communist International, which was based in Moscow, and defined it as anti-democratic, according to the 1946 Constitution. The document accused the party of 'inciting class warfare and encouraging strikes, with an aim to creating an atmosphere of confusion and disorder'.[38] In January 1948 the National Congress decided to repeal the mandates of all the deputies elected by the Communist Party. Deprived of their democratic rights and isolated in the party system, the communists once again found themselves faced with the risk of government persecution and were forced to return to the harsh reality of underground militancy.

General Dutra's presidency was politically inept and economically disastrous. To fight the inflation of the war years, the government not only allowed an indiscriminate amount of imports but also subsidized them through an overvalued exchange rate. The medicine almost killed the patient. The inflation rate slowed down, but at the cost of using up the sterling and dollar reserves the country had accumulated during the war. President Dutra burnt the nation's reserves with an import policy that inundated the domestic market with superfluous items and leftovers from the war – plastic goods, Cadillacs, yo-yos and hula hoops – while he took no measures to expand the country's industrial capacity. The government tried to repair the damage in 1948 by announcing a plan to concentrate investments in key segments – health, food, transport and energy; but the plan made little progress and some of it was not even implemented.[39]

President Dutra considered himself austere; he was a man of few words and regular habits. But he was also a moralist with limited vision. In April 1946, shortly after he took office, he signed a decree banning gambling throughout the country and closed all the casinos. The measure was supposedly taken under pressure from his wife, a devout Catholic, who had earned the soubriquet *Dona Santinha* ('the little saint'). The government's justification was that it had a duty to preserve the morality of national customs.[40] Brazil had more than seventy officially registered casinos located in Rio de Janeiro, Niterói and Petrópolis, and in the spas where people took the waters in Minas Gerais and São Paulo. Some of them were magnificent. Rio de Janeiro's three main casinos – the Atlântico, the Copacabana Palace and the Urca Casino – were extremely glamorous. The Atlântico was located in a beautiful art deco building with an unforgettable view of Copacabana beach. The casino in the Copacabana Palace hotel was the most sumptuous: all the furniture – and the croupiers – came from France, the grill could fit six hundred people, there was a fresh orchid on every table, the dance floor was made of glass that was all lit up, and no one was allowed in if they were not in full evening dress. The casino in Urca had three orchestras which came up and down to the stage on moving platforms originating in the basement, a dazzling curtain of mirrors, and the greatest musical attractions in town – including Carmen Miranda.

The casinos were much more than just roulette and baccarat. They represented splendour, music, light; they were the perfect place for people to enjoy themselves and mix with different groups. They were frequented by the middle classes, rich businessmen, politicians and diplomats. Traditional families played side by side with the nouveau riche, expensive prostitutes, local celebrities and members of the jet set. But above all the casinos were an important work market, essential for Brazilian musicians. With President Dutra's decree, around 40,000 people all over the country lost their jobs. Many people tried to persuade the president that the loss to the country would be great and that gambling would continue clandestinely, but he would not change his mind. There was no alternative. The Dutra government was very attentive to prayers, but was impermeable to social demands.

THE RETURN TO CATETE

Getúlio Vargas openly broke with President Dutra in December 1946. Out of the limelight, he had withdrawn almost into self-imposed exile on his ranch in São Borja. But he continued to live and breathe politics, and remainded popular. In 1946 he was elected as both deputy and senator with a record-breaking number of votes. The fact that he had deliberately maintained his distance from the Congress and the work of the Constituent Assembly – he did not even go to Rio de Janeiro to sign the final text of the new constitution – made no difference at all to his prestige and capacity to mobilize the workers to support his new presidential campaign. But his political stance changed a great deal. Getúlio Vargas had left the presidency and joined the opposition. He needed to patch up his differences with President Dutra and the liberals of the National Democratic Union (UDN) and gain support for his future programme: increasing government intervention in the industrialization process, guaranteeing full employment, and combating poverty without sacrificing economic growth.[41]

In 1949, when the time came for officially nominating the candidates for the 1950 presidential elections, Getúlio Vargas was ready. He had already modified the main points of his old nationalist programme to accommodate the demands of the new international context. His new programme had two central aims: development and social welfare. The goal was nothing less than economic independence for the country, one of the greatest aspirations of the Brazilian people, especially during the Cold War. Furthermore, his focus on fighting inflation and increases in the cost of living identified his campaign with the segments most affected by President Dutra's economic policy. Furthermore, he managed to get the business community's support for his industrialization policy, which prioritized the industrial base. At sixty-seven years of age, Getúlio Vargas was in a hurry. He had every intention of returning to the presidential palace, the Catete, democratically elected, 'in the arms of the people'. The campaign slogan was a triumphant piece of political communication: 'He will return!' The campaign began with his parading in an open car along the Rua da Praia, at the time the most elegant shopping street in Porto Alegre and often the scene of political protests. In the following two months Getúlio Vargas visited every single state and all of the largest cities in the country. He also made the most astonishing agreements and alliances. To attract votes from the north and the northeast, for example, he chose as his vice-president a politician who was virtually unknown in the south: a lawyer called Café Filho who had actively participated in the National Freedom Alliance and was a fierce opponent of the *Estado Novo*.

Getúlio Vargas was more concerned with striking agreements than with being tied down to a party. In Pernambuco he made an alliance with the National Democratic Union. In São Paulo he worked with Governor Ademar de Barros, who had once been a political opponent. Ademar de Barros had a great capacity for communication with the masses, was politically ambitious, and controlled the small but very efficient Social Progress Party (PSP), which was well organized in the interior of the state. Getúlio Vargas's strategy of alliances was intended to produce short-term results, but it was risky, and he would pay a high price for it later on. Nonetheless, in the short term it worked: his candidacy was not identified with any one party; it brought new and old politicians together; it was supported by businessmen who were interested in the benefits of industrialization; and it had the electoral strength of the working class, as well as that of the new lower middle class, which was emerging in the country's major cities.

Furthermore, his adversaries showed little resilience. The National Democratic Union still had not got over being defeated by General Dutra, and once again nominated Eduardo Gomes as their candidate. But the Brigadier was incorrigible. For the second time, with a single declaration, he put an end to any chances he might have had of winning. At a political rally in June he announced he was against the minimum wage, and in favour of contractual freedom.[42] Meanwhile, the Social Democratic Party (PSD) had nominated its own candidate, the *Mineiro* Cristiano Machado, whom they soon realized had no chance of winning. Their solution was typical: while maintaining him as their official candidate, they worked on getting votes for Getúlio Vargas, leaving Cristiano Machado stranded, with very little support and even fewer votes.

Members of the National Democratic Union were disappointed, but Carlos Lacerda was enraged. 'Mr. Getúlio Vargas is a senator!' he ranted. 'He can't be a candidate for the presidency. As a candidate, he shouldn't be elected. Once elected, he shouldn't take office. Once in power we will have to resort to revolution to prevent him from govern-ing.'[43] Mr Lacerda meant what he said: during the following years he continued his tirades using the newspaper that he owned, the *Tribuna da Imprensa*, to attack the Vargas government. But there was no deny-ing Getúlio Vargas's victory. He received almost four million votes, 48.7 per cent of the total, as compared to 29.7 per cent received by Eduardo Gomes and 21.5 per cent by Cristiano Machado. On 31 Janu-ary 1951, Getúlio Vargas entered the Catete presidential palace once again, this time as the democratically elected president of Brazil.[44]

At the end of 1951, President Vargas sent the draft law creating Petrobras to Congress.[45] It was this legislation, more than any other, that convinced his contemporaries (and future generations) that his aim was indeed to guarantee Brazil's independence by creating an inde-pendent economy. The law was central to the entire government policy. The demand for oil and its derivatives made them Brazil's largest imports; the benefits of the country no longer having to depend on them were self-evident. The campaign for the nationalization of oil and minerals had started in the 1930s and had the ardent support of all Brazilians.

In the words of the Brazilian novelist Monteiro Lobato, at the begin-ning everything is either madness or a dream. And at times it can even be both. In 1937 when Monteiro Lobato wrote his children's tale *The Viscount's Well*, the idea of state-run oil prospecting and exploration in Brazil seemed like a dream, or at most, a good plot for a storybook. 'The discovery of oil on Dona Benta's farm has shocked the whole country,' Monteiro Lobato jokingly declared.[46] Perhaps he was not addressing the adults, but only the children, on whom Brazil's future economic independence depended:

> Nobody looked for petrol there because no one believed that petrol existed in that enormous area of eight and a half million square kilometres, all of it surrounded by the petrol wells of its republican neighbours. But as soon as the petrol burst out of Caramonguá n° 1, they all looked like fools and murmured 'Well I'll be damned! We had it all the time.'[47]

Monteiro Lobato, who died in 1948, did not live to see the expression on the faces of those who had denied the existence of petrol. Nor did he live to see the oil exploitation become the central issue of Brazil's political and economic life. However, by 1951, things had radically changed: the defence of a state monopoly of oil exploration had been transformed into one of the largest public opinion campaigns in Brazil's history. The Petrol Campaign, as the movement became known, took the form of major civic mobilization in defence of Brazil's national resources. Vast numbers of people from different segments of society united around the idea that Brazil's economic independence depended entirely on the political will of the Brazilians.

The subject of natural resources and oil in particular penetrated deeply into the collective imagination of the Brazilian people. It also contributed to the emergence of a sense of national sovereignty. This was one of the few mass movements in the country's history that brought together everyone on the ideological spectrum. It attracted military officers, communists, socialists, Catholics, members of the Brazilian Labour Party (PTB), and even a few from the National Democratic Union, chanting in unison the National Students' Union slogan: 'The petrol is ours.'[48]

Petrobras started operating in January 1954, while Getúlio Vargas was still president, as a state-owned company with a monopoly of the prospecting and exploration of oil. The oil industry represented one side of President Vargas's offensive to speed up the process of industrialization; the other was the generation of electric power. But whereas he had been successful in founding a state-owned oil monopoly, President Vargas did not succeed in completing the necessary procedures for the establishment of a state electricity holding. Eletrobrás was only to begin operating in 1962. But it was the Vargas administration that provided the infrastructure and financial support that allowed the country to increase its electric power generation throughout the following decade.

Hydroelectric plants require at least five years of operation before producing results. This was the reason why the national consumption of electricity did not increase more during the Vargas government: it was 5.8 million kilowatts when he took power in 1950, and had risen to 8.3 million kilowatts by the end of his term.[49] But it did not prevent his administration from executing a far-reaching industrialization programme, with special emphasis on two areas. The first of these was the expansion of key industries, especially steel. The second was the production of trucks and tractors, made possible through an agreement between the National Motor Factory and a group of international companies.

The agreement foresaw the gradual nationalization of production and had a very positive impact on the vehicle industry in the country, which was implemented by President Vargas's successor.[50] However, the proposal to create state companies in strategic areas, such as prospecting for and exploration of oil and the production of electric power, meant clashing with deeply entrenched interests, mostly those of foreign companies: Standard Oil, in the case of petrol, and the Light and Power Co. and the American & Foreign Power Co. in the case of electric power generation. With its successes and its failures, the Vargas government highlighted the clash between two proposals for modernization – his own, which was nationalist, and that of the opposition, which was in favour of an association with international capital. These were the two fundamentally different ways of looking at the role of the state which would divide Brazilian society during the following decades.

The first issue that divided these two approaches was the extent to which the state should implement social inclusion policies through legislation to bring thousands of new workers into the market. The second was the question of to what extent the country should rely on foreign capital as the driving force for its economic development. The ideology of the Vargas government was one of nationalist development,[51] state intervention in economic activities considered to be of national interest, and prioritizing industries that would lead to a diversification of the domestic market.

Brazil urgently needed to create a new role for itself on the international market that would free the country from reliance on agricultural exports – this was the *raison d'être* of the Vargas programme. The political costs were considerable: the programme clashed with the interests of foreign companies as well as with those of local industries and finance and that were associated, or about to become associated, with international capital. It also alienated important landowners who still had political power in their regions. All of these groups were hostile to government intervention and to regulatory measures in the economy. Nor did they want policies that led to the concentration of wealth and to the limitation of foreign capital in areas of the economy that were strategic for national development. Furthermore, they believed labour legislation constituted an excessive burden on companies.

Getúlio Vargas was a highly skilled politician, but he was authoritarian. Accustomed to dictatorial solutions, confident in his own charisma, widely experienced in uprisings and *coups d'état,* he simply was not cut out for working in a democratic environment. His strategy of not identifying with any single party and placing himself above political parties in general, had been highly successful during the electoral campaign, but was disastrous when it came to managing the country. The Brazilian Labour Party (PTB) was torn apart by internal disputes and the Social Democratic Party (PSD) was at times unable to respect its alliance with President Vargas due to interminable regional disputes. The National Democratic Union (UDN) took advantage of the situation by aligning with a group of smaller parties – the Liberation Party, the Republican Party and the Christian Democratic Party. Essentially, they created an opposition alliance that obstructed government initiatives.

The positions of the National Democratic Union were both radical and intransigent. Detrimental economic factors affecting the day-to-day lives of Brazilians contributed to the National Democratic Union success in opposing the government: high inflation and low workers' wages played into their hands. Starting in 1952, President Vargas's economic growth programme faced problems beyond his control: the Eisenhower government began to focus its Cold War strategy on Korea, Lebanon and Egypt, all of which were under imminent threat of becoming Soviet satellites. The United States withdrew its support of the Brazilian investment programme and, as if that were not enough, the World Bank insisted on the payment of overdue instalments. The consequences were not long in coming: rising inflation, increased cost of living, growth in public spending and collapse in wages.[52] President Vargas had lost control.

Despite the deterioration of the economic situation, the workers did not decamp and move over to the opposition, but they made it clear that their support was not unconditional. On 18 March 1953, 60,000 workers marched in protest in São Paulo, from the main cathedral square in the historic centre of the city (Praça da Sé) to the governor's palace, the seat of the state executive. The March of the Empty Pans, as it became known, which condemned the high prices and demanded higher wages, was just the beginning. Ten days later the whole city came to a halt and President Vargas finally realized the workers were in earnest. The Strike of the Three Hundred Thousand[53] lasted for almost a month and was coordinated by São Paulo's five largest trade unions: textile workers, steelworkers, printers, glassmakers and carpenters.

The strike achieved an average increase in wages of 32 per cent, and provided a model for the organization of mass movements until the military coup of 1964. Support for the strike came from all around the country, including from the students, and led to the creation of the first joint trade union. This organization included trade unions from different sectors that came together in the name of political action, which was forbidden by law. It also created a trade union centre. By the end of the strike, more than one hundred trade unions in São Paulo alone had joined the recently founded Trade Union Unity Pact.

Getúlio Vargas may have been authoritarian, but he was no fool. In March there was the Strike of the Three Hundred Thousand, followed in June by a dockworkers' strike that paralysed Rio de Janeiro. Before the month was over, he appointed João Goulart as Minister of Labour.[54] João Goulart, president of the Brazilian Labour Party (PTB), was an excellent speaker and a patient negotiator, and his party maintained very close ties with the trade union movement. President Vargas intended to show the workers the significance this appointment had for him: Jango, as Goulart had been nicknamed since he was a child, was his chosen political successor. When the new minister took office at the presidential palace after the end of the dockworkers' strike, President Vargas declared to a committee of trade union leaders 'I am Jango!' And he continued, 'He will be representing me in everything he says. You can trust in him as if he were me.'[55]

President Vargas appointed João Goulart to work with the social sectors that had supported him since the 1930s. The last thing that he wanted was to lose the political backing of the workers while he was battling for the economic and social development of the country. And the appointment was a success. João Goulart managed to bring the trade union movement and the government together again, to decrease employer pressure on the trade unions, and to build strong backing for President Vargas's policies. However, with the aggravated economic situation, the new minister's role was restricted to one of negotiation; it was impossible to prevent the outbreak of further strikes. And João Goulart was targeted by the opposition. With every step he made towards bringing the trade unions and the government together, he suffered an avalanche of criticism and denunciations by the press.

The National Democratic Union had a great deal of support in the media.[56] Newspapers and radios, especially in Rio de Janeiro and São

Paulo, had backed the candidacy of Brigadier Eduardo Gomes, both in 1945 and in 1950, and were fiercely opposed to President Vargas's proposals. Until that time, João Goulart had been seen as a provincial politician – young, wealthy and inexperienced. But his appointment as minister revealed his political skills. It was only then that the National Democratic Union understood the significance of President Vargas's choice of the younger man as his chosen successor. From then on the press frequently denounced him, accused him of organizing strikes in an attempt to create a 'Trade Unionist Republic': a union-controlled dictatorship, sustained by a new constitution, protected from its adversaries by the mass mobilization of the trade union movement, and legitimized by a worker-controlled Parliament.

Of course, members of the National Democratic Union were appalled at the prospect of a 'Trade Union Republic'. In reality, however, no such project existed. Nevertheless, Mr Goulart never managed to escape the notoriety of being the greatest proponent and beneficiary of such a plan. On the eve of the 1964 military coup, this much-repeated accusation was used against him – and became somewhat threatening, due to the polarization of the country and the broad mobilization of the masses. Carlos Lacerda, for his part, never missed an opportunity to maliciously mock João Goulart in the pages of the *Tribuna da Imprensa*. After all, João Goulart was not only Getúlio Vargas's protegé, but he was also thirty-four years old, single, handsome, a ladies' man and a bohemian! 'Little, slick João should should leave the ministry and go back to the cabaret, which is his university, his barracks and his sanctuary [. . .] Being a minister is not the same as dancing the tango.'[57]

João Goulart managed to hold onto the post for eight months. In January 1954, in reply to a demand from the trade unions, and with President Vargas's approval, he introduced a proposal to double the minimum wage, which, if approved, would rise to 2,400 cruzeiros.[58] Members of the National Democratic Union were in uproar in Congress, opposition newspapers had a field day, but the threat to democratic stability came from neither of these quarters. It came from the armed forces. In mid-February, forty-two colonels and thirty-nine lieutenant-colonels from the army delivered a manifesto severely criticizing the government to their commanding officers, who in turn publicly released the documents, which were in turn taken up by the National Democratic Union and the opposition newspapers.

The Colonels' Manifesto revealed the discontent in the army and was clearly seditious in intent.[59] It accused the Vargas government of accepting the 'atmosphere of illicit deals, fraudulent negotiations and mismanagement of public funds', stated that the crisis in leadership was affecting the armed forces, warned of riots in the streets, and condemned João Goulart's proposal for doubling the minimum wage which, they said, would put an excessive burden on the Treasury and invert the current status between civilians and the military. In hindsight, the manifesto is a clear indication that the armed forces already constituted a risk to Brazil's democratic institutions. It had been drawn up by the then Colonel Golbery do Couto e Silva, who, ten years later, would be one of the masterminds behind the *coup d'état*. It was also signed by other hardline officers who participated in planning the coup and running the military regime: Sylvio Frota, Ednardo d'Ávila Melo, Antônio Carlos Muricy, Adalberto Pereira dos Santos, Sizeno Sarmento and Amauri Kruel.

In 1954 there was no way that President Vargas could have foreseen what would happen ten years later, but he was in no doubt that the armed forces wanted more than just salaries and equipment. The Colonels' Manifesto expressed dissatisfaction and resentment, and worst of all, it was a flagrant act of indiscipline – its authors were one step away from conspiracy. Given the gravity of the situation, President Vargas took action. He dismissed his Minister of War, General Espírito Santo Cardoso, and made an agreement with Mr Goulart that he should resign. With João Goulart ousted and in the belief that he had neutralized the colonels' opposition, Getúlio Vargas now felt free to act. On the workers' day holiday, 1 May, when he always made a public pronouncement, President Vargas gave a further example of his way of doing politics: calculated moves, playing his cards very close to his chest, and always ahead of the game. He announced the doubling of the minimum wage as João Goulart had proposed. In his speech to the workers, after praising the work of his former labour minister, he went in for the counterattack: 'As citizens you have weight in the ballot boxes. As a class your votes will be decisive due to their force in numbers. You are the majority. Today you stand with the government. Tomorrow you will be the government.'[60]

GETÚLIO IS DEAD.
LONG LIVE GETÚLIO!

It was probably already too late for President Vargas to regain the upper hand – the opposition were in a stronger position to overthrow his government than the workers were to protect it. And things were to get even worse for the president. In the early hours of the morning of 5 August, the Minister of Justice, Tancredo Neves, was woken by a telephone call. On the other end of the line a colonel from the police headquarters, Milton Gonçalves, informed him that the journalist Carlos Lacerda had been the victim of an attack and had been slightly wounded in the foot. 'Is that all? It could be worse,' was Tancredo Neves's reaction. But after a short pause the colonel informed him that Carlos Lacerda had been accompanied by an officer from the air force, Major Rubens Vaz, who had been killed. With this information Tancredo Neves's reaction changed: 'Nothing could be worse.'[61]

It is not known whether these were his exact words, but Tancredo Neves was certainly not exaggerating. The attack on Carlos Lacerda's life was a catastrophe for the government: it could spark off a military crisis without precedent in the history of Brazil, further isolate the president and undermine his authority. And the media would have a field day, as they always did when there was a government crisis.[62] Mr Lacerda was an extremely influential figure in the press, and even though his newspaper the *Tribuna da Imprensa* had a limited daily edition of around 10,000 copies – and never made the slightest attempt at impartiality – Carlos Lacerda held great prestige and a single word from him could create newspaper headlines for days on end.

Carlos Lacerda's attacks on Getúlio Vargas had become more and more ferocious. Unable to bring about a *coup d'état*, he invested all his energy in destabilizing the government through the press. He denounced a sequence of scandals, some real and others imaginary, that compromised the Vargas administration – the cronyism and exchanging of favours, illegal loans, government corruption and its anti-Americanism. With constant newspaper and radio coverage, these denunciations created public outrage for weeks and put the government under considerable pressure, corroding its credibility and increasingly contributing to its political and social isolation. Although some of the denunciations were forged, others seriously compromised the government. After 1953, when there was a scandal involving the newspaper *Última Hora*, President Vagas had lost his battle with the press. Even so, and much to Carlos Lacerda's frustration, no matter how much effort he put into bringing down the Vargas government, he could not reach the president himself.

The press played a decisive role in weakening Getúlio Vargas's base of support, above all from the urban middle classes. But after the scandal involving *Última Hora*, Brazil's leading newspapers – *Correio da Manhã*, *Diário de Notícias*, *Diário Carioca*, *O Globo*, *O Jornal*, *O Estado de S. Paulo* and the *Folha da Manhã* – became openly involved in the political crisis that was to topple Getúlio Vargas's second government. The *Última Hora* had been founded as per an agreement between President Vargas and the journalist Samuel Wainer – one of the stars of the *Diários Associados*,[63] the most powerful communication group in the country. It was the newspaper that had managed to secure the interview with Getúlio Vargas, on his ranch in São Borja, during which he had announced his candidacy for the presidency.[64] During the electoral campaign the two men came to an agreement on how the newspaper would be run. President Vargas, a great proponent of the *Última Hora*, was only too aware of the importance of a direct channel for government propaganda and communication with the people. Meanwhile, Mr Wainer constantly took advantage of his position as owner of the newspaper that was, in effect, the spokesperson for the president.

Although Samuel Wainer was partial to government priorities and the relationship between the newspaper and the administration was dubious, the *Última Hora* was also the most innovative newspaper of its time. It was modern, creative – with coloured printing, and published pithy articles and photographs of the daily life in the big cities. It also paid high salaries. Its success was immediate and circulation was extraordinary. The small group of entrepreneurs who controlled the country's leading communications vehicles felt threatened: they blamed President Vargas for intervening directly in the communications market and changing the rules of the game in his favour. As a result they joined forces and confronted the government. With the vast majority of the press against him, Samuel Wainer came under heavy attack and a Congressional Enquiry (CPI) was set up to investigate him. It was established at the request of the National Democratic Union with the aim of proving illicit use of government funds. Carlos Lacerda also accused Samuel Wainer – who was Jewish and had been born in Bessarabia, then a part of the Russian Empire – of having falsified his nationality. According to the 1946 Constitution, it was illegal for foreigners to own newspapers. The Congressional Enquiry found Mr Wainer guilty. It was determined that the loans the newspaper had received were the result of the traffic of influence. The illegal loans could be traced as far as Ricardo Jafet, the president of the Banco do Brasil – but no further. The National Democratic Union's minute investigations and Carlos Lacerda's determination to involve the president were all in vain: neither the press nor the parliamentary inquiry's final report were able to establish any direct connection to the president.

However, the above-mentioned crisis that began on 5 August was a far more serious matter. The attack on Carlos Lacerda occurred outside his apartment building, on Rua Tonelero, in Copacabana.[65] Major Rubens Florentino Vaz, mortally wounded in the attempt, was a part of a group of young air force officers, supporters of the National Democratic Union (*udenista*),[66] who rotated as Mr Lacerda's bodyguards. Major Vaz's murder placed the armed forces at the heart of the crisis. The air force opposed President Vargas, and the officers venerated Brigadier Eduardo Gomes. This was an opportunity they could not afford to miss. With little concern for either the constitution or the military hierarchy, they established an inquiry of their own into Major Vaz's death.

Although Tancredo Neves was the Minister of Justice and the investigation of the crime was the responsibility of the Civil Police, neither he nor his subordinates were able to undertake an autonomous investigation of the crime. Instead, the air force installed a group of officers to study the occurrence at the Galeão airbase. The officers were given full powers, and the air force also organized a military operation to arrest the assassins. The 'Galeão Republic', as the group was called by Getúlio Vargas's supporters (*getulistas*)[67] – initially with irony, but later with dread – was a government within the government. The air force inquiry discovered that the attempted assassination of Carlos Lacerda had been planned by amateurs and carried out by hired gunmen. The getaway vehicle was a taxi from the rank outside the Catete presidential palace, waiting for passengers on a nearby corner. Before the crime, the very same taxi had followed Carlos Lacerda all around town until the gunmen finally decided where the ambush would take place. The air force had no difficulty in locating the driver and discovering who had ordered the crime. The demise of Getúlio Vargas's government began with the gunmen's confession that they had been hired by the head of the presidential guard, Gregório Fortunato. The *coup de grâce* came when officers from the air force entered the presidential palace, removed all of Gregório Fortunato's files and sent the contents to the press. The files revealed the extent of the corruption that surrounded President Vargas. There were large-scale illegal transactions recorded involving numerous advisers and leading government figures, as well as a member of Getúlio Vargas's family – his son Manuel Vargas.

Carlos Lacerda became obsessed with the idea that Getúlio Vargas had been directly or indirectly involved in the attempt to kill him, and was vociferous in making his view known before the police investigation began. 'Before God, I accuse just one man for this crime – the protector of thieves Getúlio Vargas,'[68] he thundered in the *Tribuna da Imprensa* the day after the attack. It is probable that Gregório Fortunato, a vain man with little education, and blindly devoted to Getúlio Vargas, had allowed himself to be corrupted. This is not surprising, given his proximity to the president. He was able to establish a kind of parallel power structure within the palace and had taken matters into his own hands. It is possible – as even the opposition and Carlos Lacerda might concede – that the president was an honest man, that he had not been involved in any of the misconduct. But there can be no doubt that corruption was rife in the government and that President Vargas, even if he was unaware of his bodyguard's criminal enterprise, was not exempt from personal responsibility.

President Vargas passed his final days confined to the presidential palace. Public opinion was against him, demands for his resignation were increasing, and his traditional supporters were beginning to abandon him. In the early hours of 24 August the president called a meeting of his ministers. If he still nurtured any hopes for resistance, they now disappeared. All his ministers – with the exception of Tancredo Neves – suggested that he either resign or temporarily vacate the presidency.[69] The alternatives were even worse. The president could no longer count on the support of the army as he had in 1937, nor on the mobilization of the workers who had come to his aid in 1945. If he negotiated his resignation, he would be demoralized; if he resisted, he would be deposed. When the meeting was over and he had withdrawn to his private quarters, his brother Benjamin came to inform him that a subpoena had been issued for him to appear before the Committee of Inquiry at Galeão. It was only then that he knew it was over. He closed the door and lay down on the bed. At some point between 8:30 and 8:40 on the morning of 24 August 1954, Getúlio Vargas put a pistol to the left side of his chest and pulled the trigger.

About an hour later, *Repórter Esso* – the most important news programme on Brazilian radio – went on the air in a special edition to inform the Brazilian people of Getúlio Vargas's suicide. The country went mad. People were stunned. They left their houses and embraced each other in tears. Gradually the situation spun out of control. In Porto Alegre, Belo Horizonte, Salvador and São Paulo angry, bitter crowds marched through the streets armed with stones, clubs and their fury.[70] Thousands of protesters occupied the centre of Rio de Janeiro and converged on *Cinelândia*,[71] destroying everything along the way that had any connection to the opposition against Getúlio Vargas.

The crowd tore National Democratic Union (UDN) propaganda off the lamp posts, smashed the Standard Oil building windows, threw stones at the façade of the American Embassy and at the buildings that housed the newspapers O *Globo* and *Tribuna da Imprensa*. They also attacked the newpaper delivery trucks – the following day only the *Última Hora* appeared. And the crowd did not forget Carlos Lacerda; they chased him down and he took refuge in the American Embassy. Luckily for him, when they threatened to invade the building, the air force sent a helicopter that managed to make a rooftop rescue and take him to safety aboard the navy cruiser *Barroso*, anchored in Guanabara Bay.

Around one million people gathered in front of the Catete presidential palace in an attempt to see the body. Many were weeping and some actually fainted. Others, after entering the room where the wake was taking place, clung to the coffin. At 8:30 on the morning of 25 August the crowd that accompanied Getúlio Vargas's body to Santos Dumont airport formed an immense funeral cortege filling the streets from Flamengo beach to the city centre. When the plane carrying the president's body back to his ranch in São Borja had taken off, the crowd suddenly realized that they were gathered right in front of the general headquarters of the Third Air Zone. It was unavoidable: grief turned into fury. As the multitude advanced, the terrified air force soldiers and officers opened fire on the unarmed crowd. The firing went on for fifteen minutes. In the panic, women and children were trampled underfoot, one person was killed and many others were wounded by grenade splinters, sabres and gunfire. The crowd fled, but regrouped in the city centre, where it was joined by thousands more protesters, and the conflicts continued throughout the night.

Getúlio Vargas's suicide frustrated the opposition. They were left without direction, thwarted in their attempt to worsen the political crisis, demoralize the president and force him to resign, thereby making way for a military coup. It was President Vargas's final political triumph. His epistolary will left no doubt as to how he intended his suicide to be understood: international groups, in alliance with Brazilian partners, were conducting an underground campaign to block his programme for development. 'If the birds of prey want someone's blood, if they want to continue sucking the Brazilian people's, I offer my own life in sacrifice,'[72] he declared. Otávio Mangabeira, one of the leading lights of the National Democratic Union, still in a state of shock, recognized that the opposition's political gains had now slipped through their fingers: 'He has beaten us once again,' he said.[73] Before committing suicide Getúlio Vargas had written: 'I have chosen this means to always be with you. [. . .] I fear nothing. I serenely take the first step on the path of eternity and exit life to enter history.' Taking his own life was a powerful gesture that managed to immobilize the opposition. But it was the people in the streets who kept fighting for democracy and managed to prevent a *coup d'état*.[74]

16

The 1950s and 1960s: Bossa Nova, Democracy and Underdevelopment

COUP AND COUNTER-COUP

The early morning of carnival Saturday, 1956, two air force officers, Major Haroldo Veloso and Captain José Chaves Lameirão, arrived at the Afonsos Airbase in Rio de Janeiro, walked past the guards, overpowered the officer on duty, and broke into the munitions deposit. They forced their way into the hangar, stole a combat plane laden with arms and explosives, and took off for the landing strip at Jacareacanga, a tiny air force garrison in the middle of the Atlantic Forest, on the border of Pará and Mato Grosso. The two officers were fanatical supporters of the National Democratic Union (*udenistas*), who venerated Carlos Lacerda and were indignant at the victory of Getúlio Vargas and his supporters (*getulistas*) in the October 1955 elections. Their intention was nothing less than to ignite a rebellion in central Brazil and to start a civil war.[1]

The uprising of Jacareacanga lasted fewer than twenty days – by the end of February it had been crushed. However, the episode was a grave indication of the country's political instability. The president whom the air force officers were so determined to overthrow had taken office less than a month prior: Juscelino Kubitschek. 'JK', as he became fondly known, was a politician of considerable prestige who had risen through the ranks of the Social Democratic Party (PSD) in Minas Gerais. He had been federal deputy, mayor of Belo Horizonte and governor of the state. But despite his experience and the fact that he had won the election, he faced a considerable struggle ahead before he could actually take office. After the commotion caused by Getúlio Vargas's suicide and the ensuing public uproar, the National Democratic Union was determined to stop the presidential elections set to take place on

3 October 1955 – which they had very little chance of winning.[2] However, they were outmanoeuvred by the Social Democratic Party and the Brazilian Labour Party (PTB), which quickly formed an alliance to defend Getúlio Vargas's legacy by presenting two remarkable candidates: Juscelino Kubitschek for president and, as his vice-president, João Goulart.

João Goulart's candidacy was anathema to members of the National Democratic Union. Nonetheless, since they failed to dig up any scandals about him, their only alternative was to put up a rival candidate. Once again, the party relied on moralistic discourse, choosing a candidate from the armed forces – this time from the army, General Juarez Távora. The general was one of the leaders of the 1930 revolution and had broken with Getúlio Vargas before the *Estado Novo*. As was their wont, the party chose a slogan that was so bad it was hard to believe: 'Vote for General Juarez Távora, the white-haired lieutenant'. Even so, the election was close. Juscelino Kubitschek won with 36 per cent of the votes, as compared to 30 per cent for Juarez Távora, 26 per cent for Ademar de Barros and 8 per cent for Plínio Salgado, the former leader of the *integralistas*. There was a separate election for the vice-president in which João Goulart won hands down, receiving more votes than Juscelino Kubitschek: 3,591,409 compared to 3,077,411.

Carlos Lacerda, who knew his party had lost the elections even before the first votes were counted, had no intention of standing by and watching yet another victory for Getúlio Vargas's political successors. Instead, he launched a campaign to prevent the winning candidates from taking office and, with the support of the armed forces, tried to impose an emergency government on the country, preferably a parliamentary one.[3] He wanted a government capable of 'reforming democracy and freeing Brazil of political bandits'.[4] The National Democratic Union's justification for contesting the election result was brazenly opportunistic. They claimed Juscelino Kubitschek's victory was invalid since he had not received an overall majority of the votes, although neither the 1946 Constitution nor the electoral legislation of the time demanded an absolute majority. The National Democratic Union wanted to move the goalposts after the game had already begun. Nevertheless, their arguments received a lot of attention in the press and had the army's support. Before long the political temperature was approaching boiling point. It is still not known whether the National Democratic Union or the military started the conspiracy, but one thing is certain: a *coup d'état* was being planned. It had the discreet support of the current vice-president, Mr Café Filho – who had taken over the presidency after Getúlio Vargas's suicide – and of a group of powerful ministers, including Prado Kelly, Minister of Justice, Amorim do Vale, Minister of the Navy, and Eduardo Gomes, Minister of the Air Force. But they had one formidable opponent: General Henrique Batista Duffles Teixeira Lott, the Minister of War.[5] The thorn in their side was an impeccable legalist who was obsessed with discipline and had the unswerving loyalty of the troops. As long as General Lott was in command there was no chance that a *coup d'état* planned from inside the army would succeed.

In early November the political situation suddenly changed. Mr Café Filho claimed to have fallen ill and his doctors prescribed complete rest. Although leaders of the Social Democratic Party, including Tancredo Neves and José Maria Alkmin, did not believe the vice-president was truly ill, a situation that favoured the conspirators, the constitution had to be followed, and the president of the Chamber of Deputies, Carlos Luz, became interim president.[6]

Carlos Luz did not conceal his support for the conspirators. He was certain he would be able to dismiss General Lott without creating a backlash from the army. As soon as Carlos Luz had taken office he summoned his Minister of War to the presidential palace. He kept General Lott waiting for almost two hours. When Carlos Luz finally received General Lott, it was with the news that he had overturned one of the general's recent decisions, thereby forcing the general to submit his resignation. In the early hours of 11 November thirty generals and a group of sergeants from the garrisons in Rio de Janeiro arrived at General Lott's house, where they found him still in his pyjamas. They had come to offer him their support, and General Lott must have thought, let's fight fire with fire. He went straight to his office, confirmed over the radio that the barracks in Espírito Santo, Minas Gerais, Paraná, Mato Grosso and São Paulo were all behind him, summoned the president of the Senate and the majority leader of the Chamber and told them his plans. He then ordered the tanks to occupy the streets. General Lott's counterattack was devastating. The civilian leaders were in a state of uproar, and there were even deputies who whispered in the general's ear that he should take power himself. But General Lott, the exemplary legalist, provided Congress with a way out. An extraordinary session was convoked and Carlos Luz was deposed. During his mere three days as president, he had brought the country to the verge of civil war. The deputies appointed the president of the Senate, Nereu Ramos, as the new interim president. No one was arrested and the conspirators suffered no consequences.

No sooner had the political situation been normalized than Mr Café Filho was released from hospital and declared he was ready to assume the presidency again. Things were back to square one. The National Democratic Union started conspiring, the army sent the tanks back onto the streets of Rio de Janeiro, and a special emergency session of Congress was convoked. This time the deputies realized that they could no longer collude with the conspirators. They refused to reappoint Mr Café Filho, reaffirmed Nereu Ramos as interim president, and confirmed that the president-elect would take office on 31 January 1956. They extended the state of siege until that date. Both Juscelino Kubitschek and João Goulart were able to breathe a sigh of relief. For his part, General Lott never accepted the idea that he had been the leader of a counter-coup. He had, rather, been the leader of a 'movement to return to the established constitutional order'. His argument made absolute sense. Yet there is no denying that he had rebelled against a legitimately constituted authority, however ill-intentioned that authority may have been. And it was not only a question of a break in the chain of command. The military intervention of November 1955 – the 'Novembrada' – revealed to the country that within the armed forces there was support for a whole range of political beliefs, including nationalism and even democracy.[7]

The sergeants were the first to form ties with the labour movement, and they were later followed by the navy and the marines. It was here that the Brazilian Labour Party made its greatest mistake. Instead of insisting on strictly apolitical, professional military institutions, subordinated to a civilian government, the labour movement took the same path that had already been trodden by the National Democratic Union. Their ideal army was interventionist, reformist, and able to represent the interests of the people – like the *tenentes'* movement during the First Republic. The political parties of the period, on both the left and the right, made the same mistake: they encouraged the involvement of the armed forces in politics, accepted their interference in a democratic regime, and gave them a place on the public stage. They only realized the gravity of their error when it was too late to be rectified – in March 1964.

THE HAWKER OF DREAMS

When Juscelino Kubitschek took office as determined by the constitution, his first act was to confirm General Lott as Minister of War. For his part, although the general was not wholly successful in preventing political debate inside the barracks, he was at least able to keep the armed forces under control. He integrated the activists in the military into its hierarchy, which was decisive in ensuring political stability. After all, the legitimacy of his government had been questioned from the outset, having been established in an atmosphere of crisis. Nonetheless, Juscelino Kubitschek consolidated his position. He treated the armed forces with kid gloves.[8] He granted amnesty to all officers who had been involved in insurrections, including Jacareacanga – for which he reaped political rewards, without perhaps reflecting on the dangers of a culture of impunity. He was persuasive with the military, explaining to the high command the advantage to the military of his economic development programme. It would allow them to continue building a weapons industry and would meet their demands for modernization, reorganization and rearmament. President Kubitschek was good with words and even better at winning people over. For the exclusive use by the air force, he bought a modern Vickers Viscount aircraft, fully equipped with comfortable seats, not to mention the pressurized cabin and 600-mph cruising speed. To keep the peace with the admirals, he purchased an aircraft carrier from the British navy, which they rebaptized the *Minas Gerais* in tribute to the president. But, perhaps most significantly, President Kubitschek appointed military officers to an increasing number of strategic posts in the federal administration and planning areas, notably in the oil and public safety sectors.

There is no doubt the president knew how to make the best of every situation, and to make it work to his advantage. But he also had an unbeatable card up his sleeve: the Targets Plan.[9] It was thanks to this plan that President Kubitschek, in his first year of office, built a successful alliance between social groups with widely differing interests, all of whom were keen to participate in his major economic plan. The Targets Plan was revealed at a ministerial meeting on 1 February 1956, his second day in office, and was published in the *Official Gazette* the following day. It was the most ambitious modernization programme ever introduced in Brazil. The plan allowed Juscelino Kubitschek to transform his campaign slogan – should he be elected, Brazil would grow 'fifty years in five' – into reality, and to alter the structure of the country's productive capacity. The Targets Plan made President Kubitschek's government a success. With the plan, states were made responsible for implementing rapid economic growth programmes. The process of industrialization with emphasis on consumer durables was broadened, which transformed the habits and daily routine of the Brazilian people, who were thrilled with the latest household appliances – washing machines, electric grills, portable radios, electric fans, electric cookers, floor polishers, stereos and televisions. These were accompanied by equally wonderful household items such as soap flakes, insect spray and batteries, and by a whole range of utensils and articles of clothing mass produced from cheap, brightly coloured synthetic materials with fascinating names: nappa, polymer, nylon, rayon, acrylic, Formica, vinyl and linoleum.[10]

The Targets Plan defined thirty-one objectives distributed in four special priorities. The first of these was to invest in transportation, especially highways, and boost the car industry – the other three were to channel resources into energy, heavy industry and food. In 1958 two novelties appeared on the streets of Brazil: the DKW-Vemag which, although noisy, was the first vehicle to leave the assembly line with 50 per cent of its parts made in Brazil; and the Rural Willys, the first four-wheel drive vehicle to be produced in Brazil. Perhaps the plan's greatest achievement was the expansion of the road network. Between 1956 and 1960 the Kubitschek government paved 6,000 kilometres of new highway, in a country that until then had had a road network of just 4,000 kilometres. This improved the circulation of merchandise between the rural areas and the industrialized cities and created new markets.[11] In January 1958, with the international price of oil relatively low and Brazil's new automobile industry taking hold, President Kubitschek decided it would be a worthwhile challenge to carve out new highways in the red earth of the central plateau. He summoned the agronomist Bernardo Sayão, an engineer from the Ministry of Agriculture – a man with film-star looks and a spirit of adventure – and suggested they 'cut down the forest and unite the country from north to south'.[12] During the construction of the highway from Brasília to Belém, Mr Sayão was crushed to death by an enormous falling tree. But the road he had engineered linked the states of Goiás, Maranhão and Pará, incorporating Amazônia into the Brazilian market. There was now a new alternative for offsetting regional inequalities.[13]

Mr Sayão was not the only one who collaborated with Juscelino Kubitschek on projects that to many seemed crazy. This was the president's style: a talented negotiator, an astute politician and a man with entrepreneurial vision who recognized the capacity of others and had an irresistible smile.[14] In his own time and on his own ground the president seduced, insisted, persuaded. Even Carlos Lacerda, his main opponent, could not entirely conceal his admiration: Juscelino Kubitschek was 'an extremely astute politician and the nicest person in the world,'[15] he conceded.

Juscelino Kubitschek's inimitable style made all the difference when dealing with problems and engaging the sympathy of different social groups, but it only partially explains his success. The other important aspect of his success was most likely the Targets Plan itself, which became symbolic of Brazil reaching its full potential. The government programme was emblematic of a new optimism, an enthusiasm about being Brazilian. It was a programme that could heal the injustices of the past – Brazil's historical heritage of poverty and social inequality – and open the doors to modernity. The key to constructing this new country was called 'developmentalism', which implied an understanding that Brazilian society – lagging behind and dependent on more advanced countries – had split into two: one part of the country had remained backward and traditional while the other was rapidly developing and becoming modern. Both of these, the centre and the periphery, formed part of the same country. It was a duality that could only be addressed by industrialization and urbanization.[16] President Kubitschek's confidence in his project for Brazil was contagious, and it is not hard to understand why. The JK project was based on the belief that the construction of a new society depended on the will of the state and on the collective will of the people who, through its implementation, could finally meet their destiny.

WANTED: A BRAZILIAN PEOPLE

A project of such scope had great potential for bringing people together – and many intellectuals were attracted to it. The Kubitschek government maintained close ties with a range of intellectuals of different origins and specialities, all of whom believed in a modern Brazil, a country not based on the North American model. One of these groups was the Brazilian Institute for Further Studies (Iseb). Based in Rio de Janeiro, it was subordinated to the office of the Presidential Chief of Staff.[17] The Institute provided a venue where politicians, intellectuals, students and artists could socialize. Members included many of the leading thinkers of the day: Álvaro Vieira, Alberto Guerreiro Ramos, Nelson Werneck Sodré and Hélio Jaguaribe. This group provided the theoretical basis for high-level government projects and contributed to a more global approach to Brazil and the industrialization process. The group also argued in favour of an unorthodox form of nationalism that was not anti-American but rather based on an objective definition of Brazil's national interests.

The Brazilian Institute for Further Studies was not the only think tank affiliated with the Kubitschek government. In 1954 the economist Celso Furtado, who was just over thirty, had recently published his first book, *The Brazilian Economy*. The book was the result of his study of the formulas drawn up by the Economic Commission for Latin America and the Caribbean (ECLAC). This United Nations body was established in Chile in 1949, and Mr Furtado himself was a member until 1957. The ECLAC analyses contributed to the Targets Plan, but Celso Furtado's book went further. It introduced new ways of thinking about the country and provided government technicians with a keyword – 'underdevelopment' – to describe the dilemmas of Brazilian society.[18] Underdevelopment was characteristic of societies like Brazil, whose economy had historically served to support the wider colonial system and had therefore not developed an economy that adequately supported its own population. Despite the advance of the industrialization process, the fundamental problems still remained: the archaic agrarian structure, the subservience of monoculture exports to international capitalism, the duality of Brazil's production structure, and the profound inequality in the ownership of the means of production.

According to Mr Furtado, moving beyond such a situation could only be achieved by a series of state-implemented 'core reforms' (*reformas de base*) in the areas of agriculture, finance, banking, urbanization, taxation, administration and university education. These core reforms were supported by Brazil's left-wing nationalist parties. By 1962, during the João Goulart administration, they became a central element of their political platform. The word 'underdevelopment' thus found its way into popular vocabulary. More importantly, it continued to be used in the context Celso Furtado had intended: in order to confront underdevelopment it must first be identified.

The push for developmental reformism – the key concept of underdevelopment – and the idea that the Brazilian people must be the agent for their own transformation, began to take hold among government technocrats and intellectuals. This emphasis on agency and reform coincided with a flourishing of the arts, where these concepts also rapidly became influential. For example, São Paulo's Teatro de Arena, opened in 1953, maintained a permanent cast of young actors and scenic artists who were committed to modernism and dramatic realism in order create a 'truly Brazilian form of dramaturgy'.[19] In February 1958 the group presented Gianfrancesco Guarnieri's play *Eles não usam black tie*[20] in a small, downtown makeshift space with approximately one hundred seats. Against the background of the daily routine of factory workers, the play discussed the power of capital and the right to strike for higher wages. It was a huge success and was seen as a genuinely new form of Brazilian drama.

Other vanguard theatrical groups emerged, such as the *Oficina* (Workshop) and *Opinião* (Opinion), but the commitment to modernism and dramatic realism was by no means restricted to the theatre; it spread to the cinema where it assumed a variety of forms. Companhia Cinematográfica Vera Cruz, in São Paulo, set out to produce films of European and North American calibre, following Hollywood aesthetics, but with essentially Brazilian characteristics.[21] Unfortunately, the experience was a failure. Although the company dealt with local themes – Lima Barreto's[22] *O cangaçeiro*[23] was a huge success – the production system was too expensive and the characters tended to become stereotyped. The return on the company's financial investments was too slow in coming, and the Vera Cruz Film Company went bankrupt in 1954.

However, a similar experiment in Rio de Janeiro was highly successful. Atlântida Studios produced a continuous stream of films that were low-budget, unpretentious, and completed very quickly. The critics turned up their noses, but the public adored the films and a new type of popular comedy – the *chanchada* – became the hallmark of Atlântida and drew massive crowds to the cinema.[24] It is not hard to understand why. The *chanchadas* parodied the great Hollywood successes using popular language reminiscent of the circus, revues and stand-up comics. In many cases the cast had previously worked in the circus or in radio, or both – Grande Otelo, Oscarito, Dercy Gonçalves, Zé Trindade and Ankito. The characters spoke directly to the audience, and there was always the addition of a little samba, a few jokes, and beautiful girls. The plots seemed ingenuous, but were inspired by the lives of ordinary Brazilians, who saw themselves reflected in these films. There was always a happy ending and the *chanchada* was enormously popular: people could see and hear themselves on the screen.

In 1955 the young filmmaker Nelson Pereira dos Santos was the first to depict the reality of Brazilian poverty on the screen. He converted Celso Furtado's stance into the language of film: underdevelopment must be identified in order to be confronted. The film *Rio, 40 graus* (*Rio, 40°C*) abandoned the Hollywood aesthetic. It was produced quickly and cheaply, and shot on location all over Rio de Janeiro – the zoo, Maracanã Stadium, the Sugarloaf, Copacabana, the Christ statue. The cast was made up of amateur actors.[25] The director had a clear idea of what he wanted to depict: the living conditions in the *favelas*. He approached the subject with delicacy, without prejudice and with unprecedented realism, but also with subtlety, leaving room for the imagination. The film showed the beauty of Rio de Janeiro on a sweltering Sunday, but what most impressed the spectator was the reality of a city plagued by poverty and violence. The opening scene is unforgettable: a broad panorama of Rio de Janeiro closes in on the *morro do Cabuçu favela*. In the next shot, five boys appear walking down through the *favela* hillside, as if the city below belonged to them – a scene that is full of lyricism. Rio de Janeiro had never been so forcefully depicted. Many viewers did not understand the director's vision or did not agree with it. Among these was Colonel Geraldo de Meneses Cortes, head of the Federal Department of Public Safety, who banned the film from being shown throughout Brazil. He justified his decision by saying that the official temperature of the city had never reached 40°C – the maximum that had ever been registered was 30.7°C – and that the director was not only a liar but a communist whose film was an unforgivable mockery of the federal capital.

When Mr Café Filho withdrew from the government, Colonel Cortes lost his post and the film was allowed to be shown again. From then on Nelson Pereira dos Santos was recognized as a groundbreaking filmmaker in Brazil, and *Rio, 40 graus* became the source of inspiration for the vanguard movement: *Cinema Novo*. The most emblematic films of the *Cinema Novo* were released in the aftermath of Juscelino Kubitschek's government. They include *Vidas secas* (1963), also directed by Nelson Pereira dos Santos; *Os fuzis* (1964) by Ruy Guerra,[26] and the first showing of *Deus e o diabo na terra do sol* (1964) (*Black God, White Devil*), written and directed by Glauber Rocha.[27] The precursor of all these films was *Rio, 40 graus*, which Glauber Rocha had referred to as 'the first revolutionary film exploded in the Third World prior to the Cuban Revolution'.[28]

Glauber Rocha was both the great leader of *Cinema Novo* and the most talented among the movement's artists. *Deus e o diabo na terra do sol* is not his first work, but it is without doubt the most eloquent: a landmark for Brazil, and an international example of 1960s vanguard cinema. The film draws on historical, literary and musical elements mixed with popular culture and plunges into the violence and mysticism that emerge from the inner depths of Brazil. This is filtered through a narrative of great aesthetic effect. *Deus e o diabo na terra do sol* has iconic moments: the relentless eye of the camera following protagonists Manuel and Rosa to the sound of the aria from Villa-Lobos's *Bachianas Brasileiras no. 5* is one of the great scenes in Brazilian cinema.[29]

The three main objectives of *Cinema Novo* can be summarized as follows: to change the history of Brazilian cinema, to change Brazil, and, time permitting, to change the world as well.[30] The movement produced a generation of filmmakers: Cacá Diegues, Joaquim Pedro de Andrade, Nelson Pereira dos Santos, Ruy Guerra, Gustavo Dahl, Paulo César Sarraceni, Leon Hirszman, Walter Lima Jr, Arnaldo Jabor and, of course, Glauber Rocha. The connection between art, violence and history, used as a means to explain Brazil, is the distinguishing mark of the films produced by this generation. They sought to identify the problems of ordinary Brazilians and saw themselves as nothing less than the incarnation of the nation's conscience. But the language adopted by these films was accessible to a limited public only. In *Cinema Novo* aesthetic and political content override commercial considerations – the film is an end in itself. But from the point of view of the creation of a cinematographic language, the works of the movement remain unsurpassed in Brazilian cinema.

Whereas *Rio, 40 graus* and others in its genre depicted the reality of a poverty-stricken urban population, the Bossa Nova revealed a completely different Brazil – one that was young, happy and luminous. It was a breath of fresh air for the country's cultural life, and for the political atmosphere too. At first hearing, many people failed to grasp its rhythmic subtlety and the relationship between Bossa Nova and Brazil. Some thought the dissonance was a sign of alienation of the composers, who did not discuss politics; others interpreted it as an attempt by the *Carioca* middle class to Americanize samba. But whether for or against, no one was indifferent. As a musical movement, Bossa Nova was short-lived, at least at that moment. It started in 1958 and lasted until around 1963.[31] Nevertheless, in that short time a new musical genre was created, whose rhythmical patterns turned samba on its head and whose dissonant harmonies inaugurated a new, concise style of interpretation. The precursors of the movement were a group of musicians who admired the freedom of American jazz – Dick Farney, Lúcio Alves, Johnny Alf, and the band *Os Cariocas* – and it was brought to fruition by a group of young composers who wanted to create a very different sonority from that of the omnipresent samba and the sensibility of conventional music. These included Tom Jobim, João Gilberto, Vinicius de Moraes, Carlos Lyra, Roberto Menescal, Ronaldo Bôscoli, Newton Mendonça, Sérgio Mendes and Eumir Deodato. The muse of Bossa Nova was Nara Leão, who became its definitive interpreter, hostess and, eventually, its adversary. Bossa Nova's greatest composers were Tom Jobim, who created the characteristic harmonies that accompanied the dissonant vocal line, and João Gilberto, who created its distinctive rhythm.[32] Mr Gilberto offset the rhythm of the vocals against his millimetric precision on the guitar.

In 1958 when the two men recorded João Gilberto's first LP, the public's reaction was largely unfavourable. Still, people understood a new and different form of music was emerging, with a simplified rhythm that allowed for more sophisticated harmonies. The movement took off, both as a musical language that people wanted to sing, and as a social movement, and became the seed that produced the musical forms of the 1960s – the afro-sambas of Baden Powell, the protest songs against the dictatorship, *Tropicalismo* and the *Clube da Esquina*. Bossa Nova also became a commercial craze, both in Brazil and the United States. It became a brand name for associating products – trousers, glasses, powdered milk and even a particular way of combing one's hair – with the idea of youth, modernity and daring.[33]

And Bossa Nova conquered the world: it was assimilated by popular music in innumerable countries, starting in Europe and the United States, and recorded by leading international artists, including Frank Sinatra, who in 1967 recorded an entire LP of Bossa Nova songs, *Francis Albert Sinatra & Antonio Carlos Jobim*.[34] Bossa Nova expressed the best of Brazil and confirmed its viability: modern, cosmopolitan, sophisticated, beautiful and free. For Brazilians it was a jump ahead – advancing 'fifty years in five' – a way of distancing Brazil from its underdevelopment, at least in the area of culture.

Meanwhile, in the economy, there was less cause for optimism. The Targets Plan was failing to overcome the obstacles that impeded development.[35] The first evidence of this failure was the plan's negative impact on economic growth. Although President Kubitschek, like President Vargas before him, was investing heavily in infrastructure, unlike his predecessor he was not a nationalist, but rather a very astute pragmatist. In his memoirs, the economist Roberto Campos, a member of Juscelino Kubitschek's technocratic team and an ardent believer in international capital, wrote that the president valued 'where the factory was' and not 'where the shareholder lived'.[36]

Not everyone shared Roberto Campos's faith in the benefits of internationalizing the Brazilian economy. Trade unions, students, intellectuals and above all communist militants were highly critical of an economic development process that could lead to local industry becoming dependent on the intermediation of multinationals. The historian Caio Prado Jr, for example, was unforgiving: 'Brazil has never had a government as submissive to international interests as that of Mr Juscelino Kubitschek,' he wrote.[37] The consequences of internationalization may well have been inevitable for a country that had depended for so long on the export of raw materials, but there can be no doubt that the critics were right about one thing: the damage caused was considerable.

The Targets Plan allowed Brazil to increase its industrial capacity significantly. However, the plan did not sustain the industrialization. In his haste to advance the country in just five years, Juscelino Kubitschek improvised. He invested in accelerated growth without evaluating how the process was to be financed. He used shortcuts, such as facilitating the entry of foreign capital into the country through the concession of fiscal and economic privileges and depending on international funding for the accelerated industrialization. These shortcuts were prejudicial to the country in three ways: the first was the relative ease with which foreign companies took over the control of developing sectors of the Brazilian economy; the second was the constant increase in the country's balance of trade deficit, with the consequent increase in its foreign debt; and the third was the decision to create growth while ignoring inflation.

Juscelino Kubitschek knew all too well that any programme to fight inflation would have political costs – imposing restrictions on wages, credit and government spending. In the short term, the government exerted some control over demands for wage increases, largely due to the negotiating skills of João Goulart, who was extremely popular with urban workers and the trade unions. In fact the Kubitschek/Goulart duo was not only the personification of the alliance between the Social Democratic Party (PSD) and the Brazilian Labour Party (PTB) and the continuity of the Vargas political legacy; it was also the key to maintaining good relations between the government and the trade unions. The alliance was crucial to sustaining the precarious balance between the opposing political forces[38] that characterized the Kubitschek government.

Naturally, containing government spending in order to control inflation would have meant imposing restrictions on the Targets Plan. Between slowing down the rate of growth and relying on funding that worsened inflation, President Kubitschek chose the latter without hesitation. He argued that some degree of inflation was inevitable and that the economy would gradually stabilize. He left his successor the task of dealing with an inflation rate that had reached alarming proportions: in 1957 it was 7 per cent; in 1958, 24.4 per cent; and in 1959, 39.4 per cent.[39]

The other major impediment to development was political in nature. Juscelino Kubitschek introduced his Targets Plan, the most ambitious modernization programme in the history of the country, but implementing a project of such magnitude did not include any measures to reduce social and political inequality. The strategy also relied on a certain degree of 'improvisation'. President Kubitschek created a 'parallel administration' within the state bureaucracy.[40] The intention was to circumvent the political patronage system – the practice of distributing favours and jobs to those who helped the government get the votes it needed in Congress – without having to openly contest it. This 'parallel administration' was made up of a number of centres for planning and carrying out government policies. These centres were sophisticated and received generous funding. Their purpose was twofold. For one thing, through the centres, the government was able to recruit dynamic administrators capable of rapidly implementing the Targets Plan, and for another, strategies could be thereby implemented while bypassing the inefficiency of public administration in Brazil – political patronage and the trading of government posts in return for political favours.

As far as the question of agrarian reform was concerned, the Targets Plan went no further than rhetoric. The immense estates were the greatest symbol of underdevelopment; but the ownership of land was a source of power, meant representation in Congress, and sustained regional support for the Social Democratic Party. The estate owners had never been challenged, not even by Getúlio Vargas, and Juscelino Kubitschek was cautious enough not to interfere with the status quo.[41] In the 1950s, 70 per cent of the Brazilian population still lived in rural areas. The urban population was only to overtake the rural population at the end of the 1960s. The difference between the poverty and social inequality in the country and in the cities was enormous. In the interior the situation of the poor remained unchanged: schools, basic sanitation and healthcare were in scarce supply and rural workers continued to be excluded from the labour benefits introduced by Getúlio Vargas. The intervention goals of the Kubitschek government in this sector were limited to palliative measures: the expansion of rural credit, food distribution, help for the victims of the 1958 drought and the construction of wells.

While Juscelino Kubitschek focused on the urban world, on the cities he believed would produce a new, modern society, by the early 1960s the rural workers began to organize themselves into a major political force. The rural workers' movement had started demanding land and rights in the 1940s, prior to President Kubitschek's government. Initially, the movement was motivated by the increasing number of rural workers expelled from their land due to real estate speculation and the system of *grilagem* – a long-established practice of forging documents in order to claim landownership. The practice caused social upheaval: large-scale migration to the cities, the rapid and disorderly growth of city outskirts, and the exponential growth of *favelas*. This pattern of migration was to last until the 1980s. Meanwhile, the demands for land and rights in rural areas intensified. Armed uprisings began in 1946, with a revolt in Porecatu, a settlement in the state of Paraná, where hundreds of armed peasants demanded the return of land that had been fraudulently occupied. Eight years later, in 1954, the revolt of Trombas and Formoso in the state of Goiás erupted. The troubles continued until 1961, during which time the peasants founded the 'Republic of Trombas and Formoso', governed by institutions of their own design. The Trombas and Formosa regions obtained legal registration of land for 10,000 small farmers and their families. In 1956 peasants in municipalities in the southwest of Paraná took to the town streets, expelled local authorities, and invaded the offices of colonizing real estate companies involved in land speculation. The rural workers destroyed IOUs, promissory notes and title deeds – many of which had been forged by the companies.[42]

By the end of the 1950s, the struggle of the rural workers had consolidated around the issue of agrarian reform. A number of workers' organizations were founded, such as the Union of the Agricultural Workers of Brazil (Ultab). In 1955 the first *Ligas Camponesas* (Rural Workers' Leagues) were re-established in the northeast.[43] Between 1945 and 1947 rural workers' associations had been founded by the Communist Party to address the demands of the rural workers. There was an attempt to unite rural workers' associations with urban workers' associations. The experiment was interrupted in 1947 under the growing repression of the Dutra regime. As mentioned above, at that time, the Communist Party was banned and communist federal deputies had their right to engage in politics revoked. In 1955, however, the establishment of the Society of Planters and Cattle Raisers of Pernambuco (SAPPP) gave new impetus to the movement. The society was established at the Galileia Plantation and Sugar Mill in Vitória de Santo Antão, the heart of Pernambuco's sugar-producing region. The goal of the organization was to protect tenant farmers from being expelled from plantation lands. But it quickly grew and expanded into a far-reaching social movement – *Ligas Camponesas* – which between 1950 and 1960 brought the issue of agrarian reform into the centre of the national political debate.

By the beginning of the 1960s, the *Ligas Camponesas* were fighting for both civil and social rights. Their principal strategy was through legal action: by representing the rural workers in court, the leagues' lawyers transformed a social conflict into a legal one, and their clients into citizens. This strategy began in 1955 under the direction of the then state deputy Francisco Julião, who had considerable success and became the leagues' most important leader.[44] In 1959, after the expropriation of the Galileia plantation where the Society of Planters and Cattle Raisers of Pernambuco had been founded, the leagues began to spread throughout the northeastern states, and then to the rest of the country. In 1961 they adopted a radical proposal for agrarian reform – 'Legally or by force, with flowers or with blood', according to the announcement made by the six hundred or so delegates who attended the First National Congress of Agricultural Workers in Belo Horizonte. The members of the movement began invading and occupying farms. A dissident group within the movement established guerrilla training camps. The most well known among these camps was located in Dianópolis, in Goiás, which was shut down by the army in 1962.[45] But most of those involved were less radical. They attempted to find political means for the leagues to represent rural workers with the same efficacy that the trade unions represented their city counterparts.

Rural Brazil had become a space of inexorable political dispute, involving the Communist Party and the Catholic Church. The communists systematically sent militants into the interior to help establish rural unions. The Church was divided on the issue: part of the clergy wanted to promote Christian doctrine and neutralize the influence of left-wing groups in the interior; others were interested in strengthening the ties between the Church and the workers. In an unprecedented move for the Church, the latter group used an educational radio programme to initiate the process of rural unionization – *Movimento de Educação de Base* (MEB – Movement for Basic Education). The programme taught rural workers to read and write so that they could acquire greater control over their own affairs. It was a part of the Radiophonic Schools system and used a series of textbooks inspired by the literacy method developed by Paulo Freire.[46] The programme was a success. By 1963 the Movement for Basic Education was transmitting in fourteen Brazilian states.[47]

Members of the rural workers' movements demanded land and rights. Yet the Kubitschek government still viewed the interior of Brazil as conservative and backward. The administration did not formulate a solution for the question of agrarian reform. The only alternative the government considered was to relocate people from rural areas into the cities. The inequalities were enormous and difficult to address. As early as 1956, President Kubitschek decided that the construction of a new capital for Brazil would be the crowning success of the Targets Plan. Brasília was to be a planned city that would represent Brazilian nationalism, the transition from the traditional to the modern. The new capital was meant to integrate the interior of the country to the urban centres, and Brazil into the international community. Brasília became a symbol of the Kubitschek government and the Targets Plan with which people could identify.[48] Brazilians were fascinated by the idea of building a city of the future, based on new architectural and urban concepts, erected on Brazil's central plateau in a vast, empty region of the country – the population density of the area was less than one person per square kilometre. The idea of transferring the capital of the country to the interior was by no means new: it had first been discussed in the nineteenth century and was foreseen in both the 1934 and 1946 constitutions. But, before Juscelino Kubitschek, no one had been prepared to take it seriously: apart from the astronomic cost, the transfer of the capital was not a political priority; it had not even been an issue in the election campaign.

As soon as the members of the National Democratic Union (UDN) discovered President Kubitschek was planning to build Brasília in a semi-arid region, easily accessible only by air, they acted at once. After all, the region contained nothing but stunted vegetation, red clay and a few jaguars, so they voted in favour of the law authorizing the transfer of the capital and sat back delightedly to await the disaster. But once again, the National Democratic Union got it wrong. Juscelino Kubitschek had Brasília built in three years. He hired Oscar Niemeyer as architect and Lúcio Costa for the urban planning. The record time of construction was due to the president having slashed the red tape by setting up NOVACAP – the Urbanization Company for the New Capital of Brazil – one of the most powerful nuclei of his 'parallel administration'. Furthermore, he appointed a man he trusted implicitly to be the director of the new urbanization company, the engineer Israel Pinheiro, from Minas Gerais. President Kubitschek expedited a law through Congress that allowed him to build the new capital without legal challenges. And he would hear nothing about the cost. The opposition played its usual role of seizing their weapons, taking aim, and hoping to hit something. The National Democratic Union were implacable: not a day went by when they did not express their horror at the waste of public money in a country with so many other priorities, the monumental nature of the project, the extremely suspicious urgency and the inevitable outcome – President Kubitschek's failure to complete the project during his administration. As the construction speeded up and Brasília became a reality, the opposition began to protest that it was too far away, the region was hostile, the land porous, the artificial lake would not fill up, and the telephones would never work.

President Kubitschek always maintained that the decision to build Brasília had come out of nowhere, that it was the outcome of a vision he had incorporated into his government programme. But it is improbable that the idea developed as he claimed it did: Brasília served too many useful purposes. It was the bridge between the old and the new Brazil, it made the Targets Plan comprehensible to the people, gave the president unprecedented bargaining power with groups of adversaries who wanted to participate in such a highly lucrative business, and deflected society's attention away from the problems of inflation and agrarian reform. Brasília simultaneously became a national monument and a national symbol, not to mention that it transformed Juscelino Kubitschek into one of the most exceptional leaders in the history of Brazil. Furthermore, while he was mayor of Belo Horizonte, Juscelino Kubitschek had revealed his vocation for construction and willingness to invest in daring, futuristic urban projects. When he built the lakeside residential district of Pampulha, that was where it all began.[49] Brasília became the government's absolute priority. President Kubitschek knew he had to finish the work, as no other administration would ever commit the country's resources to it. The construction project appeared to be the height of insanity. At least that was the opinion of the journalist Otto Lara Resende,[50] who wrote: 'Brasília was the product of a rare conjunction of four types of madness: Juscelino's, Israel's, Niemeyer's and Lúcio Costa's.'[51]

What the four men produced was so extraordinary it seemed as if Mr Lara Resende were right. The city appeared out of nowhere, had a strange kind of beauty, and was unlike anything Brazilians had seen before. The outline of the Pilot Plan invokes two images, superimposed: a cross that founds a new Brazil and a plane that lands on the Central Plateau, bringing the country into the future 'as if it were en route to an impossible utopia', in Lúcio Costa's famous words.[52] The city is divided by two axes that cross at right angles – the Monumental Axis and the Highway Axis – which separate the residential area and its facilities from the area occupied by government buildings. The ministries are purposefully identical, bordering the Monumental Axis and accentuating the grandeur of the *Praça dos Três Poderes*,[53] the palaces built of reinforced concrete, which nevertheless appear to float above the ground. The first residents joked that the human body of Brasília was composed of three parts – the head, the torso and wheels! The new capital does not have streets, squares, pavement or even pedestrians. Its construction is also emblematic of the ambivalence of the Targets Plan. It has never been known how much it cost to build Brasília. Nor is it known how many workers died in the haste to get it built; whether it is true that their bodies were buried by excavators alongside the buildings; whether corporal punishment was actually inflicted on the workers, and if they really protested for better working and living conditions. All that is known is that the thousands of workers, most of whom came from the northeast, Goiás and the north of Minas Gerais – the *candangos* – only lived in Brasília for as long as it remained a building site. Once the new capital was ready and the government had been established, they had two options: either they were sent back to their state of origin, or they went to live in segregated camping sites, similar to *favelas*, in the outskirts. These campsites were the origin of the 'satellite towns', which have grown steadily ever since. Ten years after Brasília was built, 100,000 migrants were already living in *favelas* around the city.[54]

Brasília expelled the poor to the outskirts and segregated civil servants, bureaucrats and members of Congress in virtually identical residential units – the *superquadras* (superblocks). The city is based on hierarchical and segmented principles of social organization, which accentuate the overpowering presence of the state as an employer. Juscelino Kubitschek, who was aware of *everything* in politics, must have realized that the transference of the capital would bring serious drawbacks – one of which was the isolation of the centre of power, which distanced the government both from increasing social unrest and from direct contact with the people. After more than fifty years, Brasília is the modern city that has integrated the interior of Brazil with the rest of the country, just as Juscelino Kubitschek promised. It has kept its ambivalent atmosphere – the palaces remain impeccably conserved, as President Kubitschek and Oscar Niemeyer planned, 'suspended, weightless and white, in the unending nights of the Planalto'; and it remains a centre of power that is more aseptic, isolated and arrogant.

THE SOWER OF THE WIND

The new federal capital was inaugurated on 21 April 1960. Nine months later, President Kubitschek handed over the office of president to his elected successor, Jânio Quadros. He could have had no idea that the next time a civilian president, elected by popular vote, would pass the presidential sash on to another elected civilian would be in 2003. Juscelino Kubitschek travelled to Europe on holiday confident that he would be re-elected to office in 1965 (the 1946 Constitution did not permit re-election for consecutive terms). His electoral campaign began there and then, as he made his farewells. The city was adorned in banners and posters with the slogan 'JK-65' and at the airport a multitude waited to bid him a temporary farewell. President Kubitschek had spent the last year of his mandate with one eye on the urgency of finishing Brasília, and the other on creating favourable conditions for his return to power. He even constructed a strategy to ensure that his party *lost* the election.[55] The country was in a critical situation, the government had no control over its expenses, and his successor would have to adopt rigorous austerity measures. The problem as far as President Kubitschek was concerned, was how to transfer this burden to the opposition. He wanted to make sure that the National Democratic Union (UDN) would win the elections and spend the next four years implementing unpopular measures to combat inflation. Thus the way would be prepared for him to return in 1965 with a new programme for economic growth.

President Kubitschek was manoeuvring in his own interests, and not without a touch of omnipotence. It was unlikely that the National Democratic Union would support a candidate appointed by him. Nevertheless, there was a chance that the manoeuvre could work. After all, the president was a master of conspiracy and behind-the-scenes politics and he had ended his mandate at the height of his popularity – his strategy could produce a broad centre-right coalition, which would offset the growing strength of the left-wing parties, above all the Brazilian Labour Party. To further facilitate the situation, the Social Democratic Party had no one who was suitable to succeed him. The only thing that President Kubitcheck was not prepared to consider was any interference from the *Paulistas*. São Paulo had been the greatest beneficiary of his government: industrial growth was concentrated in the state, easy credit was made available to its entrepreneurs, and the dizzy rate of its expansion indicated that the city was well on the way to becoming the most important state capital in the country. But on the national political scene São Paulo was not in a position to make alliances: neither the Social Democratic Party, nor the National Democratic Union, nor the Brazilian Labour Party were strong in the state, where political power was still disputed between the smaller political parties at the service of regional leaders, as exemplified by Ademar de Barros's Social Progress Party (PSP).

In May 1959 a group of these small parties made an alliance with the National Democratic Union to support the candidacy of Jânio Quadros for the presidency. This was a candidate over whom President Kubitschek had no control and who thus neutralized his strategy.[56] Since his first mandate as city councillor in 1948, Jânio Quadros had risen through the ranks at incredible speed, having been successively elected as state deputy, mayor and then governor – winning three elections in five years, all in São Paulo. He had a reputation as an honest and competent administrator, and although he had no ties to Getúlio Vargas's political legacy he was not considered *anti-getulista*. The tone of his campaign was music to the ears of the National Democratic Union. He attacked corruption, inflation, the high cost of living, and the waste of public money on monumental constructions in Brasília, while promising economic growth and austerity in government spending. Jânio Quadros never offered any convincing explanation for how his government would achieve better results than President Kubitschek's, nor how he would tackle the fundamental problems of Brazilian development. His message was anti-political. He presented himself as a candidate who was above political parties, showing complete disdain for traditional politicians and their way of doing politics. He only insisted on one thing: that the people give him their trust and believed personally *in him*. And he repeated that he was the only independent candidate, the only one who was dedicated to political activity out of civic vocation and the love of public service – and was thus the only one capable of pointing the country in a new direction.

Carlos Lacerda was one of the first to realize that, with or without the National Democratic Union, Jânio Quadros's candidacy was irresistible, and that the party must endorse him. Jânio Quadros was inspiring hope and receiving support from all the social classes – especially from middle-class voters, who, tormented by the effects of inflation, considered the candidate an energetic administrator, well equipped to manage a turbulent, expanding economy. Jânio Quadros was a very unusual candidate, and the speed at which his popularity grew should have set off an alarm. In short, a door had been left open and a clever intruder had slipped in. His rapidly rising popularity was a sign of society's discontent with the high cost of living and falling wages, and of the increasing power of the electorate to express its anxieties. It also revealed disenchantment with the main political parties, which seemed unable to adapt to and absorb new popular demands.

But the candidate's appeal was not limited to his words. Jânio Quadros had enormous talent for the theatrical.[57] At political rallies he would simulate fainting from hunger, have injections to recover his strength, and wear an old suit whose shoulders were strategically sprinkled with powder – supposedly dandruff. His tie was always crooked and he would sit down on the pavement to eat a mortadella sandwich and a banana – he wanted to be seen as one of the people, a man who understood the suffering of the working poor. He would walk onto the stage gesticulating wildly – skinny, indignant, scruffily dressed – waving a broom (the symbol of his campaign) and, assuming a grave tone of voice, promise to sweep away the corruption that permeated the government. He used pretentious language, full of old-fashioned expressions, emphasizing every syllable of the words, leaving the crowd astonished by his grandiloquent professorial tone – even though at times they understood nothing at all. But Jânio Quadros's timing was perfect, and he knew just when to say what they all wanted to hear. He attended rallies everywhere – in the streets, factories, *favelas* and in the outskirts of the cities, attracting thousands of supporters with brooms in their hands, hypnotized by the rhetoric of the campaign.

It is hard to know whether, at any point, Juscelino Kubitschek was sympathetic towards Jânio Quadros's campaign. It could not have been easy to know how to respond to such a messianic, histrionic and irascible candidate. The Social Democratic Party eventually decided to support the presidential candidate put forth by the nationalist groups in Congress, Henrique Teixeira Lott, who by then had been promoted to marshal. This was perhaps a strategy to consolidate their support within the armed forces.[58] Then the party renewed their alliance with the Brazilian Labour Party by choosing João Goulart to complete the ticket as vice-president. Marshal Lott had great political prestige, was respected within the armed forces, and was generally admired as a legalist and democrat. But as a candidate he inspired no enthusiasm. As soon as it became evident to the Social Democratic Party that their candidate was a lost cause, they abandoned him to his own resources and, along with the Brazilian Labour Party – and with the support of Jânio Quadros himself – campaigned for the 'Jan-Jan' team: Jânio Quadros for president and, for vice-president, Jango (João Goulart).

The election results had little effect on the Social Democratic Party, strengthened the Brazilian Labour Party, and confirmed the popularity of the 'Jan-Jan' duo. Jânio Quadros received a record-breaking number of votes, 5,636,623, compared to 3,846,825 for Marshal Lott.[59] João Goulart was re-elected with a total of 4,547,010 votes – in fact, more than those received by Marshal Lott. The result also produced a few novelties. The first was that the vice-president was from the opposition. The second was the boost that Jânio Quadros's candidacy gave to the National Democratic Union, whose candidates for governor won in six out of the eleven states where elections for governor were held. These included Magalhães Pinto, who was elected governor of Minas Gerais, and Carlos Lacerda, who became the first governor of the newly created state of Guanabara – of which Rio de Janeiro was the capital. The state had been created by President Kubitschek to replace what had been the federal district, in an attempt to compensate the *Cariocas* for the transference of the capital to Brasília.

Those who had voted for Jânio Quadros, however, were soon to discover that he was far better equipped to get votes than he was to run the country. It is true that he was successful in renegotiating international debts. He also implemented the most extensive plan to combat inflation since President Vargas. He was also effective in conducting an independent foreign policy, which he did in collaboration with Afonso Arinos de Melo Franco, the Minister for Foreign Affairs, from the National Democratic Union Party in Minas Gerais. Brazil modified its alignment with the interests of North America, established diplomatic and commercial ties with socialist countries, renegotiated its debts with Europe, the United States and the Soviet bloc, and created closer ties with countries of the Third World.[60]

But Jânio Quadros was a provincial politician. He had few connections with the national political parties and disdained any opportunity to create his own parliamentary base, even though the government had a minority in Congress.[61] He showed equal disregard for negotiating with the opposition; instead, he was a master at exacerbating conflicts. He set himself on a collision course with Congress, with the press, with the civil service and with the vice-president of the country. And he ended up breaking with the National Democratic Union, who were indignant at his foreign policy which, at the height of the Cold War, they saw as leaning dangerously far to the left. Within a few months Jânio Quadros managed to create a generalized sense of confusion, underestimate his allies, and isolate himself in the presidency. With no long-term plan, a limited understanding of and vision for the country, a narrowly moralistic outlook on public life, an authoritarian profile and the soul of a bureaucrat, he administered Brazil as though it were some minor government department. He centralized decisions, controlled the minutest of details, and scribbled an endless stream of notes to ministers and advisers, unable to differentiate between insignificant issues and matters of great import. As soon as he had taken office he launched his witch-hunt against corrupt officials, establishing investigative committees with instructions to comb through the finances of public bodies. Then, without proof, he released the so-called results to the press, where they made glaring headlines. His scribbled notes disappeared into the immensity of the administrative machine, and government policy oscillated every which way. Nonetheless Jânio Quadros continued to interfere in everything. He abolished the requirement for wearing ties in the presidential palace and created a khaki uniform for civil servants, based on the 'safari'-style outfits used by the British in their empire – in his opinion far more appropriate for a tropical country. To eliminate any doubts, he published details in the *Official Gazette* of how the new uniforms were to be made – 'Fabric: Brazilian linen. Colour: Beige.'[62] In fewer than seven months of government President Quadros signed an astonishing number of decrees: banning horse races on working days, outlawing cockfighting, forbidding the use of poppers during carnival balls, banning the use of bikinis on the beaches, and specifying the length for swimming costumes used in televised beauty contests. To top it all off, he brought two donkeys from the northeast to eat the grass in the immense gardens of the *Palácio da Alvorada*,[63] providing the creatures with straw hats to protect them from the scorching sun of the Central Plateau and surrounding the gardens with railings to prevent them from wandering off.[64]

Jânio Quadros was a political intruder at the head of a government that had no clear definition, yet he still intended to govern on his own terms. And in his opinion, he was constrained by the 1946 Constitution and a Congress that was suspicious and uncooperative. This was not true; or, at least, it was not entirely true. He had no commitment to democratic institutions and felt that his hands were tied by the limitations imposed on him by the constitution. He created an artificial situation that led to an impasse between the powers, increasing the hostility of Congress and isolating himself even further. Opposition to his government increased, especially from the labour movement. This opposition was creating closer ties with the communists and had the backing of the unions. They repudiated President Quadros's economic policy, which devalued the currency, doubled the price of bread, increased the price of public transport, restricted credit and froze wages. Nevertheless, there were apparently no insurmountable obstacles – nothing that could not be solved by negotiation.

In late July 1961, Jânio Quadros invited Vice-President João Goulart to head the first Brazilian trade mission to the People's Republic of China. Relations between the two men were on the brink of rupture and João Goulart, who had been one of the first targets of Jânio Quadros's investigative committees, viewed the invitation with suspicion. Since it was impossible for the vice-president to refuse, he ended up agreeing to head the mission to China. While he was negotiating trade agreements in Beijing, in Brasília Jânio Quadros was awarding the Grand Cross of the Order of the Southern Cross, Brazil's highest decoration, to the Cuban Minister for the Economy, Ernesto Che Guevara.

There was outrage. Opinions were divided over the Cuban Revolution. The president's gesture increased the fears of the United States that Brazil's foreign policy was becoming pro-Cuban. The National Democratic Union reacted with indignation and military officers who had been decorated threatened to return their medals.[65] President Quadros had good reasons for wanting to create closer ties with Cuba; there was a possibility that the island country could act as an intermediary for the trade of goods and machinery between Brazil and the Soviet bloc. But in the opinion of Carlos Lacerda, this time the government had gone too far, so he took a plane to Brasília to confront the president. There are numerous versions of what was actually said when they met. But there was no reconciliation: Carlos Lacerda returned to Rio de Janeiro, denounced the government on radio and television, called the president irresponsible, and accused the Minister of Justice, Oscar Pedroso Horta, of planning a *coup d'état* and of having invited him to take part. The political temperature rose to boiling point.

On the morning of Friday, 25 August 1961, Soldier's Day, Jânio Quadros attended the military parade in the Esplanade of Ministries, reviewed the troops, listened to the reading of the order of the day, saluted the flag – everything according to the book. Then he returned to the palace, summoned the military ministers and officially communicated that he was resigning the presidency. When the astonished officers asked him for his reason, he replied: 'I can't govern with this Congress. Organize a *junta* and govern the country.'[66] He signed his letter of resignation and gave instructions to the Minister of Justice to send it to Congress at 3 p.m. At 11 a.m. he boarded the presidential plane for the Cumbica Airbase in São Paulo. As he left Brasília, he instructed the adjutant who was travelling with him to bring the presidential sash.

IN THE BASEMENT OF THE PIRATINI PALACE

Jânio Quadros never gave a clear explanation for why he resigned. But there is consensus among historians. His gesture was intended to cause a national commotion and to bring about his triumphant return to office with greater presidential powers – preferably without Congress to get in his way. Resigning was a way of exiting the stage without losing face. He had used the threat of renunciation in the past, and it had always succeeded. And it could work again now: Jaõa Goulart was not popular with the military, and anyway, he was too far away in China to negotiate taking office. President Quadros's resignation would only be examined by Congress after the weekend, and before that the people would be on the streets defending his mandate, perhaps – who knew? – forming a new type of *queremismo*, the movement that had earlier clamoured for a permanent Vargas presidency. 'There is no one left, after me,' Jânio Quadros is reported to have said at the Cumbica Airbase. And he added: 'I shan't do anything to return, but I consider my return inevitable.'[67]

If that was his plan, it all went wrong. The people did not rise up, the state governors said nothing, Congress accepted his resignation two hours after receiving the letter, considering it a unilateral act. The deputies were fed up with a government they accused of trying to demoralize the legislature. No one in the chamber supported him. Ranieri Mazzilli, the president of the Chamber of Deputies, was appointed as interim president until João Goulart arrived back from China. On 28 August, Jânio Quadros ordered the presidential sash to be returned and embarked for Europe from the port of Santos in the state of São Paulo. But there was still one obstacle to a smooth transition: the ministers of the armed forces.[68] The resignation was one thing; they had ratified it without discussion. But the succession was quite another. At that point, the military ministers took stock of the situation and decided to intervene. On 28 August, three days after President Quadros's resignation, Mr Mazzilli informed Congress that the military ministers were not prepared to accept João Goulart's return to the presidency. And they went further: if he were to disembark in Brazil, he would be arrested. The ministers were not acting according to their role as military officers. Instead, they were playing a political card. They were betting on the success of a sort of constitutional coup, which would come at little cost to the armed forces.[69] The plan was to intimidate Congress into declaring João Goulart ineligible. But not even the National Democratic Union agreed. This was a political crisis with unpredictable results and the country was drawing dangerously close to civil war.

But that was not what fate intended. In Rio de Janeiro, Marshal Lott, reflecting the divisions within the armed forces, published a manifesto to the nation in which he defended constitutional order. Then the governor of Rio Grande do Sul, Leonel Brizola, decided it was time to act. His idea was to bring João Goulart to Porto Alegre and to ensure he take office at any cost.[70] Mr Brizola was the political leader of forces further to the left than the Brazilian Labour Party. He was also João Goulart's brother-in-law. Leonel Brizola had been elected governor in 1959 and his fame had begun to spread, especially after an audacious piece of legislation that expropriated the goods and services of the *Companhia Telefônica Nacional*, a subsidiary of the International Telephone & Telegraph (IT&T). By the end of his government, Leonel Brizola was planning to implement two measures that went even further: the expropriation of farms in order to distribute land to the *Agricultores sem Terra* (Landless Farmers), and the state government takeover of the *Companhia de Energia Elétrica Rio-Grandense*, a subsidiary of American & Foreign Power, part of the Electric Bond & Share group.[71]

Silencing Marshal Lott was relatively easy – the Minister of War ordered his arrest and he was imprisoned on an island in Guanabara Bay between Rio de Janeiro and Niterói. But silencing Governor Brizola was quite another matter. He summoned the powerful Rio Grande do Sul military brigade and ordered that the studios of Rádio Guaíba be transferred to the basement of the governor's palace – Palácio Piratini. He then posted special-guard soldiers with three heavy machine guns to protect the transmission tower on the Ilha da Pintada, twelve miles outside Porto Alegre. He instructed the announcer to open the transmission with the words: 'This is Radio Legality [*Rede da Legalidade*], transmitting from the basement of the Piratini Palace, in the capital of Rio Grande do Sul.' With microphone in hand, Leonel Brizola incited the state to revolt and mobilized the rest of the country to act in defence of the constitution. Radio Legality transmitted on shortwave twenty-four hours a day, linked to the transmissions of some 150 other radio stations, and was heard all over Brazil and in some of its neighbouring republics.[72]

Governor Brizola knew all too well the risk he was running. He armed the population for resistance, summoned the people to occupy the *Praça da Matriz*, the plaza in front of the palace, and simulated a blockade in the Rio Grande port. He installed machine guns on the roof of the palace and in the tower of the Metropolitan Cathedral, which was under still construction. He climbed up onto barricades made from sacks of sand, benches wrenched up from the *Praça da Matriz*, and cars and trucks, all piled up around the palace. He distributed guns to the civil servants and went everywhere with a machine gun slung over his shoulder. He was right to be prepared: the military ministers sent a navy task force to Rio Grande do Sul and sent planes from the Canoas Airbase with instructions to bombard the palace. But the sergeants at the airbase rebelled, let down tyres, removed weapons, and prevented pilots from taking off. On 28 August the situation began to turn around. The commander of the Third Army, General José Machado Lopes, accompanied by his joint chiefs of staff, entered the Piratini Palace and, to everyone's surprise, told Governor Brizola that he was in favour of João Goulart taking office. The Third Army was based in Rio Grande do Sul and was the most powerful division of the land forces. From then on, Leonel Brizola could count on the support of 40,000 soldiers, 13,000 men from the military brigade, and approximately 30,000 volunteers. He was the first civilian leader to have openly resisted a military *coup d'état*, and he could no longer be underestimated.

The military ministers began to realize it would not be as simple as they had thought to prevent João Goulart from taking office. In Goiás the governor, Mauro Borges, decided to join Leonel Brizola in the resistance.[73] He declared that the capital had rebelled, ordered the military police to occupy all the strategic points of the city, and instituted an 'Army of Legality' made up of volunteers. And he issued a warning: if João Goulart wanted to land in the state, he would be provided with all the security he required to travel from Goiânia to Brasília. Further support came from all around the country. The Brazilian Lawyers' Association (OAB) and the All National Students' Union – which had moved its head office to Porto Alegre – demanded that constitutional order be respected. Protests in favour of legality were organized in a number of states. It was only the *Estado de S. Paulo* newspaper and the governor of Guanabara, Carlos Lacerda, who openly declared themselves to be in favour of the military veto and against the investiture of João Goulart.

The military ministers now knew their options were limited. They would either have to negotiate a way out or be prepared to fight a civil war. However, Congress came up with a solution that would prevent their loss of face: the immediate adoption of a parliamentary regime. It was an artificial solution that would never solve the problem, but it certainly solved the short-term crisis. João Goulart would be allowed to take office, but without full powers. All that was needed was his agreement. The task of bringing him the proposal fell to Tancredo Neves, who had been in Getúlio Vargas's Cabinet. Mr Goulart had been informed of Jânio Quadros's resignation when he was in Singapore and had made the long journey back to Montevideo, where he waited for news from Brazil. Tancredo Neves then had the unenviable task of persuading him to accept the proposal, which he finally did. On the night of 1 September, João Goulart disembarked at Porto Alegre. The amendment instituting the parliamentary system was voted by Congress in the early hours of the following day. Leonel Brizola was indignant and refused to accept the agreement. In his opinion João Goulart should proceed to Brasília overland, at the head of the Third Army, and assume the government with no restrictions to his presidential powers.

It is hard to know what Mr Goulart's reasons were for accepting the formula of a parliamentary regime. Civil war was a real possibility; one that, without any doubt, he wanted to avoid. He also had no intention of missing the opportunity of becoming president. It is possible that he planned to assume the government and, in the short term, disarm his adversaries, and expand his political support by winning over the Social Democratic Party. He could then overturn the parliamentary system and regain full presidential powers – which is virtually what occurred in 1963. He knew that he could not march on Brasília. The popular rebellion that had started in Rio Grande do Sul and spread throughout Brazil was in his favour, but not under his command. Even if this battle were fought and won, the person who would emerge victorious would be Leonel Brizola.[74] Whatever his reasons, that evening João Goulart went out onto the balcony of the Piratini Palace and waved to the crowd, without saying a word. Three days later he left for Brasília.

He did not know what was waiting for him.

17

On a Knife Edge: Dictatorship, Opposition and Resistance

A PRESIDENT ON A TIGHTROPE

On 7 September 1961, Brazil's Independence Day, João Goulart arrived at the National Congress to be sworn in as president of Brazil. He was forty-three years old, and he arrived impeccably dressed in a navy blue summer suit and disguised his anxiety with a broad smile. It was the third time that a president had taken office that year.[1] The atmosphere was festive and the general feeling a mixture of euphoria and relief. The situation in the country was extremely difficult. Inflation was high and on the rise, public expenses were out of control, and an alarmingly high payment on the foreign debt was due in the first months of 1962. The incoming President Goulart was already prepared to implement an emergency plan. He had drawn up a draft for the core reforms, but had not had time to plan a full strategy. And the system was parliamentary; a system that had been hurriedly invented as a convenient solution that gave powers to the Legislature and left the Executive with little scope for action. Congress resolved the political crisis in its own way: to govern, the new president would need to obtain a solid majority in the Federal Chamber.[2]

The key to creating an alliance in Congress that would allow the government to legislate was the Social Democratic Party (PSD). The party was the most representative of the country as a whole, with effective leaders and a strong electoral base. It was also the central force in the day-to-day activities of Congress, balancing the parties with its combination of support for both conservative and moderate proposals and its capacity for negotiation. President Goulart planned to reconstruct the alliance between the Social Democratic Party and the Brazilian Labour Party (PTB), which had provided political stability during the Kubitschek administration. His goal was to create a base of support for the Executive in the centre of the political spectrum. Yet it was equally important that, as well as garnering the support of the other left-wing parties, he should not lose control of the Brazilian Labour Party.

Time was short and the president was in a hurry: he negotiated the appointment of Tancredo Neves of the Social Democrats as prime minister and encouraged him to put together a Cabinet that included the three main political parties – the Social Democratic Party, the Brazilian Labour Party and the National Democratic Union (UDN) – which he appropriately baptized the 'Cabinet of national conciliation'. During the sixteen months of parliamentary regime – during which time two further cabinets were formed – President Goulart remained on the defensive, searching for a way to implement his proposal for core reforms.

In foreign policy, the main problem was the negotiations with the United States, specifically regarding the foreign debt and the regulation of foreign capital in the Brazilian economy. In April 1962, President Goulart travelled to Washington to discuss the issue with President Kennedy. The reception was cordial and the American press enthusiastic; but Brazil's creditors were cautious, and preferred to wait and see the direction the Goulart government would take before proceeding with the negotiations. Suspicion in Washington persisted. Santiago Dantas, the new chancellor, had maintained Jânio Quadros's independent foreign policy, which – at the height of the Cold War – was unacceptable to the Americans. Brazil did not agree to align with one of the two superpowers – the United States and the Soviet Union – and insisted on diversifying its trade partners. As for Latin America, Brazil opposed the sanctions against Cuba proposed by the United States at the Organization of American States (OAS).[3]

President Goulart returned to Brazil widely praised, empty-handed, and faced with a multitude of problems. Some, like inflation and the end of the cycle of investment associated with the Targets Plan, had been inherited from the previous government. Others, however, like the question of agrarian reform, had much deeper roots – the extreme inequality of Brazilian society. In the early 1960s, Brazil's northeast became the virtual heart of the country and agrarian reform was at the top of the political agenda. Landowners, rural workers and the government wrangled over which type of reform should be adopted. In 1961, Francisco Julião, the lawyer who had become the main leader of the

Ligas Camponesas (Rural Workers' Leagues), made it clear that the rural workers' movement understood agrarian reform as the expropriation of all unproductive farms of over 500 hectares; the payment of compensation by the issue of government debt bonds, the registration of the title deeds in the names of the new owners, and government support for cooperatives. The Social Democratic Party was prepared to discuss agrarian reform – and this was a very positive sign considering the party's regional support base was sustained by local landowners. But they had a stipulation that agrarian reform had to be carried out within the terms of the constitution: expropriation with immediate cash compensation, or in public debt bonds adjusted according to inflation. The landowners, however, were completely against the reform and were terrified over the idea of rural trade unions. In 1963 they withdrew from negotiations and prepared to fight.[4]

On the left, the parties did not agree that compensation in cash or in debt bonds adjusted to inflation constituted reform. In their opinion that was a business transaction. Negotiations with the Social Democratic Party ended in stalemate. Meanwhile, the Rural Workers' Leagues occupied farms in Pernambuco, Maranhão, Paraíba, Goiás, Rio Grande do Sul, Rio de Janeiro, Minas Gerais and Bahia. In the interior of Pernambuco starving crowds looted warehouses and League leaders were assassinated. The most famous of these was João Pedro Teixeira, the head of the Rural Workers' Leagues in Sapé, in Paraíba, which had around 10,000 members. After one month as president, João Goulart reacted by creating the Department for Agrarian Policy (Supra), with powers to implement agrarian reform and expropriate land. And to rein in the Leagues, while simultaneously stimulating government support in rural areas, the government organized agricultural worker unions and extended trade union and labour law benefits to small farm owners, leaseholders, squatters and independent producers.

In the big cities, the activities of the increasingly organized trade unions led to the creation of the centralized *Comando Geral dos Trabalhadores* (CGT – General Workers' Command), and political upheaval began to permeate everyday life. High inflation, loss of purchasing power, and the increased cost of living (which grew from 51.6 per cent in 1962 to 79.9 per cent in 1964) sparked off strikes all over Brazil.[5] Apart from alarming business owners, the proliferation of strikes empowered left-wing activists, both inside and outside the trade unions, which were now breaking away from the state control imposed under Getúlio Vargas.

The activities of the left were far-reaching, active and multifaceted. The group included communists, socialists, nationalists, Catholics, workers and numerous alliances. These included parties, associations of sergeants, sailors and marines; of students, trade unions, federations of urban and rural workers, as well as revolutionary groups.[6] Despite the disparity between the groups and the obvious difficulties of coming to an agreement, what had previously seemed virtually impossible actually happened: by late 1961 the left-wing parties had formed an unprecedented coalition in order to immediately implement a programme of core reforms. They wanted to start with agrarian reform. The increasing radicalization of groups within the coalition – which refused to negotiate and were determined to implement the reforms by any means available – further complicated the situation. They brought crowds onto the streets to put pressure on the deputies and they directly confronted those who were undecided in Congress. However, with no agreement of terms, the Legislative would not approve a programme that adversely affected the government powerbase, promoted the redistribution of wealth, and advocated social inclusion. Agrarian reform measures would affect the large estates and the volume of agricultural production from the interior. Urban reforms would help control the chaotic growth of the cities, with public transport providing access to the suburbs; real-estate speculation would also be contained. The reform of the banking system foresaw a new state-controlled financial structure. The proposed electoral reform, giving the vote to the illiterate – who made up 60 per cent of the adult population – and to soldiers threatened the political status quo. Electoral reform also included the legalization of the Communist Party. The planned reform of the foreign capital statute imposed limits on the transfer of profits overseas and nationalized the strategic industrial sector. And finally, the planned reform of the universities would curtail the discretionary power of full professors and reorganize teaching and research programmes to meet Brazil's national needs.[7]

The elections in October 1962 brought in new congressmen. Also, eleven new state governors came into office. A warning had been sent to the government: the chances of gradually introducing a moderate reform programme were now virtually non-existent. Not one of the new governorships had been the result of a Social Democratic Party/ Brazilian Labour Party (PSD/PTB) alliance; and only one left-wing governor was elected, Miguel Arraes,[8] in Pernambuco.[9] Despite Leonel Brizola's victory – he was elected to the Chamber of Deputies with 269,000 votes, the highest number received by any candidate – the balance of power in Congress remained virtually unaltered.

The 1962 elections signalled something else too: the possibility of a *coup d'état*. The election campaigns had received funding from a number of non-party organizations. The most dangerous among these was the Brazilian Institute for Democratic Action (IBAD), which had been established in Rio de Janeiro in 1959 by the American Central Intelligence Agency. IBAD had poured money into the campaigns of 250 federal deputies and 600 state deputies, as well as those of eight candidates for governor – a practice that was completely illegal under the election laws. The funds came from multinational companies, or companies that were associated with foreign capital, and from United States government sources happy to invest 'one or two American dollars' in the conspiracy against President Goulart, as was confirmed some years later by the American ambassador.[10] The objective was strategic: to create strong opposition in Congress, block government initiatives, and prepare the way for a *coup d'état*. After a congressional inquiry had confirmed the presence of widespread electoral corruption and the illegal activities of the Brazilian Institute for Democratic Action, João Goulart closed the institute in 1963. But IBAD had not acted alone. They were aided by an institution with ambiguous, concealed intentions and sophisticated methods: the Research and Social Studies Institute (IPES), founded in 1961 by a group of businessmen from Rio de Janeiro and São Paulo, and a handful of officers linked to the *Escola Superior de Guerra* (ESG – National War College).

In 1949 the joint chiefs of staff of the armed forces had founded the National War College based on the model of the North American college of the same name. The mission was to bring military officers and businessmen together, for them to join forces in support of Brazil's industrial growth.[11] During the 1950s the National War College developed a plan for economic growth and national security specific to the Cold War context. This plan was not restricted to national defence. It was geared towards internal conflict and redefined the role of the army, now considered essential to the maintenance of control over the population. Intelligence and information-gathering was considered essential to the efficiency of the state.

The Research and Social Studies Institute, on the other hand, was an organization with strictly controlled membership and a dual purpose.[12] Officially it was a conservative political institution whose mission was to study the political and economic situation in Brazil. It was based in a suite of thirteen rooms on the 27th floor of Edifício Central, in Rio de Janeiro, and had offices in São Paulo, Rio Grande do Sul, Minas Gerais and Pernambuco, which were considered the most strategic states. Members included the country's richest businessmen, directors of multinational companies with operations in the country, representatives of the most important business associations, military officers, journalists, intellectuals and a group of young technocrats. All of them were active, publishing books, producing films or giving lectures.[13] But there was more to the institute's activities. Its real task was to undermine President Goulart, for which there were two strategies. The first was to undertake a well-orchestrated destabilization plan, which included financing an anti-communist propaganda campaign, funding anti-government protests, and promoting the opposition and the extreme right in politics as well as in business. The second was to draw up the plans for a new government – authoritarian in nature – based on development and the free flow of international capital. Contrary to popular belief, the Research and Social Studies Institute was not just a propagator of anti-communist propaganda, nor a group of right-wing extremists stockpiling arms. It was the nucleus of a *coup d'état* conspiracy whose members had their own agenda. They were well informed and were very well placed among the conspirators who were to overthrow President Goulart, as they were in the occupation of the state after March 1964.

But the activities of the Research and Social Studies Institute alone were not enough to bring about a *coup d'état*. Businessmen and military officers could conspire, but with no real support from the masses there was no campaign, propaganda or ideological conviction that could destabilize the Goulart government. A *coup d'état* was on the horizon, although it was not a realistic option in the short term. By late 1962, however, things began to change, the parliamentary system seemed increasingly vulnerable, and not without help from the president himself. A referendum on the form of government was held on 6 January 1963. The result was an overwhelming victory for the presidential system, which received

9.5 million out of a total of 11.5 million votes.[14] For President Goulart, winning the referendum was much the same as having won a new election. And he was not entirely wrong. But he had overlooked an important detail. The victory was not his per se, it was a vote for the presidential system, which had been supported by a number of political parties and their leaders who had an eye to winning the 1965 presidential elections. Even so, the president's popularity was high and his government was being given the chance to start again. But then, surprisingly, in a year that had begun with so much promise, João Goulart stumbled irrevocably.

THE IDES OF MARCH

In 1963 there were two political agendas in Brazil, one on the left and one on the right, competing to transform the country. Yet there was only limited space for manoeuvre, and even less political will, to resolve political differences democratically. The government had very little power of persuasion and there were too many radical movements, both within and outside Congress. In April that year, on the instructions of President Goulart, the Brazilian Labour Party proposed a constitutional amendment for agrarian reform. Congress delayed six months, and then rejected it. With the defeat of the amendment, the president lost his second opportunity to implement his government's programme. Nevertheless, he still underestimated the forces aligned against him.

Among the left-wing parties there was a general feeling of self-sufficiency, and a consensus that things were not moving fast enough. The leader of the coalition, Leonel Brizola, was in no way making things any easier for President Goulart. Mr Brizola wanted the government to confront the problem of foreign capital and to summon a new Constituent Assembly whose members would include trade union members, rural workers, and subaltern officers from the armed forces. He claimed Congress had to be bypassed in order to implement core reforms. There is no doubt that Leonel Brizola was hard-headed, but the left-wing parties united under his leadership and he enjoyed unprecedented popularity, particularly among the sergeants in the armed forces and the military police, as well as in the navy and the marines. In 1963 there were 40,000 sergeants in the army, of whom 22,000 declared their support for Leonel Brizola.[15] Mr Brizola's rhetoric, already pretentious, became dangerously radical. And his was not the only revisionist voice. By late 1963 members of the left-wing parties considered their position so strong they denounced Congress as excessively conservative, determined the 1946 Constitution obsolete, and referred to all political activity in Brazil as superficial propaganda.

At the other end of the spectrum, Carlos Lacerda continued stirring things up in his attempt to destabilize the president. In October he gave a long interview to a North American journalist – reproduced in the *Tribuna da Imprensa* – which exacerbated the political situation even further. He declared that the situation in Brazil was so serious that the military were debating whether it were better to 'patronize him [João Goulart], control him until the end of his term or remove him from office altogether'.[16] For someone who had learnt the art of politics from Getúlio Vargas, President Goulart overreacted to the declarations: he summoned his ministers and sent a message to Congress requesting the declaration of a state of siege, which would allow him to intervene in the state of Guanabara.[17] The reaction was hostile all around. The state governors informed President Goulart that none of them would accept federal intervention in their states. Left-wing leaders feared the same measures might be used against them. And the three major parties – the Brazilian Labour Party, the National Democratic Union and the Social Democratic Party – joined forces and informed the Executive that the state of siege would not be approved.

João Goulart had no choice but to admit defeat and accept that his authority had been weakened. And it was not for the first time. A month earlier he had also lost face over the government's handling of a military crisis – the Rebellion of the Sergeants.[18] The crisis had begun with the decision of the Federal Supreme Court that sergeants who had run for office in 1962 were ineligible for public office. The decision was followed by an unexpected act of military insubordination. In Brasília, air force and navy sergeants, and soldiers from the marine corps, invaded the airforce base and the naval ministry, blockaded the roads and the airports, invaded the National Congress, occupied the Supreme Court building, and kidnapped the Supreme Court president, Victor Nunes Leal, whom they kept under arrest for several hours.

Before the movement could spread, the military commanders sent troops into the streets of Brasília and suppressed the rebellion. But the political ramifications were to be disastrous for the government. For the army command, the incident came as a shock, both for its infringement of military discipline and for the ease with which the sergeants had virtually isolated the capital. But they were even more astounded at President Goulart's reaction: he remained neutral, neither defending nor attacking the rebels. Nor did he respond to the left-wing parties that had supported the sergeants. His silence allowed the conspirators to take on the role of guarantors of legality, which in turn lent credibility to the Research and Social Studies Institute sponsored anti-Goulart campaign. As from October the Goulart government's political and administrative instability became increasingly evident. The Executive virtually came to a halt due to the constant replacement of ministers, the absence of a majority in Congress, and the heightened radicalization of political forces on both sides of the political spectrum. Annual inflation reached 79.9 per cent, economic growth was 1.5 per cent a year, and there was a generalized feeling that the government had lost control. Brazil's international creditors stopped all further loans while the American government tipped money into the pockets of the state governors of Minas Gerais, São Paulo and Guanabara, who were planning a *coup d'état*.[19]

As the Ides of March of 1964 approached, President Goulart brought things to a head. The first unequivocal sign that his government was on a collision course with the National Congress came on a Friday the 13th. *O Comício da Central* – the political rally held outside Rio de Janeiro's central train station – was carefully planned, even down to the symbolism. The stage was set up in the same location where Getúlio Vargas had held ceremonies during the *Estado Novo*, in a show of unity between all the left-wing forces, the workers' movements and the government. It attracted a multitude, estimated between 150,000 and 200,000 people, and lasted for more than four hours. Thirteen speeches were given in all. João Goulart was the last to speak, beside his beautiful young wife, Maria Thereza, who appeared nervous. The president gave an improvised, emotional speech in which he declared that the time for the reforms had come and the time for compromise was over.[20]

Two days later President Goulart sent the president's annual address to Congress. Therein were his agenda for reforms, a proposed referendum for their approval, a request to delegate legislative powers to the Executive, and recommended alterations to the text of the 1946 Constitution.[21] The presidential message terrified Congress. For many it confirmed the worst fears of the Research and Social Studies Institute and of the National Democratic Union, that sooner or later the president would impose his policies, dissolve Congress, grant special powers to the Executive, change the election rules for his own benefit, and permit Leonel Brizola to run for office. (Under the 1946 Constitution, as João Goulart's brother-in-law, Mr Brizola was not allowed to stand as a candidate.) In fact, Leonel Brizola made no secret of his ambition to rule the country, and João Goulart probably did covet re-election. It is also true that the two of them planned significant alterations to the constitution. But until then, there had only been rhetoric, a political game. But with the annual address to Congress, everything changed. People began to focus on Leonel Brizola and President Goulart's activities, realizing there was nothing to prevent the two of them from carrying out the president's plans. At any moment President Goulart could annul the legislation that sustained his presidency. There was widespread suspicion, in the press and public opinion, as to the government's intentions.

On 19 March, in São Paulo, a large crowd left the Praça da República and marched to the Praça da Sé carrying banners, flags and a profusion of rosaries, to save Brazil from João Goulart, Leonel Brizola and communism, as they shouted in chorus. The Family with God March for Freedom had been organized by the Research and Social Studies Institute through the Women's Civic Union, one of the many women's groups set up by the institute all over Brazil to increase political pressure. The march attracted around half a million people and had two main objectives. It was both a response to the rally at the Central do Brazil as well as a powerful appeal on the part of society for intervention by the armed forces.[22] Due to an excess of self-confidence, President Goulart and the coalition of left-wing parties remained unfazed by the fact that half a million people had protested in the streets of Brazil's most important city. 'These aren't "the people",' they said disdainfully.[23] But they were wrong. The march in São Paulo proved that a strong government opposition coalition had been formed, willing and able to mobilize people from all walks of life. Their shared aversion to the increasing political activity of the trade unions and rural workers was one of their main uniting forces. Furthermore, financial stress and uncertainty with respect to the future had stirred the urban middle classes into action. They were well aware that a radical process of redistribution of income and power would affect their traditional position in that brutally inequitable society. Taking all of this into account facilitates the understanding of the intensity and breadth of the opposition movement. Between 19 March and 8 June 1964 crowds marched *with* God and *against* João Goulart – or, after 31 March, to commemorate the *coup d'état* that had deposed him – in at least fifty cities all around the country, from state capitals to small towns.[24]

Deposing President Goulart required unification in the barracks. And the armed forces, after all, had promised to uphold the constitution when João Goulart took office in 1961. On 25 March, when the president was spending the Easter weekend on his farm in São Borja, the Minister of the Navy sparked off a crisis that was to have an irrevocable effect on the government's authority over the military. In fact, it provided justification for the coup. The minister ordered the arrest of forty sailors and corporals who were organizing the commemorations for the second anniversary of the Brazilian Association of Sailors and Marines (AMFNB).[25] For all intents and purposes, the association was a trade union whose purpose was to achieve better working conditions for navy personnel, who survived on very low wages and poor food aboard their ships. Furthermore, they had to submit to absurd regulations – they were not allowed to get married without authorization or wear civilian clothing in the streets. As the guest of honour for the event, they had invited João Cândido, who had led the Revolt of the Whip in 1910 in protest against the practice of flogging in the navy. In many ways the sailors' situation had remained unchanged since the days of the First Republic. After the arrests were ordered, more than 3,600 sailors rebelled. They took refuge in the offices of the Metalworkers Union (Palácio do Aço) in downtown Rio de Janeiro, and for three days refused to come out. They demanded that the navy recognize the association and revoke all punishments. Sailors aboard ship in the bay joined the movement, conducting acts of sabotage that prevented other ships from leaving the port.[26] The minister was further demoralized when he sent five hundred Marines and thirteen tanks to invade the building and remove the rebels. Twenty-six of the soldiers put down their weapons, entered the building, and joined the rebels.

In the early hours of 27 March, President Goulart rushed back to Rio de Janeiro, appointed a new naval minister, personally took charge of the negotiations, and put everything on the line. The next morning he organized the rebels' exit from the building, from where they were taken to army barracks. On the very same day he ordered their release and declared an amnesty. The sight of the delighted sailors marching through the streets of Rio de Janeiro towards the War Ministry came as a shock to the armed forces. The high command was indignant. Their response was unanimous: what had happened in the navy was nothing less than a collapse in discipline, a breach of hierarchy, and the demoralization of the command. The episode caused an uproar in the barracks and members of the Research and Social Studies Institute conceded that a military coup was imminent. The coup was to begin in São Paulo, probably on the night of 10 April. All that was needed to finalize the plans was agreement among the chief military commanders. Meanwhile, at the United States military base of Norfolk, Virginia, a naval task force was waiting for authorization to head for Brazil. The task force was part of Operation Brother Sam, which had been prepared in Washington with the complicity of the Brazilian military to provide support for the coup. The plan was for the ships to set sail on 1 April and to divide into three groups upon entering Brazilian waters. The first group would head to the port of Santos, the second to Rio, and the third to Carapebus near Vitória, in Espírito Santo. Their orders were to offer logistical support, above all in the case of prolonged resistance.[27]

On the night of 30 March, President Goulart left the presidential residence in Rio de Janeiro (Palácio de Laranjeiras) to follow advice expressed in a popular idiom, '*manda brasa!*' (shoot the works). Leftists had transformed it into a slogan, '*manda brasa, Presidente!*' And the president did just that. He was to give a speech at a party in honour of the investiture of the new Board of Directors of the Sergeants' Association, in the auditorium of the Automóvel Clube, in Cinelândia.[28] João Goulart entered the room, filled with sergeants, sailors and Marines, and took the stage. At his side was able seaman Corporal Anselmo (José Anselmo dos Santos), the president of the Brazilian Association of Sailors and Marines, who had led the sailors' revolt – and who later became a notorious double agent, passing information to the navy and the CIA.[29]

It is not known exactly when Corporal Anselmo became a double agent: whether it was while he was still president of the AMFNB or whether it was after the coup of 1964. What is known is that his activities resulted in the death of a number of militants who were fighting the military dictatorship, including that of his own wife, Soledad Viedma. However, on 30 March his popularity was irrepressible and his photograph was constantly in the newspapers. Corporal Anselmo was twenty-five, with boyish good looks, and had no idea that evening that he was witnessing João Goulart's last appearance in public as president. At dawn the following morning, General Olímpio Mourão Filho, commander of the Fourth Military Region (based in Juiz de Fora, Minas Gerais), having run out of patience awaiting instructions from the Brazilian Association of Sailors and Marines, led his troops towards Rio de Janeiro. He intended to occupy the War Ministry and depose the Goulart government.

Between 31 March and 4 April, when João Goulart went into exile in Uruguay, there were still several possible ways he could have dealt with the coup. The first, with a good chance of success, and with little cost and little risk, would have been to prevent General Mourão from advancing. The troops were moving slowly, clearly visible, along the União e Indústria highway. They were badly equipped and many were recent recruits. The second would have been to stay put in Rio de Janeiro, make an announcement to the nation, and take personal command of the resistance, with the support of the garrisons that remained loyal to the government. Instead, his sudden departure from Rio de Janeiro to Brasília confused his supporters, who interpreted it as flight. The third opportunity would have been to then remain in Brasília and mobilize congressional support. He could have proposed democratic elections. In addition to the support of the Brazilian Labour Party and the left-wing coalition, the chances were high of getting the support of the Social Democratic Party. The last possibility – and certainly the most reckless – was proposed by Leonel Brizola when President Goulart was already in Porto Alegre. The plan was based on the 1961 campaign for legality, when Mr Brizola had mobilized civilians and General Ladário Telles, the commander of the Third Army, led the military operations.[30]

Historians are still debating how the conspirators were so easily victorious. Obviously, one of the reasons was that João Goulart did not lead a resistance. But nor did anyone else from the left take the initiative to resist the coup – neither the Communist Party, the General Workers' Command (CGT), the Rural Workers' Leagues (*Ligas Camponesas*), nor Leonel Brizola. It is probable that all of them, including

President Goulart, thought that the coup would follow the pattern of previous military interventions, such as those of 1945, 1954, 1955 and 1961.[31] In all these cases the armed forces had acted as both protagonist and moderating power, and after a cooling-off period had called elections and returned power to the civilians. It is also possible that João Goulart saw his position as analogous to that of Getúlio Vargas in 1945. He would retreat to his farm in São Borja from where he would watch events unfold and prepare to stand for re-election in 1965.

After all, General Mourão's act of insubordination was fairly typical. He was nearing retirement and believed that if he sent the troops out, the military command might be jolted into action. The governor of Minas Gerais in turn, Magalhães Pinto, wanted to run for president in 1965. And he knew that he had very little chance of being his party's candidate – the National Democratic Union would in all likelihood choose Carlos Lacerda. Magalhães Pinto thus supported General Mourão's plan with an eye to increasing his own political power. He intended to offer Minas Gerais to the conspirators as a base for their campaign.[32] No one, neither Magalhães Pinto nor Carlos Lacerda nor Ademar de Barros, imagined the movement would lead to anything but a short military intervention. Even Juscelino Kubitschek, who had been senator for the state of Goiás since 1962, agreed with them. Typical of his political style, Juscelino Kubitschek declared he was not in favour of the *coup d'état*, but nor would he support President Goulart – he would not take a stand against his own state, Minas Gerais.[33] The president of the Senate, Auro de Moura Andrade, was yet another leader who did not foresee a prolonged military dictatorship. Faced with the disintegration of the government, he decided to anticipate events by deposing President Goulart. In the early hours of 2 April he called a secret session of both Houses and declared the presidency vacant. When Tancredo Neves protested vehemently that João Goulart was still in Brazil and was thus still invested with the full powers of president, Mr Moura Andrade disconnected the sound and turned off the lights. The *coup d'état* was consummated.[34] Nonetheless, everyone believed there would be elections in 1965. They were all wrong. A faction among the conspirators had its own agenda and the military government was to last for twenty-one years. Brazil's military dictatorship was about to begin.

WHEN A COUP BECOMES A GOVERNMENT

On the afternoon of 11 April 1964 the National Congress met to elect the new president of Brazil. The deputies of the left-wing coalition were no longer present. The day before, the first list was published of deputies whose mandates had been annulled. The term in Portuguese is actually *cassado*, a derogatory term for those whose political rights were revoked for a period of ten years. There were to be other lists. By March 1967, four hundred mandates had been annulled. What remained of the Congress participated in the indirect election, for which there was only one candidate – General Humberto de Alencar Castello Branco. The deputies were required to announce their votes, one by one – only seventy-two had the courage to abstain, including Tancredo Neves and Santiago Dantas. At the end of the afternoon the general was elected with 361 votes – including Juscelino Kubitschek's – to complete João Goulart's term. General Castello Branco took office in Congress a few days later. He swore to defend the 1946 Constitution, promised to hand over the presidency to his successor in 1965, and guaranteed there would be no more annulments of political rights and mandates.[35]

In his speech the general said what everyone wanted to hear, but he kept none of his promises. The coup that brought General Castello Branco to power had very little in common with the military uprising commanded by General Mourão and Magalhães Pinto, except that both were exceptions, arbitrary and violent. Between 30 March and 11 April military officers and business leaders from the Research and Social Studies Institute (IPES) competed with each other to neutralize the various forces that had acted independently to depose President Goulart. And, as journalists look back on those times in Rio de Janeiro, they note with irony that people could even conduct those discussions safely by telephone!

While the political world was thinking of the elections for the next president and ratified general Costa e Silva to hold the post until then, members of the Research and Social Studies Institute were concentrating on how to transform the military uprising into a *coup d'état*, and the *coup d'état* into a government. The associates and collaborators of the institute manoeuvred to fill key positions in the ministries and other state administrative departments.[36] The main goal was to outline the programme of the new government and define its political economy – with the immediate establishment of the Ministry of Planning and Economic Coordination. Other top priorities included the decision-making bodies in Planalto[37] and the various ministries – starting with the Civil and Military Cabinets. Equal importance was given to the control and collection of information on questions of domestic security, which led to the creation of the National Information Service (SNI) in June.

None of this resembled the traditional form of intervention by the armed forces that had occurred so frequently in the history of Brazil. The investiture of General Castello Branco was a prelude to a complete change in Brazil's political system. This transformation was brought about by collaboration between the military and sectors of civilian society that wanted to implement a modernization project based on industrialization and economic growth, sustained by an openly dictatorial regime. This implied far-reaching changes to the structure of the state. It required the creation of a new legal framework, the implementation of a new model for economic development, the creation of a secret service for political repression and information gathering and, of course, censorship to silence dissent.

The most sensitive area of the new political system was the control of the armed forces over the presidency. The military took over the government by unconstitutional methods. They granted themselves emergency powers and 'elected' five army generals in succession to head the Executive – Castello Branco (1964–7), Costa e Silva (1967–9), Garrastazu Médici (1969–74), Ernesto Geisel (1974–9) and João Figueiredo (1979–85). There was also a short period during which the country was governed by a Military Junta (August to October 1969), made up of ministers of the three components of the armed forces. Throughout the dictatorship, however, there were disputes between factions within the armed forces over who should control the Executive. The armed forces had a long tradition of involvement in government and were home to a wide variety of political ideologies. There were also differences of opinion between the three forces, between the generations and within the hierarchy. Furthermore, although the armed forces had the will and the capacity to take power, they had never exercised it for long. In 1964 the situation was very different. The generals considered themselves ready to take over the government. Various groups of rival officers with convictions and strategies of their own intended to intervene during the course of the dictatorship which, after all, they had helped to create, and for which they felt responsible.[38] Despite their differences all these groups agreed that domestic security should take priority as the mission of the armed forces. They also insisted that the source of sovereignty of the new political system was military and originated in the armed forces – it did not only stem from the hierarchical authority of the generals.

The disagreements between the rival factions within the armed forces were not over power per se, but about what should be done with it. In the periods leading up to the selection of a new president, these rivalries intensified.[39] General Castello Branco was no exception. Every single one of the military presidents succeeded to the presidency and left office amid a serious crisis. In spite of what is often said, President Castello Branco's government was anything but moderate. It institutionalized the limitations imposed on the Legislature and the Judiciary and constructed the basis for the political repression that was to give the dictatorship such a long life. Even so, there were sections of the army that were dissatisfied. The Minister of War, General Artur da Costa e Silva, became the leader of the faction in favour of a more authoritarian government and stricter societal control. It was these dissidents who successfully aided General Costa e Silva in promoting his own candidacy.

President Castello Branco died on 18 July 1967, soon after he had left government. As he was returning from a trip to Ceará, he was in an aeroplane crash stemming from a strange coincidence. The small twin-engine plane he was travelling in entered into a collision course with a squadron of air force jets.[40] His successor, General Costa e Silva, built a government seemingly tailor-made to meet the aspirations of those officers interested in determining the future of Brazil. Among his nineteen ministers, ten were from the armed forces and one of them, the Minister of Interior, General Albuquerque Lima, was the leader of the most radical faction in the army. Nevertheless, President Costa e Silva's mandate was to end amid an even more serious military crisis.[41] In August 1969 he suffered a stroke and was officially removed from the presidency due to illness. The armed forces now faced an impasse.

They could swear the vice-president into office, the National Democratic Union deputy from Minas Gerais, Pedro Aleixo, but they rejected him on the grounds that he was a civilian, and also because he was a moderate with democratic tendencies. Rumours were rife, the various factions competed with each other to influence the next step. Pedro Aleixo was put under house arrest, and finally a solution was found. The Executive was handed over to a junta formed by the three military ministers. The solution only lasted for three months. Meanwhile the crisis had deepened. The navy and the air force refused to accept that the next president be appointed by the army; meanwhile, more radical factions supported the candidacy of General Albuquerque Lima.

Before the situation degenerated into anarchy, the army suggested General Émilio Garrastazu Médici, the director of the National Information Service, the national intelligence agency set up by President Castello Branco. He was a taciturn military bureaucrat, virtually unknown, and with no popularity among the troops. Brazilians only became aware of his existence on 6 October 1969, when his name was confirmed by the high command[42] of the armed forces as president of Brazil.

When he completed his term of office in March 1974, President Médici chose his successor seamlessly: General Ernesto Beckmann Geisel. The last major crisis of the dictatorship occurred at the end of President Geisel's mandate, in 1979. His War Minister, Sylvio Frota, aimed to succeed him.[43] General Frota behaved as if he were the official representative of the army's position. He disagreed with President Geisel's policies. He had made himself the self-appointed spokesman for the officers who, diverted from their original functions, were required to work in the state apparatus for dissident repression. President Geisel came from a family of German immigrants. He had an explosive personality and was feared among his colleagues. He dismissed General Frota, forbade the generals from participating in the succession, and decided himself who the next president would be. Once again the candidate, General João Figueiredo, was the director of the National Information Service. There were no complaints from the barracks. The recurring crises within the armed forces no doubt influenced the choice of the military presidents, although they did not alter the dynamics of the dictatorship. The period was marked by the emergency powers, repression, controlled public information, and a conservative development and modernization economic plan.

The years of the dictatorship were a sombre time for Brazil.

THE DICTATORSHIP

Although the dictatorship was a succession of generals exercising the presidency with imperial powers, between 1964 and 1985, that power was shared with the ministries of Planning and of Finance. All the ministers were civilians from the Research and Social Studies Institute, and they controlled the entire economy: Roberto Campos, Octávio Gouvêa de Bulhões, Antônio Delfim Netto, Hélio Beltrão and Mário Henrique Simonsen.[44] 'The channel between the government and the business sector was entirely open,'[45] Delfim Netto – Finance Minister between 1967 and 1974, and Planning Minister between 1979 and 1985 – confirmed fifty years later. The Finance Minister had complete control of the budget, which, in ordinary circumstances, would have been subject to approval by Congress. 'The Finance Minister had the power to authorize any expense he thought fit,' former minister Maílson da Nóbrega recalled, and added that Delfim Netto had 'powers that would make a mediaeval king die of envy'.[46] The dictatorship's economic development project facilitated foreign investment, reduced the active role of the state, and increased the rate of growth. 'We did it all. There was no force, neither the legislature nor the judiciary that could oppose our economic policies,'[47] former minister Ernane Galvêas later confirmed. President Castello Branco's government had built the economic and financial foundation that sustained the development model. It prioritized an incentive programme for foreign investment and for exports. This was achieved through the devaluation of Brazil's currency, the *cruzeiro*, against the dollar. The programme was based on a strict stabilization policy: wage control, reduced minimum working age, elimination of 'job security',[48] repression of trade unions and prohibition of strikes.[49]

In 1967, when General Costa e Silva took over the government, the economy began to grow. However, by that time working-class wages and middle-class salaries were feeling the impact of the economic squeeze. With the cost of living going up and wages frozen, in April 1968 around 1,200 workers at the Companhia Siderúrgica Belgo-Mineira occupied the plant and demanded a salary increase, above the government-established wages.[50] The Companhia Siderúrgica Belgo-Mineira is a steel mill located in Contagem, an industrial town seventeen kilometres outside Belo Horizonte in Minas Gerais. The workers occupied the largest plant in the complex. Three days later the whole of Contagem came to a halt, with the number of workers on strike reaching 16,000. The Minister of Labour, Jarbas Passarinho, was forced to travel to the town and negotiate with the workers in person. As he left the plant, he was booed. The town was occupied by the military police, workers were arrested, the trade union closed down and, from then on, the company provided workers transportation directly to the plant from their homes. Anyone who refused the transportation was fired. The strikers had taken the military by surprise and the government had to negotiate. The strike had been planned in such a way as to make immediate repression logistically more difficult. The strikers did not picket, did not call meetings, and had very few conspicuous leaders. The only known participants were Ênio Seabra and Imaculada Conceição de Oliveira from the city's steel workers' union. The mobilization of the workers took place inside the factories, in a semi-clandestine way, in committees of between five and ten people, linked to each other through an internal network. The strike in Contagem ended fifteen days after it had begun with a wage increase of 10 per cent and some hope that it would be possible to confront the government's wage policies in the future.

Three months later, in Osasco, in the São Paulo industrial belt, the workers at Cobrasma, whose main activity was steel and mechanical construction, laid down their tools.[51] The strike organizers intended to set off a chain reaction among workers' movements and trade unions all around the country to protest the dictatorship's economic policies. As had been the case in Contagem, the Cobrasma workers had been mobilized through committees inside the factory and the support was massive. On the first day 10,000 workers went on strike. But this time the military had no intention of losing face. On the second day of the strike, Cobrasma was invaded by soldiers with machine guns and two tanks. After the invasion, the military police occupied the town of Osasco and around four hundred workers were arrested. Those leaders who managed to escape from prison went into hiding – including the president of the Metalworkers' Trade Union of Osasco, José Ibrahim.

The brutality worked, both as an instrument of coercion and dissuasion. For the next ten years there were no more strikes in Brazil.

The military were improving their methods of repression – inside the factories and in society at large – the economy had expanded and inflation, instead of rising, began to fall. The cycle of economic growth began which, at its height, surpassed anything that had been seen before. The government began to refer to it as 'the Brazilian economic miracle'.[52] There is no denying the miracle occurred; but it had a more mundane explanation. The 'miracle' was the result of a combination of factors, including the repression of the opposition and censorship of the media to prevent any criticism of the economic model; government subsidies for exports and their consequent diversification; privatization of the economy with an increasing number of foreign companies entering the market; and centralized government control of prices and wages.

Automobile industry production tripled, the supply of cement for civil construction dried up, and people earned a small fortune on the stock exchange – there was a month in 1970 in Rio de Janeiro when the volume of trade surpassed that of the entire year of 1968. However, the 'economic miracle' came with a price tag. The process was accompanied by an ever-increasing concentration of income in the hands of the few as a result of the strict wage controls that prevented any productivity gains from being shared with the workers. Another result was the dramatic increase in the foreign debt, which made the country more vulnerable to instability in the international market. Brazil had taken out loans in hard currency, with longer terms and lower interest rates, and the industrial sector had received credit from private international banks at floating interest rates. Brazilians would only grasp the extent of the country's economic vulnerability in 1973, when the Organization of Petroleum Exporting Countries (OPEC) reduced the supply of oil, and the price multiplied by four times. There was no alternative but to continue buying it, and the 'miracle' came to an end. Unlike most Brazilians, the generals in the Executive and the technocrats in the Ministry of Planning knew the economic growth could not be maintained and that consequences such as these were inevitable. But no one took any action. In fact, the dictatorship benefited enormously from the results. From the somewhat cynical viewpoint of General Médici, who was president at the height of the growth cycle, the country was fine; it was the people who were not.

Dictatorships are a combination of arbitrary leadership, tenacious opposition, and a population that needs to survive – part of which remains silent either out of fear or resignation. While the 'economic miracle' lasted, the cost of income concentration was latent. Many people, especially among the urban middle classes, benefited from easy credit, new professional opportunities, and incentives to consume new products, including colour televisions, cassette tapes, Super-8 cameras and cars – the Corcel, Opala, Galaxie and Chevette. And to complete the happy expectations of Brazilians, wage earners could finally plan to buy their own home, with a mortgage from the recently created National Housing Bank (BNH). The 'economic miracle' reached its peak between 1970 and 1972. This economic success explains President Médici's popularity, in spite of his leading the country during the worst period of political violence in Brazilian history. He received very little criticism and much applause. The increase in the state apparatus for repression during his government was immense, but that alone would not have been enough to keep him in office. Every government needs support in order to survive, and in Brazil's case the 'economic miracle' was the source of citizens' satisfaction with the administration. Three days after he took office, in 1969, President Médici restructured a communications department created by his predecessor – the Special Agency for Public Relations (AERP) – and turned it into a formidable political propaganda machine. The agency's propaganda was creative, with no ostensive signs of political marketing. Their productions emphasized optimism, pride and national greatness. They celebrated Brazil's racial diversity, integration and social harmony. All of these messages were contained in short films communicated directly to the public with artfully chosen imagery and popular, catchy melodies.[53] The agency's television propaganda was equally successful.

The military had a development project of major proportions and were determined to integrate the whole of the country. Brazil was transformed into an enormous building site, all duly noted and celebrated by the Special Agency for Public Relations. The most famous of these construction projects – the Transamazônica[54] – was part of the economic development project conceived by the Research and Social Studies Institute and the National War College programme of internal security. It was a gigantic highway, planned to be 4,997 kilometres long, of which 4,223 kilometres were built (although the work was of very poor quality). It was intended to cut across the Amazon Basin from east to west, connecting Brazil's northeast to Peru and Ecuador. The construction of the Transamazônica was the basis of an ambitious plan to settle the area, which included the dislocation of close to a million people in the region. The goal was to leave no part of the country uninhabited and, for the first time, to control the frontiers. The highway was inaugurated by President Médici on 27 September 1972,[55] and used to promote a triumphant image of a country fully geared toward modernization whose population had a strong sense of identity. But the reality was rather different. The construction of the Transamazônica destroyed the forest, consumed billions of dollars, and even today there are many parts of it that are impassable due to rains, landslides and flooding rivers.

The project burned money that did not exist, which Brazilians would only discover in 1980, when the 'miracle' was over and inflation reached three digits – 110 per cent. In 1985, when the military regime finally came to an end, it left behind a huge national debt and a 235 per cent annual rate of inflation. In 1978 the economist Edmar Bacha, cautiously avoiding the censors, had baptized the country Belíndia (a combination of Belgium and India) in an article entitled 'The Economist and the King of Belíndia: A Fable for Technocrats'.[56] In Belíndia, national wealth was calculated such as to conceal both the extent of the concentration of wealth in developed areas ('Belgium'), as well as the backwardness of those areas that were underdeveloped ('India'), where hunger, abject poverty, low life expectancy and high levels of infant mortality prevailed.

SUFFOCATING TEMPERATURE

On 14 December 1968 the *Jornal do Brasil*, one of the most important daily newspapers, published an edition especially planned to surprise its readers. Among other oddities the newspaper published a headline on the front page that read 'Yesterday was the Day of the Blind'. The weather forecast also appeared on the front page: 'Stormy weather. Suffocating temperature. Air unbreathable. The country is being swept by strong winds.' The day was actually hot and sunny with a bright blue sky. The weather forecast was the paper's way of warning readers that the censors had been in their offices. That night the military government had begun an operation to stifle the Brazilian press.

The newspaper also warned readers that the situation had gone from bad to worse. At 10 o'clock on the previous night, 13 December 1968, the Minister of Justice, Luís Antônio da Gama e Silva, had addressed the nation on national radio and television. After a brief introduction he passed the microphone to Alberto Curi,[57] who proceeded, in a grave monotone, to read the entire text of the Institutional Act no. 5. The act had twelve articles and was accompanied by Complementary Act no. 38, which closed the National Congress for an indeterminate period of time. The AI-5 suspended habeas corpus, freedom of expression and freedom of reunion; it permitted peremptory dismissals, the annulment of mandates and citizens' rights; and it determined that political trials would be conducted by military courts, with no right of appeal. It was imposed at a time of political unrest and increasingly hostile opposition activity. There had been student protests, strikes, pronouncements by pre-1964 political leaders, and the beginning of armed resistance by the revolutionary left. The pretext for these acts was the refusal on the part of Congress to carry out judicial proceedings against Deputy Márcio Moreira Alves. Mr Moreira Alves was accused of offending the armed forces in a speech given in the Chamber of Deputies on 3 September that year. He was a courageous man who had denounced in the Chamber – based on proof – dozens of cases of torture that had occurred in military barracks during President Castello Branco's government.[58] 'When will the army cease to be a refuge for torturers?' he asked. There had been no repercussions for him at the time because Deputy Moreira Alves had spoken to a virtually empty house. But it served as an excellent pretext for the military. The Minister of Justice asked for permission to take legal action against the deputy, but Congress refused, and the crisis was solved with the issue of the AI-5.[59]

The AI-5 was an instrument intended to intimidate people. There was no stipulation as to how long it was to remain in effect. It allowed the dictatorship to repress all opposition and dissent. However, it was by no means the first emergency measure created by the armed forces, nor did it represent a 'coup within a coup' carried out by a radical faction of officers to increase their powers of political repression. The AI-5 was part of a whole range of emergency measures that were, in fact, legal. The military had spent a great deal of time and energy creating a legal framework for their arbitrary measures – the 'legality of a state of emergency'.[60] These measures imposed severe limitations on the freedom of action of the other powers. They legalized the punishment of dissidents, prevented the opposition from organizing, and restricted any kind of political participation. The first Institutional Act had been drawn up in secret and promulgated eight days after the *coup d'état*. It was signed by the self-proclaimed Supreme Command of the Revolution – formed by General Costa e Silva, Admiral Rademaker and Brigadier Correia de Mello – and contained eleven articles. It transferred part of the powers of the Legislature to the Executive, limited the powers of the Judiciary, suspended individual guarantees, and allowed the president to annul mandates – and deny political rights to those whose mandates had been cancelled for a period of ten years – and to dismiss civil servants and members of the armed forces. In order for this measure to have some sort of legal basis, the military granted themselves constitutional powers and included the manipulation of the Judiciary in the 'Introduction' of the First Institutional Act: 'The victorious Revolution [. . .] is the most radical form of expression of the Constituent Power.'[61]

To this day, the armed forces employ the term 'revolution' to refer to the *coup d'état*. This is due to the first Institutional Act, which guaranteed the legitimacy of the system and institutionalized repression. Because of the number of other Institutional Acts that were to follow, it became known as the Institutional Act no. 1 and gave General Castello Branco the legal means to imprison thousands of people, as well as to create detention centres out of football stadiums, such as Caio Martins stadium in Niterói, and to transform merchant ships and warships into prisons.[62] The AI-1 also allowed the military police to arrest people en masse, close off streets, conduct individual and house-to-house searches, all of which occurred in 1964 – in Minas Gerais, Rio Grande do Sul, São Paulo and Pernambuco – when around 50,000 people were detained in a deployment that the police baptized 'Operation Cleanup'.

The AI-1 also provided the government with the legal means to purge the civil service. There were two main procedures. In the first, the military set up Special Inquiry Commissions at all levels of government administration, including ministries, government bodies and state-owned companies. In the second, they set up Military Police Inquiries (IPMs) to investigate the activities of civil servants in the public administration.[63] The Military Police Inquiries were usually conducted by army colonels, chosen for their ideological radicalism. Being appointed to the post was a sign of prestige. The colonels were invested with police powers of a new type: they were not required to submit proof, and, above all, they were encouraged to hand down arbitrary punishments. In the first weeks after the *coup d'état*, 763 inquiries were established. In one year 10,000 defendants and 40,000 witnesses were submitted to inquiries that showed complete contempt for the rules of justice.

Between 1964 and 1973 thousands of Brazilians were victims of the purges. It is estimated that 4,841 people lost their political rights, had their mandates annulled, were forced into retirement or lost their jobs under the dictatorship – 2,990 of these under the AI-1 alone. In the army, navy and air force, 1,313 soldiers were transferred to the reserves. These included 43 generals, 532 officers of all ranks, 708 subaltern officers and sergeants, and 30 soldiers and sailors.[64] These people were treated with particular cruelty: they were declared 'dead'. They thus lost everything acquired during a long career – promotion, retirement, health care and benefits. Their wives received a widow's pension. The AI-1 was applied for a limited period, until 1 April 1964, the last day of President João Goulart's mandate. However, in October 1965, President Castello Branco laid to rest any doubts over whether or not the dictatorship was temporary. He prolonged his mandate and imposed the AI-2 by decree. Apart from measures to strengthen the Executive, the AI-2 changed the rules for elections. Direct presidential elections by popular vote were abolished and all political parties were forbidden.

After the AI-2, Carlos Lacerda returned to the opposition, and in great style. In October 1966 he launched the Broad Front, an implausible opposition group that, in addition to Mr Lacerda, included Juscelino Kubitschek and João Goulart.[65] The idea of an understanding between the three political enemies was Mr Lacerda's. The Broad Front united almost all the political forces that had been active before 1964 – including the communists. There were, however, two exceptions. Leonel Brizola, exiled in Uruguay, refused to meet with Carlos Lacerda; and Miguel Arraes – the main leader of the left in the northeast – wanted nothing to do with the Broad Front. Mr Arraes was one of two governors who had been arrested by the dictatorship (Governor Seixas Dória, of Sergipe, was the other).

If the idea behind the Broad Front was to choose a candidate for the presidency, then the main beneficiary was Carlos Lacerda himself: João Goulart was in exile and Juscelino Kubitschek, despite his lack of hostility towards the military, had been the subject of a parliamentary inquiry regarding his misappropriation of public funds. Despite the fact that there was no proof, his mandate was annulled and his political rights were suspended for ten years. But the Broad Front represented a genuine alternative to the military. It brought together three of the most important national leaders, and provided an opportunity for political participation by organizing rallies, public meetings and street protests. Furthermore, they developed a plan to defeat the dictatorship through the vote. Their goal was to obtain the restoration of civilian power, general amnesty, the creation of political parties, the right to strike, a Constituent Assembly and direct elections. It was too good to last. In April 1968, President Costa e Silva declared the Broad Front illegal and forbade its activities. The military never forgave Carlos Lacerda, whom they considered a traitor. In December 1968 his name headed the list of politicians whose mandates had been annulled under the AI-5 and he was arrested. He was never to return to political life.

The Institutional Act no. 3 had been signed by General Castello Branco in February 1966 to directly eliminate elections for state governor. A complementary act changed the correlation of political forces in Congress and the State Assemblies by founding just two political parties: one that supported the government, the National Renewal Alliance (Arena), and the other that represented the opposition, the Brazilian Democratic Movement (MDB). Thus, the period of multiple political parties that began in 1946 came to an end. At the same time, the Brazilian people lost their democratic rights. For the next seventeen years there were no elections for governors, and elections for president had to wait for another twenty-three years. Those who wanted to stay in politics, and had not been arrested or had their mandates annulled, had to choose a party. It was not easy to create the Brazilian Democratic Movement – most politicians who had remained active ran to take shelter in the National Renewal Alliance (Arena). The government party united the conservative elite. Virtually all the National Democratic Union (UDN) deputies joined, as did a good many from the Social Democratic Party (PSD), and even a few from the Brazilian Labour Party (PTB).[66] The National Renewal Alliance (*Aliança Renovadara*

Nacional, or ARENA) was incapable of acting as a real political party would, nor did it produce alternative policies. Members were incurably subservient to the military, approving virtually every project the Executive sent to Congress. The party had offices throughout Brazil and was rapidly established as a broad-based political party, sustained by an extensive network of politicians, sympathizers, militants and voters. It guaranteed civilian support for the government and was a source for generating consent.

The National Renewal Alliance entered history as the 'yes, sir' party, and the military likewise expected the Brazilian Democratic Movement to be docile, to at least feign agreement. After all, had they not gone along with the idea of playing the role of opposition? In fact, between 1966 and 1970, when real opposition to the dictatorship began to consolidate, those activists saw no reason to trust the Brazilian Democratic Movement.[67] Many doubted the sincerity of a weak party that was playing the dictatorship's game. When the time came for parliamentary elections, the revolutionary left led a campaign to abstain from voting, or to leave one's vote blank, which was highly successful.[68] In 1966 the combination of annulled and blank votes accounted for 21 per cent of the total; in 1970 they reached 30 per cent, in an evident sign that the electors rejected the puppet two-party system that had been imposed by the military.

Members of the Brazilian Democratic Movement now realized they had been backed into a corner. Nevertheless, between dissolving the party and continuing to operate despite the annulment of mandates and the suspension of political rights, the party leadership chose the latter. This leadership was composed of politicians from the Brazilian Labour Party and the Social Democratic Party, and they brought the party together around a single issue – the return to democracy. Eventually, they took the risk of becoming a true opposition. Between 1967 and 1968 deputies and senators from the Brazilian Democratic Movement took part in protest marches and strikes and began to denounce the government's arbitrary measures, the removal of political rights and the predominance of foreign capital in Congress. They paid a high price: the AI-5 devastated the party – out of 139 representatives, 60 had their mandates annulled. By 1970 the party had been reduced to 89 deputies.

THE MACHINE FOR KILLING PEOPLE

In the first days of June 1964, General Golbery do Couto e Silva left the offices of the Research and Social Studies Institute, and walked a few blocks to his new office on the twelfth floor of the Finance Ministry in downtown Rio de Janeiro. The general had a budget the equivalent of $260,000 – of which half of the funds were secret – and, with his new appointment, he had the status of a government minister. He had access to data on 400,000 Brazilians compiled by the Situation Analysis Group,[69] a secret department of the Research and Social Studies Institute of which he was the director. General Couta e Silva then used this data as the foundation for the National Information Service, yet another agency. The general's idea was to put this intelligence-gathering agency at the disposition of the Executive and – more importantly – to use it for obtaining information at all levels of public administration, as well as in society as a whole.[70] General Couta e Silva had a true vocation for political conspiracy.[71] He was extremely reserved, which only added to the mythology surrounding him. He never spoke in public, never gave interviews, always acted behind the scenes, and was the *éminence grise* behind the dictatorship. Behind his back he was called 'The satanic Dr Go', an allusion to the villain of the James Bond film *The Satanic Dr No*.[72] General Golbery do Couto e Silva's notoriety was well deserved. Within ten years of the National Information Service being created, it had become the centre for the collection and analysis of information that was to feed the repression apparatus created by the military.

In 1966 the most secret department of the dictatorship's intelligence services was created under the auspices of the National Information Service and linked to the Ministry of Foreign Relations. It was called the Centre of Information from Abroad (CIEx).[73] The centre's agents worked in foreign countries. They were employed as staff at the Brazilian embassies and their task was to collect as much information as possible on the activities of Brazilian exiles. The apparatus set up by the military to identify and liquidate their opponents was highly complex, the National Information Service was in charge of the entire system, and the CIEx was just a part of the picture.

Until May 1967 the dictatorship simply used the repression structure that already existed in Brazilian states. This included the Departments of Political and Social Order (Dops), which were subordinated to the state Secretaries of Public Security, and the civil police. The latter worked in police stations designated to investigate theft (*Delegacias de Furtos e Roubos*), which were notorious for their corruption and use of violence. But in 1967 there was a new addition: the Army Information Centre (CIE). The Army Information Centre was involved both in the collection of information and in direct repression. Actually, it was probably the most lethal of the repression mechanisms. Equally dreaded was the Navy Information Centre (Cenimar), which had been formed in 1957, and the Air Force Information Centre, which was created later, in 1970.[74]

Starting in 1969, the military regime's repression mechanisms became even more sophisticated with the creation in São Paulo of the *Operação Bandeirante* (Oban – Operation Bandeirante), made up of officers from the three armed forces and the civil and military police. Their mission was to collect information, interrogate suspects, and organize military deployments to combat armed opposition forces. Operation Bandeirante was financed by *Paulista* businessmen as well as executives from multinational companies – Ultragaz, Ford, Volkswagen, Supergel and Copersucar. At a meeting with the then minister Delfim Netto, organized by the owner of the Banco Mercantil, Gastão Vidigal, a system of fixed contributions to the organization was negotiated.[75] The details of this system are among the dictatorship's most well-kept secrets. Operation Bandeirante was also the model for Operation Centres for Internal Defence (Codi), created in 1970, and the Internal Operation Detachments (DOI). These two organizations were under the direct command of the Army Minister, Orlando Geisel (President Geisel's older brother). They were responsible for most of the repression operations in the cities and always acted together as planning and coordination units. The Internal Operation Detachments was the operational wing of the Operation Centres for Internal Defence.[76] But even before these various departments the dictatorship regularly engaged in illegal emergency measures and acts of repression. These occurred in at least three circumstances. The first circumstance, beginning in 1969, was in the cases of 'disappearances'. The vast majority of these so-called disappearances involved cover-ups, either of the murder of a prisoner, or of the destiny of the individual concerned, which increased uncertainty among the opposition. The second circumstance, beginning in 1970, was when evidence was destroyed that could have identified the bodies of individuals tortured at the army's clandestine centres. This was done by removing fingerprints and teeth, then cutting up the bodies and burning them in piles. The third circumstance, which began in 1964, was when torture was used systematically as an interrogation technique.[77]

The army used torture from the beginning of General Castello Branco's government. The practice spread like a virus, thanks to the silent collusion of those in power – both civilians and military. Between 1964 and 1978 the use of torture was state policy. Torturers became 'untouchable' and the practice moved far beyond the walls of the barracks. For a systematic policy of torture to work, there must be judges who overlook obviously fraudulent prosecutions and accept forced or unreliable confessions and falsified technical findings. Staff in hospitals have to be willing to collude, by forging death certificates and records of the circumstances of death. They also have to treat prisoners who have been the victims of physical violence. A government that relies on torture must also be able to count on people in business who are prepared to make unofficial donations so that the political repression machine can operate efficiently. In Brazil the practice of political torture was not the result of the actions of a few sadistic individuals, and this is precisely what makes the situation so scandalous and painful. It was a killing machine conceived according to the logic of combat: liquidate the enemy before it acquires the capacity to fight. Torture and physical repression were undertaken in a methodical and coordinated way, with various degrees of intensity, in different environments and locations. In the first years of the dictatorship, the priority targets were left-wing activists who had fought for social change during the Goulart government. But from 1966 on, when the students returned to the streets and led the great protest marches of 1967 and 1968, they too became targets of the military government.[78]

It had never been so dangerous to be a student in Brazil. In 1968 news that the police had shot high-school student Edson Luís de Lima Souto at point-blank range during a protest in his high-school canteen (the Calabouço) in Rio de Janeiro affected people all over the country. His death marked the transformation of student protests into a mass social movement. More than six hundred people attended the seventh-day Mass, which was celebrated in Rio de Janeiro by Dom José de Castro Pinto, the vicar general of the diocese. With the Candelária church surrounded by hundreds of Marines and mounted police, the priests held hands and formed a corridor to allow the congregation to leave in safety. As he left, the literary critic Otto Maria Carpeaux[79] murmured emotionally, 'Unforgettable, Fathers.'[80]

This was far from the only occasion when a group of courageous priests protected people from violence and from arbitrary acts of the security forces.[81] The undeniable evidence that the military were routinely torturing people led a group of Catholic bishops to join the opposition and to use the Church's communication channels to disclose internationally what was going on in Brazil. In 1970 the Saint-Germain-des-Prés church in Paris displayed a handcuffed Christ on the altar with a tube in His mouth and a magneto[82] on the top of the cross. Above the cross the words 'Ordem e Progresso'[83] were inscribed. In May 1969, Father Antônio Henrique Pereira Neto was kidnapped, tortured and killed in Recife. He was the personal assistant to Dom Helder Câmara,[84] the Archbishop of Olinda and Recife, internationally recognized for his work in human rights. Father Peireira Neto's death was the first time in Brazil that a priest had been murdered for political reasons.

When it became clear the left-wing forces were really prepared to take up arms, the dictatorship showed all its savagery. In January 1969, Carlos Lamarca, an officer from the Fourth Infantry Regiment based in São Paulo, robbed an army weapons deposit and escaped in a van full of rifles, submachine guns and ammunition. Mr Lamarca had left the army to join guerrillas of the Popular Revolutionary Vanguard (VPR), one of several left-wing revolutionary movements created since the coup. Some of these organizations were tiny, very few of them had the strength or the structure to confront the military, and most of their members came from the Communist Party, which had been eliminated without resistance in 1964. The vast majority of these movements chose armed resistance.[85]

Mr Lamarca intended to organize a guerrilla base in the interior. He was killed by the army in 1971 near the tiny village of Buriti Cristalino, in the backlands of Bahia – the hamlet had four streets, mud and straw houses, a marketplace and around two hundred inhabitants. Carlos Marighella, another important leader of the revolutionary left, used urban guerrilla warfare and planned to confront the dictatorship with columns of guerrillas from all over the country, converging on the south of Pará. Carlos Marighella had fought against the Estado Novo, had been a deputy in the Constituent Assembly of 1946, and formed the largest group of opposition to the military – the National Liberation Front (ALN).[86] He was also a football enthusiast, loved samba, and was an amateur poet. In 1969, in São Paulo, he was shot to death in a military ambush.

Carlos Marighella's death marked the beginning of the military offensive against the revolutionary left. The death of Carlos Lamarca marked the beginning of the left's decline. By 1976 opposition groups had been decimated. During the dictatorship there were a series of armed attacks, to which the military reacted by intensifying repression and adopting a policy of extermination. Opposition moves included bank robberies, attacks on armoured cars, companies, weapon stores and the installation of guerrilla bases. The most spectacular feat of the revolutionary left was the kidnap of the American ambassador, Charles Burke Elbrick, in Rio de Janeiro in 1969. The kidnap was planned by two young militants – Franklin Martins and Cid Benjamin – from the Dissident Movement of the University of Guanabara, a minuscule but daring organization. In return for the ambassador's release they obtained the freedom of fifteen political prisoners.[87] This type of action had far-reaching repercussions. It made the armed struggle, the practice of torture and the existence of political prisoners – all of which were denied by the military – into international news, and undermined the dictatorship.

There were also forceful movements in rural areas. The *Guerrilha do Araguaia* – a guerrilla group – was made up of about a hundred guerrillas, including some rural workers. They ended up in a massacre.[88] Between 1972 and 1974 the armed forces sent approximately 4,000 men to the Parrot's Beak region in the southwest of Pará. In October 1973 the government issued orders for no prisoners to be taken. The sending of military and police forces to areas where it was thought there were guerrilla training bases was one source of repression; the landowners in the south of Pará were also known for their brutality. Apart from Pará, which was a sort of epicentre for violence against rural workers, consistent throughout the dictatorship, rural repression during the dictatorship occurred mainly in two critical periods. The first was during the years immediately preceding and following the 1964 coup, and the second was from 1975 to the mid-1980s, when the violence reached its peak, with approximately 1,100 murders.[89] The majority of these deaths occurred during land disputes, during which the local landowners hired local thugs and paramilitary militias, although they counted on the collusion (or omission) of the state. In many of these cases there was no investigation and the criminals were not even identified. In those that were investigated the circumstances of the crime were never fully clarified.

But nothing can be compared to the crimes committed by the dictatorship against Brazil's indigenous peoples. The most important document denouncing these crimes – the Figueiredo Report – was produced by the government in 1967. It then disappeared for forty-six years, allegedly destroyed in a fire. In 2013 the report was found, virtually intact. Twenty-nine volumes containing 5,000 pages were found – of the thirty volumes with 7,000 pages contained in the original. In order to write it, Attorney General Jader de Figueiredo Correia and his team had travelled more than 16,000 kilometres and visited 130 Indian reserves in the country.

The report was terrifying: Indians were tortured with appalling cruelty and entire tribes murdered by landowners and state agents. Mr Figueiredo's investigative work was a considerable feat. The report included accounts by dozens of witnesses, presented hundreds of documents, and identified every crime that he unearthed: murders, Indian women and girls forced into prostitution, ill-treatment, slave labour, and the misappropriation of Indian land and funds. It reported the hunting of Indians with machine guns and dynamite thrown from aeroplanes, the inoculation of isolated groups with the smallpox virus, and donations of sugar laced with strychnine.[90] The Indians living in areas the military had decided were strategic for their occupation of the whole of Brazilian territory, according to the plan conceived by the Research and Social Studies Institute and the National War College, paid a very high price indeed.

SHUT UP!

In 1973 the composer and musician Francisco Buarque de Hollanda (Chico Buarque) and the film director Ruy Alexandre Coelho Pereira

(Ruy Guerra) wrote a play called *Calabar: In Praise of Treason*.[91] The play cast doubt on the official version of Brazil's independence and was put on to coincide with the celebrations for the 150th anniversary of independence organized by the dictatorship. The play was banned the day before the first performance. The writers were informed that the censor would not allow any mention of the name 'Calabar', and therefore the whole play had been censored.[92] As a result the producers went bankrupt.

This was by no means an isolated case. Censorship was the fastest growing of all the government's activities. It was used to control the flow of information, public opinion and cultural production, as well as to manipulate the coverage of events and the interpretation of the national reality. The censorship of 'moral content' had existed since the 1946 Constitution, and was exercised by the Entertainment Censorship Division (DCDP). The military government simply expanded the role of the division, transforming it into an instrument of repression that banned any anti-government ideas and cultural manifestations.[93] Scenes were removed from films, or else the movie was banned altogether; popular songs were mutilated or forbidden and plays were vetoed by the authorities, sometimes on the eve of their first performance, as was the case with *Calabar*.

A law implementing advanced censorship was passed in 1970, requiring all editors to send the original texts and books to Brasília before publication. But in practice the law was impossible to implement due to the huge number of censors that would be required: in 1971 alone 9,950 new books were published. But the press was gagged and journalists were pursued and imprisoned. Works were removed from art exhibitions, such as from the *IV Salão de Arte do Distrito Federal* and the *I Salão de Ouro Preto*, in 1967, and from the Bahia Biennale in 1968. The country's leading popular singers, including Caetano Veloso, Gilberto Gil, Nara Leão, Geraldo Vandré, Odair José and Chico Buarque all went into exile. The government kept a close watch on intellectuals and university professors, many of whom were forced into early retirement. A group of ten researchers at the Instituto Oswaldo Cruz[94] were forbidden to work in Brazil, and one of the country's leading historians, Caio Prado Jr, was arrested.

To avoid censorship, those in the cultural world had to invent strategies of resistance, between the lines, making the most of any tiny opportunity to protest. These were 'the stratagem of the weak',[95] small acts of rebellion that would burst unexpectedly on the scene. Perhaps the first of these, a protest in front of the Gloria Hotel in Rio de Janeiro on 18 November 1965, was born of this need for stealth. At the time, the II Extraordinary Inter-American Conference of the Organization of American States (OAS) was being held at the hotel. Although the protest became known as the 'Gloria Eight', in fact there were nine protesters present. These included the journalists and writers Antonio Callado, Márcio Moreira Alves and Carlos Heitor Cony; film directors Glauber Rocha, Mário Carneiro and Joaquim Pedro de Andrade; recently dismissed Ambassador Jayme de Azevedo Rodrigues; set designer Flávio Rangel and poet Thiago de Mello. As soon as President Castello Branco got out of his car to enter the hotel to preside over the opening ceremony, the protesters waved banners with phrases written in gigantic letters: 'Down with the dictatorship', 'Bienvenidos a nuestra dictadura' ('Welcome to our dictatorship') and 'Viva la liberdade' ('Long live freedom'). They were all arrested. The government received hundreds of protests against the arrests, from intellectuals and artists including Luis Buñuel, Jean-Luc Godard, Alain Resnais, Michelangelo Antonioni, Pier Paolo Pasolini and Alberto Moravia.[96]

The military was soon to learn that arresting intellectuals or silencing artists was not always simple. In February 1968 the theatre where Tennessee Williams's A Streetcar Named Desire was being performed was closed down, and the leading actress, Maria Fernanda Meirelles Correia Dias, was banned from acting for thirty days. The reaction was overwhelming. There was a strike in protest against censorship that closed all theatres in Rio de Janeiro and São Paulo for seventy-two hours, and an unforgettable vigil was held on the steps of the Rio de Janeiro Opera House. Among those who participated were the poet Carlos Drummond de Andrade, composers Chico Buarque and Vinicius de Moraes, popular TV host Chacrinha, playwright Nelson Rodrigues, actors Paulo Autran, Cacilda Becker and Tônia Carrero, film director Glauber Rocha, architect Oscar Niemeyer, literary critic Otto Maria Carpeaux, and painters Emiliano Augusto Cavalcanti de Albuerquerque Melo (Di Cavalcanti) and Djanira da Motta e Silva.[97]

The arts were a thorn in the dictatorship's side. In 1970 the artist Antonio Manuel exposed his own body at the opening of the Salão Nacional de Arte Moderna in Rio de Janeiro's Museum of Modern Art.

The installation was entitled *The body is the work*. It was provocative and had been refused by the jury. Years later the artist declared: 'At the time the body was in the front line. It was submitted to the violence of street protests and to the torture of political prisoners by the military regime.'[98] The same year Cildo Meireles created his work *Insertions into Ideological Circuits*, which invited the spectators to participate in a type of artistic guerrilla warfare, writing information and critical opinions on the labels of Coca-Cola bottles and banknotes, which were passed from hand to hand. The same year, at the exhibition *Do Corpo à Terra*, which opened at the Palácio das Artes in Belo Horizonte, Cildo Meireles burned chickens alive in a work called *Tiradentes: Totem-monument to the political prisoner*, which denounced the torture and murder of those who opposed the military government. Artur Barrio threw bloody bundles of animal bones and meat into the Arrudas river that flows through the capital of Minas Gerais, in an allusion to the crimes of the dictatorship – the bundles suggested human bodies cut into pieces and abandoned anonymously in the open. The event attracted around 5,000 people and ended with the arrival of the military police and the fire brigade who forced those present to accompany them to the police station.[99] The cartoon strip *Rango* – a starving character created by Edgar Vasques – became a symbol of criticism of the military. But it was Henrique de Souza Filho (Henfil) who best demonstrated that the power of communication of cartoons is vital for the political struggle, due to the speed and clarity with which they transmit ideas and opinions. The concision of his texts, the caustic criticism and the levity of his lines gave life to the famous trio Capitão Zeferino, Graúna and the goat Francisco Orelana. They formed an indignant, ironic and anarchic threesome from the Bahia scrublands and reflected both the poverty and the courageous resistance of the Brazilian people.[100]

The *canção de protesto* (protest song) was the first attempt by popular composers to create systematic criticism of the dictatorship. Setting the cosmopolitan sophistication of Bossa Nova aside, the *canção de protesto* rooted political denunciation and resistance in the everyday cultural life of Brazilians. The establishment of a direct relationship between art and social context, and the belief in the revolutionary power of singing, led to the incorporation of broad political themes into music during the 1960s. These popular compositions incorporated a wide variety of aesthetic and musical components, such as Geraldo

Vandré and Théo de Barros's *Disparada* (1966); *Terra de ninguém*, by the Valle brothers (1965); Padeirinho and Jorginho's *Favela* (1966); Gilberto Gil's *Procissão* (1968); Carlos Lyra and Nélson Lins de Barros's *Maria do Maranhão* (1965); *O comedor de gilete*, which Carlos Lyra wrote in partnership with Vinicius de Moraes (1964), and Sidney Miller's *A estrada e o violeiro* (1967).[101] *Tropicália* emerged in 1968, the musical movement that brought together popular singer-composers including Caetano Veloso, Gilberto Gil, Tom Zé, Torquato Neto, Capinam, Rogério Duprat and the revolutionary rock band Mutantes. *Tropicália* invaded the theatre, visual arts and cinema. Stylistically, it was a combination of traditional popular songs, international pop and avant-garde experiments, evoking stereotyped images of Brazil. A tropical paradise undermined by political repression, social inequality and poverty would illustrate the *Tropicália* movement.

Some *Tropicália* singer-composers incorporated elements of rock, especially from the Beatles, into their songs. The movement influenced a parallel group of musicians, *Clube da Esquina* (Corner Club), associated mainly with Milton Nascimento, whose new and quite sophisticated songs evoked images of disappearances, the death of friends and the suppression of freedom. Romantic songs – seen by some as a form of kitsch – sold in record numbers. They were constantly played on the radio, exposing themes such as racism and social segregation, the reality of the poor.[102]

Whatever form they took, many popular songs of the period aimed, in one way or another, to oppose the dictatorship, avoid the censors, irritate those in power, and combat the official narrative of events. After all, everything leaves a trace, nothing can be completely extinguished and no one disappears completely without someone remembering their name. As Chico Buarque foresaw:

> O que hoje é banal
> Um dia vai dar no jornal.
> The banal of today
> Will be in journals someday.[103]

18

On the Path to Democracy: The Transition to Civilian Power and the Ambiguities and Legacy of the Military Dictatorship

'NAVEGAR É PRECISO'[1]

On 15 March 1985 the last general to govern Brazil, President João Figueiredo, refused to hand over the presidential sash to his successor and to ceremoniously walk down the ramp from the presidential palace according to protocol.[2] Instead, he left the palace by a back door. Fewer than two months before, in January, in a television interview, he had expressed what was seemingly his own assessment of his term as president. Addressing the Brazilian people he said, 'I want you to forget me.'[3] President Figueiredo was ill-tempered, explosive and extraordinarily vulgar.[4] By the time he left office, he had alienated virtually everyone, including the group of generals who had supported his appointment six years earlier. His prestige was low. He was notorious for having been at the helm of the most unpopular administration in twenty years. Most significantly, his government had failed to free the Executive from the control of the military without endangering the developmental project the military had been implementing since 1964. This is what had been expected of his presidency.

President Ernesto Geisel and General Golbery do Couto e Silva had begun to gradually dismantle the dictatorial regime in 1975. Both were convinced that the emergency powers could be revoked without undue upheaval.[5] The two generals, along with various other commanders in the armed forces, believed it was time for the military to relinquish the presidency. The wear and tear of political life and the requirement to guarantee Brazil's domestic safety was taking a toll on the army and beginning to put the interests of the institution at risk. Furthermore, the years of dictatorship had seriously damaged the structure of the armed forces. Countless officers had been removed from the hierarchy of command, from the routine of training and from their professional environments, to work as policemen and interrogators. And worse: those who had remained in the barracks were envious. After all, torturers were being decorated with the Peacemaker's Medal – awarded for acts of bravery or exceptional service to the army – and received regular promotions and salary increases. The bureaucracy created to administer the violence had taken over the armed forces and become the source of power in the military hierarchy.

The policy of controlled *abertura*,[6] which started in 1975 during General Geisel's government, could also be seen as a strategy to keep the opposition away from the presidency, to make certain that civilian allies of the regime would come to power. In 1977, when questioned by journalists about the instruments of control that had been created to maintain an authoritarian political system, President Geisel retorted, 'Everything in the world, except God, is relative.' And he added, 'Relatively speaking, Brazil's system is democratic.'

The arbitrary measures issued by his government in April 1977, which became known as the *Pacote de Abril* (April Package), postponed indirect elections for governors until 1982 and altered the composition of the electoral college in favour of the National Renewal Alliance (*Aliança Renovadora Nacional*, or ARENA). For the radio and television campaigns, President Geisel created what the Brazilian Democratic Movement (MDB) referred to as the 'deaf-mute' rules. On television the candidates were only allowed to show a passport-size photograph, with their name and a brief curriculum vitae – no message of any type was allowed. The April Package also changed the composition of the Chamber of Deputies, increasing the number of representatives from the smaller states, where National Renewal Alliance support was stronger. President Geisel also created what became popularly known as the 'bionic senator' – a senator who was indirectly elected by the same electoral college that chose the state governors. The nickname was a reference to the television series 'The Six Million Dollar Man', whose hero, a cyborg, had artificial powers created by advanced technology.

Back in 1973, when President Geisel was waiting to be appointed president of Brazil by an electoral college selected for precisely that purpose, a group of twenty congressmen – known as the 'authentic group' of the Brazilian Democratic Movement – out of determination to form a true opposition party, used the very rules of the dictatorship to nominate one of their party leaders, Ulysses Guimarães, to run against General Geisel.[7] It was an act of astuteness that showed a great sense of opportunity, even though the sole purpose of the electoral college was to ratify the government candidate. The nomination of a Brazilian Democratic Movement candidate appeared a waste of time. And worse, it ran the risk of demoralizing the party, should the nomination be viewed as capitulation, and unintentionally legitimizing the emergency powers of the dictatorship. And yet, the congressmen were right to make the nomination. It was clear that the Brazilian Democratic Movement strategy was not to really win the election, but rather to reaffirm its status as the opposition, find loopholes in the campaign rules, and mobilize the public at political rallies. Ulysses Guimarães adopted the Portuguese poet Fernando Pessoa's line 'Navegar é preciso, viver não é preciso' ('Navigation is vital, living is not') as the slogan for his 'anti-candidacy', as he defined it in a memorable speech given at the party convention. Then he and his candidate for vice-president, Barbosa Lima Sobrinho – a liberal-minded politician and journalist who had been federal deputy and governor of Pernambuco – travelled around Brazil calling for the restoration of democratic values. They visited fourteen states, helped to structure the Brazilian Democratic Movement nationwide – the number of party offices increased from 786 to 3,000 – and increased coverage of the opposition's activities in newspapers and magazines. The anti-candidacy required conviction and personal courage when it came to confronting the truculence of the National Renewal Alliance governors. In Salvador, Bahia, for example, the airport was surrounded by armed military police with dogs. But the threats did not work. Ulysses Guimarães's anti-candidacy put an end to the former opposition strategy of protest, casting blank votes, and opened the way for the victory of the Brazilian Democratic Movement in the 1974 congressional elections. The party got four million votes more than the National Renewal Alliance for the Senate, and won 161 seats in Congress, compared to 203 for the National Renewal Alliance. The Brazilian Democratic Movement obtained a majority in the Legislative Assemblies of important states, including São Paulo, Rio de Janeiro and Rio Grande do Sul. The role of the Brazilian Democratic Movement was no longer in doubt, and when General Geisel's victory in the electoral college was announced, Ulysses Guimarães turned to the deputy beside him and said with a wry smile, 'Now the fun begins.'

The Brazilian Democratic Movement confronted the dictatorship with a handful of courageous deputies, a remarkable president – Ulysses Guimarães – and a very clever slogan: 'Vote for the MDB – you know why.' The reform of the political party system, in 1979, was the last chance for the Geisel-Golbery team to phase out the plebiscite, the result of the extreme polarization between the government and the opposition. Their goal was to weaken the opposition by splitting it into a number of different parties, and to open the way for a new party, one that would not be so closely associated with the military government. Five new parties participated in the 1982 elections: the PMDB (the MDB under its new name, the Party of the Brazilian Democratic Movement); the Social Democratic Party, essentially a revamped version of the National Renewal Alliance; the Brazilian Labour Party (PTB), reinvented as a government sidekick; and two new opposition parties, the Workers' Party (*Partido dos Trabalhadores*, or PT) and the Democratic Labour Party (*Partido Democrático Trabalhista*, or PDT), founded by Leonel Brizola to combine the principles of the 1960s socialist movement of social democracy.[8] In the 1982 elections the military finally got a dose of their own medicine: for the first time since the 1964 coup, they had lost their majority in Congress.

President Geisel's style may have been imperious and authoritarian, but he knew exactly how he wanted to handle the *abertura* – the transition. For this he relied on two very able political operators, General Golbery de Couto e Silva and Petrônio Portella, then senator for Piauí and president of the Senate. The former worked from the inside, creating the strategy for a controlled *abertura*, while the latter – long-winded but crafty and discreet – knew the inside workings of Congress well and was a skilled negotiator. He became the intermediary between the government and moderate sectors of the opposition. Starting in 1978, Mr Portella and General Couto e Silva began a series of meetings, both with leaders of the Brazilian Democratic Movement and with representatives of civil institutions such as the National Congress of Brazilian Bishops (CNBB), the Brazilian Lawyers' Association (OAB) and the Brazilian Press Association. They wanted to open negotiations over the opposition's most urgent demands, and to assess the feasibility of a gradual re-democratization process, to be conducted in stages.

The armed forces intervened in public life in 1964, and remained in power for twenty-one years, because they thought it was in their interest as an institution, but also – and this is still the case – because they believed they acted in the best interest of Brazil. Such conviction lends the armed forces a sense of autonomous authority. While evaluating how to relinquish direct control of the Executive, they were also concerned with protecting their own interests. One of their demands was that the intelligence-gathering institutions be maintained. They also stipulated that all those who had engaged in political repression remain untouchable – there would be no retaliation. They required that weapons industry incentives that had been in effect since 1964 be maintained, as well as those incentives considered of key importance for state security, such as telecommunications and information technology.[9]

No one laid a finger on the military when they left power, nor has anyone done so since. But the armed forces lost prestige and legitimacy in the public mind. Moreover, their strategy failed. They did not maintain control over the process of re-democratization, nor did they substitute their government with a civilian government aligned with their ideas. None of the generals engaged in the *abertura* process had ever intended a complete return to democracy. Using the argument that Brazil had never had a truly democratic government, General Golbery de Couto e Silva, for example, refused to discuss democratization proposals and would not hear of restoring aspects of the 1946 Constitution. General Figueiredo agreed with him, but his approach was more didactic, 'There are sweet oranges, blood oranges and navel oranges. They all have different flavours, but that doesn't mean they're not oranges [. . .] There are different democracies too,' he explained to newspaper reporters from *Folha de S. Paulo* in 1978. And he concluded, 'You tell me, are the people ready to vote? [. . .] Can Brazilians vote properly when they have no notion of hygiene?'[10]

There were a number of reasons why the military failed to replace the dictatorship with another authoritarian regime. The most obvious is that they lost their trump card – a successful economy. At the end of the Geisel government, Brazil had one of the largest and most integrated industrial economies of any developing country, but the country had suffered the impact of the increase in oil prices and all its consequences: the volume of exports fell and international interest rates rose, accompanied by the foreign debt. Inflation was astronomic: in 1983 it reached an annual 211 per cent, and in 1984, towards the end of the Figueiredo government, 223 per cent. This had a severe effect on the daily lives of wage earners and the middle classes: prices were shooting up, government spending was out of control, the economy was in recession, and unemployment was rampant.[11]

FOR DEMOCRATIC FREEDOMS

The economic situation aggravated the polarization of society, but the opposition had also changed the rhythm, form and language of political confrontation with the dictatorship. In March 1973 a student, Alexandre Vannucchi Leme, was kidnapped, tortured and killed in a building that housed the Internal Operation Detachments (DOI) and the Operation Centres for Internal Defence (Codi) in São Paulo.[12] He was a student at the University of São Paulo, a leader among university students in the city, and active in a revolutionary organization – the ALN. He was kidnapped while on the University of São Paulo campus (Cidade Universitária). His death caused a general outcry and the student movement took to the streets again. Three thousand students attended the Mass in memory of their murdered colleague, which was celebrated in the main São Paulo cathedral (Catedral da Sé) by the highly respected cardinal Dom Paulo Evaristo Arns, one of the leading human rights activists in Brazil.[13] The police surrounded the University of São Paulo, put up barriers in strategic points of the city, and set up a war apparatus in front of the cathedral. However, those who managed to get through the blockade and into the cathedral had an unforgettable experience. Twenty-four priests celebrated Mass with Cardinal Arns, a Mass that touched the entire country. Just before the communion, singer-composer João Lufti (Sérgio Ricardo) walked up to the altar and, accompanying himself on the guitar, sang the song 'Calabouço' for the first time, thus associating the murder of Mr Vannucchi with that of Edson Luís de Lima Souto, who had been shot dead five years previously in the Calabouço student canteen in Rio de Janeiro.

Although the events of 1973 marked the beginning of the more systematic organization of the opposition, the real turning point came in early November 1975, a week after the death of the journalist Vladimir Herzog, once again in the DOI-Codi building in São Paulo. Mr Herzog was a respected professional who directed the news department at São Paulo's TV Cultura. When the police came to arrest him on 24 October, he said he would proceed to the Internal Operation Detachments the following morning, because he needed to finish the next edition of the news. At 8 o'clock the following morning, Mr Herzog arrived at the DOI-Codi building. That same day, in the afternoon, he was found dead in his cell.[14] Vladimir Herzog died under torture and this time the military had no way of getting rid of the body – all the staff at TV Cultura knew he had gone of his own accord to the Internal Operation Detachments building. The military officials had no alternative but to forge a suicide. The commander of the Second Army issued an official note informing the country that Vladimir Herzog had committed suicide in his cell, using a strip of cloth – which he did not have with him – with his knees bent and his feet on the ground.

By 1975 the fraudulent suicides announced by the military had become routine. Almost five months prior to Mr Herzog's death, Lieutenant José Ferreira de Almeida had supposedly committed suicide in the same cell, also using a strip of cloth that he did not possess, and with his body in the same position. Approximately two months after Vladimir Herzog's murder, the police produced an identical story to explain the death of factory worker Manoel Fiel Filho in the DOI-Codi building. Mr Fiel Filho was the thirty-ninth case of a political prisoner who had committed suicide during the dictatorship, and the nineteenth to hang himself – in two of these cases the detained men had apparently hanged themselves sitting down.[15] Vladimir Herzog, Lieutenant José Ferreira de Almeida and Mr Manoel Fiel Filho were victims of a major repression offensive carried out by the Army Intelligence Centre (CIE) aimed at neutralizing the Communist Party.[16] During the campaign, more than two hundred people were arrested in São Paulo and sixteen of the party leaders killed. The offensive was a part of President Geisel's strategy to control the *abertura* process and to expose the connections between the Communist Party and deputies of the Brazilian Democratic Movement. But Mr Herzog's death led to a large-scale reaction, led by the Professional Journalists' Union of the state of São Paulo, which denounced the farce of the alleged suicide and launched a protest movement against illegal imprisonment, torture and murder. Mr Herzog's widow, Clarice, and their two sons, Ivo and André, refused to bury the body immediately and remain silent, as the army had instructed them. Rabbi Henry Sobel reaffirmed the denunciation that Vladimir Herzog had, in fact, been assassinated by having his body interred at the centre of the Israelite Cemetery of São Paulo, and not against the walls as dictated in cases of suicide. Mr Hertoz came from a Jewish family that had emigrated from Yugoslavia to Brazil to escape the advance of Hitler's troops.

The shot backfired. Approximately 30,000 students brought São Paulo's main universities to a standstill. A broad front began to mobilize against the dictatorship, formed by the Brazilian Democratic Movement, the Journalists' Trade Union (ABI), the students' movement, the Brazilian Lawyers' Association and the National Congress of Brazilian Bishops. With virtually no planning, the mobilization went on for several days and resulted in an ecumenical worship held at the cathedral. The service was officiated by four religious leaders – rabbis Henry Sobel and Marcelo Rittner, Dom Paulo Evaristo Arns and Presbyterian minister Jaime Wright, in addition to a special guest who officiated from the altar, Dom Helder Câmara, Archbishop of Olinda and Recife. Around 8,000 people openly defied the dictatorship by attending the service. A silent, indignant multitude filled the nave, the steps and the square. At the same time, in Rio de Janeiro, 700 journalists squeezed into the auditorium at the Journalists' Trade Union, in a silent tribute to the memory of Vladimir Herzog. 'There are moments when silence speaks louder,' Dom Helder Câmara told a journalist after the religious ceremony. And in a single sentence, he summed up the strength of what had just happened: 'Today the ground beneath the dictatorship began to shake. It's the beginning of the end.'[17] Dom Helder was not mistaken. The ecumenical service in memory of Vladimir Herzog was a turning point. Brazilian society began to recover access to public space and the forces of the opposition began to form a network of alliances to fight against the dictatorship. The key demand that united the opposition forces was for a return to a legally constituted state and for the restoration of citizens' rights. From that point on the opposition movements were to advance persistently towards democracy, not towards the controlled *abertura* proposed by the generals.

The opposition united under a single slogan: 'For democratic freedoms'. Emphasis shifted from the armed struggles of the 1960s to a return to legal forms of conducting politics.[18] From this point on, the opposition began to outline the direction that re-democratization would take, gradually adopting a different view of democracy itself. Democracy was no longer considered a means to an end – socialism, for example – but an end in and of itself. People began to advocate democracy as the best form of government for Brazil.

It took another ten years for the last generals of the dictatorship to depart from the seat of the federal government – the *Palácio do Planalto*. And the re-democratization process jogged along in fits and starts, but the opposition was changing the path of transition. First, they incorporated many diverse voices from across society, apart from underground organizations and groups from the left. Second, the core of the opposition movement had become less rigid and more accommodating to distinct forms of activism.

One of the most active citizens' rights movements emerged in the outskirts of São Paulo, from associations that were almost invisible to the government, but typical of communities completely abandoned by the authorities. These associations included mothers' clubs, residents' groups and health committees. Meetings generally took place in the parish halls of local churches and were supported and protected by the structure of the *Comunidades Eclesiais de Base* (CEBs – Basic Christian Communities).[19] The communities were first organized in 1970 and they soon became centres for the dissemination of Liberation Theology. They were made up of small groups of Christians led by a priest. There were Bible readings meant to awaken a sense of community and encourage group participation in constructive actions for change. By the mid-1970s there were thousands of Basic Christian Communities active throughout Brazil, in cities and in the interior. They often took on leadership roles in their communities. These organizations spawned new social movements throughout the decade – the Cost of Living Movement, the Friends of the District Society, the *Favela* Associations – and were essential for organizing participation in large-scale campaigns to put pressure on the dictatorship.

Encouraged by the civil rights movement, several political activist groups emerged in the 1970s, including the Unified Movement of Blacks against Racial Discrimination (MMUCDR), the Centre for Brazilian Women (CMB) and *Somos* (We are), a gay rights group. Such organizations added a new dimension to the fight for democracy. Many of them produced publications that combined the demand for recognition of diversity with the introduction of new categories, such as gender and sexual orientation: *Nós Mulheres, O Lampião da Esquina* and *Sinba*.[20] These publications were just a small part of a far broader journalistic and political movement whose common denominator was the intransigent opposition to the military dictatorship. Between 1964 and 1980 about 150 such small-scale newspapers were published in Brazil. Many of them had innovative layouts and provocative texts, although not all of them had regular editions. They were called the 'dwarf press' due to their limited circulation and diminutive size, and 'alternative' since they expressed critical positions that contrasted with the editorial line of the country's major newspapers.[21] But they were also 'alternative' in the sense that these publications opted for political confrontation in a difficult scenario.

The decade of the 1970s was actually a high point for the alternative press, following in the tradition of the satirical and irreverent pamphlets of the Regency period and the anarchist publications of the First Republic. The writers, artists and publishers were passionate about their point of view, sought a new direction for the political process, and proposed social, cultural and behavioural transformation. Some of these publications were aligned with political organizations or clandestine groups of the left, such as *Opinião, Movimento, Hora do Povo* and *Em Tempo*. Others originated from cooperatives formed by journalists, as was the case with *Coojornal, De Fato* and *Ex*. There were also small-scale newspaper publications that combined humour, behaviour and social criticism, the most famous of which was *O Pasquim*.[22] In addition, there were publications featuring new cartoonists, a long tradition in Brazilian journalistic humour, such as *O Bicho* and *Humordaz*. And there were the iconoclastic magazines such as *Beijo*, and its anarchistic companion, *O Inimigo do Rei*.[23] Many of their readers were university students, and they helped bring about a radical transformation in the concept of 'revolution' – the possibility that it could be a revolution in behaviour, customs and culture. The student movement began to undergo a significant change. There was now a new generation of students that joined the 1970s opposition, young people who had not experienced the 1964 and 1968 defeats. Instead, they witnessed the victory of the Brazilian Democratic Movement in 1974. They rejected the notions of older leftist groups that had believed in an armed struggle.

The quintessence of this generation was a Trotskyite organization that had no more than a thousand student members all over the country, but that ignited the spark of all the cultural, aesthetic, behavioural and political experiments that occurred in the 1970s. It was called *Liberdade e Luta* (Freedom and Struggle), and was nicknamed *Libelu*. Members of this organization completely rejected anything reminiscent of the rigid and authoritarian line adopted by the Stalinist Communist Party. They were mainly students at universities in São Paulo, Minas Gerais, Rio Grande do Sul, Paraíba and Bahia. There were not very many of them, but they made a lot of noise. They listened to the Rolling Stones, Pink Floyd, Lou Reed and Caetano Veloso, read Walter Benjamin and venerated the Dadaists. Unafraid of the dictatorship – they were convinced that it was the dictatorship that was afraid of them – they used every possible opportunity to repeat their slogan, created by one of their sympathizers, the poet Paulo Leminski: 'We will overcome – without thinking about it' (*Distraídos venceremos*).[24]

But it was not necessary to be a member of *Libelu* to realize that both the student movement and the alternative press were voicing a new type of countercultural subversion in the 1970s.[25] The Brazilian offshoot of the countercultural movement began four years after the 1966 Flower Power happenings in San Francisco. There was a great deal of interest in drugs, especially hallucinogens, pacifism, oriental mysticism and communes. Their clothes also transgressed the norms. Originally based on the kind of clothes worn by Native Americans and gypsies, in Brazil they adopted Afro-Brazilian and African styles. The counterculture movement wanted paradise here and now. They brought the dream of a small community, a mythical space held together by ties of solidarity, by people working and living together, and creating art compatible with their philosophy. A whole generation of poets sold verses from door to door, outside cinemas, bars, museums and theatres – short poems expressing facts and feelings about daily life, characterized by bewilderment and good humour. For example, the *Nuvem Cigana* (Gypsy Cloud) collective in Rio de Janeiro would hold book launchings that were veritable spectacles, a new kind of 'happening' – the *Artimanhas*[26] – which sometimes lasted for days and included dramatized poetry readings and almost always ended with a party or at the police station.[27]

These cultural events redefined the political movements in the universities and, from 1977, when the movement returned to the streets in full force, student activists definitively adopted the slogan 'For democratic freedoms'. The students always wanted to be in the frontline, but there were others who were equally keen to join the opposition. In August 1977, during a public event to celebrate the 150th anniversary of the University of São Paulo Law School (USP – São Francisco), Professor Goffredo da Silva Telles read out his 'Letter to the Brazilians' in a courtyard packed with students. It was a protest in the form of a speech that defended a legally constituted state.[28] He was lifted up by the students and carried away in triumph. The Brazilian Lawyers' Association then used the professor's speech as a manifesto. In a meeting in Brasília, when asked by President Geisel what he expected from his administration, the president of the Brazilian Lawyers' Association, Raimundo Faoro – a lawyer who was not engaged in political militancy, and author of the classic *Os donos do poder*[29] – replied, 'I want very little, Mr President: just the restoration of habeas corpus, the extinction of the Institutional Acts and the end of torture in the dungeons of DOI-Codi.' And he concluded, 'So that Your Excellency does not go down in history as a bloody dictator.'[30]

Mr Faoro's remarks surprised even Ulysses Guimarães, who in 1975 had compared General Geisel to the dictator of Uganda, Idi Amin Dada – and almost lost his mandate as a result.[31] And the military were to receive a similar surprise in 1978, with the dissemination in the press of the 'Manifesto of the Group of Eight', which showed the extent and the social visibility of the opposition alliance. The manifesto argued for re-democratization, brought together a group of the country's most powerful entrepreneurs: Antônio Ermírio de Moraes (Grupo Votorantim), Jorge Gerdau (Grupo Gerdau), Paulo Villares (Indústrias Villares S.A.),[32] Severo Gomes (Cobertores Parahyba), Laerte Setúbal Filho (Itaú S.A.), José Mindlin (Metal Leve), Claudio Bardella (Bardella Indústrias Mecânicas S.A.) and Paulo Vellinho (Grupo Springer-Admiral).[33]

The year 1978 was surprising. On 12 May, a decade after the strike in Osasco had been crushed, around 3,000 workers entered the Saab-Scania truck factory in São Bernardo do Campo, near São Paulo,[34] on what appeared to be an ordinary work day. They clocked in, sat down in front of the machines and crossed their arms. Two weeks later, 77,950 workers went on strike in Santo André, São Bernardo, São

Caetano and Diadema, the industrial heart of the country, where the new consumer-durables and capital-goods sectors consolidated during the 'economic miracle' were located.[35] The strike appeared to be motivated by economic causesand it was. But it signified much more. São Bernardo sparked off a cycle of strikes – the metalworker strikes of 1979 and 1980, also in the ABC Paulista,[36] and others throughout the country. Strikes affected more than four million workers in fifteen of the twenty-three states over the course of the following two years. They continued virtually uninterrupted until 1980, and these in turn encouraged collectivization in other areas, including the construction workers in Belo Horizonte, the sugar planters in Pernambuco, and the so-called *boias-frias* – temporary sugarcane harvest cutters – in the interior of Sao Paulo.[37]

Although the strikes and the organizing of the workers were largely due to the activism of the metalworkers' union, they were joined by other sectors in what became known as Brazil's 'new trade unionism'.[38] The expression was used to describe a trade union movement that not only opposed the dictatorship, but was also autonomous, free from the state controls established during the Vargas administration; unions that could negotiate collective contracts directly with employers and act independently of the Labour Courts. These trade unions started on the factory floor, took their decisions at large assemblies, and proved that it was not only football that could fill a stadium in Brazil. During the strikes of 1979 and 1980 more than 100,000 workers attended the famous assemblies in the Vila Euclides Stadium in São Bernardo. The cycle of strikes that began with the metalworkers in 1978 led to the consolidation of two major labour movements that emerged at the turn of the decade. The first, the Centralized Workers' Union (CUT), founded in 1983, was a near-deployment of the 'new trade unionism'. This organization represented a broad spectrum of workers, including rural labourers, and it advocated agricultural reform. It was democratically run and supported autonomy for organized unions, and the freedom to form them inside the factories.[39] The second major labour movement was represented by the Workers' Party (*Partido dos Trabalhadores*, or PT).[40] It was founded in 1980, from the bottom up, and drew support from the trade unions and other mass movements. Members of the Workers' Party planned to capture the vote of the impoverished populations in the city outskirts and the interior.[41] The party was founded by workers to give shape to the social struggle and to the principle of an egalitarian society, within a democratic context. In the words of Lula (Luiz Inácio Lula da Silva), one of the party's founders, it grew quickly, spreading 'like *tiririca*,[42] sprouting up everywhere'.[43] The Workers' Party was formed from a wide range of political forces. It incorporated the trade unionist and workers' movements, the progressive wing of the Catholic Church (via the Basic Christian Communities – CEB), the remaining revolutionary armed resistance groups, the Trotskyites, and a wide range of artists and intellectuals.

The Workers' Party brought out the popularity and leadership of Lula, a factory worker and two-term president of the Metalworkers' Union of São Bernardo do Campo and Diadema, who became famous throughout the country as the leader of the strikes in 1978, 1979 and 1980. In 1980, when he was thirty-five, Lula was extremely charismatic and thought of nothing but politics. He could never have imagined, however, that in 2002 he would be elected president of Brazil. The cycle of strikes that began in 1978 exposed the limitations of the government's controlled *abertura* policy, which ignored the political participation of the workers. In 1979, as soon as the strike began, the Ministry of Labour decided to intervene in the Metalworkers' Union in São Bernardo. As a result, the company bosses locked down the factories, and the governor of São Paulo, Paulo Maluf, ordered the military police to repress the pickets, the meetings – including those in the churches – the rallies and the street protests. The police violence was in stark contrast to the official discourse of gradual re-democratization. On 30 October 1979, Santo Dias da Silva, a trade union leader and member of the Pastoral Workers' Association,[44] was shot dead by the *Paulista* military police during a metalworkers' protest march.[45]

During the 1980 strike, the Figueiredo administration abandoned its rhetoric and went on the attack. Photographs of two army helicopters, with the doors open and eight armed soldiers in each one, aiming their machine guns at the crowd in the Vila Euclides Stadium, were published in the press all around the world. In São Bernardo, troops occupied the trade union's headquarters, the Praça da Matriz[46] and the stadium itself. The companies were not permitted to negotiate with the strikers and fifteen union leaders were arrested – including Lula.

IN THE STREETS – WEARING
YELLOW SHIRTS

The process of gradual re-democratization led to a reduction in political repression, which occurred slowly, and not always continuously. But President Geisel kept his promises: at midnight on 31 December 1978 the AI-5 was annulled. At the end of the same year the government modified the National Security Law, reducing the number of acts defined as crimes against the state and shortening the prison terms. But at the same time, the government decreed a series of authoritarian measures – the so-called 'State protection measures'. They allowed the Executive to suspend legal guarantees, declare a state of siege, appoint governors and employ censorship without authorization from Congress.

Also in December 1978, President Geisel took the first step towards political reconciliation by revoking the banishment decree that had affected 120 exiled politicians. Then in June 1979, General João Figueiredo, his successor, continued moving forward in fits and starts when he sent Congress a draft of a government proposal for a general amnesty. Brazil had around 7,000 exiles and 800 political prisoners, and more time was needed before it could be discovered how many people had been killed, or whose whereabouts remained unknown, as a result of the activities of government authorities. A recent estimate for the period 1964 to 1985 puts the figure at around 434 people.[47]

The public demand for an amnesty had begun in 1975, with the creation of the Women's Amnesty Movement (MFPA), in São Paulo. The movement was led by Therezinha Zerbini, a courageous lawyer and the wife of General Euryale Zerbini – a legalist officer who had refused to support the 1964 coup and had been forced into the Reserve.[48] The movement soon had centres all over Brazil, was supported by the Party of the Brazilian Democratic Movement (PMDB) and the Catholic Church, and encouraged those in exile to unite around a single cause. In 1979 there were about thirty amnesty committees operating outside Brazil, the most active of which were in Portugal, France and Switzerland. It was only a question of time before the opposition forces realized that demand for an amnesty was at the root of the process of reconstructing Brazilian democracy. In February 1978, in Rio de Janeiro, the first Brazilian Amnesty Committee (CBA) was founded, and what had previously been seen as the restoration of justice became an affirmation of a basic right – 'a vital part of democratic liberties', according to the Charter of Principles of the *Paulista* CBA, which was founded in May the same year.

The Brazilian Amnesty Committees were the spark that ignited an unforgettable movement – the campaign for broad, general and unrestricted amnesty. This cause brought everyone within the opposition together. It was supported by artists and intellectuals, as well as the general public. The amnesty cause motivated large-scale street protests and political rallies, but its popularity was confirmed on 11 February 1979, in São Paulo's Morumbi Stadium. During a match between Santos and Corinthians, the *Gaviões da Fiel*,[49] a huge banner was unfurled on which the words 'Broad, general and unrestricted amnesty' appeared in gigantic letters. The scene was shown on nationwide television and printed by the newspapers on their front pages. There could no longer be any doubt what the Brazilian people were demanding.[50]

The draft legislation that President Figueiredo sent to Congress might have been an attempt to change the political environment, but it was also a measure of pragmatic compromise.[51] It permitted the exiles' return (including Leonel Brizola and Luís Carlos Prestes), freed political prisoners, and allowed those who had gone underground to reassume their identities. President Figueiredo's legislation, however, proposed limited amnesty, restricted and reciprocal. It did not include the 195 political prisoners who had been condemned for armed attacks – officially known as 'blood crimes' – nor did it guarantee that those who had been forcibly retired or dismissed from public office during the dictatorship would be reinstated. In both of these cases, the law was eventually changed. What has never been changed, however, is the reciprocity clause whereby the military, who also committed political crimes, or were accessories to them, have been granted immunity. Today, more than thirty years later, this law prevents holding anyone to account who perpetrated state-sponsored crimes during the dictatorship. These crimes include torture, murder and forced disappearances. The amnesty law granted judicial immunity to the armed forces, making them unaccountable. Even so, this was not enough to appease certain sectors within the army that did not accept the *abertura* – especially those responsible for the violence and mechanisms of repression. This nucleus of authoritarian, reactionary officers blocked the progress of President Geisel and General Golbery do Couto e Silva – and after them, of President Figueiredo – as they attempted to administer a controlled transition. In addition to preventing the politicization of Brazilian society and neutralizing the opposition, they had to confront resentment from within the armed forces.

Those who had been involved in the violent political repression tried to justify their actions with vehement protests against the process of *abertura*.[52] Their political identity was at stake; they simply could not abide the thought of losing their institutional role. The first signs of discontent were manifested in pamphlets. These circulated inside the barracks for ten years, between 1975 and 1985, attacking the strategy of re-democratization and making numerous accusations against General Golbery do Couta e Silva. This open rebellion within the military created a problem for the armed forces, and was a disaster for the government. After all, the president needed the unrestricted support of the barracks in order to successfully control the process of re-democratization. To make the situation worse, when these sectors confronted the *abertura*, they had a powerful weapon in their hands: the mechanisms of repression. President Geisel had considered Vladimir Herzog's murder a provocation to the government and an outrage. Manoel Fiel Filho's death a few months later represented nothing less than a political manifesto and a show of strength to the president. President Geisel may have been quite capable of justifying torture, as he demonstrated during an historic interview at the Research Centre for the Documentation of Brazilian Contemporary History (CPDOC),[53] when he said 'I think torture is necessary in certain cases, to obtain confessions' – but he would not tolerate lack of discipline, nor would he have his presidential authority challenged. Manoel Fiel Filho's death was offensive on both counts, and the president responded by dismissing the head of the Army Intelligence Centre, exonerating the commander of the Second Army and, much to his displeasure, allowing the country to catch a glimpse of the divisions within the armed forces.[54]

Although President Geisel reacted to the deaths that had occurred in the dungeons of the DOI-Codi in São Paulo, he made no attempt to restrict the apparatus of repression. After all, it formed an important part of the state's power, which he considered necessary – and at times convenient. He granted immunity to those who had committed the crimes, turned a blind eye to the denunciations of torture, and the political violence continued. There were still twenty-four more murders, fifty-one disappearances and 1,022 denunciations of torture.[55] And in a very short period of time, three of the country's most important civilian political leaders, active prior to the coup, had died: Juscelino Kubitschek, João Goulart and Carlos Lacerda. In August 1976, Juscelino Kubitschek died in a car accident on the Via Dutra, the highway that connects São Paulo to Rio de Janeiro. In December 1976, João Goulart died on his farm in Argentina, allegedly of a heart attack. Carlos Lacerda died in May 1977, in Rio de Janeiro, one day after being hospitalized in the São Vicente clinic with symptoms of flu. Although the National Truth Commission concluded in 2014 that Juscelino Kubitschek's death was a genuine accident, the suspicion that both João Goulart and Carlos Lacerda were poisoned by repressive elements prevails to this day.[56]

The policy of impunity created increasing difficulties for President Geisel and then for President Figueiredo. Between 1976 and 1981 the officers involved in the political repression executed terrorist attacks, bombing newspaper offices, bookshops, universities and institutions identified with the opposition.[57] Members of the opposition were kidnapped and tortured. Between August and September 1976 bombs were exploded – or in some cases found and defused by the police – in the offices of the National Congress of Brazilian Bishops, the Brazilian Lawyers' Association and the Journalists' Trade Union – in addition to one that exploded in the residence of Roberto Marinho, the media magnate who owned the *Globo* newspaper and television channel. Mr Marinho had been one of President Geisel's most powerful allies. In one of the dormitory towns in the greater Rio de Janeiro area, Nova Iguaçu, the bishop of the diocese, Dom Adriano Hipólito, was kidnapped and later abandoned, naked and tied up, in the middle of a street in the *Carioca* suburb of Jacarepaguá. Within the first eight months of 1980, during General Figueiredo's government, there were forty-six terrorist attacks. Newspaper stands that sold alternative publications were blown up in the middle of the night, the legal specialist Dalmo Dallari was kidnapped in São Paulo, a bomb was found in the hotel room where Leonel Brizola was staying, and the house of the rural labour leader, Manuel da Conceição, was attacked and vandalized. On 27 August 1980, the eve of the first anniversary of the Amnesty Law, three bombs were exploded in a period of twelve hours in the centre of Rio de Janeiro. The first destroyed the offices of the pro-labour newspaper *Tribuna da Luta Operária*; the second wounded six people in the Municipal Chamber; and the third exploded at the head offices of the Brazilian Lawyers' Association, mutilating a servant, José Ribamar, and killing Lyda Monteiro da Silva, the secretary of the association.

Then on the night of 30 April 1981 something went horribly wrong. A bomb accidentally exploded in the lap of a parachute brigade sergeant, Guilherme Rosário, while he was sitting inside a car, a metallic grey Puma, beside infantry captain Wilson Machado, who was sitting in the driver's seat. The car was parked in the parking lot of the Riocentro – Rio de Janeiro's largest venue for events and conferences. The sergeant died and the captain was seriously wounded – he was lucky to have survived. Both worked in the Internal Operation Detachments of the First Army. Inside the car there were three other bombs and two grenades. The two men were part of a group of fifteen soldiers from the Internal Operation Detachments and the Army Information Centre, distributed among six cars, who were there to execute a large-scale terrorist attack. If the attack had been successful, the devastation would have been indescribable. That night the venue was hosting a musical event to celebrate Workers' Day, which had attracted an audience of 20,000 people to hear thirty of Brazil's most popular singers. The event had been organized by the Centre for a Democratic Brazil (Cebrade), an institution with ties to the opposition. The plan was to explode a bomb in the electric generator, leaving everything in the dark, and then set off two more bombs close to the stage. Before detonating the bombs the terrorists had padlocked twenty-eight of the thirty emergency exits. They intended to blame the attack on the Popular Revolution Vanguard, an armed group that had been decimated by the army ten years earlier.

General Figueiredo had learnt about the plan a month before, and had done nothing to prevent it.[58] The army had no time to remove the evidence before the press arrived, and was thus forced to divulge the identity of the men who had been in the car, but alleged reasons of national security for giving no further explanation. The military also issued an official statement that convinced no one: the two officers had got into the car without noticing the bomb – a two-and-a-half-litre tin full of TNT – that had allegedly been put under the seat by left-wing armed militants. President Figueiredo maintained the official version and kept close watch over the investigations and the Military Police inquiry. No one was arrested. Sergeant Guilherme Rosário and Captain Wilson Machado were depicted as victims of left-wing insurgents and the case was shelved.

Politically this was the end of the Figueiredo government. Its double game was exposed during the investigation of the Riocentro bombing and the president lost his ability to conduct controlled *abertura*. The opposition now decided to mobilize the masses.[59] They needed to unite. In 1983 the leadership of the Party of the Brazilian Democratic Movement and the Workers' Party united to demand a change in the rules for the election of General Figueiredo's successor. They wanted a constitutional amendment to re-establish the direct vote for the president of Brazil. Draft legislation for the amendment had been prepared in March 1983 by a Brazilian Democratic Movement deputy who was unknown at the time, Dante de Oliveira, a deputy from Mato Grosso. It was a mere fifteen lines of proposed amendment, and the likelihood that it would not pass was extremely high. But it was picked up by the National Executive of the party. The Dante de Oliveira Amendment, as the law became known, led to the creation of a broad-based alliance between the parties – the Brazilian Democratic Movement, the Workers' Party, the Democratic Labour Party and even the Brazilian Labour Party – as well as trade unions and workers' movements. And, for the first time, there were dissidents from within the government party who supported an opposition initiative. Public demonstrations in favour of the law took place across the entire country in the largest display of popular opinion ever seen in Brazil.[60]

Despite the growing pressure from the public for direct elections, there was no chance whatsoever that the government would agree. It had a majority in the electoral college, made up of 660 deputies, and a majority in the National Congress. For a constitutional amendment to pass, a two-thirds majority was needed – 320 votes. There was only one thing the opposition could do to try to prevent President Figueiredo's successor from being elected by an indirect vote: get the masses onto the streets. And this is precisely what they did. The '*Diretas Já*' ('Direct Elections Now') campaign started in June 1983, with a political rally in Goiânia, the capital of Goiás. Around 5,000 people attended, which was enough to show the viability of a campaign to have the Dante de Oliveira Amendment pass in Congress.

The opposition had several advantages. The president's credibility was further undermined by the extremely high inflation, which reached 211 per cent in 1983, and the consequent collapse in purchasing power. The government position was then dogged by a series of financial scandals that affected President Figueiredo and his closest advisers. Fraud had been proven in Brazil's largest building society, the Grupo Delfin. There had been misappropriation of public funds by the financial conglomerate Coroa-Brastel, a scandal involving two of the government's most powerful ministers, Delfim Netto and Ernane Galvêas, as well as the president of the Central Bank, Carlos Langoni. And there were irregularities in paying back a loan to Poland; there were suspicions that employees of the Planning Secretary had received money.[61] This went down in history as the Polonetas scandal.

The opposition had also been strengthened by the 1982 elections, which were the first direct elections for state governors since 1965. Governors from the Brazilian Democratic Movement were elected in nine states, including the four wealthiest, São Paulo, Minas Gerais, Rio Grande do Sul and Paraná. And, much to the government's chagrin, Leonel Brizola was elected leader of the Liberal Workers' Party (PLT) and governor of the state of Rio de Janeiro, although there had been attempts to steal the victory for the government candidate, Moreira Franco,[62] who was running for the Social Democratic Party. The attempted fraud was known as the 'Proconsult scandal'.[63] It had been planned by the National Information Service (SNI) and the Federal Police, with the assistance of the *Globo* newspaper and television channel, which initially divulged the fraudulent result. According to the plan, those reported results would then be confirmed by the Electoral Court.[64]

Mr Brizola was suspicious of the vote count and widely broadcast his lack of confidence. The result was that he won the election and twice – once in the vote and the other time by force, as he liked to say. Now that the opposition controlled ten key states and had the people's support, they had both the resources and the capacity to act. The first sign that the campaign was really going to take off came in February 1984, when Ulysses Guimarães, Lula, and the president of the Democratic Labour Party, Doutel de Andrade, left Brasília at the head of the Direct Elections Caravan, travelling 22,000 kilometres across fifteen states in the north, northeast and midwest, attracting almost a million people to their rallies. The campaign of '*Diretas Já*' was a civic celebration of republican values. The editor Caio Graco Prado – son of the historian Caio Prado Jr – conceived the idea of making the colour for the campaign yellow. The idea caught on. People took to the streets wearing yellow T-shirts. Journalists from TV Globo arrived at work sporting bright yellow ties in protest at the television station's official policy of ignoring the mass rallies. The artist Alex Chacon created the Direct Elections Dragon, made out of bamboo, printed cotton and papier maché and operated by nine people who danced in a zigzag pattern along the streets. Before the Direct Elections campaign, the directors of the Globo television network had believed that anything that they did not show on the news simply did not exist. The campaign woke them up to reality and they started to cover it. But neither TV Globo nor the opposition parties, not even Ulysses Guimarães – who had earned the nickname *Sr Diretas* – had any idea of the avalanche they had triggered. The first rally, in Belo Horizonte's Praça Rio Branco, was attended by 300,000 protesters. During the second rally, in Rio de Janeiro, a million people descended on Candelária.[65] And in the last rally, which took place in São Paulo, the crowd was estimated at one and a half million people.

An array of opposition leaders appeared on the stage of these rallies: Ulysses Guimarães, Leonel Brizola, Lula, Tancredo Neves, Fernando Henrique Cardoso[66] and Franco Montoro.[67] The crowds were in a state of euphoria. Many of Brazil's leading intellectuals and artists made public their support, including Antonio Candido, Lygia Fagundes Telles and Celso Furtado, Chico Buarque, Maria Bethânia, Paulinho da Viola, Juca de Oliveira and Fafá de Belém, Fernanda Montenegro. Football players such as Sócrates and Reinaldo showed the public that they too supported the direct elections. The backing of these public figures was decisive in diffusing the ideals of a democratic project. The success of the campaign generated widespread optimism. People began to believe it could be victorious.

But however much credibility the government had lost, the armed forces remained determined not to allow any change in the rules. The Dante de Oliveira Amendment was put to the vote in the early hours of 26 April 1984. The atmosphere in Congress was one of apprehension. President Figueiredo had decreed a state of emergency in ten cities in the state of Goiás, and Brasília was surrounded by troops, 6,000 army soldiers occupied the Monumental Axis,[68] and Congress was surrounded by troops from the Planalto Military Command. Although the amendment received more votes for it than against, it failed to receive the required two-thirds majority. There were 298 votes in favour, 63 against and 3 abstentions. A total of 113 deputies were absent. The amendment only needed another 22 votes to pass. The government party deputies had vetoed a political transition that they could no longer control.

STARTING TO PLAY THE DEMOCRATIC GAME (BUT WITH SOME DIFFICULTIES)

During the vote count, a huge election panel was erected to display the votes for and against the amendment. When it failed to pass, there was tremendous disappointment and frustration. If it had passed, Ulysses Guimarães would have been the opposition candidate for president. As a candidate he would have been virtually unbeatable. He had a popular base and was in a strong position to refashion the country's political power structure. But in an indirect election he had little chance of winning. The Brazilian Democratic Movement decided it would participate in the elections, despite the fact that the next president was to be chosen by an electoral college. It chose the governor of Minas Gerais, Tancredo Neves, as its candidate.

Initially Ulysses Guimarães refused to accept the defeat of the Dante de Oliveira Amendment and wanted public pressure on the government to be maintained, forcing a second vote in Congress. But Tancredo Neves, who was determined to be a candidate whatever form the election took, thought differently. He thwarted the direct vote movement on more that one occasion. In April 1984, the day before the vote on the amendment, all the parties had agreed that if it failed to pass they would join forces to find an alternative solution. Tancredo Neves called a press conference at which he announced that he would be happy to take the lead in negotiating with the military government, if, as a result, the generals agreed to receive a delegation from the Brazilian Democratic Movement.[69]

Compared to Ulysses Guimarães, who never missed an opportunity to needle the government, Mr Neves must have seemed like a relatively palatable candidate to President Figueiredo and his supporters. Nevertheless, to do him justice, he was a moderate politician who, since 1964, had been consistent in his opposition to the dictatorship. He had not had his mandate annulled nor had he been deprived of his political rights. He proved to be an astute and experienced leader of the opposition, having been elected federal deputy from Minas Gerais in the 1960s and 1970s, senator in 1978 and state governor in 1982. He had been in politics for fifty-one years – his first elected post was as a town councillor for São João del-Rei. Moreover, he had an impeccable curriculum vitae: Minister of Justice in the last Vargas government and prime minister during the parliamentary government of João Goulart. He was always loyal to those who had helped him in his political career.[70] And he was a master in the art of politics in the Minas Gerais style. He was a skilled negotiator who knew exactly when to come out of the shadows and seize an opportunity.

It is difficult to know whether Tancredo Neves foresaw the amendment would not pass, or whether he was playing a balancing act: concealing his agenda, to be named the opposition candidate, while actively engaging in the rallies and planning his next move. But one thing is certain: he knew that if he were to be the compromise candidate, he would be successful. He must have calculated that the 298 votes in favour of the amendment were a clear indication the opposition could achieve a majority; moreover, the vote revealed the government party was no longer united, and the dissent could be worsening. Thus, he concentrated on winning the election in the electoral college, and to this end he set about getting the support of deputies from the Democratic Social Party (PDS) in an attempt to upset the government's parliamentary base and establish his own channel for negotiations with the military.[71] The circumstances were in his favour. First, General Figueiredo was trying to find some means to extend his term of office and had rejected all the potential candidates suggested by the Democratic Social Party. Second, there was no candidate capable of uniting the government supporters. Internal feuds were tearing the Democratic Social Party apart. Third, the candidate they finally chose, Paulo Maluf, was a disaster. Mr Maluf was a product of the dictatorship: a voracious and reactionary politician who had become synonymous with corruption during his terms as mayor and governor of São Paulo, but who nevertheless had been elected federal deputy in 1983 with a record number of votes. He had his own method of making friends and convincing traditional politicians from the Democratic Social Party that he should be the next president of the Republic. He worked aggressively, one on one, to get each deputy's vote. It was simple: he distributed gifts, pledged government posts, and made generous promises for the future.

Not everything went as Tancredo Neves would have wished, but he had calculated correctly that his chances of winning were greater than his chances of losing. He achieved what had previously seemed impossible, which was to reach an agreement with a faction of government supporters. He persuaded enough deputies to vote against their party to ensure his victory in the electoral college. As a result, in 1985 a group of deputies from the Democratic Social Party split away and founded the Popular Liberal Front (PFL). The Popular Liberal Front party was conservative, with an uncontrollable appetite for opportunism.[72] Meanwhile, Tancredo Neves networked with important members of the military. He spoke directly with General Geisel, who was now in the Reserve, and was still greatly respected within the armed forces. And he announced publicly that his government would not question the armed forces, nor investigate the crimes that had been committed during the dictatorship. While welcoming the support of the dissident faction of the Democratic Social Party, Mr Tancredo built a broad-based political alliance among the opposition called the Democratic Alliance. This strong alliance included members of the Party of the Brazilian Democratic Movement, the Democratic Labour Party, the Brazilian Labour Party, and even members of the Brazilian Communist Party (PCB).[73] He prudently introduced his programme as a change in government rather than a clean break with the political system. And the programme included three strategic points essential to the opposition in the re-democratization process: direct elections at federal, state and municipal levels; the summoning of a Constituent Assembly; and the promulgation of a new constitution. For vice-president, Mr Neves chose Senator José Sarney from Maranhão, who called a press conference and declared that he was resigning as president of the Democratic Social Party to join the Democratic Alliance. Tancredo Neves then adopted the slogan 'Change Brazil' and began to travel the country promoting his candidacy and accepting any support that came his way, from whatever quarter.

Ulysses Guimarães was reconciled to the situation, claiming that Tancredo Neves championed indirect elections precisely so he could overturn that system once he got into power.[74] To a certain extent, he was right, but he still could not persuade the Workers' Party to collaborate with what it considered a conservative transition, nor to participate in the electoral college. But Tancredo Neves was successful in putting an end to the cycle of military governments. On 15 January 1985 he was elected – along with his vice-president Senator Sarney – as president of Brazil. The result was a triumph: 480 votes for Tancredo Neves as against 180 for Paulo Maluf. The president-elect had three months before taking office to consolidate his victory, set up a new government, and turn the rhetoric into reality. The transition plan for the 'New Republic', as it was called, was ambiguous. It was politically conservative and based on compromise, but nevertheless it was an extraordinary change. The way was now open for the reconstruction of democracy and the establishment of economic and institutional stability.

On the eve of his investiture, Tancredo Neves was rushed to hospital for an emergency operation. He was seventy-five years old, and had known he was ill. He had hidden the fact from even his closest advisers, convinced that he would be able to take office and afterwards seek medical help. He was fearful that the generals would find a way to prevent him from taking office for health reasons. For important public figures, illness was a taboo, and the military could allege that medical treatment – however long it took – would incapacitate him from running the country. Everything went wrong. The hospital where the operation took place, the Hospital de Base in Brasília, was badly equipped to prevent sepsis. The doctors were negligent, the infection spread, and the patient's condition became increasingly serious. Tancredo Neves would never take office. He was transferred to the Instituto do Coração in São Paulo, where he underwent seven more operations. His death was announced on 21 April 1985.[75]

While Mr Neves was undergoing his first operation the whole country experienced a state of shock. Meanwhile the Brazilian Democratic Movement acted quickly to guarantee the transfer of the post of president. The constitution determined that if the president was unable to take office, he would be replaced by the vice-president. The next in the line of succession was the president of the Chamber of Deputies, who in this case was Ulysses Guimarães. It was the only time General

Figueiredo and the 'authentic group' from the Brazilian Democratic Movement came to an agreement: if Tancredo Neves did not take office, his legal successor would be Ulysses Guimarães. But Mr Guimarães refused. He said that the doctors' prognosis was that Tancredo Neves would be able to take office in forty-eight hours, as his personal secretary Aécio Neves[76] had announced on television. He insisted that José Sarney take office and temporally be in charge of the government.[77] Everyone was convinced.

There is no way of knowing what a government led by Tancredo Neves would have been like. With his death, the New Republic began as a tremendous disappointment and offered very little that was new. José Sarney had supported the dictatorship in 1964. In 1965 he had been elected governor of Maranhão by direct vote, and in 1970 he had successfully stood as senator for the National Renewal Alliance. He had changed horses at the very last moment. Mr Sarney had an extraordinary capacity for adapting to the ideology of the government of the moment, just as long as he could maintain his position – that is, in power. In Maranhão he was all powerful – and that would remain the case until 2014. Like many other Brazilian politicians he was an incarnation of a new type of *coronelismo*, which continued many of the practices characteristic of the First Republic. These included a disregard for the rules of democracy, a strong sense of being above the law, an incapacity to distinguish between what is public and what is private property, and the use of power to obtain jobs, contracts, subsidies and other favours for family and friends.[78]

Life for the opposition was not easy during President Sarney's government. Ministers were appointed and then summarily dismissed as he manoeuvred to maintain political support for his government from whoever was prepared to offer it. Tancredo Neves's plans for the transition did not enter the political equation. Conflicts between the Palácio do Planalto (the Executive offices) and the National Congress became frequent as soon as the Constituent Assembly began its work.[79] While Ulysses Guimarães, as president of the Assembly, was trying to mediate between the commitment of the Brazilian Democratic Movement to the re-democratization process, the socialist platform of the Workers' Party, and the manoeuvring of the conservative groups to protect their own interests, President Sarney concentrated on stitching up a political agreement that allowed him to extend his term of office to five years.

Not only that, he abandoned all that still remained of the programme that had been projected for the New Republic.

The Constituent Assembly was inaugurated on 1 February 1987, and the constitution was promulgated the following year, on 5 October 1988. The overriding purpose of the new constitution was to guarantee the end of the dictatorship and to establish democracy. Two main concerns are reflected therein: to create democratic institutions solid enough to survive political crises, and to ensure that the rights and freedoms of the Brazilian people would be respected. It was baptized the 'Citizens' Constitution'. It is by far the longest of all the Brazilian constitutions, with 250 clauses and an additional 98 contingency provisions, and is in effect to this day.[80] The text was the collaborative work of a remarkable group of congressmen: Fernando Henrique Cardoso, Florestan Fernandes, José Serra, Lula, Mário Covas and Plínio de Arruda Sampaio, and it was the outcome of the most democratic constitutional debate in the history of Brazil.

For a year and eight months Congress became the centre of public life. Many Brazilians engaged in the constitutional debate through the associations, popular committees, activists' assemblies and trade union groups. Several forms of manifestation emerged. The most innovative, the 'popular amendments' accommodated a wide gamut of themes, and were a sort of instrument of participatory democracy. When all was said and done, the people had sent a total of 122 popular amendments to the Constituent Assembly, with more than 12 million signatures.

Like Brazil, and like democracy itself, the 1988 Constitution is imperfect. Its composition involved contradictory movements and formidable clashes between unequal political forces. Furthermore, several times it missed the point. The agrarian structure remained intact, as did the freedom of the armed forces to decide on all internal matters. The forty-hour week was rejected and illiterate people were prevented from running for office, although they could vote. Out of a concern to regulate the minutest details of the electoral system and of social life in general – unsurprising considering the historical context – parts of the text were obsolete by the time they took effect. Nevertheless, the 1988 Constitution is a fine example of a nation making use of its history to build a future, based on a solid commitment to democracy. It was signed by all the political parties, including the Workers' Party. The constitution is modern in its approach to rights, attentive to political minorities, advanced in environmental questions, committed to establishing legal constitutional instruments for popular and direct participation, determined to limit the power of the state over the citizen and to demand public policies directed at solving the gravest problems faced by the people. When Ulysses Guimarães presented the final text, he told the *Jornal do Brasil* it should be passed by Congress with '[. . .] hatred for the dictatorship. Hatred and disgust.'[81] The 1988 Constitution provided the foundations for a period of consistent, long-lasting freedoms and solid democratic institutions. Since then, all the presidents of Brazil have been elected through the ballot box, none of their mandates have been interrupted, and none of the election results have been contested.

But everything has its price. The Constituent Assembly marathon to write the constitution ended up creating divisions in the Brazilian Democratic Movement. The party divided into two major groups, the Progressives and the Democratic Centre. The latter, popularly known as the *Centrão* (the big centre), was a conservative agglomeration that was not in fact restricted to members of the party. The former Party of the Brazilian Democratic Movement (PMDB), which had fought against the dictatorship, fell apart. Half of the party joined the *Centrão*, which became hostage to the bargaining power that President Sarney knew how to wield so well. It was the beginning of the formation of a conservative Brazilian Democratic Movement party that was no longer a true opposition party. It transformed into a front to support the government in Congress, no matter which party that government belonged to.[82] The split in the Brazilian Democratic Movement was inevitable. Finally in June 1988, in Brasília, a group of left-wing PMDB dissidents formed a new party: the Brazilian Social Democratic Party (PSDB).

As is the case with almost all political parties in Brazil, the Brazilian Social Democratic Party was created by professional politicians. The party was initially represented in Congress by eight senators and forty federal deputies from seventeen states.[83] Their symbol was the toucan, a Brazilian bird with a yellow chest, an allusion to the colour of the campaign for direct elections. The party attracted both Social Democrats and progressive liberals. Their programme was to consolidate democracy in Brazilian; uphold a parliamentary system; reform the state for efficiency, transparency and accessibility; privatize some of the state-owned companies; gradually relax the impediments to foreign capital and investment in technology towards the development of key economic sectors, especially microelectronics. Despite the name, it was not a Social Democratic party in the European sense, because the party did not have close ties to the trade unions and workers' movements. The strongest electoral base of the Brazilian Social Democratic Party was in São Paulo, the home state of the party's most important leaders: Franco Montoro, José Serra, Fernando Henrique Cardoso and Mário Covas. With these strong founders, the party was immediately popular among the urban middle classes and the number of votes it attracted grew rapidly.

Even so, no one could have imagined that six years later one of the party's most outstanding politicians – sociologist Fernando Henrique Cardoso – would be elected president of Brazil for two terms. Fernando Henrique was born in Rio de Janeiro but lived and worked in São Paulo where he was a professor at the University of São Paulo (USP), until he was forced to retire under the AI-5 and went into exile in Chile. He went on to teach in Europe and in the United States. When he returned to Brazil in 1969 he formed a group with twenty-seven other intellectuals, and together they created the Brazilian Analysis and Planning Centre (Cebrap) – a highly prestigious research institute for the study of political, social and economic issues in the country.[84] Fernando Henrique Cardoso had been involved in politics all his life, but had only considered running for office in 1983, against the advice of his wife, Ruth Cardoso – an anthropologist with independent and strong opinions – who thought her husband would be more influential as an independent intellectual. Maybe she was wrong. Once elected as senator for the Brazilian Social Democratic Party, Fernando Henrique Cardoso soon gained enough support to be nominated for the presidency – and with him, the generation that had fought against the dictatorship finally obtained control of the Executive.

Meanwhile, Ulysses Guimarães was preparing for the promulgation of the constitution, the Brazilian Social Democratic Party was taking shape, and the Sarney government was going from bad to worse. There was high inflation, a decline in the government's popularity, and an increasing number of denunciations for corruption. The government had begun to lose credibility after the failure of its first plan to stabilize the economy – the *Plano Cruzado*. In 1986, President Sarney was faced with the following circumstances: he had been elected by no one, the government had begun the year with an inflation rate of 16 per cent, and he was under increasing attack from Senator Fernando Henrique Cardoso for his government's failed economic policies. In short, the president urgently needed a plan that was simple and would produce quick results to control inflation.

The *Plano Cruzado* was his magic wand.[85] Under the plan, the old currency, the *cruzeiro*, was replaced with a new one, the *cruzado*, after removing three zeros – so that one *cruzado* was worth a thousand of the old *cruzeiros*. The plan addressed unemployment by increasing the minimum wage by 15 per cent, granting a pay rise of 8 per cent to all government employees, creating a 'trigger' whereby wages would be adjusted according to inflation every time it reached 20 per cent, and providing for unemployment insurance. But the plan's trump card was freezing the prices of all goods, tariffs and services. Inflation plummeted, people's purchasing power increased, and President Sarney revelled in his success. With a table of the frozen prices, which applied all over the country, and armed with a calculator, Brazilians could programme their spending, remodel their homes, consume more and travel abroad – the future looked good. And people participated enthusiastically in the maintenance of the plan. They would check prices at supermarkets to make sure they had not gone up – and if they had, they would denounce the market in question. They were 'Sarney's inspectors'.

But there were troubles on the horizon. The price freeze could only be maintained for so long before it needed adjustments, which would be unpopular – allowing price increases, cutting costs and reducing consumption. But President Sarney was so pleased with the popularity and political benefits the plan was bringing him, he refused to make any changes and maintained the price freeze until the November 1986 gubernatorial elections. The results were extraordinary. On the one hand, the Brazilian Social Democratic Party won a landslide victory, electing all but one of the state governors – the exception was Sergipe – and winning a large majority in Congress. On the other hand, the Plano Cruzado began to fall to pieces. Products disappeared from the shelves and the Federal Police made themselves ridiculous by undertaking the *Operação Boi Gordo* – the Fat Bull Operation – to confiscate cattle kept on farms, and taking the beef and the milk in order to guarantee supply. To top it off, a strategy was developed, called *agio*, the illegal overpricing that Brazilian people were subjected to for everyday items.

On 21 November, less than a week after the election victory of the Brazilian Social Democratic Party, President Sarney, forced to recognize the economy was in trouble, launched the Plano Cruzado II. The new plan made adjustments that should have been introduced when the first version of the plan had been implemented. Public service tariffs were increased and price hikes were authorized, with the result that the inflation rate exploded. When President Sarney summoned a group of businessmen to a meeting at the Finance Ministry, in order to announce the end of the price freeze, it was obvious to the people that he had delayed the announcement of the second plan until after the elections. He was accused of electoral fraud and his government's credibility was destroyed.

The voters had showed their frustration in the presidential elections of 1989, the first direct elections for president since 1961. They had been disillusioned, first by the defeat of the Dante de Oliveira Amendment, and then by the unexpected death of Tancredo Neves. This time the disillusion was to be even greater. With hyperinflation imminent, many people no longer believed the problem could be solved through conventional measures. The country needed a saviour. And that saviour appeared in the form of candidate Fernando Collor, the governor of Alagoas. He was forty years old, and had an arrogant, alert and fixated gaze. He set out to win the elections by aggressively attacking President Sarney and leading a moral crusade against cronyism and the practice in the Legislature and the Judiciary of the so-called *maharajas*, who increased their own salaries through bureaucratic manoeuvres.[86] Fernando Collor insisted on the urgency of changing Brazil. Some voters liked it when he attacked President Sarney's plan. Mr Collor would say his plan was to modernize Brazil, put an end to corruption, and make sure government employees did a full day's work. With five months to go before the election, Fernando Collor's popularity was sufficient to ensure him a place in the run-off.

There were over twenty candidates for president. Ulysses Guimarães paid a heavy price for having supported José Sarney: he had the highest level of rejection, right after Paulo Maluf. The Brazilian Social Democratic Party withdrew their support from Mr Guimarães, alleging he was too old to run for president. And since Ulysses Guimarães could not be the anti-Collor candidate, that role fell to Leonel Brizola and Lula. Lula received 500,000 more votes than Mr Brizola, a defeat that the gaucho found hard to swallow. When Lula approached him for his support in the run-off, Leonel Brizola suggested that, since the result had been a tie, they should both renounce in favour of Mário Covas, the candidate of the Brazilian Social Democratic Party, who had come fourth. 'It wasn't a tie, Brizola! I got 500,000 more votes than you,'[87] Lula retorted furiously.

Right up until his death, in 2004, Leonel Brizola clashed numerous times with Lula. They were suspicious of each other, competed and occasionally exchanged blows. Perhaps they were fighting due to the qualities that each perceived in the other. But in the end, Mr Brizola accepted his loss. He supported Lula in the run-off and ensured that his votes would transfer to the Workers' Party candidate – not an easy thing to do in politics. The run-off began with Mr Collor at an advantage, but by the end of the campaign the two candidates were neck and neck. Polls showed that Lula had 46 per cent of the vote, against 47 per cent for Collor. The election was only decided in the final week, by which time it had polarized the country. Fernando Collor had money and the backing of the media. The only newspaper that commented how, as governor of Alagoas, Ferando Collor had never practised what he had preached was the *Folha de S. Paulo*. The rest of the press was unanimous in backing Mr Collor, above all the media controlled by Roberto Marinho, the owner of the Globo media empire. For Mr Marinho, the idea of Leonel Brizola or Lula in the presidency was anathema. With the support of Globo media, President Sarney was no longer the target – the focus was on attacking the Workers' Party. The middle class, which already felt robbed every day by galloping inflation, was terrified when Fernando Collor played on their fears of communism by suggesting that Lula would expropriate their houses and confiscate their savings accounts.

It was a dirty campaign. The president of the São Paulo Federation of Industries (Fiesp), Mario Amato, declared that 800,000 businessmen would leave Brazil if Lula won. Mr Collor discovered a former girlfriend of Lula's, Miriam Cordeiro, with whom he had had a daughter, who was prepared to go on television and say that he had offered her money to have an abortion. It was a lie, but the effect on the voters was devastating. Three days before the election, the news programme with the highest audience in the country – Globo TV's *Jornal Nacional* – showed a shortened version of the last debate between Fernando Collor and Lula, which had been specially edited to show the former as decisive and confident and the latter insecure and hesitant. It was seen by 60 million people.

The last event to influence the outcome occurred on the eve of the elections, a Saturday, when the police in São Paulo rescued a leading businessman, Abilio Diniz, who had been kidnapped. There was only one Brazilian in the group who had committed the crime – the others were Chilean and Argentinean – but the police reported that they had links to the Workers' Party. Although none of the party militants had been involved, the Sunday edition of the *Estado de S. Paulo* printed an interview with Abilio Diniz's brother who said that the Workers' Party had indeed taken part in the kidnapping.

Fernando Collor won the election with 50 per cent of the votes, compared to 44 per cent for Lula. He took office on 15 March 1990, and the next day called a meeting of his economic advisers and instructed the new Minister of the Economy, the economist Dr Zélia Cardoso de Mello, to announce to the press the details of his plan for combating inflation: the *Plano Brasil Novo*, which became known as the *Plano Collor*.[88] The plan would prove fragile. It had a strong voluntary component, and the reform package announced by the government – fiscal, banking, property ownership – could not be implemented by decree. The minister saved the worse news for the last part of her presentation. In the banks, part of the money in checking accounts, investment accounts and savings accounts was blocked. Account holders could withdraw up to a maximum of 50,000 cruzeiros (the old currency, which the plan had rehabilitated), the equivalent of $1,250. The amount withheld would be returned after eighteen months, and even then in twelve instalments, with a considerable reduction in real value. Twenty years later, 890,000 individual court cases and 1,030 class actions are still waiting for a judicial decision. In addition, wages were frozen, public service tariffs were increased and the Central Bank decreed a three-day Bank Holiday. The newspapers calculated that savings and current account deposits in Brazil amounted to around $120 billion and that the government was confiscating around 80 per cent of all the money in the banking system, approximately $95 billion.

It was a cataclysm. No one could buy anything, consumption came to a standstill, and thousands of workers lost their jobs. Companies went bankrupt, no one had savings, and people's only recourse was to trust their luck. They cancelled their plans, negotiated to pay doctors and hospitals in instalments, and realized they had no way of paying their debts. But, extraordinary as it may seem, Brazilians accepted the confiscation. To put the situation in context, people were exhausted by the consequences of hyperinflation, and the president, who had just been elected by the popular vote, was adamant in his claim that there was no alternative. For the time being, most people believed him when he said that the confiscation was the only possible way to put an end to inflation. 'Either we'll win, or we'll win,' the president declared.

DEMOCRACY HAS NO END

But President Collor lost. Ten months later inflation was back, the economic crisis had become endemic, and workers across the country were demanding wage increases. The government introduced a second economic plan – Collor II. At the same time, the administration prepared the privatization of state-owned companies, closed government sponsored agencies and foundations, and opened the doors to the international market. The economic policy continued to be erratic. Every time prices went up, the government adopted a new measure – freezing wages, increasing taxes, raising tariffs – all as ineffectual as they were pugnacious. Little after a year upon taking office, Dr Zélia Cardoso de Mello, the Minister of Economy, resigned. The government had no credibility left and the Brazilian people were fed up with anti-inflationary plans.

Although Brazilians did not make the comparison, Fernando Collor was very like Jânio Quadros – only younger. They both had an inclination for histrionics, contempt for politicians, disdain for Congress, a moral vision for the country, and an authoritarian style. During Mr Collor's presidency, the theatrical spectacle included descending the ramp of the Planalto Palace in the company of athletes, comedians and television personalities, wearing T-shirts stamped with pseudo-philosophical phrases and promoting his image as an athlete. To reaffirm his role as the representative of youth and modernity, the president had himself photographed doing practically anything: riding a motorcycle, on a jet ski and even inside a fighter jet – as if he were a co-pilot – dressed in camouflage uniform. As president his tone was artificial and his attitude imperious. He ignored group interests, stayed aloof from politics, was unaware of how precarious his government was, and behaved as if nothing could touch him. Jânio Quadros had done all of the same things, and had fallen when he resigned, and his bluff was called. The cause of Fernando Collor's fall was corruption.

The rumours had begun with the confiscation of the country's savings, when stories spread that there had been exceptions: certain groups and individuals were able to keep their money. But the extent of the abuses only reached the public when the press investigated Paulo César Farias, who had been President Collor's campaign treasurer, and discovered that he was at the centre of a systematic corruption scheme within the government, a scheme in which the president himself was his partner.[89] From then on it was just a question of time. In May 1992, *Veja* magazine exploded a bombshell. In a seventeen-page interview, Pedro Collor, the president's younger brother, accused Paulo César Farias of being a front man for the president, not only in the administration of illegal funds that had been raised during the election campaign – around $60 million – but also by acting as an intermediary in illicit deals involving the exchange of political favours and government posts, in return for bribes. In June, Congress began a Parliamentary Commission of Inquiry, which, although it had little credibility at the outset, soon began to expose the scandals. Through the inquiry, it was discovered that Mr Farias's interference reached into every level of federal administration. All the president's personal expenses were paid by him, including the rental of cars for use by the president. It is still not known where the funds misappropriated by Paulo César Farias – estimated at between $300 million and $1 billion – were deposited.[90] Up until the very last minute, President Collor did not believe the scandal could destroy him. However, on Thursday 13 August 1992, during an informal speech to two thousand taxi drivers who had come to thank him for government assistance, he lost his composure – right there in front of the government offices, the Palácio do Planalto. He vehemently denied all the denunciations, claiming they were false. He called on the people to take to the streets the following day, wearing the national colours – green and yellow – in a massive show of support for his government. The president was very angry, but the Brazilians were sick and tired, and Sunday ended up being a day for demonstrations. With one detail: people dressed in black. With no prior organization, all over the country, people spontaneously came onto the streets – but they were all wearing black, with black mourning bands around their arms and black strips of cloth tied to the antennas of their cars. Fernando Collor had underestimated Brazilians.

People were determined to expose the president. Street protests irrupted with full force, but this time they were characterized by good humour and a carnival spirit. People carried gigantic dolls modelled after the president, wearing prison garb, and of Paulo César Farias dressed up as a rat with a moustache and glasses. And they carried coffins bearing the names of President Collor and Dr Zélia Cardoso de Mello. The students, who were already restless, painted their faces black, or green and yellow – the *caras-pintadas* (painted faces) – and called for a nationwide protest with the slogan 'Collor Out! Impeachment Now!'

Ulysses Guimarães's last great contribution to Brazilian politics was to lead the impeachment process in the National Congress. But on 12 October 1992 he died in a helicopter accident and his body was lost at sea – once again Brazil was in mourning.[91] On 29 December the Senate met to vote on the impeachment of the president. This was the first great test of the 1988 Constitution: the removal from office of the first president elected by the people since 1961. The request for impeachment had been presented to the Chamber of Deputies by Marcelo Lavenère, the president of the Brazilian Lawyers' Association, and Barbosa Lima Sobrinho, president of the Journalists' Trade Union – the two national institutions most committed to re-democratization – and had been accepted. President Collor had been temporarily removed from the presidency in September. On the morning of the Senate vote he attempted a last manoeuvre to avoid a conviction that would ban him from politics for eight years: he resigned. The session in the Senate was suspended and the vice-president, Itamar Franco, was sworn in as the new president of Brazil. The following day, the Senate met again and passed the impeachment with seventy-six votes in favour and three against. Fernando Collor's political rights were suspended and he was prevented from holding public office until the end of 2000.

It is hard to believe that Itamar Franco would have agreed to run as

Fernando Collor's vice-president because he believed in his moral discourse and modernizing mission. Mr Collor had selected Mr Franco as his running mate because he needed the votes from Minas Gerais, the second-largest electoral college in the country. Not only that, but election results in Minas Gerais tend to predict the results of the rest of the country. The state is centrally located and mirrors the different faces of Brazil. Mr Franco probably accepted because his term of office as senator was coming to an end and he had failed to get re-elected. The two men were in complete disagreement about everything from the beginning of the election campaign to the end of the government. Mr Collor made no attempt to conceal his contempt for his vice-president, who was a traditional politician from the provinces, with nationalist leanings. For his part, Itamar Franco was quarrelsome and unstable. Despite having been the governor of Minas Gerais, he was virtually unknown to the Brazilian people and took over the presidency in the middle of a general crisis. He knew Brazilians had misgivings about him, and that most people were only accepting the situation because they wanted to maintain the democratic order. He surprised everyone.

When Itamar Franco became president, the situation in the country was calamitous.[92] The GDP (gross domestic product) was decreasing and, in the metropolitan area of São Paulo alone, 15 per cent of the economically active population was unemployed. Inflation was back to over 20 per cent a month, in spite of Fernando Collor's promises. And the rate of inflation had been the same for the two previous years. Inflation affected all the social classes, but its affect on the poor was particularly severe. Since they generally did not hold bank accounts, their money did not receive the benefits of daily monetary correction. Inflation not only sabotaged their future, but had lethal collateral effects including food shortages, unemployment and violence – unbelievable violence. It is no coincidence that in 1993 two of the worst acts of urban barbarity in the country's history took place. On 23 July six military police officers jumped out of two cars in front of the Candelária church in the centre of Rio de Janeiro and opened fire on forty adolescents and street children who were sleeping on the church steps. On 29 August the same year a group of thirty-six armed men wearing hoods opened fire on twenty-one youths in the *favela* of Vigário Geral in Rio de Janeiro's north zone.[93]

Brazil was experiencing the paradox of being a country where democracy coexisted with social injustice. The cruelty of this paradox was best expressed by the voices from the *favelas*.[94] Rap music became the instrument for expressing the chaos, poverty and violence that characterized everyday life in the *favelas* and the suburbs. It exposed police violence, a discriminatory justice system, abandonment by the state, and the lack of opportunities – all the damage wrought by social inequality. It was to the credit of members of the Itamar Franco government that they attempted to understand how a democratic system had become the hostage of social injustice, and how inflation had become its ally. After changing his Finance Minister three times, the president appointed Fernando Henrique Cardoso to the post and asked him to develop a new plan to combat inflation. The request sent a shiver down the spine of government leaders – between 1980 and 1993 Brazil had had four different currencies, prices had been frozen five times, and nine anti-inflation plans had been implemented. There were a total of eleven indexes that measured inflation.

This time everything was done with transparency. The *Plano Real* was submitted to public discussion, the nation understood how it worked, and the National Congress voted for its implementation.[95] In the embryo of the new currency, the *real*, was an inflation index: the Unit of Real Value (URV). Although people gradually gained confidence, they were suspicious when the full transfer to the new currency took place. Many thought the government could be planning to freeze prices again or that the plan was another ruse to win the next elections, in 1994. But what the people of Brazil wanted most was to have a stable currency – preferably equal to the value of the dollar – which would allow them to plan for the future. The *real* offered all of this. This time the plan resulted from a partnership between the cosmopolitan sociologist Fernando Henrique Cardoso and the provincial engineer Itamar Franco. Fernando Henrique Cardoso became the official candidate to succeed Itamar Franco to the presidency and beat Lula in the first round of the elections in 1994. The *Plano Real* was his ticket to the presidency.

Such is the nature of democracy, conquests are slow, hard to achieve and easily lost. But the struggle against the dictatorship taught Brazilians that democracy is a value in and of itself and it needed to be attained. The 1988 Constitution consolidated the country's democratic institutions and the *Plano Real* gave it a stable currency – an essential element for democracy to grow. In the twenty years that followed, Brazil began to confront the issue of social inequality, with only moderate success. The task will not be easy. Three presidents in a row were elected for two consecutive terms: Fernando Henrique Cardoso, Luiz Inácio Lula da Silva and Dilma Rousseff. At the turn of the twenty-first century Brazil had accumulated five hundred years of history and, along the way, a certain degree of self-knowledge. History is the only resource Brazil can rely on to lend a future to the country's past, and, for that reason, our history draws to a close here – although we, the authors, suspect it is incomplete. This history ends with another intuition too: we believe democracy will never be extinguished in Brazil. One never knows. The future could be bright.

Conclusion: History Is Not Arithmetic

When the Portuguese arrived
In the pouring rain
He dressed the Indian
What a pity!
If it'd been a sunny day
The Indian would have undressed
The Portuguese.

Oswald de Andrade, Portuguese Error

Tupi or not tupi, that is the question.

Oswald de Andrade, Manifesto antropófago

What makes brasil, Brasil – or Brazil, Brasil? Ever since the Portuguese arrived, every generation has asked themselves this question. Some have come to more positive conclusions than others. It is not an easy question, and history is not the only key to the answer. Brazil has a short history, just five hundred years – at least if we adhere to the official narrative that it began with the arrival of the Portuguese – and a troubled one. Once aroused, history tells all and loves to engage in controversy. History rewrites concepts and myths, questions many of the assumptions about Brazil, and reveals trends and reoccurrences truly worthy of a new interpretation. And history plays with time, entangles, orders and reorders the thread. With one eye on the past, history keeps the other wide open to the present, and even to the future.

Since Brazil has been Brasil – since the country first created its identity as a nation – there has been a long history of internal conflict, violence, attempts at self-government and demands for equality – accompanied by the gradual development of human rights and citizenship. The story of

Brazil is common, yet distinct. There is nothing evolutionary about Brazil's history, in the sense of following a predictable progression of facts and data. From one side, this process looks very similar to that of all modern countries, with the struggle for individual freedoms during the seventeenth, eighteenth and nineteenth centuries; and the struggle for collective freedoms during the twentieth century. In addition, there has been a gradual perception of a new type of right, neither individual nor collective – the right to a sustainable environment and to a national cultural heritage. But there is another side to Brazil's story. In Brazil, the fight for political rights lagged far behind the fight for social rights. It took until the 1970s for the country to be proactive in defending civil rights, with movements for Afro-Brazilians, women and LGBTs – and for the environment, and, even then, at least initially, those movements were tentative. The exercising of some rights does not necessarily lead to the exercising of others. Nevertheless, without the guarantee of civil rights, whose normative principle is individual liberty, and without understanding that law-abiding people must have equal rights – no matter what their differences are – there is no citizenship.[1]

Rights are never acquired simultaneously by all social groups. The sense of what those rights are is in constant flux, as are reactions to civil rights victories. Brazilian history is inextricably linked with the ongoing fight to win rights and gain citizenship.[2] As a colony the country experienced a fundamental duality – great landholdings on one side, and on the other, slavery. As an independent country, in 1822 Brazil became the only monarchy on a continent of republics. Despite its purported liberalism, the first constitution, imposed by the emperor in 1824, actually permitted a direct vote only to a small portion of freed men, it led to the concentration of power in the hands of the emperor, and it left the structure of a slave-based society untouched.

If historical remembrance is our mission, the deep-rooted and long experience of slavery cannot be overlooked. Its scars remain to this day, even in our architecture. Residential apartment buildings have a back entrance for servants and are still built with a minuscule room for the maid. Social and racial discrimination is reflected in our vocabulary – and poor people, especially those of African descent, are the constant targets of discrimination and injustice in contemporary Brazil. The very definition of slavery meant the denial of the fundamental rights of freedom and equality. In legal parlance, a slave was a person without rights, *servus non habet personam*[3] – with no name and no past, according to the classical definition of the Romans.[4] A person who has no origin is a foreigner wherever he or she goes. Of course, slaves in Brazil rewrote that dictum, through rebellion, activism and negotiation. But at the heart of our community the notion remains, and persists stubbornly, that there are men and women who are by nature different – that they are separate because of their history, their biology and their condition. The destiny of Brazil's poor and mixed-race underclass – the vast majority of the population – has followed much the same pattern, entrapped in a structure of domination, the strong against the weak, *coronelismo*. The system has sustained the dependence of individuals on the powerful, rather than promoting the gradual acquisition of civil and social rights. 'The favour', virtually a national currency in Brazil, is in fact the denial of individual rights.[5] It confers inflated powers on a handful of individuals to the enormous detriment of legitimate government.

Although during the Second Reign the construction of a national identity[6] became a priority – in the form of Romantic Indianism – it was only under the Republic that the idea of 'Brazilianness' began to take root: the feeling of belonging to a community, a society which recognized that its unity stemmed from the collective experience of being Brazilian.[7] Brazilians were no longer subjects, they were now citizens of the Republic – a group of individuals united under one law and by their collective existence. It was a process that had begun during the First Republic when a form of sub-citizenship was first introduced.[8] After the abolition of slavery in 1888, the former slaves were not recognized as equals and were referred to either as freedmen or as '13th of Mays', in a derogatory reference to the date of the Lei Áurea.[9] The assumption was that the law had decreed freedom but not equality,[10] an assumption that was justified by the racial theories of the time, put forth in the name of science. On the other hand, the republican experience started in that context, with the first struggles for equality, labour rights and full citizenship. If the political moment resulted in strikes and public demonstrations, led by Brazilians and immigrants, policies of social exclusion also showed the new face of the regime – which had only just begun.

With the ascension of Getúlio Vargas during the 1930s, extensive social legislation was introduced guaranteeing legal protection for workers. But there was a paradox: it was offered at the cost of individual freedoms. Getúlio Vargas's dictatorship promoted social rights while suppressing political ones. The 1946 Constitution marked the beginning of a period of democracy, the first in Brazilian history. This period maintained the social advances of the Vargas era while reintroducing individual and political rights as the basis for the exercise of citizenship.

Then, there was to be one more dictatorship, this time military, brought on by the *coup d'état* of 1964, which would once again block the path to civil and political rights. Since that time, Brazilians have tended to think of dictatorships as being exclusively military, but President Vargas's *Estado Novo* – which suppressed all political rights and maintained the arbitrary rule of its governors by force – clearly refutes this idea. It was only after the 1988 Constitution – appropriately called the 'Citizens' Constitution' – that a consistent and lasting period of solid democratic institutions and full civil liberties was under way. In the opening ceremonies of the 1987 Constituent Assembly, Ulysses Guimarães unequivocally declared, 'The nation wants to change; the nation must change; the nation will change.' He was right, Brazil changed. Thirty years ago, no one could have imagined the country would elect a cultured academic like Fernando Henrique Cardoso, a labour leader like Lula, or a woman and former guerrilla like Ms Dilma Rousseff as presidents of Brazil.

But at the investiture of the first civilian president after twenty-one years of military rule, in 1985, no one could foresee the direction that the re-democratization of the country would take. The creation of contemporary Brazil has been a task of painstaking reconstruction. Political institutions have been consolidated, there is a separation of the powers, elections are free and regular, and people can express their political views freely. Democracy is no longer seen as a means to an end, but as an end in itself. Equal rights are now at the centre of public debate, affirming the rights of all citizens within a context of social inequality, all the while incorporating new, individualized rights for the equal treatment of minority groups – the elderly, the LGBT community and children.

Nevertheless, extreme social injustice still exists alongside democracy in Brazil. Although the country now has the seventh-largest economy in the world, social inequality is among the most acute in Latin America when measured in terms of education, wages and life expectancy.[11] The system is very far from being truly republican. Politics is still largely based on cronyism, within both the political system and the country's public institutions. Although the number of voters has grown exponentially, this has not been accompanied by a change in the unethical procedures that characterize the electoral system and the workings of the political parties. Corruption runs the risk of becoming endemic due to the constant misappropriation of public funds and the lack of control over government policies.

Brazil entered the twenty-first century with one certainty: the consolidation of democracy is our greatest legacy for future generations. There is no political regime that is entirely democratic; democracy is a concept that is constantly shifting, being adapted and expanded along the way. If Brazil wants to move forward alongside the other modern democracies around the world, the main challenge is the present. What is the agenda going forward? Which path will Brazil choose to take?

During his two consecutive terms as president, Fernando Henrique Cardoso, who governed Brazil from 1995 to 2002, was successful in fighting inflation and in the restructuring of government funds, which led to economic growth. He is also one of the founders of the Brazilian Social Democratic Party (PSDB), and has contributed to its consolidation and strength. His government stands out, among other reasons, for having invested in strategic public sector careers, in a clear break with President Vargas's project. The Cardoso administration implemented the first programme of wealth redistribution, which gave benefits to poor families so they could keep their children in school. President Fernando Henrique Cardoso's government was also active in the social arena, with a programme of food grants and the eradication of child labour. The first lady, anthropologist Dr Ruth Cardoso, worked with her husband and was behind many social projects that attended to the poor population, such as *Comunidade Solidária*, *Capacitação Solidária* and *Alfabetização Solidária*.

With the election of Luiz Inácio Lula da Silva in 2002, for the first time Brazil's working classes became a power to be reckoned with. In a smooth transition of power, a working-class man who had left the drought-stricken interior of Pernambuco for São Paulo as a child – accompanied by his illiterate mother and seven siblings – became president of Brazil. Lula is a left-wing leader with a trade union background, who won the elections at the head of the Workers' Party (PT), which he had helped to found during the years of repression in the 1970s.

With President Lula's election, democracy in Brazil was extended to many sectors of the population that had previously been excluded.

President Lula's government reduced poverty, inequality and social exclusion. The improvement of working conditions included registered employment, increased credit and a higher minimum wage, which grew by almost 60 per cent between 2000 and 2013. The Family Benefit programme, which was created in 2004, permitted the direct redistribution of wealth to the poor and extremely poor. In 2013, 50 million people – 26 per cent of the population – received benefits. Democratic procedures continued unaltered and large-scale policies were implemented to expand the network of social protection measures to vast numbers of Brazilians.[12]

Although democracy has moved forward, the Republic has stayed on the drawing board. A republic is not only a political regime – it is the *res publica*: that which belongs to the public, that which is in the public domain, that which is in the common interest, as opposed to the interests of private parties. The main virtue of a republic is its affirmation of the value of political freedom, of equality among its citizens and their right to participate in public life. Its greatest enemy is corruption.

Corruption is by no means exclusive to Brazil; it exists of course in most countries. But it has always been a part of Brazilian history, in one form or another.[13] That is perhaps why, within Brazil, corruption is generally seen as an intrinsic characteristic of the country, as if it were endemic, an unavoidable destiny. This notion is reaffirmed by common practices – getting away with whatever you can, entering politics to misappropriate public funds – which have supposedly become a part of the Brazilian character and of a national 'culture of corruption'. This viewpoint, quite apart from being harmful, is an oversimplification. It is a stereotype that actually impedes the fight against a phenomenon that is highly complex. Most importantly, it is a viewpoint that underestimates the outrage most Brazilians feel about such practices.

Brazil has been changing its public and private behaviour with regards to corruption. The country has progressed in terms of prosecuting both government employees and private-sector individuals, and diverse control practices have been implemented. There is now an independent Federal Prosecutor's Office with guaranteed administrative and functional autonomy; Courts of Auditors to oversee the collection and distribution of public funds; and Congressional Committees of Inquiry, which institutionalize Legislative authority over the other powers of the Republic, and over society itself. In addition, the Controller General of the Union investigates irregularities and oversees government employee activity in order to maintain legality. It also standardized the *Quarentena*, a set of norms that limits the participation of formal civil servants in the management of situations where he or she may benefit from that condition.

However, there is undeniable evidence that corruption is deeply rooted in Brazilian public life. Recent denunciations of the involvement of top government officials have shown that corruption continues and that successive governments have been ineffective in combating the practice. Recent history is littered with examples. During Fernando Henrique Cardoso's two terms of office there were accusations of the manipulation of figures and the misappropriation of funds, above all during the privatization of state-owned companies – the National Development Bank (BNDES), Telebrás and the Companhia Vale do Rio Doce – and of the bribery of congressmen to pass the law that permitted the president's re-election (and that of all future presidents). During President Lula's first term of office the scandal of the 'monthly payments' erupted: the systematic payment to deputies from various political parties for their support of the government in Congress. The scandal involved the highest echelons of the Workers' Party and resulted in the imprisonment of members of the country's political and economic elite.

Those accused during the scandal were found guilty by the Supreme Court, after four months of debates that were broadcast live. There was unprecedented interest shown by the Brazilian people, who agreed with the verdict of guilty handed down by the court. Then, at the end of Dilma Rousseff's first term in the presidency, the Petrobras scandal erupted. This involved conspiracy, corruption, money laundering and administrative incompetence in Brazil's most valuable state-owned company, previously the proud symbol of economic independence. The investigations, which are still under way, have led to the imprisonment of leading executives from six of the country's largest companies, Camargo Correia, UTC Engenharia, OAS, Mendes Júnior, Engevix and Galvão Engenharia, which are all construction companies. The executives have been found guilty of under-the-table deals involving millions and for distributing bribes to politicians in all the political parties. For the first time both sides – those who offered the bribes and those who received them – are being investigated by the Federal Prosecutor's Office and the Federal Police, in what may, with hindsight, be seen as a turning point in the history of the Republic.

There has been public outrage that corruption on such a scale has become routine. The outrage has grown steadily as these acts have remained part of the national political scene. There is, however, a risk of the indignation over corruption becoming the raison d'être of political engagement. People could turn away from politics and participation in public life, which would lead to a loss in credibility of the democratic institutions. Corruption can only be combated through strict public controls, transparency in government, and an educational process. The average Brazilian needs to incorporate republican values. We need to live with a clear sense of the definition of public rights. This means showing respect to others – to anyone and to everyone.

The exercising of public rights was on full display in mid-2013. Many Brazilians woke up one June morning astonished to learn that an increase in bus fares in the city of São Paulo had sparked an explosion of public fury all over the country. Thousands of people, mostly young, protested on the streets of the largest cities, with an agenda that went far beyond the question of the cost of public transport. They vehemently expressed their generalized dissatisfaction and, albeit unfocused, desire for change. There were no leaders and no political speeches at the *Manifestações de Junho* (June Protests), as they became known. They were organized on social networks by a variety of independent movements without connections to political parties. They led to waves of consecutive protests that lasted for a short time but had a significant impact. They revealed that the government and the political system were out of touch with national sentiment. Those marching demanded improvements in education, health and basic services, and noisily denounced government corruption. The protests reconfirmed the importance of public space as an arena for citizens to demand direct participation.

But above all, the June Protests made it clear that the period of re-democratization was over. It was now a question of taking a step towards strengthening Brazil's public institutions and expanding its democracy – which includes new claims for gender, sexual, ethnic, regional and generational equality. This is the only path to full citizenship. One of the greatest recent developments has been the demand for civil rights, for the 'right to be different', defended by movements of feminists, blacks, *quilombolas* and members of the LGBT community. For many Brazilians, citizenship is no longer defined by the right to equality, but includes the right to be different within that equality.

An important step on the path to democracy was the establishment of the National Truth Commission (CNV) in November 2011, to investigate the violations of human rights committed by government agents between 18 September 1946 and 5 October 1988.[14] On 10 December 2014 the National Truth Commission delivered its final report to President Dilma Rousseff. It was a deeply symbolic act. The report – now part of Brazil's collective memory – affirmed the rights of Brazilian citizens to address the grave human rights violations committed during the military dictatorship. The National Truth Commission questioned the reciprocal clause in the Amnesty Law and recommended that the torturers be punished, because torture is not a crime eligible for amnesty. The report, however, did not address the central point, did not uncover the truth about the facts and events, which would have revealed the truth about politics under the military dictatorship. The files have been kept by the armed forces, especially files that have been transferred to microfilm since 1972. This project has been undertaken by the information and repression agencies of the three forces. Accessing this material is still virtually impossible, thus a great opportunity has been missed. The frustration resulting from this loss is significant because it had aggravated the already challenging circumstances facing those in government posts since 1985. Among these leaders is President Dilma Rousseff, a former *guerrilheira* who was arrested and tortured. The lack of transparency makes it difficult for Brazilian leaders to uphold the pre-eminence of civilian rule within the democratic government.

History is not the same as putting two and two together, nor is the historian a clairvoyant. History has very little to do with the accumulation of data, nor is it a linear process, and it is certainly not predictable. Characteristics of the past remain interwoven in the fabric of today's society and cannot be removed by goodwill or by decree. A large portion of the population still lives in abject poverty and, despite the progress that has been made, Brazil is still one of the world champions of social inequality. In many parts of the country women earn less than men for doing the same work, and the violence of men against women continues at very high levels, often euphemistically referred to as 'crimes of passion'. New types of family, formed by single mothers or same-sex couples, coexist with widespread sexism and homophobia, expressed in violent attacks on women and gay people. People of African descent – no matter how dark or light they are – despite new affirmative-action policies, are still subject to racial discrimination, which is all too evident in labour and education statistics, mortality rates and criminalization. The playing field is still uneven and racial prejudice is ubiquitous in public venues such as restaurants, clubs, theatres and football stadiums, not to mention in private ones. The rights of the indigenous peoples to differential treatment and the ownership of land are gradually being recognized, but when economic interests intervene, these hard-earned rights fall by the wayside.

Lastly, although since 1980 torture has no longer been an official policy of the state, it is still widely practised (and covered up) by the police, especially in the *favelas* and poorest residential districts, where the violence and the humiliation of the population – especially young black people – are at their worst. These situations reveal the precarious nature of the citizenship of certain social groups and the segregation to which they are still subjected. There is no democracy in such cases. Brazil's history of slavery and its twentieth-century dictatorships seem to have left an indelible mark. Personal scores are still being settled by hired henchmen or with the help of authorities. And such practices are by no means restricted to any one social class or group.

This book leaves many questions unanswered. Will Brazil consolidate the Republic and the values enshrined in the 1988 Constitution? Will the country manage to maintain sustainable growth without destroying its natural resources? What role will Brazil play on the international stage? History is open-ended and is open to many interpretations. This book has come to an end, but not to a conclusion. It is not a definitive textbook, but herein we have tried to describe the long road toward Brazilian citizenship. The challenges for transforming the country's imperfect republic are many. Institutions continue to be fragile, corruption is deep-rooted, and public funds are used for private ends. The great utopia may be the embracing of truly republican values that will lead to a country for all Brazilians. This could be the beginning of a new chapter in Brazilian history. After all, now that Brazil has achieved democracy, the Republic awaits.

Afterword to the English Edition

Like people, countries occasionally experience abrupt changes – that which was seemingly calm yesterday is now in turmoil. The manuscript of *Brazil: A Biography*, in its original Portuguese version, was completed in January 2015. We ended the book with no categorical predictions regarding Brazil's future; nonetheless, our outlook was full of expectations and hope. The political gains gradually accrued over the course of the longest period of democracy in Brazil's history (since 1988, when the current constitution became law) seemed irreversible. In our Conclusion, we mentioned several positive indicators: an increasing approximation between public policy and the reality of the Brazilian people; a decrease in social and economic disparity; improvement in the standard of living among the poorest in the country, and progress in civil rights. Brazil's democracy was strong, borne of choices made by the Brazilian people during the long transition from military dictatorship to democracy and of the weight of the 1988 Constitution. In our opinion, the three governmental powers – the Legislative, the Executive and the Judicial – were sound and well balanced. Strong institutions are the sign of a healthy democracy, and that was our sense of the state of affairs in Brazil upon finishing our book.

In fact, by early 2015, progress in Brazil had been considerable, although not altogether flawless. We observed that, while democracy had taken hold and the Republic enjoyed a constitutional regime, citizens were still not fully participating in topics of general interest to the country. Appropriate public administration mechanisms were not in place – it was therefore challenging to fully support their initiatives to meet public service needs. At that time, and to this day, the Brazilian government has failed to guarantee rights, especially civil rights. All too frequently there have been acts of racism, homophobia and femicide. There have also been aggressive attacks on Brazil's indigenous populations and on their land rights, as well as on *quilombo* residents. In addition, policies and infrastructure for people living with all sorts of handicaps are still lacking.

It is safe to say that our assessment three years ago was correct: the Republic was a work in progress. But we were mistaken in our somewhat euphoric belief that Brazil was firmly established on the road to democracy.

At least up until 2014, according to the usual short-term indicators of the quality and strength of democracy – procedural, comparative and historical – Brazil seemed to be on track. The country was heading into the twenty-first century with a vigorous, albeit new, democracy. After all, the two strongest political parties – the Brazilian Social Democracy Party (Partido da Social Democracia Brasileiro, PSDB) and the Workers' Party (Partido dos Trabalhadores, PT) – alternated their terms in power. It was broadly understood and accepted that the popular vote was the only legitimate means to political leadership. Institutions were sound, elections took place at regular intervals and the transference of power was seamless. In fact, there was more transference of power between 1985 and 2015 than there had been in any other period of republicanism in Brazil. Furthermore, public policies adopted by governing bodies had to be submitted to the popular vote, including economic inequality legislation. The list of rights, mainly civil rights, was greatly lengthened. In terms of the economy, Brazil's democracy allowed for increased stability, with hyperinflation under control and a stronger currency.[1] All of this occurred during a period of thirty years, which left the Brazilian people with a sense of optimism.

But something went wrong between 2015 and 2017. In spite of the fact that, by mid-2014, there were constant reports in the press of government corruption and the Judiciary was plagued with the same issue, there was still a sense of control. The ability to face the problem of corruption seemed greater than its propensity to become a pervasive issue. Unfortunately, that assessment was erroneous. Dizzying changes were to come. The strength of Brazil's democracy has been put to the test. Democratic procedures have been in crisis, and facts have become ever more difficult to ascertain. All of this has been going on while Brazil's economy has plunged into a downward spiral right before our very eyes.

Historians tend to be cautious, often warning resignedly that history is only predictable with hindsight. They have learned that time does not run a straight course, nor does it necessarily evolve. From the viewpoint of the present, blurred by the unfolding of contemporaneous circumstances, very little can be seen on the horizon beyond the familiar twists and turns. Naturally, current events had repercussions on the writing of our book, but in the following few pages we would like to point to several processes now under way that we had no way of predicting at the time.

The truth is, looking back, we can say that something was already amiss in the country. Starting in 2012, the signs were increasingly evident, especially in the economy.[2] Until then, there had been full employment and a healthy labour market. Nonetheless, there were some indications that public finances were in trouble, due to the high fiscal deficit. Still, the government had its own agenda for the economy and was determined to stay the course. In a televised broadcast in April 2012, then President Dilma Rousseff announced a decrease in real interest rates and an increase in lines of credit to consumers, through public sector banks. In May, consumer electricity costs were reduced; and in August a public works package was announced, involving the railways, highways and airports. The plans were meant to increase investment, generate jobs and improve the country's infrastructure and logistical capabilities.

The economic programme adopted during President Dilma Rousseff's first term relied on State participation in the stimulation of Brazil's industrial sector. The National Bank of Economic and Social Development (Banco Nacional de Desenvolvimento Econômico e Social, BNDES) was called upon to invest in companies determined by the government. The strategy was to relieve their tax burden and to control capital inflows from abroad to protect Brazilian industry. The plan was called New Economic Matrix (Nova Matriz Econômica).

But the results of the plan were grave. While it is true that Brazil was severely impacted by the second phase of the international financial crisis, whose epicentre was in Europe, as well as by the initial economic slowdown in China, the major cause of the negative effect can be blamed on government economic policy. By forcing interest rates down, President Rousseff put herself at loggerheads with the financial sector, which generally faced increased credit risk and the expectation of reduced profits. Meanwhile, the tax exemptions granted to stimulate business activity expended public resources without obtaining the benefits of renewed growth.

The problems that had been building up during the period before President Rousseff's term in office snowballed into an avalanche. For example, the National Treasury (Tesouro Nacional) had to come up with the funds to back the decreased cost of electrical power the government had promised; Petrobras (Brazil's national oil company) faced terrifying losses – close to 50 billion US dollars by year-end 2014 – because of government-enforced artificial price controls on petrol established by President Rousseff; deterioration of the country's fiscal situation adversely affected international investors' confidence in the future of Brazil's economy; and inflation increased. In 2015, the economy was in free fall: the country went into recession; inflation persisted; the cycle of high interest rates started all over again – reaching 14.25 per cent a year; investment collapsed; and the shrinking economy began to threaten the labour market. The warning signs came from abroad as well, with international credit-rating agencies and international multilateral institutions such as the International Monetary Fund (IMF) and the World Bank sounding the alarm.

The problems in the economy were an issue. Yet there was another pressing complication in dialogue with the economic predicament: civic unrest, which manifested itself in a series of demonstrations held throughout Brazil revealed a tremendous amount of pent-up frustration. On 7 June 2013, the Free Pass Movement (Movimento Passe Livre, MPL), made up of militants from various political parties on the left, took to the streets in São Paulo demanding that recent price increases in public transport be revoked. Surprisingly, the demonstrations, initially thought to be local, washed over the country in a great wave, carrying with them enormous crowds, plans and hopes. In June 2013, the protests took place in yet more venues, uniting thousands of people who seemingly appeared from nowhere – and yet they came from everywhere. Four hundred and seventy protests swept through twelve capitals and every large city in Brazil, exposing extreme dissatisfaction and frustration, in addition to promoting a somewhat chaotic agenda for change. The latter questioned everything, from the high salaries of footballers to the low salaries of teachers. There was to be no impunity for politicians and corruption, government spending policies were criticized for the lack of investment in Brazil's infrastructure and there were demands for educational reforms. The only thing inviolable was the exclusion of major political parties as a source of reform.[3] The plans included a disruption of the mega events scheduled for the following years: the 2013 FIFA Confederations Cup; the 2014 FIFA World Cup; and the 2016 Olympics. According to the astonishing announcement in the 18 June 2013 edition of the *Folha de S. Paulo* newspaper, 'Thousands will take to the streets in protest against everything.'

In the heat of the moment, one had the impression the bottle had popped and there was no getting the cap back on. The last straw was São Paulo governor Geraldo Alckmin's[4] violent police crackdown, which on 13 June led to 128 injured protesters among the throng on the main avenue of the city, Avenida Paulista. The brutality of the police repression altered public opinion and had national repercussions. The demonstrations became larger and larger – on 13 June approximately 6,500 people had turned out for the protest on Avenida Paulista; on 17 June, there were 65,000.

The alarm had been sounded, but it was difficult to interpret. 'Within two weeks, the Brazil everyone had held up as a success story – the country that had checked inflation, integrated the marginalized and was eliminating abject poverty; in short, the country that had become an international model – had been substituted by another country all together, where public transportation, education and health care were a disaster and whose politicians were an embarrassment, without even taking the rampant corruption into consideration. Which of the two countries was real?' asked essayist and literary critic Roberto Schwarz.[5] And he was not the only one confused. The government delayed its response for nearly an entire month. It took until the end of June for President Rousseff, her popularity at an all time low, to go on television to present a rather abstract series of policies (of complex implementation) with regards to the protests. She spoke about fiscal responsibility, controlling inflation, a plebiscite to create a new assembly to conduct political reform, and new investment in transportation, healthcare and education – but virtually nothing was put into practice.

It was also disheartening to observe a new streak within these protests. In fact, they were radically distinct from any type of turmoil previously seen. They went far beyond previous demonstrations over administrative lethargy and government obtuseness. In broad terms, at the outset these protests were initiated by a libertarian flurry, a sort of self-absorbed activism. A strong sense of individual militancy and a regressive political imaginary surrounded the movement. That was the novelty. Antagonistic ideals permeated the atmosphere, leading to proposals and types of mobilization that at once separated and brought people together.

In part, the difference in the demonstrations that began in 2015 was their form. They were mainly organized through movements, groups and individuals that acted autonomously and manifested various types of militancy. They did not rely on structured rallies with established chains of command. Instead, they were mainly set up over social media. But there was another side to this, soon to emerge: the so-called 'black blocs'. These protesters wore masks and looked militaristic in their dark clothing. They claimed to be libertarian, but their attitude was standardized, violent and aggressive in an attempt to imitate the self-defence demonstrators in Seattle and Berlin. They entered the scene shattering windows in shops, banks and government buildings and attacking the riot police with rocks and clubs.[6] And there was yet another part of this drama, less evident and more difficult to visualize, at least at that time: homogeneous groups with clearly defined goals joined together to take part in the demonstrations.

By 2013, there were already signs of this individualistic activism on the fringes of the protests. It was characterized by intransigence tempered with hatred and an increasing aversion to dialogue.[7] The joining together of various interest groups – collectives, feminist movements, LGBT groups, anti-racist organizations, student groups, and so on – seemed to have been displaced, to have lost the position of power. These groups were formerly an integral part of the demonstrations and had lent them an aura of innovation. Unexpectedly, the politics of the protesters emerged as very different and divided, and their type of participation changed. The previous dynamic of the movement disappeared; the Free Pass Movement (Movimento do Pass Livre) lost control over both the demonstrators and their demands.

It was quite a reversal. There had already been signs of divisions in Brazil but, over the course of the 2015–2016 demonstrations, those dividing lines became irreparable.[8] The Rousseff administration was by then the main target; and corruption, the major source of discontent. Certain groups, previously silent, made themselves heard. These were characterized by conservatism and regressive opinions, such as the idea of a return to a military dictatorship, and a regressive civil and social rights agenda. Furthermore, these groups, which moved to the fore-front of the protests began to control much of what went on. The consequences were astounding: the left lost control over the protests; the moderate centre withdrew, or else aligned with the right; and a pervasive hatred directed towards politicians surfaced, and exploded.

The demonstrations continued, attracting thousands of people, but the changes were now crystal clear. The demonstrators were divided, with conflicting agendas. People got involved to protest either in favour of *or* against the government. The type of polarization often seen abroad now took hold in a unique manner – tropical and Brazilian. Demonstrations in favour of the government always took place on weekdays, generally starting after 6 p.m. Protesters filled the streets with the colour red: their clothing, flags and sashes, ready to defend the Workers' Party at any cost. Protests against the government usually occurred in the morning, preferably on Sundays, and participants wore mainly green and yellow, like Brazil's national football team jersey. They demanded that President Rousseff be impeached and they accused Lula and the Workers' Party of corruption. They also carried blow-up dolls of Lula and President Rousseff, dressed in prison garb.[9]

By all indications, Brazil was headed for trouble. Still, the government managed to distance itself from the problems, at least for the time being, even though the signs were everywhere. In March 2014, the Federal Police (Polícia Federal, PF) discovered that a gas station in Brasília was a front for illegal financial activities. The realization that the same gas station washed cars *and* laundered money was irresistible: the investigation conducted by the Federal Police in conjunction with the Federal Ministry of Public Affairs (Ministério Público Federal) soon came to be known as operation 'Car Wash' (Lava Jato).[10] The money trail ended in Brasília, but it started in a company based in the city of Londrina, in the State of Paraná. The operation was under the jurisdiction of Judge Sérgio Moro of the 2nd Lower Federal Court[11] in Curitiba, Paraná. This federal court is one of several throughout Brazil established by the Federal Board of Justice in 2003 to investigate cases of money laundering. This was no small incident, and it did not take long for Brazilians to realize the gravity of the situation, and how much money was involved. The investigation uncovered a billion-dollar corruption scheme in Petrobras involving several people at the highest levels of the company, the sixteen largest construction companies in the country organized into a cartel and the five main political parties in Brazil – PMDB, PP, PSD, PT, PSDB.[12] Everything was interconnected: construction projects, contracts and bribes to politicians, political parties and public employees. The construction companies would meet regularly to agree on collusive bidding schemes for Petrobras projects. They would settle on prices, divide contracts and agree on the amount of bribe money to set aside for political parties and for the politicians in on the scheme.

The investigation uncovered the involvement of all kinds of people in the enormous corruption scheme – public servants, dollar buyer-sellers, businessmen and women and politicians – and demonstrated how, during the previous thirty years, corruption had become a viable form of governing in Brazil at all levels of public life, federal, state and municipal.[13] Never before had so many top executives and large business owners been sent to jail. This list included the presidents of the following construction companies: Andrade Gutierrez, Camargo Corrêa, OAS, Queiroz Galvão and UTC Engineering; in addition to the vice-presidents of Engevix and Mendes Júnior engineering firms. And, as if this were not enough, in June 2015 the Federal Police sent Marcelo Odebrecht to jail. Mr Odebrecht, an engineer, was the president of the largest construction company in the country, and the second largest privately owned corporation in Brazil.

Along with the construction and engineering companies, the Curitiba investigation disclosed the breadth and depth of the relationship between the business community and the political system in Brazil. One government administration leaves, the next one comes in and companies alone or in cartels pay for benefits, from both state-owned companies and powerful government departments. In exchange for tolerance and access, they finance political parties and pay politicians individually. The tip of the iceberg was exposed by the dollar dealers arrested by the Federal Police in Paraná, Alberto Youssef, Carlos Habib Chater, Nelma Kodama – and Paulo Roberto da Costa, a former director at Petrobras, who was also sent to prison. According to several of them, Petrobras senior managers had been accomplices in the pillage of the company, each of them representing a political party. Others were in charge of the money laundering and distribution of proceeds.

The presidential electoral campaign began in June 2014. It was a tough race, which resulted in a very close outcome, leaving no doubt as to how divided the country had become. Only two candidates remained in the second round, Dilma Rousseff of the Workers' Party and Aécio Neves of the Brazilian Social Democracy Party. Both parties claimed victory before the ballots had been counted. But on 26 October 2014, Dilma Rousseff was re-elected with 54,501,118 votes (51.64%) to Aécio Neves's 51,041,155 (48.36%).[14] Brazil was, indeed, divided.

Four days after the results were announced, Aécio Neves and the Brazilian Social Democracy Party formally asked the Superior Electoral Court for a recount. They wanted the electoral process to be audited and verified by specialists chosen by a coalition from the losing parties. They alleged that the election results were false, but the intention was to cast doubt over the legitimacy of Dilma Rousseff's mandate, to have her victory annulled. It was the first time since the military dictatorship that a losing candidate had challenged election results and attempted to veto a majority vote. The country was becoming increasingly radicalized. Several factions played up the dichotomy, which rendered dialogue – previously difficult – impossible. In the public arena, and even in the most private spaces, political discussions had become highly contentious, and ugly.

President Rousseff was slow to realize the severity of the crisis, and the speed with which it was unfolding. Throughout the campaign, she had promised that upon her re-election she would keep economic policies on track. She pledged her government would not adopt restrictive or recessive measures – it was precisely the opposite of what her adversaries were promising. President Rousseff underscored economic policies she considered inviolable. She declared she would maintain government investment in education, healthcare, housing and social work and would also safeguard social programmes, including the right to holidays and to social security (including the annual extra month, the '13th salary'). Nonetheless, for three weeks after being sworn in, President Rousseff was holed up inside the Planalto Palace in Brasília; then finally, in January 2015, she did exactly the opposite of what she had promised. The administration began the new mandate with a complete about-turn: the developmentalist agenda for which she had been elected was discarded. They took aim at unemployment insurance, survivor pensions and salary allowances, among other policies. The administration adopted a plan that was both anti-interventionist and orthodox, in practice very similar to what the opposition had proposed. It was a plan that, during her campaign, President Rousseff had referred to as a quick road to 'recession, unemployment, salary decreases and an increase in socio-economic inequality'.[15]

The president's disastrous manoeuvres led to an economic policy entirely in opposition to what she had promised. It seemed as if she believed that, given the fiscal problems and the economic crisis, there was nothing left to be done except to rely on traditional solutions. The government paid dearly for this about-turn. President Rousseff had managed to destabilize her base and provide ammunition to the opposition, who were still trying to delegitimize her mandate.

It was probably at this juncture that a window of opportunity appeared. Between the start of President Rousseff's second term in January 2015 and the impeachment vote in the Senate in August 2016, an increasing number of people adhered to the idea that democratic presidential elections could be vetoed, that their own will could be imposed on society. It is one thing to criticize and question poor government management which led to a rampant increase in public debt; it is another thing entirely to attempt an institutional change through frankly dubious legal manoeuvres, with the clearly defined goal of removing the president from office.

This group brought together a wide variety of interests hostile to the federal government, including business people, industrialists, bankers, members of parliament, journalists, judges and some sectors of the middle class. They favoured legislation that served their immediate interests, and organized an opposition coalition that put forth unified objectives, while operating independently.[16] And beyond that, they had a goal in common, which was to topple the government. This coalition was able to instigate protests and to bring together a handful of parliamentary leaders willing to act against the interests of the government, from within and from outside of congress, among whom were Eduardo Cunha, then president of the Chamber of Deputies; Michel Temer, then vice-president of Brazil and the president of the Brazilian Democratic Movement Party, and Senador Aécio Neves, then president of the Brazilian Social Democracy Party. Over the course of a year and a half, an unbelievable series of crises befell the Rousseff administration. It was a very long list: unemployment increased and the economic situation deteriorated; accusations of corruption flowed in from Curitiba, initially focused on the Workers' Party, especially on the former president, Lula; protests and intolerance were ever more common; Congress systematically boycotted the administration's initiatives; meanwhile, the vice-president openly conspired to take over the leading role. Matters went from bad to worse when the Fundão dam burst, leading to several deaths in Mariana, in the State of Minas Gerais. It was the worst environmental disaster Brazil had ever experienced. On the heels of that calamity, there was an outbreak of the Zika and dengue viruses, the handling of which proved how ill-prepared the government was to cope with such emergencies, not to mention the lack of policy.[17] Not even Brazil's defeat in the 2014 World Cup match against Germany could further upset the country. If up till then the major crises seemed to happen mainly on the football field, they were now a part of daily life.

The opposition coalition armed themselves with pragmatism. Their plan was to champion the government's downfall and to determine who should take over in the interim and which changes should be implemented in the short term. They came up with a scripted policy wherein the crisis in Brazil was, in essence, inextricably linked to the government in general and to President Rousseff in particular. And yet there was something different in this assault; it remained strictly within the boundaries of democratic ritual. Making use of the tools of democracy and following the law to the letter in order to oppose democratically established values and institutions was a manoeuvre entirely unheard of in Brazilian history.

The foundation of the manoeuvre was the so-called 'fiscal pedalling', the term used by economists to describe government postponement of a given payment from one month to the next, or from one year to the next. The recourse inflates the Treasury's cash position and artificially ameliorates the primary surplus, which allows the government to present fictitiously improved financial results. The system had been used by previous administrations; in fact, the metaphor could not be more appropriate – after all, if the cyclist stops pedalling, the bicycle falls over.[18]

In December 2015, the call for impeachment was taken up by then president of the Chamber of Deputies, Eduardo Cunha.[19] Mr Cunha proved to be a very strong leader. He managed to take congressional corruption to an entirely new level by obtaining illegal campaign funding for nearly 100 candidates to the Chamber of Deputies. His political power derived from his position of leadership over a cohesive block of nearly 250 parliamentarians from eight different political parties, whose relationship in some cases was one of cronyism. This group was known as the 'blocão' – big block. Mr Cunha, an adversary of the administration since 2014, regularly relied on blackmail and threats to his opponents. The call for the impeachment of President Rousseff was passed in the Chamber of Deputies on 17 April 2016 and confirmed by the Senate on 31 August 2016. Mr Cunha was arrested and sent to jail and later sentenced to fifteen years in prison for corruption, illegal remittances of moneys offshore and money laundering, as determined by Curitiba Federal Judge Sérgio Moro.[20]

It will take some time before we are able to fully access what took place in Brazil over the course of 2015 to 2017. Routine procedures in adherence to the rule of law were used to serve interests contrary to the democratic values preserved in our public institutions. This manoeuvre was undertaken and accepted by a portion of the Brazilian population without due critical judgement and without recognizing the cost to Brazil's democracy.[21]

Today everyone, or nearly everyone, acknowledges that President Rousseff committed grave administrative infractions. Furthermore, she did not fulfil her administration's fiscal obligations and, during an election year, she approved highly irresponsible government spending. It is also true, however, that the impeachment was justified by a congress whose members were in large part accused of corruption. The government's infraction was serious, but the opposition had a clear agenda: to remain in power using the very same methods that they had accused President Rousseff of employing. This leaves us with an unavoidable question: is the use of these methods to remove an elected official justifiable in the name of the public good? The legal mechanisms used by the opposition deputies were utilized for the same reasons – or even more spurious ones – than those of President Rousseff, accused of governing ineptly.

Senator Rose de Freitas,[22] leader of Mr Michel Temer's provisional government, went straight to the point in an interview just days before the impeachment vote: the so-called 'fiscal pedalling' technique was a mere formality, a pretext. President Rousseff's demise was based not on those accusations alone; it was the entire scenario. 'Why did the government topple? In my opinion, it had nothing to do with this "pedalling" business, [that] was beside the point. Quite simply, the government was in a state of paralysis, with no direction and without any basis to govern. People were fed up and Congress wouldn't give her the necessary votes to pass legislation.'[23] The senator was being sincere, but the justification of the 'pedalling' accusation had become difficult to sustain. There was no unanimity of public opinion as there had been in the case of former President Fernando Collor de Mello's impeachment proceedings and subsequent resignation in 1992. Brazilian citizens remained divided: on 13 March approximately 500,000 protesters demonstrated on Avenida Paulista (São Paulo), screaming, 'Out with Dilma!' and beating pots and pans from their apartment windows. Five days later, a significantly smaller number, approximately 100,000, took to the same avenue with placards reading, 'There will be no coup'.

A telling sign of the times was the two-metre-high metal fence built around the Ministries Esplanade (the location of many important federal government buildings in Brasília), ordered by the Federal Secretariat of Public Safety precisely on the day of the impeachment vote. There was a clear, quasi-didactic meaning behind the move: to separate those demonstrating in favour of impeachment from those demonstrating against. The wall transferred the divide in Brazil from the realm of the symbolic to that of the real, right inside the capital city. As far as the opposition was concerned, the solution to the national crisis was to attack the Workers' Party government, which they blamed for the chaotic state of affairs. They believed Vice-President Michel Temer could work a miracle, that he could put together a team capable of ending the crisis in the short term. Government backers, on the other hand, denounced what they called a *coup d'état* and what they saw as the attempt to obstruct the democratic process. There were also those who questioned the probity of the entire process. 'Paralysis, lack of direction and of ability to manage the country may be motives to want to overturn the government – and thousands took to the streets demanding precisely that, but they are unjustifiable causes for impeachment,' noted journalist Elio Gaspari in his *Folha de S. Paulo* newspaper column, the day before the impeachment vote. He explained it didactically: it was not constitutional.[24]

The impeachment of President Dilma Rousseff laid bare just how serious the crisis was in Brazil. The situation was made worse by the prevailing loss of faith in politics and in politicians. As a matter of fact, what followed only increased the cynicism, as example upon example of poor governance came to light. Instead of behaving with transparency and honesty, in keeping with the democratic values so painstakingly incorporated into the system, many politicians who came into power behaved in the same old ways. They did not preserve the social gains of previous governments; instead many of them went back to (or had never given up) former habits – patrimonialism, political patronage and cronyism – with ever increasing boldness.

Is democracy in Brazil at risk? The question cannot yet be answered. One thing is certain: democracy is always vulnerable if and when society turns a blind eye to the protection of rights. In a profoundly unequal society, such as Brazil's, the focus of the distortion must be immediately on human rights and the guaranteeing of said rights, which comes through government financial support.[25]

Institutions cannot protect themselves, and using the rules of democracy to undermine them destroys them from the inside out. This cannot be overstated. After all, one of the first measures undertaken by the Temer administration was to eliminate the various ministerial secretariats dealing with civil and human rights, whose principle goal was to decrease inequality in Brazil and to promote social inclusion. These were the former departments for the protection of women, indigenous peoples, people of African descent and inhabitants of the *quilombos*. And with the make-up of his Cabinet, President Temer revealed the full extent of his indifference to a pluralistic society. The photo op for his new Cabinet was of white males exclusively, mainly of his generation and socioeconomic group.

A certain imbalance has resulted in the way power is exercised in Brazil. The dynamic has radically changed among the agencies in charge of the balance of power. Especially notable (in such a short time frame) has been the dramatic decrease in authority in the Executive and Legislative branches, as they have failed to curb practices of clientelism and corruption. Currently in Brazil, both the Executive and the National Congress have suffered great losses in their administrative capability, legitimacy and reputation. The situation of the Judiciary, on the other hand, has been diametrically opposed – its sphere of influence has expanded significantly. The risk of this imbalance is that members of any one of the powers begin to view themselves as the sole and virtuous mirror of society. If it is truly fundamental that corruption – so entrenched right now as to be virtually a natural phenomenon – be confronted, it is also crucial that the balance of power among the branches of government be re-established. Otherwise there is a risk there will be untoward intrusion among them as they carry out their responsibilities. And there is a single means by which to prevent the abuse of power. It is called the Constitution.

While the proceedings, practice and context for fighting corruption have greatly changed over the past thirty years, at the same time moral codes have become increasingly rigid and there has been a trend to blame the individual, which is not – in and of itself – wrong. But personal blame should not be at the expense of recognizing a broader political culture that needs to be confronted equally earnestly. This reduction of the political sphere to one that is moralistic, individual and characterized by cronyism can be seen in displays of noisy activism. It is as if Brazilian citizens have grown accustomed to living their daily lives on some sort of roller coaster, consuming the news as if it were a mini-series or soap opera. Nevertheless, the fact that Brazilian citizens' indignation has apparently subsided is the most shocking thing of all. The anger that led citizens to take to the streets between 2015 and 2016, claiming that the only solution to corruption in Brazil would be through criminal law proceedings, seems to have ben extinguished. Either that, or it was entirely spent in August 2016. No one is protesting on the streets any more.

Even though not very much time has passed, it is still difficult to understand why the enormous protests against corruption have disappeared. Nor do we know why this has happened precisely when there have been so many accusations of cronyism and embezzlement of public funds. On the one hand, the Workers' Party, a major participant in building democracy in Brazil, has systematically failed to re-establish its reputation as a party that is above corruption. Nor have members of the party provided answers to accusations of corruption directed at several party leaders. On the other hand, the government is far from being in the clear. Less than one year after the vote to impeach then President Rousseff, Supreme Court Minister Edson Fachin started an investigation of eight ministers in the current administration. The list of those being investigated also includes the presidents of the Chamber of Deputies and the Senate, twenty-four senators, forty federal deputies, three governors and all of the former presidents of Brazil elected since 1988, with the exception of former presidents Tancredo Neves and Itamar Franco. Former President Rousseff's opponent Aécio Neves is among those being investigated. The investigation includes charges of corruption, ideological falsehoods, money laundering, fraud and the formation of cartels. Brazil's major political parties are also involved in accusations of embezzlement of public funds and illicit campaign financing, including the Democrats (Democratas, DEM), the Democratic Labour Party (Partido Democrático Trabalhista, PDT), the Brazilian Democratic Movement Party, the Progressive Party and the Brazilian Social Democracy Party. President Temer himself has done everything he can to exonerate himself and to block the Attorney General's investigation of his possible passive participation in corruption. To that end, he substituted deputies on the Constitution and Justice Commission, agreed to amendments to the federal budget, negotiated positions in the second and third tiers of his government, and made concessions to deputies from every political party, including those affecting the environment.[26]

At the time of writing, the crisis is acute. Nevertheless, it may lead to the posing of very serious questions that have yet to be asked. This crisis may even promote changes, giving rise to meaningful words and actions – in the public sphere, and in the world of politics.

We have already written that the history of Brazil is not a destiny – it is made up of choices, projects and their consequences. We all know this is not the first time the country has faced a crisis of great magnitude and proportion. Everything seen at close range seems to be gigantic, with no future and no possible escape. But if history helps us to recall the past, it must also reveal the many times over the years Brazil has relied on periods of introspection. And, incidentally, the country has always found its way.

Belo Horizonte/São Paulo, August 2017

Notes

The full bibliography for the book in Portuguese can be found in the original Brazilian edition.

INTRODUCTION

1. This book was originally written in 2014. In the Afterword we address changes that have occurred since that time.

1: FIRST CAME THE NAME

1. Pseudonym of Sérgio Porto (1923–1968), Brazilian essayist, journalist and composer.
2. At the command of their Catholic Majesties, Ferdinand and Isabella of Spain, Christopher Columbus captained the first expedition to reach the Americas, on 12 October 1492.
3. The semantic distinction between anthropophagy and cannibalism is explained later in this chapter.
4. The Genesis account (9:20–9:27) is confusing. Noah cursed Ham's son Canaan and not Ham himself. There are also many controversial interpretations of the act that provoked the curse, thought by many scholars to have been a far more serious offence.
5. Noah's curse on Ham allegedly included the black people of Africa who were said to be his descendants. The verses in Genesis that list his descendants (10:6–10:20) give no explanation for this. The Midrash states that Cush, one of Ham's sons, was a sub-Saharan African and it was through him that the curse was passed on.
6. Lorenzo di Pierfrancesco de' Medici (1463–1503) was educated under the tutelage of his cousin Lorenzo il Magnifico. One of his teachers was Amerigo Vespucci's uncle, Giorgio Antonio Vespucci. Amerigo himself was Lorenzo's fellow student and became both a friend and an employee. In the early 1500s Amerigo Vespucci sent most of his famous letters from the New World to Lorenzo.
7. Francisco Bethencourt, *Racisms: From the Crusades to the Twentieth Century*. Princeton: Princeton University Press, 2013, pp. 102–4.

8. Dom Afonso III (King Alphonse III) of the House of Burgundy, King of Portugal from 1248 to 1279.

9. See also, among others, Júnia Ferreira Furtado, *O mapa que inventou o Brasil*. Rio de Janeiro: Versal, 2013.

10. Dom Afonso V (King Alphonse V), of the House of Aviz, King of Portugal from 1438 to 1481.

11. Dom João II (King John II), of the House of Aviz, King of Portugal from 1481 to 1495.

12. The comments that follow on life at sea during the great discoveries are taken from Paulo Miceli, *O ponto onde estamos: Viagens e viajantes na história da expansão e da conquista*. Campinas: Editora da Unicamp, 2008.

13. Meaning the crates were not permitted to be overloaded.

14. *Quintal*, from the Latin *centenarius* – a historical unit of mass equivalent to 100 pounds (45.35 kilos).

15. Miceli, *O ponto onde estamos*, p. 77.

16. Padre Fernando Oliveira, *A arte da guerra do mar*. Lisbon: Naval Ministry, 1969, p. 77.

17. A mysterious disease cured by St Cosmas. The twin saints Cosmas and Damian were doctors to whom miraculous cures were attributed. During Diocletian's persecution they were arrested and decapitated in Cilicia around 300 CE.

18. Joaquim Romero de Magalhães, 'Quem descobriu o Brasil', in Luciano Figueiredo (Org.), *História do Brasil para ocupados*. Rio de Janeiro: Casa da Palavra, 2013.

19. Miceli, *O ponto onde estamos*, p. 171.

20. Pêro Vaz de Caminha (c.1450–1500) was a Portuguese knight who had accompanied Cabral to India in 1500. He wrote the official report of the discovery of Brazil by Cabral's fleet in April 1500 (*Carta de Pêro Vaz de Caminha*). He died in a riot in Calcutta later that year.

21. 'Land of the True Cross' (from the Latin *Vera Crux*).

22. Portuguese for 'bay'. The state is named after 'All Saints' Bay' (*Bahia de Todos os Santos*) where the capital Salvador is located.

23. Dom Manuel I (King Emmanuel I), of the House of Aviz, King of Portugal from 1495 to 1521.

24. Paracelsus (1493–1541) was a Swiss-German Renaissance physician, occultist, alchemist and astrologer. His insistence on using observations from nature rather than consulting ancient texts was a radical departure from the medical practices of his day.

25. Gerolamo Cardano (1501–1576) was an Italian mathematician, physician, philosopher and astrologer. He was an inveterate gambler who formulated the first rules of the theory of probability and the author of over two hundred books on medicine, mathematics, philosophy and music.

26. Pêro Vaz de Caminha, *Carta de Pêro Vaz de Caminha*, April 1500.

27. François I, of the Angoulême branch of the House of Valois, King of France from 1515 to 1547.

28. Dom João III (King John III), of the House of Aviz, King of Portugal from 1521 to 1557.

29. The term, currently used for the semi-arid scrubland in the interior of Brazil's northeast, had a much wider application in the early days of the colony when it referred to the vast unchartered interior of the territory.

30. A coastal town 211 kilometres ('as the crow flies') to the south of Salvador.

31. For the name 'Brazil' see, among others, 'O nome Brasil' (*Revista de História*, n. 145, pp. 61-86, 2. sem. 2001), and *Inferno Atlântico* (São Paulo: Companhia das Letras, 1993, pp. 29-32), both by Laura de Mello e Souza.

32. *Pau-Brasil.*

33. Fernando de Noronha (c.1470-c.1540) claimed to be the first European to discover the paradisiacal island named after him, the largest of an archipelago situated in the Atlantic 545 kilometres to the northeast of Recife. There is controversy surrounding who first arrived on the island, which was initially named *Sao João* after St John the Baptist.

34. See S. D'Agostini et al., 'Ciclo econômico do pau-brasil'. Available at: <http://www.biologico.sp.gov.br/docs/pag/v9_1/dagostini.pdf>. Accessed on 15/12/2014.

35. João de Barros with Laura de Mello e Souza, *Inferno Atlântico*, p. 24.

36. Pero de Magalhães Gândavo (c.1540-c.1580) was a Portuguese scholar and historian. His *History of Santa Cruz Province, commonly known as Brazil* was published in 1576. The book describes the discovery of Brazil and the first years of its colonization, as well as its exotic fauna and flora that were unknown to Europeans. It even describes a sea monster that supposedly appeared off the coast of the Captaincy of São Vicente (the modern-day State of São Paulo) and was killed by the local inhabitants.

37. The National Archive of Torre do Tombo is one of the oldest institutions in Portugal. Originally installed in one of the towers of Lisbon Castle in 1378 (*tombo* 'register of charters', *torre* 'tower'), it has been one of the central archives of the Portuguese state.

38. Sérgio Buarque de Holanda, *Visão do Paraíso: Os motivos edênicos no descobrimento e colonização do Brasil.* 6th edn. São Paulo: Brasiliense, 2002.

39. De Mello e Souza, *Inferno Atlântico.*

40. The following passage about the reports of fifteenth-century travellers is based on research undertaken for the book *O sol do Brasil: Nicolas-Antoine Taunay e as desventuras dos artistas franceses na corte de d. João* by Lilia Moritz Schwarcz (São Paulo: Companhia das Letras, 2008).

41. 'Voyage of Saint Brendan the Abbot', a ninth-century account of the legendary journey of St Brendan (c.484-c.577) to the Isle of the Blessed.

42. Aethicus Ister (Aethicus of Istria) was the protagonist of the seventh- to eighth-century *Cosmographia* written by a churchman, Hieronymus Pres-

byter (pretending to be St Jerome), that purports to be a Latin translation of the original Greek. It describes Aethicus' travels from Ireland to India and his encounters with strange foreign peoples.

43. Pierre d'Ailly (1351–1420), a French theologian, astrologer and cardinal, was the author of 170 books. In *Imago mundi*, a work that influenced Christopher Columbus, he discusses the form of the Earth.

44. The (probably fictional) compiler of the immensely popular *Travels of Sir John Mandeville*, an account of his supposed travels around the world.

45. Information taken from José Roberto Teixeira Leite, 'Viajantes do imaginário: A América vista da Europa, século XVII' (São Paulo, *Revista Usp*, no. 30, pp. 32–45, June/August 1996). See also Guilhermo Giucci, *Viajantes do maravilhoso: O Novo Mundo* (São Paulo: Companhia das Letras, 1992); Howard Rollin Patch, *El otro mundo en la literature medieval* (Mexico: Fondo de Cultura Económica, 1956); Joaquín Gil Aléxis Chassang, *Historia de la novela y de sus relaciones com la antigüedad griega y latina* (Buenos Aires: Poseidon, 1948).

46. Teixeira Leite, 'Viajantes do imaginário'.

47. See Laura de Mello e Souza, *O diabo e a terra de Santa Cruz*. São Paulo: Companhia das Letras, 1986.

48. Antonio Pigafetta (1491–1534) was an Italian scholar and traveller from the Republic of Venice who travelled with the Portuguese explorer Ferdinand Magellan (Fernão de Magalhães) on his first expedition to the Indies. They entered the Bay of Guanabara in 1519 (before the city of Rio de Janeiro existed). As Magellan's assistant, he kept an accurate journal of the voyage in which he noted extensive data concerning the geography, climate, flora and fauna, and the inhabitants of the places that the expedition visited.

49. Dom Sebastião I (King Sebastian I), of the House of Aviz, King of Portugal from 1557 to 1578.

50. *Treatise on the Land of Brazil* and *History of the Province of Santa Cruz.*

51. The French attempt to establish the colony of France Antarctique on the shores of Guanabara Bay is discussed later in this chapter. Their foundation of the city of São Luis in the northern captaincy of Maranhão is discussed in chapter 2.

52. Ibid.

53. F, L and R in the original (*Fé, Lei* and *Rei*).

54. Pero de Magalhães Gândavo, *Tratado da terra & história do Brasil*. Org. de Leonardo Dantas Silva. Recife: Fundação Joaquim Nabuco, Massangana, 1995, pp. 19 and 24.

55. Gândavo, ibid., pp. 24, 27 and 29.

56. The translation of the title is *History of Santa Cruz Province, commonly known as Brazil*. The book has not been published in English.

57. Serge Gruzinski, *La colonisation de l'imaginaire: Sociétés indigènes et occidentalisation dans le Mexique espagnol, XVIe–XVIIIe siècle*. Paris: Gallimard, 1988.

58. Pierre de Ronsard (1524–1585) was a French Renaissance poet, known to his generation as the 'Prince of poets'. He wrote his *Complainte contre Fortune* after reading André Thevet's *Singularitez de la France antarctique*. He refers to the Indians as 'happy people' who should be left in peace 'without anguish or worry' (*'sans peine et sans souci'*). (*Encyclopaedia Universalis*)

59. Ronsard with Manuela Carneiro da Cunha, 'Imagens de índios do Brasil', op. cit., p. 4.

60. Henri II, of the House of Valois, King of France from 1547 to 1559. He married Catherine de' Medici in 1533 when they were both fourteen years old.

61. Ferdinand Denis, *Une fête brésilienne célébrée à Rouen en 1550*. Paris: Techener Librarie, 1850.

62. Carneiro da Cunha, 'Imagens de índios do Brasil', op. cit, p. 5.

63. Denis Diderot (1713–1784) was the editor (along with Jean de Rond d'Alembert, until 1759) of the *Encyclopédie, ou dictionnaire raisonné des sciences, des arts et des metiers*, which was published in France between 1751 and 1772.

64. Claudius Ptolemy (c.90–c.168 CE) was a Greco-Egyptian writer from Alexandria whose *Geographia* was a compilation of the geographical knowledge of the second-century Roman Empire. During the Renaissance a sequence of new editions was published with updated maps.

65. Sebastian Münster (1488–1552) was a German cartographer and cosmographer whose *Cosmographia*, published in 1544, was the earliest German description of the world.

66. '[. . .] persistent legends before the voyages of Columbus and Vespucci that feed [. . .] an association between cannibals and the mythical dog-headed inhabitants of Africa, as in the definition appended to Rabelais' Gargantua and Pantagruel'. (*African Cultures and Literatures* edited by Gordon Collier)

67. Quoted by Carneiro da Cunha, 'Imagens de índios do Brasil', p. 5.

68. The proponents of literary Romantic Indianism were the novelist José de Alencar (1829–1877) and the poet Gonçalves Dias (1823–1864). The movement sought to create a national identity through the romantic portrayal of Brazil's indigenous peoples in the early years of the colony.

69. Montaigne, 'The Cannibals', *Essays*. Translated into Portuguese by Sérgio Milliet. São Paulo: Abril Cultural, 1972, pp. 101–6. (Coleção Os Pensadores)

70. The title in translation is *The Singularities of Antarctic France*.

71. André Thevet, *As singularidades da França Antártica*. Lisbon: [n.p.], 1878, pp. 146–80.

72. Jean de Léry (1536–1613) was a Calvinist who joined the colony of France Antarctique in 1556. Nicolas Durand de Villegaignon, the French admiral who had founded the colony, originally accepted the Protestants. However, after eight months he accused them of heresy and had them expelled. Léry and the other Protestants took refuge with the Tupinambá. Three of them later returned to the colony and were executed by Villegaignon. Léry and the other missionaries returned to France on an old, unseaworthy vessel. Later, Léry wrote his *History of the Martyrs* (1564), in which he dedicated a chapter to his three murdered colleagues, entilted 'Persecution of the Faithful in the Lands of America'.

73. See Carneiro da Cunha, 'Imagens de índios no Brasil'

74. The title in English is *History of a Voyage to the Land of Brazil*.

75. Jean de Léry, 'Preface', in *Histoire d'un voyage fait en la terre du Brésil, autrement dite Amerique*. Genebra: A. Chuppin, 1580, pp. 2–9.

76. Ibid., p. 227.

77. Léry related the history of these killings in his *Memorable History of the Town of Sancerre*, in which he accuses the French of being more barbarous than the cannibalistic Indians he had met in Brazil.

78. See Frank Lestringant, 'De Jean de Léry a Claude Lévi-Strauss: Por uma arqueologia de *Tristes Trópicos*', *Revista de Antropologia*, São Paulo, vol. 43, no. 2 (2000).

79. Located on the coastline of the present-day state of São Paulo, to the northeast of the Island of São Vicente.

80. Hans Staden, *Duas viagens ao Brasil*. São Paulo: Hans Staden Society Publications, 1942 [1557], ch. 42, part 1.

81. Ibid., pp. 161 and 185.

82. Ibid., pp. 196–8.

83. Carneiro da Cunha, op. cit., p. 14.

84. The whole passage about indigenous legislation is based on the excellent article 'Índios livres e índios escravos' by Beatriz Perrone Moisés, in Manuela Carneiro da Cunha's (Org.) *História dos índios no Brasil* (São Paulo: Companhia das Letras, 1992, pp. 115–32).

85. St José de Anchieta (1534–1597; canonized by Pope Francis in 2014) was a Spanish Jesuit missionary, one of the first priests to introduce Christianity in Brazil and one of the founders of Sao Paulo (1554). He is considered one of the most influential figures of the first century of the colony.

86. Oswald de Souza Andrade (1890–1954) was one of the founders of *Paulista* Brazilian modernism. The quote is from his *Manifesto Antropófago* (1928) in which he attacks the legacy of the Portuguese and of the missionaries.

87. Much of the subsequent commentary is based on *Os índios antes do Brasil* (Rio de Janeiro: Zahar, 2000) by Carlos Fausto, and from the already

cited *História dos índios no Brasil*, organized by Manuela Carneiro da Cunha.

88. Arid grasslands interspersed with stunted vegetation, characteristic of Brazil's central plateau (where Brasília, the capital of the country, is located today).

89. Examples of Aratu ceramics – pear-shaped funeral urns – have been found at archaeological sites in Brazil's northeast. Aratu ceramics were influenced by the Uru tradition of the Carajá. See Gabriela Martin, *Pré-história do nordeste do Brasil*.

90. *Oca* – one of the names used for indigenous habitation. Normally made of wood or bamboo and thatched with straw or palm fronds.

91. *Ocara*.

92. Eduardo Viveiros de Castro, *A inconstância da alma selvagem*. São Paulo: Cosac Naify, 2002.

93. The Ducks' Lagoon (*Lagoa dos Patos*) is the largest in Brazil.

94. Today the highly polluted river that runs through the city of São Paulo. The source is in the Serra do Mar, and it ends at the Jupiá dam on the Paraná river, in the interior of the state.

95. The river that forms the boundary between the state of São Paulo and its immediate neighbour to the south, the state of Paraná.

96. The division between the groups is also based on Fausto, *Os índios antes do Brasil*, pp. 68–70.

97. Piratininga (Tupi-Guarani for 'fish to be dried') is the name of the plateau where the first settlement was located, from which the city of São Paulo was to grow. It was founded in 1554 on a steep hilltop between the Anhangabaú and Tamanduateí rivers by a group of twelve Jesuits, including Manuel de Nóbrega and José de Anchieta, around a Jesuit college built of rammed earth (the *Colégio de São Paulo de Piratininga*). See chapter 3.

98. These reflections on the exploitation of the Indians in São Paulo are based on John Monteiro, *Negros da terra: Índios e bandeirantes nas origens de São Paulo* (São Paulo: Companhia das Letras, 1994).

99. Fausto, *Os índios antes do Brasil*, pp. 78–9.

100. Pierre Clastres, op. cit.

101. Father Antonio Vieira – born 1608 in Lisbon, died 1697 in Bahia – a great Catholic pulpit-orator, was one of the few sources who described the conditions in the early days of the colony.

102. See Viveiros de Castro, *A inconstância da alma selvagem*.

2: THE SUGAR CIVILIZATION

1. Beet sugar made its appearance even more recently, only becoming part of the Western diet from the nineteenth century onward.

2. This introductory section on the history of sugar is largely based on the seminal work by Sidney Mintz, *Sweetness and Power: The Place of Sugar in Modern History* (New York: Penguin, 1985).

3. The Infante Henrique, of the House of Aviz, later to become Dom Henrique I (Henry I), King of Portugal from 1578 to 1580.

4. A historical unit of weight used in Portugal and Spain, originally a quarter of a *quintal* (25 pounds, 11.33).

5. *Muscovado* or *mascavado* – past participle of *mascavar*, the term used for separating sugar of inferior quality – used figuratively to mean 'adulterated'. (*Dicionário Aurélio*).

6. Stuart Schwartz, *Sugar Plantations in the Formation of Brazilian Society: Bahia, 1550–1835*. Cambridge: Cambridge University Press, 1986.

7. The first two kings during the period of political union between the Crowns of Spain and Portugal known as the Iberian Union or the Philippine Dynasty. Philip II, of the House of Hapsburg, was King of Spain from 1556 to 1598 and succeeded to the Portuguese throne as Felipe I in 1581. He was also Lord of the Seventeen Provinces of the Netherlands, and, during his marriage to Mary I of England (1554–8), King of England and Ireland. He was succeeded by his son, King Philip III of Spain and Dom Felipe II of Portugal (1598–1621).

8. See Marshall Sahlins, 'Cosmologias do capitalismo: O setor transpacífico do "sistema mundial"', in *Cultura na prática*. Rio de Janeiro: Editora da Ufrj, 2004, chapter 13.

9. Dom Manuel I (King Emmanuel I), of the House of Aviz, King of Portugal from 1495 to 1521.

10. See Vera Lúcia Amaral Ferlini, *A civilização do açúcar: Séculos XVI a XVIII*. São Paulo: Brasiliense, 1984.

11. Dom João III (King John III), son of Dom Manuel, King of Portugal from 1521 to 1557.

12. 'Holy war' – a war motivated by religion.

13. A region of the captaincy (present-day state) of Bahia comprising the area of fertile land along the coast of the *Baia de Todos os Santos* (where the colony's first capital, Salvador, is located).

14. *Jaguaripe* (from the Tupi-Guarani 'River of the Jaguars'), the first town to be built in the Reconcâvo baiano.

15. The cult remained active until the second decade of the seventeenth century, although it was promptly repressed by the Portuguese. See Ronaldo Vainfas, *A heresia dos Índios: Catolicismo e rebeldia no Brasil colonial*. São Paulo: Companhia das Letras, 1995.

16. Porto Seguro, in the south of Bahia, is the municipality immediately south of Santa Cruz Cabrália where Cabral arrived in 1500.

17. The low-lying lands around the port of Santos in the captaincy of São Vicente (present-day state of São Paulo). Nowadays, Santos is the port that

serves the state capital, São Paulo, which is located approximately 70 kilometres inland, 790 metres above sea level, on the Piratininga Plateau.

18. Gilberto Freyre (1900–1987) was a famous Brazilian sociologist and anthropologist whose best-known work, *Casa-Grande & Senzala* (*The Masters and the Slaves*; 1933), is still considered a Brazilian classic, despite a lot of polemic generated by some of its racial premises.

19. Quoted by Manuel Diegues Junior in *O engenho de açúcar no Nordeste*. Rio de Janeiro: Ministério da Agricultura; Serviço de Informação Agrícola, 1952.

20. An old Portuguese arroba was equivalent to 32 pounds, or 14.5 kilograms.

21. See Engel Sluiter, 'Os holandeses antes de 1621', *Revista do Instituto de Arqueológico, Histórico e Geográfico de Pernambuco*, Recife, vol. 46 (1967), pp. 188–207.

22. Boris Fausto, *História do Brasil*, 4th edn. São Paulo: Edusp, 1996.

23. Schwartz, *Sugar Plantations in the Formation of Brazilian Society*, p. 159. For pirates, see Jean Marcel Carvalho França and Sheila Hue, *Piratas no Brasil: As incríveis histórias dos ladrões dos mares que pilharam nosso litoral*. São Paulo: Globo, 2014.

24. Andréia Daher, 'A conversão dos Tupinambá entre a oralidade e a escrita nos relatos franceses dos séculos XVI e XVII', *Horizontes antropológicos*, Porto Alegre, vol. 10, no. 22 (July/December 2004).

25. A reference to the *Ile de Saint-Louis* (*Ilha de São Luís*) in St Mark's Bay (*Baía de São Marcus*) on the coast of northern Brazil, where the French founded a settlement in 1612. In 1615 it was conquered by the Portuguese and renamed São Luís, the capital of the captaincy (present-day state) of Maranhão.

26. Paul Louis Jacques Gaffarel, *Histoire du Brésil français au seizième siècle*. Paris: Maison Neuve, 1878.

27. The greatest specialist on Dutch Brazil is the diplomat and historian Evaldo Cabral de Mello. The text that follows is approximately based on information taken from his books *O negócio do Brasil: Portugal, os países baixos e o Nordeste, 1641–1669* (Rio de Janeiro: Topbooks, 2003), *Rubro veio: O imaginário da restauração pernambucana* (Rio de Janeiro: Topbooks, 2005), and *Nassau: Governador do Brasil holandês* (São Paulo: Companhia das Letras, 2006).

28. Salvador was founded by Tomé de Souza (1503–1579), the first Governor-General of Brazil, in 1549. In 1763 the capital was transferred to Rio de Janeiro and in 1960 to Brasília.

29. Brazil's coastline, adjacent to the Atlantic Ocean, measures 7,491 kilometres.

30. The adopted name of Italian Jesuit Giovanni Antonio (André João Antonil) – born Italy 1649, died Bahia, 1716. His 'Culture and Opulence of Brazil through its Drugs and Mines', published in Lisbon in 1711, is considered one of the most important sources of information on the social and economic conditions in Brazil at the beginning of the eighteenth century.

31. Wolfgang Lenk, 'Guerra e pacto colonial: Exército, fiscalidade e administração colonial da Bahia (1624–1654)'. Campinas: Unicamp, 2009. Thesis (PhD in Economic Development).

32. See Hugo Coelho Vieira, Nara Neves Pires Galvão and Leonardo Dantas Silva, *Brasil holandês: História, memória, patrimônio compartilhado*. São Paulo: Alameda, 2012.

33. Rômulo Luiz Xavier Nascimento, '"Entre os rios e o mar aberto': Pernambuco, os portos e o Atlântico no Brasil holandês'. Also in Vieira, Galvão and Silva, *Brasil holandês*, p. 193.

34. The New Christians were Sephardim (Iberian Jews) who had, with some exceptions, been forced to convert to Roman Catholicism.

35. José Antonio Golsalves de Mello, *Tempo dos flamengos: Influência da ocupação holandesa na vida e na cultura do Norte do Brasil*. São Paulo: José Olympio, 1947, p. 61.

36. The residue (*bagaço*) after the juice has been extracted from the sugarcane.

37. A glossy-black, pheasant-like bird, formerly originally found in the forests of northeastern Brazil but now extinct in the wild.

38. Sérgio Buarque de Holanda (ed.), *A época colonial*. São Paulo: Bertrand Brasil, 2003, p. 271. vol. 1: *Do descobrimento à expansão territorial* (Coleção História Geral da Civilização Brasileira).

39. Dom João IV (King John IV), King of Portugal from 1640 to 1656.

40. The Portuguese *Cortes*, or 'Courts' – from the Latin *cohors* – date back to the Middle Ages. They were political assemblies convoked by the king for consultation and deliberation, reaching the height of their power in the fourteenth and fifteenth centuries.

41. See Cabral de Mello, *Rubro veio*, 2005.

42. See Evaldo Cabral de Mello, *O Brasil holandês* (São Paulo: Companhia das Letras, 2010), *Rubro veio* and *Nassau*; and Pedro Puntoni, *Guerras do Brasil (1504–1604)* (São Paulo: Brasiliense, 1992). (Coleção Tudo é História)

43. *Escravizados*, according to the criteria adopted by Alberto da Costa e Silva, are Africans of the first generation. The term emphasizes the compulsory nature of enslavement and thus corresponds better to the notion that they were not in the situation voluntarily.

44. Inhabitants of the province of São Paulo. (The inhabitants of the city of São Paulo are called *paulistanos*.)

45. John Monteiro, Pedro Puntoni and Hal Langfur show the persistence of Indian slavery in Minas Gerais during the eighteenth and nineteenth centuries, and thus one cannot speak of a transition from one system to the other.

46. Alberto da Costa e Silva. *A enxada e a lança: A África antes dos Portugueses*. Rio de Janeiro: Nova Fronteira, 2010.

47. *Cachaça*, made from distilled sugarcane, is nowadays Brazil's national drink.

48. Schwartz, *Sugar Plantations in the Formation of Brazilian Society*, p. 73.
49. The *casa-grande*, literally translated 'big house', and the *engenho*, which included the *casa-grande*, the *senzala* (slave quarters), the sugar mills and the surrounding plantations, were both emblematic of the power of the slave-owning sugar barons. The word *senzala* is equally emblematic of the forced submission of the slaves.
50. A tall grass, still used in Brazil for thatching rustic homes. The Tupi called it *ssa'pé*, 'that which lights up', due to the ease with which it catches fire.
51. Both quotes are taken from Schwartz, *Sugar Plantations in the Formation of Brazilian Society*, p. 209.
52. The habit of wealthy households adopting outsiders and treating them as family members continued into the twentieth century. These people were referred to as *agregados* or *agregadas*.
53. Genipap is a reddish-brown fruit that yields a dark blue dye used as body paint by the Indians. The mangaba tree grows in the scrublands of Brazil's northeast.
54. Gilberto Freyre, *Açúcar: Uma sociologia do doce, com receitas de bolos e doces do Nordeste do Brasil*. São Paulo: Companhia das Letras, 1987.
55. Junior, *O engenho de açúcar no Nordeste*; Leila Mezan Algranti, 'Os livros de devoção e a religiosa perfeita (normatização e práticas religiosas nos recolhimentos femininos do Brasil colonial)', in Maria Beatriz Nizza da Silva (ed.), *Cultura portuguesa na Terra de Santa Cruz* (Lisboa: Estampa, 1995, pp. 109–24), and Leila Mezan Algranti, 'Mulheres enclausuradas no Brasil colonial', in Heloisa Buarque de Holanda and Maria Helena Rolim Capelato (eds.), *Relações de gênero e diversidades culturais na América Latina* (Rio de Janeiro and São Paulo: Expressão Cultural/Edusp, 1999, pp. 147–62. *Coleção América 500 Anos*, 9).
56. By northern European standards Brazilians have a 'sweet tooth' – a tradition of preparing desserts with large amounts of sugar that originated in the sugarcane cycle.
57. For an analysis of the expression, see Ricardo Benzaquen, *Guerra e paz: Casa-grande & Senzala e a obra de Gilberto Freyre nos anos 30* (São Paulo: Editora 34, 1994).
58. Kimbundu is the Bantu language spoken by the Ambundu in northwest Angola.
59. Schwartz, *Sugar Plantations in the Formation of Brazilian Society*, p. 125.
60. The *boçais* were new arrivals (considered 'the ignorant ones') and the *ladinos* were second generation or later (considered 'the clever ones').
61. Francisco Bethencourt, *Racisms: From the Crusades to the Twentieth Century*. Princeton: Princeton University Press, 2013.
62. Ibid., p. 173.
63. For a fundamental analysis of dependence and the policies of favour in Brazil, see Roberto Schwarz, *Ao vencedor as batatas: Forma literária e*

processo social nos inícios do romance brasileiro (São Paulo: Duas Cidades, 1977 [5th edn. rev. São Paulo: Duas Cidades; Editora 34, 2000]).

64. Sugar mills propelled by animal traction; in the former, oxen, in the latter, horses.

65. André João Antonil, *Cultura e opulência do Brasil*, 3rd edn. Belo Horizonte and São Paulo: Itatiaia/ Edusp, 1982.

66. Water that 'stings' or 'burns'.

67. Schwartz, *Sugar Plantations in the Formation of Brazilian Society*, p. 146.

68. 'Molasses white', 'dirty white', 'almost white', 'whitish', 'slightly mestizo'.

69. For the 1976 PNAD data (National Research per Sample of Domiciles) see, among others, Lilia Moritz Schwarcz, *Nem preto nem branco, muito pelo contrário: Cor, raça e sociabilidade brasileira* (São Paulo: Claro Enigma, 2013).

70. Fausto, *História do Brasil*, p. 48.

3: TIT FOR TAT

1. Herbert S. Klein, *O tráfico de escravos no Atlântico: Novas abordagens para as Américas*. Ribeirão Preto: FUNPEC-Editora, 2006, pp. 6–7.

2. Luiz Felipe de Alencastro, 'As populações africanas no Brasil'. Available at: <http://www.casadasafricas.org.br/wp/wp-content/uploads/2011/08/As-Populacoes-Africanas-no-Brasil.pdf>. Accessed on 2/06/2014.

3. Ciro Flamarion Cardoso, *A afro-América: A escravidão no novo mundo*, 2nd edn. São Paulo: Brasiliense, 1984. (Coleção Tudo é História)

4. At the Battle of Ambuila (or Mbwila) on 29 October 1665, Portuguese forces defeated the forces of the Kingdom of Congo and decapitated Dom Antonio I (also called Nvita a Nkanga). Hostility between the two countries, previously trading partners, had increased since the establishment of the Portuguese colony of Angola in 1575.

5. Klein, *O tráfico de escravos no Atlântico* , p. 18.

6. 'Tomb ships'. *Tumbeiro* means 'pallbearer' – the person who carries the coffin to the tomb.

7. Herbert S. Klein, 'Novas interpretações do tráfico de escravos do Atlântico', *Revista de História*, São Paulo, vol. 120 (January/July 1989), pp. 3–25. Available at: <http://www.revistas.usp.br/revhistoria/article/view/18589>. Accessed on 02/06/2014.

8. Ibid., p. 16.

9. Ibid., p. 12.

10. Wlamyra R. de Albuquerque and Walter Fraga Filho, *Uma história do negro no Brasil*. Salvador: Centro de Estudos Afro-Orientais; Brasília: Fundação Cultural Palmares, 2006.

11. Sidney Mintz and Richard Price, *O nascimento da cultura afro-americana: Uma perspectiva antropológica*. Rio de Janeiro: Pallas; Centro de Estudos Afro-Brasileiros, 2003.

12. Klein, 'Novas interpretações do tráfico de escravos do Atlântico', pp. 16–17.

13. *Santeria* is a syncretic religion that developed mostly in the Spanish colonies. Today it is practised in Hispanic America and in the Caribbean, notably Cuba.

14. See, among others, Clarival do Prado Valladares and his article 'A iconologia africana no Brasil', in *Revista Brasileira de Cultura* (Rio de Janeiro, MEC, year 1, July/September 1999, pp. 37–48), and Reginaldo Prandi, *Mitologia de orixás* (São Paulo: Companhia das Letras, 2004).

15. Charles R. Boxer, *O império marítimo português: 1415–1825*. São Paulo: Companhia das Letras, 2002, pp. 117–18.

16. The Colônia do Sacramento was founded by Portugal in 1680. Its possession of the colony was disputed by the Spanish, who settled on the opposite bank of the River Plate at Buenos Aires. Until the creation of the state of Uruguay in 1828 the colony was to alternate between Spanish and Portuguese control no fewer than six times.

17. He was named after Dom João II (John II), King of Portugal from 1477 to 1495.

18. The *Costa da Mina*, comprising the coastline of the present-day states of Ghana, Benin, Togo and Nigeria.

19. David Eltis and David Richardson, *Atlas of the Transatlantic Slave Trade*. New Haven and London: Yale University Press, 2010.

20. Schwartz, *Sugar Plantations in the Formation of Brazilian Society*, pp. 280–1.

21. Albuquerque and Fraga Filho, *Uma história do negro no Brasil*.

22. Ambrósio Fernandes Brandão, *Diálogo das grandezas do Brasil* (1618).

23. Schwartz, *Sugar Plantations in the Formation of Brazilian Society*, p. 288.

24. See Manolo Florentino and José Roberto Góes, *A paz das senzalas: Famílias escravas e trafico atlântico, Rio de Janeiro, c.1790–c.1850* (Rio de Janeiro: Civilização Brasileira, 1997), and Robert Slenes, *Na senzala, uma flor: Esperanças e recordações na formação da família escrava* (Rio de Janeiro: Nova Fronteira, 1999).

25. Jorge Benci, *Economia cristã dos senhores no governo dos escravos*. Rome: Antonio de Rossi, 1705.

26. Amaral Ferlini, *A civilização do açúcar*.

27. *Quilombos* (explained later in this chapter) were settlements founded by escaped enslaved people that existed all over Brazil. The inhabitants were called *Quilombolas*.

28. Didier Fassin, *La Force de l'ordre: Une anthropologie de la police des quartiers*. Paris: Seuil, 2012. (Coleção La Couleur des Idées)

29. See Schwartz, *Sugar Plantations in the Formation of Brazilian Society*.

30. Lilia Moritz Schwarcz and Maria Helena P. T. Machado, 'Um pouquinho de Brasil: Por que deveríamos nos reconhecer nas cenas de *12 anos de*

escravidão', *Folha de S. Paulo*, São Paulo (February 2014). Caderno Ilustrada, Ilustríssima, p. C-2.

31. There is a vast bibliography on the subject. We suggest reading Stuart Schwartz, Reis and Slenes.

32. See Letícia Vidor de Sousa Reis, *O mundo de pernas para o ar: A capoeira no Brasil*, 3rd edn. (Curitiba: CRV, 2010), and Carlos Eugênio Líbano Soares, *A capoeira escrava e outras tradições rebeldes no Rio de Janeiro, 1808–1850*, 2nd edn. (Campinas: Editora da Unicamp, 2004).

33. Pedro Paulo de Abreu Funari, 'A arqueologia de Palmares; sua contribuição para o conhecimento da história da cultura afro-americana', in João José Reis and Flávio dos Santos Gomes (eds.), *Liberdade por um fio: História dos quilombos no Brasil*. São Paulo: Companhia das Letras, 1996.

34. See Kátia de Queirós Mattoso, *Ser escravo no Brasil*. São Paulo: Brasiliense, 1982.

35. For *quilombos* as the 'third margin' of the slavery system, see João José Reis and Eduardo Silva, *Negociação e conflito: A resistência negra no Brasil escravista*. São Paulo: Companhia das Letras, 1989.

36. For access to the land and its cultivation in the *quilombos*, see Flávio dos Santos Gomes and João José Reis, 'Roceiros, camponeses e garimpeiros quilombolas na escravidão e na pós-emancipação', and Heloisa Maria Murgel Starling, Henrique Estrada Rodrigues and Marcela Telles (eds.), *Utopias agrárias*. Belo Horizonte: UFMG, 2008.

37. 'The armadillo's burrow'.

38. Now a district of the city of Salvador, the capital of Bahia.

39. For the *Buraco do Tatu*, see Reis and Silva, *Negociação e conflito*.

40. The term *campo negro*, coined by Flávio Gomes, is used to analyse the complex network of social relations surrounding the *quilombos*. See Flávio dos Santos Gomes, *Histórias de quilombolas: Mocambos e comunidades de senzalas no Rio de Janeiro, século XIX*. São Paulo: Companhia das Letras, 2006.

41. The *quilombos*' names are given in the text: Maravilha ('Wonder'), Inferno ('Hell'), Cipoteua (from the Tupi – a type of tropical creeper) and Caxangue (a region of Africa on the *Costa da Mina*).

42. For the *quilombos* of the Lower Amazon, see Eurípedes Funes, 'Nasci nas matas, nunca tive senhor; história e memória dos mocambos do baixo Amazonas', in Reis and dos Santos Gomes (eds.), *Liberdade por um fio*.

43. *Babaçu* – a tall pinnate-leaved palm.

44. A flowering vine that puts out a red berry with medicinal qualities.

45. In the colony most of the major cities were on the coast. The coastal plains were separated from the interior by mountains covered in forest – the *Zona da Mata* ('coastal wooded zone').

46. For Palmares, see Flávio Gomes (ed.), *Mocambos de Palmares: História e fontes (séculos XVI–XIX)* (Rio de Janeiro: 7Letras, 2010); Edison Car-

neiro, *O quilombo de Palmares* (São Paulo: Nacional, 1988); Décio Freitas, *Palmares: A guerra dos escravos*, 5th edn. rewritten, revised and expanded (l. Porto Alegre: Mercado Aberto, 1984).

47. The Royal Circle of the Monkey.

48. For the use of the term 'república', see 'Relação das guerras feitas aos Palmares de Pernambuco no tempo do governador dom Pedro de Almeida (1675–1678)', quoted in Gomes (ed.), *Mocambos de Palmares*, pp. 220 ff. See also Sebastião da Rocha Pita, *História da América portuguesa* (São Paulo and Belo Horizonte: Edusp/Itatiaia, 1976, vol. 8, p. 215). For the use of the term 'república' in Portuguese political culture, see Heloisa Maria Murgel Starling, 'A liberdade era amável ou como ser republicano na América portuguesa (séculos XVII e XVIII)'. Belo Horizonte: UFMG, 2013. PhD (Brazilian history).

49. For data on the population, see Ronaldo Vainfas, *Antônio Vieira: Jesuíta do rei*. São Paulo: Companhia das Letras, 2011, p. 270.

50. Antônio Frederico de Castro Alves (1847–1871) was an abolitionist poet who died of tuberculosis at the age of twenty-four. He was known as the 'Slaves' Poet' for his ardent condemnation of slavery in such poems as *Os Escravos* ('The Slaves') and *O Navio Negreiro* ('The Slave Ship').

51. Castro Alves, 'Saudação a Palmares', in *Obra completa*. Rio de Janeiro: Nova Aguilar, 1960.

52. Slavery was abolished in Brazil on 13 May 1888.

53. For a compilation of the various versions of Palmares in the Brazilian popular imagination, see Jean Marcel Carvalho França and Ricardo Alexandre Ferreira, *Três vezes Zumbi: A construção de um herói brasileiro*. São Paulo: Três Estrelas, 2012.

54. The word *capitão* means 'captain', and *mato* ('wood', 'brush' or 'forest') referred to the country in opposition to the city.

55. For the *capitão do mato*, see Silvia Hunold Lara, 'Do singular ao plural: Palmares, capitães do mato e o governo dos escravos', in Reis and Dos Santos Gomes (eds.), *Liberdade por um fio*.

56. For the use of St Anthony for the repression of escaped slaves, see Luiz Mott, 'Santo Antônio, o divino capitão do mato', in Reis and Dos Santos Gomes (eds.), *Liberdade por um fio*.

57. For the 'tomadia', see Carlos Magno Guimarães, *Uma negação da ordem escravista: Quilombos em Minas Gerais no século XVIII*. São Paulo: Ícone, 1988.

58. For acts of sabotage of the sugar industry, see Schwartz, *Sugar Plantations in the Formation of Brazilian Society*.

59. *Terreiro* (from the Latin *terrarium*) is an area of beaten earth. It is still the name for the area where the ceremonies of Afro-Brazilian cults are performed.

60. See, for example, Zeca Ligiéro, *Corpo a corpo: Estudo das performances brasileiras*. Rio de Janeiro: Garamond, 2011, especially chapter 3.

61. For *candomblé*, see Reginaldo Prandi, *Segredos guardados: Orixás na alma brasileira*. São Paulo: Companhia das Letras, 2005.
62. Gregório de Matos (1636–1696) was the colony's most famous baroque poet, best known for his satirical verses attacking the Catholic Church.
63. *Não há mulher desprezada/galã desfavorecido/que deixe de ir ao quilombo/ dançar o seu bocadinho.*
64. Gregório de Mattos, 'Preceito 1', in *Obra poética completa*. Rio de Janeiro: Record, 1984.
65. For the practice of *calundu*, see José Ramos Tinhorão, *Os sons dos negros no Brasil: Cantos, danças, folguedos – Origens*. São Paulo: Ed. 34, 2008.

4: GOLD!

1. For 'Cataguás', see Ricardo Ferreira Ribeiro, *Florestas anãs do sertão: O cerrado na história de Minas Gerais* (Belo Horizonte: Autêntica, 2005, vol. 1, p. 113); for the context of the discovery of gold in Portuguese America, see Sérgio Buarque de Holanda, 'A mineração: Antecedentes luso-brasileiros' (*História geral da civilização brasileira*. São Paulo: Difusão Europeia do Livro, 1960, 1: A época colonial, vol. 2); Charles R. Boxer, *A idade de ouro do Brasil: Dores de crescimento de uma sociedade colonial*, 3rd edn. (Rio de Janeiro: Nova Fronteira, 2000), especially chapter 2 (Original title: *The Golden Age of Brazil 1695–1750: Growing Pains of a Colonial Society*. Berkeley: University of California Press, 1962); Lucas Figueiredo, *Boa ventura! A corrida do ouro no Brasil (1697–1810) – A cobiça que forjou um país, sustentou Portugal e inflamou o mundo*, 5th edn. (Rio de Janeiro: Record, 2011).
2. Sérgio Buarque de Holanda, *Visão do Paraíso: Os motivos edênicos no descobrimento e colonização do Brasil*. São Paulo: Companhia das Letras, 2010.
3. The sentence is quoted from Sérgio Buarque de Holanda', see his *Visão do Paraíso*, p. 99.
4. The *Serra do Mar* (the coastal mountain chain) is a 1,500-kilometre-long system of mountain ranges and escarpments in southeastern Brazil.
5. For the first discoveries of gold and the importation of llamas, see Buarque de Holanda, *Visão do Paraíso*, p. 237.
6. André João Antonil, *Cultura e opulência do Brasil por suas drogas e minas*, 3rd edn. Belo Horizonte: Itatiaia; São Paulo: Edusp, 1982.
7. Diogo de Vasconcelos, *História antiga das Minas Gerais*, 4th edn. Belo Horizonte: Itatiaia, 1999, p. 123.
8. *Ouro Preto* – 'Black Gold' – was the name given to the capital of the then province of Minas Gerais, previously called Vila Rica, by Emperor Dom Pedro I, in 1823, a year after Brazilian independence.

9. For the expression 'ouro preto', see the letter from the *sertanista* Bento do Amaral Coutinho to the governor of Rio de Janeiro, Artur de Sá e Menezes, dated 16 January 1709, quoted by José Soares de Mello in *Emboabas: Crônica de uma revolução nativista – Documentos inéditos* (São Paulo: São Paulo Editora, 1929, pp. 239 ff).

10. Dom Pedro II (King Peter II) of the house of Bragança, King of Portugal from 1683 to 1706.

11. See 'Carta de d. João de Lencastro ao rei. Bahia, 7 de janeiro de 1701', in Orville A. Derby, 'Os primeiros descobrimentos de ouro nos distritos de Sabará e Caeté', *Revista do Instituto Histórico e Geográfico de São Paulo*, vol. 5 (1889–1900). See also 'Copia do papel que o Sr Dom Joam de Lancastro fez sobre a recadaçam dos quintos do ouro das minas que se descobrirão neste Brazil na era de 1701. Bahia, 12 janeiro 1701', in André João Antonil, *Cultura e opulência do Brasil por suas drogas e minas: Texte de l´édition de 1711, traduction française et commentaire critique par Andrée Mansuy* (Paris: Institut des Hautes Études de l'Amérique Latine, 1965).

12. Antônio Vieira, *Sermões: Obras completas do padre Antônio Vieira.* Porto: Lello e Irmão, 1959, vol. 5, p. 271.

13. The expression is a quote from Sérgio Buarque de Holanda, *Caminhos e fronteiras*, 3rd edn. São Paulo: Companhia das Letras, 2001.

14. For the origins of São Paulo, see Mário Neme, *Notas de revisão da história de São Paulo* (São Paulo: Anhambi, 1959); Jaime Cortesão, *A fundação de São Paulo, capital geográfica do Brasil* (Rio de Janeiro: Livros de Portugal, 1955); see also Roberto Pompeu de Toledo, *A capital da solidão: Uma história de São Paulo das origens a 1900* (Rio de Janeiro: Objetiva, 2003).

15. For the capture and imprisonment of Indians, see John Manuel Monteiro, *Negros da terra: Índios e bandeirantes nas origens de São Paulo* (São Paulo: Companhia das Letras, 1994). For the practice of catechizing the indigenous people and their resistance, see Vainfas, *Antônio Vieira.*

16. For the inspiration of the exploratory journeys of the Royal Ordnance Regiment, see Jaime Cortesão, *Introdução à história das bandeiras* (Lisbon: Portugália, 1964, vol. 1, pp. 55 ff). See also Pedro Puntoni, *A guerra dos bárbaros: Povos indígenas e a colonização do sertão nordeste do Brasil, 1650–1720* (São Paulo: Fapesp; Hucitec; Edusp, 2012, pp. 196 ff).

17. For the argument that the discovery of gold in Minas was the result of a deal between the Crown and the *Paulista bandeirantes*, above all see Francisco Eduardo de Andrade, *A invenção das Minas Gerais: Empresas, descobrimentos e entradas nos sertões do ouro da América portuguesa* (Belo Horizonte: Autêntica; Editora PUC Minas, 2008).

18. Rocky plateaus.

19. See, for example, Domingos Vandelli, 'Memória III: Sobre as Minas de ouro do Brasil', *Anais da Biblioteca Nacional do Rio de Janeiro*, Rio de Janeiro, vol. XX (1898), pp. 265–6.

20. See Waldemar de Almeida Barbosa, *Dicionário histórico-geográfico de Minas Gerais*. Belo Horizonte: Itatiaia, 1995. (Série Reconquista do Brasil, 181)

21. 'Swallows' Waterfall'.

22. Our Lady of Mount Carmel.

23. Our Lady of the Immaculate Conception.

24. For the installation of civil government and the foundation of the first towns, see Cláudia Damasceno Fonseca, *Arraiais e vilas d'el Rei: espaço e poder nas Minas setecentistas* (Belo Horizonte: Editora UFMG, 2011). For the discovery of gold in Minas, see Sérgio Buarque de Holanda, 'Metais e pedras preciosas', *História geral da civilização brasileira*; Antonil, *Cultura e opulência do Brasil por suas drogas e minas*; Vasconcelos, *História antiga das Minas Gerais*.

25. Inhabitant of the state of Minas Gerais.

26. For the Emboaba conflict, above all see Adriana Romeiro, *Paulistas e emboabas no coração das Minas: Ideias, práticas e imaginário político no século XVIII*. Belo Horizonte: Editora UFMG, 2009.

27. For a biography of Fernão Dias, see Afonso de E. Taunay, *A grande vida de Fernão Dias Pais*. Rio de Janeiro: José Olympio, 1955.

28. For the myth of the Sabarabuçu Mountains, see Buarque de Holanda, *Visão do Paraíso*.

29. Quoted in ibid., p. 84.

30. '*ao findar das chuvas, quase à entrada/do outono, quando a terra em sede requeimada/bebera longamente as águas da estação*'.

31. Olavo Bilac (1865–1918) was a Brazilian journalist consecrated as the country's most important Parnassian poet.

32. Olavo Bilac, 'O caçador de esmeraldas', *Obra reunida*. Rio de Janeiro: Nova Aguilar, 1996.

33. For the myth of Lake Vapabuçu, see Buarque de Holanda, *Visão do Paraíso*.

34. '*E as esmeraldas/Minas que matavam/de esperança e de febre/e nunca se achavam/e quando as achavam/eram verde engano?*', from Carlos Drummond de Andrade, 'Canto mineral', *Poesia completa e prosa*. Rio de Janeiro: Nova Aguilar, 1988.

35. Carlos Drummond de Andrade (1902–1987) was one of the great modernist poets.

36. For the importance of the undertaking and discovery by Fernão Dias, see Andrade, *A invenção das Minas Gerais*, above all chapter 2. For the strategy of food allotments, see also Buarque de Holanda, *Caminhos e fronteiras*.

37. The Mantiqueira Mountains (*Serra da Mantiqueira*) cross three southeastern states – São Paulo, Rio de Janeiro and Minas Gerais – starting from the banks of the Paraíba do Sul river and extending northeastwards for 320 kilometres.

38. Respectively the *General Route to the Interior*, the *Old Route* and the *São Paulo Route*.

39. For the roads that led into Minas during the seventeenth and eighteenth centuries, see Heloisa Maria Murgel Starling, 'Caminhos e descaminhos das Minas', in Heloisa Maria Murgel Starling, Gringo Cardia, Sandra Regina Goulart Almeida and Bruno Viveiros Martins (eds.), *Minas Gerais* (Belo Horizonte: Editora UFMG, 2011).

40. A large knife or machete.

41. *Garganta* is a geological term for a ravine or abyss. The ordinary meaning of the word is 'throat'.

42. For the adventures of Pedro Hanequim, see C. Adriana Romeiro, *Um visionário na corte de d. João V: Revolta e milenarismo nas Minas Gerais*. Belo Horizonte: Editora UFMG, 2001.

43. 'Copia do papel que o Sr Dom Joam de Lancastro fez sobre a recadaçam dos quintos do ouro das minas que se descobrirão neste Brazil na era de 1701. Bahia, 12 janeiro 1701', in Antonil, *Cultura e opulência do Brasil por suas drogas e minas*, p. 587.

44. Antonil, *Cultura e opulência no Brasil por suas drogas e minas*.

45. A woodworm that feeds off bamboo (*bicho*, 'insect'; *taquara*, a species of small bamboo).

46. 'O sertão era outro mar ignoto', from Raimundo Faoro, *Os donos do poder: Formação do patronato político brasileiro*. São Paulo: Globo, 1991, vol. 2. p. 154.

47. 'Representação de Pedro Barbosa Leal questionando as ordens de erigir duas casas de fundição, uma em Jacobina e outra em Rio das Contas, explicando que isso não evita o descaminho do ouro, e sugerindo que sejam construídas em Pernambuco, Bahia e Rio de Janeiro'. Rio de Janeiro: Fundação Biblioteca Nacional, Divisão de Manuscritos, 11–31, 25, 009, pp. 36–40.

48. For a description of the roads, see Antonil, *Cultura e opulência no Brasil por suas drogas e minas*; Teodoro Sampaio, *O rio São Francisco e a Chapada Diamantina* (Salvador: Livraria Progresso, 1955). For the smuggling routes, above all see 'Representação de Pedro Barbosa Leal questionando as ordens de erigir duas casas de fundição, uma em Jacobina e outra em Rio das Contas, explicando que isso não evita o descaminho do ouro, e sugerindo que sejam construídas em Pernambuco, Bahia e Rio de Janeiro', op. cit.

49. Originally a term for the quantity of grain that could be loaded into the bags carried by donkeys or mules, it is thought that during the colonial period an *alqueire* corresponded to about twenty-five kilograms.

50. At the end of the eighteenth century the value of one *réis* corresponded to approximately fifty cents of a real today.

51. Eduardo Frieiro, *Feijão, angu e couve*. Belo Horizonte: Imprensa da Universidade Federal de Minas Gerais, 1966, pp. 56–7.

52. A short musket with wide bore and flared muzzle that scattered lead shot at close range.

53. See José Vieira Couto, *Memória sobre a capitania das Minas Gerais: Seu território, clima e produções metálicas*, ed. Júnia Ferreira Furtado. Belo Horizonte: Fundação João Pinheiro, 1994.

54. *Fluminense*, from the Latin for 'river', refers to the people and the land of the state of Rio de Janeiro. The *Baixada Fluminense* is the name of the low-lying lands between the coast and the mountains.

55. Passage from Sir Richard Burton's *Exploration of the Highlands of Brazil* (1869).

56. *Minhocas*, 'earthworms'; *macaúba*, Tupi-Guarani for a species of palm tree; *jaguara*, originally Tupi-Guarani for 'jaguar'. (*Dicionário Houaiss*)

57. For the entry of merchandise into Minas, see, for example, Angelo Alves Carrara, *Minas e currais: Produção rural e mercado interno de Minas Gerais, 1674–1807*. Juiz de Fora: Editora da UFJF, 2007.

58. For the *quilombo* of São Bartolomeu, see Waldemar de Almeida Barbosa, *Negros e quilombos em Minas Gerais* (Belo Horizonte: n.p., 1972); see also Carlos Magno Guimarães, *Uma negação da ordem escravista: Quilombos em Minas Gerais no século XVIII* (São Paulo: Ícone, 1988).

59. Quoted in Almeida Barbosa, *Negros e quilombos em Minas Gerais*, p. 121. For the black women who sold food and vegetables in the streets in Minas, see Laura de Mello e Souza, *Desclassificados do ouro: A pobreza mineira no século XVIII* (Rio de Janeiro: Graal, 1982).

60. Quoted in Donald Ramos, 'O quilombo e o sistema escravista em Minas Gerais do século XVIII', in João José Reis Flávio dos Santos Gomes (eds.), op. cit., p. 186. For food shops in general, see also Mello e Souza, *Desclassificados do ouro*.

61. 'Carta de dom Pedro Miguel de Almeida ao rei de Portugal, 13 de junho de 1718', *Revista do Arquivo Público Mineiro*, Belo Horizonte (1898), vol. III, pp. 251–66.

62. 'Bando sobre quilombolas, 20 de dezembro de 1717', *Arquivo Público Mineiro*, Belo Horizonte, Seção Colonial, códice SC 11, p. 269. See also Boxer, *A idade de ouro do Brasil*, pp. 196–7.

63. See Magno Guimarães, *Uma negação da ordem escravista*; Queirós Mattoso, *Ser escravo no Brasil*.

64. For the gangs of thieves, above all see Carla Maria Junho Anastasia, *A geografia do crime: Violência nas Minas setecentistas*. Belo Horizonte: Editora UFMG, 2005.

65. For the population of poor people and vagrants in Minas, above all see Mello e Souza, *Desclassificados do ouro*.

66. Nowadays considered a national hero and leading propagandist of the 1789 conspiracy known as the *Inconfidência mineira* ('The Minas Disloyalty').

67. For mining techniques, see Sérgio Buarque de Holanda, 'A mineração: antecedentes luso-brasileiros', op. cit.; Buarque de Holanda, 'Metais e pedras preciosas'; Antonil, *Cultura e opulência do Brasil por suas drogas e minas*; Boxer, *A idade de ouro do Brasil*, especially chapters 2 and 7.

68. For data on the slave labour force, see Douglas Cole Libby, 'As populações escravas das Minas setecentistas: Um balanço preliminar', in Maria Efigênia Lage de Resende e Luiz Carlos Villalta (eds.), *História de Minas Gerais: As Minas setecentistas*. Belo Horizonte: Autêntica; Companhia do Tempo, 2007, vol. 1.

69. Antonil, *Cultura e opulência do Brasil por suas drogas e minas*, p. 167.

70. For taxation in Minas, see João Pandiá Calógeras, *As minas do Brasil e sua legislação* (Rio de Janeiro: Imprensa Nacional, 1905, 3 vols.); Virgílio Noya Pinto, *O ouro brasileiro e o comércio anglo-português* (São Paulo: Companhia Editora Nacional, 1979); Diogo Pereira de Vasconcelos, 'Minas e quintos do ouro', *Revista do Arquivo Público Mineiro*, Belo Horizonte, vol. 6, nos. 3/4 (July/December 1901), pp. 855–965.

71. For the statistics of gold production, see Noya Pinto, *O ouro brasileiro e o comércio anglo-português*, p. 114. See also Figueiredo, *Boa ventura!*

72. The expression is from Fritz Teixeira de Sales quoted in Mauro Werkema, *História, arte e sonho na formação de Minas*. Belo Horizonte: DUO Editorial, 2010.

73. José Joaquim da Rocha, *Geografia histórica da capitania de Minas Gerais*. Belo Horizonte: Fundação João Pinheiro; Centro de Estudos Históricos e Culturais, 1995.

74. For Vila Rica, see Cláudia Damasceno Fonseca, *Arraiais e vilas d'El Rei: espaço e poder nas Minas setecentistas* (Belo Horizonte: Editora UFMG, 2011); Laura de Mello e Souza, *Cláudio Manuel da Costa: O letrado dividido* (São Paulo: Companhia das Letras, 2011); Figueiredo, *Boa ventura!*; Manuel Bandeira, *Guia de Ouro Preto* (Rio de Janeiro: Ediouro, 2000); Lúcia Machado de Almeida, *Passeio a Ouro Preto* (Belo Horizonte: Editora UFMG, 2011).

75. The Counting House.

76. The poet, however, concludes the verse by saying that the churches of Vila Rica rival the beauty and permanence of the temples of Rome: *Presentes tem talvez os Santuários/Em que se hão de esgotar tantos erários/Onde Roma há de ver com glória rara/Que debalde aos seus templos disputara/A grandeza, o valor e a preeminência*. Cláudio Manuel da Costa, 'Vila Rica', in Domício Proença Filho (ed.), *A poesia dos inconfidentes: Poesia completa de Cláudio Manuel da Costa, Tomás Antônio Gonzaga e Alvarenga Peixoto* (Rio de Janeiro: Nova Aguilar, 1996), 'Canto x', p. 443. For the poetry of Cláudio Manuel da Costa, see Sérgio Alcides, *Estes penhascos: Cláudio Manuel da Costa e a paisagem das Minas* (São Paulo: Hucitec,

2003). For the importance of urban space in the work of the Minas poets of the seventeenth century, above all see Reinaldo Martiniano Marques, *Poeta e poesia inconfidentes: Um estudo de arqueologia poética* (Belo Horizonte: Universidade Federal de Minas Gerais, 1993). (PhD thesis)

77. The 'Letters from Chile' were satirical poems in blank verse that were critical of the governor and administration of Minas. They circulated in manuscript form. The narrator is an inhabitant of Santiago do Chile, a metaphor in the poem for Vila Rica.

78. Tomás Antônio Gonzaga, 'Cartas chilenas', in Proença Filho (ed.), *A poesia dos inconfidentes*, letters 3, 5, 6, 12). See also Sérgio Buarque de Holanda, 'As Cartas chilenas', in Sérgio Buarque de Holanda, *Tentativas de mitologia* (São Paulo: Perspectiva, 1979), and Tomás Antônio Gonzaga, 'Cartas chilenas', in Proença Filho (ed.), *A poesia dos inconfidentes*, letter 3, pp. 815, 818–19.

79. For the concession of freedom to slaves and the mixture of races in Minas, see Eduardo França Paiva, *Escravos e libertos nas Minas Gerais do século XVIII* (São Paulo: Annablume, 1995); Laura de Mello e Souza, 'Coartação; problemática e episódios referentes a Minas Gerais no século XVIII', and Laura de Mello e Souza, *Norma e conflito: Aspectos da história de Minas no século XVIII* (Belo Horizonte: Editora UFMG, 1999).

80. For the social structure in Minas, see Mello e Souza, *Desclassificados do ouro*.

81. For the Baroque in Minas, see Rodrigo Almeida Bastos, 'O barroco, sagrado e profano; o regime retórico das artes em Minas Gerais no século XVIII', in Starling, Cardia, Almeida and Viveiros Martins (eds.), *Minas Gerais; Brasil barroco: Entre céu e terra* (Paris: União Latina; Petit Palais, 1999); Benedito Lima de Toledo, *Esplendor do Barroco luso-brasileiro* (São Paulo: Ateliê Editorial, 2012); Afonso Ávila, *Resíduos setecentistas em Minas: Textos do século do ouro e as projeções do mundo barroco*, 2 vols. (Belo Horizonte: Arquivo Público Mineiro, 2006).

82. The Fraternity of Our Lady of the Rosary.

83. For the orders and lay fraternities, see Caio Boschi, *Os leigos e o poder*. São Paulo: Ática, 1986.

84. Rodrigo José Ferreira Bretas, *Traços biográficos relativos ao finado Antônio Francisco Lisboa, distinto escultor Mineiro, mais conhecido pelo apelido de Aleijadinho* (Belo Horizonte: Editora UFMG, 2013); André Guilherme Dornelles Dangelo and Vanessa Brasileiro, *O Aleijadinho arquiteto e outros ensaios sobre o tema* (Belo Horizonte: Escola de Arquitetura da UFMG, 2008).

85. The expression is from Laura de Mello e Souza. See Mello e Souza, *Desclassificados do ouro*, p. 38.

5: REVOLT, CONSPIRACY AND SEDITION

1. *Banda*, a strip or area of land; *além*, 'on the other side', 'beyond', 'over there'. An area distant from the city, across the bay, the other side of the river.

2. *Praça XV* is the shortened version used for *Praça XV de Novembro* – '15 November Square' – in the heart of Rio de Janeiro.

3. For Rio de Janeiro during the seventeenth century, see Vivaldo Coaracy, *O Rio de Janeiro no século XVII* (Rio de Janeiro: José Olympio, 1965); Maurício de Almeida Abreu, *Geografia histórica do Rio de Janeiro (1502–1700)* (Rio de Janeiro: Andrea Jakobsson Estúdio, 2010, 2 vols.). For the Guanabara Bay, see Bia Hetzel, *Baía de Guanabara* (Rio de Janeiro: Manati, 2000).

4. Our Lady of the Immaculate Conception.

5. For the revolt of 1660 in Rio de Janeiro, see Luciano Raposo de Almeida Figueiredo, 'Revoltas, fiscalidade e identidade colonial na América portuguesa; Rio de Janeiro, Bahia e Minas Gerais, 1640–1761' (PhD in history. São Paulo: FFLCH-USP, 1995, vol. 1); Miguel Arcanjo de Souza, 'Política e economia no Rio de Janeiro seiscentista: Salvador de Sá e a Bernarda de 1660–1661' (MA in history. Rio de Janeiro: CFCH-UFRJ, 1994); Antônio Felipe Pereira Caetano, 'Entre a sombra e o sol: A Revolta da Cachaça, a freguesia de São Gonçalo do Amarante e a crise política fluminense' (MA in history. Niterói: UFF, 2003).

6. The Fortress of Santa Cruz is located opposite the Sugar Loaf in the district of Jurujuba, Niterói, protecting the entrance to the bay. The Portuguese occupied the location in 1584, making it the oldest fort in the state of Rio.

7. The estimate is from Frei Vicente do Salvador, *Historia do Brazil 1560–1627* (Rio de Janeiro and São Paulo: Versal/Odebrecht, 2008). For the sugar culture, see Roberto Simonsen, *História econômica do Brasil (1500–1820)* (São Paulo: Companhia Editora Nacional, 1962); Tamás Szmrecányi (ed.), *História econômica do período colonial* (São Paulo: Hucitec, 1996); Celso Furtado, *Economia colonial no Brasil nos séculos XVI e XVII* (São Paulo: Hucitec, 2001); Luiz Felipe de Alencastro, *O trato dos viventes: Formação do Brasil no Atlântico sul séculos XVI e XVII* (São Paulo: Companhia das Letras, 2000).

8. For the trade and smuggling of slaves, see Manolo Florentino (ed.), *Tráfico, cativeiro e liberdade: Rio de Janeiro, séculos XVII–XIX* (Rio de Janeiro: Civilização Brasileira, 2005).

9. *Carioca* – an inhabitant of the city of Rio de Janeiro.

10. Individuals with one black and one Indian parent.

11. See Luís da Câmara Cascudo, *Prelúdio da cachaça: Etnologia, história e sociologia da aguardente no Brasil* (Belo Horizonte: Itatiaia, 1986).

12. For Sá e Benevides, see Charles R. Boxer, *Salvador de Sá e a luta pelo Brasil e Angola 1602–1686* (São Paulo: Edusp, 1973); Francisco Adolfo de Varnhagen, 'Biografia de Salvador Correia de Sá' (Rio de Janeiro, *Revista do IHGB*, vol. 3, 1841).

13. Alencastro, *O trato dos viventes*, p. 197.

14. 'Governor's Island' and 'Galleon Point'. The latter is now the location of Rio de Janeiro's International Airport, Galeão.

15. 'Carta dos oficiais da Câmara do Rio de Janeiro dirigida ao rei, em 31 de dezembro de 1660', in José Vieira Fazenda, 'Antiqualha e memórias do Rio de Janeiro', Rio de Janeiro, *Revista do IHGB*, vol. 89 (1921), pp. 9–33.

16. See Carl E. H. Vieira de Mello, *O Rio de Janeiro no Brasil quinhentista*. São Paulo: Giordano, 1996.

17. The *Fortaleza de São Sebastão* (St Sebastian Fortress) was build on the *Morro de Castelo* (Castle Hill), to which the town was transferred in 1567, two years after its foundation by Estácio de Sá on the *Morro Cara de Cão* (Dog-faced Hill) at the foot of the Sugarloaf at the entrance to the bay.

18. Jerônimo Barbalho Bezerra (1616–1661).

19. For the revolts, see Almeida Figueiredo, 'Revoltas, fiscalidade e identidade colonial na América portuguesa'.

20. Silvia Hunold Lara (ed.), *Ordenações Filipinas: Livro V*. São Paulo: Companhia das Letras, 1999.

21. Almeida Figueiredo, 'Revoltas, fiscalidade e identidade colonial na América portuguesa', pp. 277 ff. For the common motives behind most of the settlers's revolts, see idem, 'Além de súditos: notas sobre revoltas e identidade colonial na América portuguesa', Niterói, *Tempo*, vol. 5, n. 10 (2000), pp. 81–95.

22. *St Benedict Street.*

23. For the revolt of 1666 in Pernambuco, see Evaldo Cabral de Mello, *A fronda dos mazombos: Nobres contra mascates, Pernambuco, 1666–1715*. São Paulo: Ed. 34, 2003.

24. Antônio Vieira, *Sermões*, vol. 1. São Paulo: Hedra, 2003.

25. '*Esta é a causa original das doenças do Brasil: tomar o alheio, cobiças, interesses, ganhos e conveniências particulares por onde a Justiça se não guarda e o Estado se perde. Perde-se o Brasil (digamo-lo em uma palavra) porque alguns ministros de Sua Majestade não vêm cá buscar nosso bem, vêm cá buscar nossos bens'.*

26. The present-day state of Sergipe.

27. For a chronology of the revolts and armed uprisings in colonial America in the seventeenth and eighteenth centuries, see Luciano Figueiredo, *Rebeliões no Brasil Colônia* (Rio de Janeiro: Jorge Zahar, 2005). For an overview of these movements, see Laura de Mello e Souza, 'Motines, revueltas y revoluciones en la America portuguesa de los siglos XVII y XVIII', in J. H. Lehuedé (ed.), *História general de America Latina* (Madrid: Trotta, 2000, vol. 4).

28. For the Beckman revolt, see Milson Coutinho, *A revolta de Bequimão* (São Luís: Geia, 2004); João Francisco Lisboa, *Crônica do Brasil colonial: Apontamentos para a história do Maranhão* (Petrópolis and Brasília: Vozes/Instituto Nacional do Livro, 1976).
29. 'The trading Company of Maranhão and Grão-Pará'. The latter refers to the present-day Amazonian state of Pará, which borders Maranhão to the north.
30. *Nosso Senhor dos Passos* – referring to the *Passos da Via Sacra* (Stations of the Cross).
31. The Company of Jesus.
32. Where the São Luís Council Chamber and the Customs House were located.
33. A citizen of the captaincy (later the province and today the state) of Bahia.
34. For the Maneta uprisings and their causes, see Sebastião da Rocha Pitta, *História da América portuguesa* (Belo Horizonte and São Paulo: Itatiaia/Edusp, 1976); Braz do Amaral e Ignácio Accioli, *Memória histórica e política da província da Bahia* (Salvador: Imprensa Oficial do Estado, 1931, vol. 3). For the meaning of *motins*, see Jean Delumeau, *História do medo no ocidente 1300–1800* (São Paulo: Companhia das Letras, 1989).
35. In Salvador a steep, almost vertical hillside rises up behind the port. The district along the front of the bay is called the Lower City (*Cidade Baixa*) and the old town on the top of the hill the Upper City (*Cidade Alta*). They are connected by sharply sloping streets, many with hairpin bends that descend the hillside.
36. *Dízimo* – a 10 per cent tax levied on produce.
37. See George Rudé, *Ideology and Popular Protest* (New York: Pantheon, 1980). See also Delumeau, *História do medo no ocidente 1300–1800*, especially chapter 4.
38. *Discurso histórico e político sobre a sublevação que nas Minas houve no ano de 1720*. Belo Horizonte: Fundação João Pinheiro/Centro de Estudos Históricos e Culturais, 1994, p. 59. The author is anonymous, attributed by Laura de Mello e Souza to Don Pedro Miguel de Almeida Portugal and to the two Jesuits who accompanied him during their stay in Minas: José Mascarenhas and Antônio Correia. See Laura de Mello e Souza, 'Estudo crítico', in *Discurso histórico e político sobre a sublevação que nas Minas houve no ano de 1720*, op. cit.
39. For the rebellions in Minas during the first half of the eighteenth century, see Carla Maria Junho Anastasia, *Vassalos rebeldes: Violência coletiva nas Minas na primeira metade do século XVIII* (Belo Horizonte: Editora C/Arte, 1998). For Catas Altas and Pitangui, see Vagner da Silva Cunha, *A 'rochela' das minas de ouro? Paulistas na vila de Pitangui (1709–1721)*. MA theses in history (Belo Horizonte: UFMG, 2009).
40. For the causes of the Vila Rica Sedition, see 'Termo que se fez sobre a proposta do povo de Vila Rica na ocasião em que veio amotinado a Vila do

Carmo, 2 de julho de 1720', *Arquivo Público Mineiro*, Belo Horizonte, seção colonial, códice SC 06, pp. 95–7. For a history of the Sedition, see Feu de Carvalho, *Ementário da história mineira: Felipe dos Santos Freire na sedição de Villa Rica em 1720* (Belo Horizonte: Edições Históricas, 1933); Diogo de Vasconcelos, *História antiga das Minas Gerais* (Belo Horizonte: Itatiaia, 1999).

41. In colonial Brazil the *ouvidor* was the senior judge who presided over the legal system of the captaincy (from the verb *ouvir*, 'one who listens').

42. The *Morro do Arraial do Ouro Podre* (the Hill behind Rotten Gold Village).

43. For the Revolts in the Backlands, see Diogo de Vasconcelos, *História média de Minas Gerais* (Belo Horizonte: Itatiaia, 1974); Junho Anastasia, *Vassalos rebeldes*, especially chapter 3.

44. 'Carta do governador Martinho de Mendonça para Gomes Freire de Andrade, 23 de julho de 1736', *Arquivo Público Mineiro*, Belo Horizonte, seção colonial, códice SG 55, fl. 91–2.

45. 'Carta do governador Martinho de Mendonça para o secretário de Estado Antônio Guedes Pereira, 17 de outubro de 1737', Belo Horizonte, *Revista do Arquivo Público Mineiro*, vol. 1 (1896), p. 662.

46. See Almeida Figueiredo, 'Revoltas, fiscalidade e identidade colonial na América portuguesa'.

47. The singularity is pointed out by Evaldo Cabral de Mello in a comparative analysis of the emboaba uprising and the Pernambuco uprisings in 1710 and 1711. Cabral de Mello, *A fronda dos mazombos*, pp. 358–9.

48. The War of the *Mascates* – 'street hawkers' or 'itinerant street sellers' – a derogatory term used by the 'refined' Brazilian inhabitants of Olinda for the 'uncouth' Portuguese inhabitants of Recife.

49. For the complex story of the characters and events in the *Guerra dos Mascates*, see, especially, Cabral de Mello, *A fronda dos mazombos*.

50. See Joaquim Dias Martins, 'Os mártires pernambucanos, vítimas da liberdade nas duas revoluções ensaiadas em 1710 e 1817, Recife, 1853', pp. 272–3, and Maximiano Lopes Machado, 'História da província da Paraíba' (Paraíba: Imprensa Oficial, 1912, p. 366), quoted in Cabral de Mello, *A fronda dos mazombos*, pp. 308–9 and 311–12.

51. Referred to at the time as 'men of letters' – *letrados*.

52. For a description of the conspirators, see Márcio Jardim, *A Inconfidência mineira: Uma síntese factual* (Rio de Janeiro: Biblioteca do Exército Editora, 1989). For a biography of Gonzaga, see Adelto Gonçalves, *Gonzaga, um poeta do Iluminismo* (Rio de Janeiro: Nova Fronteira, 1999). For Cláudio Manuel da Costa, see Sérgio Alcides, *Estes penhascos: Cláudio Manuel da Costa e a paisagem das Minas* (São Paulo: Hucitec, 2003); Laura de Mello e Souza, *Cláudio Manuel da Costa* (São Paulo: Companhia das Letras, 2011).

53. José da Silva e Oliveira Rolim (1747–1835).

54. *Capangueiros* – men who purchased gold and gems directly from the miners.

55. For a biography of Padre Rolim, see Roberto Wagner de Almeida, *Entre a cruz e a espada: A saga do valente e devasso padre Rolim* (São Paulo: Paz e Terra, 2002). For the interests and activities of the Minas elite considered illegal by the Crown, see Kenneth Maxwell, *A devassa da devassa: A Inconfidência mineira Brasil-Portugal (1750–1808)* (São Paulo: Paz e Terra, 2009).

56. Francisco de Paula Freire de Andrade, '2a Inquirição: Rio, Fortaleza da Ilha das Cobras – 25 de janeiro de 1790', in *Autos da Devassa da Inconfidência Mineira*, vol. 5. Brasília and Belo Horizonte: Câmara dos Deputados/Imprensa Oficial de Minas Gerais, 1982, p. 180.

57. For the causes of the movement, see Maxwell, *A devassa da devassa*; Roberta Giannubilo Stumpf, *Filhos das Minas, americanos e portugueses: Identidades coletivas na capitania de Minas Gerais (1763–1792)*. São Paulo: Hucitec, 2010.

58. See 'Inquirição de Testemunhas (1). Testemunha 4a', in *Autos da Devassa da Inconfidência Mineira*, op. cit., p. 156, vol. 1.

59. Kenneth Maxwell (ed.), *O livro de Tiradentes: Transmissão atlântica de ideias políticas no século XVIII*. São Paulo: Penguin Classics Companhia das Letras, 2013.

60. For Tiradentes' skills in the art of healing, see Junia Ferreira Furtado, 'Dos dentes e seus tratamentos: A história da odontologia no período colonial', in Heloisa Maria Murgel Starling, Betânia Gonçalves Figueiredo, Júnia Ferreira Furtado and Lígia Beatriz de Paula Germano (eds.), *Odontologia: História restaurada* (Belo Horizonte: Editora UFMG, 2007, pp. 49 ff). For Tiradentes' activities as commander of the Caminho Novo, see Carla Maria Junho Anastasia, *A geografia do crime: Violência nas Minas Setecentistas* (Belo Horizonte: Editora UFMG, 2005), especially chapter 3. For further biographical information on Tiradentes, see Lúcio José dos Santos, *A Inconfidência mineira: Papel de Tiradentes na Inconfidência mineira* (Belo Horizonte: Imprensa Oficial, 1972).

61. José Joaquim Maia e Barbalho (1757–1788).

62. For the lack of international support for the Minas Conspiracy, see Kenneth Maxwell, 'A Inconfidência mineira: Dimensões internacionais', in Kenneth Maxwell, *Chocolate, piratas e outros malandros: Ensaios tropicais*. São Paulo: Paz e Terra, 1999.

63. For the Embuçado, see 'Ofício do Visconde de Barbacena a Luís de Vasconcelos e Souza, vice-rei, sobre o início da repressão em Minas', in *Autos da Devassa da Inconfidência Mineira*, op. cit., vol. 8, pp. 170–1. See also 'Inquirição das testemunhas, Casa do Ouvidor, 11-01-1790', in *Autos da Devassa da Inconfidência Mineira*, op. cit., vol. 2, pp. 237 ff.

64. For the denunciations, see *Autos da Devassa da Inconfidência Mineira*, op. cit., vol. 1.
65. Dona Maria I became Queen of Portugal in 1777.
66. The *Tribunais da Relação* were the Portuguese High Courts. *Cadeia* means 'gaol'. The prisoners were held in the prison of the High Court that had jurisdiction over the district *(comarca)* of Rio de Janeiro.
67. *Ilha das Cobras* – 'Snake Island' – an island in Guanabara Bay at a short distance from the city centre. Initially fortified in the early seventeenth century to protect the city from invasion, in 1789 there were three fortresses located on the island.
68. For the death of Cláudio Manuel da Costa, see Jardim, *A Inconfidência mineira*; Mello e Souza, *Cláudio Manuel da Costa*.
69. Counting House.
70. New Prison.
71. Santiago's book was published in 1994, when the 'suicides' of political prisoners tortured during the military regime (1964–85) were still very much alive in the national memory.
72. *Modinhas* are short rhymed poems that were sung to a guitar in the streets and at family gatherings.
73. In 1890, one year after the foundation of the Republic, the *Largo da Lampadosa* – one of the oldest squares in the city centre – was renamed *Praça Tiradentes* and 1 April declared a national holiday.
74. As noted by Vilhena, an important chronicler of colonial Brazil, in *A Bahia no século XVIII*, vol. 2 (Salvador: Editora Itapuã, 1969, p. 425). The term 'pasquim' was used in Portugal for a certain type of pamphlet.
75. The central square in the old town where the pillory (or whipping post) was located. For the date and locations where the pamphlets were fixed, see, especially, Luís Henrique Dias Tavares, *História da sedição intentada na Bahia em 1798 ('A conspiração dos alfaiates')* (São Paulo and Brasília: Pioneira/ Instituto Nacional do Livro, 1975).
76. There are eleven pamphlets in all. The originals can be found in the Arquivo Público do Estado da Bahia (Seção Histórica, maços 578 and 581). There are also copies in the manuscript section of the Biblioteca Nacional (1–28; 23/nos. 1–12, Coleção Martins). They were published in their entirety by Dias Tavares, *História da sedição intentada na Bahia em 1798*, pp. 22–40; Kátia de Queirós Mattoso, *Presença francesa no movimento democrático baiano de 1798* (Salvador: Editora Itapuã, 1969, pp. 144–59).
77. For a history of the Bahia Conspiracy, see István Jancsó, *Na Bahia contra o Império: História do ensaio da sedição de 1798*. São Paulo and Salvador: Hucitec; EDUFba, 1996.
78. Defamatory pamphlets began to be documented in Portuguese America by the Tribunal do Santo Ofício (the Portuguese Inquisition) between 1587

and 1591. See Emanuel Araújo, *O teatro dos vícios: Transgressão e transigência na sociedade urbana colonial* (Rio de Janeiro: José Olympio, 2008), esp. pp. 330 ff.

79. For the targets of the pamphlets, see Kátia de Queirós Mattoso, 'Bahia 1789: Os panfletos revolucionários – Proposta de uma nova leitura), in Osvaldo Coggiola, *A Revolução Francesa e seu impacto na América Latina* (São Paulo: Nova Stella Editorial/Edusp, 1990, pp. 346 ff).

80. See 'Panfleto 50 Prelo', in Queirós Mattoso, *Presença francesa no movimento democrático baiano de 1798*, p. 151.

81. The uprising is often referred to as the Tailors' Revolt (*A revolta dos Alfaiates*).

82. 'Perguntas a Antônio Ignacio Ramos: A Inconfidência da Bahia em 1798 – Devassas e Sequestros', Rio de Janeiro, *Anais da Biblioteca Nacional*, vols. 43–4 (1920–1), pp. 130–4. See also Dias Tavares, *História da sedição intentada na Bahia em 1798*, p. 100.

83. A cowrie shell. *Búzios* are used in African religions for divination.

84. 'Continuação das perguntas a José de Freitas Sacoto, pardo, livre e preso nas cadeias desta Relação: Autos da Devassa do Levantamento e Sedição Intentados na Bahia em 1798', *Anais do Arquivo Público da Bahia*, Salvador: Imprensa Oficial da Bahia, vol. XXXV (1961), p. 129.

85. For the inscription and the conspiracy flag, see Bráz Hermenegildo do Amaral, 'A conspiração republicana da Bahia de 1798', in Bráz Hermenegildo do Amaral, *Fatos da vida do Brasil*. Salvador: Tipografia Naval, 1941, p. 14.

86. 'Assentada: Autos da Devassa do Levantamento e Sedição Intentados na Bahia em 1798', op. cit., vol. XXXVI, p. 406.

87. 'Perguntas a Joaquim José de Santa Anna: A Inconfidência da Bahia em 1798 – Devassas e Sequestros', *Anais da Biblioteca Nacional*, Rio de Janeiro, vol. 45 (1920–1), p. 119.

88. For the suppression of the conspiracy, see Patrícia Valim, 'Da contestação à conversão: a punição exemplar dos réus da Conjuração Baiana de 1798'. *Topoi*, Niterói, vol. 10, n. 18, pp. 14–23, January/June 2009; István Jancsó, 'Teoria e prática da contestação na colônia', in Jancsó, *Na Bahia contra o Império; história do ensaio da sedição de 1798*.

6: SHIP AHOY!

1. This chapter is based on the research undertaken for the book *A longa viagem da biblioteca dos reis: Do terremoto de Lisboa à Independência do Brasil* (São Paulo: Companhia das Letras, 2002) by Angela Marques da Costa, Paulo Cesar de Azevedo and Lilia Moritz Schwarcz.

2. For the period before his acclamation as king (in 1818), we refer to Dona Maria I's son as Don João, and after his mother was declared incapable, as

the Prince Regent Don João. His full name was João Maria José Francisco Xavier de Paula Luís Antônio Domingos Rafael de Bragança.

3. Fernando Novais, *Portugal e Brasil na crise do antigo sistema colonial* (*1777–1808*). São Paulo: Hucitec, 1989, p. 18.

4. Fernando Pó (now called Bioko) and Ano Bom (Annobón), along with São Tomé and Principe, are islands in the Gulf of Guinea.

5. Ana Cristina Bartolomeu de Araújo, 'As invasões francesas e a afirmação das ideias liberais', in José Mattoso, *História de Portugal*. Lisboa: Estampa, (1989), p. 17, vol. 5: o liberalismo, 1807–90.

6. *Luto cerrado*, literally 'closed mourning', during which dressing in black was mandatory even indoors and all forms of entertainment were banned; and *luto aliviado*, literally 'alleviated mourning', when the dress code and other restrictions were relaxed.

7. Luiz Carlos Villalta, *1789–1808: O império luso-brasileiro e os Brasis* (São Paulo: Companhia das Letras, 2000), p. 126. For the Portuguese neutrality policy and the fear provoked by the French Revolution, see Lúcia Maria Bastos Pereira das Neves, *Napoleão Bonaparte: Imaginário e política em Portugal – c. 1808–1810* (São Paulo: Alameda, 2008).

8. According to Pedro Penner da Cunha, *Sob fogo: Portugal e Espanha entre 1800 e 1820* (Lisbon: Horizonte, 1988), p. 138. (Coleção Horizonte Histórico, 14)

9. Bartolomeu de Araújo, 'As invasões francesas e a afirmação das ideias liberais', p. 19.

10. J. B. F. Carrère, *Panorama de Lisboa no ano de 1796*. Lisboa: Biblioteca Nacional/Secretaria do Estado da Cultura, 1989, p. 60.

11. Carl Israel Ruders, *Viagem a Portugal: 1798–1802*. Lisbon: Biblioteca Nacional/Secretaria de Estado da Cultura, 1981, p. 36.

12. Bartolomeu de Araújo, 'As invasões francesas e a afirmação das ideias liberais', p. 21.

13. Carrère, *Panorama de Lisboa no ano de 1796*, p. 56.

14. Olivença (in Spanish, Olivenza), on the disputed border between Spain and Portugal, was ceded to Spain at the Treaty of Badajoz (1801). Although it has been administered by Spain ever since, Portugal claims the treaty should be revoked and the town, with the surrounding territory, returned.

15. Bartolomeu de Araújo, 'As invasões francesas e a afirmação das ideias liberais', p. 22.

16. Oliveira Lima, *Dom João VI no Brasil*, 3rd edn. (Rio de Janeiro: Topbooks, 1996), pp. 177–89. See also Francisca L. Nogueira de Azevedo, *Carlota Joaquina na corte do Brasil* (Rio de Janeiro: Civilização Brasileira, 2003).

17. José Hermano Saraiva, *História de Portugal*. Mem Martins: Publicações Europa-América, 1998, p. 300.

18. Lima, *Dom João VI no Brasil*, p. 43.

19. Alexandre José de Mello Moraes, *História da transladação da Corte portuguesa para o Brasil em 1807–1808*, vol. 1. Rio de Janeiro: E. Dupont, 1982, p. 112.

20. Dom João V (King John V), King of Portugal from 1706 to 1750.

21. Luís da Cunha, born Lisbon 1662, died Paris 1749, was a Portuguese diplomat during the reign of Dom João V. He was considered an 'Estrangeirado' (from *estrangeiro*, 'a foreigner') due to the influence exerted on him by foreign ideas.

22. Kátia de Carvalho, *Travessia das letras*. Rio de Janeiro: Casa da Palavra, 1999, p. 156.

23. 'Relato de d. Rodrigo de Sousa Coutinho, conde de Linhares'. Rio de Janeiro: Biblioteca Nacional, ms. 11 30, 35, 60.

24. Dom Pedro Miguel de Almeida Portugal e Vasconcelos (1688–1756) inherited the title of third Count of Assumar in 1718, a year after his appointment as governor of the captaincy of Minas Gerais, where he became famous for his repression of the 'Vila Rica Sedition' (also known as the 'Felipe dos Santos Revolt') in 1720 (see chapter 4).

25. Carta de 30 de maio de 1801, Arquivo Público do Rio de Janeiro', in Lima, *Dom João VI no Brasil*, p. 45. The subsequent quotes, attributed to the Marquis of Alorna, are from the same document.

26. Joel Serrão, *Cronologia de Portugal*. Lisboa: Iniciativas Editoriais, 1971, p. 376.

27. Lima, *Dom João VI no Brasil*, p. 46; see also Maria Graham, *Journal or a Voyage to Brazil and residence there, London, 1824* (London: Longman, 1824).

28. The monumental palace-monastery of Mafra was built between 1717 and 1755.

29. Anônimo, 'Jornada do sr. d. João VI ao Brasil em 1807', in Ângelo Pereira, *Os filhos d'el Rei d. João VI*. Lisbon: Empresa Nacional de Publicidade, 1946, p. 101.

30. Lima, *Dom João VI no Brasil*, p. 49.

31. Anônimo, 'Jornada do sr. d. João VI ao Brasil em 1807', p. 101.

32. The Prince Regent and Carlota Joaquina had eight children: Maria Teresa, the Princess of Beira, the infantas Maria Isabel, Maria da Assunção, Maria Fransisca de Assis and Anna de Jesus Maria, and their two brothers, the eight-year-old Pedro, future Emperor of Brazil (and, for a few weeks, King of Portugal), and his six-year-old brother Dom Miguel.

33. Lima, *Dom João VI no Brasil*, p. 47.

34. Alan K. Manchester, 'A transferência da corte portuguesa para o Rio de Janeiro', in H. Keith and Edward S. F. (eds.), *Conflito e continuidade na sociedade brasileira*, trs. José Laurênio de Melo. Rio de Janeiro: Civilização Brasileira, 1970, p. 67.

35. *Carta do Visconde de Anadia ao Príncipe Regente, de 29 de setembro de 1807*. Rio de Janeiro: Arquivo Nacional/Fundo Negócios de Portugal, 1807, caixa 714.

36. The Collect, from Latin *collecta* (the gathering of people together), is a Marian litany (a form of prayer to the Blessed Virgin Mary) used in church services and processions.

37. Camilo Luís Rossi, *Diário dos acontecimentos de Lisboa, por ocasião da entrada das tropas, escrito por uma testemunha*. Lisbon: Oficinas Gráficas da Casa Portuguesa, 1944, p. 6.

38. Manchester, 'A transferência da corte portuguesa para o Rio de Janeiro', p. 68.

39. 'Carta do frei Matias de São Bruno sobre notícias militares contra a Inglaterra. Cartuxa, 2 de novembro de 1807', in Enéas Martins Filho, p. 51.

40. Martins Filho, p. 16.

41. 'Parecer do Marques de Pombal, 2 de novembro de 1807', in ibid., p. 59.

42. João Rodrigues de Sá e Melo (born Aveiro 1755, died Rio de Janeiro 1809), Viscount and later Count of Anadia.

43. Ibid., p. 62.

44. Manchester, 'A transferência da corte portuguesa para o Rio de Janeiro', p. 181.

45. Lima, *Dom João VI no Brasil*, p. 37.

46. Mello Moraes, *História da transladação da Corte portuguesa para o Brasil em 1807–1808*, p. 53.

47. Rossi, *Diário dos acontecimentos de Lisboa*, p. 9.

48. Domingos de Sousa Coutinho, *Cartas a Sua Alteza Real*. Rio de Janeiro: Biblioteca Nacional, 1807, ms., 10, 3, 29. All subsequent quotes are from this document.

49. Dom Pedro José Joaquim Vito de Meneses Coutinho, born Lisbon c. 1775, died Paris 1823.

50. 'Assento tomado em Conselho de Estado no Real Palácio da Ajuda em 8 de Novembro de 1807 na presença de S.A.R.O Príncipe Regente Nosso Senhor', in Martins Filho, op. cit., p. 68.

51. Manchester, 'A transferência da corte portuguesa para o Rio de Janeiro', p. 181.

52. Penner da Cunha, *Sob fogo*, p. 76.

53. Manchester, 'A transferência da corte portuguesa para o Rio de Janeiro', p. 71.

54. The entire passage can be found in Francisco Adolfo de Varnhagen, 'História da independência do Brasil', *Revista do IHGB*, Rio de Janeiro, vol. 173 (1962), pp. 58–9.

55. Joaquim José de Azevedo (1761–1835) was a Portuguese aristocrat and court official in both Portugal and Brazil.

56. João Manuel Pereira da Silva, *História da fundação do Império brasileiro*, vol. 1. Rio de Janeiro: L. Garnier, 1865, pp. 114–15.

57. The *Palácio de Nossa Senhora da Ajuda* – the Palace of Our Lady of Divine Assistance – was initially built by Dom José I in 1761, in the wake of the

earthquake that destroyed most of Lisbon in 1755, as a temporary structure. Construction began in 1802, and parts of the project were still incomplete when the royal family left for Brazil.

58. *Exposição analítica e justificativa de conduta* . . . Rio de Janeiro: Biblioteca Nacional, 1821, Rare words section, 37, 17, 1, p. 5.

59. Rossi, *Diário dos acontecimentos de Lisboa*, p. 11.

60. Mello Moraes, *História da transladação da Corte portuguesa para o Brasil em 1807–1808*, p. 61.

61. The Irish lieutenant Thomas O'Neil, an officer aboard one of the British ships that accompanied the Portuguese fleet to Rio de Janeiro, published his notes in 1810. Although widely consulted, both the facts and the style are also thought by many to be exaggerated.

62. Rio de Janeiro: Biblioteca Nacional, Seção de Obras Raras, 32, 1, 11.

63. See Marques da Costa, Azevedo and Schwarcz, *A longa viagem da biblioteca dos reis*.

64. Emílio Joaquim da Silva Maia, Rio de Janeiro, Instituto Histórico e Geográfico Brasileiro, lata 245, doc. 7, [n.d.], and Pereira da Silva, *História da fundação do império brasileiro*, p. 118.

65. The hereditary title of Dom Nuno da Silva Telo de Meneses Corte Real (1746–1813), seventh Count of Aveiras.

66. Mello Moraes, *História da transladação da Corte portuguesa para o Brasil em 1807–1808*, p. 6.

67. Emílio Joaquim da Silva Maia, 'Embarque, séquito e viagem da família real portuguesa. Arribada à Bahia. Estado do Brasil no tempo de colônia. Desembarque no Rio de Janeiro. Primeiro Ministério Português que funcionou no Brasil', Rio de Janeiro, Instituto Histórico e Geográfico Brasileiro, lata 345, doc. 7 [n.d.].

68. Pereira da Silva, *História da fundação do império brasileiro*, p. 121.

69. *Exposição analítica e justificativa da conducta e vida pública do visconde do Rio Seco* . . . Rio de Janeiro: Imprensa Nacional, 1821, pp. 3–4.

70. As described by Pereira da Silva, *História da fundação do império brasileiro*, p. 119.

71. Tobias do Rego Monteiro, *História do Império: A elaboração da independência*, vol. 1. Belo Horizonte and São Paulo: Itatiaia/Edusp (1981), p. 66. See also Oliveira Martins, *Don João VI no Brasil* (Brasília: Fundação Projeto Rondon, 1987), p. 8.

72. Pereira da Silva, *História da fundação do império brasileiro*, p. 287. The ships under the command of Graham Moore were the *Marlborough*, *London*, *Bedford* and *Monarch*.

73. Ibid., p. 289.

74. Kenneth Light, p. 110.

75. Manchester, 'A transferência da corte portuguesa para o Rio de Janeiro', p. 188. The ships that transported the royal family were: the *Príncipe Real* –

the ship with the largest tonnage – 84 guns, *Afonso de Albuquerque*, 64 guns, and *Rainha de Portugal*, 74 guns. Also included in the squadron were the *Príncipe do Brasil*, 74 guns, *Meduza*, 74 guns, *Conde D. Henrique*, 74 guns, *Martim de Freitas*, 64 guns, and *D. João de Castro*, 64 guns. There were also frigates – the *Minerva*, 44 guns, *Golfinho*, 36 guns and *Urânia*, 32 guns – and brigs – the *Vingança*, 20 guns, *Voador*, 22 guns and *Lebre*, 22 guns – as well as the freight ship for supplies, the *Thetis*. Rio de Janeiro: Biblioteca Nacional, mss. 1, 31, 30, 63.

76. Pereira da Silva, *História da fundação do império brasileiro.*

77. *Relação das pessoas que saíram desta cidade para o Brasil, em Companhia de S. A.R, no dia 29 de novembro de 1807*. Lisboa, 29 de novembro de 1807. Rio de Janeiro: Instituto Histórico e Geográfico Brasileiro, lata 490, pasta 29. 15 fls.

78. *Papéis particulares do conde de Linhares*. Rio de Janeiro: Instituto Histórico e Geográfico Brasileiro, mss. 1, 29, 20, 1, doc. 7.

79. Allan K. Light, pp. 110 and 112.

80. Nireu Oliveira Cavalcanti, *A cidade de São Sebastião do Rio de Janeiro: As muralhas, sua gente, os construtores, 1710–1810* (Rio de Janeiro: UFRJ, PhD thesis in history, p. 160), quotes the work of Antonio Marques Esparteiro, 'Transmigração da família real para o Brasil', which gives detailed figures for the number of crew members on-board all the vessels, in *História Naval Brasileira*. Rio de Janeiro: Ministério da Marinha, 1979, pp. 325–51, book 2, vol. 2.

81. Pereira da Silva, *História da fundação do império brasileiro*, p. 121. Mello Morais gives the number as 30,000 (Rio de Janeiro: Biblioteca Nacional, mss. 2, 30, 23, 6, n. 5); O'Neill says that between 16,000 and 18,000 subjects embarked, including 4,000 soldiers. José Vieira Fazenda ('Antiqualha e memórias do Rio de Janeiro', *Revista do IHGB*, Rio de Janeiro, vol. 142, book 88 [1920]) calculates that in three months the population of Rio increased by 20,000 people. Cavalcanti concludes that it was about 5,000 people (1997). Jurandir Malerba (*A corte no exílio: Civilização e poder no Brasil às vésperas da independência, 1808–1821*. São Paulo: Companhia das Letras, 2000) calculated an average of 15,000, citing other authors and figures in a footnote: according to Rocha Martins 13,800 people, and according to Soriano, 15,000. Alan K. Manchester, in 'A transferência da corte portuguesa para o Rio de Janeiro', aware of the discrepancies, opts for 10,000. Luiz Edmundo calculates the number as 15,000.

82. 'Rodrigo José Ferreira Lobo, Capitão de Mar e Guerra Comandante – Bordo da fragata Minerva, 31 de janeiro de 1808', *Papéis relativos à vinda . . .*, (1808), pp. 19 and 21.

83. Mello Moraes, *História da transladação da Corte portuguesa para o Brasil em 1807–1808*, p. 72, and Kenneth Light, p. 112. For details on the calendar and conditions of the journey, see Kenneth Light.

84. Traditional card games of the period: *faraó* (Faro or Farabank, which used a banker and several players); *espenifre* (a game in which the two of clubs was the highest card); *pacau* ('four fingers'); and *chincalhão* ('chaffinch').
85. As he arrived in Lisbon, it seems General Juno could actually see the fleet in the distance.
86. Varnhagen, 'História da independência do Brasil', p. 59.
87. The Rossio has been one of Lisbon's main squares since the Middle Ages, the scene of popular uprisings, celebrations, bullfights and executions. It was rebuilt in the Pombaline style after the earthquake.
88. Domingos Alves Branco Barreto, *Memória dos sucessos acontecidos na cidade de Lisboa, desde vinte e nove de novembro de 1808.* BN/Mss/I 13-4-no. 7
89. Rossi, *Diário dos acontecimentos de Lisboa*, p. 15.
90. Varnhagen, 'História da independência do Brasil', pp. 58-9.
91. Rossi *Diário dos acontecimentos de Lisboa*, p. 29.
92. Pereira, *Os filhos d'el Rei d. João VI*, p. 120.
93. The Palace of Queluz was known in Portugal as the Portuguese Versailles, situated in the town of Queluz (between Lisbon and Sintra). It was built as a summer retreat for Dom Pedro de Bragança, Dom João VI's father. Later on the palace was used as a discrete residence for Queen Dona Maria I.
94. Arquivo Nacional Torre do Tombo, Ministério do Reino, maço 279.
95. Rio de Janeiro, Biblioteca Nacional, mss. 10, 3, 29.
96. See Lúcia Maria Bastos Pereira das Neves, *Napoleão Bonaparte: Imaginário e política em Portugal – c. 1808–1810.* Rio de Janeiro: Alameda, 2008.
97. Dom Sebastião I (1554–1578) was king from 1557 to 1578. He disappeared (thought to have been killed in action) fighting the Moors in Morocco. He became known as *O Desejado* (the 'Desired One') as after his death the succession crisis led to the decline of Portugal's power during the Iberian Union.

7: DOM JOÃO AND HIS COURT

1. This chapter is partly based on the text written for the book *A longa viagem da biblioteca dos reis* by Angela Marques da Costa, Paulo Cesar de Azevedo and Lilia Moritz Schwarcz.
2. The information here is based on the account of Maria Graham, who arrived in Bahia two years later. Maria Graham, *Diário de uma viagem.* Belo Horizonte and São Paulo: Itatiaia/Edusp, 1990, p. 164. (Coleção Reconquista do Brasil, 157)
3. A measurement equivalent to an outstretched arm.
4. Luís dos Santos Vilhena, *Recopilação de notícias soteropolitanas e brasílicas.* Bahia: Imprensa Oficial do Estado, 1922 [1802].

5. Arquivo Nacional (981.42 v 711). *Cartas de Vilhena: Notícias soteropolitanas e brasílicas por Luís dos Santos Vilhena*. Bahia: Imprensa Oficial do Estado, 1922, p. 36.

6. Graham, *Diário de uma viagem*, pp. 167–8.

7. *Óleo de Dendê* – a palm oil extracted from the Dendezeiro palm – an indispensable ingredient in the typical Afro-Brazilian dishes from Bahia.

8. Pierre Verger, *Fluxo e refluxo do tráfico de escravos entre o Golfo do Benin e a Bahia de Todos os Santos: Dos séculos XVII a XIX*. São Paulo and Brasília: Corrupio/Ministério da Cultura, 1987, p. 8.

9. Sergio Buarque Holanda, 1976, pp. 71–2.

10. Ibid., p. 76.

11. The Treaty of Peace and Friendship was annulled by the Congress of Vienna in 1815.

12. *Relação das festas que se fizeram no Rio de Janeiro quando o Príncipe Regente N. S. e toda a sua Real Família chegaram pela primeira vez àquela capital*. Lisbon: Impressão Régia, 1810, p. 4.

13. *Sé* is an abbreviation for *Sedes Episcopalis* ('the Episcopal Seat'), the church that serves as the cathedral in Brazilian cities.

14. Gastão Cruls, *Aparência do Rio de Janeiro: Notícia histórica e descritiva da cidade*, vol. 1. Rio de Janeiro: José Olympio, 1952, p. 238.

15. Norbert Elias, *A sociedade da corte: Investigação sobre a sociologia da realeza e da aristocracia de corte*. Rio de Janeiro: Zahar, 2001.

16. Luís Edmundo, *O Rio de Janeiro no tempo dos vice-reis*. Brasília: Senado Federal, 2000, p. 34. (Coleção Brasil 500 Anos)

17. This description is based on ibid., pp. 123–30. (Coleção Brasil 500 Anos)

18. The *Beija-mão* was a tradition of reverence from the 'common people' to the Portuguese Crown that originated in the Middle Ages. It was a public ceremony in which the vassals had direct contact with the monarch from whom, after the hand-kissing, they could solicit a royal favour. It was of great symbolic importance for the role of the king as a father and a protector.

19. Luís Gonçalves dos Santos (1767–1844) was a teacher and churchman whose writings provide an important source of information on Brazilian life in the first half of the nineteenth century. Luís Gonçalves dos Santos, *Memórias para servir à história do Brasil*. Belo Horizonte and São Paulo: Itatiaia/Edusp, 1981, p. 175.

20. Luiz Edmundo, *A corte de d. João no Rio de Janeiro (1808–1821)*, vol. 1. Rio de Janeiro: Conquista, 1939, pp. 84, 113, 164, 226 and 228.

21. Royal Palace.

22. *Para a Glória esmaltar do novo Mundo/Manda o sexto João o Céu amigo.*

23. *Negras nuvens longe exalem,/Morte, estrago, horror, veneno,/E entre nós sempre sereno,/Seja o Céu, a Terra, o Mar.*

24. The rural region of São Cristóvão was separated from the centre of the town by a swampy terrain which, later during Dom João's reign, was

land-filled and incorporated into the town as the *Cidade Nova* (New Town).

25. Cruls, *Aparência do Rio de Janeiro*, pp. 241–2.

26. 'Toma-larguras' in the Portuguese jargon of the time. According to the historian Nireu Oliveira Cavalcanti, no more than 140 houses were actually requisitioned as lodgings. Luís Marrocos, an employee of the Royal Library, commented in a letter to his father: 'We are awaiting the battleship *S. Sebastião* loaded with people [. . .], And I am sorry for them all, because not even a house will they find here [. . .]' (Luís Joaquim dos Santos Marrocos, 'Carta n. 14, Rio de Janeiro, 27 de fevereiro de 1812', *Anais da Biblioteca Nacional do Rio de Janeiro*, vol. LVI. Rio de Janeiro: Ministério da Educação, 1934, p. 61.)

27. Lilia Moritz Schwarcz, *As barbas do Imperador: D. Pedro II, um monarca nos trópicos*. São Paulo: Companhia das Letras, 1998, p. 159.

28. The *Ordem da Espada* and the titles of *Grã-cruz*, *Comendador* and *Cavaleiro*.

29. Faoro, *Os donos do poder*.

30. Lima, *Dom João VI no Brasil*, p. 54.

31. Luiz Norton, *A corte de Portugal no Brasil* (São Paulo: Companhia Editora Nacional, 1938), p. 40. The comparison supposedly originated with Hipólito da Costa and was published in the *Correio Braziliense*, a reflection on the influence of the journal, as will be seen below.

32. Faoro, *Os donos do poder*, vol. 1, p. 251. Quotation attributed to Hipólito da Costa.

33. *Quem furta pouco é ladrão/Quem furta muito é barão/Quem mais furta e esconde/Passa de barão a visconde*.

34. Faoro, *Os donos do poder*, vol. 1, p. 251.

35. *Ordenações filipinas*, Book III, título 75, paragraph 1, with Silvia Hunold Lara (ed.), *Ordenações filipinas: Livro V*. São Paulo: Companhia das Letras, 1999, p. 30.

36. Tribunal da Relação – see chapter 5, note 44.

37. Casa da Suplicação.

38. Ibid., p. 33.

39. Desembargo do Paço.

40. Mesa da Consciência e Ordens.

41. Manuel Luís Salgado Guimarães, 'Cronograma avulso, 1750–1808', in *Nação e civilização nos trópicos*. Rio de Janeiro: Vértice, 1985.

42. Lima, *Dom João VI no Brasil*, p. 162.

43. Attempts at setting up a printing press were made in Recife in 1706, and in Rio de Janeiro in 1746. For details, see Carlos Rizzini, *O livro, o jornal e a tipografia no Brasil: 1500–1822*. São Paulo: Imprensa Oficial, 1988, p. 310.

44. Leila Mezan Algranti, *D. João VI: Bastidores da Independência* (Rio de Janeiro: Ática, 1987); idem, 'Os bastidores da censura na corte de d.

João', Seminário Internacional d. João VI, um Rei Aclamado na América, *Anais da Biblioteca Nacional* (Rio de Janeiro: Museu Histórico Nacional, 2000), p. 83.

45. Ana Maria Camargo and Rubens Borba de Moraes, *Bibliografia da Impressão Régia do Rio de Janeiro*, vol. 2. São Paulo: Edusp/Kosmos, 1993, p. 229.

46. Tereza Maria R. Fachada L Cardoso, 'A Gazeta do Rio de Janeiro: Subsídios para a história da cidade', *Revista do IHGB*, Rio de Janeiro, vol. 371 (April/June 1991).

47. Rizzini, *O livro, o jornal e a tipografia no Brasil*, p. 332.

48. The lagoon is named after Rodrigo de Freitas de Carvalho (1684–1748), a Portuguese cavalry officer whose wife was heiress to an estate that included many districts of Rio de Janeiro.

49. *Jambo.*

50. *Carambola.*

51. Rizzini, *O livro, o jornal e a tipografia no Brasil*, p. 257.

52. Lilia Moritz Schwarcz, *O espetáculo das raças: Cientistas, instituições e questão racial no Brasil do século XIX*. São Paulo: Companhia das Letras, 1993, p. 70.

53. See Schwarcz, Marques da Costa and Cesar de Azevedo, *A longa viagem da biblioteca dos reis*.

54. Faoro, *Os donos do poder*, vol. 1, p. 252; Varnhagen, 'História da independência do Brasil', pp. 102–3.

55. Varnhagen, 'História da independência do Brasil', pp. 102–3.

56. Lima, *Dom João VI no Brasil*, pp. 478–9.

57. In the 'Almanac histórico da cidade de S. Sebastião do Rio de Janeiro' (*Revista do IHGB*, Rio de Janeiro, book XXI, 1. trim. 1858, pp. 5–7) there are references to at least twenty institutions. See Graça Salgado (ed.), *Fiscais e meirinhos: A administração no Brasil Colonial* (Rio de Janeiro and Brasília: Nova Fronteira/Instituto Nacional do Livro, 1985).

58. An expression used by Lima in *Dom João VI no Brasil*, p. 71.

59. There are no precise figures for the number of inhabitants. Whereas Boris Fausto mentions 100,000, other travellers put it at 80,000. Even so, in 1817, Spix and Martius calculated the population of the city at 100,000. According to the calculations of Pizarro, in 1789 the population of the city was 43,780 inhabitants. Pohl (who lived in Brazil from 1817 to 1821) mentions 82,000 residents. Renault calculates the number at 80,000 people in 1808 and 112,695 in 1821. The official 1799 census counted 43,376 inhabitants.

60. Johann Baptist von Spix and Carl Friedrich Phillip von Martius, *Reise in Brasilien*. São Paulo: Companhia Editora Nacional, 1938, p. 91, part 1, vol. II.

61. John Luccock was a tradesman from Yorkshire who arrived in Brazil in June 1808, three months after the royal court. He stayed in the country for

ten years doing business and making somewhat acidic comments, which he published in his *Notes on Rio de Janeiro and the Southern Parts of Brazil* in 1820.

62. Seção de Obras Gerais da Biblioteca Nacional, 294, 5, 17. Francisco José da Rocha Martins, *A Independência do Brasil: No rumor duma epopeia o levedar duma nação forte* (Lisbon: Lvmen, 1922).

63. Delso Renault, *O Rio antigo nos anúncios de jornais (1808–1850).* Rio de Janeiro: José Olympio, 1969, p. 26.

64. Maria Beatriz Nizza da Silva, *Vida privada e quotidiano no Brasil: Na época de d. Maria I e d. João VI,* 2nd edn. Lisbon: Estampa, 1993, p. 243.

65. Theodor von Leithold (1771–1826) was a relative of one of the Prince Regent's counsellors. He came to Brazil with his nephew Ludwig Von Rango with the intention of acquiring a coffee plantation. They soon gave up the idea and returned to Europe, where they published *Rio de Janeiro seen by two Prussians in 1819.*

66. Nizza da Silva, *Vida privada e quotidiano no Brasil,* p. 244.

67. The Campo de Santana, named after the church that was demolished in 1854 to make way for Rio's first railway station, was the city's largest recreation area at the time, and the main location for religious and state commemorations.

68. T. von Leithold and L. von Rango, *O Rio de Janeiro visto por dois prussianos em 1819.* São Paulo: Companhia Editora Nacional, 1966, p. 97.

69. Padre José Maurício Nunes Garcia (1767–1830), a grandson of enslaved people, was a composer of baroque sacred music and also an organ and harpsichord virtuoso. In 1819 he conducted the first performance of Mozart's *Requiem* in the colony, and in 1821, of Haydn's *Creation.*

70. Benedicto Freitas, *Santa Cruz, fazenda jesuítica, real e imperial,* 3 vols. Rio de Janeiro:, 1985–7, p. 131.

71. Marcos Antônio Portugal (1762–1830) was a Portuguese classical composer of operas and sacred music. He came to Rio at the express invitation of Dom João.

72. The Santa Cruz Estate was originally a convent and farm, covering a vast area of land, founded in 1570 by the Jesuits, who began the long tradition of training its enslaved as musicians. With the expulsion of the Jesuits in 1759 the Marquis of Pombal claimed the property for the Crown.

73. *O Paiz,* Rio de Janeiro, 10 October 1908, quoted by Freitas, *Santa Cruz, fazenda jesuítica, real e imperial,* vol. 1, p. 140.

74. Barreto Filho and Hermeto Lima, *História da polícia do Rio de Janeiro: Aspectos da cidade e da vida carioca,* 3 vols. Rio de Janeiro: A Noite, 1939–43, vol. 2, 1831–1870, p. 199.

75. Royal Decree dated 13 May 1808, by which Dom João authorized the governor of Minas to go to war against the Botocudo ('Carta régia ao governador e capitão general da capitania de Minas Gerais sobre a guerra

aos índios botocudos', Rio de Janeiro: Biblioteca Nacional, mss. 11, 36, 05, 47, 6 pp.).

76. Viterbo Sousa, *Dicionário histórico e documental dos arquitectos, engenheiros e construtores portugueses*. Lisbon: Casa da Moeda/Imprensa Nacional, 1988, p. 65.

77. $000 is the symbol for *mil-réis*. The amount here is forty mil-réis.

78. See Gilberto Freyre, *O escravo nos anúncios de jornais brasileiros do século XIX: Tentativa de interpretação antropológica, através de anúncios de jornais brasileiros do século XIX, de característicos de personalidade e de formas de corpo de negros ou mestiços, fugidos ou expostos à venda, como escravos, no Brasil do século passado*, 2nd edn (São Paulo and Recife: Companhia Editora Nacional/Fundaj, 1979). For the same subject but in the newspapers of São Paulo, see Lilia Moritz Schwarcz, *Retrato em branco e negro: Jornais, escravos e cidadãos em São Paulo no final do século XIX* (São Paulo: Companhia das Letras, 1987).

79. *Sinhô branco também furta/Nosso preto furta galinha/furta saco de feijão/Sinhô branco quando furta/Furta prata e patação/Nosso preto quando furta/Vai parar na [Casa de] Correção/Sinhô branco quando furta/Logo sai sinhô baron.*

80. Nizza da Silva, *Vida privada e quotidiano no Brasil*, p. 267.

81. J. F. Almeida Prado, *D. João VI e o início da classe dirigente do Brasil: 1815–1889*. São Paulo: Companhia Editora Nacional, 1968, p. 240. (Brasiliana, 345)

82. Manolo Florentino calculates a total of 706,870 Africans set ashore in the port of Rio de Janeiro between 1790 and 1830. Mary C. Karasch, on the other hand, establishes the number as a minimum of 602,747 divided as follows: 225,047 between 1800 and 1816, and 377,700 between 1817 and 1843.

83. Filho and Lima, *História da polícia do Rio de Janeiro*, vol. 2, 1831–1870, p. 186.

84. Jean-Baptiste Debret, *Voyage pittoresque et historique au Brésil*. Paris: F. Didot Frères, 1835.

85. Lima, *Dom João VI no Brasil*, p. 241.

86. Filho and Lima, *História da polícia do Rio de Janeiro*, vol. 2, 1831–1870, p. 211.

87. Notes based on the letter that Luís Marrocos sent his father on 30 March 1816.

88. The description of the funeral ceremonies for Dona Maria were mostly taken from Lima, *Dom João VI no Brasil*, pp. 583–90.

89. *Paul et Virginie*, a popular children's book, written in 1787 by the French writer Jacques-Henri Bernardin de Saint-Pierre (1737–1814).

90. Lúcia M. Bastos Neves, 'O privado e o público nas relações culturais do Brasil com França e Espanha no governo Joanino', Seminário Interna-

cional d. João VI, um Rei Aclamado na América, *Anais da Biblioteca Nacional*. Rio de Janeiro: Museu Histórico Nacional, 2000, pp. 100-1.

91. See Lilia Moritz Schwarcz, *O sol do Brasil: Nicolas-Antoine Taunay e as desventuras dos artistas franceses na corte de d. João*. São Paulo: Companhia das Letras, 2008.

92. Nicolas-Antoine Taunay returned to France in 1821 and Pradier in 1818. Lebreton withdrew to a house on the Praia do Flamengo where he died in May 1819.

93. See Maria Odila Dias Leite, 'A interiorização da metrópole (1808-1853)', in Carlos Guilherme Mota, *1822: Dimensões*, 2nd edn. São Paulo: Perspectiva, 1985.

94. Mary C. Karasch, *A vida dos escravos no Rio de Janeiro (1808-1850)*. São Paulo: Companhia das Letras, 2000, p. 75.

95. *Correio Brasiliense*, London, vol. XVIII, no. 108 (May 1817).

96. Caetano Pinto Montenegro (born Portugal, 1748, died Rio de Janeiro 1827), captain-general and governor of the captaincy of Pernambuco from 1804 to 1817.

97. Carlos Guilherme Mota, *Nordeste 1817*. São Paulo: Perspectiva, 1972.

98. Evaldo Cabral de Mello, *A outra independência: O federalismo republicano de 1817 a 1824*. São Paulo: Ed. 34, 2004.

99. Carlos Guilherme Mota, 'O processo de independência no Nordeste', in idem, *1822: Dimensões*, p. 227.

100. *Gazeta do Rio de Janeiro*, Rio de Janeiro, vol. 11, no. 1 (7 February 1818).

101. Ibid., vol. 12, no. 2 (10 February 1818).

102. See Iara Lis Carvalho e Souza, 'D. João VI no Rio de Janeiro: Entre festas e representações', Seminário Internacional d. João VI, um Rei Aclamado na América, *Anais da Biblioteca Nacional*. Rio de Janeiro: Museu Histórico Nacional, 2000, pp. 58-60.

103. Adolfo Morales de los Rios, *Grandjean de Montigny e a evolução da arte brasileira*. Rio de Janeiro: A Noite, 1941.

104. Marc Ferrez (born France 1788, died Rio de Janeiro, Brazil, 1850) and his brother Zéphryn Ferrez (born France 1797, died Rio de Janeiro, Brazil, 1851), sculptors and engravers.

105. See the document 'Sobre a aclamação do sr. d. João Sexto no Rio de Janeiro, 1818', in the Arquivo Nacional.

106. See Filho and Lima, *História da polícia do Rio de Janeiro*, vol. 2, 1831-1870, p. 212.

107. The wedding took place in Vienna without the presence of the prince, before she travelled to Brazil. See below.

108. Lima, *Dom João VI no Brasil*, p. 539.

109. Almeida Prado, *D. João VI e o início da classe dirigente do Brasil*, p. 9.

110. Quoted by Malerba, *A corte no exílio*, p. 63.

111. See Filho and Lima, *História da polícia do Rio de Janeiro*, vol. 2, 1831–1870, pp. 213–14.

8: THE FATHER LEAVES, THE SON REMAINS

1. Part of the research for this chapter is based on *A longa viagem da biblioteca dos reis* by Angela Marques da Costa, Paulo Cesar de Azevedo and Lilia Moritz Schwarcz.

2. José Antonio de Miranda, *Memória constitucional e política: Sobre o Estado presente de Portugal e do Brasil, 1821*. Rio de Janeiro: Biblioteca Nacional, Seção de Obras Raras, 37, 18, 11, pp. 37–8.

3. For the Portuguese Revolution and its consequences in Brazil, see Pereira das Neves, *Napoleão Bonaparte*.

4. *O Português*, vol. I (30 April 1814), pp. 11–12, quoted by Mattoso, *História de Portugal*, vol. v, p. 48.

5. *O Campeão*, vol. II (16 June 1820), p. 412, quoted by ibid., vol. IV, p. 50.

6. Lima, *Dom João VI no Brasil*, p. 21.

7. *As Cortes Constitucionais.*

8. The assembly in ancient Israel that acted as both the judiciary and the legislature.

9. On the Sanhedrin see, among others, Mattoso, *História de Portugal*, vol. V, pp. 54–5.

10. Dom Pedro de Sousa Holstein (born Turin, Kingdom of Sardinia, 1781, died Lisbon, 1850) had remained in Portugal where he fought against the Napoleonic invasions. In 1811, Dom João appointed him as ambassador to Madrid, in 1812 to London and in 1815 he represented Portugal at the Congress of Vienna. He travelled to Rio de Janeiro in 1817 when he was appointed as Minister of Overseas Trade.

11. See José Murilo de Carvalho and Lúcia Bastos, known as Francisco de Sierra y Mariscal, 'Ideas geraes sobre a revolução do Brasil e suas consequencias', *Anais da Biblioteca Nacional*, Rio de Janeiro, 1926, vols. 43–4.

12. Boris Fausto, *História do Brasil* (São Paulo: Edusp, 2001, p. 130). An association dating back to the Middle Ages, by the modern era the Masons had become a secret society that was anti-absolutist and was linked to national liberation movements.

13. Rio de Janeiro: Impressão Régia, 1820, 17 pp. Rio de Janeiro: Biblioteca Nacional, Seção de Obras Raras, 37, 15, 5.

14. Otávio Tarquínio de Sousa, 1988, p. 139.

15. See José Murilo de Carvalho, Lúcia Bastos and Marcelo Basile, *Às armas, cidadãos! Panfletos manuscritos da independência do Brasil (1820–1823)*. São Paulo and Belo Horizonte: Companhia das Letras/Editora UFMG, 2012.

16. Portugal was effectively a British protectorate from 1808 to 1821 under the increasingly despotic rule of William Beresford (1768–1856).

17. Maria Graham, *Journal of a Voyage to Brazil and Residence there.* London: [n.p.], 1824.

18. Quoted by José Alexandre de Mello Moraes, *História do Brasil-Reino e do Brasil-Império.* Belo Horizonte and São Paulo: Itatiaia/Edusp, 1982, p. 124.

19. The people of 1820. From *vinte*, Portuguese for 'twenty'.

20. *Gazeta Universal* (1823), quoted by Pereira, *Os filhos d'el Rei d. João VI.*

21. Lima, *Dom João VI no Brasil*, p. 30.

22. Fausto, *História do Brasil*, p. 130.

23. Lima, *Dom João VI no Brasil*, pp. 149–50. Data relating to other overseas possessions is taken from António Henrique Rodrigo de Oliveira Marques, *História de Portugal*, vol. III. Lisbon: Palas, 1986, pp. 58–9.

24. Francisco Muniz Tavares (born Recife, 1793, died Recife, 1876), a priest and one of the leaders of the 1817 revolution in Pernambuco.

25. Pedro de Araújo Lima, Marquis of Olinda (born Sirinhaém, 1793, died Rio de Janeiro, 1870).

26. Francisco Vilela Barbosa, first Marquis of Paranaguá (1769–1846), was later Minister of the Navy under Dom Pedro I and during the regency, and a senator of the empire.

27. Cipriano José Barata de Almeida (born Salvador, 1762, died Natal, 1838). A member of Brazil's first Masonic Lodge, the Loja Cavaleiros da Luz (founded in Salvador in 1798), he had taken part in the Conspiracy of Bahia in 1798 and the revolution of Pernambuco in 1817.

28. Francisco Agostinho Gomes was a priest who was later to found a pro-independence periodical called *Escudo da Liberdade do Brasil.*

29. There were five deputies for Rio de Janeiro, six for São Paulo, one for Santa Catarina, nine for Bahia, eight for Pernambuco, three for Paraíba, three for Rio Grande do Norte, four for Ceará, two for Piauí, two for Maranhão, four for Pará, two for Goiás, two for Rio Grande do Sul, eleven for Minas and one for Espírito Santo. There were also two for Alagoas, two for Rio Negro and one for Cisplatina.

30. José Bonifácio de Andrada e Silva (1763–1838). As we shall see, he will play an important part in the Brazilian Independence movement.

31. Fausto, *História do Brasil*, p. 132.

32. Joaquim Gonçalves Ledo (1781–1847) was a Brazilian journalist, politician and freemason, leader of the liberal and democratic faction during the period of independence.

33. Letter from Dom Pedro, 8 June 1821, quoted in Tarquínio,, vol. II, p. 236.

34. Letter of 10 December 1821, quoted in Lima, *Dom João VI no Brasil*, pp. 149–50.

35. Oliveira Martins, p. 185.

36. These letters from Leopoldine were published in the *Revista do Instituto Histórico* under the title 'Cartas inéditas da 1a Imperatriz D. Maria Leopoldina (1821–1826)', *Revista do IHGB*, vol. 75 (1912), book 126, part II, pp. 109–27.

37. *Desorganizadores*.

38. *'Diga ao povo que fico'*. The declaration, where the verb is in the present tense, is known as 'the *Fico*'.

39. These are Dom Pedro's words, according to official Brazilian history, that have been taught in schools and memorized by children ever since.

40. Passages quoted by Lima, *Dom João VI no Brasil*, p. 197. See also in IHGB (DL.480.18), 'Centenário do 'Fico' (9 January 1822). 'Prefeitura do Distrito Federal' (January 1922), p. 30. 'Facsímile dos documentos do Senado da Câmara do Rio de Janeiro existentes no Arquivo Municipal' (January/August 1822), 1922.

41. Lima, *Dom João VI no Brasil*, p. 218.

42. *Correio do Rio de Janeiro*, no. 56 (19 June 1822), p. 2.

43. Among them, Antônio Carlos Ribeiro de Andrada Machado e Silva (born Santos 1773, died Rio de Janeiro 1845), a politician and journalist, nephew of José Bonifácio and known for his criticism of despotism.

44. Diogo Antônio Feijó (born São Paulo, 1784, died São Paulo 1843). See below.

45. José Lino dos Santos Coutinho (born Salvador, 1784, died Salvador, 1836).

46. For an overview of this situation and the activities of the more radical groups, see Renato Lopes Leite, *Republicanos e libertários: pensadores radicais no Brasil da Independência*. Rio de Janeiro: Civilização Brasileira, 2000.

47. Isabel Lustosa, *Insultos impressos: A guerra dos jornalistas na Independência*. São Paulo: Companhia das Letras, 2000, p. 134.

48. For further information on this data and the election procedures, see Oliveira Martins, pp. 309–11.

49. 'D. Pedro I, Príncipe Regente. Manifesto de independência. Rio de Janeiro, 1 de agosto de 1822', Rio de Janeiro: Biblioteca Nacional, ms. 1, 36, 28, 009, p. 1.

50. Fernando Novais e Carlos Guilherme Mota, *A independência do Brasil*. São Paulo: Hucitec, 1996, p. 54.

51. 'Manifesto do Príncipe Regente do Brasil aos governos e nações amigas. 6 de agosto de 1822', *Código Brasiliense ou Coleção das Leis, alvarás, decretos, cartas régias etc. promulgadas no Brasil desde a feliz chegada do príncipe Regente Nosso Senhor a estes estados com um índice cronológico (1808–1837)*. Rio de Janeiro: Biblioteca Nacional, Seção de Obras Raras, 4, 1, Impressão Régia, Tipografia Nacional e Imperial, 1811–38.

52. *Ouviram do Ipiranga às margens plácidas* – the first line of Brazil's national anthem.

53. The Marquesa de Santos was later to become the prince's favourite lover. See below.

54. riding boots.

55. Tarquínio, vol II, p. 33.

56. Quoted in Tarquínio, vol. II, p. 36.

57. 'Memória sobre a Independência do Brasil pelo Major Francisco de Castro Canto e Mello, gentil homem da Imperial Câmara'. Rio de Janeiro: Instituto Histórico e Geográfico Brasileiro, box 400, doc. 8, 1864.

58. 'Memória . . . Castro Canto e Mello', in ibid.; see also 'Fragmento de uma memória sobre a independência do Brasil, onde se encontram alguns trechos sobre os serviços do Conselheiro José Joaquim da Rocha', Rio de Janeiro, Arquivo Nacional, codex 807, vol. 3, 1864.

59. Quoted in Tarquínio, vol. II, p. 37.

60. Memória . . . Castro Canto e Mello', op. cit.

61. BN/PR SOR 92 (1) O Espelho.

62. Quoted by Lustosa, Insultos impressos, p. 242.

63. Iara Lis Carvalho Souza, A independência do Brasil. Rio de Janeiro: Zahar, 1999, p. 257.

64. Antônio Augusto de Lima Júnior, Cartas de D. Pedro I a D. João VI relativas à independência do Brasil. Rio de Janeiro: Gráfica do Jornal do Comércio, 1941, p. 74.

65. See Cabral de Mello, A outra independência.

66. Maria Odila Leite da Silva Dias, 'Historicidade da condição feminina no Brasil Colonial para o curso de pós-graduação Problemas Brasileiros', lecture given on 22 August 1986, p. 165.

9: INDEPENDENCE HABEMUS

1. José Murilo de Carvalho, A construção da ordem: A elite política imperial, 2nd edn. Rio de Janeiro: UFRJ/Relume Dumará, 1996.

2. Luiz Felipe de Alencastro and Fernando A. Novais (eds.), História da vida privada no Brasil. São Paulo: Companhia das Letras, 1997, vol. 2: Império – A corte e a modernidade nacional.

3. The Brazilian Empire, although it covered a vast region, did not, obviously, have any overseas dominions, although this is what the word 'empire' in English implies.

4. Ilmar Rohloff de Mattos, 'O gigante e o espelho', in Keila Grinberg and Ricardo Salles (eds.), O Brasil imperial. Rio de Janeiro: Civilização Brasileira, 2009, vol. II: 1831–1870.

5. In Latin the Pontificale Romanum, the Latin Catholic liturgical book that contains the rites performed by bishops, the first versions of which date back to the ninth century. A standard version was published by Clement

VIII (r.1592–1605) for use by the entire Roman Rite. This is the version mentioned here.

6. Ricardo Salles, *Nostalgia Imperial*. Rio de Janeiro: mimeo [n.d.], p. 74.

7. Debret, *Voyage pittoresque et historique au Brésil*, p. 326.

8. Ibid., pp. 327–9.

9. 'Memória estatística do Império do Brasil', *Revista do IHGB*, Rio de Janeiro, 1987, in Grinberg and Salles (eds.), *O Brasil imperial*, p. 210.

10. Mariza de Carvalho Soares and Ricardo Salles, *Episódios da história afro-brasileira*. Rio de Janeiro: DP&A, 2005.

11. Mary C. Karash, *Slave Life in Rio de Janeiro: 1808–1850*. Princeton: Princeton University Press, 1987, p. 335.

12. 'Portugal e o Brazil', *O Campeão Portuguez em Lisboa*, vol. I, no. 6 (11 May 1822), p. 83.

13. Lúcia Bastos Neves, 'Estado e política na independência', in Grinberg and Salles (eds.), *O Brasil imperial*, p. 130.

14. 800,000 mil réis (units of 1,000 réis).

15. Marques da Costa, Azevedo and Schwarcz, *A longa viagem da biblioteca dos reis*.

16. Ilmar Rohloff de Mattos, *O tempo Saquarema*. São Paulo: Hucitec/MinC/Pró-Memória/Instituto Nacional do Livro, 1987, p. 88. (Coleção Estudos Históricos, 10)

17. Luiz Felipe de Alencastro, 'L'Empire du Brésil', in Maurice Duverger (ed.), *Le Concept d'empire*. Paris: Presses Universitaires de France, 1980.

18. Luiz Felipe de Alencastro, 'Le Commerce des vivants: Traites d'esclaves et "pax lusitana" dans l'Atlantique Sud'. Paris Nanterre: Université Paris x, 1986. PhD.

19. Manolo Florentino, *Em costas negras: Uma história do tráfico de escravos entre a África e o Rio de Janeiro*. São Paulo: Companhia das Letras, 1997.

20. Beatriz Gallotti Mamigonian, 'A proibição do tráfico atlântico e a manutenção da escravidão', in Grinberg and Salles (eds.), *O Brasil imperial*, pp. 207–33.

21. Alcir Lenharo, *As tropas da moderação: O abastecimento da Corte na formação política do Brasil*, 2nd edn. Rio de Janeiro: Secretaria Municipal de Cultura, 1992.

22. See Marcello Otávio Neri de Campos Basile, *Anarquistas, rusguentos e demagogos: Os liberais exaltados e a formação da esfera pública imperial (1829–1834)*. Rio de Janeiro: IH-UFRJ, 2000. (Master's dissertation in Social History)

23. In Rio de Janeiro and the northern states an *alqueire* was equal to 27,225 m². Although in Minas Gerais the measure was larger (48,400 m²), in all probability it was the former that the Assembly adopted.

24. Sérgio Buarque de Holanda, *O Brasil monárquico*, 4th edn. São Paulo: Difel, 1986, vol. 3: O processo de emancipação. (Coleção História Geral da Civilização Brasileira)

25. Ronaldo Vainfas (ed.), *Dicionário do Brasil imperial: 1822–1889*. Rio de Janeiro: Objetiva, 2008.
26. See the letters of Santos Marrocos (Biblioteca Nacional) in Marques da Costa, Azevedo and Schwarcz, *A longa viagem da biblioteca dos reis.*
27. Henri-Benjamin Constant de Rebecque (1767–1830), or Benjamin Constant, was a Swiss-French political activist and writer.
28. Richard Graham, *Clientelismo e política no Brasil do século XIX.* Rio de Janeiro: Editora da UFRJ, 1997.
29. Lustosa, *Insultos impressos*, pp. 231–3.
30. See João Armitage, *História do Brasil.* Belo Horizonte and São Paulo: Itatiaia/Edusp, 1981, pp. 205–8.
31. John Armitage (1807–1856) was a British traveller who wrote *History of Brazil*, which narrates the story of the independence process from a foreigner's point of view.
32. *Sempre-viva* is a special flower. Its petals close in cold weather and open up when the temperature rises, giving the impression that it is always alive. Hence the name.
33. Basile, *Anarquistas, rusguentos e demagogos.*
34. Ibid., pp. 20–3.

10: REGENCIES

1. For this debate and the significance of federalism during the process of independence, see Cabral de Mello, *A outra independência.*
2. Joaquim Nabuco (1849–1910), statesman and abolitionist.
3. Marco Morel, 'O pequeno monarca', *Nossa História*, Rio de Janeiro: Vera Cruz, 3, no. 26 (December 2005), pp. 14–17.
4. *Aurora Fluminense*, Rio de Janeiro, no. 470 (11 April 1831), p. 2.
5. On Dom Pedro's childhood, see, among others, Schwarcz, *As barbas do Imperador.*
6. Murilo de Carvalho, *A construção da ordem.*
7. Miriam Dolhnikoff, *O pacto imperial: Origens do federalismo no Brasil.* São Paulo: Globo, 2005, pp. 89–93.
8. The yellow-headed caracara, a member of the falcon family.
9. Yellow parrot, from the Tupi *aîuruîuba* (*aîuru* = parrot + *îuba* = yellow).
10. Ragamuffins. Supporters of the Ragamuffins' War. See note 4.
11. The origin is the Tupi word for Moray Eel – *karamu'ru.*
12. An island in Guanabara Bay.
13. Rio's twin city, on the other side of Guanabara Bay.
14. *Urucum* ('red colour' in Tupi) is a tropical shrub from which an orange-red dye is extracted.
15. *Guaraná* is a climbing plant of the maple family that grows in the Amazon.

16. Maria Januária Vilela Santos, *A balaiada e a insurreição de escravos no Maranhão*. São Paulo: Ática, 1983. (Coleção Ensaios, 101)

17. Dom José, the fifth king of the Bragança dynasty, reigned in Portugal between 1750 and 1777.

18. Dona Maria I, Queen of Portugal from 1777 to 1816, whose son became regent after she was declared mentally incapable. See chapters 6 and 7.

19. See Manuel Valentim Alexandre, *Os sentidos do império: Questão nacional e questão colonial na crise do Antigo Regime português*. Porto: Afrontamento, 1993.

20. The tupi name for an Amazonian tree whose seeds contain an oil with medicinal properties.

21. The plant from whose root the dye is extracted.

22. Arthur César Ferreira Reis, 'O Grão-Pará e o Maranhão', in Sérgio Buarque de Holanda (ed.), *História Geral da Civilização Brasileira*, 4th edn. São Paulo: Difel, 1978, vol. II: O BRASIL monárquico.

23. Magda Ricci, 'Cabanos, patriotismo e identidades: Outras histórias de uma revolução', in Grinberg and Salles (eds.), *O Brasil imperial*.

24. The term used to designate groups of Indians who didn't speak the Tupi language.

25. See Ricci, 'Cabanos, patriotismo e identidades', pp. 189–90.

26. Euclides da Cunha (1866–1909) was a *Paulista* engineer, geologist and journalist whose book *Os Sertões* (*The Backlands*) documented the Canudos War (1896–7 – see chapter 13).

27. Euclides da Cunha, 'Da independência à República', in ibid., *À margem da história*. Porto: Lello e Irmão, 1926, p. 63.

28. For the uprising in the *quilombo do Urubu*, see João José Reis, *Rebelião escrava no Brasil: A história do levante dos Malês em 1835* (São Paulo: Companhia das Letras, 2003, pp. 100 ff). For the use of the word 'candomblé', see Reis and Silva, *Negociação e conflito*, p. 41.

29. For the political context in Bahia between the end of the eighteenth century and the first half of the nineteenth, see Reis, *Rebelião escrava no Brasil*, especially part 1.

30. For the conspiracy of 1807, see ibid., pp. 71 ff.

31. For the conspiracy of 1814, see Stuart B. Schwartz, 'Cantos e quilombos numa conspiração de escravos Haussá; Bahia, 1814', in Reis and dos Santos Gomes (eds.), *Liberdade por um fio*.

32. *Crioulos* were slaves who had been born in Brazil, and were thus Brazilians, as opposed to first-generation slaves who had been imported from Africa.

33. For the uprising of 1835, see Reis, *Rebelião escrava no Brasil*.

34. Most deportations were to Africa, above all Angola.

35. In Portuguese, 'um partido desorganizador'.

36. Paulo César Souza, *A Sabinada: A revolta separatista da Bahia* (São Paulo: Companhia das Letras, 2009). For the description of the revolt we used this book, as well as Luiz Vianna Filho, *A Sabinada: A república baiana de 1837* (Rio de Janeiro: José Olympio, 1938).

37. Keila Grinberg, 'A sabinada e a politização da cor na década de 1830', in Grinberg and Salles (eds.), *O Brasil imperial*, p. 275.

38. Hendrik Kraay, 'As Terrifying as Unexpected: The Bahian Sabinada, 1837–1838', *The Hispanic American Historical Review*, Durham, NC, vol. 72, no. 4 (November 1992), p. 521.

39. The passages on the previous history of this region were mostly taken from the text by Sandra Jatahy Pesavento, 'Uma certa revolução farroupilha', in Grinberg and Salles (eds.), *O Brasil imperial*, pp. 235–40.

40. The seven missions founded by the Jesuits on their return.

41. *Sesmaria* (from the Portuguese *sesma*, derived from the Latin *sexima*, a sixth part) was a Portuguese legal institution for the distribution of land to be used for production.

42. See, among others, Spencer Leitman, *Raízes socioeconômicas da Guerra dos Farrapos*. Rio de Janeiro: Graal, 1979.

43. See, among others, Maria Medianeira Padoin, *Federalismo gaúcho: Fronteira platina, direito e revolução*. São Paulo: Companhia Editora Nacional, 2002.

44. For an overview of the region, see César Augusto Barcellos Guazzelli, *O horizonte da província: A república rio-grandense e os caudilhos do rio da Prata, 1835–45*. Rio de Janeiro: IH-UFRJ, 1998. PhD thesis in History.

45. The *Liberal Summarizer*.

46. See Sandra Jatahy Pesavento, *A revolução farroupilha*. São Paulo: Brasiliense, 1985, p. 12. (Coleção Tudo é História, 101)

47. A small town 344 kilometres from the capital of the province, Rio Grande do Sul.

48. Paraná, Santa Catarina and Rio Grande do Sul.

49. Part of this information was researched by Matheus Gato de Jesus, whom we thank. See, in this context, the account 'Intelectuais negros maranhenses na formação do Brasil moderno (1870–1939)'. São Paulo: FFLCH-USP, July 2013. Relatório de qualificação.

50. See, among others, Fabiano Vilaça dos Santos, *O governo das conquistas do norte: Trajetórias administrativas no Estado do Grão-Pará e Maranhão (1751–1780)*. Available at: <http://www.teses.usp.br/teses/disponiveis/8/8138/tde-06072008-140850/pt-br.php>. São Paulo: FFLCH-USP, 2008, p. 37. PhD thesis in Social History. In book form: Fabiano Vilaça dos Santos, *O governo das conquistas do norte: Trajetórias administrativas do Grão-Pará e Maranhão* (São Paulo: Annablume, 2011).

51. The largest tributary on the left bank of the Amazon river.

52. *Bem-te-vi* is a songbird found throughout Brazil, including in the towns. In English it is called the Great Kiskadee. Both names imitate the sound of its call. The words *Bem-te-vi* mean 'I saw you!'

53. Claudete Maria Miranda Dias, *Balaios e bem-te-vis: A guerrilha sertaneja*, 2nd edn. Teresina: Instituto Dom Barreto, 2002.

54. See, among others, Maria Janotti de Lourdes Mônaco, *A Balaiada* (São Paulo: Brasiliense, 1987) (Coleção Tudo é História, 117); Maria Villela Santos, *A Balaiada e a insurreição de escravos no Maranhão* (São Paulo: Ática, 1983).

55. Mentioned above as the Baron of Caxias, he was to become the most famous military figure in the history of Brazil.

56. See Lúcia Maria Paschoal Guimarães, 'Sociedades políticas', in Vainfas (ed.), *Dicionário do Brasil imperial*.

57. Gilberto Freyre, *Sobrados e mucambos: Decadência do patriarcado rural no Brasil*, 8th edn. Rio de Janeiro: Record, 1990, pp. 389–90.

11: THE SECOND REIGN

1. Tobias Barreto series, Rio de Janeiro: National Library Archives.

2. Papers relating to the consecration and coronation of Dom Pedro II, Arquivo Nacional, Fundo Casa Imperial.

3. *Rio da Prata*, the River Plate.

4. When Dom Pedro returned to Portugal he fought a war against his brother Dom Miguel, who had seized the throne with the aid of the Absolutist Party. Dom Miguel and his supporters were finally defeated in 1834, and Maria, Dom Pedro's daughter, reigned as Maria II until her death in 1853.

5. See the document 'Descripção do Edificio construido para a solemnidade da coroação e sagração de S. M. O Imperador O Senhor D. Pero II', Publicações do Arquivo Nacional, 1925.

6. See the edition of 15 July 1841 of the *Jornal do Commercio*.

7. The Guianan cock of the rock (*Rupicola rupicola*), a species of South American passerine.

8. *Manual de acompanhamento do Imperador no dia de seu aniversário e aclamação*. Thypografia Nacional, 1841.

9. The custom of kissing the king's hand came from Portugal, representing the servile character of the court with the gesture of bowing to the monarch. Dom João had incorporated it into the Brazilian ritual: every night – with the exception of Sundays and holidays – at eight o'clock, he received the public in the Palace of São Cristóvão.

10. Paulo Barbosa worked as the imperial steward until his death in 1868.

11. Letters from Dom Pedro II to Paulo Barbosa, Biblioteca Nacional, 26 February 1863.

12. 3,555 *contos de réis*, the equivalent of 3,555,000 réis.

13. Alencastro, 'L'Empire du Brésil', p. 502.

14. Manolo Fiorentino, *Em costas negras*. São Paulo: Companhia das Letras, 2008.

15. Luiz Felipe de Alencastro, *Le Commerce des vivants: traites d'esclaves er 'pax lusitana' dans L'Atlantique Sud*. Paris: Universite de Paris X, 1986. PhD thesis, Murilo de Carvalho, *A construção da ordem*.

16. Jorge Caldeira, *Mauá: Empresário do Império*. São Paulo: Companhia das Letras, 1995, p. 241.

17. 11,171.52 *contos de réis*, or 11,171,520 réis.

18. Irineu Evangelista de Sousa , the Viscount of Mauá (1813–1889), a Brazilian entrepreneur, industrialist, banker and politician. He was called the Rothschild of the South American continent by *The New York Times* in 1871. He received the titles of baron (1854) and *visconde com grandeza* (1874) of Mauá.

19. The question of immigration was only resolved when, from the decade of the 1870s, the government began to finance it, withdrawing the exclusive initiative from the farmers. See the preface to Sérgio Buarque de Holanda's *Memórias de um colono no Brasil (1850)* by Thomas Davatz (Belo Horizonte and São Paulo: Itatiaia/Edusp, 1980), and Murilo de Carvalho, *A construção da ordem*, p. 316.

20. In *O espetáculo das raças* (op. cit.) there is an analysis of the impact of the racial theories in the selection of predominantly white groups of immigrants. For further details see *Raça, ciência e sociedade,* eds. Marcos Chor Maio and Ricardo Ventura Santos (Rio de Janeiro: Fiocruz/Centro Cultural Banco do Brasil, 1996).

21. Alencastro, *Le Commerce des vivants*, p. 515.

22. For further details on the subject, we suggest Sidney Chalhoub, *Cidade febril: Cortiços e epidemias na corte imperial*. São Paulo: Companhia das Letras, 1996.

23. The 'court' here, as in most other cases, refers to the city of Rio de Janeiro, rather than to the court itself.

24. This passage on urban slavery is based on the texts that Maria Helena Machado Lilia Schwarcz presented at the International Seminar *Emancipação, Inclusão e Exclusão: Desafios do Passado e do Presente*, organised in partnership with the Instituto Moreira Salles in October 2013.

25. Joaquim Maria Machado de Assis (1839–1908), poet and novelist, founder of the Brazilian Academy of Letters, is considered to be one of Brazil's greatest writers.

26. *Fulano* is a generic name, something like 'John Doe' in American usage. *Fulano, Betrano, Sicrano* is the exact equivalent of 'Tom, Dick and Harry'.

27. Machado de Assis, *Papéis avulsos*. Rio de Janeiro and Belo Horizonte: Garnier, 1989, pp. 118 and 120.

28. José de Alencar, *O tronco do ipê*. São Paulo: Ática, 1995, p. 14.

29. Carlos Gomes (1836–1896) was an important classical composer during the empire. He studied in Italy and composed operas in Verdian style that became immensely popular during his lifetime. One of his most well-known operas is 'O Guarani'.

30. Martins Pena (1815–1848), one of Brazil's funniest playwrights. His 'comedies of manners' earned him the nickname of the Brazilian Molière.

31. 'The Barman'.

32. Darcy Damasceno (ed.), *Martins Pena: Comédias*. São Paulo: Ediouro, 1968, p. 78.

33. Wanderley Pinho, *Salões e damas do Segundo Reinado*. São Paulo: Martins, 1942, p. 5.

34. João Maurício Wanderley (1815–1889), Baron of Cotegipe, was an important politician, senator and minister of the Second Reign.

35. 'Father against mother'.

36. Machado de Assis, *Relíquias da Casa Velha*. Rio de Janeiro and Belo Horizonte: Garnier, 1990, pp. 17 and 27.

37. The *Almanak Laemmert* was produced by the German brothers Eduard and Heinrich Laemmert, and was issued by the imperial court every year between 1844 and 1889. It contained appointments of court officials, ministers and officials in the provinces, statistics, information on legislation and advertisements for goods and services.

38. Ibid.

39. Campos dos Goytacazes is located on the northern coast of the present-day state of Rio de Janeiro.

40. The respective populations for these capitals at the time were 354,396, 1,083,039 and 1,398,097 (Murilo de Carvalho, *A construção da ordem*, p. 104).

41. José Murilo de Carvalho, *Teatro de sombras: A política imperial*. Rio de Janeiro: Vértice/Iuperj, 1988; Murilo de Carvalho, *A construção da ordem*, p. 84.

42. Murilo de Carvalho, *A construção da ordem*, p. 210. See also José Murilo de Carvalho, *Dom Pedro* II (São Paulo: Companhia das Letras, 2007).

43. Ilmar Rohloff de Mattos, *O tempo de Saquarema*, p. 51.

44. Murilo de Carvalho, *A construção da ordem*, p. 56.

45. Ibid.

46. Silvio Vasconcelos da Silveira Ramos Romero – Sílvio Romero (1851–1914) – was a literary critic, poet, philosopher and politician who attended law school in Recife.

47. *Doctrine against Doctrine*.

48. Sílvio Romero, *Doutrina contra doutrina: O evolucionismo e o positivismo na República do Brasil*. Rio de Janeiro: Lucta, 1895, p. 38.

49. See Murilo de Carvalho, *A construção da ordem*.

50. In 1847, with the introduction of a president of the Council de Conselho, Dom Pedro II only appointed the president, who, in turn, appointed the other members (Murilo de Carvalho, *A construção da ordem*, p. 49).

51. 800 *contos de réis.*

52. Murilo de Carvalho, *A construção da ordem*, p. 84.

53. Afonso Celso de Assis Figueiredo (1860–1938) was a Brazilian politician, historian, poet and journalist.

54. Afonso Celso de Assis Figueiredo, *Oito annos de parlamento: Poder pessoal de d. Pedro II*. São Paulo: Melhoramentos, 1928, p. 21.

55. 'Medallion Theory'.

56. A political party that believes in the absolute power of the pope in all spiritual matters and questions of faith. The name originated in France.

57. Machado de Assis, *Papéis avulsos*, p. 74.

58. The *Revolta Praieira*, the Beach rebellion.

59. Murilo de Carvalho, *Teatro de sombras*, p. 374.

60. Afonso Arinos de Melo Franco, *A câmara dos deputados: Síntese histórica*. Brasília: Centro de Documentação e Informação, 1978, p. 114.

61. Honório Carneiro Leão, Marquês de Paraná (1801–1856), was one of the founders of the Conservative Party and President of the Council of Ministers in 1853.

62. Benedict Anderson, *Comunidades imaginadas: Reflexões sobre a origem e a difusão do nacionalismo*. São Paulo: Companhia das Letras, 2008.

63. Anne-Marie Thiesse, *La Création des identités nationales*. Paris: Seuil, 1999.

64. See the article by José Augusto Pádua, 'Natureza e sociedade no Brasil monárquico', in Grinberg and Salles (eds.), *O Brasil imperial*, and Schwarcz, *As barbas do Imperador*.

65. Antonio Candido, *O romantismo no Brasil*, 2nd edn. São Paulo: Humanitas, 2004, p. 81.

66. Francisco Adolfo de Varnhagen (1816–1878), a Brazilian soldier, diplomat and historian. He obtained recognition as an historian with his two-volume *General History of Brazil*, written between 1854 and 1857.

67. Manuel José de Araújo Porto Alegre (1806–1879), writer, painter and art critic, was also director of the Imperial Academy of Fine Arts.

68. Joaquim Norberto de Sousa e Silva (1820–1891) was part of the circle of intellectuals and artists who were close to the emperor.

69. Joaquim Manuel de Macedo (1820–1882), a Brazilian doctor and politician and noted writer from the Romantic movement, was the secretary of IHGB. He is also remembered as the author of the immensely popular *A Moreninha* (1844).

70. In 1817 von Martius (1794–1868) and Johann Baptist von Spix were sent to Brazil by Maximilian I Joseph, the King of Bavaria. They travelled from Rio de Janeiro through several of the southern and eastern provinces of Brazil and also to the Amazon.

71. Peter Wilhelm Lund (1801–1880) moved from his native Denmark to Brazil in 1833 where for ten years he undertook excavations of limestone caves in the Rio das Velhas valley in Minas Gerais.

72. Louis Couty (born France 1854, died Rio de Janeiro 1884) was a French physician and physiologist. Shortly after his arrival in Brazil, in 1876, he began to study curare, a plant poison, at the laboratory of the National Museum.

73. Émil August Goeldi (1859–1917) was a Swiss-Brazilian naturalist and zoologist. In 1884 he was invited to be the director of a new museum located in Belém, Pará.

74. Adalbert Derby (1851–1915) was an American geologist who worked with Charles Frederick Hartt in the first Geological Commission of the Empire of Brazil. In 1877, with the end of the Commission, Derby decided to stay in Brazil and accepted a post at the National Museum of Rio de Janeiro.

75. Charles Frederick Hartt (1840–1878), a Canadian-American geologist, palaeontologist and naturalist who specialized in the geology of Brazil.

76. Auguste François Marie Glaziou (1828–1906), a French landscape designer and botanist. In 1858, at the request of Dom Pedro II, he moved to Rio de Janeiro as director of parks and gardens, and was responsible for the landscape design of the gardens of the *Palácio de São Cristóvão*.

77. Simon Schwartzman, 'A ciência no Império', in *Um espaço para a ciência: A formação da comunidade científica no Brasil*, 2001. Available at: <http://www.schwartzman.org.br/simon/spacept/pdf/capit3.pdf>. Accessed on 30 January 2015.

78. The following passage, on Romantic Indianism, is based on the book *As barbas do Imperador* by Lilia Moritz Schwarcz.

79. Candido, *O romantismo no Brasil*, p. 27.

80. Pedro Puntoni, 'Gonçalves de Magalhães e a historiografia do Império', *Novos Estudos Cebrap*, São Paulo, no. 45 (1996).

81. Baltasar da Silva Lisboa (1761–1840) was a magistrate and historian from Bahia.

82. Antônio Gonçalves Dias (1823–1864) was not just a Romantic poet but also a well-known playwright.

83. Gonçalves Dias, *Poesias completas*, 2nd edn. São Paulo: Saraiva, 1957, p. 525.

84. José de Alencar (1829–1877) was a Brazilian politician and prolific writer.

85. Gonçalves de Magalhães, *A confederação dos Tamoios*, 3rd edn. Rio de Janeiro: Garnier, 1864, pp. 353–4.

86. Simplício Rodrigues de Sá (born Cape Verde 1785, died Rio de Janeiro 1839), a Portuguese-born painter and art professor who emigrated to Brazil in 1809. He was named a court painter and private art tutor to Princess Maria da Glória, the future Queen of Portugal.

87. Félix-Émile Taunay, Baron of Taunay (1795–1881), was the son of Nicolas-Antoine Taunay, and travelled to Brazil with his father in 1816.

Three years later Nicolas-Antoine returned to France, leaving Félix his post at the *Academia Imperial de Belas Artes*. In 1835 he was appointed as the young emperor's Greek, drawing and literature tutor.

88. Victor Meirelles de Lima (1832–1903) was one of the protected painters of the emperor and was particularly recognized for his magnificent historical scenes.

89. *The First Mass in Brazil*.

90. José Maria Medeiros (1849–1925), a Portuguese painter who became a Brazilian citizen. In 1868 he entered the *Academia Imperial de Belas Artes* where he studied with Victor Meirelles. In 1884 the emperor granted him the Imperial Order of the Rose in recognition of his painting *Iracema*.

91. Gabriel Soares de Sousa (1540–1591), a Portuguese explorer and naturalist.

92. Sebastião da Rocha Pita (1660–1738), a Brazilian poet and historian. In 1730 he published *History of Portuguese America from the Year 1500 of its Discovery to the Year 1724*.

12: THE END OF THE MONARCHY IN BRAZIL

1. Francisco Fernando Monteoliva Doratioto, *O conflito com o Paraguai: A grande guerra do Brasil*. São Paulo: Ática, 1996, p. 7.

2. Francisco Inácio de Carvalho Moreira, Baron of Penedo (1815–1906), was an important politician and diplomat during the Second Reign. In 1852 he was appointed as ambassador to the United States and then as Minister Plenipotentiary to Great Britain.

3. Zacarias de Góis e Vasconcelos (1815–1877) was president of the provinces of Piauí and Sergipe and the first president of the new sate of Paraná; provincial deputy for Bahia and later deputy general and senator for Bahia (from 1864 to 1877), Minister of the Navy, of Justice and of Finance, and three times president of the Council of Ministers.

4. Eusébio de Queirós Coutinho Matoso da Câmara (born Luanda 1812, died Rio de Janeiro 1868) was Minister of Justice from 1848 to 1852 and the author of the law that abolished the slave traffic in 1850, known as the Eusébio de Queirós Law.

5. Robert W. Slenes, ' "Malungu, Ngoma vem!": África coberta e descoberta no Brasil', *Cadernos do Museu de Escravatura*, Luanda, vol. 1 (1995); Chalhoub, *Visões da liberdade*.

6. Hebe Mattos, 'Raça e cidadania no crepúsculo da modernidade escravista no Brasil', in Grinberg and Salles (eds.), *O Brasil imperial*, vol. 3: 1870–1889, pp. 20–2.

7. It is not possible here to explain all the complexities of these events. For further information see Doratioto, *O conflito com o Paraguai*; Ricardo

Salles, *Guerra do Paraguai: Escravidão e cidadania na formação do Exército* (Rio de Janeiro: Paz e Terra, 1990); André Toral, *Adeus, Chamigo brasileiro: Uma história da guerra do Paraguai* (São Paulo: Companhia das Letras, 1997); Evangelista de Castro Dionísio Cerqueira, *Reminiscências da campanha do Paraguai, 1865–1870* (Rio de Janeiro: Biblioteca do Exército, 1979); Milda Rivarola, *Vagos pobre y soldados* (Assunção: Centro Paraguaio de Estudos Sociológicos, 1994); John Schulz, *O Exército na política: Origens da intervenção militar: 1850–1894* (São Paulo: Edusp, 1994); and Luiz Alberto Moniz Bandeira, *O expansionismo brasileiro e a formação dos estados na Bacia do Prata* (Brasília: UnB; São Paulo: Ensaio, 1995).

8. Mate (sometimes written 'maté' in English) is a traditional South American caffeine-rich infused drink, particularly popular in Argentina, southern Chile, Uruguay, Paraguay, the Bolivian Chaco and southern Brazil.

9. Uruguaiana is the region on the eastern frontier of the state of Rio Grande do Sul, which shares a border with Argentina and Uruguay.

10. Doratioto, *O conflito com o Paraguai*, p. 22.

11. For the development of the Brazilian Army, see Schulz, *O Exército na política*, Nelson Werneck Sodré, *História militar do Brasil* (Rio de Janeiro: Civilização Brasileira, 1965), among others.

12. Machado de Assis, *Iaiá Garcia*. Rio de Janeiro and Belo Horizonte: Garnier, 1988, p. 72.

13. The naval Battle of Riachuelo was fought on 11 June 1865. The Brazilian fleet commanded by Admiral Barroso destroyed the Paraguayan navy.

14. Machado de Assis, *Histórias sem data*. Rio de Janeiro and Belo Horizonte: Garnier, 1989, p. 117.

15. Joaquim Marques Lisboa, Marquis of Tamandaré (1807–1897), a member of the Liberal Party, was Brazil's first native admiral.

16. José Antônio Pimenta Bueno, Marquis of São Vicente (1803–1878), was Chief of Police, High Court Judge in Maranhão and Rio de Janeiro, Minister of Foreign Trade, Minister of Justice and President of the Council of Ministers. In 1849, Pimenta Bueno left the Liberal Party and joined forces with the Conservatives.

17. José Tomás Nabuco de Araújo Filho (1813–1878) was deputy general, president of the province of São Paulo, Minister of Justice and senator of the empire.

18. IHGB, tin 322 – file 317, report by Councillor Nabuco de Araújo. See Lilia Moritz Schwarcz, Lúcia Klück Stumpf and Carlos Lima Junior, *A Batalha do Avaí: A beleza da barbárie – A Guerra do Paraguai pintada por Pedro Américo* (Rio de Janeiro: Sextante, 2013).

19. José Maria da Silva Paranhos, the Viscount of Rio Branco (1819–1880), was an important monarchist, politician, diplomat and journalist during the empire (1822–1889).

20. *Atas do Conselho de Estado Pleno*, Terceiro Conselho de Estado, 1865–7, 2 April 1867. Available at: <http://www.senado.gov.br/publicacoes/anais/pdf/ACE/ATAS6-Terceiro_Conselho_de_Estado_1865–1867.pdf>. Accessed on 30 January 2015; see also Ricardo Salles, 'La Guerra de Paraguay, la cuestión servil y la cuéstion nacional en Brasil (1866–1871)', in Ana María Stuven and Marco A. Pamplona (eds.), *Estado y nación en Chile y Brasil en el siglo XIX* (Santiago: Ediciones Universidad Católica de Chile, 2009), p. 123.

21. Grinberg and Salles (eds.), *O Brasil imperial*, p. 133.

22. On the morning of 6 December 1868, Caxias led 16,999 infantrymen, 926 cavalrymen and 742 artillerymen to take the Paraguayan town of Villeta. The plan was to attack the rear of the Paraguayan army. But Solano discovered that the allies had landed in the rear of his army and sent 5,000 men to stop the enemy at a narrow passage over a stream called Itororó.

23. The Battle of Avaí was fought in December 1868 beside the small river of that name in Paraguayan territory. Many consider it to be the bloodiest battle in the history of South America.

24. Caxias left Villeta at two in the morning on 21 December 1868, and by noon was ready to storm the Lomas Valentinas fortifications on the banks of a small tributary of the Paraguay river. The Paraguayan defences were finally taken on 27 December. López managed to make his escape with his cavalry.

25. The Fortress of Humaitá was a defensive system near the mouth of the Paraguay river.

26. Manuel Luís Osório, Marquis of Herval (1808–1879), was the most prestigious officer in the Plate region, having fought in every campaign since the *Guerra dos Farrapos* (in which he initially supported the rebels). He played an important role in retaking Uruguaiana. During the Battle of Avaí, after successfully taking the enemy's artillery position, he was wounded in the face, thereafter concealing the wound with his poncho.

27. Literally, 'his body was closed'. This generalized belief originated with the Afro-Brazilian sects, where it is believed that the body can be preserved from all external harm by the invocation of an Orisha.

28. Ibid., p. 177.

29. During the battle – known as *Acosta-Ñu* by the Paraguayans – as he had lost so many men, Solano resorted to the use of boys, who fought wearing false beards, carrying old weapons.

30. Doratioto, *O conflito com o Paraguai*, p. 94.

31. See Schulz, *O Exército na política*, p. 60.

32. *A Vida Fluminense*, Rio de Janeiro, no. 128 (1870).

33. Francisco Manuel Barroso da Silva, Baron of Amazonas (born Lisbon 1804, died Montevideo 1882), was the commander who led the Brazilians to victory at the naval Battle of Riachuelo.

34. Pedro Américo de Figueiredo e Melo (1843–1905) moved to Rio de Janeiro in 1854, where he was granted a scholarship to study in the Academia Imperial de Belas Artes.

35. The Battle of Guararapes came in the wake of the Restoration War that put an end to the Iberian Union and restored Portuguese independence in 1640 against the Dutch, who finally capitulated in 1654. Meirelles tried to compare this 'glorious' battle with the Paraguayan War.

36. Louis Moreau Gottschalk (1829–1869) was an American composer and pianist. He travelled extensively throughout his life, to Cuba, Puerto Rico, and Central and South America.

37. Bernardo Joaquim da Silva Guimarães (1825–1884) was a poet and novelist. He is the author of the novels *A Escrava Isaura* and *O Seminarista*.

38. 'O adeus do voluntário'.

39. See Sidney Chalhoub, *A força da escravidão*. São Paulo: Companhia das Letras, 2012.

40. See Carvalho, *Teatro de sombras* and *A construção da ordem*, p. 290.

41. For the theme of gradualism see the article by Maria Helena P. T. Machado, 'Teremos grandes desastres se não houver providências enérgicas e imediatas: a rebeldia dos escravos e a abolição da escravidão', in Grinberg and Salles (eds.), *O Brasil imperial*, vol. 3: 1870–1889, pp. 371–3.

42. Renato Lemos, 'A alternativa republicana e o fim da monarquia', in Grinberg and Salles (eds.), *O Brasil imperial*, vol. 3: 1870–1889, p. 411.

43. José Murilo de Carvalho, 'República, democracia federalismo: Brasil 1870–1891', *Varia História*, Belo Horizonte, vol. 27, no. 45 (January/June 2011), pp. 146–7.

44. See Lemos, 'A alternativa republicana e o fim da monarquia', p. 414.

45. *Harper's Weekly*, New York (1876), p. 16.

46. See Sergio Goes de Paula, *Um monarca da fuzarca: três versões para um escândalo na corte*. Rio de Janeiro: Relume Dumará, 1993.

47. Raul Pompéia (1863–1895) was a Brazilian journalist and writer well known in the country for his novel *O Ateneu*.

48. Gilberto Freyre, *O perfil de Euclides da Cunha e outros perfis*, 2nd edn. Rio de Janeiro: Record, 1987, p. 123.

49. For Castro Alves, see Alberto da Costa e Silva, *Castro Alves: Um poeta sempre jovem*. São Paulo: Companhia das Letras, 2006. (Coleção Perfis Brasileiros)

50. Pedro Calmon, *História de dom Pedro II*. Rio de Janeiro: José Olympio, 1975, p. 1398.

51. Antônio da Silva Jardim (1860–1891) was an abolitionist and republican, whose speeches drew large crowds.

52. Luís Gonzaga Pinto da Gama (1830–1882), the son of a black mother and white father, was enslaved at the age of ten and remained illiterate until he was seventeen. He obtained his own freedom through the courts and became a lawyer who defended slaves.

53. José Carlos do Patrocínio (1854–1905), writer, journalist, activist and orator.

54. Antônio Bento de Sousa e Castro (1843–1898) was a judge and abolitionist. He had an abolitionist newspaper called *A Redenção*.

55. *Jornal do Commercio, A Onda, A Abolição, Oitenta e Nove, A Redenção, A Vida Semanária, Vila da Redenção, A Liberdade, O Alliot, A Gazeta da Tarde, A Terra da Redenção, O Amigo do Escravo, A Luta, O Federalista.*

56. See Angela Alonso, *Joaquim Nabuco: Os salões e as ruas.* São Paulo: Companhia das Letras, 2012. (Coleção Perfis Brasileiros)

57. Machado, 'Teremos grandes desastres se não houver providências enérgicas e imediatas', p. 380.

58. For the abolitionist *quilombos* and their relationship with the abolitionist movement, see Eduardo Silva, *As camélias do Leblon e a abolição da escravatura: Uma investigação de história cultural* (São Paulo: Companhia das Letras, 2003). See also Chalhoub, *Visões de liberdade.*

59. For Quilombo Jabaquara, see Maria Helena P. T. Machado, *O plano e o pânico*, especially chapter 4.

60. Olavo Brás Martins dos Guimarães Bilac (1865–1918) was a Parnassian poet celebrated for the publication of his *Poems* in 1888.

61. Coelho Neto (1864–1934) was a politician and a prolific writer.

62. André Pinto Rebouças (1838–1898) was a military engineer and writer. Rebouças became famous in Rio de Janeiro during the Second Reign by solving the city's water-supply crisis, piping it from sources outside the town. He served as a military engineer during the Paraguayan War. In the 1880s he began to participate actively in the abolitionist cause, creating the Brazilian Anti-Slavery Society.

63. Francisco de Paula Nei (1858–1897) was a poet and journalist and a member of bohemian society during Rio de Janeiro's *belle époque*.

64. For the Leblon *quilombo* and its idealizer, see especially Silva, *As camélias do Leblon e a abolição da escravatura.*

65. Coleção Tobias Monteiro, Rio de Janeiro: Acervo Biblioteca Nacional.

66. Besouchet, *Pedro II e o século XIX*, p. 495.

67. *Hail!*

68. José Maria da Silva Paranhos Júnior, Baron of Rio Branco (1845–1912) and son of the Viscount of Rio Branco.

69. Oliveira Lima, *O Império brasileiro.* São Paulo: Melhoramentos, 1927.

70. Rui Barbosa (1849–1923) was a very influential politician at this moment in time.

71. Heitor Lyra, *História de dom Pedro II*, 3 vols. (Belo Horizonte and São Paulo: Edusp/Itatiaia, 1977), 1st edn. (São Paulo: Companhia Editora Nacional, 1938–40), p. 387.

72. Adriano do Vale was set free, without trial, in the first month of the Republic.

73. João Alfredo Correia de Oliveira (1835–1919) was a conservative politician.

74. Ilha Fiscal is a small island in Guanabara Bay. Its name (*fiscal* means 'inspector') derived from the fact that it was the base for the port authority.

75. For an excellent analysis of the ball, see Carvalho, *A construção da ordem*, pp. 388–91.

76. Marshal Deodoro da Fonseca (1827–1892), a military man who would became the first president of the Republic.

77. Benjamin Constant (1836–1891) was one of the spokesmen of the republican uprising in 1889 and responsible for drawing up the provisional constitution of 1891.

78. Frederico Sólon de Sampaio Ribeiro (c.1839–1900) was a Brazilian politician who had fought in the Paraguayan War. On the eve of the foundation of the Republic he is said to have spread a rumour that Deodoro and Benjamin Constant had been arrested by the imperial police.

79. Quintino Antônio Ferreira de Sousa Bocaiúva (1836–1912) was a journalist and politician who was a central figure in the process that led to the Proclamation of the Republic.

80. Francisco Glicério de Cerqueira Leite (1846–1916) was a politician who also played a central role in the foundation of the Republic.

81. Aristides da Silveira Lobo (1838–1896) was an abolitionist, republican politician and journalist.

82. A *jangada* is a primitive wooden fishing boat with a triangular sail, which is still used by fishermen – called *jangadeiros*.

83. Pedro Calmon, *O rei filósofo: a vida de dom Pedro II*. São Paulo: Companhia Editora Nacional, 1938, p. 203.

84. Besouchet, *Pedro II e o século XIX*, p. 542.

85. Machado de Assis, *Esaú e Jacó*. Rio de Janeiro: Garnier, 1988, p. 142.

13: THE FIRST REPUBLIC

1. Alencastro and Novais (eds.), *História da vida privada*, vol. 2: *Império – A corte e a modernidade nacional*.

2. See Carvalho, *A formação das almas*.

3. Leopoldo Américo Miguez (1850–1902) was a Brazilian conductor and composer.

4. Antonio Candido, 'A literatura durante o Império', in Sérgio Buarque de Holanda (ed.), *História Geral da Civilização Brasileira*. São Paulo: Difel, 1976, book II: O BRASIL monárquico, vol. 3: Reações e transições.

5. The title refers to the tacit agreement that the presidency of the Republic would alternate between the candidate from São Paulo (the coffee-producing state) and Minas Gerais (with its dairy farms).

6. For the constitution, see Jairo Nicolau, *Eleições no Brasil: Do Império aos dias atuais* (Rio de Janeiro: Zahar, 2012); Américo Freire e Celso Castro, 'As bases republicanas dos Estados Unidos do Brasil', in Ângela de Castro Gomes, Dulce Pandolfi and Verena Alberti (eds.), *A República no Brasil* (Rio de Janeiro: Nova Fronteira; CPDOC-FGV, 2002).

7. For the armed forces and, in particular, the army, see Frank D. McCann, *Soldados da pátria: História do exército brasileiro 1889–1937* (São Paulo: Companhia das Letras, 2007); Schulz, *O Exército na política*.

8. For Floriano and *florianismo*, see Lincoln de Abreu Penna, *O progresso da ordem: O florianismo e a construção da República* (Rio de Janeiro: 7Letras, 1997); Suely Robles Reis de Queiros, *Os radicais da República: Jacobinismo, ideologia e ação – 1893–1897* (São Paulo: Brasiliense, 1986).

9. Steven Topik, *A presença do Estado na economia política do Brasil de 1889 a 1930*. Rio de Janeiro: Record, 1987.

10. Inhabitants of the state of Rio Grande do Sul.

11. For the 'governors' policy' and the institutional engineering of the First Republic, see Renato Lessa, *A invenção republicana: Campos Sales, as bases e a decadência da Primeira República brasileira*. Rio de Janeiro: Vértice/Iuperj, 1988.

12. For the system of fraud, see Nicolau, *Eleições no Brasil*; Carvalho, *Cidadania no Brasil*.

13. From the word *coronel*, meaning 'colonel'; literally, 'colonelism'.

14. For *coronelismo*, see Victor Nunes Leal, *Coronelismo, enxada e voto: O município e o regime representativo no Brasil* (São Paulo: Companhia das Letras, 2012); José Murilo de Carvalho, 'Mandonismo, coronelismo, clientelismo: Uma discussão conceitual', in José Murilo de Carvalho, *Pontos e bordados: Escritos de história e política* (Belo Horizonte: Editora UFMG, 1998); and Maria Isaura Pereira de Queiroz, *O mandonismo local na vida política brasileira e outros ensaios* (São Paulo: Alfa-Ômega, 1976).

15. The passage on immigration was largely based on the research undertaken by Lilia Moritz Schwarcz for the third volume of the series *História do Brasil Nação: 1808–2010* (Rio de Janeiro: Objetiva/ Mapfre, 2012), of which she was the coordinator.

16. Zuleika Alvim, 'Imigrantes: A vida privada dos pobres do campo', in Nicolau Sevcenko (ed.), *História da vida privada* (São Paulo: Companhia das Letras, 2001), vol. 3: República: Da belle époque à era do rádio, p. 220.

17. Ibid., p. 221.

18. Ibid., pp. 283–4.

19. Maria Thereza Schorer Petrone, 'Imigração', in Boris Fausto (ed.), *História geral da civilização brasileira* (Rio de Janeiro: Difel, 1977), vol. III: O Brasil republicano, p. 97.

20. Fernando Henrique Cardoso, 'Dos governos militares a Prudente-Campos Sales', in Fausto (ed.), *História geral da civilização brasileira*, vol. 1: Estrutura de poder e economia (1889–1930), p. 20.

21. Belo Horizonte, the capital of Minas Gerais.

22. The description of the three capitals – São Paulo, Belo Horizonte and Rio de Janeiro – is based on the research carried out for the book *1890–1914: No tempo das certezas* by Lilia Moritz Schwarcz and Angela Marques da Costa. São Paulo: Companhia das Letras, 2000.

23. The equivalent of something like 'flea pits'.

24. See Lima Barreto, *Marginália*. São Paulo: Brasiliense, 1961, p. 33.

25. A *caixotim* is a compartment of a cardboard box.

26. For Belo Horizonte, see Beatriz de Almeida Magalhães and Rodrigo Ferreira Andrade, *Belo Horizonte: Um espaço para a República*. Belo Horizonte: UFMG, 1989.

27. For the Revolt of the Vaccine, see José Murilo de Carvalho, *Os bestializados: O Rio de Janeiro e a República que não foi*. São Paulo: Companhia das Letras, 1987.

28. See Gilberto Hochman, 'Saúde pública ou os males do Brasil', in André Botelho and Lilia Moritz Schwarcz (eds.), *Agenda brasileira: Temas de uma sociedade em mudança*. São Paulo: Companhia das Letras, 2011.

29. See, among others, Schwarcz, *O espetáculo das raças*.

30. *Barbeiro* in Portuguese. Its scientific name is *Triatominae*.

31. Hochman, 'Saúde pública ou os males do Brasil'.

32. For the Revolt of the Whip, see Edmar Morel, *A Revolta da Chibata: subsídios para a história da sublevação na Esquadra pelo marinheiro João Candido em 1910*, 5th ed. (Rio de Janeiro: Paz e Terra, 2009); Carvalho, 'Os bordados de João Cândido', in *Pontos e bordado*.

33. For the military, see McCann, *Soldados da pátria*; Carvalho, *Forças Armadas e política no Brasil*.

34. See below – the modernists and the *Semana de Arte Moderna* of 1922.

35. Mário de Andrade, *O turista aprendiz*. São Paulo: Livraria Duas Cidades, 1976, p. 20.

36. For Euclides da Cunha, see Roberto Ventura, *Euclides da Cunha: Esboço biográfico – Retrato interrompido da vida de Euclides da Cunha*. São Paulo: Companhia das Letras, 2003.

37. *Os Sertões* literally means *The Arid Lands* or *The Backlands*. It is published by Penguin Classics.

38. For *Os sertões*, see Euclides da Cunha, *Os sertões: Campanha de Canudos* (Rio de Janeiro: Francisco Alves, 1923); Ventura, *Euclides da Cunha*; Luiz Costa Lima, *Terra ignota: A construção de Os sertões* (Rio de Janeiro: Civilização Brasileira, 1997); Walnice Nogueira Galvão, *Correspondência de Euclides da Cunha* (São Paulo: Edusp, 1997).

39. For Canudos, see Henrique Estrada Rodrigues, Bruno Pimenta Starling and Marcela Telles, 'O novo continente da utopia', in Delsy Gonçalves de Paula, Heloisa Maria Murgel Starling and Juarez Rocha Guimarães (eds.), *Sentimento de reforma agrária, sentimento de República* (Belo Horizonte: UFMG, 2006); Pauliane de Carvalho Braga, Raissa Brescia dos Reis and Ana Letícia Oliveira Goulart, 'Canudos', in Heloisa Maria Murgel Starling and Pauliane de Carvalho Braga (eds.), *Sentimentos da terra* (Belo Horizonte: PROEX/UFMG, 2013).

40. Euclides da Cunha, *Os Sertões* (1902). São Paulo: Cultrix, 1973, p. 392.

41. Duglas Teixeira Monteiro, 'Um confronto entre Juazeiro, Canudos e Contestado', in Boris Fausto (ed.), *História geral da civilização brasileira* (Rio de Janeiro: Difel, 1977), vol. 2: Sociedade e instituições (1889–1930).

42. For the working class and industrialization, see Francisco Foot Hardman and Victor Leonardi, *História da indústria e do trabalho no Brasil: Das origens aos anos 1920* (São Paulo: Ática, 1991); Lúcio Kowarick, *Trabalho e vadiagem: A origem do trabalho livre no Brasil* (São Paulo: Brasiliense, 1987); Paulo Sérgio Pinheiro and Michael Hall, *A classe operária no Brasil: 1889–1930 – Documentos* (São Paulo: Alfa-Ômega, 1979, vol. 1).

43. For further details, see José Antonio Segatto, *A formação da classe operária no Brasil*. Porto Alegre: Mercado Aberto, 1987.

44. For anarchism in Brazil, see Francisco Foot Hardman, *Nem pátria, nem patrão! Memória operária, cultura e literatura no Brasil* (São Paulo: Editora Unesp, 2002); Daniel Aarão Reis Filho and Rafael Borges Deminicis (eds.), *História do anarquismo no Brasil* (Niterói: Editora UFF, 2006, vol. 1); Boris Fausto, *Trabalho urbano e conflito social* (Rio de Janeiro: Difel, 1977); Edilene Toledo, *Anarquismo e sindicalismo revolucionário: Trabalhadores e militantes em São Paulo na Primeira República* (São Paulo: Fundação Perseu Abramo, 2004).

45. *The Friend of the People, The Worker's Voice, The Land of Freedom, The Working Class, The Lantern.*

46. Boris Fausto, 'Expansão do café e política cafeeira', in Boris Fausto (ed.), *História geral da civilização brasileira* (Rio de Janeiro: Difel, 1977), vol. 1: Estrutura de poder e economia (1889–1930). See also Fausto, *Trabalho urbano e conflito social*, especially chapter 6.

47. Nísia Trindade Lima, 'Campo e cidade: Veredas do Brasil moderno', in Botelho and Schwarcz (eds.), *Agenda brasileira*.

48. See Milton Lahuerta, 'Os intelectuais e os anos 20: Moderno, modernista, modernização', in Helena Carvalho de Lorenzo and Wilma Peres da Costa (eds.), *A década de 1920 e as origens do Brasil moderno*. São Paulo: Editora Unesp, 1997.

49. Alessandra El Far, *A encenação da imortalidade: Uma análise da Academia Brasileira de Letras nos primeiros anos da República (1897–1924)*. Rio de Janeiro: Fundação Getúlio Vargas, 2000.

50. *Brazilwood Poetry.*

51. *The Anthropophagy Magazine.*

52. Mário de Andrade, *Macunaíma: O herói sem nenhum caráter.* Brasília: CNPQ, 1988, pp. 37–8.

53. Alfredo Bosi, 'Situação de Macunaíma', in ibid.

54. André Botelho, *De olho em Mário de Andrade: Uma descoberta intelectual e sentimental do Brasil.* São Paulo: Companhia das Letras, 2012.

55. For *Tia Ciata*, see Carlos Sandroni, *Feitiço decente: Transformações do samba no Rio de Janeiro (1917–1933).* Rio de Janeiro: Zahar/Editora UFRJ, 2001.

56. Each initiate of the Afro-Brazilian religions is the son or daughter of an Orisha Oxum (pronounced *Oshung*), a female deity of Yorubá origin who governs sweet water.

57. *On the phone.*

58. Alfredo da Rocha Viana Jr, better known as Pixinguinha (1897–1973), was a composer, arranger, flautist and saxophonist born in Rio de Janeiro.

59. Heitor dos Prazeres (1898–1966) was one of the pioneers of *carioca* samba and a self-taught naïve painter.

60. *Corta-Jaca* – literally 'Cut the Jackfruit'.

61. The presidential palace in Rio's Catete district.

62. Manuel Bastos Tigre (1882–1957) was a man of many talents. He was a journalist, poet, composer, dramatist, satirist, engineer and librarian, as well as working in advertising.

63. *The comical fraternity.*

64. The Parrot Café.

65. Mônica Pimenta Velloso, *Modernismo no Rio de Janeiro: Turunas e quixotes.* Rio de Janeiro: FGV, 1996).

66. Manuel Maria Barbosa du Bocage (1765–1805) was a Portuguese poet, famed for his satirical verses.

67. Brito Broca, *A vida literária no Brasil – 1900*, 5th edn. Rio de Janeiro: José Olympio, 2005, p. 44.

68. Gilberto Freyre, *Casa-grande & senzala.* Rio de Janeiro: Maia & Schmidt/ José Olympio, 1933, p. 307.

69. Ricardo Benzaquen, *Guerra e paz.* São Paolo, Ed.34, 1994.

70. João Batista Lacerda, *Sur les métis au Brésil.* Paris: Imprimerie Devougue, 1911.

71. Aluísio Tancredo Gonçalves de Azevedo (1857–1913) was a writer who was part of the Naturalist movement in Brazil.

72. Lima Barreto, *Contos completos de Lima Barreto*, ed. and introduction by Lilia Moritz Schwarcz. São Paulo: Companhia das Letras, 2010.

73. See Antonio Sérgio Alfredo Guimarães, 'La République de 1889: Utopie de l'homme blanc, peur de l'homme noir', *Brésil(s): Sciences Humaines et Sociales*, Paris, vol. 1 (2012), pp. 149–68, and 'A República de 1889: Uto-

pia de branco, medo de preto', *Contemporânea – Revista de Sociologia da UFSCar*, São Carlos, vol. 1, no. 2 (2011), pp. 17–36.

74. Maria Cristina Cortez Wissenbach, 'Da escravidão à liberdade: Dimensões de uma privacidade possível', in Nicolau Sevcenko (ed.), *História da vida privada* (São Paulo: Companhia das Letras, 2001), vol. 3: República: Da belle époque à era do rádio.

75. Ibid.

76. Antonio Candido, *Os parceiros do Rio Bonito*, 9th edn. São Paulo: Editora 34, 2001.

77. José Bento Renato Monteiro Lobato (1882–1948) was a very important writer, critic and editor.

78. Lima, 'Campo e cidade'.

79. Manioc flour boiled in water that has been used for cooking fish; manioc or corn flour boiled in water; roasted and crushed peanuts mixed with sugar and manioc flour.

80. Manuela Carneiro da Cunha, 'Política indigenista no século XIX', in idem, *História dos índios no Brasil*.

81. Information taken from Carneiro da Cunha, *História dos índios no Brasil*, p. 133.

82. Barreto, 'Três gênios da secretaria', in idem, *Contos completos de Lima Barreto*.

83. For the lieutenants, see McCann, *Soldados da pátria*; Carvalho, *Forças Armadas e política no Brasil*; Mário Cleber Martins Lanna Júnior, 'Tenentismo e crises políticas na Primeira República', in Lucilia de Almeida Neves Delgado and Jorge Ferreira (eds.), *O Brasil republicano: O tempo do liberalismo excludente* (Rio de Janeiro: Civilização Brasileira, 2007), vol. 1: Da Proclamação da República à Revolução de 1930.

84. The fort stands on a headland at the end of Copacabana beach.

85. For Coluna Prestes/Miguel Costa, see McCann, *Soldados da pátria*; Domingos Meirelles, *As noites das grandes fogueiras: Uma história da Coluna Prestes* (Rio de Janeiro: Record, 1995).

86. General Eurico Gaspar Dutra, President of Brazil from 1946 to 1951.

87. Maria Alice Rezende de Carvalho, *Quatro vezes cidade*. Rio de Janeiro: 7Letras, 1994.

88. Roberto Schwarz, 'Nacional por subtração', in idem, *Que horas são?* São Paulo: Companhia das Letras, 2009.

14: *SAMBA, MALANDRAGEM,* AUTHORITARIANISM

1. *Malandro* ('rogue') and *malandragem* ('roguery') are words that have no direct equivalent in English. A *malandro* is a *carioca* type, a charming, seductive man who generally does nothing.

2. For the 1910 election, see Borges, *A batalha eleitoral de 1910*.

3. Between the constitution of 1891 and the revolution of 1930, the state governors were called 'presidents'. In 1930, Vargas substituted most of the state presidents with federal interveners. The current title of 'governor' for the head of the state executives was established in the constitution of 1946.

4. For the workers' movement and the repressive measures of the 1920s, see Boris Fausto, *Trabalho urbano e conflito social* (São Paulo: Difel, 1977); Everardo Dias, *História das lutas sociais no Brasil* (São Paulo: Alfa-Omega, 1977). For the Coluna Prestes/Miguel Costa, see Meirelles, *As noites das grandes fogueiras*.

5. For the agreement between Minas and São Paulo, its tensions and the stability of the political system, see Cláudia Maria Ribeiro Viscardi, *O teatro das oligarquias: Uma revisão da 'política do café com leite'* (Belo Horizonte: C/Arte, 2011); John Wirth, *O fiel da balança: Minas Gerais na federação brasileira (1889–1937)* (Rio de Janeiro: Paz e Terra, 1982).

6. The neoclassical palace had been built in 1855 on Rio's Praia de Flamengo as a family residence by the Barão de Novo Friburgo. In 1897 it was purchased by the government and converted into the presidential palace.

7. Gilberto de Lima Amado de Faria (1887–1969), federal deputy and senator for the state of Sergipe.

8. Gilberto Amado, *Depois da política*. Rio de Janeiro: José Olympio, 1968.

9. For the options of Washington Luís, see Cláudia Maria Ribeiro Viscardi, *O teatro das oligarquias: Uma revisão da 'política do café com leite'*; Boris Fausto, *A Revolução de 1930: História e historiografia* (São Paulo: Brasiliense, 1994). On the importance of coffee, see Sérgio Silva, *Expansão cafeeira e origem da indústria no Brasil* (São Paulo: Alfa-Omega, 1986).

10. For Antônio Carlos, see Lígia M. L. Pereira and Maria Auxiliadora Faria, *Presidente Antônio Carlos: Um Andrada da República*. Rio de Janeiro: Nova Fronteira, 1998.

11. For Rio Grande do Sul, see Joseph Love, *O regionalismo gaúcho* (São Paulo: Perspectiva, 1975); for Paraíba, see Leda Lewin, *Política e parentela na Paraíba: Um estudo de caso da oligarquia de base familiar* (Rio de Janeiro: Record, 1993). See also Ângela Maria de Castro Gomes et al., *Regionalismo e centralização política: Partidos e Constituinte nos anos 30* (Rio de Janeiro: Nova Fronteira, 1980).

12. For biographical details of Vargas and João Pessoa, see Lira Neto, *Getúlio: Dos anos de formação à conquista do poder (1882–1930)*. São Paulo: Companhia das Letras, 2012, vol. 1.

13. For the Liberal Alliance and its programme, see Boris Fausto, *A Revolução de 1930: História e historiografia*; Lúcia Lippi de Oliveira (ed.), *Elite intelectual e debate político nos anos 30: Uma bibliografia comentada da Revolução de 1930* (Rio de Janeiro: Fundação Getulio Vargas, 1980); Milton Lahuerta, 'Os intelectuais e os anos 20: Moderno, modernista,

modernização', in Helena Carvalho de Lorenzo e Wilma Peres da Costa (eds.), *A década de 1920 e as origens do Brasil moderno* (São Paulo: Unesp, 1997).

14. *Caravanas* are groups of people travelling in large numbers.

15. For the *caravanas* and the Liberal Alliance platform, see Fausto, *A Revolução de 1930*.

16. Franklin Martins, *Quem inventou o Brasil?* Rio de Janeiro: Nova Fronteira (forthcoming).

17. Antônio Evaristo de Morais (1871–1931) was one of the founders of the Brazilian Socialist Party in 1902.

18. Maurício Paiva de Lacerda (1888–1959) was a member of the Communist Party. After the war he rejected communism and joined the conservative União Democrática Nacional (UDN).

19. For Sinhô, see Martins, *Quem foi que inventou o Brasil?*; J. B. da Silva (Sinhô), 'Eu ouço falar (Seu Julinho)' (Rio de Janeiro: Odeon, 1929).

20. For the election results, see Neto, *Getúlio*.

21. For Prestes, see Domingos Meirelles, *1930: Os órfãos da Revolução*. Rio de Janeiro: Record, 2005.

22. For the murder of João Pessoa, see Meirelles, *1930*; see also José Joffily, *Anayde Beiriz: Paixão e morte na revolução de 30* (Niterói: CBAG, 1980).

23. For the Princesa Uprising, see Inês Caminha Lopes Rodrigues, *A Revolta de Princesa: Uma contribuição ao estudo do mandonismo local* (João Pessoa: A União, 1978); Meirelles, *1930*.

24. Quoted in Meirelles, *1930*, p. 532.

25. For the military operations during the revolt of 1930, see Frank D. McCann, *Soldados da pátria: História do Exército brasileiro – 1889–1937* (São Paulo: Companhia das Letras, 2007); José Murilo de Carvalho, *Forças Armadas e política no Brasil* (Rio de Janeiro: Zahar, 2005).

26. Pedro Nava, *O círio perfeito*. São Paulo: Ateliê Editorial, 2004.

27. For the episode of Távora's escape, see Neto, *Getúlio*, p. 415.

28. For the reaction and fall of Washington Luís, see Meirelles, *1930*; Neto, *Getúlio*.

29. Quoted in Meirelles, *1930*, p. 619.

30. For a review of the historiography, see Marieta de Moraes Ferreira and Surama Conde Sá Pinto, 'A crise dos anos 1920 e a Revolução de 1930', in Delgado and Ferreira (eds.), *O Brasil republicano*, vol. 1.

31. For the measures of the Provisional Government, see Dulce Pandolfi, 'Os anos 1930: As incertezas do regime', in Delgado and Ferreira (eds.), *O Brasil republicano*, vol. 2; Neto, *Getúlio*.

32. Quoted in Neto, *Getúlio*, p. 520.

33. For Vargas's labour policies, see Carvalho, *Cidadania no Brasil*; Ângela Maria de Castro Gomes, *Cidadania e direitos do trabalho* (Rio de Janeiro: Zahar, 2002).

34. For the 1932 electoral law, see Carvalho, *Cidadania no Brasil*; Jairo Nicolau, *Eleições no Brasil: Do Império aos dias atuais* (Rio de Janeiro: Zahar, 2012).

35. For Elvira Komel, see Lélia Vidal Gomes da Gama, *Elvira Komel: Uma estrela riscou o céu*. Belo Horizonte: Imprensa Oficial do Estado de Minas Gerais, 1987.

36. For the political forces, see Ângela Maria de Castro Gomes, 'Confronto e compromisso no processo de constitucionalização', in Boris Fausto (ed.), *O Brasil republicano*. São Paulo: Difel, 1981, vol. 3.

37. For the 1932 *Paulista* Uprising, see Hélio Silva, *A guerra Paulista: O ciclo de Vargas* (Rio de Janeiro: Civilização Brasileira, 1976, vol. 2); Maria Helena Capelato, *O movimento de 1932: A causa Paulista* (São Paulo: Brasiliense, 1981); Lira Neto, *Getúlio: Do governo provisório à ditadura do Estado Novo (1930–1945)* (São Paulo: Companhia das Letras, 2013, vol. 2).

38. Oswald de Andrade, *Marco zero: A revolução melancólica*. Rio de Janeiro: Civilização Brasileira, 1978.

39. Quoted in Silva, *A guerra paulista*.

40. For the absence of factory workers, see Capelato, *O movimento de 1932*; Leôncio Basbaum, *Uma vida em seis tempos* (São Paulo: Alfa Omega, 1978).

41. For the 1932 military operations, see McCann, *Soldados da pátria*; Neto, *Getúlio*.

42. For the Vargas measures, see McCann, *Soldados da pátria*; Neto, *Getúlio*.

43. For the Constituent Assembly and the 1934 Constitution, see Carvalho, *Cidadania no Brasil*.

44. For Vargas's observation, see Neto, *Getúlio*, p. 189.

45. The expression is taken from Norbert Frei. See Norbert Frei, *L'État Hitlérien et la société allemande: 1933–1945* (Paris: Seuil, 1994), p. 95.

46. For the AIB, see Marcos Chor Maio and Roney Cytrynowicz, 'Ação Integralista Brasileira: Um movimento fascista no Brasil (1932–1938)', in Lucilia de Almeida Neves Delgado and Jorge Ferreira (eds.), *O Brasil republicano: O tempo do liberalismo excludente – da proclamação da República à Revolução de 1930*. See also Marilena Chaui, 'Apontamentos para uma crítica da Ação Integralista Brasileira', in André Rocha (ed.), *Escritos de Marilena Chaui: Manifestações ideológicas do autoritarismo brasileiro* (Belo Horizonte: Autêntica; São Paulo: Fundação Perseu Abramo, 2013, vol. 2).

47. Plínio Salgado (1895–1975) was one of the founders of the Brazilian Fascist Party.

48. Miguel Reale (1910–2006) was a philosopher, poet and legal scholar.

49. For fascism in the Brazilian armed forces, see McCann, *Soldados da pátria*.

50. For the ANL, see Francisco Carlos Pereira Cascardo, 'A Aliança Nacional Libertadora: Novas abordagens', in Jorge Ferreira and Daniel Aarão Reis

(eds.), *A formação das tradições (1889–1995)* (Rio de Janeiro: Civilização Brasileira, 2007); Marly Vianna, 'A ANL (Aliança Libertadora Nacional)', in Antonio Carlos Mazzeo and Maria Izabel Lagoa (eds.), *Corações vermelhos: Os comunistas brasileiros no século XX* (São Paulo: Cortez, 2003).

51. Miguel Alberto Rodrigo da Costa (1885–1959) was a military officer who fought in the *tenente* uprising of 1924, in the Revolution of 1930 and the Constitutionalist Revolution of 1932.

52. For the PCB, see Marly de Almeida Gomes Vianna, 'O PCB: 1929–43', in Ferreira and Reis (eds.), *A formação das tradições*; John W. Foster Dulles, *Anarquistas e comunistas no Brasil (1900–1935)* (Rio de Janeiro: Nova Fronteira, 1977).

53. Quoted in Neto, *Getúlio*, p. 235.

54. Quoted in Francisco Carlos Pereira Cascardo, 'A Aliança Nacional Libertadora: Novas abordagens', in Ferreira and Reis (eds.), *A formação das tradições*, p. 475.

55. For the Communist International and its participations in the uprisings of 1935, see William Waack, *Camaradas. Nos arquivos de Moscou: A história secreta da revolução brasileira de 1935* (São Paulo: Companhia das Letras, 2004).

56. For the uprising in Natal and Pernambuco, see Marly de A. G. Vianna, *Revolucionários de 1935: Sonho e realidade* (São Paulo: Companhia das Letras, 1992); Hélio Silva, *1935: A revolta vermelha* (Rio de Janeiro: Civilização Brasileira, 1969); Paulo Cavalcanti, *O caso eu conto como o caso foi: Da Coluna Prestes à queda de Arraes* (Recife: Cepe, 2008, vol. 1), chapter 6.

57. For the uprising in Rio de Janeiro, see McCann, *Soldados da pátria*; Vianna, *Revolucionários de 1935*; Silva, *1935*.

58. For the repression under Vargas, see Dulles, *Anarquistas e comunistas no Brasil (1900–1935)*; Vianna, *Revolucionários de 1935*; Waack, *Camaradas*.

59. Graciliano Ramos (1892–1953) is a very well-known Brazilian writer.

60. *Prison Memoirs*.

61. Graciliano Ramos, *Memórias do cárcere* (Rio de Janeiro: Record, 2007), vol. II, pp. 69–70. On Graciliano, see Wander Melo Miranda, *Graciliano Ramos* (São Paulo: Publifolha, 2004).

62. For the double agent, see R. S. Rose and Gordon D. Scott, *Johnny: A vida do espião que delatou a rebelião comunista de 1935* (Rio de Janeiro: Record, 2010).

63. For Vargas's preparations for the coup, see Neto, *Getúlio*; Boris Fausto, *Getúlio Vargas* (São Paulo: Companhia das Letras, 2006).

64. Quoted in Fausto, *Getúlio Vargas*, p. 75.

65. For the Cohen Plan, see McCann, *Soldados da patria*.

66. Alberto Martins Torres (1865–1917) was a prolific writer and critic.

67. For the common traits, see Fausto, *Getúlio Vargas*.

68. Ramos, *Memórias do cárcere*, vol. 1, p. 34.

69. For the repression apparatus, see Fausto, *Getúlio Vargas*; McCann, *Soldados da pátria*; Neto, *Getúlio*.

70. The name of the state investigative police force.

71. For the exchanges with the Gestapo, see Neto, *Getúlio*, p. 263.

72. Ibid., p. 264.

73. For the propaganda apparatus and the legitimacy of the *Estado Novo*, see Lúcia Lippi Oliveira, Mônica Pimenta Velloso and Ângela Maria de Castro Gomes, *Estado Novo: Ideologia e poder* (Rio de Janeiro: Zahar, 1982); Dulce Pandolfi, *Repensando o Estado Novo* (Rio de Janeiro: Fundação Getulio Vargas, 1999).

74. For Noel Rosa, see João Máximo and Carlos Didier, *Noel Rosa: Uma biografia*. Brasília: Editora UnB/ Linha Gráfica Editora, 1990.

75. Brazilian serenades.

76. For the censorship, see Robert M. Levine, *Pai dos pobres? O Brasil e a era Vargas* (São Paulo: Companhia das Letras, 2001, p. 94).

77. For the activities of DIP, see Magno Bissoli Siqueira, *Samba e identidade nacional: Das origens à era Vargas* (São Paulo: Unesp, 2012).

78. For the Ministry of Education under the direction of Capanema, see Helena Bomeny (ed.), *Constelação Capanema: Intelectuais e políticas*. Rio de Janeiro: Fundação Getulio Vargas, 2001.

79. Candido Portinari (1903–1962) was a very important painter in Brazil.

80. For the procedures of promoting a mixed-race culture and the construction of nationality based on regional cultural products associated with popular art, see Lilia K. M. Schwarcz, 'Complexo de Zé Carioca: Notas sobre uma identidade mestiça e malandra', *Revista Brasileira de Ciências Sociais*, no. 29:10 (1995); Lilia M. Schwarcz, 'Nem preto nem branco, muito pelo contrário: Cor e raça na intimidade', in Lilia M. Schwarcz, *História da vida privada no Brasil* (São Paulo: Companhia das Letras, 2006, vol. 4). See also Hermano Vianna, *O mistério do samba* (Rio de Janeiro: Zahar, 2012).

81. For Carmen Miranda, see Ruy Castro, *Carmen: Uma biografia* (São Paulo: Companhia das Letras, 2005). See also Eneida Maria de Souza, 'Carmen Miranda: Do kitsch ao cult', in Heloisa Starling, Berenice Cavalcante and José Eisemberg (eds.), *Decantando a República: Retratos em branco e preto da nação brasileira* (Rio de Janeiro: Nova Fronteira; São Paulo: Fundação Perseu Abramo, 2004, vol. 2).

82. In Portuguese it was called *Serenata Tropical*.

83. The noun *bossa* is hard to translate. It means a mixture of style, talent and charm.

84. Castro, *Carmen*, p. 322.

85. For the Good Neighbor Policy and its cultural products, see Antônio Pedro Tota, *O imperialismo sedutor: A americanização do Brasil na época da Segunda Guerra*. São Paulo: Companhia das Letras, 2000.

86. 'Watercolour of Brazil' or 'Brazilian Watercolour'.

87. For Zé Carioca, see Ruy Castro, 'Nascido no Copacabana Palace, Zé Carioca completa 70 anos', *Serafina, Folha de S. Paulo*, São Paulo (25 November 2012).

88. The expression is taken from Camila Ferreira. See Camila Manduca Ferreira, 'Zé Carioca: Um papagaio na periferia do capitalismo', *Novos Rumos*, vol. 49, no. 1 (January–June 2012).

89. For the song by Noel Rosa, see Mayra Pinto, *Noel Rosa: O humor na canção*. São Paulo: Ateliê, 2012.

90. In fact the *pandiero*, similar to a tambourine – it has a tuneable drumhead and metal cymbals around the rim – which is used to accompany samba.

91. Gilberto Freyre, *Casa-grande & senzala* (Rio de Janeiro: José Olympio, 1981). On Freyre, see Schwarcz, 'Complexo de Zé Carioca'; Vianna, *O mistério do samba*.

92. *Roots of Brazil*.

93. Sérgio Buarque de Holanda, *Raízes do Brasil* (São Paulo: Companhia das Letras, 2006). For Sérgio Buarque de Holanda, see Robert Wegner, 'Caminhos de Sérgio Buarque de Holanda', in André Botelho and Lilia Moritz Schwarcz (ed.), *Um enigma chamado Brasil: 29 intérpretes e um país* (São Paulo: Companhia das Letras, 2009).

94. Caio Prado Jr, *Formação do Brasil contemporâneo* (São Paulo: Brasiliense, 1979). For Caio Prado Jr, see Bernardo Ricúpero, 'Caio Prado Junior e o lugar do Brasil no mundo', in André Botelho and Lilia Moritz Schwarcz (ed.), *Um enigma chamado Brasil: 29 intérpretes e um país*. For the impact of the three authors on the cultural production of the 1930s and 1940s, see Antonio Candido, 'A Revolução de 30 e a cultura', in Paula Monteiro e Álvaro Comin (ed.), *Mão e contramão e outros ensaios contemporâneos*.

95. For labour legislation and the achievement of social rights, see Carvalho, *Cidadania no Brasil*; Luiz Werneck Vianna, *Liberalismo e sindicato no Brasil* (Belo Horizonte: Editora UFMG, 1999, chapter 5).

96. For *malandragem*, see Antonio Candido, 'Dialética da malandragem', in Antonio Candido, *O discurso e a cidade* (São Paulo: Duas Cidades; Rio de Janeiro: Ouro sobre Azul, 2004); Cláudia Matos, *Acertei no milhar: Samba e malandragem no tempo de Getúlio* (Rio de Janeiro: Paz e Terra, 1982).

97. Wilson Batista and Ataulfo Alves, 'O bonde São Januário'. Performer: Cyro Monteiro. Victor 34.691-a, 1940. For Wilson Batista, see Rodrigo Alzuguir, *Wilson Batista: O samba foi sua glória!* (Rio de Janeiro: Casa da Palavra, 2013).

98. For Vargas's political activities during the war and the modernization project, see Fausto, *Getúlio Vargas*; McCann, *Soldados da patria*; Neto, *Getúlio*.

99. For the telegram, see Levine, *Pai dos pobres?*, p. 100.

15: YES, WE HAVE DEMOCRACY!

1. For Vargas's political manoeuvres, see Neto, *Getúlio*.

2. The two lines of the original rhyme: '*Vote no Brigadeiro, que ele é bonito e é solteiro.*'

3. For the candidates, see Maria Victoria de Mesquita Benevides, *A UDN e o udenismo: Ambiguidades do liberalismo brasileiro (1945–1965)* (Rio de Janeiro: Paz e Terra, 1981); Jorge Ferreira, *O imaginário trabalhista: Getulismo, PTB e cultura política popular 1945–1964* (Rio de Janeiro: Civilização Brasileira, 2005), especially chapter 1.

4. For the two episodes, see Michelle Reis de Macedo, *O movimento queremista e a democratização de 1945*. Rio de Janeiro: 7Letras, 2013, p. 105.

5. For the transformations inside the armed forces, especially the army, see McCann, *Soldados da patria*; Carvalho, *Forças Armadas e política no Brasil*.

6. Portuguese has one word for 'politics' and 'policy': *política*.

7. Quoted in Carvalho, *Forças Armadas e política no Brasil*, p. 82.

8. See especially ibid.

9. For Prestes, see Jorge Ferreira, *Prisioneiros do mito: Cultura e imaginário político dos comunistas no Brasil (1930–1956)* (Rio de Janeiro: Editora da UFF; Niterói: Mauad, 2002), especially chapter 9; Dênis de Moraes and Francisco Viana, *Prestes: Lutas e autocríticas* (Petrópolis: Vozes, 1982).

10. For the São Januário stadium rally, see Moraes and Viana, *Prestes*; Mário Magalhães, *Marighella: O guerrilheiro que incendiou o mundo* (São Paulo: Companhia das Letras, 2012).

11. For the growth of the Communist Party, see Magalhães, *Marighella*, p. 157.

12. For the São Paulo rally, see Macedo, *O movimento queremista e a democratização de 1945*.

13. *Sé* is an abbreviation for *sede episcopalis* – the seat of the bishopric. Hence the *Praça da Sé* is the square where the cathedral is located.

14. For the end of the *Estado Novo* and simultaneous growth of Vargas's popularity, see Ângela de Castro Gomes, *A invenção do trabalhismo*. Rio de Janeiro: Vértice; Iuperj, 1988.

15. For the *queremista* movement, see Macedo, *O movimento queremista e a democratização de 1945*; Ferreira, *O imaginário trabalhista*, especially chapter 1.

16. Quoted in Neto, *Getúlio*, pp. 466 ff.

17. Quoted in Ferreira, *O imaginário trabalhista*, p. 75.

18. For the restrictions, see Nicolau, *Eleições no Brasil*, pp. 89–90.

19. For the UDN, see Benevides, *A UDN e o udenismo*.

20. For Lacerda, see Carlos Lacerda, *Depoimento* (Rio de Janeiro: Nova Fronteira, 1978). See also Rodrigo Lacerda, *A República das abelhas* (São Paulo: Companhia das Letras, 2013); Otávio Frias Filho, 'O tribuno da imprensa', *piauí*, no. 91 (April 2014).

21. Quoted in Claudio Bojunga, *JK: O artista do impossível* (Rio de Janeiro: Objetiva, 2001), p. 389.

22. For the PSD, see Lúcia Hipólito, *PSD: De raposas e reformistas* (Rio de Janeiro: Paz e Terra, 1985).

23. Quoted in Bojunga, *JK*, p. 166.

24. Ibid.

25. Literally 'PSDsters' – in other words, members of the party.

26. For the PTB, see Lucilia de Almeida Neves Delgado, *PTB: Do getulismo ao reformismo* (São Paulo: Marco Zero, 1989).

27. For the labour movement as a political project, see Gomes, *A invenção do trabalhismo*. See also Macedo, *O movimento queremista e a democratização de 1945*; Ferreira, *O imaginário trabalhista*, especially chapter 1.

28. For the labour movement after Vargas's death, see Ângela de Castro Gomes, 'Trabalhismo e democracia: O PTB sem Vargas', in Ângela de Castro Gomes (ed.), *Vargas e a crise dos anos 50*. Rio de Janeiro: Ponteio, 2011.

29. For details of the PTB, see Delgado, *PTB*.

30. For the episode of the rally and its consequences, see Macedo, *O movimento queremista e a democratização de 1945*, pp. 144 ff.

31. For the election results, see Boris Fausto, *História do Brasil* (São Paulo: Edusp, 2012), p. 340; Thomas E. Skidmore, *Brasil: de Getúlio a Castello (1930-1964)* (São Paulo: Companhia das Letras, 2010), p. 97.

32. For the 1946 Constitution, see Nicolau, *Eleições no Brasil*; Carvalho, *Cidadania no Brasil*.

33. The expression is taken from Ângela de Castro Gomes. For Brazil's democratic experience between 1946 and 1964, see Jorge Ferreira e Ângela de Castro Gomes, *1964: O golpe que derrubou um presidente, pôs fim ao regime democrático e instituiu a ditadura no Brasil* (Rio de Janeiro: Civilização Brasileira, 2014).

34. For the Cold War, see Martin Walker, *The Cold War: A History*. New York: Henry Holt and Co., 1993.

35. For the PC growth figures see Skidmore, *Brasil*, p. 100.

36. Quoted in Fausto, *História do Brasil*, p. 343. On the repression of the workers, see Fernando Teixeira da Silva and Antonio Luigi Negro, 'Trabalhadores, sindicatos e política (1945-1964)', in Lucilia de Almeida Neves Delgado and Jorge Ferreira (eds.), *O Brasil republicano: O tempo da experiência democrática – da democratização de 1945 ao golpe civil-militar de 1964* (Rio de Janeiro: Civilização Brasileira, 2008, vol. 3); Ronald H. Chilcote, *O Partido Comunista Brasileiro: Conflito e integração – 1922-1972* (Rio de Janeiro: Graal, 2002).

37. For Prestes's response and the suspension of the Communist Party, see Magalhães, *Marighella*, pp. 182 ff.

38. Quoted in Nicolau, *Eleições no Brasil*, p. 90.

39. The plan was known as the SALTE Plan (formed from the initial letters of *Saúde, Alimentação, Transporte* and *Energia*).

40. For Dutra's decision and the decree that banned gambling and closed the casinos, see João Perdigão and Euler Corradi, *O rei da roleta: A incrível vida de Joaquim Rolla* (Rio de Janeiro: Casa da Palavra, 2012); Isabel Lustosa, *Histórias de presidentes: A República no Catete (1897–1960)* (Rio de Janeiro: Agir, 2008).

41. For the efforts of the Legislature and Vargas's presidential campaign, see Fausto, *Getúlio Vargas*; Levine, *Pai dos pobres?*

42. Quoted in Fausto, *Getúlio Vargas*, p. 164.

43. Ibid., p. 166.

44. For the election numbers, see Boris Fausto, *História do Brasil* (São Paulo: Edusp, 2012, p. 346); Skidmore, *Brasil*, p. 113.

45. For energy policy, see Hildete Pereira de Melo, Adilson de Oliveira and João Lizardo de Araújo, 'O sonho nacional: Petróleo e eletricidade (1954–94)', in Gomes (ed.), *Vargas e a crise dos anos 50*. See also Maria Antonieta P. Leopoldi, 'O difícil caminho do meio: Estado, burguesia e industrialização no segundo governo Vargas (1951–1954)', in Gomes (ed.), *Vargas e a crise dos anos 50*.

46. Dona Benta was the kindly old lady who owned Yellow Woodpecker Farm, the location for the writer's successful children's books of the same name.

47. Monteiro Lobato, *O poço do visconde* (São Paulo: Brasiliense, 1960), p. 204. For Lobato's political campaigns, including on oil, see Carmen Lúcia de Azevedo, Márcia Camargos and Vladimir Sacchetta, *Monteiro Lobato: Furacão na Botocúndia* (São Paulo: Senac, 2000), pp. 147 ff.

48. For the engagement of UNE in the oil campaign, see Arthur Poerner, *O poder jovem: História da participação política dos estudantes brasileiros*. Rio de Janeiro: Booklink, 2004.

49. For the increase in electric energy production, see Maria Antonieta P. Leopoldi, 'O difícil caminho do meio: Estado, burguesia e industrialização no segundo governo Vargas (1951–1954)', in Gomes (ed.), *Vargas e a crise dos anos 50*, p. 185.

50. For the steel industry and transportation, see Leopoldi, 'O difícil caminho do meio'.

51. For Getúlio Vargas's nationalist development programme, see Pedro Paulo Zahluth Bastos, 'Ascensão e crise do projeto nacional-desenvolvimentista de Getúlio Vargas' and 'A construção do nacionalismo econômico de Vargas', in Pedro Paulo Zahluth Bastos and Pedro Cezar Dutra Fonseca (eds.), *A era Vargas: Desenvolvimentismo, economia e sociedade*. For the development project associated with it, see René Armand Dreifuss, *1964: A conquista do Estado* (Petrópolis: Vozes, 1981), especially chapters 1, 2, and 3.

52. For the economic crisis, see Bastos, 'Ascensão e crise do projeto

nacional-desenvolvimentista de Getúlio Vargas'. On the emphasis of the Cold War, see Walker, *The Cold War*.

53. For the Strike of the Three Hundred Thousand, see Paul Singer, 'A política das classes dominantes', in Octavio Ianni et al., *Política e revolução social no Brasil* (Rio de Janeiro: Civilização Brasileira, 1965); Delgado, *PTB*.

54. For Goulart, see Jorge Ferreira, *João Goulart: Uma biografia* (Rio de Janeiro: Civilização Brasileira, 2011), especially chapters 2 and 3.

55. Quoted in Ferreira, *João Goulart*, pp. 103–4.

56. For the support of the communication vehicles for the UDN and their activities during the period, see Alzira Alves Abreu and Fernando Lattman-Weltman, 'Fechando o cerco: A imprensa e a crise de agosto de 1954', in Gomes (ed.), *Vargas e a crise dos anos 50*.

57. Quoted in Paulo Markun and Duda Hamilton, *1961: O Brasil entre a ditadura e a guerra civil*. São Paulo: Benvirá, 2011, p. 61.

58. In Brazil the amount given for the minimum wage is always the value per month.

59. For the Colonels' Manifesto, see Ferreira, *João Goulart*; Skidmore, *Brasil*.

60. See Paulo Bonavides and Roberto Amaral, *Textos políticos da história do Brasil: República: Terceira República (1945–1955)* (Brasília: Senado Federal, 2002, p. 677); Skidmore, *Brasil*, p. 169.

61. For the dialogue with Tancredo, see Carlos Heitor Cony, *Quem matou Vargas: 1954, uma tragédia brasileira* (São Paulo: Planeta, 2004), p. 208.

62. For the press, see Alzira Alves Abreu and Fernando Lattman-Weltman, 'Fechando o cerco: A imprensa e a crise de agosto de 1954', in Gomes (ed.), *Vargas e a crise dos anos 50*; Markun and Hamilton, *1961*.

63. *Associated Dailies*.

64. For the *Última Hora* episode, see also Ana Maria de Abreu Laurenza, *Lacerda x Wainer: O corvo e o bessarabiano* (São Paulo: Senac, 1998). For Wainer, see Samuel Wainer, *Minha razão de viver: Memórias de um repórter* (Rio de Janeiro: Record, 1988).

65. For the attack and its consequences, see Skidmore, *Brasil*; Claudio Lacerda, *Uma crise de agosto: O atentado da rua Toneleros* (Rio de Janeiro: Nova Fronteira, 1994); Fausto, *Getúlio Vargas*; Ferreira, *João Goulart*.

66. Literally 'UDNists'.

67. Supporters of Getúlio Vargas and what he represented.

68. Quoted in Ferreira, *João Goulart*, p. 127.

69. For the last ministerial meeting and the suicide, see Skidmore, *Brasil*; Fausto, *Getúlio Vargas*. See also Cony, *Quem matou Vargas*; Rubem Fonseca, *Agosto* (São Paulo: Companhia das Letras, 1990).

70. For the protests, see Jorge Ferreira, 'O Carnaval da tristeza: Os motins urbanos do 24 de agosto', in idem, *O imaginário trabalhista*.

71. *Cinelândia* was, and still is, the popular name for Praça Marechal Floriano Peixoto, the square in the centre of Rio de Janeiro.
72. Quoted in Fausto, *Getúlio Vargas*, p. 195.
73. Quoted in Bojunga, *JK*, p. 258.
74. The argument is Jorge Ferreira's. See Ferreira, 'O Carnaval da tristeza', in idem, *O imaginário trabalhista*.

16: THE 1950S AND 1960S

1. For the Jacareacanga uprising, see Bojunga, *JK*.
2. For the presidential elections of 1955, see Benevides, *A UDN e o udenismo*; Skidmore, *Brasil*; Bojunga, *JK*.
3. Under a parliamentary system, with the appointment of a prime minister, the president would have reduced powers.
4. Quoted in Ferreira, *João Goulart*, p. 148.
5. For the Café Filho government, see Skidmore, *Brasil*. For the coup and counter-coup, see Ferreira, *O imaginário trabalhista*, especially chapter 4; Flávio Tavares, *O dia em que Getúlio matou Allende e outras novelas do poder* (Rio de Janeiro: Record, 2004), especially chapter 3.
6. In Brazil, the president of the Chamber of Deputies is the third in the line of succession.
7. For the ties between subaltern officers and the labour movement, see Ferreira, *O imaginário trabalhista*, especially chapter 4.
8. For Juscelino's relationship with the military, see Bojunga, *JK*; Ricardo Maranhão, *O governo Juscelino Kubitschek* (São Paulo: Brasiliense, 1984); Maria Victoria Benevides, *O governo Kubitschek: Desenvolvimento econômico e estabilidade política* (Rio de Janeiro: Paz e Terra, 1976).
9. For the Targets Plan, see Benevides, *O governo Kubitschek*; Miriam Limoeiro Cardoso, *Ideologia do desenvolvimento: Brasil JK-JQ* (Rio de Janeiro: Paz e Terra, 1977); Clovis de Faro and Salomão L. Quadros da Silva, 'A década de 50 e o Programa de Metas', in Ângela de Castro Gomes (ed.), *O Brasil de JK* (Rio de Janeiro: Fundação Getulio Vargas, 1991).
10. For daily life in the 1950s, see Joaquim Ferreira dos Santos, *1958: O ano que não devia terminar* (Rio de Janeiro: Record, 1997).
11. Por the paved highways, see Bojunga, *JK*, p. 407.
12. Quoted in ibid., p. 398.
13. For the construction of the Belém–Brasília highway, see Bojunga, *JK*.
14. For JK's style of doing politics, see ibid.; Skidmore, *Brasil*.
15. For Lacerda's observation, see Lacerda, *A República das abelhas*.
16. For developmentalism, see Cardoso, *Ideologia do desenvolvimento*; Celso Furtado, *Desenvolvimento e subdesenvolvimento* (Rio de Janeiro: Fundo

de Cultura, 1961); Francisco de Oliveira, *A economia brasileira: Crítica à razão dualista* (Petrópolis: Vozes, 1981).

17. For Iseb, see Caio Navarro de Toledo (ed.), *Intelectuais e política no Brasil: A experiência do Iseb*. Rio de Janeiro: Revan, 2005.

18. For underdevelopment, see Furtado, *Desenvolvimento e subdesenvolvimento*; Maria da Conceição Tavares (ed.), *Celso Furtado e o Brasil* (São Paulo: Fundação Perseu Abramo, 2001); Oliveira, *A economia brasileira*; Marcelo Ridenti, *Brasilidade revolucionária* (São Paulo: Unesp, 2010).

19. For the Teatro de Arena, see Izaías Almada, *Teatro de Arena: Uma estética de resistência* (São Paulo: Boitempo, 2004); Sábato Magaldi, *Um palco brasileiro: O Arena de São Paulo* (São Paulo: Brasiliense, 1984).

20. *They don't wear evening dress.*

21. For Vera Cruz, see Sidney Ferreira Leite, *Cinema brasileiro: Das origens à retomada* (São Paulo: Fundação Perseu Abramo, 2005); Maria Rita Galvão, *Burguesia e cinema: O caso Vera Cruz* (Rio de Janeiro: Civilização Brasileira, 1981).

22. Not to be confused with the writer of the same name (to whom he was not related).

23. The *cangaçeiros* were the armed bandits who terrorized the scrublands in the interior of the northeast.

24. For *chanchadas*, see Suzana Ferreira, *Cinema Carioca nos anos 30 e 40: Os filmes musicais nas telas da cidade* (São Paulo: Annablume, 2003); Sérgio Augusto, *Este mundo é um pandeiro* (São Paulo: Companhia das Letras/Cinemateca Brasileira, 1989).

25. For Nelson Pereira dos Santos and *Rio, 40 graus*, see Helena Salem, *Nelson Pereira dos Santos: O sonho possível do cinema brasileiro* (Rio de Janeiro: Record, 1996); Leite, *Cinema brasileiro*.

26. Ruy Guerra was born in Mozambique, then still a Portuguese colony, in 1931. He is best known as an actor and film director.

27. Glauber Rocha (1939–1981) is the author of the same vanguard of very influential films. Notably *Deus e o diabo na terra do sol* (1964) and *Terra em transe* (*Entranced Earth* – 1967).

28. Glauber Rocha, *Revolução do Cinema Novo*. Rio de Janeiro: Alhambra/Embrafilme, 1981, pp. 393–4.

29. The *Bachianas Brasileiras* is a series of nine suites written by Heitor Villa-Lobos for different combinations of instruments and voices.

30. For Glauber Rocha and the Cinema Novo, see Ismail Xavier, *Cinema brasileiro moderno* (São Paulo: Paz e Terra, 2001); Rocha, *Revolução do Cinema Novo*; Raquel Gerber et al., *Glauber Rocha* (São Paulo: Paz e Terra, 1977); Lucia Nagib, *A utopia no cinema brasileiro: Matrizes, nostalgia, distopias* (São Paulo: Cosac Naify, 2006), especially chapter 1; Eduardo Escorel, 'Deus e o diabo – ano 1: Glauber Rocha no turbilhão de 1964', *piauí*, no. 90 (March 2014).

31. For Bossa Nova as a movement, see Ruy Castro, *Chega de saudade: A história e as histórias da Bossa Nova* (São Paulo: Companhia das Letras, 1990); idem, *A onda que se ergueu no mar: Novos mergulhos na Bossa Nova* (São Paulo: Companhia das Letras, 2001).

32. For Bossa Nova as a musical language, see Luiz Tatit, *O século da canção* (Cotia: Ateliê, 2004); Walter Garcia, *Bim Bom: A contradição sem conflitos de João Gilberto* (São Paulo: Paz & Terra, 1999).

33. For Bossa Nova as a commercial product, see José Gave, *Momento Bossa Nova*. São Paulo: Fapesp/Annablume, 2006.

34. For the internationalization of Bossa Nova, see Castro, *Chega de saudade* and *A onda que se ergueu no mar*.

35. For the bottlenecks in the Targets Plan, see Carla Maria Junho Anastasia, 'From Drummond to Rodrigues: Venturas e desventuras dos brasileiros no governo JK', in Wander Melo Miranda, *Anos JK: Margens da modernidade* (São Paulo: Imprensa Oficial do Estado de São Paulo; Rio de Janeiro: Casa de Lúcio Costa, 2002); Skidmore, *Brasil*; Maria Antonieta P. Leopoldi, 'Crescendo em meio à incerteza: A política econômica do governo JK', in Gomes (ed.), *O Brasil de JK*.

36. Roberto Campos, *A lanterna na popa*. Rio de Janeiro: Topbooks, 1994, 2 vols.

37. *Revista Brasiliense*, nos. 35–36 (1961), p. 29. Cited in Bojunga, *JK*, p. 340.

38. The expression is taken from Maria Victoria Benevides. See Benevides, *O governo Kubitschek*.

39. For inflation figures, see Maria Antonieta P. Leopoldi, 'Crescendo em meio à incerteza: A política econômica do governo JK', in Gomes (eds.), *O Brasil de JK*.

40. For the 'parallel administration', see Benevides, *O governo Kubitschek*.

41. For the limitiations of the Targets Plans and the rural question, see Vânia Maria Losada Moreira, 'Os anos JK: Industrialização e modelo oligárquico de desenvolvimento rural', in Delgado and Ferreira (eds.), *O Brasil republicano*; Skidmore, *Brasil*.

42. For the revolts, see Thiago Lenine Tito Tolentino, 'Margens da marcha para o Oeste: Luta pela terra em Trombas e Formoso, Porecatu e sudoeste do Paraná', in Heloisa Marcia Murgel Starling and Pauline de Carvalho Braga (eds.), *Sentimento da terra*. Belo Horizonte: Proex, 2013.

43. For the *Ligas Camponesas*, see Antônio Montenegro, 'As Ligas Camponesas e os conflitos no campo', in Rita de Cássia Araújo and Túlio Velho Barreto (eds.), *1964: O golpe passado a limpo* (Recife: Fundação Joaquim Nabuco/Massangana, 2007); Joseph Page, *A revolução que nunca houve: O Nordeste do Brasil (1955–1964)* (Rio de Janeiro: Record, 1972).

44. For Francisco Julião, see Cláudio Aguiar, *Francisco Julião: Uma biografia*. Rio de Janeiro: Civilização Brasileira, 2014.

45. For the military training camps, see Flávio Tavares, *Memórias do esquecimento: Os segredos dos porões da ditadura* (Rio de Janeiro: Record,

2005); Aguiar, *Francisco Julião*; and Claudia Moraes de Souza, *Pelas ondas do rádio; cultura popular, camponeses e o rádio nos anos 1960* (São Paulo: Alameda, 2013).

46. Paulo Neves Freire (1921-1997) was a Brazilian educator and philosopher and a leading advocate of critical pedagogy, which he called Pedagogy of the Oppressed.

47. For the MEB, see Ana Emília de Carvalho and Bruno Viveiros Martins, 'MEB, MCP, UNE e CPC: Cultura e educação no campo na década de 1960', in Starling and Braga (eds.), *Sentimentos da terra*. For the PCB, see Angelo Priori, 'O PCB e a questão agrária: Os manifestos e o debate político acerca de seus temas', in Antonio Carlos Mazzeo and Maria Izabel Lagoa (eds.), *Corações vermelhos: Os comunistas brasileiros no século XX* (São Paulo: Cortez, 2003).

48. For the project and construction of Brasília, see James Holston, *A cidade modernista: Uma crítica de Brasília e sua utopia* (São Paulo: Companhia das Letras, 1993); Bojunga, *JK*; Lauro Cavalcanti, 'Brasília: A construção de um exemplo', in Miranda, *Anos JK*; Tavares, *O dia em que Getúlio matou Allende e outras histórias*, especially chapter 4.

49. For the relation between Belo Horizonte and Brasília, see Helena Bomeny, 'Utopias de cidades: As capitais do modernismo', in Gomes (eds.), *O Brasil de JK*.

50. Otto Lara Resende (1922-1992) was a writer of histories (*cronicas*) for various newspapers.

51. Quoted in Bojunga, *JK*, p. 398.

52. The phrase comes from Manuel Bandeira, in a column entitled 'Lúcio Costa', *Jornal do Brasil*, Rio de Janeiro (24 March 1957), p. 5.

53. The Square of the Three Powers.

54. For the workers and the satellite towns, see Holston, *A cidade modernista*; for the workers during the construction of Brasília, see Tavares, *O dia em que Getúlio matou Allende e outras histórias*, especially chapter 4.

55. For JK's strategy, see Sheldon Maran, 'Juscelino Kubitschek e a política presidencial', in Gomes (ed.), *O Brasil de JK*.

56. For the candidacy of Jânio Quadros, the campaign and UDN support, see Benevides, *A UDN e o udenismo*; Skidmore, *Brasil*; Dulci, *A UDN e o antipopulismo no Brasil*.

57. For Jânio Quadros, see Ricardo Arnt, *Jânio Quadros: O Prometeu de Vila Maria* (Rio de Janeiro: Ediouro, 2004); Tavares, *O dia em que Getúlio matou Allende e outras histórias*, especially chapter 4.

58. For the candidacy of Marshal Lott, see Hippolito, *PSD*; Ferreira, *João Goulart*.

59. For the election results, see Skidmore, *Brasil*, p. 233; Ferreira, *João Goulart*, p. 213.

60. For foreign policy, see Brás José de Araújo, *A política externa do governo Jânio Quadros*. Rio de Janeiro: Graal, 1981

61. For Jânio's presidency, see Skidmore, *Brasil*; Ferreira, *João Goulart*.

62. See Arnt, *Jânio Quadros*, p. 154.

63. The president's residential palace.

64. See Tavares, *O dia em que Getúlio matou Allende e outras histórias*, p. 167.

65. For Jango's trip and the conflicts with Jânio, see Ferreira, *João Goulart*. For the decoration of Che Guevara, see Markun and Hamilton, *1961*, especially chapter 4.

66. Quoted in Amir Labaki, *1961: A crise da renúncia e a solução parlamentarista* (São Paulo: Brasiliense, 1986, p. 47). For the resignation, see also Arnt, *Jânio Quadros*; Skidmore, *Brasil*.

67. Quoted in Labaki, *1961*, pp. 51–2.

68. At this time there was a separate military minister for each of the armed forces.

69. The argument is taken from Argelina Figueiredo. See Argelina Cheibub Figueiredo, *Democracia ou reformas? Alternativas democráticas à crise política – 1941–1964* (São Paulo: Paz e Terra, 1993).

70. For the political crisis and the resistance to the coup, see Figueiredo, *Democracia ou reformas?*; Labaki, *1961*; Markun and Hamilton, *1961*; Ferreira, *João Goulart*; Flávio Tavares, *1961: O golpe derrotado – Luzes e sombras do Movimento da Legalidade* (Porto Alegre: L&PM, 2011).

71. For Brizola, see F. C. Leite Filho, *El caudillo: Leonel Brizola – Um perfil biográfico*. São Paulo: Aquariana, 2008.

72. For the Rede da Legalidade, see Tavares, *1961*; Juremir Machado da Silva, *Vozes da legalidade: Política e imaginário na era do rádio* (Porto Alegre: Sulina, 2011); Aloysio Castelo de Carvalho, *A rede da democracia: O Globo, O Jornal e Jornal do Brasil na queda do governo Goulart (1961–1964)* (Niterói: Editora da UFF, 2010).

73. For Goiás, see Maria Dulce Loyola Teixeira, *Mauro Borges e a crise político-militar de 1961: Movimento da legalidade*. Brasília: Senado Federal, 1994.

74. For Jango, see Ferreira, *João Goulart*, especially chapter 6.

17: ON A KNIFE EDGE

1. Jânio Quadros in January, Raniero Mazzilli (interim) in August and Jango (João Goulart) in September.

2. For the Jango administration, see Ferreira, *João Goulart*; Moniz Bandeira, *O governo João Goulart e as lutas sociais no Brasil (1961–1964)* (Rio de Janeiro: Civilização Brasileira, 1978); Marco Antonio Villa, *Jango: Um perfil (1945–1964)* (São Paulo: Globo, 2004).

3. For foreign policy, see Miriam Gomes Saraiva and Tulio Vigevani, 'Política externa do Brasil: Continuidade em meio à descontinuidade, de 1961 a

2011', in Daniel Aarão Reis, Marcelo Ridente and Rodrigo Patto Sá Motta (eds.), *A ditadura que mudou o Brasil*. Rio de Janeiro: Zahar, 2014.

4. For the various projects of agrarian reform, see Mario Grynspan, 'O período Jango e a questão agrária: Luta política e afirmação de novos atores', in Marieta de Moraes Ferreira (ed.), *João Goulart: Entre a memória e a história* (Rio de Janeiro: Fundação Getúlio Vargas, 2006); Leonilde Servolo de Medeiros, *Reforma agrária no Brasil: História e atualidade da luta pela terra* (São Paulo: Fundação Perseu Abramo, 2003); Aguiar, *Francisco Julião*. For the landowners, see Heloisa Maria Murgel Starling, *Os senhores de Gerais: Os novos inconfidentes e o golpe de 1964* (Petrópolis: Vozes, 1986). For land occupation, raids and murders, see Page, *A revolução que nunca houve*.

5. For the trade unions and workers' strikes, see Lucília de Almeida Neves, *CGT no Brasil (1961–1964)* (Belo Horizonte: Vega, 1981).

6. For the diversity of the left in the country, see Jorge Ferreira and Daniel Aarão Reis (eds.), *Nacionalismo e reformismo radical (1945–1964)* (Rio de Janeiro: Civilização Brasileira, 2007, vol. 2); Ferreira, *João Goulart*.

7. For the core reforms, see Daniel Aarão Reis, *Ditadura e democracia no Brasil: Do golpe de 1964 à Constituição de 1988* (Rio de Janeiro: Zahar, 2014); Ferreira, *João Goulart*.

8. Miguel Arrães Arraes (1916–2005), Leonel Brizola and Luis Carlos Prestes were to be considered by the military the most radical – and consequently dangerous – left-wing politicians during the dictatorship (1964–85), and there were those who initially wanted to exclude them from the general amnesty of 1979. Arrães was first elected governor of Pernambuco in 1962. After the military coup he refused to stand down, was arrested and imprisoned for eleven months, and then went into exile in Algeria. After his return he was re-elected twice as governor of Pernambuco, in 1986 and 1994. His grandson, Eduardo Campos (1964–2014), governor of Pernambuco for two terms, was candidate for the presidency in the 2014 general election. His death in an aeroplane accident, during the campaign, caused national commotion.

9. For the elections of 1962, see *Revista Brasileira de Estudos Políticos*, Belo Horizonte: UFMG (16 January 1964); Skidmore, *Brasil*. For Miguel Arraes, see Antonio Torres Montenegro and Taciana Mendonça dos Santos, 'Lutas políticas em Pernambuco: A Frente do Recife chega ao poder (1955–1964)', in Ferreira and Reis (eds.), *Nacionalismo e reformismo radical (1945–1964)*, vol. 2.

10. See Roberto Garcia, 'Castello perdeu a batalha', *Veja*, no. 444 (9 March 1977), p. 6.

11. For the ESG, see Alfred Stepan, *Os militares na política* (Rio de Janeiro: Artenova, 1975); Eliezer R. de Oliveira, *As Forças Armadas: Política e ideologia no Brasil (1964–1969)* (Petrópolis: Vozes, 1976).

12. For the IPES, see Dreifuss, *1964*; Starling, *Os senhores das Gerais*; Thiago Aguiar de Moraes, *Entreguemos a empresa ao povo antes que o comunista a entregue ao Estado. Os discursos da fração vanguardista da classe empresarial gaúcha na revista Democracia e Empresa do Instituto de Pesquisas Econômicas e Sociais do Rio Grande do Sul (1962–1971)* (Porto Alegre: FFCH-PUC-RS, 2014). MA dissertation in History. Mimeographed.

13. For the films produced by IPES, see Denise Assis, *Propaganda e cinema a serviço do golpe (1962–1964)*. Rio de Janeiro: Mauad/Faperj, 2001.

14. For the numbers of votes in the referendum, see Ferreira, *João Goulart*, p. 323.

15. For the support for Brizola among subaltern officers, see Filho, *El caudillo*. See also Ronaldo Vainfas, 'A luz própria de Leonel Brizola: Do trabalhismo getulista ao socialismo moreno', in Jorge Ferreira and Daniel Aarão Reis Filho (eds.), *As esquerdas no Brasil: Revolução e democracia* (Rio de Janeiro: Civilização Brasileira, 2007, vol. 3).

16. Quoted in Villa, *Jango*, p. 118. For the request to Congress and its consequences, see Ferreira, *João Goulart*; Skidmore, *Brasil*.

17. The state of Guanabara, of which Carlos Lacerda was governor, was created in 1960 after the transfer of the government to Brasília, with Rio de Janeiro as its capital.

18. For the Sergeants' Revolt, see Almoré Zoch Cavalheiro, *A legalidade, o golpe militar e a rebelião dos sargentos*. Porto Alegre: AGE, 2011.

19. For the Executive paralysis, see Wanderley Guilherme dos Santos, *Sessenta e quatro: Anatomia da crise* (São Paulo: Vértice, 1986). For the consequences of radicalization, see José Murilo de Carvalho, 'Fortuna e Virtù no golpe de 1964', in Carvalho, *Forças Armadas e política no Brasil*. For the economic crisis and American funding, see Ferreira, *João Goulart*, pp. 351 and 376.

20. For the Central do Brasil rally, see Alberto Dines et al., *Os idos de março e a queda em abril* (Rio de Janeiro: José Alvaro, 1964). For Jango's speech, see Ferreira, *João Goulart*, pp. 425 ff.

21. For the presidential message, see Ferreira, *João Goulart*; Skidmore, *Brasil*.

22. For the March of the Family in São Paulo, see Solange de Deus Simões, *Deus, patria e família: As mulheres no golpe de 1964* (Petrópolis: Vozes, 1985); Dines et al., *Os idos de março e a queda em abril*.

23. Quoted in Ferreira, *João Goulart*, p. 438.

24. For the marches throughout the country, see Aline Presot, 'Celebrando a "Revolução": As Marchas da Família com Deus pela Liberdade e o golpe de 1964', in Denise Rollemberg and Samantha Viz Quadrat (eds.), *A construção social dos regimes autoritários: Brasil e América Latina*. Rio de Janeiro: Civilização Brasileira, 2010, vol. 2.

25. For the sailors' revolt and its consequences, see Dines et al., *Os idos de março e a queda em abril*; Elio Gaspari, *A ditadur envergonhada* (São

Paulo: Companhia das Letras, 2002); Avelino Bioen Capitani, *A rebelião dos marinheiros* (São Paulo: Expressão Popular, 2005).

26. For the sailors aboard ship, see Anderson da Silva Almeida, 'A grande rebelião: Os marinheiros de 1964 por outros faróis', in Reis, Ridente and Motta (eds.), *A ditadura que mudou o Brasil*.

27. For the date of the coup, see Starling, *Os senhores de Gerais*. For the United States, the task force and Operation Brother Sam, see Phyllis R. Parker, *1964: O papel dos Estados Unidos no golpe de Estado de 31 de março* (Rio de Janeiro: Civilização Brasileira, 1977); Carlos Fico, *O grande irmão: Da operação Brother Sam aos anos de chumbo – O governo dos Estados Unidos e a ditadura militar brasileira* (Rio de Janeiro: Civilização Brasileira, 2008); Flávio Tavares, *1964: O golpe* (Porto Alegre: L&PM, 2014).

28. For the slang, the speech and its consequences, see Dines et al., *Os idos de março e a queda em abril*; Gaspari, *A ditadura envergonhada*; Ferreira, *João Goulart*.

29. For Cabo Anselmo, see Marco Aurélio Borba, *Cabo Anselmo: A luta armada ferida por dentro* (São Paulo: Global, 1981); Urariano Mota, *Soledad no Recife* (São Paulo: Boitempo, 2009).

30. For Jango's journey from Rio de Janeiro, Brasília and Porto Alegre to Montevideo, see Ferreira, *João Goular*. For Brizola's resistance plan, see Filho, *El caudillo*.

31. When the military removed Vargas from power; when they intervened after his suicide; when they intervened to permit the investiture of JK; and when they decided to allow Jango to take power under a parliamentary regime.

32. For Minas and the uprising, see Starling, *Os senhores de Gerais*. For the justifications of the conspirators, see Olympio Mourão Filho, *Memórias: A verdade de um revolucionário* (Rio de Janeiro: L&PM, 1978); Carlos Luís Guedes, *Tinha que ser Minas* (Rio de Janeiro: Nova Fronteira, 1979).

33. For Juscelino, see Ferreira, *João Goulart*, p. 256.

34. For Tancredo Neves and the session of Congress, see Ferreira, *João Goulart*.

35. For Castello Branco's election, see Lira Neto, *Castello: A marcha para a ditadura* (São Paulo: Contexto, 2004). For the lifting of the punishments, see Lúcia Klein and Marcus Figueiredo, *Legitimidade e coação no Brasil pós-64* (Rio de Janeiro: Forense-Universitária, 1978); Maria Helena Moreira Alves, *Estado e oposição no Brasil (1964–1984)* (Petrópolis: Vozes, 1984).

36. For the occupation of the state by IPES, see Dreifuss, *1964*, especially chapter 9.

37. That is, that came under the presidency of the Republic.

38. For the intramilitary groups, see Maud Chirio, *A política nos quartéis: Revoltas e protestos de oficiais na ditadura militar brasileira*. Rio de Janeiro: Zahar, 2012.

39. For the crises, see Carlos Chagas, *A guerra das estrelas (1964–1984): Os bastidores das sucessões presidenciais*. Porto Alegre: L&PM, 1985.

40. For Castello's death, see Neto, *Castello*.

41. For the Costa e Silva government and the succession crisis, see Carlos Castello Branco, *Os militares no poder. O Ato 5* (Rio de Janeiro: Nova Fronteira, 1978, vol. II); Carlos Chagas, *A ditadura militar e os golpes dentro do golpe (1964–1969)* (Rio de Janeiro: Record, 2014).

42. A council formed of the military ministers, the heads of the chiefs of staff of the three forces and the head of the military cabinet.

43. For the crisis, see Gaspari, *A ditadura envergonhada*, especially the introduction; Maria Celina D'Araujo and Celso Castro (eds.), *Ernesto Geisel* (Rio de Janeiro: Fundação Getulio Vargas, 1997); Sylvio Frota, *Ideais traídos* (Rio de Janeiro: Zahar, 2006).

44. For the participation of the IPES, see Dreifuss, *1964*.

45. For Delfim Netto's declaration, see Rafael Cariello, 'O chefe', *piauí*, no. 96 (September 2014), p. 23.

46. For Maílson da Nóbrega's declaration, see Cariello, ibid., p. 24.

47. For Ernane Galvêas's declaration, see Cariello, ibid., p. 22.

48. 'Stable employment' was a right enjoyed by the majority of civil servants who were admitted via examination and could not be dismissed, except in extreme circumstances.

49. For the economic policy of the Castello government, see Francisco Vidal Luna and Herbert S. Klein, 'Transformações econômicas no período militar (1964–1985)', in Reis, Ridente and Motta (eds.), *A ditadura que mudou o Brasil*; Alves, *Estado e oposição no Brasil (1964–1984)*.

50. For Contagem, see Edgard Leite Oliveira, *Conflito social, memória e experiência: As greves dos metalúrgicos de Contagem em 1968*. Belo Horizonte: UFMG, 2010. MA dissertation in Education.

51. For the strike in Osasco, see Marta Gouveia de Oliveira Rovai, *Osasco 1968: A greve no feminino e no masculino*. São Paulo: USP, 2012. PhD dissertation in History.

52. For the 'economic miracle', see Luna and Klein, 'Transformações econômicas no período militar (1964–1985)'; Gaspari, *A ditadura envergonhada*; Luiz Carlos Delorme Prado e Fábio Sá Earp, 'O "milagre" brasileiro: Crescimento acelerado, integração internacional e concentração de renda (1967–1973)', in Lucilia de Almeida Neves Delgado and Jorge Ferreira (eds.), *O Brasil republicano: O tempo da ditadura – Regime militar e movimentos sociais em fins do século XX* (Rio de Janeiro: Civilização Brasileira, 2007).

53. For the AERP, see Carlos Fico, *Reinventado o otimismo: Ditadura, propaganda e imaginário social no Brasil* (Rio de Janeiro: Fundação Getulio Vargas, 1997). Copies (16 mm) of the films produced by the Aerp can be found in the Centro de Produção Cultural, Decanato de Extensão, Universidade de Brasília.

54. For the Transamazônica, see Daniel Drosdoff, *Linha dura no Brasil: O governo Medici (1969–1974)* (São Paulo: Global, 1986); Murilo Melo Filho, *O milagre brasileiro* (Rio de Janeiro: Bloch, 1972).

55. See *Anais do Senado Federal*, vol. 3 (1972), p. 93.

56. Edmar L. Bacha and Roberto M. Unger, *Participação, salário e voto: Um projeto de democracia para o Brasil.* Rio de Janeiro: Paz e Terra, 1978.

57. A TV presenter of the time.

58. See Márcio Moreira Alves, *Tortura e torturados.* Rio de Janeiro: Idade Nova, 1966.

59. For the political situation in 1968 and Márcio Moreira Alves's speech, see Zuenir Ventura, *1968: O ano que não terminou* (Rio de Janeiro: Nova Fronteira, 1988); Gaspari, *A ditadura envergonhada.*

60. The argument is Anthony Pereira's. See Anthony W. Pereira, *Ditadura e repressão: O autoritarismo e o estado de direito no Brasil, no Chile e na Argentina* (Rio de Janeiro: Paz e Terra, 2010).

61. Arthur da Costa e Silva et al., 'À nação. Ato Institucional' (9 April 1964), in Carlos Fico, *Além do golpe: Versões e controvérsias sobre 1964 e a ditadura militar.* Rio de Janeiro: Record, 2004, pp. 339 ff.

62. See Alves, *Estado e oposição no Brasil (1964–1984)*; Heloisa Starling et al., *Relatório parcial de pesquisa: Instituições e locais associados a graves violações de direitos humanos* (Brasília: Comissão Nacional da Verdade, 2014).

63. For the IPMS, see Chirio, *A política nos quartéis*; Alves, *Estado e oposição no Brasil (1964–1984).*

64. For the data, see Lúcia Klein and Marcus Figueiredo, *Legitimidade e coação no Brasil pós-64* (Rio de Janeiro: Forense-Universitária, 1978).

65. For the Frente Ampla, see Célia Maria Leite Costa, 'A Frente Ampla de oposição ao regime militar', in Moraes Ferreira (ed.), *João Goulart.*

66. For Arena, see Lucia Grinberg, *Partido político ou bode expiatório: Um estudo sobre a Aliança Renovadora Nacional (Arena), 1965–1979* (Rio de Janeiro: Mauad X, 2009).

67. For the MDB, see Maria Dalva Gil Kinzo, *Oposição e autoritarismo: Gênese e trajetória do MDB.* São Paulo: Idesp/Vértice, 1988.

68. The vote in Brazil was, and still is, compulsory.

69. *Grupo de Levantamento da Conjuntura.*

70. For the SNI and the information and repression system, see Dreifuss, *1964*; Lucas Figueiredo, *Ministério do silêncio: A história do serviço secreto brasileiro de Washington Luís a Lula (1927–2005)* (Rio de Janeiro: Record, 2005); Carlos Fico, *Como eles agiam: Os subterrâneos da ditadura militar – espionagem e polícia política* (Rio de Janeiro: Record, 2001); Samantha Viz Quadrat, *Poder e informação: O sistema de inteligência e o regime militar no Brasil* (Rio de Janeiro: UFRJ/PPGHIS, 2000).

71. For Golbery, see Elio Gaspari, *A ditadura derrotada* (São Paulo: Companhia das Letras, 2003); Dreifuss, *1964.*

72. *O Satânico Dr No* was the title that the distributors gave to the film *Dr No* in Brazil and the rest of Latin America.

73. For CIEX, see Claudio Dantas Sequeira, 'O serviço secreto do Itamaraty'. A series of seven reports published in the *Correio Brasiliense* between 23 and 26 July 2007.

74. For Dops and police stations, see Mariana Joffily, 'O aparato repressivo: Da arquitetura ao desmantelamento', in Reis, Ridenti and Motta (eds.), *A ditadura que mudou o Brasil*. For CIE, Cenimar, Cisa, see Heloisa Starling, 'Relatório de acompanhamento e avaliação de resultados de consultoria especializada para fornecer subsídios para as atividades de pesquisa da Comissão Nacional da Verdade' (Brasília: Comissão Nacional da Verdade, 15 July 2013).

75. For companies and the meeting with Delfim Netto, see Gaspari, *A ditadura escancarada*, pp. 62 ff; Antonio Carlos Fon, *Tortura: A história da repressão política no Brasil* (São Paulo: Global, 1979), pp. 54 ff; Marcelo Godoy, *A casa da vovó: Uma biografia do DOI-Codi (1969–1991), o centro de sequestro, tortura e morte da ditadura militar* (São Paulo: Alameda), pp. 220 and 412–13.

76. For the Oban, see Mariana Joffily, *No centro da engrenagem: Os interrogatórios na Operação Bandeirante e no DOI de São Paulo (1969–1975)* (São Paulo: Edusp, 2013); Godoy, *A casa da vovó*. On Codi-DOI, see Ministério do Exército, Centro de Operações de Defesa Interna (Codi/I Ex.), 1970, seventeen typed pages. Acervo Projeto República: núcleo de pesquisa, documentação e memória da UFMG. Arquivo Cenimar.

77. For disappearances and clandestine centres, see Heloisa Starling et al., 'Centros clandestinos de violações de direitos humanos. Relatório preliminar de pesquisa' (Brasília: Comissão Nacional da Verdade, March 2014). For torture, see Heloisa Starling and Danilo A. Marques, 'Tortura em quartéis e instituições militares. Relatório preliminar de pesquisa' (Brasília: Comissão Nacional da Verdade, May 2013); Elio Gaspari, *A ditadura escancarada* (São Paulo: Companhia das Letras, 2002).

78. For students, see Maria Ribeiro do Valle, *1968: O diálogo é a violência – Movimento estudantil e ditadura militar no Brasil* (São Paulo: Editora da Unicamp, 2008).

79. Otto Maria Carpeaux (1900–1978) was born in Vienna to a Jewish family. Despite not being a native speaker, his eight-volume *History of Western Literature* used to be considered a reference work.

80. Quoted in Ventura, *1968*, p. 123. See also Mylton Severiano (ed.), *A ditadura militar no Brasil: A história em cima dos fatos* (São Paulo: Caros Amigos, 2007).

81. For the Church, see Paulo César Gomes, *Os bispos católicos e a ditadura militar brasileira: A visão da espionagem* (Rio de Janeiro: Record, 2014); Kenneth P. Serbin, *Diálogos na sombra: Bispos e militares, tortura e justiça social na ditadura* (São Paulo: Companhia das Letras, 2002).

82. A small generator for applying electric shocks.
83. The words that appear on the Brazilian flag.
84. Dom Hélder Câmera (1909–1999) was a proponent of Liberation Theology and best known for his lifelong fight against poverty.
85. For Lamarca, see Oldack Miranda and Emiliano José, *Lamarca: O capitão da guerrilha* (São Paulo: Global, 2004); Judith Lieblich Patarra, *Iara: Reportagem biográfica* (Rio de Janeiro: Rosa dos Tempos, 1993). For the left-wing revolutionary movements, see Marcelo Ridenti and Daniel Aarão Reis (eds.), *História do marxismo no Brasil: Partidos e movimentos após os anos 1960* (Campinas: Editora da Unicamp, 2007, vol. 6).
86. For Marighella, see Magalhães, *Marighella*.
87. For the kidnapping, see Silvio Da-Rin, *Hércules 56: O sequestro do embaixador americano em 1969* (Rio de Janeiro: Zahar, 2008); Alberto Berquó, *O sequestro dia a dia* (Rio de Janeiro: Nova Fronteira, 1997).
88. For the *Guerrilha do Araguaia*, see Elio Gaspari, 'A floresta dos homens sem alma', in Elio Gaspari, *A ditadura escancarada* (São Paulo: Companhia das Letras, 2002); Leonencio Nossa, *Mata! O major Curió e as guerrilhas no Araguaia* (São Paulo: Companhia das Letras, 2002).
89. For the rural labourers, see Heloisa Starling et al., 'Mortos e desaparecidos na área rural. Relatório final de pesquisa'. Brasília: Comissão Nacional da Verdade, November 2013.
90. Jader de Figueiredo Correia, 'Relatório' (Brasília: Ministério da Justiça, 1967). Acervo Projeto República: núcleo de pesquisa, documentação e memória da UFMG. Arquivo: Indígenas.
91. Domingos Fernandes Calabar (c. 1600–1635) is traditionally considered a traitor in Brazilian history.
92. For *Calabar*, see Ministério do Exército, 'Parecer "Calabar o elogio da traição"', 1973, eight typed pages. Acervo Projeto República: núcleo de pesquisa, documentação e memória da UFMG. Arquivo CIE.
93. For the censorship, see Heloisa Starling and Ana Marília Carneiro, 'Política de censura. Relatório preliminar de pesquisa'. Brasília: Comissão Nacional da Verdade, July 2014.
94. The Oswaldo Cruz Foundation is a scientific institute for research and development in the biomedical sciences.
95. The expression is from Michel de Certeau. See Michel de Certeau, *A invenção do cotidiano: Artes de fazer*. Petrópolis: Vozes, 2002.
96. For the 'Oito do Glória', see José Rubens Siqueira, *Viver de teatro: Uma biografia de Flávio Rangel*. São Paulo: Nova Alexandria, 1995.
97. For the vigil, see Ventura, *1968*, pp. 95–6. For theatre, see Yan Michalski, *O teatro sob pressão: Uma frente de resistência* (Rio de Janeiro: Zahar, 1985).
98. Quoted in Claudia Calirman, *Arte brasileira na ditadura: Antonio Manuel, Artur Barrio, Cildo Meireles*. Rio de Janeiro: Réptil, 2013, p. 49.

99. For the visual arts, see Calirman, *Arte brasileira na ditadura*; Paulo Sérgio Duarte, *Anos 60: Transformações da arte no Brasil* (Rio de Janeiro: Campos Gerais, 1998).

100. Henfil – Henrique de Souza Filho (1944–1988) – drew cartoons that captured the imagination of Brazilians.

101. *Stampede*; *No man's land*; *Favela*; *Procession*; *Maria from Maranhão*; *The razor-blade eater*; *The road and the guitar player.*

102. For popular songs, see Heloisa Maria Murgel Starling, 'Canção popular e direito de resistência no Brasil', in Heloisa Maria Murgel Starling, Newton Bignotto, Leonardo Avritzer, Fernando Filgueiras and Juarez Guimarães (eds.), *Dimensões políticas da Justiça* (Rio de Janeiro: Record, 2012). For Tropicália, see Christopher Dunn, *Brutalidade jardim: a Tropicália e o surgimento da contracultura brasileira* (São Paulo: Unesp, 2009). For the Clube da Esquina, see Bruno Viveiros Martins, *Som imaginário: A reinvenção das cidades nas canções do Clube da Esquina* (Belo Horizonte: UFMG, 2009). For kitsch songs, see Paulo César de Araújo, *Eu não sou cachorro, não: Música popular cafona e ditadura militar* (Rio de Janeiro: Record, 2002).

103. The meaning being 'the horrors that are being committed around us may seem banal (to those who commit them) – but one day they'll be headline news (exposed and condemned)'.

18: ON THE PATH TO DEMOCRACY

1. 'Navegar é preciso' is the title of a poem by the Portuguese poet Fernando Pessoa. Literally translated it means 'To navigate is necessary', but the phrase has multiple levels of meaning.

2. The Planalto Palace, designed by Oscar Niemeyer in 1959, has a main concrete ramp that is used for ceremonial occasions.

3. *Senhor* (1987).

4. For the Figueiredo government, see Alexandre Garcia, *Nos bastidores da notícia* (São Paulo: Globo, 1990), especially the second part; Saïd Farhat, *Tempo de gangorra: Visão panorâmica do processo político-militar no Brasil de 1978 a 1980* (São Paulo: Tag et Line, 2012); Lucas Figueiredo, *Ministério do silêncio: A história do serviço secreto brasileiro de Washington Luís a Lula (1927–2005)* (Rio de Janeiro: Record, 2005).

5. For the military project of decompression of the political system, see Alfred Stepan, *Os militares: Da abertura à Nova República* (Rio de Janeiro: Paz e Terra, 1986); Brasilio Sallum Jr, *Labirintos: Dos generais à Nova República* (São Paulo: Hucitec, 1996); Gaspari, *A ditadura derrotada*; Elio Gaspari, *A ditadura encurralada* (São Paulo: Companhia das Letras, 2004).

6. *Abertura* literally means 'opening' or 'opening up'. The term is used for the process of gradual re-democratization of the country.

7. For the anti-candidacy of Ulysses Guimarães, see Luiz Gutemberg, *Moisés: Codinome Ulysses Guimarães – Uma biografia* (São Paulo: Companhia das Letras, 1994). See also Kinzo, *Oposição e autoritarismo: Gênese e trajetória do MDB*; Ana Beatriz Nader, *Autênticos do MDB, semeadores da democracia: História oral de vida política* (São Paulo: Paz e Terra, 1998).

8. For Brizola and the PDT, see João Trajano Sento-Sé, *Brizolismo: Estetização da política e carisma* (Rio de Janeiro: Fundação Getulio Vargas, 1999).

9. For the demands, see Stepan, *Os militares*; Sallum Jr, *Labirintos*.

10. *Folha de S. Paulo* (5 April 1978), pp. 4–5. For Golbery, see Gutemberg, *Moisés*.

11. For the economic crisis during the Geisel government, see Luna and Klein, 'Transformações econômicas no período militar (1964–1985)'.

12. For Vannucchi's murder and its consequences, see Caio Túlio Costa, *Cale-se: A saga de Vannucchi Leme, a USP como aldeia gaulesa, o show proibido de Gilberto Gil*. São Paulo: Girafa, 2003.

13. For Dom Paulo Evaristo Arns, see Ricardo Carvalho (ed.), *O cardeal da resistência: As muitas vidas de dom Paulo Evaristo Arns* (São Paulo: Instituto Vladimir Herzog, 2013).

14. For Herzog's murder, see Hamilton Almeida Filho, *A sanguequente: A morte do jornalista Vladimir Herzog* (São Paulo: Alfa-Omega, 1978); Audálio Dantas, *As duas guerras de Vlado Herzog: Da perseguição nazista na Europa à morte sob tortura no Brasil* (Rio de Janeiro: Civilização Brasileira, 2012); Fernando Pacheco Jordão, *Dossiê Herzog: Prisão, tortura e morte no Brasil* (São Paulo: Global, 2005).

15. See Gaspari, *A ditadura encurralada*, pp. 177 and 215.

16. For the offensive against the Communist Party, see Gaspari, *A ditadura encurralada*; Figueiredo, *Ministério do silêncio*.

17. For Dom Helder, see Dantas, *As duas guerras de Vlado Herzog*, pp. 318–19.

18. For the opposition alliance and the defence of democratic freedoms, see Mário Sérgio de Moraes, *O ocaso da ditadura: Caso Herzog* (São Paulo: Barcarolla, 2006).

19. For the CEBS, see Maria Victoria de Mesquita Benevides, *Fé na luta: A Comissão de Justiça e Paz de São Paulo, da ditadura à democratização* (São Paulo: Lettera.doc, 2009); Marcos Napolitano, *1964: História do regime militar brasileiro* (São Paulo: Contexto, 2014).

20. For the minority political movements, see Céli Regina Jardim Pinto, *Uma história do feminismo no Brasil* (São Paulo: Fundação Perseu Abramo, 2003); João Silvério Trevisan, *Devassos no paraíso: A homossexualidade no Brasil, da Colônia à atualidade* (Rio de Janeiro: Record, 2007); Lucy Dias, *Anos 70: Enquanto corria a barca* (São Paulo: Senac, 2001); James

Green, 'Mais amor e mais tesão: A construção de um movimento brasileiro de gays, lésbicas e travestis', *Cadernos Pagu*, no. 15 (2000), pp. 271–95.

21. For the alternative press, see Bernardo Kucinski, *Jornalistas e revolucionários nos tempos da imprensa alternative* (São Paulo: Edusp, 2003); Maria Paula Nascimento Araujo, *A utopia fragmentada: As novas esquerdas no Brasil e no mundo na década de 1970* (Rio de Janeiro: Fundação Getulio Vargas, 2000).

22. *Pasquim* – the name for the satirical pamphlets of the nineteenth century – had a similar format and editorial line to that of the British publication *Private Eye*.

23. Respectively: *The Animal*; *Biting Humour* (a combination of the words humour – *humor* – and biting – *mordaz*); *Kiss*; *The Enemy of the King*.

24. For the student movement, see Gaspari, *A ditadura encurralada*; Costa, *Cale-se*. See also Paulo Leminski, *Distraídos venceremos* (São Paulo: Brasiliense, 1987).

25. For the counterculture and its relation to Brazil, see Ken Goffman and Dan Joy, *Contracultura através dos tempos* (Rio de Janeiro: Ediouro, 2007); Santuza Cambraia Naves and Maria Isabel Mendes de Almeida (eds.), *'Por que não?' Rupturas e continuidades da contracultura* (Rio de Janeiro: 7Letras, 2007); Luiz Carlos Maciel, *O sol da liberdade* (Rio de Janeiro: Vieira & Lent, 2014); Dias, *Anos 70*.

26. Artifice, in the sense of *trick* or *ruse*.

27. For the poets of the alternative culture, see Heloisa Buarque de Hollanda, *Impressões de viagem: CPC, vanguarda e desbunde – 1960/70* (São Paulo: Brasiliense, 1980). For Nuvem Cigana, see Sérgio Cohn (ed.), *Nuvem Cigana: Poesia e delírio no Rio dos anos 70* (Rio de Janeiro: Beco do Azougue, 2007).

28. For the 'Letter to the Brazilians', see Napolitano, *1964*.

29. *The Owners of Power*.

30. Quoted in Cezar Britto, 'O herói da redemocratização', *Folha de S. Paulo* (17 October 2008), p. A3.

31. For the reference to Idi Amin, see Gutemberg, *Moisés*.

32. 'S.A.' stands for *Sociedade anónima* – a limited liability company.

33. For the 'Manifesto of the Group of Eight', see Napolitano, *1964*.

34. The industrial belt of São Paulo is often referred to as the *ABC Paulista*, as it includes the industrial towns of Santo André, São Bernardo do Campo and São Caetano.

35. For the strike of 1978 and its consequences, see Laís Wendel Abramo, 'O resgate da dignidade: A greve metalúrgica em São Bernardo', in Zilah Abramo e Flamarion Maués (ed.), *Pela democracia, contra o arbítrio: A oposição democrática do golpe de 1964 à campanha das Diretas Já* (São Paulo: Fundação Perseu Abramo, 2006); Ricardo Antunes, *A rebeldia do trabalho: O confronto operário no ABC paulista: As greves de 1978/80*

(Campinas: Ed. da Unicamp, 1988); Paulo Markun, *O sapo e o príncipe: Personagens, fatos e fábulas do Brasil contemporâneo* (Rio de Janeiro: Objetiva, 2004).

36. ABC Paulista refers to the three districts on the outskirts of São Paulo, Santo André, São Bernardo and São Caetano.

37. The *boias-frias* are rural workers, who are transported by truck, at dawn, to the sugar plantations. They bring their lunch with them, in a tin (or plastic) box – for which the slang word is *boia* – which doesn't keep the food warm.

38. For the 'new trade unionism', see Antunes, *A rebeldia do trabalho*; Ricardo Antunes and Marco Aurélio Santana, 'Para onde foi o "novo sindical-ismo"? Caminhos e descaminhos de uma prática sindical', in Reis, Ridenti and Motta (ed.), *A ditadura que mudou o Brasil*; Markun, *O sapo e o príncipe.*

39. For the creation of CUT, see Gelsom Rozentino de Almeida, *História de uma década quase perdida: PT, CUT, crise e democracia no Brasil – 1979-1989* (Rio de Janeiro: Garamond, 2011); Leôncio Martins Rodrigues, *CUT: Os militantes e a ideologia* (Rio de Janeiro: Paz e Terra, 1990).

40. Often referred to in English as the Brazilian Labour Party.

41. For the creation of the PT, see Zilah Abramo and Maués (eds.), *Pela democracia, contra o arbítrio*; Markun, *O sapo e o príncipe*; Lincoln Secco, *História do PT* (São Paulo: Ateliê, 2011).

42. Coco grass or Java grass (*Cyperus rotundus*).

43. Quoted in Markun, *O sapo e o príncipe*, pp. 227-8.

44. *Pastoral Operária* – a Liberation Theology church organization.

45. For the death of Santo Dias, see Benevides, *Fé na luta*.

46. The *Matriz* is the parish church; the *Praça da Matriz* is the parish church square.

47. For the data, see 'Relatório final', *Brasil Nunca Mais* (São Paulo: Arquidi-ocese de São Paulo, 1985); *Direito à verdade e à memória* (Brasília: Comissão Especial sobre Mortos e Desaparecidos, 2007); *Tribunale Ber-trand Russel II* (Rome: Fundação Lelio Basso, 1974, 1975, 1976).

48. For Therezinha Zerbini, see Paulo Moreira Leite, *A mulher que era o gen-eral da casa: Histórias da resistência civil à ditadura*. Porto Alegre: Arquipélago, 2012.

49. The *Gaviões da Fiel* ('Corinthian Hawks') is the official fan club of the Corinthians, a very popular *Paulista* soccer team.

50. For the MFPA, the CBAs and the campaign for amnesty, see Abramo and Maués (eds.), *Pela democracia, contra o arbítrio*; Haike R. Kleber da Silva (ed.), *A luta pela anistia* (São Paulo: Ed. Unesp; Arquivo Público dos Estados de São Paulo; Imprensa Oficial, 2009).

51. For the Amnesty Law, see Glenda Mezarobba, 'Anistia de 1979: O que restou da lei forjada pelo arbítrio?', in Cecília MacDowell Santos, Edson

Teles and Janaína de Almeida Teles (eds.), *Desarquivando a ditadura: Memória e justiça no Brasil* (São Paulo: Hucitec, 2009, vol. 2); Carlos Fico, Maria Paula Araujo and Monica Grin (eds.), *Violência na história: Memória, trauma e reparação* (Rio de Janeiro: Ponteio, 2012), especially pp. 25–7; Da Silva (ed.), *A luta pela anistia*.

52. For these sectors in action, see Chirio, *A política nos quartéis*.

53. For Geisel's declaration, see D'Araujo and Castro (ed.), *Ernesto Geisel*, p. 225.

54. For the confrontation, see Gaspari, *A ditadura encurralada*.

55. For the number of deaths and torture denunciations, see 'Relatório final' (Brasília: Comissão Nacional da Verdade, December 2014); 'Relatório final', *Brasil Nunca Mais*; 'Direito à verdade e à memória'.

56. For the suspicions, see Anna Lee and Carlos Heitor Cony, *O beijo da morte* (Rio de Janeiro: Objetiva, 2003); Ferreira, *João Goulart*. For JK, see 'Laudo referente à análise dos elementos materiais produzidos em virtude da morte do ex-presidente Juscelino Kubitschek de Oliveira e de Geraldo Barros' (Brasília: Comissão Nacional da Verdade, 2014).

57. For the increase in terrorist activity, see Gaspari, *A ditadura encurralada*; Figueiredo, *Ministério do silêncio*; Chirio, *A política nos quartéis*; José A. Argolo, Kátia Ribeiro and Luiz Alberto M. Fortunato, *A direita explosiva no Brasil: A história do grupo secreto que aterrorizou o país com suas ações, atentados e conspirações* (Rio de Janeiro: Mauad, 1996).

58. For Figueiredo, see José Casado, '50 anos do golpe/Riocentro', *O Globo*, Caderno especial (6 October 2014), pp. 2–5.

59. For the paralysis in the Figueiredo government, see Stepan, *Os militares*; Sallum Jr, *Labirintos*.

60. For the Dante de Oliveira Amendment and the 'Diretas Já' campaign, see Alberto Rodrigues, *Diretas Já: O grito preso na garganta* (São Paulo: Fundação Perseu Abramo, 2003); Domingos Leonelli and Dante de Oliveira, *Diretas Já: 15 meses que abalaram a ditadura* (Rio de Janeiro: Record, 2004).

61. For the financial scandals, see Rodrigues, *Diretas Já*.

62. Moreira Franco, governor of the state of Rio de Janeiro from 1987 to 1991.

63. Proconsult was the company hired to count the votes, using what was at the time sophisticated software, which served as the means for vote rigging.

64. For the Proconsult scandal, see Paulo Henrique Amorim and Maria Helena Passos, *Plim-Plim: A peleja de Brizola contra a fraude eleitoral*. São Paulo: Conrad, 2005.

65. A large neoclassical church in the centre of Rio de Janeiro, one of the symbols of the city.

66. Later to be president of the Republic for two consecutive terms.

67. Governor of São Paulo from 1983 to 1987; see below.

68. The central avenue of Brasília.

69. Quoted in Leonelli and De Oliveira, *Diretas Já*, pp. 518–19. On the two candidacies, see Gutemberg, *Moisés*.

70. For Tancredo, see José Murilo de Carvalho, 'Ouro, terra e ferro: Marcas de Minas', in Heloisa Maria Murgel Starling, Gringo Cardia, Sandra Regina Goulart Almeida and Bruno Viveiros Martins (eds.), *Minas Gerais* (Belo Horizonte: UFMG/Fapemig, 2011); Vera Alice Cardoso Silva and Lucilia de Almeida Neves Delgado, *Tancredo Neves: A trajetória de um liberal* (Petrópolis: Vozes, 1985).

71. For Tancredo's strategy, see Gilberto Dimenstein et al., *O complô que elegeu Tancredo* (Rio de Janeiro: Editora JB, 1985); Figueiredo, *Ministério do silêncio*.

72. For the PFL and Maluf, see Eliane Cantanhêde, *O PFL*. São Paulo: Publifolha, 2001.

73. For the Democratic Alliance, see Dimenstein et al., *O complô que elegeu Tancredo*; Cantanhêde, *O PFL*; Sallum Jr, *Labirintos*.

74. Quoted in Gutemberg, *Moisés*, p. 204.

75. For Tancredo's illness and death, see Antônio Britto, *Assim morreu Tancredo: Depoimento a Luís Claudio Cunha* (Porto Alegre: L&PM, 1985); Figueiredo, *Ministério do silêncio*.

76. Aécio Neves (born 1960) is Tancredo's grandson.

77. For Ulysses and the PMDB, see Gutemberg, *Moisés*.

78. For Sarney, see Malu Delgado, 'Maranhão 2014', *piauí*, São Paulo, no. 98 (November 2014), pp. 25–30; Cantanhêde, *O PFL*. For the contemporary *coronelismo*, see José Murilo de Carvalho, 'As metamorfoses do coronel', *Jornal do Brasil*, Rio de Janeiro (6 May 2001), p. 4.

79. For the Constituent Assembly and the 1988 Constitution, see Marcos Emílio Gomes (ed.), *A constituição de 1988: 25 anos* (São Paulo: Instituto Vladimir Herzog, 2013); Carvalho, *Cidadania no Brasil*; Nicolau, *Eleições no Brasil*; Adriano Pilatti, *A Constituinte de 1987–1988: Progressistas, conservadores, ordem econômica e regras do jogo* (Rio de Janeiro: Lúmen Júris, 2008).

80. Available at < http://www.planalto.gov.br/ccivil_03/constituicao/constituicaocompilado.htm>. Accessed 3 February 2015.

81. Ulysses Guimarães, 'A Constituição Cidadã'. Speech delivered in the National Congress on 5 October 1988, in Gomes (ed.), *A Constituição de 1988*, pp. 270–1.

82. For the PMDB, see Marcos Nobre, *Imobilismo em movimento: Da abertura democrática ao governo Dilma*. São Paulo: Companhia das Letras, 2013.

83. For the PSDB, see Jales R. Marques and David V. Fleischer, *PSDB: De facção a partido* (Brasília: Instituto Teotônio Vilela, 1999).

84. For Fernando Henrique Cardoso, see Markun, *O sapo e o príncipe*. For Cebrap, see Flávio Moura and Paula Montero (eds.), *Retrato de grupo: 40 anos do Cebrap* (São Paulo: Cosac Naify, 2009).

85. For the Cruzado Plan, see Carlos Alberto Sardenberg, *Aventura e agonia: Nos bastidores do cruzado* (São Paulo: Companhia das Letras, 1987); Miriam Leitão, *Saga brasileira: A longa luta de um povo por sua moeda* (Rio de Janeiro: Record, 2011).

86. For Collor and the electoral campaign, see Mario Sergio Conti, *Notícias do Planalto: A imprensa e o poder nos anos Collor* (São Paulo: Companhia das Letras, 2012); Carlos Melo, *Collor: O ator e suas circunstâncias* (São Paulo: Novo Conceito, 2007); Markun, *O sapo e o príncipe*.

87. Quoted in Markun, *O sapo e o príncipe*, p. 229.

88. For the *Plano Collor* and its consequences, see Leitão, *Saga brasileira*.

89. For corruption in the Collor government, see Conti, *Notícias do Planalto*; Luciano Suassuna and Luís Costa Pinto, *Os fantasmas da Casa da Dinda* (São Paulo: Contexto, 1992); Markun, *O sapo e o príncipe*. For Paulo César Farias, see Lucas Figueiredo, *Morcegos negros* (Rio de Janeiro: Record, 2013).

90. Paulo César Farias was murdered on 23 June 1996, at his beach house in Maceió, the capital of Alagoas. Pedro Collor died of brain cancer on 19 December 1994, at the age of forty-two.

91. For Ulysses and the impeachment, see Gutemberg, *Moisés*; Conti, *Notícias do Planalto*.

92. For the Itamar Franco government, see Ivanir Yazbeck, *O real Itamar: Uma biografia* (Belo Horizonte: Gutemberg, 2011).

93. For the mass murders, see Eugenia Paim, Márcia Lathmaher and Rosilene Alvim (eds.), *Uma noite tão comprida* (Rio de Janeiro: 7Letras, 2011); Geraldo Lopes, *O massacre da Candelária* (Rio de Janeiro: Scritta, 1994).

94. For rap, see Wivian Weller, *Minha voz é tudo o que eu tenho: Manifestações juvenis em Berlim e São Paulo*. Belo Horizonte: UFMG, 2011.

95. For the *Plano Real*, see Leitão, *Saga brasileira*; Markun, *O sapo e o príncipe*; Luiz Filgueiras, *História do Plano Real* (São Paulo: Boitempo, 2000).

CONCLUSION

1. André Botelho and Lilia Moritz Schwarcz (eds.), *Cidadania, um projeto em construção: Minorias, justiça e direitos* (São Paulo: Companhia das Letras, 2013); see also Carvalho, *Cidadania no Brasil*.

2. See Lynn Hunt, *A invenção dos direitos humanos: Uma história* (São Paulo: Companhia das Letras, 2009).

3. 'A slave has no persona' – in other words, a slave is a non-person.

4. Marcel Mauss, *Sociologia e antropologia*, 4th edn. São Paulo: Cosac Naify, 2011.

5. Roberto Schwarz, 'As ideias fora do lugar', in *Ao vencedor as batatas: Forma literária e processo social nos inícios do romance brasileiro*. São Paulo: Duas Cidades, 1988.

6. Anderson, *Comunidades imaginadas*.
7. See Ridenti, *Brasilidade revolucionária*.
8. The Constitution of 1824 didn't recognize slaves and granted the vote to landowners, thus conferring the status of 'sub-citizen' on the majority of the population.
9. Maria Helena P. T. Machado, 'Os caminhos da Abolição: Os movimentos sociais e a atuação dos escravos'. Manuscript. San Francisco: Latin American Studies Association, 2012.
10. Guimarães, 'La République de 1889'.
11. In the 2015 Human Development Index (HDI), released in the United Nations Human Development Report, an index based on life expectancy, literacy, education and standard of living, Brazil comes in eighth place for Latin American countries, below Uruguay, Panama, Cuba, Costa Rica, Venezuela and Mexico. In the world ranking Brazil is in 75th place.
12. For the policies of the Lula government, see Carvalho, *Cidadania no Brasil*; José Maurício Domingues, *O Brasil entre o presente e o futuro: Conjuntura interna e inserção internacional* (Rio de Janeiro: Mauad X, 2013).
13. For corruption, see Heloisa Maria Murgel Starling, Newton Bignotto, Leonardo Avritzer and Juarez Guimarães (eds.), *Corrupção: Ensaios e críticas* (Belo Horizonte: Editora UFMG, 2008); Célia Regina Jardim Pinto, *A banalidade da corrupção: Uma forma de governar o Brasil* (Belo Horizonte: Editora UFMG, 2001).
14. For CNV, see Napolitano, *1964*; Fico, Araujo and Grin (eds.), *Violência na história*.

AFTERWORD TO THE ENGLISH EDITION

1. For indicators and the quality of Brazil's democracy, see Leonardo Avritzer, *Impasses da democracia no Brasil* (Rio de Janeiro: Civilização Brasileira, 2016); Fabiano Santos and José Szwako, 'Impasses políticos e institucionais no cenário atual', in André Botelho and Heloisa Murgel Starling, *República e democracia: Impasses no Brasil contemporâneo* (Belo Horizonte: Editora UFMG, 2017); Robert Dahl, *Polyarchy: Participation and Opposition* (New Haven: Yale University Press, 1971).
2. For the economic scenario and the explanation of economic policies, see: André Singer, 'A (falta de base) política para o ensaio desenvolvimentista', in André Singer and Isabel Loureiro, *As contradições do lulismo: a que ponto chegamos?* (São Paulo: Boitempo, 2016); André Singer, 'Cutucando onças com varas curtas: o ensaio desenvolvimentista no primeiro mandato de Dilma Rousseff (2011–2014)', *Novos estudos*, São Paulo, Cebrap, no. 102 (July 2015); Claudia Safatle, João Borges and Ribamar Oliveira, *Anatomia de um desastre: Os bastidores da crise econômica que*

mergulhou o país na pior recessão de sua história (São Paulo: Portfolio-Penguin, 2016); Brasílio Sallum Jr, 'A crise política de 2015–16: para além da conjuntura', in Botelho and Starling, *República e democracia*; Miriam Leitão, *A verdade é teimosa* (Rio de Janeiro: Intrínseca, 2015).

3. For the 2013 demonstrations, and those that followed through August 2016, see Angela Alonso, 'Protestos em São Paulo de Dilma a Temer', in Botelho and Starling, *República e democracia*; André Singer, 'Brasil, junho de 2013: classes e ideologias cruzadas', *Novos Estudos*, São Paulo, Cebrap, no. 97 (November 2013); Marcos Nobre, *Choque de democracia: Razões da revolta* (São Paulo: Companhia das Letras, 2013); Eugênio Bucci, *A forma bruta dos protestos: Das manifestações de junho de 2013 à queda de Dilma Rousseff em 2016* (São Paulo: Companhia das Letras, 2016); João Feres Jr et al., 'A mídia impressa na cobertura das manifestações de junho' (Caxambu: Anpocs, 2014).

4. Of the Brazilian Social Democracy Party – Partido da Social Democracia Brasileiro, PSDB.

5. Roberto Schwarz, 'Sobre Cidades rebeldes', in Raquel Rolnik et al., *Cidades rebeldes: Passe Livre e as manifestações que tomaram as ruas do Brasil* (São Paulo: Boitempo, 2013), p. 3.

6. For *black blocs*, see Bucci, *A forma bruta dos protestos*; Francis Depuis-Déri, *Black blocs* (São Paulo: Veneta, 2014). For a different point of view on these groups, see Luiz Eduardo Soares, 'Entrevista com um vândalo', 2014.

7. For autonomist activism and the conflicts in the antagonist movement's repertory, see Alonso, 'Protestos em São Paulo de Dilma a Temer', in Botelho and Starling, *República e democracia*.

8. To contextualize the turnaround, see Avritzer, *Impasses da democracia no Brasil* (especially chapter 3); Alonso, 'Protestos em São Paulo de Dilma a Temer', in Botelho and Starling, *República e democracia*.

9. For the Sunday demonstrations, see Bucci, *A forma bruta dos protestos*.

10. For Operation Car Wash and the outcome, see Rodrigo de Almeida, *À sombra do poder: os bastidores da crise que derrubou Dilma Rousseff* (São Paulo: Leya, 2016); Safatle, Borges and Oliveira, *Anatomia de um desastre*; Vladimir Netto, *Lava Jato: O juiz Sergio Moro e os bastidores da operação que abalou o Brasil* (Rio de Janeiro: Primeira Pessoa, 2016); Paulo M. Leite, *A outra história da Lava Jato* (São Paulo: Geração Editorial, 2015).

11. 2a Vara da Justiça Federal.

12. Brazilian Democratic Movement Party/Partido do Movimento Democrático Brasileiro, PMDB; Progressive Party/Partido Progressista, PP; Socialist Democrat Party/Partido Social Democrático, PSD; Workers' Party/Partido dos Trabalhadores, PT); Brazilian Social Democratic Party/Partido da Social Democracia Brasileira (PSDB).

13. For the corruption phenomenon and the Brazilian context, see Leonardo Avritzer, Newton Bignotto, Juarez Guimarães and Heloisa Starling, *Corrupção: ensaios e críticas* (Belo Horizonte: Editora UFMG, 2012); Célia Regina Jardim Pinto, *A banalidade da corrupção: uma forma de governar o Brasil* (Belo Horizonte: Editora UFMG, 2011); Bruno Wanderley Reis, 'Financiando os que vão ganhar', *Folha de S. Paulo*, 18 September 2016, pp. 4–5.

14. For the 2014 elections and consequences, see de Almeida, *À sombra do poder*; Safatle, Borges and Oliveira, *Anatomia de um desastre*.

15. Marcos de Moura e Souza, 'Dilma diz que PSDB quer "trazer de volta recessão e desemprego"', *Valor Econômico*, 30 May 2014. For the shift in economic policy and the consequences, see Singer, 'A (falta de base) política para o ensaio desenvolvimentista'; Sallum Jr, 'A crise política de 2015–16', in Botelho and Starling, *República e democracia*.

16. For opposition political agents and the creation of their mechanisms of intervention, see Wanderley Guilherme dos Santos, *A democracia impedida: o Brasil no século XXI* (Rio de Janeiro: Editora FGV, 2017); Fábio Wanderley Reis, 'Crise política: a "opinião pública" contra o eleitorado', in Luis Felipe Miguel and Flávia Biroli, *Encruzilhadas da democracia* (Porto Alegre: Zouk, 2017).

17. For the crises in Dilma Rousseff's second term, see de Almeida, *À sombra do poder*.

18. For 'fiscal pedalling' and the impeachment process, see de Almeida, *À sombra do poder*; Safatle, Borges and Oliveira, *Anatomia de um desastre*.

19. Of the Brazilian Democratic Movement Party (PMDB).

20. At the time of writing, the deputy is still incarcerated. On Eduardo Cunha, see de Almeida, *À sombra do poder*; Leonardo Avritzer, 'Democracia no Brasil: do ciclo virtuoso à crise política aberta', in Botelho and Starling, *República e democracia*.

21. For the utilization of the democratic ritual and its origins in Brazil, see dos Santos, *A democracia impedida*; Santos and Szwako, 'Impasses políticos e institucionais no cenário atual'.

22. Of the Brazilian Democratic Movement Party (PMDB).

23. Marina Dias, 'Líder do governo rejeita pedaladas e defesa de Dilma usará fala em processo', *Folha de S. Paulo*, 25 June 2016.

24. Elio Gaspari, 'Há golpe', *Folha de S. Paulo*, 29 June 2016. On the metal fence and its political symbolism, see Alonso, 'Protestos em São Paulo de Dilma a Temer', in Botelho and Starling, *República e democracia*.

25. For undermining democratic institutions in Brazil from the inside, see Newton Bignotto, 'O fascismo no horizonte', *Cult*, no. 212, 6 May 2016.

26. For the investigations, see 'Oito ministros, comando do Congresso e 24 senadores são investigados no stf', *Folha de S. Paulo*, 12 April 2017, pp. A1–A11. Michel Temer's negotiations were reported nearly every day, especially in the newspapers *O Globo* and *Folha de S. Paulo* between June and August 2017.

Index

CPSIA information can be obtained
at www.ICGtesting.com
Printed in the USA
LVHW020146200121
676902LV00007B/712